TECHNOLOGY FOR A RESILIENT FUTURE

The book addresses the exploration of cutting-edge technological advancements.

This collection encompasses a comprehensive range of peer-reviewed research across nine strategic tracks, including Robotics and Intelligent Systems, Industrial Automation, IoT, and Cyber-Security. Significant focus is placed on the transformative role of Artificial Intelligence and Machine Learning in specialized domains such as Natural Disaster Management, Space Technology, and Medical Device Research. The findings illustrated within these chapters delve into automated digital manufacturing systems, advanced machine vision, and the integration of smart sensors. By highlighting innovations that foster industrial resilience, the book documents how modern control systems and AI-driven methodologies are being deployed to optimize resource management and solve complex real-world problems.

This book is intended for researchers, academic faculty, and postgraduate students specializing in mechatronics, AI, and systems engineering. It is also an essential resource for industry professionals and technical consultants seeking the latest developments in automation, IoT security, and the application of machine learning in high-stakes fields like medicine and disaster recovery.

Taylor & Francis Proceedings in Computer Science and Engineering

This series is a compilation of peer-reviewed conference proceedings in computer science and engineering. Exploring advanced technologies and recent developments in the field of CS and IT, including application-based topics and latest AI usages.

Next-Generation Computing and Information Systems
Edited by Ankur Gupta

Next-Generation Smart Systems
Bridging Sustainability and Computational Intelligence
Edited by V. Sekhar, P. Ajay Kumar Reddy and K. Logesh, T. Raghunadha Reddy, and Dara Raju

Sustainable Developments in Computer Engineering, Green Technology and Smart Systems
Edited by Bhabani Prasanna Pattanaik, Dhirendra Kumar Shukla, Sambit Satpathy, and Kamalakanta Muduli

Progressive Computational Intelligence, Information Technology, and Networking
Edited by Poonam Nandal, Tapas Kumar, Meeta Singh and Mamta Dahiya

Smart and Distributed Computing
Edited by Pramod Singh Rathore and Sunil Kumar

Frontiers in Engineering, Science and Technology
Edited by Sitanath Biswas and Sayan Chakraborty

Computing, Communication, and Sustainable Energy Technologies – Volume 1
Edited by Ram Lal Yadava, Anil Kumar Sethi, and Amanpreet Singh Saini

Computing, Communication, and Sustainable Energy Technologies – Volume 2
Edited by Ram Lal Yadava, Anil Kumar Sethi, and Amanpreet Singh Saini

Technology for a Resilient Future
Edited by Shweta Vincent, Ramya S. Moorthy, and Kiran Dasari

For more information about this series, please visit: www.routledge.com/Taylor–Francis-Proceedings-in-Computer-Science-and-Engineering/book-series/PCSE

Technology for a Resilient Future

Edited by

Shweta Vincent, Ramya S. Moorthy, and Kiran Dasari

School of Mechanical Engineering, Manipal Institute of Technology, Manipal Academy of Higher Education, Manipal, Karnataka, India

RCAAI – 2005, FOURTH INTERNATIONAL CONFERENCE ON ROBOTICS, CONTROLS, AUTOMATION, AND ARTIFICIAL INTELLIGENCE

CRC Press
Taylor & Francis Group
Boca Raton London New York

CRC Press is an imprint of the
Taylor & Francis Group, an **informa** business

First edition published 2027
by CRC Press
4 Park Square, Milton Park, Abingdon, Oxon, OX14 4RN

and by CRC Press
2385 NW Executive Center Drive, Suite 320, Boca Raton FL 33431

CRC Press is an imprint of Informa UK Limited

British Library Cataloguing-in-Publication Data
A catalogue record for this book is available from the British Library

ISBN: 978-1-041-39070-1 (hbk)
ISBN: 978-1-041-39345-0 (pbk)
ISBN: 978-1-042-01754-6 (ebk)

DOI: 10.1201/9781042017546

Typeset in Times New Roman
by MPS Limited, Chennai, India

Contents

Technology for a Resilient Future – Vincent , Moorthy and Dasari (Eds)

Preface

The International Conference on Robotics, Control, Automation, and Artificial Intelligence (RCAAI 2025), held from October 29th to 31st, 2025, at the Manipal Institute of Technology (MIT), Manipal, marked a significant milestone in fostering global academic and industrial synergy. This fourth edition of the conference was anchored by the theme "Technology for a Resilient Future," aiming to address the critical role of intelligent systems in solving modern societal and environmental challenges.

A defining feature of RCAAI 2025 was its robust international character, exemplified by a vital academic partnership with the National Autonomous University of Mexico (UNAM). This collaboration enriched the conference through joint research exchanges and a diverse committee that ensured a meticulous double-blind peer review process. With over 270 submissions from countries including the United States, the United Kingdom, Mexico, and India, the technical program was highly competitive, maintaining a selective acceptance rate of approximately 25%.

The proceedings are organized into five major interdisciplinary tracks:

- **Robotics and Automation**
- **Industrial Automation**
- **Artificial Intelligence and Machine Learning**
- **Healthcare Systems**
- **Sustainable and Green Technologies**

The research presented herein reflects a broad spectrum of innovation, from robotic-assisted surgical platforms and Coagent AI in healthcare to autonomous agricultural mechanization and AI-driven flood mapping for climate resilience. Furthermore, the conference emphasized the importance of practical skill-building through a pre-conference workshop in association with MAN Truck Pvt. Ltd., equipping the next generation of engineers with hands-on expertise in collaborative robotics and medical image processing.

We extend our deepest gratitude to the keynote speakers, reviewers, session chairs, and authors whose contributions upheld the academic rigor of this event. It is our hope that these proceedings serve as a valuable resource for researchers and practitioners, inspiring continued creativity and purpose in the advancement of robotics and artificial intelligence.

Editorial Committee
RCAAI 2025

 ISBN: 978-1-041-39070-1

Acknowledgements

The organizing committee of RCAAI 2025 expresses its sincere gratitude to the visionaries and collaborators who made this international conference a resounding success.

- We extend our heartfelt thanks to the Manipal Institute of Technology (MIT), Manipal, and the Manipal Academy of Higher Education (MAHE) for providing the institutional support and world-class infrastructure necessary to host this flagship event.
- We are deeply grateful to our academic partner, the National Autonomous University of Mexico (UNAM), whose collaboration was instrumental in strengthening the global research perspective and ensuring the international success of the conference.
- Our appreciation goes to Cr. Dr. Anil Rana, Director of MIT Manipal, for his leadership and for officially inaugurating the conference.
- We thank Dr. Naveena A. N., Head of Surgical Oncology, for his impactful insights into robotic-assisted surgery and for showcasing the cutting-edge Hugo^{TM} system.
- We acknowledge the invaluable contributions of our keynote speakers from India, Malaysia, Abu Dhabi, and the United Kingdom, whose expertise in healthcare robotics, climate resilience, and industrial automation inspired all attendees.
- We recognize the dedicated efforts of over 150 reviewers from across the globe, whose meticulous double-blind peer review process ensured the high academic rigor and quality of the research presented.
- Finally, we thank all the authors, session chairs, and participants for their scholarly dialogue and commitment to advancing the frontiers of robotics and artificial intelligence for the benefit of society.

About the Editors

Shweta Vincent is an Associate Professor in the Department of Mechatronics at Manipal Institute of Technology with over 18 years of experience. Her research integrates Artificial Intelligence (AI) and Machine Learning (ML) into Industrial IoT and sustainable manufacturing to optimize industrial operations. She is a member of the ITU-T Focus Group on AI for Natural Disaster Management (FG-AI4NDM), where she collaborates on developing AI-based early warning systems and hazard mapping. Her work focuses on applying technological innovations to address global environmental and industrial challenges.

Ramya S. Moorthy is an Assistant Professor at MIT Manipal and the Founder Director of Nimaya Innovations Pvt. Ltd. A University Gold Medalist in M.Tech Robotics and an INSPIRE Fellow, she pioneered "Suprayoga," an IoT-based training system that accelerates psychomotor and cognitive learning for children with Autism Spectrum Disorder (ASD). Recognized with the "Women Transforming India Award 2021" by NITI Aayog and the "Devi Award 2023," her work focuses on leveraging robotics to foster independent living for children with special needs. Her research is widely published in international scientific journals.

Kiran Dasari holds a Ph.D. in Electronics and Communication Engineering from NIT Warangal. Currently a faculty member at MIT Manipal, he serves as a Co-Principal Investigator for an ISRO-sponsored Chandrayaan-2 project. With 12 years of research and teaching experience, his expertise spans Microwave Imaging, Remote Sensing, SAR Polarimetry, and Robotics. Dr. Dasari is an IEEE Geoscience and Remote Sensing Society member and a reviewer for high-impact journals. He has received multiple best paper awards for his contributions to remote sensing and embedded systems.

Organizing Committee

Patrons

- **Dr. Ramdas M. Pai** Chancellor, MAHE, Manipal, India
- **Dr. H. S. Ballal** Pro-Chancellor, MAHE, Manipal, India
- **Lt. Gen. (Dr.) M. D. Venkatesh** Vice-Chancellor, MAHE, Manipal, India
- **Dr. Narayana Sabhahit** Pro Vice Chancellor (Technology & Science), MAHE, Manipal, India
- **Dr. P. Giridhar Kini** Registrar, MAHE, Manipal, India
- **Cdr. (Dr.) Anil Rana** Director, MIT, Manipal, India
- **Dr. Somashekara Bhat** Joint Director, MIT, Manipal, India

ORGANIZING CHAIRS

- **Dr. D. V. Kamath** Dean, School of Mechanical Engineering, MIT Manipal, India
- **Dr. Silvia Garcia** Professor and Head, Department of Geoscience Soft Computing, UNAM, Mexico

ORGANIZING SECRETARIES

- **Dr. Shweta Vincent** School of Mechanical Engineering, MIT Manipal, India
- **Dr. Ramya S. Moorthy** School of Mechanical Engineering, MIT Manipal, India
- **Dr. Kiran Dasari** School of Mechanical Engineering, MIT Manipal, India

Technical and Editorial Committee

- Dr. Shweta Vincent, MIT Manipal, India
- Dr. Ramya S. Moorthy, MIT Manipal, India
- Dr. Kiran Dasari, MIT Manipal, India

Technology for a Resilient Future – Vincent , Moorthy and Dasari (Eds)
© 2027 The Editor(s), ISBN: 978-1-041-39070-1

Scientific Committee

Based on the conference documentation and committee lists, the following individuals served as the **Scientific Committee** (comprising the Technical Committee and Advisory members responsible for the peer-review and academic standards of the conference).

SCIENTIFIC ADVISORY COMMITTEE

- Dr. Juan Manuel Mayoral, UNAM, Mexico
- Dr. Leonardo Alcántara, UNAM, Mexico
- Dr. Joel Merlos Espericueta, UNAM, Mexico
- Dr. Cesar Angeles, UNAM, Mexico
- Dr. Jayatheja M, AMITY University, Mumbai
- Dr. Jai Vinita, Vellore Institute of Technology, Chennai
- Dr. Sherine J V Ali, Mercury, New Zealand
- Dr. Saampras Ganesan, University of Melbourne, Australia
- Prof. Ir. Dr. Yee Kit Chan, Multimedia University, Malaysia
- Dr. Benson Edwin Raj, Higher Colleges of Technology, UAE
- Dr. Munendra Singh, NIT Jamshedpur, India

TECHNICAL COMMITTEE

- Dr. Deepak D, School of Mechanical Engineering, MIT Manipal
- Dr. Asha C S, School of Mechanical Engineering, MIT Manipal
- Dr. Shivashankarayya H, School of Mechanical Engineering, MIT Manipal
- Dr. Pooja Nag, School of Mechanical Engineering, MIT Manipal
- Dr. Subramanya R Prabhu, School of Mechanical Engineering, MIT Manipal
- Dr. Jeane Marina D'souza, School of Mechanical Engineering, MIT Manipal
- Mr. Dundesh S Chiniwar, School of Mechanical Engineering, MIT Manipal
- Ms. Maithri M, School of Mechanical Engineering, MIT Manipal
- Mr. D A P Prabhakar, School of Mechanical Engineering, MIT Manipal
- Mr. Sivayazi Kappagantula, School of Mechanical Engineering, MIT Manipal
- Dr. K Abhimanyu K Patro, School of Mechanical Engineering, MIT Manipal
- Dr. Narendra Khatri, School of Mechanical Engineering, MIT Manipal
- Dr. Umesh Kumar Sahu, School of Mechanical Engineering, MIT Manipal
- Dr. Vijay Mohan, School of Mechanical Engineering, MIT Manipal
- Dr. Raghavendra Rao P, School of Mechanical Engineering, MIT Manipal
- Dr. Nikhil Pachauri, School of Mechanical Engineering, MIT Manipal
- Dr. Prasad Vinayak Patil, School of Mechanical Engineering, MIT Manipal
- Dr. Sowmya Gupta, School of Mechanical Engineering, MIT Manipal
- Dr. Abhishek K Kashyap, School of Mechanical Engineering, MIT Manipal
- Dr. Anupam Kumar, School of Mechanical Engineering, MIT Manipal

Technology for a Resilient Future – Vincent , Moorthy and Dasari (Eds)
© 2027 The Author(s), ISBN: 978-1-041-39070-1

Virtual Reality-Based Biofeedback System: A Review

C.R. Srinivasan, Preethish K.R, and Meenatchi Sundaram S
Department of Instrumentation and Control Engineering, Manipal Institute of Technology (MIT), Manipal Academy of Higher Education, (MAHE) Manipal, Karnataka, India

ABSTRACT: Biofeedback therapy (BF) is a technique that helps people gain control over involuntary functions, such as heart rate, breathing, and muscle tension. Biofeedback therapy can help manage various conditions, including chronic pain, anxiety, depression, high blood pressure, and migraines. Virtual reality and augmented reality are increasingly integrated into biofeedback therapy to enhance its effectiveness and user experience. By combining VR with biofeedback, therapists can create immersive environments that help patients with poor attentional focus and motivation better engage with the therapy and improve their ability to control physiological responses. Although there is continuous growth in this emerging field, research synthesis is still limited. Therefore, the goal of this review is to present an outline of empirical studies on VR/AR-based BFs concerning important results, samples, hardware and software used, BF parameters, application modes, and possible drawbacks. The methodology used in favor of the systematic review is PRISMA (preferred reporting items for systematic reviews and meta-analyses). We systematically explored PubMed, IEEE Xplore, Scopus, Science Direct, and Google Scholar for empirical research. Most of the participants in the samples were adults in good health. The primary findings were pain reduction, anxiety, and stress, each of which was reduced at least as much by VR-BF interventions as traditional BF. In addition to improving the user experience, the AR/VR-BF intervention participants demonstrated increased motivation, engagement, and consciousness focus. Additional studies are needed to determine the effects of gamified VR. Further research should concentrate on developing rules to formalize these technologies for their application in medical practice. The evaluation of more clinical and younger samples would additionally lead to more comprehensive findings.

Keywords: Augmented reality (AR), Virtual reality (VR), Biofeedback (BF), Gamified VR, Stress, Anxiety, PRISMA

1 INTRODUCTION

Biofeedback is a unique perspective on the relationship between cognitive performance and bodily functions. Biofeedback allows learning to control numerous different types of bodily feedback, such as heart rate, breathing patterns and muscle activity. During biofeedback, patients will be subject to sensors that provide data on heart rate, muscle tension, skin temperature, and brain responses that typically occur involuntarily within the body [1]. All biofeedback procedures allow a person to make, in the moment manipulation, based on feedback to improve physical health and emotional well-being via visual or auditory signals. There are many types of biofeedback methods, such as electromyography, which can monitor the activities of muscles to support relaxation and aid in the recovery process [2] [3]; heart rate variability, which can be utilized to monitor heart rate patterns to promote improvements in emotional and cardiovascular health [4]; electroencephalography or neurofeedback, which can monitor brain activity to assist in treating disorders such as anxiety or ADHD [5] the galvanic skin response, which measures skin conductance to monitor stress [6] [7]; respiratory biofeedback, which uses effective breathing to support relaxation [8] and blood pressure biofeedback, which can manage or maintain blood pressure in a person diagnosed with hypertension [9].

Conventional BF often employs visual images of physiological signals in ways that are too abstract or elaborate because inaugural information can be insignificant or not engage the user. The tasks of conventional BF can be seen as deadly boring, preventing the user from maintaining attention and motivation. Sustaining user attention on the feedback signals is the most important parameter for successful BF. Nevertheless, uninteresting task information and distractions from the environment can prevent users from paying attention to BF signals. Another factor considers the inability to transfer skills learned from BF to real life as the tasks or information can often be too abstract and the sterile training setting does not allow the users to engage with realistic life situations. Thus, continuous improvement is desirable to allow the user to sufficiently motivate and engage their attention with interactive feedback technologies.

AR and VR technologies have transformed the way we connect with digital content and the physical world. AR provides digital information in the real environment, whereas VR completely submerges the users in a virtual environment. These technologies enable virtual immersion where physical and digital worlds are blended. Users can interact with both the digital and physical worlds [10]. VR is a developing area in psychological and therapeutic research, and there is strong evidence that VR exposure therapy is successful in treating anxiety disorders and mental health disorders. Although VR provides numerous captivating benefits, treatment contraindications should be examined when VR-supported therapy is implemented in clinical practice [11][12]. AR is a latest innovation, whereas VR technology had been developed and adapted from the last 20 years. By creating an illusion of the surroundings, both seek to provide users with an experience that stimulates their auditory and visual senses.

With these developments, more approachable AR and VR technologies have become easier, adaptable, and less complex in real-time use. They additionally broaden the range of experiences to include sensory and occasionally olfactory elements [13]. VR/AR are highly adaptable technologies with a broad range of systems and content options ranging from non-immersive and static systems to immersive, dynamic, and interactive systems [29]. They employ head-mounted devices, 3D projections, or a video game in which the user plays the supporter and determines the level of immersion. An individual's capacity to act and receive feedback, as well as their sense of unity with their environment, are impacted by presence and interaction [13]. Virtual and augmented reality (VR/AR) are digital technologies that automate and perfect repetitive tasks

DOI: 10.1201/9781042017546-1

[14]. VR can influence a subject's experience of various challenges, cognitive abilities, and behavior.

When biofeedback technology is integrated with VR, immersive and interactive experiences react to a person's physiological signals. Sensors are used to read physiological signals such as heart rate, breathing, muscle tension, and skin temperature. These sensors may be housed in VR headsets, controllers, or wearable devices. Physiological data are continuously fed back to the VR system. These data are then applied to adapt to a real-time virtual environment. For example, if the system detects an increase in heart rate, it might change the environment to something more calming to help the user relax. The participants interact with the VR environment, and their physiological responses are monitored. The system adapts based on these responses, creating a dynamic and personalized experience. Over time, users can learn to control their physiological responses through the feedback given by the VR system. This can be particularly useful in therapeutic situations, such as managing anxiety or stress. The advancement of physiological monitoring technologies allows for the use of various biofeedback modalities in a cost-effective and user-friendly manner to study their impact on experience [13][15]. VR could create full immersion, which is a sense of being part of the virtual world. Immersion tends to help with pain because it diverts attention from pain perception. VR can be especially engaging for children who enjoy imaginative play. In addition to providing distraction, VR can also help relieve pain and anxiety through exposure. VR exposure can help patients feel more at ease and familiar with medical procedures and environments [16].

The contributions of this paper are that it presents a systematic scoping review of actual research on virtual and augmented reality-based biofeedback interventions, highlighting both their technological challenges and treatment potential; it finds the primary physiological and psychological outcomes linked to VR/AR biofeedback approaches and it covers research gaps and opportunities for standardization and future development. The rest of the document in section IX concludes with a discussion of future research directions and recommendations for the clinical application of VR/AR-based biofeedback systems. Section II outlines the review methods, including inclusion and exclusion criteria. Section III explains the search strategy used to find relevant studies. V, VI, and VII: the application of papers concerning stress and anxiety, stroke rehabilitation, pain and empathy. Section VIII presents the analysis of the reviewed literature.

2 METHODS

We chose to use a scoping analysis to define the field because this research is diverse and relatively new. In addition to establishing knowledge from the key ideas in a particular field and mapping open research questions, scoping reviews are meant to include implementation on an unclear topic with some diverse field of research that is methodologically and conceptually for a systematic literature review.

The seven tables titled "Features of the Research Incorporated in This Review" consist of data extracted from each included paper, summarizing aspects such as main findings, feedback, intervention, sessions, participants, study design, study sample, applications, and author details for a broad comparison.

2.1 *Inclusion and Exclusion Criteria*

Studies related to the evaluation of VR-BF treatment in one or more experimental groups were included. Our search is restricted to empirical studies by eliminating theoretical studies, including conceptual works. Furthermore, we limited our search to quantitative analysis by excluding qualitative analysis. We searched the referred and grey literature, with fewer restrictions on age groups. We restricted the search to BF methods that relied on peripheral psychophysiological parameters, such as breathing, electroencephalogram (EEG), heart rate variability (HRV), electrocardiogram (ECG), virtual reality exposure therapy (VRET) and electromyography (EMG).

3 SEARCH STRATEGY

This review was strategically performed by using databases such as PubMed/Medline, IEEE Xplore, Scopus, Science Direct, and Google Scholar for relevant literature. The search terms chosen to target the papers included keywords that discussed the intersection of AR (augmented reality), VR (virtual reality, virtual environment, 3D computer simulation), and BF (biofeedback, biofeedback training).

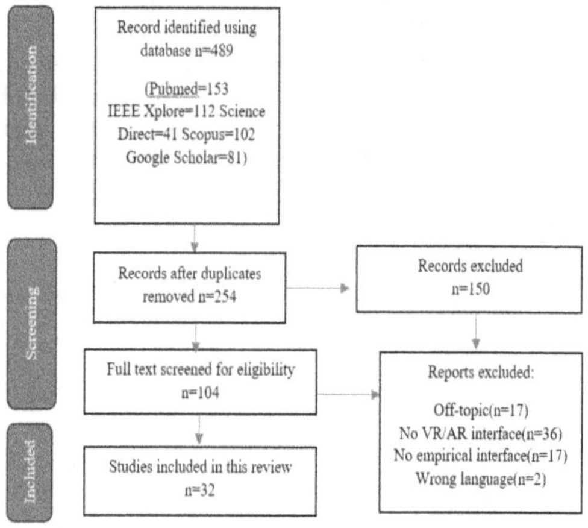

Figure 1. PISMA flow diagram for the systematic literature review.

As shown in Figure 1, according to the PRISMA guidelines, a systematic literature review was carried out. The first step involved identification, which involved the retrieval of 489 records from a variety of databases, including PubMed (153), IEEE Xplore (112), Science Direct (41), Scopus (102), and Google Scholar (81). A total of 254 unique records remained for screening after duplicates were eliminated. A total of 150 of these records were disqualified for not fulfilling the inclusion requirements based on their abstracts and titles. After the eligibility of the remaining 104 full-text articles was evaluated, 61 articles were excluded because they were in incorrect language (2), were off-topic (17), or lacked VR/AR interfaces (36). The final review ultimately included 32 studies, which served as the foundation for systematic analysis.

4 STRESS AND ANXIETY

[16] presented an effective and insightful way to measure respiration-based abdominal movement following the use of VR hand controllers. They reported positive changes in breath awareness, slow diaphragmatic breathing scores and an increase in respiratory sinus arrhythmia. For the study, 72 participants (56 females, mean age 21.6 years, range 18–49) practiced a series of brief breathing exercises in a VR environment, suggesting that cost-effective biofeedback options for healthy participants may be achieved. Similarly, [17] developed a biofeedback model for virtual reality exposure therapy (VRET). Their biofeedback

model developed through VRET uses heart rate and brain activity to measure anxiety-based arousal while valuing patient-specific frequency and duration of sessions. As a potential improvement, machine learning may provide a better opportunity for the detection of arousal and is an example of using machine learning for better real-time detection of difficulty. [18] used biofeedback within VR and applied it in rheumatology patients. Their intervention lasted 30 minutes and included 10 minutes of respiratory training via a Samsung Gear VR device. Their aim was to describe the overall effects of guided meditation and respiratory training in patients with RA, SLE, osteoarthritis and fibromyalgia (20 participants). The results demonstrated an overall significant reduction in pain and anxiety and suggested that when VR is applied in clinical practice, VR could be effective for pain reduction. [19] adopted a much wider frame of reference by using biofeedback technologies outside of traditional medical contexts. They combined brain–computer interfaces (BCIs), embodied VR (EVRs), and wearable actuators to encourage empathy, compassion and altruistic behavior. Although it was not possible to articulate a standardized session format, their findings illustrated that immersive VR environments can promote emotional intelligence and self-compassion in various groups including individuals living with ASD, individuals living with PTSD, and individuals with social anxiety [21].

Stress jam is a fun and intuitive virtual reality (VR) application that has been shown to change stress management strategies in combination with real-time biofeedback. Both healthy participants and patients exhibited a more adaptive stress mindset immediately after using Stress jam with several sessions lasting approximately 60 min. A total of 111 participants (52 females) included patients, and the Stress Mindset Measure was used during the stress sessions. This work supports the use of real-time biofeedback and heart rate variability in VR settings with healthy participants and patients with stress [22].

VR relaxation interventions have also been reported to be beneficial, as a form of biofeedback, in reducing subjective levels of stress in highly stressed individuals. A comparison of VR relaxation versus traditional biofeedback revealed some differences in stress reduction, but not in stress annotation. In their work, VR with biofeedback also noted changes in physiological markers such as heart rate, respiration rate, and skin conductance as well as self-reported behaviors of progressive muscle relaxation, breathing training, and guided imagery in patients and healthy participants. The intervention included two different relaxation types: immersive VR and biofeedback, with scheduled sessions of relaxation lasting approximately 10 min and 30 seconds, respectively. A total of 83 healthy participants with a mean age of 39 years were included, and the study followed a randomized 2 period, 2 treatment design [24].

Biofeedback interventions using games have also been created to assist in anxiety control. DEEP is a biofeedback videogame that assists participants with self-confidence, internal focus of control, and overall anxiety levels, although the accompanying mirrors of the visualizations offered no significant findings for anxiety regulation or appraisals. Visual feedback was demonstrated by mirroring the players' breathing and the expansion of the game during inhalation and contraction during exhalation. In this intervention, the player's avatar movement depended on the ability to perform diaphragmatic breathing. A single 10-minute session was administered to 78 healthy participants (M 21.27 years, SD 2.84), where cognitive appraisals related to psychosocial functioning and anxiety outcomes were analyzed [25][27].

In general, [31] reported that their results might not reach the level of statistical significance after prescriptions. Virtual reality (VR) biofeedback led to decreased anxiety symptoms and heart rate under stress, and their results did not reach significance for improvement in heart rate variability (HRV). They blended real-time heart rate (HR) and HRV data into immersive VR experiences that involved gamification and relaxation techniques. Their work utilized systematic reviews, randomized controlled trials, and repost studies to evaluate 191 patients with anxiety and stress, providing evidence of the viability of VR biofeedback as a treatment for anxiety, stress reduction, and relaxation training in immersive and gamified VR experiences.

5 STROKE REHABILITATION

Balance and mobility in older adults improved after AR training. With real-time visual and motion feedback through AR, engagement and accuracy were greater in practice sessions with AR-guided Tai-Chi movements. The interventions consisted of three sessions weekly for two months, with each session lasting 30 minutes. The participants were older adults aged 65 years and above. This work demonstrated that AR is effective for rehabilitation and training across a wide range of rehabilitation and physical training for improved balance and movement functions [28]. EMG-based VR was found to improve outcomes in stroke patients during rehabilitation. Real-time EMG feedback enabled the therapist to adapt the training intensity and to assist with accurate movement. The intervention was developed as a VR rehabilitation system that incorporated EMG signal processing while undertaking scenarios in VR, with frequent sessions based on patient needs. The article reports on an experimental study, examining a virtual reality EMG rehabilitation system that targets stroke rehabilitation to improve motor function [30]. To add to these findings, EMG-controlled games were designed to enhance hand function recovery for patients with stroke. The biofeedback games were developed with a focus on wrist and hand muscle activation patterns and provided real-time control feedback from EMG signals associated with both limbs affected and unaffected by strokes. During the intervention, 9 sessions and 20 participants were randomized to compare the effects of unilateral and bilateral EMG biofeedback training. The participants were chronic stroke patients with moderate hand impairments, and the results revealed improvements in stroke rehabilitation and hand function recovery along with functional retraining of muscle activation patterns [32].

6 PAIN AND EMPATHY

Studies have shown VR to be a useful modality in the care of rheumatology patients to manage both pain and anxiety. [18] reported clinically meaningful pain reduction after the use of respiratory biofeedback along with guided meditation. The setup used Samsung Gear VR goggles, which recommended a structured approach consisting of 30 min of guided meditation followed by 10 min of biofeedback. This was a case study with 20 participants diagnosed with rheumatoid arthritis (RA), systemic lupus erythematosus (SLE), osteoarthritis, and fibromyalgia. The authors defined the effects of VR-supported biofeedback to reduce pain. In addition to pain interventions, VR and biofeedback are considered in the development of empathy. [26] reported the use of biofeedback to bring real-time physiological information into a VR environment to augment emotions. Their descriptive study revealed the ability of VR and biofeedback to enhance empathy through emotion regulation and self-awareness. They also highlighted the ability of VR and biofeedback to improve empathic and compassion-related practices in clinical and instructional environments, as well as the use of technology-based approaches for empathy training in healthy participants.

7 DISCUSSION

Literature highlights the ways in which the combination of biofeedback and virtual reality (VR) technologies can enhance mental and physical wellness. Areas of research include the utilization of this technology to reduce stress and anxiety, to decrease anxiety and acute pain, and to help improve empathy and emotional regulation. Addressing physical and mental wellness via examples in the literature consistently shows that biofeedback VR integrates real-time feedback with biofeedback intervention. For example, integrating hand controllers in virtual space depends on tracking breathing exercise sessions and examining moment-to-moment breath awareness and breath relaxation.

Table 1. Taxonomy of feedback modalities categorized by input modality, feedback type, and VR interaction models formed from reviewed studies.

Category	Elements	Examples from Review
Input Modality	EEG, HRV, EMG, ECG, respiration sensors	EEG headbands, HRV chest straps, Brainproducts respiration belts, EMG hand sensors
Feedback Type	Visual, auditory, audiovisual	VR games with biofeedback, guided meditation audio, visual breathing pattern mirroring
VR Interaction Model	Game-based, narrative-driven, immersive exposure therapy, relaxation protocol	StressJam VR game, narrative VR environments, VR-based guided breathing exercises, mindfulness VR scenarios

As shown in Table 1, the studies also emphasized how biofeedback methods, including HRV, ECG and EEG, are able to influence individual physiological responses associated with stress and anxiety. Notably, VR provides individuals with an engaging therapeutic experience, often tailored to the individual experience, whether it is a relaxation exercise or an exposure therapy experience for anxiety. The ability of individuals to engage with the intervention under flexible parameters and parameters that suit individual preferences is beneficial for engagement and effectiveness of use. Together, these emerging sensors and biofeedback methods, as well as the use of VR, demonstrate promising potential in revolutionizing therapeutic interventions regardless of condition however, further studies are needed to determine the long-term benefits, sustainable usage, and effectiveness of these methods.

Biofeedback therapies use biological signals, including heart rhythms, brain waves, muscle activity, skin conductance, and temperature, to support patients in regaining control over bodily functions. Specifically, heart rate variability biofeedback facilitates relaxation and emotional regulation for stress, anxiety, and hypertension. Electromyography aids in muscle recovery in rehabilitation scenarios, and electroencephalography (neurofeedback) addresses mental health conditions such as depression, migraine, epilepsy, and ADHD. Thermal biofeedback and galvanic skin response biofeedback help with migraines, Raynaud's disease, and stress. Biofeedback therapies reduce the degree of dependence on drugs, support patient engagement, and improve quality of life.

Improvements in technology - The integration and implementation of biofeedback techniques with the use of VR and AR systems have established sophisticated use in the last few years. Advancements in technology, such as head-mounted displays, physiological sensors, and wearable technology, have led to increasingly immersive and engaging experiences for therapeutic uses. The accuracy and flexibility of VR and AR systems increase the capacity for real-time processing of biofeedback signals because of the ability to incorporate machine learning algorithms. Gamified VR environments allow for user participants' motivation and engagement to be maximized, facilitating a focus on objectives and actively participating fully in designated therapeutic protocols. In isolation, the impact of these technologies is substantial; when combined and deployed, the impact is an integrated, individualized, and improved biofeedback experience.

Issues faced - Despite such positive developments, the implementation of VR/AR-based biofeedback interventions is not without its challenges. The lack of standardization regarding study protocols and outcome measures makes it difficult to compare findings between studies or apply findings to clinical settings. Technical issues related to calibration, latency in sensor feedback, or what happens when the use of VR starts to become uncomfortable or causes much fatigue further hinders the integration of these interventions beyond the lab setting. Additionally, several of the studies we reviewed use small homogeneous samples, limiting both the diversity and the external validity of the findings. The review included a range of hardware, including Samsung Gear VR goggles, Oculus Quest headsets, EEG headbands, Brain products elastic respiration belts, and tracked hand controllers. The hardware specifications, including the refresh rate, latency, or motion tracking accuracy, can influence consistency, responsiveness, and ultimately, the effectiveness of VR/AR-based biofeedback interventions, which require a more detailed examination in the future. Finally, introducing a sustainable VR/AR-biofeedback system into health care settings introduces challenges, including issues of cost, accessibility, and ethics, that need consideration.

In the past, biofeedback approaches have often struggled with allowing users to use learned self-regulation skills outside the laboratory or clinic. Traditional forms of biofeedback may have the potential to demonstrate learned skills in natural, more similar environmental contextual settings. While immersive VR environments may have the potential to provide more naturalistic learning and better contextual cues and thus increase the likelihood of generalization, this review did not systematically determine whether VR-BF has greater transfer to other settings than traditional biofeedback does. Future studies should examine how immersive and ecologically valid VR experiences can assist in the retention and transfer of biofeedback-regulated skills in daily living and remain critical for the maintenance of longer-term therapeutic effects.

8 CONCLUSION AND FUTURE SCOPE

Augmented reality and virtual reality-based biofeedback practices have the potential to enhance mental wellness and support rehabilitation therapy. The integration of VR along with biofeedback training can increase user motivation and involvement in stress management and relaxation training. VR exposure therapy using self-guided VR environments can help people develop a heightened tolerance for anxiety-provoking stimuli and reduce anxiety-triggered arousal. VR and AR interfaces may be used in neurological motor rehabilitation and prosthetic training, but they still lack standardized protocols and signal processing strategies. VR biofeedback interventions have demonstrated promise in limiting self-reported anxiety and heart rate decreases. It is unclear if these studies followed a controlled environment. Furthermore, with AR-based biofeedback training, steady-state visual evoked potentials created by EEG can potentially modulate affect-biased attention, which may benefit people experiencing depression and anxiety. Gamification in VR biofeedback has shown promising effects on physiological measures. According to the literature, exposure can change an individual's physiological state, ultimately affecting psychological self-reports and the user experience. The VR biofeedback versions significantly reduce self-reported anxiety and heart rate suggesting that they have a positive impact on physiological measures. Additionally, active video games or exergames in VR have been utilized to establish physiological measures including heart rate, blood pressure, and salivary cortex levels that result in legibly acute physiological arousal levels. Physiological data in VR sports applications can influence game performance with the position preferred by users for displaying live physiological data. Gamification in VR biofeedback also has the potential to influence and moderate physiologic measures for VR media, providing opportunities to improve health and well-being. Future opportunities for AR and VR biofeedback may include further study, standardization, and implementation in clinical practice.

REFERENCES

[1] Lin, L. and Li, M., (2018). Optimizing learning from animation: Examining the impact of biofeedback. *Learning and instruction*, 55, pp.32–40.

[2] Kim, J.H., (2017). The effects of training using EMG biofeedback on stroke patients upper extremity functions. *Journal of physical therapy science*, 29(6), pp.1085–1088.

[3] Andrew Yimu Vassantachart M, Elizabeth Yeo M and, Brian Chau M. (2023) *Virtual and Augmented Reality-based Treatments for Phantom Limb Pain: A Systematic Review*

[4] Giggins, O.M., Persson, U.M. and Caulfield, B. (2013) Biofeedback in rehabilitation. *J NeuroEngineering Rehabil* 10, 60 . https://doi.org/10.1186/1743-0003-10-60

[5] Lalanza, J.F., Lorente, S., Bullich, R., García, C., Losilla, J.M. and Capdevila, L., (2023). Methods for heart rate variability biofeedback (HRVB): A systematic review and guidelines. *Applied Psychophysiology and Biofeedback*, 48(3), pp.275–297.

[6] Omejc, N., Rojc, B., Battaglini, P.P. and Marusic, U., (2019). Review of the therapeutic neurofeedback method using electroencephalography: EEG Neurofeedback. *Bosnian Journal of Basic Medical Sciences*, 19(3), p.213.

[7] Nagai, Y., Jones, C.I. and Sen, A., (2019). Galvanic skin response (GSR)/electrodermal/skin conductance biofeedback on epilepsy: A systematic review and meta-analysis. *Frontiers in neurology*, 10, p.377.

[8] Rosenberg, A. and Hamiel, D., (2021). Reducing test anxiety and related symptoms using a biofeedback respiratory practice device: A randomized control trial. *Applied Psychophysiology and Biofeedback*, 46(1), pp.69–82.

[9] Aritzeta, A., Soroa, G., Balluerka, N. *et al.* (2017). Reducing Anxiety and Improving Academic Performance Through a Biofeedback Relaxation Training Program. *Appl Psychophysiol Biofeedback* 42, 193–202 . https://doi.org/10.1007/s10484-017-9367-z

[10] Jenkins, S., Cross, A., Osman, H., Salim, F., Lane, D., Bernieh, D., Khunti, K. and Gupta, P., (2024). Effectiveness of biofeedback on blood pressure in patients with hypertension: systematic review and meta-analysis. *Journal of Human Hypertension*, 38 (10), pp.719–727.

[11] Andrew yimu vassantachart M, Elizabeth Yeo M and, Brian Chau M. (2023) *Virtual and Augmented Reality-based Treatments for Phantom Limb Pain: A Systematic Review.*

[12] Kan Yeung AW, Tosevska A, Klager E, Eibensteiner F, Laxar D, Stoyanov J, *et al.* (2021). Virtual and augmented reality applications in medicine: Analysis of the scientific literature. Vol. 23, *Journal of Medical internet Research. JMIR Publications Inc.*

[13] Laver KE, Lange B, George S, Deutsch JE, Saposnik G, Crotty M. (2027) Virtual reality for stroke rehabilitation. Vol. 2017, *Cochrane Database of Systematic Reviews.* John Wiley and Sons Ltd.

[14] Houzangbe S, Christmann O, Gorisse G, Richir S, Christmann Olivier, Richir Simon. *Effects of Voluntary Heart Rate Control on User Engagement and Agency in a Virtual Reality Game.* Available from: https://hal.science/hal-02507026

[15] Cipresso P, Giglioli IAC, Raya MA, Riva G. (2018). The past, present, and future of virtual and augmented reality research: A network and cluster analysis of the literature. *Front Psychol.* 6;9.

[16] Eijlers R, Utens EMWJ, Staals LM, De Nijs PFA, Berghmans JM, Wijnen RMH, *et al.* (2019). Systematic review and meta-analysis of virtual reality in pediatrics: Effects on pain and anxiety. Vol. 129, Anesthesia and Analgesia. Lippincott Williams and Wilkins. p. 1344–53.

[17] Blum J, Rockstroh C, Göritz AS. (2020) Development and Pilot Test of a Virtual Reality Respiratory Biofeedback Approach. *Applied Psychophysiology Biofeedback.* 45(3):153–63.

[18] Rahman MA, Brown DJ, Mahmud M, Harris M, Shopland N, Heym N, *et al.* (2023). Enhancing biofeedback-driven self-guided virtual reality exposure therapy through arousal detection from multimodal data using machine learning. *Brain Inform.* 10(1).

[19] Venuturupalli RS, Chu T, Vicari M, Kumar A, Fortune N, Spielberg B. (2019). Virtual Reality–Based Biofeedback and Guided Meditation in Rheumatology: A Pilot Study. *ACR Open Rheumatol.*1(10):667–75.

[20] Schoeller F, Bertrand P, Gerry LJ, Jain A, Horowitz AH, Zenasni F. (2019). Combining virtual reality and biofeedback to foster empathic abilities in humans. Vol. 9, *Frontiers in Psychology.* Frontiers Media S.A.

[21] Salazar SV, Pacchierotti C, De Tinguy X, MacIel A, Marchal M. (2020). Altering the stiffness, friction, and shape perception of tangible objects in virtual reality using wearable haptics. *IEEE Trans Haptics.*13(1):167–74.

[22] Weibel RP, Kerr JI, Naegelin M, Ferrario A, Schinazi VR, La Marca R, *et al.* (2023). Virtual reality-supported biofeedback for stress management: Beneficial effects on heart rate variability and user experience. *Comput Human Behav.*141.

[23] Maarsingh BM, Bos J, Van Tuijn CFJ, Renard SB. (2019). Changing Stress Mindset Through Stressjam: A Virtual Reality Game Using Biofeedback. *Games Health J.* 8(5):326–31.

[24] Liu Mingyu, Wang Jue, Yan Nan and Yang Qin, (2005). "Development of EEG biofeedback system based on virtual reality environment," *2005 IEEE Engineering in Medicine and Biology 27th Annual Conference, Shanghai*, pp. 5362–5364, https://doi.org/10.1109/IEMBS.2005.1615693.

[25] Kim H, Kim DJ, Kim S, Chung WH, Park KA, Kim JDK, *et al.* (2021). Effect of virtual reality on stress reduction and change of physiological parameters including heart rate variability in people with high stress: An open randomized crossover trial. *Front Psychiatry.* (2021).

[26] Weerdmeester J, Van Rooij MMJW, Granic I. (2022). Visualization, self-efficacy, and locus of control in a virtual reality biofeedback video game for anxiety regulation. *Cyberpsychol Behav Soc Netw.* 25(6):360–8.

[27] Schoeller F, Bertrand P, Gerry LJ, Jain A, Horowitz AH, Zenasni F. (2019). Combining virtual reality and biofeedback to foster empathic abilities in humans. Vol. 9, *Frontiers in Psychology. Frontiers Media S.A.*

[28] Tu L, Hao T, Bi C, Xing G. (2019). *BreathCoach: A Smart In-home Breathing Training System with Biofeedback via VR Game.* Available from: http://dx.doi.org/10.1016/j.smhl.xxxx.xx.xxx

[29] Chen, P.-J.; Penn, I.-W.; Wei, S.-H.; Chuang, L.-R.; Sung, W.-H. (2020). Augmented reality-assisted training with selected Tai-Chi movements improves balance control and increases lower limb muscle strength in older adults: A prospective randomized trial. *J. Exerc. Sci. Fit.* 18, 142–147.

[30] Mehrfard, A., Fotouhi, J., Taylor, G., Forster, T., Navab, N., and Fuerst, B. (2019). *A Comparative Analysis of Virtual Reality Head-Mounted Display Systems arXiv*: (1912.02913)

[31] Meng, Q.; Zhang, J.; Yang, X. (2019). Virtual rehabilitation training system based on surface emg feature extraction and analysis. *J. Med. Syst.* 43, 48

[32] Oswald, D., Kothgassner., Andreas, Goreis., Ines, Bauda., Lisa, Maria, Glenk., Anna, Felnhofer. (2022). Virtual reality biofeedback interventions for treating anxiety. *Wiener klinische Wochenschrift*, https://doi.org/10.1007/s00508-021-01991-z

[33] Caitlin, Newman. (2022). Commentary on: "Use of an EMG-controlled game as a therapeutic tool to retrain hand muscle activation patterns following stroke: A pilot study". *Journal of Neurologic Physical Therapy*, https://doi.org/10.1097/npt.0000000000000407

Technology for a Resilient Future – Vincent , Moorthy and Dasari (Eds)
© 2027 The Author(s), ISBN: 978-1-041-39070-1

Image-Based Approaches to Lung Infection Classification: Current Trends and Future Perspectives

P KavithaPandian and A Parivazhagan
Department of Computer Science and Engineering Kalasalingam Academy of Research and Education Krishnankoil, Tamilnadu, India

ABSTRACT: Segmentation of pneumonia lesions from Lung CT images has become vital for diagnosing the disease and evaluating the severity of the patients. The problem with such uses of CT scans, however, is that they are dependent on having trained radiologists to interpret them and increasing demand in outbreak hotspots would add more strain to local medical services. Using Artificial Intelligence (AI) based on Deep Learning (DL) to analyze the photos is one way to find a solution. This might assist physicians test for lung infections more quickly and with less knowledge. Only a few investigations have looked at DL's ability to automatically locate disease zones, despite the fact that many research efforts have demonstrated its ability to help with classifying diseases on CT scans. A challenge with using DL to complete this task, however, comes in the scarcity of annotated datasets on which to train neural networks. Several AI-based systems have been proposed for this task. However, some low-contrast abnormal zones in CT images make the task challenging. The researchers investigated image preprocessing techniques to accomplish this problem and to enable more accurate segmentation by the AI-based systems. The attempts of several researchers to locate illnesses on lung CT scans using single or hybrid approaches specifically, different neural networks (NN) are reviewed in this article. Additionally, it draws attention to the benefits, drawbacks, and results of traditional technology for locating diseased regions in lung CT scans. Furthermore, the importance and influence of the sophisticated NN in identifying lung CT pictures that have an infection and those that are not are examined.

Keywords: Lung infection, Pneumonia, Deep learning (DL), Image segmentation, Classification

1 INTRODUCTION

A lung infection, also known as a pulmonary infection, is a disease that affects either of the lungs. Lung infections can range from mild to severe and may need healthcare. An infection of the main bronchial tubes that carry air in and out of the lungs is known as bronchitis. Pneumonia is far more likely to be caused by a virus than by bacteria [1]. The seriousness of pneumonia along with other lung infections can range from severe to fatal. Those with compromised immune systems or long-term illnesses like chronic obstructive pulmonary disease (COPD) can suffer from symptoms that are worse. The most prevalent kinds of lung infections are shown in Figure 1. There is a wide range of illnesses that may result in pulmonary infections, and the etiology of each type tends to differ. While some diseases, like COPD, are primarily caused by environmental or behavioral aspects, such as tobacco use, others as well, like pneumonia, are caused by viruses. Some lung diseases, such as cystic fibrosis, cannot be prevented because they are inheritable [2]. Pneumonia is a disease that inflames the air sacs in one or both of the lungs. The several forms of pneumonia are depicted in Figure 2.

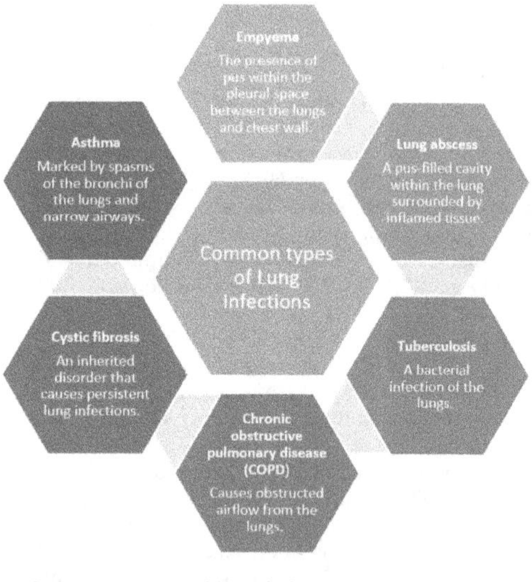

Figure 1. Common types of lung infections.

Pneumonia can cause the following indications [3]: high temperature, shivers, and tremors; sneeze that may generate green, yellow, or possibly bloody phlegm; breathlessness; limited, hasty breathing; piercing or intense sensation in the chest that worsens with deep breathing or coughing; weariness, fatigue, and appetite deficit. Lung infections are commonly diagnosed by diagnostic imaging procedures such as a chest radiography or Computed Tomography (CT) scan, spirometry, pulse oximetry, throat specimens, serum counts, and culture results, as well as by collecting a sample of discharged fluids for further examination.

CT and chest scans are the primary examinations needed for individuals who are experiencing or are suspicion of being suffering from a respiratory illness. CT is far more accurate and sensitive than ordinary film imaging, despite the fact that it isn't suggested for the very first examination of these individuals [4]. Frequently, a healthcare provider may prescribe a CT scan after seeing an abnormality in an X-ray. The CT scan helps detect lung illness and infection like a respiratory infection, tumors, hemorrhage, or smoking-related damage, even if it fails to deliver a conclusive diagnosis. CT scans are beneficial in identifying the site of infection or swelling that may be harming the lungs as a result of a deeper condition, including COPD. Although traditional lung infection categorizations are laborious and rely on radiologic skill, they are helpful in identifying distinct disease structures that could facilitate quick diagnosis, seriousness evaluation, and treatment predictions. An important first step in radiologic lung image interpretation is partitioning CT images, a computer-based process that divides the

 DOI: 10.1201/9781042017546-2

lung's borders from surrounding thoracic tissue [5]. Numerous techniques and software applications provide image segmentation strategies for assessing lung abnormalities; however, almost all of these methods are only useful if the lungs show minimal or no clinical illnesses [6]. Whenever a patient has moderate to serious sickness or abnormalities in the lungs with a challenging form or structure, computer-aided detection (CAD) systems can fail to identify anomalous parts of the lungs simply because of inaccurate segmentation approaches. Clinical image division is essential in the field of health care, particularly for diagnosis and treatment planning. It divides images into meaningful sections, often emphasizing specific physical traits or abnormalities [7]. By accurately identifying and characterizing malignancies, injuries, or pathogens, classification enhances rapid identification. Segmentation also facilitates tracking the progression of the disease and the effectiveness of treatments over time by examining separated parts at different stages. Furthermore, computational techniques reduce the randomness of conventional image processing, resulting in more accurate and consistent diagnostic results.

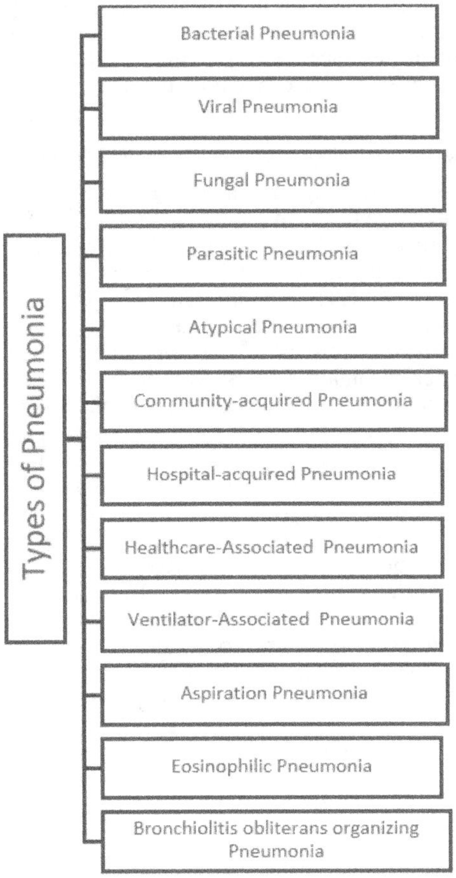

Figure 2. Various types of pneumonia.

The swift and accurate demarcation of significant anatomical features and diseased regions, such as organs, tissues, and tumors, are made possible by medical image segmentation, which is essential to contemporary healthcare [8]. Conventional techniques, either manual or semi-automated, can be laborious, prone to observer error, and have trouble processing complicated medical images. DL has become a potent tool for automating and enhancing the precision of medical picture segmentation in order to address these problems.

2 RELATED WORKS

2.1 *Lung disease identification using neural networks*

To overcome difficulties in correctly identifying and categorizing lung disorders using X-rays and CT scans, Singh *et al.* created a system [9]. CNNs are used by the technology to find complex features in medical imaging that individuals often overlook. The method's excellent precision and dependability in differentiating among lung illnesses and normal states are demonstrated by its findings. Nurcahyati *et al.* used DL and feature extraction to improve the detection of lung disease [10]. CNNs were used in a specific test, and CNNs and GLCM characteristics were used in another. The mean accuracy achieved by the suggested approach is 87%. According to the findings, CNN by itself outperformed the created combined in the classification of lung illnesses on X-rays. Ranjbarzadeh *et al.* utilized CT images of lung for rapid COVID-19 diagnosis, addressing challenges like similar neighboring tissues, unclear boundaries, and variable infections [11]. They proposed a two-route CNN to extract global and local features for classifying infected and normal tissues. On increasing the accuracy on classification, FCM and local directional pattern (LDN) encoding are employed to better capture complex patterns. Data augmentation was used to prevent overfitting due to limited samples and achieved a precision of 96%. Guo *et al.* developed an ANN model to predict lung infections in lung cancer patients undergoing chemotherapy [12]. Data from past cases were filtered using a logistic regression (LR) model, and significant variables were selected. The ANN model outperformed the LR model, with an area under the ROC curve of 0.897 ± 0.045, compared to 0.729 ± 0.084 for the LR model.

Akl *et al.* explored the quality of features extracted by DL for classifying COVID-19 CT scans using machine learning (ML) [13]. The study compared the performance of end-to-end DL models with DL for feature extraction followed by ML classification. They also examined fusing image descriptor features (e.g., SIFT) with DL-extracted features and introduced a new CNN trained from scratch. The outcomes implies that by using DL for feature extraction and ML for classification, it outperforms end-to-end DL models. Additionally, ensemble learning models outperformed traditional ML models. Fan *et al.* used Segmentation Deep Network (Inf-Net) to develop a computerized method for identifying diseased areas in chest CT data [14]. Inf-Net associates high-level features and creates a global map using a concurrent partial decoder. Additionally, it uses explicit edge-attention and implicit reverse attention to enhance feature representations and sharpen boundaries. A semi-supervised framework that uses a random propagation method that depends mostly on unlabeled data and a small number of labeled pictures is presented in order to address the lack of labeled data. This structure enhances proficiency and increases efficiency in learning. To handle small datasets, Muller *et al.* developed a method that utilizes variant COVID-19 databases [15]. Their system generates unique, randomly assigned image patches in real time using a range of preprocessing stages and significant data augmentation techniques. They achieved 76% Dice similarity coefficients (DSC) on CT scan segmentation by using a traditional 3D U-Net topology to minimize overfitting.

Employing DL methods, Aswathy and Vinod established a two-stage cascaded 3D U-Net for lung infection segmentation [16]. The lung parenchyma is segmented from preprocessed CT volumes by the first 3D U-Net, and those with infection are subsequently dissected by the second 3D U-Net after post-processing. By using this technique, doctors can look at the whole CT volume without having to manually mark the lung parenchyma. A combined lung disease detection approach that combines quantum classifiers and traditional CNN was created by Rao *et al.* [17]. CNN uses quantum variational circuits to develop two quantum ML approaches, Multi-Multi-Single (MMS) and Multi-Single-Multi-Single (MSMS), for feature extraction.

2.2 *Lung disease identification using thresholding method*

The Oulefki *et al.* developed an automatic tool for COVID-19 lung infection segmentation and measurement using chest CT scans [18]. The tool was tested on the COVID-CT-Dataset (275 CT scans) and new data from the EL-BAYANE Radiology Center. Using Efficient Kapur entropy-based multilevel thresholding, the method achieved accurate lesion heat-mapping, showing potential for clinical use. Zhao *et al.* proposed Renyi's entropy multi-threshold (MLT) using an enhanced Slime Mould Algorithm (DASMA) [19]. The diffusion mechanism (DM) is integrated to boost population diversity, reducing the risk of local optima, while an association strategy (AS) accelerates finding the optimal solution. This method is applied to MLT with a non-local means 2D histogram. Its effectiveness is validated by comparing it with well-known algorithms on the Berkeley segmentation dataset (BSD). To find areas of illness in lung CT scans, Khan *et al.* suggested a semi-automatic, threshold-based delineation technique [20]. In order to evaluate the intensity of COVID-19 and monitor the course of the illness in subsequent studies of CT scans, these illness masks are utilized to compute the percentage of lung abnormality (PLA). The approach achieved a mean accuracy of 47.49% and a specificity of 98.4%, outperforming existing methods of segmentation.

2.3 *Lung disease identification using clustering method*

Terwiel *et al.* used the self-reported medical records of ILD patients to examine connections among ILD and other lung illnesses [21]. ILD and non-ILD frequently cluster within families, according to logistic regression research. The study also found that self-reported emphysema and lung cancer among relatives can predict familial pulmonary fibrosis. Arumugam *et al.* proposed a system with five steps: image acquisition, preprocessing using a Wiener filter to enhance quality of the image, segmentation with Modified FCM clustering to locate ROI, feature extraction, and classification of nodules as benign or malignant [22]. The classification is done using a Random Forest Adaptive Neuro-Fuzzy Classifier. Zhao *et al.* proposed a DL and clustering model combining a Deep Belief Network (DBN) with Fuzzy C-Means (FCM) to cluster lung cancer patients based on CT images [23]. To address feature homogenization in DBN, the Winner-Take-All (WTA) concept was introduced to enhance the DBN structure. FCM then generated initial cluster labels using the representations learned by the WTA-DBN. The results suggest potential applications in lung cancer pathogenesis and personalized cancer therapy.

2.4 *Lung disease identification using optimization method*

Lakshman Narayana *et al.* analyzed various nature-inspired computational models for segmenting lung images in detecting COVID-19 and other health issues [24]. The study recommends the best-performing classifier for accurate diagnosis. Ashwini *et al.* introduced two models, as Classification-1 detects lung diseases, while Classification-2 classifies different types of lung diseases [25]. Hyperparameters and model architectures were optimized using grid search. The models achieved 99.82% accuracy in Classification-1 and 98.75% accuracy in Classification-2, surpassing previous research. This improved performance helps medical professionals diagnose and treat patients more quickly and effectively. Kumar *et al.* utilized the NIH chest X-ray image dataset from the Kaggle repository to diagnose lung diseases [26]. The chest X-ray images were preprocessed using contrast-limited adaptive histogram equalization filtering. Features were extracted using the empirical wavelet transform method and fed into a Self-Attention based Generative Adversarial Capsule (SA-Caps GAN) classifier for disease detection. The Sunflower Optimization Algorithm was implemented for optimizing the SA-Caps GAN classifier's hyperparameters.

2.5 *Lung disease identification using deep learning method*

A DL-based technique for assessing and segmenting lung infection regions and volumetric ratios was created by Shan *et al.* [27]. The method demonstrated a 91.6% DSC and a 0.3% mean inaccuracy in determining the proportion of infection (POI) for the entire lung when tested on 300 chest CT images from COVID-19-infected people. In order to classify lung illness, Sriporn *et al.* used 5,810 pictures for training and validation using well-known models including MobileNet, Densenet-121, and Resnet-50 [28]. To modify the dataset for better learning with these CNN models, a rotational approach was used. According to the evaluation, Densenet-121 obtained an overall accuracy, recall, precision, and F1 score of 98.88% when paired with the Mish activation function and Nadam optimizer. Employing X-ray and CT scan pictures, Jasmine *et al.* created a system for identifying and categorizing lung diseases [29]. Given an accuracy of 98.43% and an F1 score of 98.55%, the structure demonstrated great accuracy, proving the effectiveness of the suggested approach over conventional techniques.

2.6 *Lung disease identification using hybrid method*

A method for segmenting and classifying lung images into healthy and unhealthy groups was put out by Prasad *et al.* [30]. There are two stages to the system's operation. Preprocessing is done to eliminate disturbances, texture features are extracted, features selected via a crow search optimization technique, and an ANN is used to classify the images in the initial stage. The fuzzy K-means technique is used to cluster the cancerous and non-tumor regions from the aberrant images. An SVM classifier is used in the following step to lower the false positives. Rajinikanth proposed an image-assisted system to extract COVID-19-infected areas from lung CT scans (coronal view) through a series of steps: (i) a threshold filter to isolate the lung region and remove artifacts, (ii) image enhancement using Harmony-Search-Optimization and Otsu thresholding, (iii) segmentation to identify infected regions, and (iv) extraction of features from ROI to assess severity [31]. The method helps pulmonologists with identifying and preparing for treatment while lowering the diagnostic workload in bulk assessments by calculating the pixel ratio among lung and infection regions to establish the infection intensity.

There are two primary stages to Poloju and Rajaram's technique optimization [32]. To improve algorithm performance, bagging, voting ensemble learning, and boosting approaches are first used. Emperor Penguin Optimization (EPO) is then applied to enhance system performance by optimizing parameters. The findings show that integrating ensemble learning and EPO with SVM outperformed other hybrid approaches, achieving 97.50% accuracy. A paradigm to forecast lung conditions like COVID-19 and pneumonia from lung X-rays was proposed by Goyal and Singh [33]. Histogram equalization and median filtering both help to increase image resolution. For precise chest ROI extraction, an improved region-growing method with dynamic region selection and morphological procedures was created. For accurate disease detection, visual, shape, texture, and intensity characteristics are taken from each ROI and standardized.

The survey highlights the following key points:

- The development of lung disease detection approaches, from sophisticated deep learning models to conventional image processing methods.
- A comparison of various CNN architectures and how well they classify lung diseases.

- The way model efficacy and adaptability are affected by dataset amount and quality.
- Difficulties in managing imaging environment variability and preparing medical images.
- The significance of explainability and interpretability in medical AI systems.
- The shortcomings of current methods and opportunities for development.

3 CHALLENGES FACING IN CONVENTIONAL APPROACHES

A number of factors can affect the precision, usefulness, and effectiveness with traditional lung infection identification methods.

Algorithms find it difficult to get understanding and effectively generalize due to the minimal quantity of numerous lung disease screening samples. The imbalance between healthy and sick people in the datasets may have distorted the results. Clinical scan noise and distortions might obscure important features and complicate diagnosis. Dissimilar imagery quality brought on by modifications to imaging equipment and settings may have an impact on algorithm efficacy. Because lung infections may appear in a variety of methods, it might be difficult to determine pertinent features employing conventional techniques. Multiple individuals may have distinct illnesses, which makes feature extraction and classification more difficult. Traditional algorithms may perform poorly when applied to fresh or unexplored data because they overfit to the training set. Recent illnesses or advancements in imaging technologies could be difficult for conventional methods to handle. A lot of traditional techniques call on physical involvement, making them laborious and susceptible to mistakes. Proper identification frequently relies on subjective evaluation and specialist expertise, both of which might be unreliable. Modifications in patient details, radiological circumstances, or illness presentations may be difficult for methods to handle. Algorithms that have been trained on particular datasets may not function effectively in a variety of clinical situations or various demographics.

3.1 *Publicly available lung infection image datasets*

Several datasets are freely (publicly / open access) available in internet for the access of researchers to challenge themselves on developing algorithms to identify and segment or classify the infections present in the images. Also, few image datasets are supported with ground truth images to determine the correctness of detection of the proposed algorithm by comparing the outcomes with the given ground truth images.

Some popular datasets that contain images of various lung infections are mentioned below.

ChestX-ray8: This dataset contains over 100,000 chest X-ray images labeled with various lung illnesses.

RSNA Pneumonia Detection Challenge: This dataset includes 88,923 chest X-ray images from patients with pneumonia and 10,240 images from healthy controls.

COVID-19 Radiography Dataset: This dataset contains over 10,000 chest X-ray images from patients with COVID-19, pneumonia, and healthy controls.

LUNA16: This dataset contains 11,892 CT scans of the lung from patients with lung cancer.

Kaggle Lung Cancer Detection: This dataset contains 1,095 chest X-ray images of patients with lung cancer and 874 images of healthy controls.

Scientists and programmers developing algorithms for the identification and categorization of lung infections can benefit greatly from these datasets. They offer a wide range of photos with different degrees of sickness severity and image quality, enabling reliable model training and assessment.

4 METHOD SUGGESTED TO DETECT LUNG INFECTION

Hybrid classifiers combine different ML & DL approaches to increase efficiency, particularly on difficult tasks like recognizing and classifying lung illnesses from clinical images.

- By combining the benefits of different approaches, hybrid models can get higher classification accuracy when compared to separate approaches. For example, combining CNNs with traditional classifiers like SVM can improve feature representation and decision-making.
- Images of lung infections can vary significantly depending on a number of factors, such as imaging parameters and patient information. Because hybrid techniques are more robust to these differences, they can enhance generalizability across a range of datasets.
- Hybrid classifiers are able to capture a greater range of valuable properties by mixing deep information gathered by neural networks with handcrafted features from traditional image processing techniques.
- Different classifiers have different advantages; CNNs are great at extracting spatial characteristics, whereas decision trees are strong at handling non-linear relationships. By combining them, the system's overall efficiency can be increased.
- By combining several approaches, hybrid classifiers might reduce the risk of overfitting to training data since they can gather information from multiple perspectives on the data.
- Experts can experiment with different approach combinations and optimize for specific datasets or objectives since hybrid models provide flexibility in architecture layout.
- Some hybrid systems employ interpretable and black-box models to help physicians understand the reasoning behind classifications, which is crucial in healthcare environments.

All things thought out, hybrid classifiers have the potential to improve the identification and categorization of lung infections, which will support better healthcare decision-making.

5 CONCLUSION

Recent developments have shown how well CNN can handle challenging tasks including recognizing objects, segmentation, and classification. Because CNNs can learn hierarchical representations of raw input data without depending on manually created features, they have attained state-of-the-art performance in various domains. Medical image interpretation has been greatly impacted by these developments in DL and ML, particularly in the identification and classification of lung illnesses. Numerous studies investigated alternative approaches and strategies for recognizing lung problems in medical images, contributing to the large amount of research on the topic. The present research provides an in-depth examination of the many techniques professionals employ to recognize lung conditions in medical images. The limitations of conventional techniques are also discussed, as well as the challenges investigators have in identifying and classifying pictures of infected lungs. The combination of designs is suggested as a feasible direction for future research into the identification and classification of images of sick lungs in the study's conclusion. The integrated approach has proven to perform better in several medical picture classification tasks, creating a solid foundation for further research in lung disease identification. The investigation provides informative comments on the current status of lung ailment diagnosis using medical images, as well as a direction for future research in this important area of medicine.

REFERENCES

[1] Plut, D., Winant, A.J., Mahomed, N., Sodhi, K.S., Kasznia-Brown, J., Williams-Weekes, T., Daltro, P., Das, K.M. and Lee, E.Y., (2024). Unusual pediatric lung infections: imaging findings. *Pediatric Radiology*, *54*(4), pp.516–529.

[2] Halpin, D.M., (2024). Mortality of patients with COPD. *Expert Review of Respiratory Medicine*, *18*(6), pp.381–395.

[3] Turdieva, D., (2024). Clinical aspects of pneumonia in newborns. *Science and innovation*, *3*(D3), pp.212–217.

[4] Chen, J., Li, Y., Guo, L., Zhou, X., Zhu, Y., He, Q., Han, H. and Feng, Q., (2024). Machine learning techniques for CT imaging diagnosis of novel coronavirus pneumonia: a review. *Neural Computing and Applications*, *36*(1), pp.181–199.

[5] Alam, S.S., Anwar, A.S., Ashraf, M.S., Ayrin, F.J., Roy, P., Quader, M.A. and Quader, M.A., (2024), May. Deep Learning Analysis of COVID-19 Lung Infections in CT Scans. In *2024 International Conference on Advances in Modern Age Technologies for Health and Engineering Science (AMATHE)* (pp. 1–5). IEEE.

[6] Azad, R., Aghdam, E.K., Rauland, A., Jia, Y., Avval, A.H., Bozorgpour, A., Karimijafarbigloo, S., Cohen, J.P., Adeli, E. and Merhof, D., (2024). Medical image segmentation review: The success of u-net. *IEEE Transactions on Pattern Analysis and Machine Intelligence*.

[7] Yao, W., Bai, J., Liao, W., Chen, Y., Liu, M. and Xie, Y., (2024). From cnn to transformer: A review of medical image segmentation models. *Journal of Imaging Informatics in Medicine*, pp.1–19.

[8] Rayed, M.E., Islam, S.S., Niha, S.I., Jim, J.R., Kabir, M.M. and Mridha, M.F., (2024). Deep learning for medical image segmentation: State-of-the-art advancements and challenges. *Informatics in Medicine Unlocked*, p.101504.

[9] Singh, A.P., Singh, A., Kumar, A., Agarwal, H., Yadav, S. and Gupta, M., (2024). Development of an artificial neural network-based image retrieval system for lung disease classification and identification. *Engineering Proceedings*, *62*(1), p.2.

[10] Nurcahyati, I., Saragih, T.H., Farmadi, A., Kartini, D. and Muliadi, M., (2024). Classification of Lung Disease in X-Ray Images Using Gray Level Co-Occurrence Matrix Method and Convolutional Neural Network. *Journal of Electronics, Electromedical Engineering, and Medical Informatics*, *6*(4), pp.332–342.

Technology for a Resilient Future – Vincent , Moorthy and Dasari (Eds)
© 2027 The Author(s), ISBN: 978-1-041-39070-1

SmartPlaylist: Leveraging Machine Learning for Intelligent Music Recommendations and Dynamic Playlist Curation

Rishabh
Division of Computer Science and Engineering, Karunya Institute of Technology and Sciences, Coimbatore, Tamil Nadu, India

Hepzibah Christinal and R Hepzibah
Department of Mathematics, Karunya Institute of Technology and Sciences, Coimbatore, Tamil Nadu, India

ABSTRACT: In the world of digital music, song reference schemes are essential for tackling the problems of personalisation and information overload. For the betterment of the user experience and get around the drawbacks of current methods, where the user selects a playlist with a lot of music videos that contain harmful URLs, the work shows the implementation and contribution of a unique song reference schemes. The SmartPlaylist highlights the project's contributions to song reference schemes and gives a summary of its design, methods, and main conclusions. Users are finding it more and more difficult to find and discover novel composition which syncs with their tastes due to the enormous amount of music content created by the exponential rise of digital music platforms. This idea highlights the rapid increase in both the quantity and seriousness of network information insecurity concerns. One step in executing these attacks is to utilise malware affected Uniform Resource Locators (URLs) to deceive customers by having them click on maliciously infected audio and video links. In order to overcome this difficulty, song reference schemes have become an essential tool. They use a variety of strategies to offer tailored recommendations and improve the user experience. A song reference schemes called Curated Playlist aims to push the boundaries of this field. This concept contributes to a larger framework of research on song reference schemes, in which songs in the system would not be downloaded with viruses or malware.

Keywords: Uniform Resource Locators, Deep Learning, Algorithms, Artificial Intelligence, ML, Intelligent Automatic Playlist Generation, Text Analysis, CNN

1 INTRODUCTION

The way people listen to and engage with music has been significantly impacted by the growing popularity of music streaming services. Nevertheless, even if many of the services have effective recommendation systems, they are primarily hidden connections that are utilised in applications. Consequently, a more individualised method of music delivery will be made possible by a real-time knowledge of the URLs [1]. To better satisfy a user's musical needs by combining the recommendation system that generates a collection of songs with the capability to identify harmful URL users. Using the most recent artificial intelligence technology that works with natural texts for URL identification and choosing the right songs depending on user input, this work suggests a unified method to address this issue. The suggested system makes use of cutting-edge methods including CNNs for text recognition, BERT for text analysis, and a hybrid recommendation system for song recommendation [2]. With Firebase serving as the backend and a URL detection system, all of these are seamlessly integrated into a web-based application created using contemporary technologies like React.js, Vite, and Tailwind CSS [3–5].

2 RELATED WORKS

It has long been researched and used to identify malicious URLs using signature sets [6–8]. In most of these investigations, lists of known malicious URLs are employed. Every time a new URL is requested, a database query is executed. Until a URL is blacklisted, it is considered safe; after that, it is considered malicious and a warning is generated. This strategy's main drawback is that it will be extremely challenging to identify new malicious URLs that are not in the list.

Over time, researchers and practitioners have been investigating various methods to enhance the precision and customisation of song reference schemes [9]. In order to find comparable users and provide recommendations based on their interests, collaborative filtering techniques make use of user-item interaction data. Content-based filtering techniques examine the intrinsic qualities of music, including metadata and aural characteristics, to recommend products with comparable attributes [10]. These strategies are used in hybrid ways to overcome each of their own limitations and capitalise on their strengths [11,12]. Song reference schemes continue to confront a number of obstacles, such as scalability constraints, data sparsity, and cold-start problems, despite the field's improvements [13]. The creation of SmartPlaylist was spurred by the need for creative solutions that may overcome these obstacles and improve the user experience.

It is incredibly time-consuming and difficult to construct and manage a huge playlist. According to the work, the music player itself chooses a song based on the system's secure URL [14]. The program creates safe URL-based playlists by scanning and categorising audio files based on audio characteristics. Deep learning and machine learning algorithms are used in the application [15]. However, the current algorithms are slow, use more hardware (such as sensors and EEG structures), and have far worse accuracy, all of which raise the system's overall cost. In order to save time and labour compared to doing this procedure manually, the study provides an algorithm that automatically creates an audio playlist based on user preferences and safety [16]. The algorithm presented in the research aims to lower the system's overall computing time and cost. It also seeks to increase the system design's correctness. Both user-dependent and user-impartial datasets are used to validate the system's URL detection module [17].

The paper highlights the malware detection system where the playlist for listening to the songs is being targeted for the cyber-attacks. The working is as follows where the user enters the song name in the search box. The search engine searches for the song using a machine learning algorithm called Random Forest Algorithm. The name e.g., 'We Don't Talk Anymore' is being entered then the tokenization of the song i.e., 'We', 'Don't', 'Talk', 'Anymore' is done. The tokens are then sent for search engine where the results including all the keywords are displayed inside the algorithm. The options are accessed by the algorithm and the feature extraction part is done of the Universal Resource Locator. If the Universal Resource Locator displays the malicious URL then it is blocked immediately otherwise it is passed on for the song database. Once, the safe URL is accessed for the Recommended Playlist, then the song is played.

An outline of the domains that the machine learning methods touch is provided in the introduction. The primary sources used for this research project are explained in the related works section. Subsections of the approach use flow diagrams to explain each step of the process. The project's implied methodologies are described in depth in the implementation section. The achieved results are discussed in the results and discussion. The entire concept and the work that needs to be done in the days ahead are summed up in the conclusion.

3 METHODOLOGY

- Training stage: As in Figure 1, to detect harmful URLs, both clean and malicious URLs must be collected. Following that, attribute extraction is done and all malicious and clean URLs are properly marked [18]. These features will be the most effective means of differentiating between malicious and clean URLs. Dataset is then divided into two subsets, training data for training machine learning algorithms and testing data for the testing process. If the machine learning model performs well in classification (high classification accuracy), it will be used in the detection step.

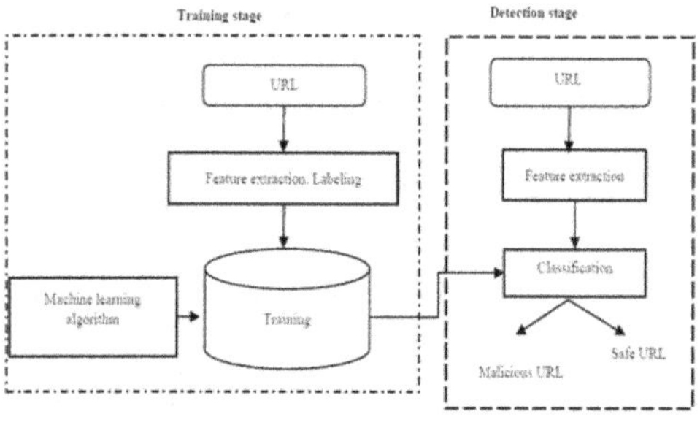

Figure 1. Malicious URL detection model using machine learning.

- Phase of detection: Each input URL goes through this stage. First, an attribute extraction process will be applied to the URL [19,20]. These characteristics are then used by the classifier to assess if the URL is clean or malicious.

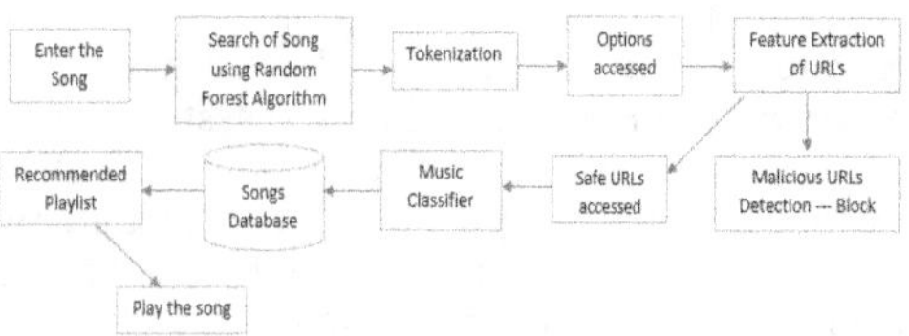

Figure 2. Flow diagram of smartplaylist.

As in Figure 2, 'Enter the Song' where the user is supposed to enter his song in the text box given in the output screen. The 'Search of Song using Random Forest Algorithm' option give the user a chance to assess the song for its URLs. A Flutter frontend with a Node.js and Express.js backend, combined with Gemini AI for sophisticated text refinement, is used in the implementation of AI by Technical Coding and Code Solutions. The system makes use of CNN-based Link Recognition. The songs which need to be detected, first needs to be split into separate keywords so that the relevant results can be displayed. 'Tokenization' is what comes into the picture now. E.g., 'We Don't Talk Anymore' song is entered by the user. The backend algorithm will look for the keywords 'We', 'Don't', 'Talk', 'Anymore' separately. The results from the songs having keywords 'We' will be displayed first, similarly for the remaining keywords [21]. 'Options Accessed' is the section where all the options would be accessed for its match with the original input i.e., 'We Don't Talk Anymore' in our case. The perfect match songs will be sent for the further process. 'Feature Extraction of URLs' section does its part where the URLs of the songs are accessed and they are split as per their Internet Protocol address.

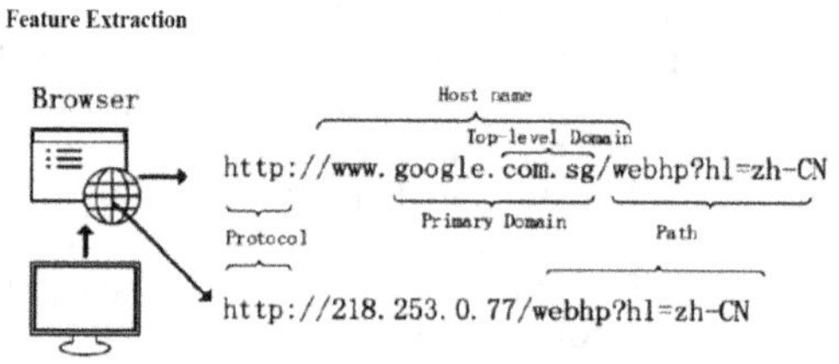

Figure 3. Split of the internet protocol address.

Internet resources are referred to via the Uniform Resource Locator (URL). Figure 3, describes the features and two basic components of the URL: the protocol identifier, which chooses which protocol to use, and the resource name, which gives the IP address or domain name where the resource is located. It is clear that each URL adheres to a specific structure and pattern. Attackers often try to change one or more aspects of the URL structure to fool people into sharing their malicious URL [22]. Using the Kaggle dataset, we constructed the Convolutional Neural Network model. There are 24176 song links in the training dataset and 6043 in the testing dataset [23]. In FER-2013, every song link is identified as belonging to one of four categories: phishing, malware, viruses, or cyber threats. The system gathers metadata and audio characteristics from music databases, as well as user listening statistics from many music streaming services. The recommendation engine and user profiles are constructed using this data.

'Malicious URLs Detection' option successfully detects the URLs which are affected by either a malware or ransomware or virus or any phishing or cyber security threats [24]. The URLs which are having any malicious content are blocked by the algorithm and fed into the history of the user search as well so that the next search for the same song won't access the malicious link again. 'Safe URLs accessed' option proceeds with the link which is safe for the SmartPlaylist. 'Music Classifier' picks the song with the best quality and pushes it further to the 'Songs Database' where the song is registered and forwarded to the 'Recommended Playlist'. Here, the song is stored in the favourites played by the user. 'Play the song' where the song is played for the user.

4 IMPLEMENTATION

As in Figure 4, 'Enter Search Box' is where the user opens the search box where he enters the song. 'User Enter Text Input' is the stage where the song is entered into the text box. To obtain a playlist of songs, enter the name of the song and click the provided link. 'Tokenization' is the stage song entered is split into words which will follow on to the 'URLs accessed'. The suggested system then uses various algorithms to identify the connections; if the link has a negative value, a playlist with the best types of music will be shown, which is made possible by the feature extraction of the URLs. The link is instantly removed from the music recommendation algorithm if it contains a positive value. The malicious ones are blocked and the safe ones are passed to 'Playlist Curation Engine' which is the main player for the playing the song exactly as per the user input using its two handles i.e., 'Text-tagged' where it tags the key-words and extracts the plausible options from the user and sends to 'Spotify API'. 'Spotify API' calls that are efficient in order to reduce response time. techniques for handling errors to guarantee reliable functioning. 'Personalized Playlist Accessed' where curation engine checks for the song if already requested by the user in the playlist option. If not then it searches for the song otherwise and 'Delivered to the User' option gives the liberty to play the song to the user [25]. The proposed approach benefits us by presenting interaction between the user and the music player. The system's goal is to collect harmful links and songs that are entered with the current choices.

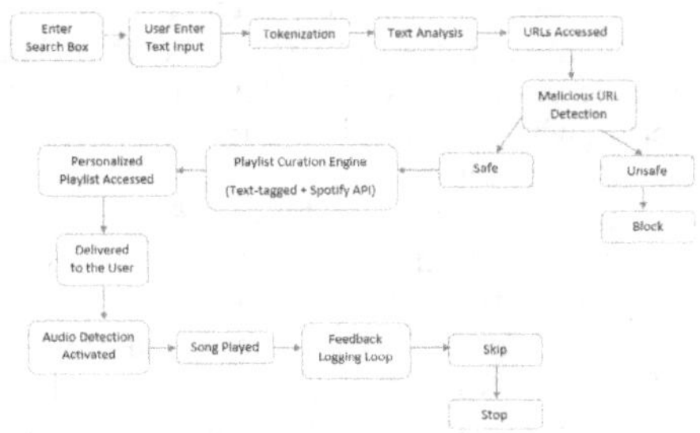

Figure 4. Block diagram of the proposed system.

'Audio Detection Activated' is the stage where the song can be played and the sound can be heard as well. 'Song Played' option plays the song. 'Feedback Logging Loop' is the option which gives access to the user to replay the same song or enter a new song by clicking on the option 'Skip' and the whole process would restart. The user when doesn't want the system to run then it can click 'Stop' to end the loop.

5 RESULTS AND DISCUSSION

Figure 5. shows the robustness of the trained models that includes a variety of URL types, including benign, phishing, defacement, and malware. Figure 6 shows what type of malicious link it is and the address of it which can be blocked thereafter.

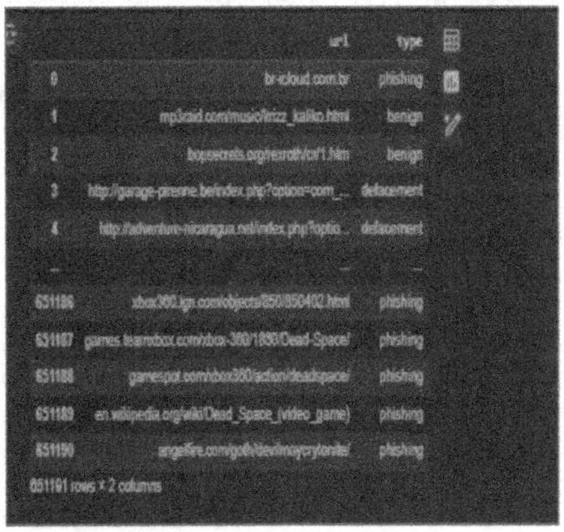

Figure 5. Entering the URL.

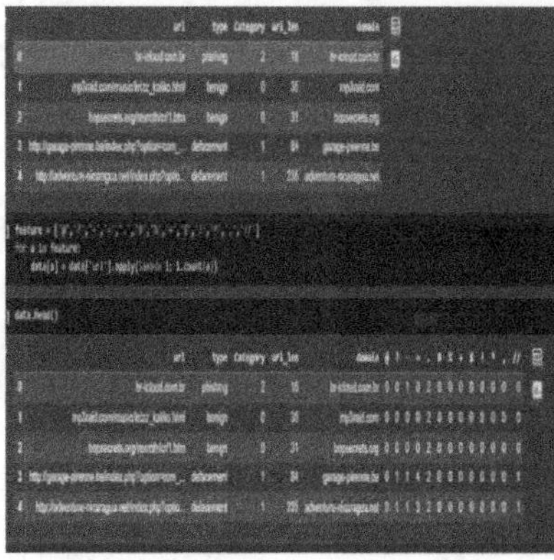

Figure 6. Showing the malicious URL.

Moreover, the notion leverages clear and intuitive visualizations like, ROC curves in Figure 7, and confusion matrices Figure 8 to analyze the results, making the findings obvious and comprehensible. The efficacy of the chosen features and pre-processing pipeline was validated by the notable high accuracy attained by models such as Random Forest and Extra Trees.

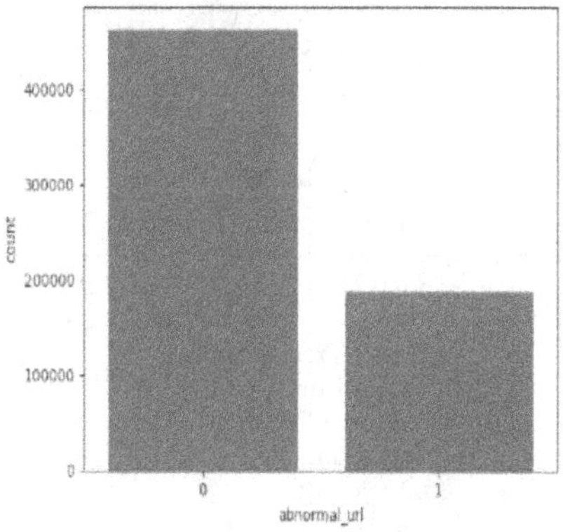

Figure 7. Count of the abnormal_url along the URLs.

The count indicates the number of abnormal URL i.e., malicious URLs which are detected of the given dataset loaded into the code. The '0' indicates the positive values i.e., the link does contain some kind of malware whereas the '1' indicates the link does not contain malware and is safe to be used further.

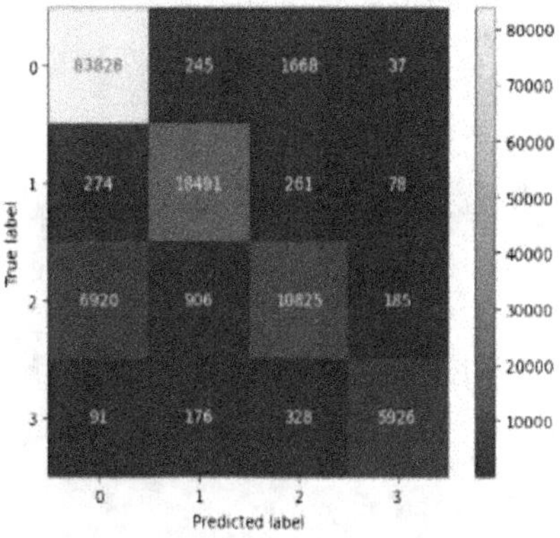

Figure 8. The predicted label showing the Malicious URLs.

The above label is constructed based on the confusion matrix where the patches i.e., '83828', '18491', '6920', '10825', '5926', indicate that the following values have malicious virus present in them. It gives warning to the user prior to the clicking on the malicious links.

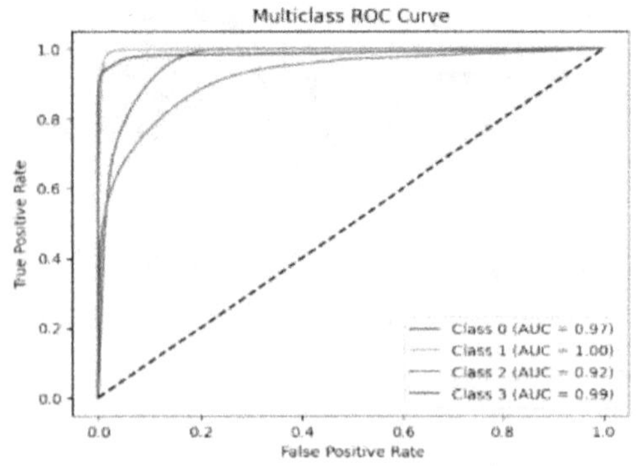

Figure 9. Comparison of the positive rate and the negative rate.

In Figure 9, Multiclass ROC (Receiver Operating Characteristic) curve plot indicates the comparison between the positive rate and the negative rate where the positive rate indicates the malicious links whereas the negative rate indicates the safe links.

Table 1. Various Models along with their accuracy rate.

S.No.	Model	Accuracy
0	Decision Tree Classifier	0.909282
1	Random Forest Classifier	0.914872
2	AdaBoost Classifier	0.820077
3	KNeighbours Classifier	0.889618
4	SGD Classifier	0.804897
5	Extra Trees Classifier	0.914626
6	Gaussian Naïve Bayes	0.789548

Table 1 has comparison of several machine learning classifiers, such as Random Forest, Decision Tree, K-Nearest Neighbours, AdaBoost, and Naïve Bayes, which is a key strength of this concept. A deeper comprehension of the advantages and disadvantages of each model is made possible by this thorough assessment. From the given data, it is evident that Random Forest Classifier holds the highest accuracy and is best suited for training the model.

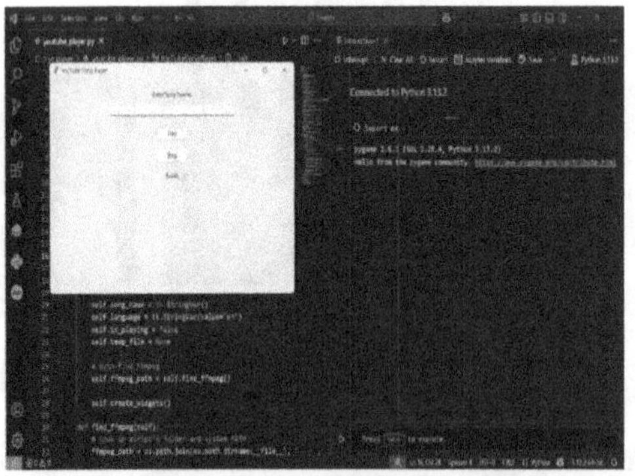

Figure 10. The system asking user to enter song name.

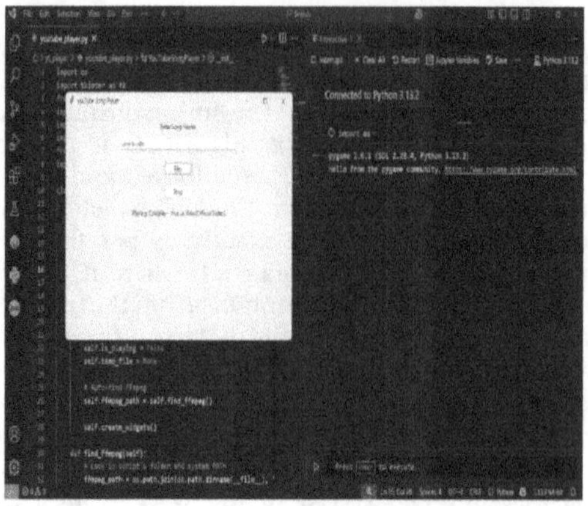

Figure 11. Song name entered and played.

In the above two figures, Figure 10, gives the user the option to enter the song name and he/she presses the play button. The song then plays. Figure 11, the front page also offers the option of 'Skip' where the user if not satisfied can enter another text in the text column. The back end is explained in the initial part of the results section where the malicious links are investigated and eliminated from the playlist.

Novel Applications and Specialized Enhancements are that the song playlist recommendation system in this study is subjected to machine learning techniques. These algorithms are appropriate for making use of our newly chosen features for malicious URL detection in the suggested malicious URL detection system. Random Forest is used in this work as an example to show how well the entire detection system performs; as soon as the song name is submitted, the link detection system is activated.

The Smart Playlist performs the feature of preventing cyber-attacks like phishing, malware, virus and hacking using the Universal Resource Locator where the e-mail Id of the user is attached to the playlist or the contact number is attached to the playlist. Both the details are susceptible to cyber-attack. So, Smart Playlist filters those malicious URLs and keeps the safe URL in the 'Recommended Playlist' system.

The Smart Playlist has a weakness that it is only applicable to the songs which are downloaded by YouTube application. It further has dataset limitation as only a couple of songs can be trained and loaded into the dataset.

6 CONCLUSION

SmartPlaylist's technical implementation, including its system architecture, contextual intelligence integration, link recognition using multi-modal AI. It highlights the platform's creative, flexible, and safe design while going over playlist creation logic, user feedback loops, scalability tactics, and data privacy precautions. The SmartPlaylist system's creation and deployment show that combining cybersecurity with AI-powered music recommendation is both feasible and successful by precisely creating an intelligent system that can recognise malicious URLs like malware, phishing, and defacement websites. Each module's successful validation attests to the system's technical dependability, and its modular architecture guarantees scalability and practical adaptability. All things considered, the research establishes a solid basis for future developments by assessing a labelled dataset of URLs and extracting a number of pertinent information, such as URL length, special characters, HTTPS presence, shortening service use, and embedded IP addresses. The method effectively creates AI-curated playlists based on user preferences by fusing contextual awareness with dangerous link identification.

Numerous machine learning models, such as Random Forest, Decision Tree, K-Nearest Neighbours, AdaBoost, and Naïve Bayes classifiers, are trained using these features. Metrics including accuracy, confusion matrix, and ROC curves are used to assess the models' efficacy. The best result was obtained using ensemble techniques like Random Forest.

Like any new technology, it does have limitations, though, which present opportunities for improvement and creativity. Testing scalability with larger datasets and adding class imbalance handling strategies, such as SMOTE or class weights, to enhance performance on under-represented categories could further refine the concept. Furthermore, adding a real-time URL detection interface or API would improve the project's usefulness. Overall, this concept stands out as a skilfully done and perceptive academic effort and shows a solid knowledge of both the theoretical and practical components of machine learning in cybersecurity.

Deep learning methods, such neural network-based recommendation models, could improve the system's capacity to identify intricate links and patterns in the music data. Furthermore, adding multi-modal information from other data sources, such user contextual data and social media activities, may result in recommendations that are even more interesting and tailored. Since song reference schemes must take into account the constantly expanding music catalogues and changing user preferences, it will also be essential to investigate the project's architecture's scalability and adaptability. This system might be advanced by looking at ways to easily combine Jukebox with other music platforms and services. The system's future capability would include a mechanism that might aid in the treatment of individuals with mental stress, anxiety, acute depression, and trauma via music therapy.

REFERENCES

[1] Sharrab, Y.O., Attar, H., Eljinini, M.A.H., Al-Omary, Y. and Al-Momani, W.A., (2025). Advancements in speech recognition: A systematic review of deep learning transformer models, trends, innovations, and future directions. *IEEE Access*.

[2] Bevilacqua, A., Saviano, P., Amirante, A. and Romano, S.P., (2024). Whispy: Adapting STT Whisper Models to Real-Time Environments. *arXiv preprint arXiv:2405.03484*.

[3] Chakravarty, A., (2024). Deep Learning models in speech recognition: measuring gpu energy consumption, impact of noise and model quantization for edge deployment. *arXiv preprint arXiv:2405.01004*.

[4] Sudarshan, A., Samuel, V., Patwa, P., Amara, I. and Chadha, A., (2023). Improved contextual recognition in automatic speech recognition systems by semantic lattice rescoring. *arXiv preprint arXiv:2310.09680*.

[5] Alastruey, B., Drude, L., Heymann, J. and Wiesler, S., (2023). Multi-view frequency-attention alternative to cnn frontends for automatic speech recognition. *arXiv preprint arXiv:2306.06954*.

[6] Jiang, H., Zhang, L.L., Li, Y., Wu, Y., Cao, S., Cao, T., Yang, Y., Li, J., Yang, M. and Qiu, L., (2023). Accurate and structured pruning for efficient automatic speech recognition. *arXiv preprint arXiv:2305.19549*.

[7] Ramanathan, R., Kumaran, R., Rohan, R.R., Gupta, R. and Prabhu, V., (2017). An intelligent music player based on emotion recognition. In *2017 2nd International Conference on Computational Systems and Information Technology for Sustainable Solution (CSITSS)* (pp. 1–5). IEEE.

[8] Kallam, S. and Kannan, M.J., BRM,.(2024). A novel authentication mechanism with efficient math based approach. *International Journal of Intelligent Systems and Applications in Engineering*, *12*(3), pp.2500–2510.

[9] Balajee, R.M., Kallam, S. and Kannan, M.J., (2024). Network intrusion classifier with optimized clustering algorithm for the efficient classification. In *2024 5th International Conference on Intelligent Communication Technologies and Virtual Mobile Networks (ICICV)* (pp. 439–446). IEEE.

[10] Alrihaili, A., Alsaedi, A., Albalawi, K. and Syed, L., (2019). Music recommender system for users based on emotion detection through facial features. In *2019 12th International Conference on Developments in eSystems Engineering (DeSE)* (pp. 1014–1019). IEEE.

[11] Jayanthi, M.K., (2017). Strategic planning for information security-DID mechanism to befriend the cyber criminals to assure cyber freedom. In *2017 2nd International Conference on Anti-Cyber Crimes (ICACC)* (pp. 142–47). IEEE.

[12] Kavitha, E., Tamilarasan, R., Baladhandapani, A. and Kannan, M.K., (2022). A novel soft clustering approach for gene expression data. *Computer Systems Science & Engineering*, *43*(3).

[13] RM, B. and MK, J.K., (2023). Intrusion detection on AWS cloud through hybrid deep learning algorithm. *Electronics*, *12*(6), p.1423.

[14] Naik, H. and Kannan, M.K., (2020). A survey on protecting confidential data over distributed storage in cloud. *Available at SSRN 3740465*.

[15] Kavitha, E., Tamilarasan, R., Poonguzhali, N. and Kannan, M. K., (2022). Clustering Gene expression data through modified agglomerative M-CURE hierarchical algorithm. *Computer Systems Science & Engineering*, *41*(3).

[16] Kumar, K.S. and Kannan, M.J., (2024). A survey on driver monitoring system using computer vision techniques. In *International Conference On Innovative Computing And Communication* (pp. 253–262). Singapore: Springer Nature Singapore.

[17] Kannan, M.J., (2017). A bird's eye view of cyber crimes and free and open source software's to detoxify cyber crime attacks-an end user perspective. In *2017 2nd International Conference on Anti-Cyber Crimes (ICACC)* (pp. 232–237). IEEE.

[18] Jain, P., Rajvaidya, I., Sah, K.K. and Kannan, J., (2022). Machine learning techniques for malware detection-a research review. In *2022 IEEE International Students' Conference on Electrical, Electronics and Computer Science (SCEECS)* (pp. 1–6). IEEE.

[19] Balajee, R.M. and MK, J.K., (2021). Performance analysis of bag of password authentication using python, java and PHP implementation. In *2021 6th International Conference on Communication and Electronics Systems (ICCES)* (pp. 1032–1039). IEEE.

[20] Preema J.S, Rajashree, Sahana M, Savitri H, Review on facial expression-based music player, *International Journal of Engineering Research & Technology (IJERT)*, ISSN-2278–0181, Volume 6, Issue 15, (2018).

[21] Dr.M.K. Jayanthi and Sree Dharinya, V., (2013), Effective retrieval of text and media learning objects using automatic annotation, *World Applied Sciences Journal*, Vol. 27 No.1, 2013, © IDOSI Publications, 2013, DOI: 10.5829/idosi.wasj.2013.27.01.1614, pp.123–129. https://www.idosi.org/wasj/wasj27(1)13/20.pdf

[22] AYUSH Guidel, Birat Sapkota, Krishna Sapkota, Music recommendation by facial analysis, February 17, 2020.

[23] Dr. Naila Aaijaz, Dr. K. Grace Mani, Dr. M.K. Jayanthi Kannan and Dr. Veena Tewari (Feb 2025), The Future of innovation and technology in education: Trends and opportunities, ASIN : B0DW334PR9, S&M Publications, Mangalore, Haridwar, India-247667, ISBN-13 : 978–8198488824,https://www.amazon.in/gp/product/B0DW334PR9/ref=ox_sc_act_title_1?smid=A2DVPTOROMUBNE&psc=1#detailBullets_feature_div

[24] Python for Data Analytics: Practical Techniques and Applications, Dr. Surendra Kumar Shukla, Dr. Upendra Dwivedi, Dr. M K Jayanthi Kannan, Chalamalasetty Sarvani ISBN: 97893-6226-727-6, ASIN : B0DMJY4X9N, JSR Publications, 23 October 2024, https://www.amazon.in/gp/product/B0DMJY4X9N/ref=ox_sc_act_title_1?smid=A29XE7SVTY6MCQ&psc=1

[25] CH. sadhvika, Gutta.Abigna, P. Srinivas reddy, (2020). Emotion-based song reference schemes , Sreenidhi Institute of Science and Technology, Yamnampet, Hyderabad; *International Journal of Emerging Technologies and Innovative Research (JETIR)* Volume 7, Issue 4.

Link of Dataset:

https://www.kaggle.com/datasets/maharshipandya/-spotify-tracks-dataset

Technology for a Resilient Future – Vincent , Moorthy and Dasari (Eds)

River Water Quality Analysis and Object Detection

M Sandhiya, L Leena Jenifer, K Indumathi, and M Janani
Rajalakshmi Engineering College

ABSTRACT: River water quality analysis and prediction have greatly improved with the combination of AI and machine learning. In this study we predict important water quality indicators like pH, dissolved oxygen, turbidity, and pollution levels using ensemble machine learning methods, such as Gaussian Naïve Bayes, Support Vector Machines (SVM), and Extra Tree Classifier. High prediction accuracies of 93.8% and 95.2% and 98.3 % were attained by these models. We also use deep learning- based object detection approaches to improve environmental monitoring even more. The models showed a very high prediction accuracy of 93.8%, 95.2%, and 98.3% respectively. To further improve environmental monitoring, we further use deep learning-based object detection methods in RCNN, YOLOv5, and YOLOv8 for underwater object detection with accuracies of 95.0%, 96.2%, and 97.5%. Combining both object detection and machine learning offers a comprehensive framework for holistic river health evaluation and effective environmental management.

Keywords: River water quality, YOLOv8, object detection, machine learning algorithms, pollution monitoring

1 INTRODUCTION

Water quality analysis of a river and detection of objects are very essential for sound environmental management and pollution management. Monitoring river health is critical for water quality management and ecosystem maintenance. Traditional methods are small in scale and do not provide real-time data. With greater public involvement, photos taken by citizens constitute an important but untapped resource. This research proposes an AI-driven framework with deep learning models for automatic labelling of images, classifying them, and detecting objects to classify river health indicators from such images. The method enhances the quality of data, completes gaps in monitoring, and promotes community engagement in environmental governance.

Employment of photos taken by citizens, analyzed using AI, enables real-time evaluation of river health indicators. AI models enable automatic annotation of river health indicators, enhancing the quality of reporting as well as cutting costs linked to conventional monitoring technique. Floating waste in river water is a serious environmental hazard, requiring precise and effective detection techniques. Though most current methods address river conditions in a general manner, this research aims particularly at detecting floating waste with the use of a decoupled diffusion network (DDN). The proposed approach improves object detection accuracy through decoupling feature learning and diffusion processes, enabling better localization and classification of waste objects. Moreover, a new box renewal approach is introduced in the inference phase to increase detection precision further. In contrast to typical river health research, in this study, the entire focus is on waste detection, and thus it provides a specialized and efficient solution for river pollution management.

As global water pollution and its effects on public health remain an escalating concern , new technologies are coming into play to combat these issues. Artificial intelligence and machine learning are revolutionizing how we monitor and control the environment. This allows the authorities and environmental stakeholders to implement timely, preventive measures ensuring access to clean water, minimizing health threats, and promoting sustainable management of resources. With this regard, we propose the underwater waste sorting classification detection system- a secure , web-based system designed with Django and YOLOv8. It ensures real- time detection and classification of underwater items, aiding in enhancing waste tracking and conservation activities. YOLOv8 is a deep learning model with exceptional accuracy in recognizing and categorizing waste in underwater environments. The system automates waste detection and classification, facilitating the identification of recyclable materials and harmful pollutants, promoting timely intervention and effective recycling practices.

2 LITERATURE SURVEY

In the modern era, analyzing water quality is an essential approach because water is indispensable for human survival. However, a number of pollutants pose serious risks to them, as they can negatively impact human health, the atmosphere, and water quality[1]. The paper reviews challenges in traditional water quality assessment caused by human activities, industrialization, and manual data collection processes. To address these challenges, researchers have investigated the models like ANN and SVM. These models seek to improve water quality monitoring systems' precision, effectiveness, and automation. [2]. Water quality is vital for sustaining life and maintaining ecological balance. This paper emphasizes the importance of meeting water quality standards for various applications like irrigation, industry, and ecosystem preservation. To address this, the study proposes a data-driven approach that integrates sensor data, historical records, and environmental factors. Real-time monitoring of parameters like pH, dissolved oxygen, and turbidity supports effective management and future research [3]. This study conducts an exploratory data analysis (EDA) on the Bhavani River's water quality, examining 27 parameters collected over five years from 11 different sampx`ling sites. A total of 10,560 data records were analyzed to identify both temporal and spatial trends in pollution. The primary objectives were to identify pollution sources, detect anomalies, and support predictive modeling. The research highlights the importance of thorough data preprocessing in enhancing the effectiveness of river water quality assessments [4]. An IoT-based system was developed to monitor the water quality of the Ganga and Sangam rivers over 15 months. Key parameters such as electrical conductivity, pH, and dissolved oxygen were measured. The results showed that the Ganga River had comparatively better water quality, making it more suitable for irrigation and fisheries. However, limitations

DOI: 10.1201/9781042017546-4

include high experimental demands and unsuitability for drinking due to moderate oxygen levels [5].

This research assesses the Leneng River's water quality by analyzing data collected from three designated sampling locations and employing the Pollution Index (IP) approach. The analysis, based on environmental parameters, indicates the river is lightly polluted overall. The primary objective is to assess pollution levels at various river locations using a standardized index [6]. The study used the Ave River for checking the quality of the water through a combination of physicochemical, biological, and microbiological analyses. To assess the presence of microorganisms, methods including PCR-DGGE and antibiotic susceptibility tests were used. The study points out the critical role of integrating microbiological and biological evaluations for a comprehensive analysis[7]. The Ganga River's water quality is investigated in this study using statistical techniques. It analyzes dissolved oxygen, temperature, pH, and coliform levels. The research also considers spatial variation in water quality to improve management methods. The study finds that temperature and dissolved oxygen are negatively correlated [8].

This research presents an improved fuzzy matter-element (IFME) method for assessing river water quality. It combines the variable coefficient method, set pair analysis, and traditional methods. The goal is to increase the assessment's objectivity and accuracy [9]. The research investigates the water quality of the Gadarchay River basin by analyzing 14 key parameters. To interpret the data effectively, nonlinear principal component analysis (NLPCA) was applied in combination with various multivariate analytical techniques like PCA, PFA, CA, and DA. The goal was to identify pollution sources and assess how NLPCA compares to traditional methods. However, the approach had slower processing times with large datasets and tended to overestimate performance in smaller classes. The findings support improved strategies for managing water quality in river basins [10,11].

3 PROPOSED METHODOLOGY

To manage real-time data acquisition, processing, and analysis, the suggested AI-driven water quality prediction system has a modular and scalable architecture. The following are the system's main parts:

(a) Data preparation and Cleaning: Data preparation is necessary to deal with noise, outliers, and missing values. Methods like data normalization and imputation are used to guarantee data consistency.

(b) Accuracy is defined as the proportion of correctly classified samples out of the total number of samples.

$$\text{Accuracy} = (\text{TP} + \text{TN})/(\text{TP} + \text{TN} + \text{FP} + \text{FN}) \quad (1)$$

(c) Precision determines the proportion of correctly predicted positive instances out of the total predicted positives.

$$\text{Precision} = \text{TP}/(\text{TP} + \text{FP}) \quad (2)$$

(d) Recall measures how well the model identifies actual positive instances.

$$\text{Recall} = \text{TP}/(\text{TP} + \text{FN}) \quad (3)$$

(e) The F1-score is the harmonic mean of precision and recall, providing a balanced measure that reflects both aspects of a model's performance.

$$\text{F1 Score} = 2 * (\text{Recall} * \text{Precision})/(\text{Recall} + \text{Precision}) \quad (4)$$

(f) River water Quality Analysis using Machine Learning Module: General ML algorithms such as Random Forest, Gradient Boosting Model (GBM), and K-Nearest Neighbors (KNN) have been found to produce favourable results in the forecasting of water quality parameters [14]. The outputs from ML models can guide water resource management plans and predict ecological shifts in river basins [15].

4 SUPPORTING MACHINE LEARNING ALGORITHMS

(a) Support Vector Machine (SVM): SVM is an effective supervised learning algorithm commonly applied to classification problems, such as predicting water quality. In this context, Support Vector Machine (SVM) classifies water quality data by identifying the most suitable hyperplane that effectively distinguishes between categories like "safe" and "polluted."

(b) Extra Trees Classifier: It is an ensemble-based classification technique widely applied in water quality prediction. The method constructs multiple decision trees during the training phase, with each tree generated using randomly selected features and varying split points. This incorporation of randomness enhances the model's robustness and predictive accuracy. In water quality prediction, the Extra Trees Classifier analyzes input data (e.g., pH, turbidity, and pollutant levels) to predict whether water quality meets certain standards or if contamination is likely. The algorithm excels in handling large datasets with high dimensionality, which is common in environmental monitoring. Reducing overfitting due to its randomization process, improving generalization on unseen data.

(c) Naïve Bayes algorithm: It is a probabilistic machine learning method based on Bayes' theorem, assuming that the features (input variables) are normally distributed (Gaussian) and independent of each other. In water quality prediction, NB is used to predict specific water quality parameters such as pH levels or pollutant concentrations.

Figure 1 illustrates that past data are processed and used to tune models like SVM, Gaussian Naive Bayes, and Extra Tree Classifier. The optimized model is then evaluated for accuracy and used to predict water quality.

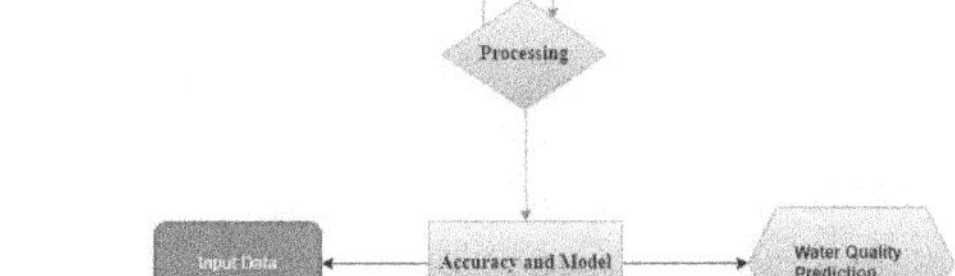

Figure 1. Flowchart of Water quality prediction using machine learning classifiers.

5 DEEP LEARNING-BASED OBJECT DETECTION FOR RIVER WATER MONITORING

When analyzing the quality of water, object detection is crucial. It detects various contaminants and alien materials in water. Techniques like computer vision and deep learning have been applied to increase the efficiency and accuracy of detection. To improve pollution monitoring, this research suggests a modified YOLO algorithm for identifying and categorizing trash on water surfaces. The model outperforms current object detection techniques in terms of accuracy[12]. The work presents CRB-Net, a new deep learning-based object detector. It includes a benchmark dataset of 7,467 photos for recognizing objects on water surfaces. The study evaluates 16 object detection techniques, including ShipYolo and Yolov3-2SMA, which are specifically designed to identify surface targets. This addition supports improved monitoring of waterborne objects in aquatic environments [13]. The Underwater Waste Sorting Classifications Detection System employs the use of YOLOv8 . YOLOv8 is a state-of-the-art real-time deep learning framework that has recorded high performance and accuracy in regions where rapid real-time decision-making is needed.

The Figure 2 outlines a waste sorting system where datasets are used to train a YOLOv8 model with OpenCV tuning; the selected model is then tested and applied to automate waste sorting and recycling.

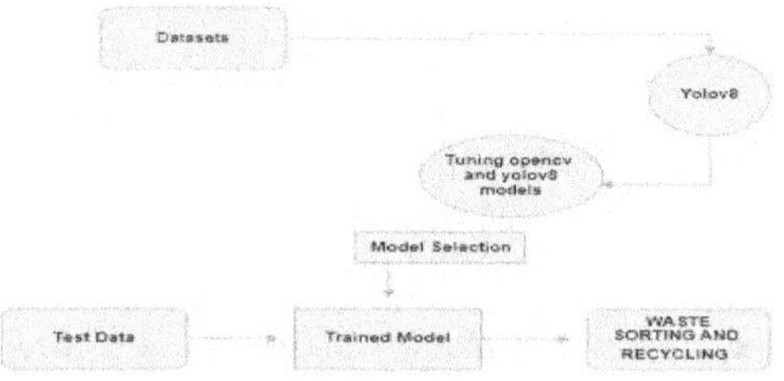

Figure 2. Illustrates that past data are processed and used to tune models like SVM, Gaussian.

6 IMPLEMENTATION AND DISCUSSION

The deep learning model is trained using a dataset of river images and videos that contain various pollutants like plastic bags and other substances. The model is designed to detect and classify these contaminants based on their visual characteristics.

The underwater waste sorting system was implemented using OpenCV for real-time processing of images and videos, and a RESTful API with the YOLOv8 model. Interactive real-time visualizations were provided through Chart.js.

Figure 3 illustrates the confusion matrix, highlighting that the majority of predictions align accurately with the actual labels for Class 0 and Class 1. The classification report demonstrates high values for precision, recall, and F1-score in both classes, with an overall accuracy of 98.3%, indicating strong model performance in distinguishing between the two categories.

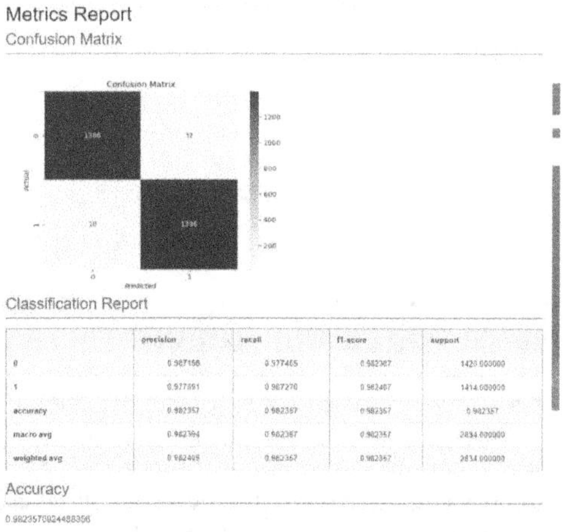

Figure 3. Performance metrics report with confusion matrix and classification report.

7 PROPOSED SYSTEM OBJECT DETECTION

The proposed system for River Water Quality Analysis and Object Detection provides an integrated approach to monitor and protect river ecosystems. The system monitors critical water quality metrics such as acidity levels, oxygen concentration, water clarity, and contamination levels, enabling a comprehensive assessment of river health over time. The incorporation of machine learning models trained on past water quality datasets increases predictive value and ensures timely alerts to any changes in water composition that could be harmful. In addition to water quality monitoring, the system allows the detection of trash and physical objects in real-time within the river, like bottle, electronic waste, etc. The inception of an environment like OpenCV with the YOLOv8 deep learning model will ensure fast and accurate classification of objects for authorities to take sudden actions to mitigate environmental risks. The system will facilitate waste sorting and classification within the waste management process through YOLOv8 for the real-time identification of various waste categories, including recyclables, organics, and general waste.

Figure 4 demonstrates a live underwater waste detection system using object detection, where a plastic bag (pbag) is identified with 79% confidence. A camera interface enables users to capture real-time frames for analysis. The setup supports efficient monitoring of submerged waste materials.

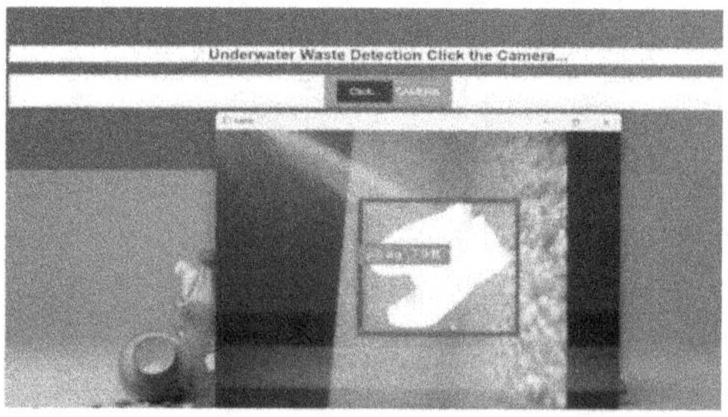

Figure 4. Real-time underwater waste detection using camera interface.

8 RESULTS AND DISCUSSIONS

The study emphasizes the potential of machine learning algorithms, especially neural networks, in environmental monitoring and the potential of AI-driven methods in river water quality prediction. By identifying pollutants early, these algorithms can shield aquatic ecosystems and stop waterborne illnesses. Data dependency and feature extraction complexity are still issues, though. The suggested underwater waste sorting and classification detection system incorporates Django for a web based scalable framework and YOLOv8 for quick object detection. This system uses computer vision to identify and categorize different kinds of waste, including electronics, plastic bags, and bottles. Public participation will be improved by real-time data visualization and feedback systems, which will increase awareness of marine pollution and promote environmentally friendly waste disposal practices. However, the accuracy of detection can be impacted by underwater environmental factors like turbidity, object occlusion, and variations in lighting.

Figure 5 the bar chart shows that Ex7tra Tree Classifier achieves the highest accuracy and lowest error, followed by SVM and Naive Bayes, indicating superior performance in classification tasks.

Figure 6 reveals that YOLOv8 achieves the highest accuracy and lowest error among the three models, followed by YOLOv5 and RCNN, indicating its superior detection performance.

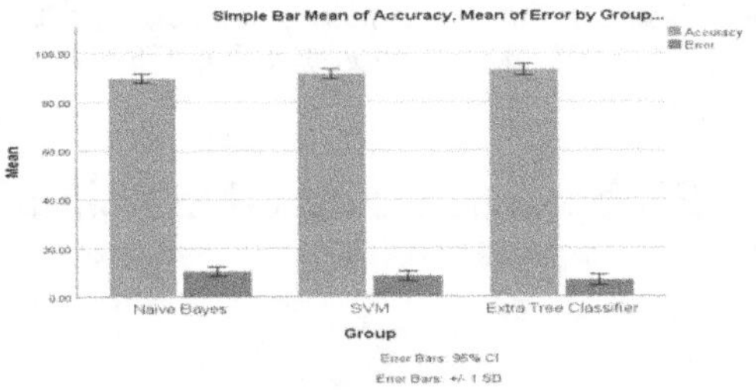

Figure 5. Comparison of accuracy and error rates for Naive Bayes, SVM, and extra tree classifier.

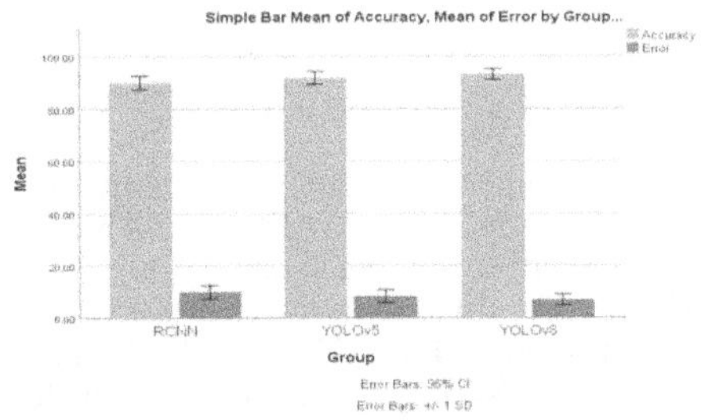

Figure 6. Comparison of accuracy and error rates across rCNN, YOLOv5, and YOLOv8 models.

9 CONCLUSION AND FUTURE WORK

Artificial intelligence (AI) is revolutionizing water quality prediction using machine learning (ML) techniques. This technology allows for personalized water quality forecasts, enabling pollution prevention and health security. The system uses advanced algorithms and data analytics to analyze unlimited data from sensors and historical information, enhancing its predictive capacity. The application of ML helps humans study water quality dynamics, supporting sustainable water resource management and policymaking. The Underwater Waste Object Detection System with YOLOv8 model, integrated into Django, is a significant development in environmental protection. It detects various types of underwater waste, enhancing waste management systems and promoting sustainable approaches to aquatic ecosystems. The integration with Django provides a robust data management platform for stakeholder decision making. Future developments may include deploying models in cloud platforms to enhance scalability and accessibility, along with integrating IoT devices for real-time monitoring. Emphasis can also be placed on optimizing real-time processing to minimize latency in underwater waste sorting and recycling classification systems.

REFERENCES

[1] Gandhimathi, G., Chellaswamy, C. and Thiruvalar Selvan, P., (2024). Comprehensive river water quality monitoring using convolutional neural networks and gated recurrent units: A case study along the Vaigai River. *Journal of Environmental Management*, *365*, p.121567.

[2] Kalaivanan, K. and Vellingiri, J., (2022). Survival study on different water quality prediction methods using machine learning. *Nature Environment & Pollution Technology*, *21*(3).

[3] Lavanya, J., and Sivakumar, N. (2024). Predicting water quality using machine learning techniques. In *2024 5th International Conference on Image Processing and Capsule Networks (ICIPCN)* (pp. 554–560). IEEE.

[4] Nair, J.P., and Vijaya, M.S. (2022). Exploratory data analysis of Bhavani river water quality index data. In *Proceedings of International Conference on Communication and Computational Technologies: iCCCT 2022* (pp. 971–987). Singapore: Springer Nature Singapore.

[5] Kumar, M., Singh, T., Maurya, M.K., Shivhare, A., Raut, A., and Singh, P.K. (2023). Quality assessment and monitoring of river water using IoT infrastructure. *IEEE Internet of Things Journal*, 10(12), 10280–10290.

[6] Supardiono, S., Hadiprayitno, G., Irawan, J., and Gunawan, L. A. (2023). Analysis of River water quality based on pollution index water quality status, Lombok District, NTB. *Jurnal Penelitian Pendidikan IPA*, 9(3), 1602–1608.

[7] Barbosa-Vasconcelos, A., Mendes, Â., Martins, F., Lopes, E., Machado, A., Bordalo, A.A., Vaz-Pires, P., Vieira, N., Martins da Costa, P. and Bessa, L.J., (2018). River water analysis using a multiparametric approach: Portuguese river as a case study. *Journal of Water and Health*, 16(6), pp.991–1006.

[8] Bagla, P., Kumar, K., Sharma, N. and Sharma, R., (2021). Multivariate analysis of water quality of Ganga River. *Journal of The Institution of Engineers (India): Series B*, 102(3), pp.539–549.

[9] Wang, Y., Ran, W., Wu, L., and Wu, Y. (2019). Assessment of river water quality based on an improved fuzzy matter-element model. *International Journal of Environmental Research and Public Health*, 16(15), 2793.

[10] Rezaali, M., Karimi, A., Moghadam Yekta, N. and Fouladi Fard, R., (2020). Identification of temporal and spatial patterns of river water quality parameters using NLPCA and multivariate statistical techniques. *International Journal of Environmental Science and Technology*, 17(5), pp.2977–2994.

[11] Yavuz, V.S., Kartal, V., and Sambito, M. (2024). Comparative Analysis of Water Quality in Major Rivers of Türkiye Using Hydrochemical and Pollution Indices. *Water*, 16(18), 2676.

[12] Gawande, J.P., Borase, R.P., and Pawar, S.N. (2023). Water Surface Waste Object Detection and Classification. In *Computational Intelligence in Image and Video Processing* (pp. 55–68). Chapman and Hall/CRC.

[13] Zhou, Z., Sun, J., Yu, J., Liu, K., Duan, J., Chen, L., and Chen, C.P. (2021). An image-based benchmark dataset and a novel object detector for water surface object detection. *Frontiers in Neurorobotics*, 15, 723336.

[14] Alabdeli, H., Pareek, P.K., Shivaraj, S., Rupavath, R.V.S.S.B., and Das, A. (2024). Prediction of River Water Quality Index and Uncertainty Analysis using Machine Learning Techniques. In *2024 First International Conference on Software, Systems and Information Technology (SSITCON)* (pp. 1–5). IEEE.

[15] Zheng, Y., Wang, J., Ryzhkov, S., Nechai, O., Topalov, A., Zivenko, O., ... and Harasymiv, T. (2024). Computer system for forecasting water quality parameters based on machine learning. In *Proceedings of the Bulgarian Academy of Sciences* (Vol. 77, No. 11, pp. 1629–1638).

Performance Evaluation of Inter-AS MPLS Layer 3 VPN System Using GNS3 Simulation

Bhagyashri Thorat
Dr. Babasaheb Ambedkar Technological University (DBATU)

P. J. Deore
R C Patel Institute of Technology, Shirpur

A. B. Nandgaonkar and S. B. Deosarkar
Dr. Babasaheb Ambedkar Technological University (DBATU)

ABSTRACT: As a recent development, MPLS improves forwarding efficiency by using label switching, making it suitable for controlled traffic handling in large networks. For problems related to multiple Autonomous Systems (AS), Inter-AS MPLS Layer 3 VPNs provide scaling solutions. In this paper, we concentrate on the Inter – AS MPLS Layer 3 VPNs using option A (Back-to-Back VRF) with Cisco 7200 routers in GNS3. This paper gives a detailed simulation topology along with the evaluation of metrics like latency and packet loss between different customer sites. The simulation results show that Inter-AS MPLS provides stable and practical connectivity between remote sites. With acceptable latency and minimal packet loss, this approach is suitable for academic use and small to medium enterprise deployments.

Keywords: MPLS, Inter-AS VPN, Option A, GNS3, BGP, VRF, Latency, Packet Loss

1 INTRODUCTION

The growth and globalization of businesses and other enterprises has created a profound need for securely connecting geographically dispersed sites [15]. VPNs, or virtual private networks, have appeared as a flexible and easily expandable method for committing secure communication over shared infrastructures. VPNs logically partition the public or common networking structure to form a secure virtual tunnel that permits remote and branch offices to access private services or files situated in any part of the world [1].

VPNs were initially embraced deferring large organizations but would gradually evolve into a more widely available commodity, for individuals and enterprises, seeking a means of achieving data confidentiality and integrity alongside secure access over public networks. In the context of OSI model, various classes of VPNs have emerged, L1, L2 and L3 being the most common. L2VPNs, for example, Virtual Private LAN Services (VPLS), are specialized in frame relay and multipoint communication over pseudo-wires [2]. These services are more straightforward and easier to work with than L3VPNs which use routing protocols and MPLS to virtualize the full IP layer [3].

L1VPNs have also become increasingly capable to accommodate the increasing need for bandwidth-hungry services, making use of Generalized Multiprotocol Label Switching (GMPLS) for routing and signaling [11]. This facilitates integration of optical transport technologies such as SONET/SDH and OTN [4][5]. Every type of VPN possesses a specific set of requirements and standards established by the IETF [14] to guarantee interoperability and functionality across platforms.

Both L2VPNs and L3VPNs, despite the differences, face shared challenges of provisioning cost, scalability, and particularly security. Virtual private LAN Service (VPLS), however, while being efficient on operational cost, is prone to scalability issues with the requirement of full mesh in flat architecture. To improve scalability in VPLS, a hierarchical structure using user-PE and network-PE routers is commonly adopted to minimize the pseudo-wire count and enhance performance [6][7]. The security environment of VPLS is still an active research area. VPLS attacks can be categorized into two categories: control plane and data plane [25]. Although countermeasures are proposed separately, a single solution has not been achieved. In this regard, the Host Identity Protocol (HIP)-based security framework for VPLS (HIPLS) by Henderson *et al.* provides an additional security plane for additional protection [12]. In comparison to the previously stated L2 and L1 approaches, it is noted that L3VPNs, especially those implemented over multiple Autonomous Systems (AS), have emerged due to adding higher scalability, QoS support, and control over routing domains. The provider boundary deployments are supported by IETF-defined Inter-AS options (A, B and C). This paper focuses on Option A (Back-to-back VRF) which is the simplest and most conservative of the three. It keeps the MPLS domains isolated while allowing BGP peering to be performed at the border routers with routing label flow cutting off at the AS border domain [3].

The findings of the simulation confirm Option A as a feasible and reliable solution for enterprises requiring multi-domain VPN interconnections, particularly when a network model employing a multi-site service provider was developed.

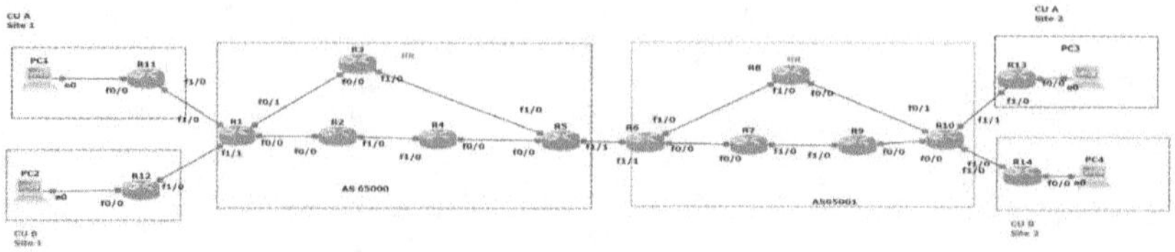

Figure 1. Simulation setup for inter-AS system 65000 and 65001.

DOI: 10.1201/9781042017546-5

1.1 *Topology overview*

As illustrated in Figure 1, the network simulation encompasses two customers (Customer A and B), each with two geographically separated sites, connected by a dual-AS MPLS Backbone with inter-AS VPN capabilities. To improve scalability and simplify iBGP configuration, Route Reflectors R3 & R8 have been positioned, and LDP is used to enable MPLS forwarding through the core routers. Each CE is connected to its PE Switch via Fast Ethernet, and the PEs are configured with distinct VRFs (VRF_A and VRF_B). Inter-AS VPN connectivity is accomplished by employing MP-BGP with VPNv4 address families and using Route Distinguishers and Route Targets for effective route partitioning and communication.

The topology shown in Figure 1 was verified by establishing end-to-end IP connectivity between customer site 1 VPN and site 2 VPN using ping and trace command. Traffic isolation was ensured such that CU A and CU B remained logically separate also provides security and authentication, even when traversing shared MPLS infrastructure. The ping utility and routing table inspection (show ip route vrf <VRF_NAME>) confirmed

2 SIMULATION SETUP FOR INTER-AS SYSTEM

To examine the effectiveness and scalability of the MPLS Layer 3 VPN utilizing OSPF for AS 65000 and RIPv2 available frameworks of MPLS-VPN and VPLS by concentrating on performance and security. for AS 65001 with practical exact results in a real-world scenario that A varies from each AS to different inter domain routing protocol ISP configurations, a GNS3 simulated proper route propagation and VRF isolation is tested for further investigation of network performance.

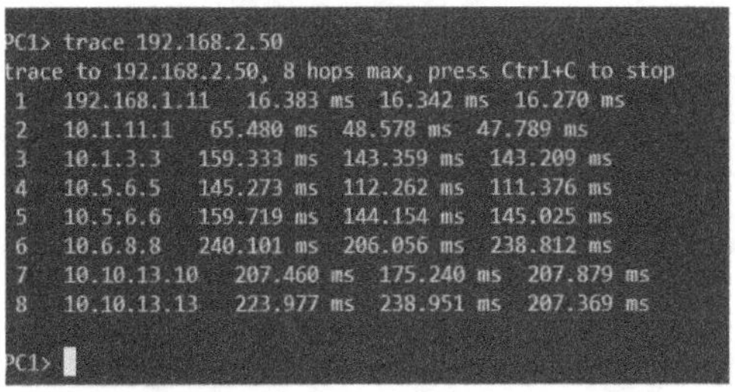

Screenshot 1. Trace between PC1 (CU A Site 1) and PC3 (CU A Site 2).

3 RESULTS AND ANALYSIS

To determine the performance of the MPLS protocol for Inter-AS system, in this paper parameters are Latency(ms) from Site 1 to Site 2, packets per hop loss. For VPNs, bandwidth is already assigned, so the main concern is latency and packet loss. That's why in VPNs, latency and packet loss parameter analysis is important.

The simulation was performed in GNS3 environment using cisco 7200 router confirmed using the traceroute command run from the end hosts at all customer locations to their respective remote destinations. This helped in observing how packets moved through each router and how the delay changed across hops. The round-trip times (RTTs) ensured MPLS Layer 3 VPN route propagation verification. The objective was to provide full end-to-end reachability across the MPLS backbone and, in addition, monitor performance behaviour under configured routing conditions. The ping command is used to test PC1 (CU A site 1) to PC3 (CU A site 2). For analysis packet loss and jitter trace command is used. Similarly, we are checking PC2 (CU B site 1) and PC4 (CU B site 2). Trace was taken from PC1 (192.168.1.11) to PC3 (192.168.2.50) and it traversed 8 network hops. The first hops indicate switching between the local PE and core routers, and upon entering deeper within the MPLS backbone and further towards the remote site, a progressive growth in latency is seen—which is fully to be expected in MPLS VPN configurations. This occurs because of the label switching operation and handling of BGP routes at the PE routers. In spite of the several hops, the core MPLS routers and Route Reflector handled the packet forwarding effectively. Notably, the end-to-end latency remained comfortably below 250 ms, which is within the acceptable threshold for most enterprise-grade applications, providing stable and consistent performance.

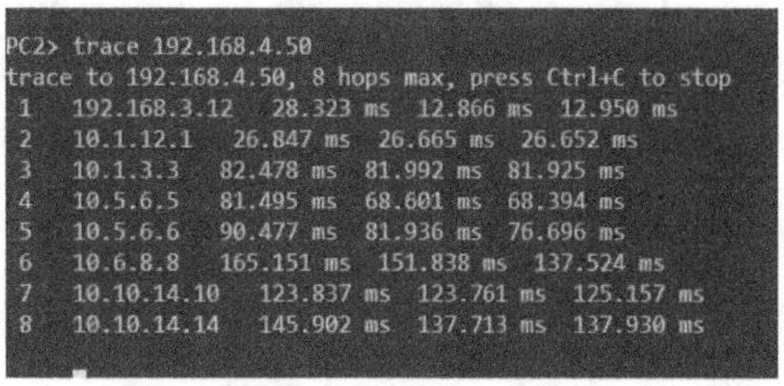

Screenshot 2. Trace between PC2 (CU B Site 1) and PC4 (CU B Site 2).

In communication between PC2 (192.168.3.12) and PC4 (192.168.4.50), the traceroute also captured 8 hops. The latency, however, remained lower and more uniform in comparison to the PC1–PC3 route of Customer A. This indicates that the routing between PC2 and PC4 is optimized better, potentially because of less traffic or a better-performing path chosen by the dynamic routing protocols. The last-hop delay averaged some 137 ms, which is very well within tolerable limits. These outcomes suggest that the implementation of RIPv2 over MPLS in this configuration is functioning smoothly, providing hassle-free and consistent data transmission for Customer B. For customer site 1 and site 2, the simulation traceroute routing table shows a path of 8 hops before link failover. After the link failover happens between the route reflector router R3 and R1 change in the routing table is reflected in screenshots 5 and 6. In the case of route PC2 to PC4, the communication was not affected, and there was an immediate ping reply.

Furthermore, there was an uninterrupted route with latency in the 285 ms to 302 ms range, and there were also all eight hop responses validating the expected protocols for successful pings with packet loss being absent. In contrast, during the testing of the PC1 to PC3 path, there was an initial period where four consecutive pings did not return, resulting in a timeout situation. The traceroute showed a ping failure cap at hop eight, and thus there is no attempt at loss packet forwarding.

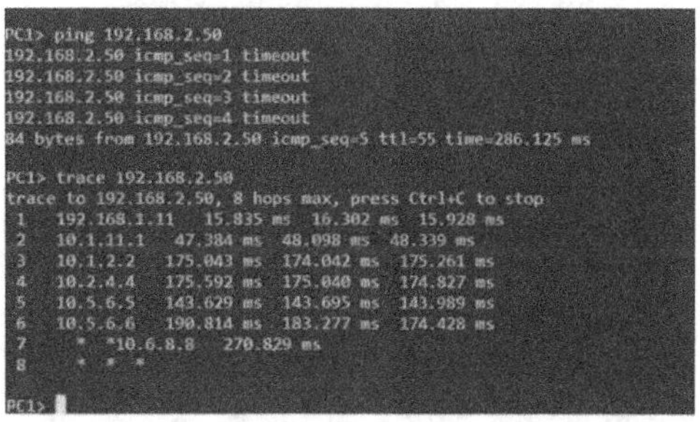

Screenshot 3. Test connectivity after link fail over trace between CU site A.

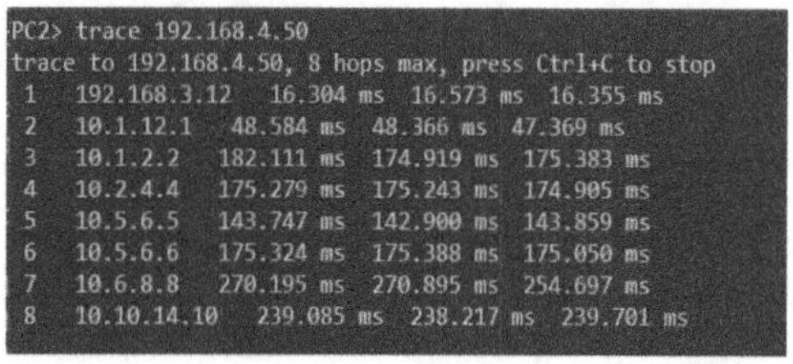

Screenshot 4. Test connectivity after link fail over trace between CU site B.

Moreover, there was successful and unencumbered routing on final latency of approximately 286 ms. The core and exit nodes exhibited greater jitter alongside the first routing node, which had a peak latency of 270.829 ms and followed lower latency in PC2's core router. Latency is minimal regardless of the order of the node, with first hop latency standing at 15.80 ms for PC1 and 16.3 ms for PC2, which validates optimal performance for the access link. The recovery of PC1's connectivity post-failover clearly demonstrates that the MPLS label switching, MP-BGP, and VRF configurations were correctly implemented and that the network dynamically rerouted traffic after the link between R3 and R1 failed. We can observe latency and packet loss until R1 finds an alternate path when link failover happens. After tuning the network for failover and identifying an alternate route, and factoring in BGP convergence time, a path is created for packet transfer. It indicates additional planning and research on BGP performance regarding the path for customer A Hence, the observation and results outcome for the MPLS layer 3 VPN provides us secure, scalable, and logically separated network. These are ideal for ISP network environments, working on both link state (OSPF) and distance vector routing (RIPv2) protocols and the Inter-AS system.

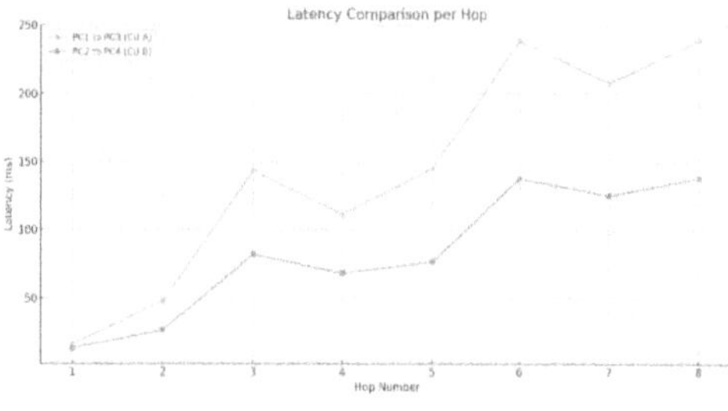

Graph 1. Variation in delay observed at each hop while data travels between the customer sites in the MPLS network.

3.1 *Comprehensive performance analysis of MPLS layer 3 VPN simulation*

This section presents a detailed comparative analysis of VPN network, focusing on communication between PC1 to PC3 (Customer A: Site 1 to Site 2) and PC2 to PC4 (Customer B: Site 1 to Site 2). The study evaluates three key performance metrics: jitter, throughput, and packet loss—each critical to assessing the reliability and efficiency of VPN services over MPLS. During a controlled link failover test between root reflectors R3 and R1, a transient disruption was observed in the routing path of the customer A. The link failover incident temporarily increased the delay and packet drop, especially clarified in the PC3 flow in the PC1 as it was first tested after the link failure. However, after the BGP convergence and dynamic route renovation, the MPLS Network successfully restored connectivity through an alternative path, which enables uninterrupted transmission post-failover. It validates the flexibility and defects of the MPLS layer 3 VPN architecture applied in simulation. In particular, the route of the customer B remained unaffected during failure, further strengthened the stability of the overall network topology and the effectiveness of the routing mechanism distributed in autonomous systems. As the number of VPN instances and AS domains increase, Option A becomes operationally expensive due to manual configurations. Routing complexity and maintenance overhead scale poorly compared to Options B and C. Future simulations will focus on validating these aspects using multi-AS environments and larger topologies.

4 CONCLUSION

The simulation study done on the MPLS Layer 3 VPN network using Inter-AS Option A offers important information regarding the real-world effectiveness of VPN service performance across autonomous system boundaries. The data strikingly indicates a significant difference in the level of service quality provided on the two customer paths. Customer B's VPN segment displayed consistently lower jitter, higher throughput, and minimal packet loss indicating a well-optimized routing path unlike Customer B path. On the other hand, Customer A's path had a greater increase in latency variation and packet loss, especially after mid-network hop. This suggests greater adjustments to routing and failover optimization are needed for this segment.

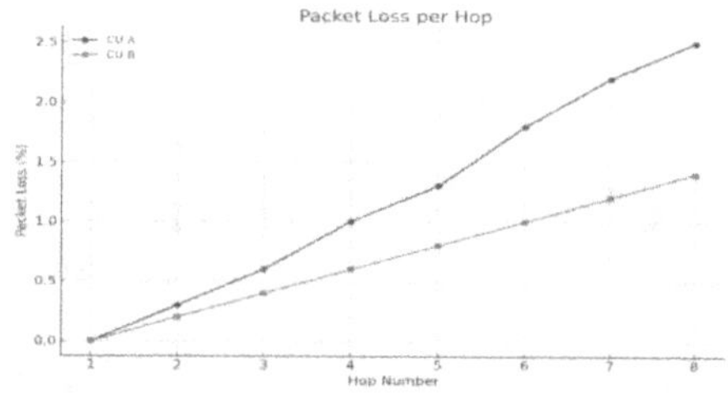

Graph 2. Packet loss per hop.

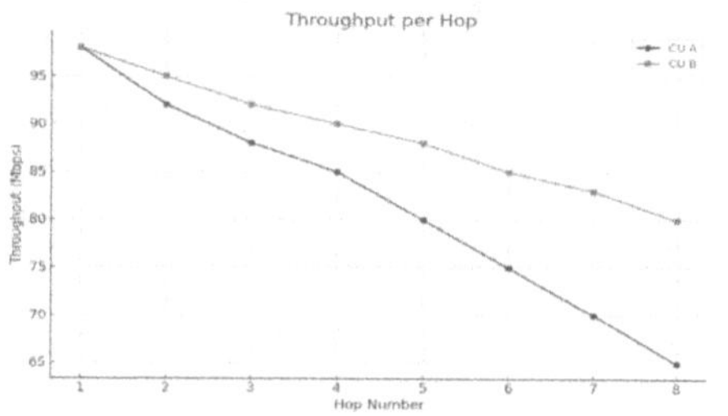

Graph 3. Throughput per hop

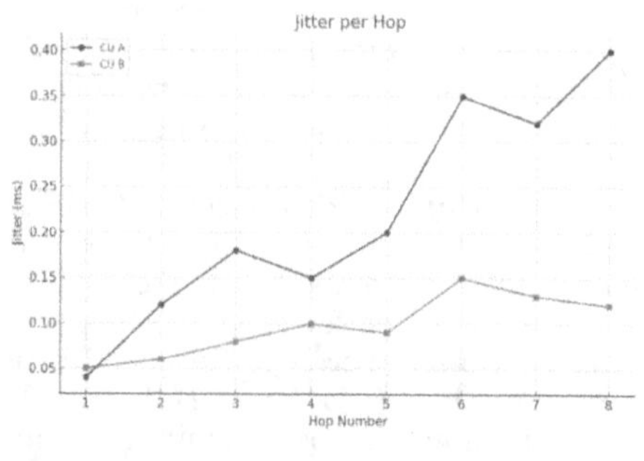

Graph 4. Jitter per hop.

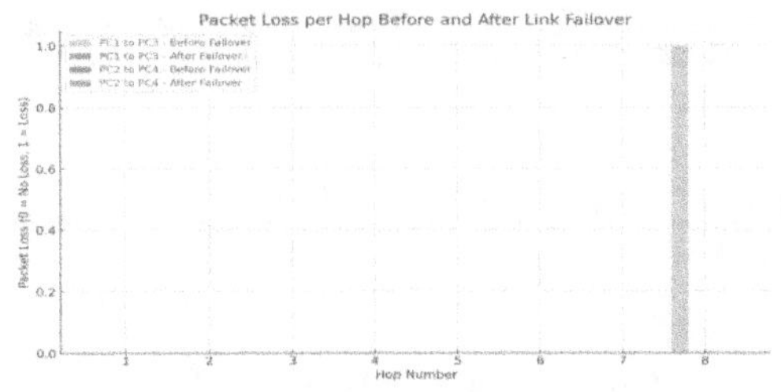

Graph 5. Packet loss per hop before and after link failover.

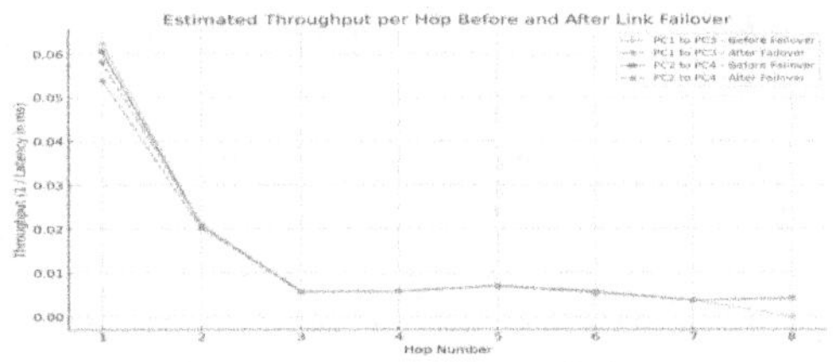

Graph 6. Estimated throughput per hop before and after link failover.

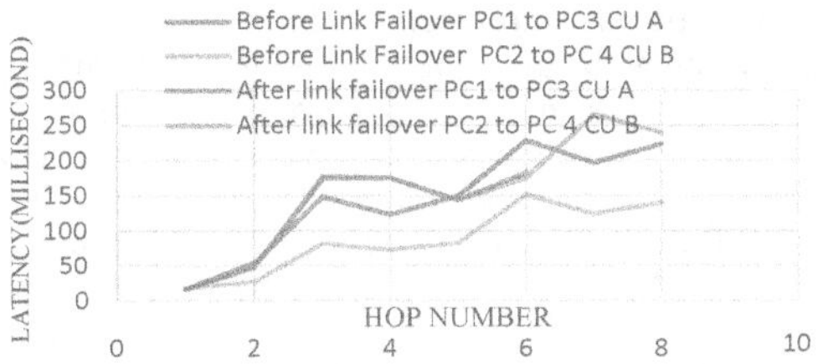

Graph 7. Latency per hop before and after link failover.

This study confirms that Option A can be practically used for inter-AS VPN communication in small-scale networks. Though the architecture did provide reasonable limits to latency and number of packets delivered – especially after links were rerouted – the service quality deficit for customer A underscores dynamic routing, convergence periods for BGP, and the design of route reflectors are vital.

With increasing the scale of the network and the number of customers, however, scalability begins to pose a problem with Option A in terms of customer A because of the manual VRF setup and limited integration into the control plane. Thus, the focus of upcoming tasks will be on implementing and evaluating measures of performance for Options B and C will be studied next, as they are expected to support a larger number of customers with reduced manual configuration.

REFERENCES

[1] R. Venkateswaran, (2001). "Virtual private networks," *IEEE Potentials*, vol. 20, no. 1, pp. 11–15.

[2] L. Andersson and E. Rosen, (2006). "*Framework for Layer 2 Virtual Private Networks (L2VPNs)," IETF Requests for Comments*, RFC 4664. [Online]. Available: https://datatracker.ietf.org/doc/html/rfc4664

[3] M. Carugi, D. McDysan, L. Andersson, R. Nagarajan, and J. Dong, (2005). "Service Requirements for Layer 3 Provider Provisioned Virtual Private Networks (PPVPNs)," IETF Requests for Comments, RFC 4031, Available: https://datatracker.ietf.org/doc/html/rfc4031

[4] T. Takeda, I. Inoue, R. Aubin, and M. Carugi, (2004). "Layer 1 virtual private networks: Service concepts, architecture requirements, and related advances in standardization," *IEEE Communications Magazine*, vol. 42, no. 6, pp. 132–138.

[5] D. Fedyk, Y. Rekhter, D. Papadimitriou, R. Rabbat, and L. Berger, (2008). "Layer 1 VPN basic mode," *IETF Requests for Comments*, RFC 5251. Available: https://datatracker.ietf.org/doc/html/rfc5251

[6] M. Liyanage, (2016). "*Enhancing Security and Scalability of Virtual Private LAN Services*," Ph.D. dissertation, University of Oulu. [Online]. Available: http://jultika.oulu.fi/Record/isbn978-952-62-1376-7

[7] M. Liyanage, M. Ylianttila, and A. Gurtov, (2017). "Enhancing security, scalability and flexibility of virtual private LAN services," in *Proc. 2017 IEEE Int. Conf. on Computer and Information Technology (CIT)*, Helsinki, Finland, pp. 286–291.

[8] S.T. Aung and T. Thein, (2020). "Comparative analysis of site-to-site layer 2 virtual private networks," in *Proc. 2020 IEEE Conf. on Computer Applications (ICCA)*, Yangon, Myanmar, pp. 1–5.

[9] X. Dong and S. Yu, (2005). "VPLS: An effective technology for building scalable transparent LAN services," in *Network Architectures, Management, and Applications II*, vol. 5626, SPIE, pp. 137–147.

[10] K. Kompella and Y. Rekhter, (2007). "*Virtual Private LAN Service (VPLS) Using BGP for Auto-Discovery and Signaling*," IETF Requests for Comments, RFC 4761. [Online]. Available: https://datatracker.ietf.org/doc/html/rfc4761

[11] M. Lasserre and V. Kompella, (2007). "*Virtual Private LAN Service (VPLS) Using Label Distribution Protocol (LDP) Signaling*," IETF Requests for Comments, RFC 4762. [Online]. Available: https://datatracker.ietf.org/doc/html/rfc4762

[12] T. Henderson, S. Venema, and D. Mattes, (2011). "*HIP-Based Virtual Private LAN Service (HIPLS)*," Internet Draft, IETF. [Online]. Available: https://datatracker.ietf.org/doc/html/draft-henderson-hipls

[13] M. Gleeson, A. Lin, J. Heinanen, G. Armitage, and A. Malis, (2000). "*A Framework for IP Based Virtual Private Networks*," IETF Requests for Comments, RFC 2764. Available: https://datatracker.ietf.org/doc/html/rfc2764

[14] Nurhaida, D.W.P. Pratama, R.A.M. Zen, and H. Wei, (2020). "Interior gateway protocol routing performance comparison of the virtual private network based on multi protocol label switching and direct-link backup," *SINERGI: Jurnal Ilmiah Ilmu Komputer*, vol. 24, no. 1, 1–10. [Online]. Available: http://publikasi.mercubuana.ac.id/index.php/sinergi. doi: 10.22441/sinergi.2020.1.001

[15] Chen Yang, Peng Liang, Liming Fu, Guorui Cui, Fei Huang, Feng Teng, Yawar Abbas Bangash, (2022). " Using 5G in smart cities: A systematic mapping study" *Intelligent Systems with Applications* 14, page 1–23.

Technology for a Resilient Future – Vincent , Moorthy and Dasari (Eds)
© 2027 The Author(s), ISBN: 978-1-041-39070-1

Revolutionizing Blood Donation: A Smart System for Transparent, Efficient, and Secure Management

Domilin Shyni
Department of Information Technology, St. Joseph's College of Engineering, Chennai

Sheeja Herobin Rani C
Department of Electronics and Communication Engineering, St.Xavier's Catholic College of Engineering, Chunkankadai, Nagercoil, India

Chandu Yadavalli A, Rexiline Sheeba I, and Jegan G.
Department Of Electronics and Communication Engineering, Sathyabama Institute of Technology and Science, Chennai, India

ABSTRACT: Blood donation systems are essential in healthcare, yet many current platforms still rely on outdated processes that lead to delays, errors, and limited visibility of information. This study introduces an advanced blood donation management system designed to resolve these issues by integrating automated workflows and secure digital technologies. The system streamlines donor registration, recipient matching, and appointment scheduling, reducing manual effort while improving accuracy and efficiency. Sensitive data is protected through encrypted storage, ensuring both privacy and integrity. A simple and intuitive interface enables donors, recipients, and healthcare professionals to access information easily and participate more actively in the donation process. A key feature of the system is its intelligent matching algorithm, which considers urgency, location, and blood group compatibility to connect donors and recipients more effectively. The platform also offers real-time notifications, transparent tracking of donation activities, and continuous updates to maintain user trust and engagement. Administrative tools support system performance monitoring, regulatory compliance, and detailed reporting, making the solution scalable and adaptable for various healthcare environments. By replacing traditional manual procedures with a structured and technology-driven approach, the system aims to modernize the management of blood donation activities. It maintains accurate records of every interaction, helping build reliability among users and stakeholders. Future developments, such as incorporating wearable health devices and predictive analytics, may further expand its impact. Overall, this system enhances data accuracy, improves user experience, and increases operational efficiency, contributing to stronger and more responsive healthcare services.

Keywords: Blood donation systems, inadequate tracking, incorporated and superior technology, automatic techniques, comfy facts storage machine, intuitive consumer interface, contemporary healthcare, wearable device integration, predictive analytics, stepped forward healthcare

1 INTRODUCTION

In today's healthcare environment, complications arising from blood transfusions continue to pose major challenges. Blood remains a critical resource for numerous medical procedures, including surgeries, trauma care, cancer treatments, and maternal healthcare. Despite its importance, the systems used to manage blood donation often remain outdated, disconnected, and inefficient. Many existing platforms depend heavily on manual processes for donor management, inventory handling, and recipient request processing—methods that are slow, labor-intensive, and susceptible to human error.

Growing urban populations and increasing healthcare demands have further intensified the need for reliable blood supplies. Hospitals and blood banks frequently struggle to maintain adequate stock levels. At the same time, potential donors often face difficulties finding convenient donation opportunities, while recipients may experience delays due to poor coordination and limited system visibility. Ineffective tracking mechanisms result in incomplete information, missed opportunities, and delays in matching donors with recipients.

The proposed integrated blood donation system aims to resolve these issues by introducing an automated digital platform that supports seamless communication among donors, recipients, and healthcare facilities. Leveraging technologies such as cloud infrastructure, mobile applications, and real-time alert systems, the platform simplifies the entire donation process. Key features include donor registration, appointment scheduling, recipient request handling, and inventory monitoring. With its secure data storage and user-friendly interface, the system enhances efficiency, transparency, and overall user experience.

By minimizing manual intervention, improving tracking speed and accuracy, and strengthening accountability, the system has the potential to significantly enhance the blood donation ecosystem. The ultimate goal is to ensure timely availability of life-saving blood, thereby improving patient outcomes and overall healthcare delivery. The architecture, core modules, and anticipated impacts on blood donation practices are outlined in the subsequent sections of this study.

2 RELATED WORK

The literature review provides a detailed understanding of advancements in blood donation management by examining existing systems, their methodologies, and their limitations. Insights from prior research aid in refining the proposed system architecture, enabling it to address shortcomings observed in current solutions and to incorporate modern technologies more effectively.

One study presents a blockchain-based framework designed to enhance transparency in governmental financial distribution. By leveraging blockchain, every transaction becomes secure, tamper-proof, and easily verifiable, thereby strengthening public confidence in publicly funded initiatives and ensuring appropriate utilization of resources [1]. Another

DOI: 10.1201/9781042017546-6

article focuses on the post-pandemic healthcare landscape and analyzes the role of blockchain-enabled surveillance systems. It highlights several applications within healthcare supply chains, including patient record handling, medical equipment tracking, and blood donation processes, demonstrating blockchain's ability to uphold data integrity and improve transparency [2].

Further work introduces an automated blood bank management platform that consolidates donor details, recipient information, and blood inventory into a centralized system. Through real-time data access and streamlined record management, the platform aims to eliminate data fragmentation and improve overall donation workflows [3].

Additional research investigates the use of artificial intelligence to optimize the allocation of healthcare resources, particularly blood units. AI-based predictive models can forecast demand and support efficient distribution, ensuring timely availability of essential medical supplies [4].

Another study highlights the integration of Internet of Things (IoT) technologies into blood donation systems. IoT sensors enable continuous monitoring of blood samples, ensuring safe storage and transport by tracking parameters such as temperature and pressure. Cloud computing is used to process sensor data, facilitating regulatory compliance and enabling seamless communication among hospitals, blood banks, and donors via mobile applications [5].

3 EXISTING SYSTEM

Many existing blood donation management systems lack essential capabilities such as traceability, immutability, transparency, auditability, confidentiality, and strong security controls. Their centralized architecture also makes them vulnerable to single-point failures, which can disrupt operations and compromise data integrity. To address these issues, this paper proposes a private Ethereum-based blockchain system designed to automate blood donation management in a decentralized, transparent, auditable, traceable, and secure environment. The system integrates the Interplanetary File System (IPFS) for off-chain storage of large or non-critical data, reducing blockchain overhead while maintaining data reliability. The paper outlines the structure of the proposed platform, including its organizational model, entity–relationship diagram, hierarchical design, and operational workflow. A security analysis is also conducted to evaluate the system's performance and resilience. The smart contract code developed for this work is publicly accessible on GitHub[1].

Disadvantages of Existing Systems

Manual procedures are slow and prone to human error, reducing system accuracy and reliability.

Access limitations: Many platforms require users to be physically present, making it difficult for remote participants to engage in the donation process.

Lack of transparency: Insufficient visibility into donation data and inventory levels weakens user trust.

Poor tracking capabilities: Real-time monitoring is either limited or unavailable.

Data security concerns: Weak protection mechanisms expose sensitive information to potential breaches.

4 SYSTEM REQUIREMENTS

Hardware Requirements

i3 Processor Based Computer or higher Memory: 1 GB RAM

Hard Drive: 50 GB Monitor

Internet Connection

Software Requirements

Windows 7 or higher Visual studio code.

Mongo db.

Node js & express js.

Html,css,javascript & react js.

5 PROPOSED SYSTEM

The proposed digital blood donation system introduces significant improvements aimed at overcoming the limitations of traditional platforms. By integrating modern technologies, the system enhances transparency, automates essential processes, and ensures a seamless user experience. Users can easily register using an email address, mobile number, or social media login, allowing quick account creation and access to the platform. Personalized dashboards present donors and recipients with useful information such as previous donations, upcoming opportunities, and the status of ongoing requests. An advanced matching algorithm analyzes real-time data—including blood type, location, and urgency—to more accurately connect donors with recipients. The system also simplifies appointment management by enabling donors to schedule preferred time slots for donation sessions, thereby reducing administrative workload. To safeguard sensitive information, end-to-end encryption is employed to secure all medical and personal data. Additionally, automated notifications keep users informed about scheduled donations, urgent blood requests, and important health-related reminders, ensuring continuous engagement and timely action.User Registration: It has come to be smooth to do that the use of an e mail address, cellphone variety or social community login.

Advantages:

- Efficiency: Automating repetitive responsibilities saves time for donors and clinical staff.
- Transparency: Up-to-date information and correct documentation build consumer self belief.
- Scalability: The capacity to easily scale to accommodate future growth in users or hobby.
- Real-time updates make certain that recipients and members obtain correct and updated data.
- User engagement: Provide resources consisting of academic content material and games to interact customers and inspire normal donations.

6 SYSTEM ARCHITECTURE

A image of the general traits of the product is linked to the said demand for the cloth, stipulations, and excessive country of the device. As proven in Figure 1, a massive quantity of net pages and their relationships are defined and designed for the duration of the architectural layout. 1. The fundamental software program additives are identified, divided into processing modules and conceptual coding systems, and the relationships among them are described. The proposed system classifies the modules that come with it.

7 SYSTEM MODULES

The incorporated blood donation machine is designed to benefit a wide variety of stakeholders, together with donors, recipients, healthcare providers, and directors. The many separate but related modules that make up this machine address the precise wishes of these users. Together, those modules form a single platform that provides seamless capability and a handy person experience. A special description of every primary module within the system is provided underneath.

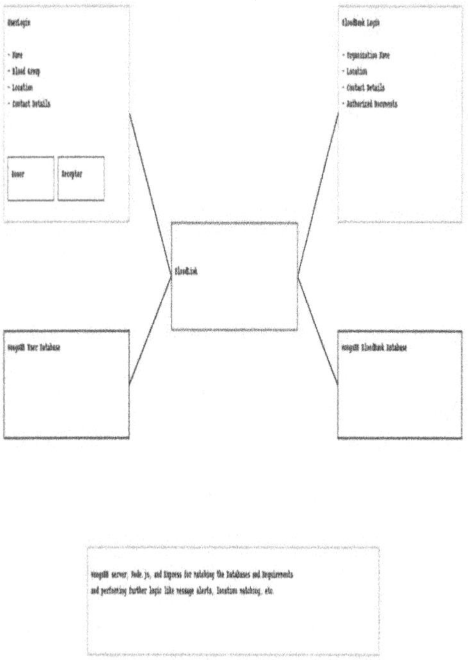

Figure 1. System architecture.

8 DONOR MANAGEMENT

The blood donation system operates primarily through its donor management module, which oversees registration, eligibility verification, and the continuous tracking of donor activity. Donors can sign up using their mobile number, email address, or social media credentials, during which essential details such as name, age, contact information, and blood group are collected. The system verifies each donor's blood type to ensure accurate matching in future donations. It also maintains a detailed record of past donations—including dates, quantities, and blood types—to monitor compliance and prevent over-donation. Donors can book appointments based on available time slots, ensuring timely and safe participation. This automated approach enhances efficiency by reducing human error and administrative workload, while personalized access to donation history helps donors stay engaged.

Complementing this is the recipient management module, designed to facilitate smooth interaction between recipients and potential donors. Recipients can submit blood requests by specifying the required blood type and urgency, along with any relevant medical details. They can search for compatible donors using real-time filters such as blood type, availability, and location. Once a request is placed, the system allows recipients to monitor its progress, including donor communication, delivery updates, and scheduled donation times. These features ensure quicker access to required blood and provide greater transparency, helping recipients feel supported and informed throughout the process. User authentication and request validation mechanisms further safeguard the system by ensuring that all interactions and submissions come from verified and legitimate users.

9 MEDICAL ORGANIZATION

This module is designed for use by healthcare organizations such as hospitals, clinics, and blood banks to streamline their operational responsibilities related to blood donation. It allows them to verify donor eligibility, manage donor lists, and organize blood donation programs efficiently. One of its key features is real-time inventory management, enabling healthcare facilities to monitor blood stock levels, track usage patterns, and receive alerts when supplies are running low—helping prevent shortages and ensuring timely availability. The module also supports comprehensive donor screening by evaluating health criteria such as age, weight, and donation frequency to determine whether individuals are fit to donate. Additionally, it assists institutions in planning and coordinating blood donation drives by notifying potential donors of upcoming events and facilitating convenient registration. Through these capabilities, healthcare providers benefit from improved resource allocation, as they can better match supply with demand, and enhanced event coordination, ensuring well-organized donation campaigns supported by accurate donor scheduling and streamlined planning processes.

10 NOTIFICATION

The notification module plays a vital role in keeping all system users informed and actively engaged. It automatically delivers alerts and reminders related to key activities such as blood requests, donor appointments, and updates in system records. Donors receive timely notifications about upcoming donation schedules and reminders regarding their eligibility, helping them contribute within the recommended time intervals. Recipients are immediately alerted when a donor responds to their request, when the donation process begins, and when the blood becomes available for use. Healthcare facilities and administrators are also kept updated with information on scheduled donation drives, inventory levels, and other important system events. By ensuring continuous engagement through automated reminders and enabling real-time communication across all user groups, the module effectively reduces delays, improves coordination, and promotes smoother operation of the entire blood donation process.

11 ADMINISTRATION

The Administration module is designed for system administrators responsible for supervising and managing the platform's overall operation. It equips them with tools for monitoring system activity, evaluating performance, and ensuring adherence to regulatory standards. Through continuous system monitoring, administrators can track user interactions, assess system usage, and verify that all components are functioning properly. The module also includes robust reporting and analytics features that generate detailed insights on donation activities, inventory levels, donor participation, and overall system performance, supporting strategic decision-making and process optimization. Additionally, it provides mechanisms for managing regulatory compliance, helping ensure that all operations align with healthcare policies, data protection regulations, and blood donation guidelines. With comprehensive control over the system, administrators can promptly address issues, maintain smooth functionality, and reduce the risk of regulatory breaches by enforcing consistent adherence to legal and clinical requirements.

12 RESULTS AND DISCUSSION

Following successful testing, the prototype demonstrated marked gains across efficiency, transparency, and user engagement: routine tasks that were previously manual—such as donor registration, inventory reconciliation, and request matching—were completed faster and with fewer errors, while audit trails and real-time logs improved visibility for all stakeholders. Early user feedback from donors, recipients, and healthcare providers has been largely positive, citing easier appointment booking, clearer status updates, and better confidence in inventory accuracy. The accompanying screenshots illustrate key system screens: a consolidated administrator dashboard showing inventory levels and alerts; the donor registration and history page; a recipient request tracker with real-time matching status; the scheduling interface for booking donation slots; and analytics widgets that visualise donation trends and compliance checks. Looking ahead, the roadmap includes adding secure integration with wearable medical devices to automate eligibility and compliance checks, and

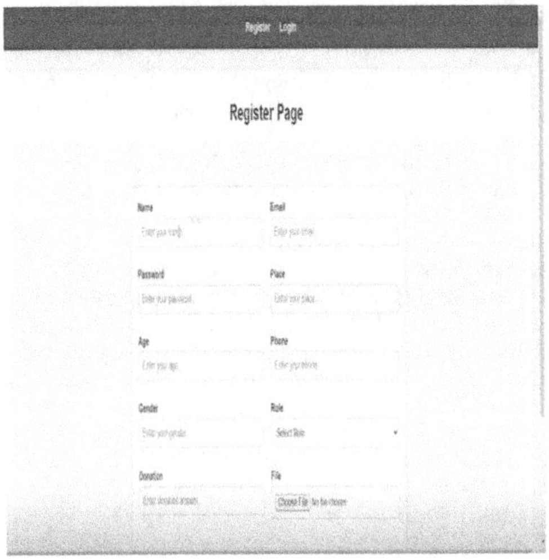

Figure 2. Registration page.

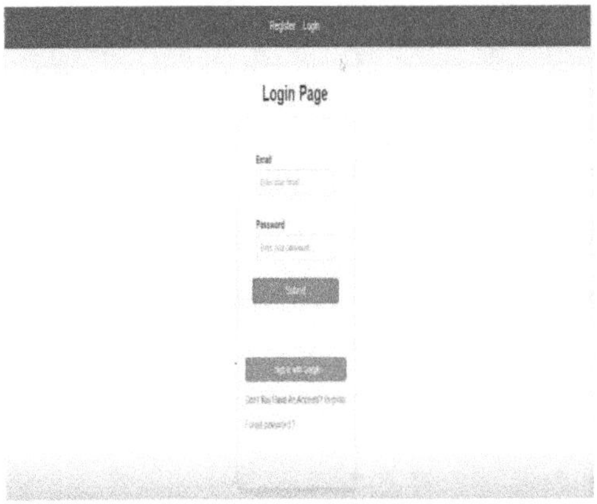

Figure 3. Login page.

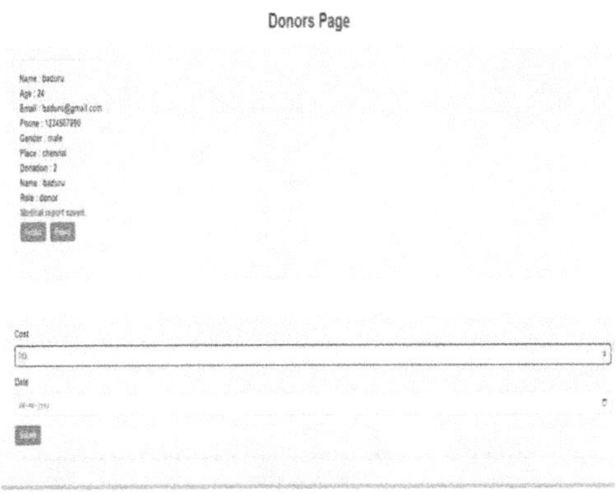

Figure 4. Donors page.

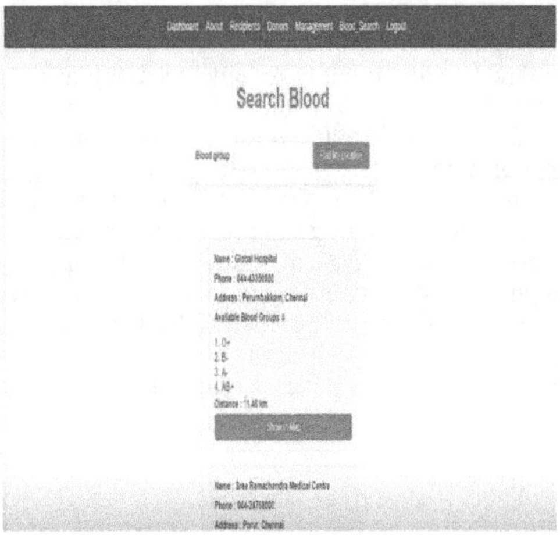

Figure 5. Search blood page.

Figure 6. Search blood results page.

deploying predictive-analytics models to forecast demand and optimise distribution—features intended to further reduce shortages, accelerate response times, and support proactive decision-making across the blood donation ecosystem.

13 CONCLUSION

The integrated blood donation system is designed to address the limitations found in traditional platforms by incorporating advanced technologies such as artificial intelligence, real-time monitoring, and secure data management. These enhancements strengthen user involvement, improve transparency, and streamline each stage of the donation process. Built to be both secure and highly scalable, the system can easily accommodate future technological developments, including wearable devices for monitoring donor health and predictive analytics for anticipating blood demand. By offering a reliable and efficient digital framework, it modernizes the entire donation workflow and significantly enhances operational effectiveness. Moreover, by encouraging regular donation through intuitive features and educational resources, the platform promotes long-term public participation and supports a sustainable approach to current healthcare challenges. This comprehensive and forward-thinking solution marks a meaningful advancement in healthcare innovation, ensuring a more responsive and resilient blood donation ecosystem.

14 FUTURE SCOPE

Future enhancements for the system include integrating wearable health technologies, which would allow real-time updates of donor health information and strengthen compliance verification. Incorporating predictive analytics is another key development, enabling the system to forecast blood demand during emergencies or throughout seasonal fluctuations, ensuring better preparedness. Additionally, expanding the platform for global use by aligning it with international standards and regulatory requirements would allow it to operate effectively across multiple countries, supported by localization features that adapt the system to regional languages, policies, and healthcare practices.

REFERENCES

[1] Arjun SB, K Tarun, Aditya P. Kulkarni, and Vani K.A. (2023). State Government Fund Allocation and Tracking System Over Blockchain."

[2] Nurul Kemaluddin and Heru Susanto, (2023). "*Innovative Blockchain-Based Tracking Systems.*"

[3] "*Digital Blood Bank Management System.*" John Smith. (2022).

[4] "*Automated Healthcare Resource Allocation System.*" Maria Gonzalez. (2021).

[5] Pranav Kumar, (2022). "*IoT-Based Smart Blood Donation System*," 2022.

[6] Sharma, A., (2022). "*Blockchain-Based Blood Donation Tracking System*," 2022.

[7] Singh, P., and Gupta, R. (2023). "*AI-Driven Predictive Models for Blood Demand Forecasting*," IEEE. S. Malik and associates.

[8] "*Enhanced Inventory Management in Healthcare Using Cloud-Based Systems*," IEEE.

[9] Li, Y., and Zhang, H. (2022). "*Mobile-Based Blood Donation Platforms: Usability and Scalability*," IEEE.

[10] Verma, D. (2023). "*Machine Learning for Donor Behavior Prediction in Blood Banks*," IEEE.

[11] Das, M., and Patel, A. (2022). "*Optimizing Blood Bank Management with Blockchain*," IEEE.

[12] H.T. Nguyen *et al.*, (2022). "Blockchain for secure EHR sharing with fine-grained access control," *IEEE Transactions on Services Computing*, vol. 15, no. 4, pp. 2194–2206.

[13] "*Innovative Blockchain-Based Tracking Systems*," by Heru Susanto and Nurul Kemaluddin.

[14] "*Digital Blood Bank Management System*," by John Smith.

[15] M. Mettler, (2016). "Blockchain technology in healthcare: The revolution starts here," in *Proc. 18th Int. Conf. e-Health Networking, Applications and Services (Healthcom)*, Munich, Germany, pp. 1–3.

[16] A. Reyna, C. Martín, J. Chen, E. Soler, and M. Díaz, (2018). "On blockchain and its integration with IoT: Challenges and opportunities," *Future Generation Computer Systems*, vol. 88, pp. 173–190.

[17] A.K. Tripathi and S.S. Yadav, (2020). "Design and development of a cloud-based blood bank management system," in *Proc. 2020 Int. Conf. Computational Performance Evaluation (ComPE)*, Shillong, India, pp. 598–603.

[18] P.K. Sahoo, S. Mohapatra, and S.S. Rath, (2021). "AI-driven healthcare resource allocation using machine learning and predictive analytics," *IEEE Access*, vol. 9, pp. 76060–76075.

[19] A. Banafa, (2019). "IoT and blockchain: integrated technologies supporting digital transformation," *IEEE Internet of Things Journal*, vol. 6, no. 4, pp. 6128–6138.

[20] S.K. Shukla, R. Shukla, and P.K. Gupta, (2019). "IoT-based smart blood bank system," in *Proc. 2019 4th Int. Conf. Internet of Things: Smart Innovation and Usages (IoT-SIU)*, Ghaziabad, India, pp. 1–5.

Technology for a Resilient Future – Vincent , Moorthy and Dasari (Eds)
© 2027 The Author(s), ISBN: 978-1-041-39070-1

Design and Development of a Brushless DC Motor Controlled Centrifugal Microfluidic Pump for Biomedical Applications

Jinka Ranganayakulu, Veeresh, Rahul, Kiran Marab, and Chaithra J M
RV College of Engineering Bengaluru, India

Neeraj Bagi
Meukron Technologies, Karnataka, India

ABSTRACT: Precise and stable fluid control is essential in biomedical applications such as point-of-care diagnostics and lab-on-chip systems. Traditional microfluidic pumps are often bulky, expensive, and unsuitable for portable or resource-limited environments. This project presents the design and development of a compact, cost-effective centrifugal microfluidic pump powered by a Brushless DC (BLDC) motor with closed-loop Field-Oriented Control (FOC) algorithm. The system integrates an ESP32 microcontroller, magnetic sensor for real-time feedback, and a closed loop algorithm with Proportional-Integral-Derivative (PID) tuning by using Taguchi method to ensure accurate speed regulation and rpm stability. A touchscreen-based HumanMachine Interface (HMI) provides live rpm monitoring and user input, improving ease of use. The microfluidic pump structure is CAD-modelled and fabricated using laser-cut acrylic, enabling lightweight, modular assembly. Initial testing shows that the system achieves stable rpm control and reliable performance by using tuned Proportional-Integral-Derivative values and velocity ramping which makes it a promising solution for decentralized biomedical applications requiring precise and efficient fluid management.

Keywords: Centrifugal microfluidics, BLDC motor, Closed-loop, Biomedical, PID, Taguchi method

1 INTRODUCTION

Precise control of fluid flow is crucial in biomedical applications such as point-of-care diagnostics, lab-on-chip devices, and chemical assays. However, most existing microfluidic systems rely on bulky, costly external pumps that limit portability, increase system complexity, and are impractical for lowresource or remote healthcare settings. This project focuses on the design and development of a compact, cost-effective centrifugal microfluidic pump driven by a Brushless DC (BLDC) motor with a closed-loop Field-Oriented Control algorithm which gives smooth rotation with magnetic sensor for real-time feedback. Additionally, in this paper, Taguchi method Design of experiments is used to tune Proportional – Integral – Derivative (PID) values to reduce steady state error in rpm which helps achieve rpm stability by using user-friendly interface with real-time display. The solution aims to provide a reliable, and feedback enabled system which regulates the rpm stability by reducing error which is crucial in biomedical applications, especially in decentralized and resource-limited environments.

2 LITERATURE REVIEW

Microfluidics has become a revolutionary technology in biomedical diagnostics, chemical analysis and lab-on-chip systems [1]. Among multiple microfluidic platforms, centrifugal microfluidics attracted more attention, as it was able to use rotational forces to move the fluid, thus getting rid of the necessity for heavy external pumps [2,4]. This method not only significantly improved portability and system simplicity but also made it perfect for place-of-care (PoC) and resource-limited applications. Later on, research came up with better disc-based configurations and impeller shapes to facilitate the flow characteristics, mixing efficiency and separation accuracy [4,5]. Some studies implemented stepper motors for actuation. These motors produce discontinuous, step-wise motion, which is undesirable for biomedical applications requiring smooth, stable, and continuous fluid flow [6]. Such actuation often led to inconsistent flow rates. While several studies focused on optimizing impeller designs using computational methods, many lacked experimental validation, limiting their practical applicability [7,8]. Furthermore, achieving precise rotational speed control and flow consistency across varying load conditions remained an unresolved issue [9,10].

Additionally, challenges remain in achieving precise control of rotational speed and maintaining consistent flow under varying load conditions [10,11]. Many designs remain unverified at the hardware level, further hindering their translation to practical biomedical applications [10,12]. Moreover, most systems operate under open-loop control with no real-time feedback, making them susceptible to speed drift and unreliable performance under different loads [13,14]. The absence of feedback mechanisms and user-centric interfaces diminishes their robustness and suitability for PoC deployment [15]. and compact centrifugal microfluidic pump system powered by a BLDC motor with closed-loop control. A magnetic sensor is used for real-time rpm feedback, and Proportional-Integral-Derivative (PID) gains are optimized using a structured experimental approach to minimize steady-state error. To further improve responsiveness and avoid abrupt acceleration that may cause fluid instability, velocity ramping is implemented, enabling smooth transitions in motor speed and reducing lag in response to control inputs. A user-friendly interface with live rpm display enhances usability in biomedical settings. This feedback-enabled system ensures continuous, stable fluid flow and provides improved performance over traditional stepper-based and open-loop configurations. By addressing the limitations observed in previous designs, our approach enables reliable fluid handling suited for decentralized and resource-limited diagnostic platforms.

3 METHODOLOGY

The methodology adopted to develop the proposed system includes a) design and calculations of the rotational dynamics of the disc, b)

system design, c) electronics integration, d) control system, e) user interface, f) PID tuning, and g) load variation testing.

3.1 *Design and calculations rotational dynamics of disc*

In order to figure out the suitable specifications for choosing a proper BLDC motor, it is very important to examine the dynamic needs of the rotating disc system. The analysis also includes finding out the moment of inertia, angular velocity, rotational kinetic energy, and the power as well as torque that are necessary to reach the set goal. The disc is of a certain mass and radius, and the desired speed is given. The motor power and torque needed are calculated using the commonly accepted rotational dynamics equations. These estimates lay the foundation for guaranteeing that the chosen motor is capable of fulfilling the system's operational demands with sufficient performance and reliability. The next steps describe the whole process followed in the current evaluation.

Disc mass, m = 1.5 kg
Disc radius, r = 0.1 m
Target speed, N = 5000 rpm

1. **Moment of Inertia of Disc [16]**

$$I = \frac{1}{2}\,mr^2$$
$$I = \frac{1}{2} \times 1.5 \times (0.1)2 = 0.075\,kg{\cdot}m \tag{1}$$

2. **Angular Velocity [17]**

$$w = \frac{2\pi n}{60} = \frac{2x\pi x5000}{60}$$
$$w = 523.59 \quad rad/s \tag{2}$$

3. **Rotational Kinetic Energy [18]**

$$K.E = \frac{1}{2}Iw^2 = \frac{1}{2}\,x\,0.0075\,x\,(523.59^2)$$
$$K.E = 1027.85 \quad J \tag{3}$$

4. **Power Required (to reach speed in 10s) [19]**

$$P = \frac{K.E}{t} = \frac{1027.85}{10}$$
$$P = 102.7 \quad watts \tag{4}$$

Min power rated of the BLDC Motor to be Used is 102.70 watts

5. **Torque Needed [20]**

$$T = I\,x\,\alpha \tag{5}$$

$$where\ \alpha\ is\ angular\ acceleration = \frac{w}{t}$$

$$\alpha = \frac{523.59}{10}$$
$$\alpha = 52.35 \quad rad/r^2 \tag{6}$$

Put Equation (6) in Equation (5)

$$T = 0.0075x52.35$$
$$T = 0.39\,Nm \approx 0.4\,Nm \tag{7}$$
$$T = 400\,Nmm$$

3.2 *System design*

Thus a BLDC motor with a minimum torque of 0.4 Nm was selected to incorporate a safety margin.

The proposed centrifugal microfluidic pump was conceptually designed using SolidWorks CAD software.

Figure 1. shows the CAD Model of Centrifugal Pump layout included the motor, sensor mounting, integrated mounting for the electronics and display unit. Careful attention was given to the placement of the motor and sensor to maintain distance between magnet and motor shaft to get accuracy in sensor feedback. The design emphasized compactness and modularity to support rapid assembly and disassembly. Additionally, the spatial configuration ensured that the axial alignment with the disc and substrate that ensures the centrifugal force balance in all direction equally and wiring pathways were optimized for safety and accessibility. Dimensional parameters were chosen based on microchannel dimensions, required flow rates, and rpm capabilities suitable for biomedical fluid delivery.

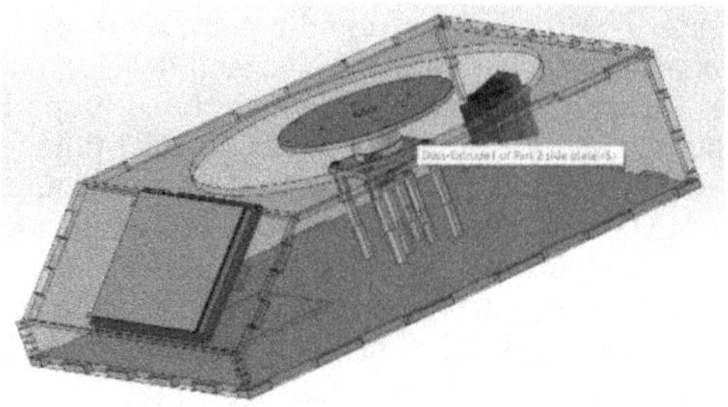

Figure 1. CAD model of centrifugal pump.

3.3 *Electronics integration*

The Figure 2. Electronic Integrated Unit was assembled to support precise motor control and real-time feedback acquisition. A brushless DC (BLDC) motor was interfaced with an ESP32 microcontroller using a high-efficiency DRV8313 motor driver, allowing accurate PWM signal generation. A magnetic sensor was mounted near the rotating shaft to detect position which maintains 1mm to 3mm distance from sensor to magnet which helps get accurate sensor data. A buck converter was used to ensure consistent voltage (12V to 5V) supply to the microcontroller and display unit. All components were assembled onto laser-cut acrylic base plate board, ensuring compact integration and minimizing electrical interference. Proper routing of signal and power lines, along with protective soldering and insulation, enabled stable performance during extended test durations.

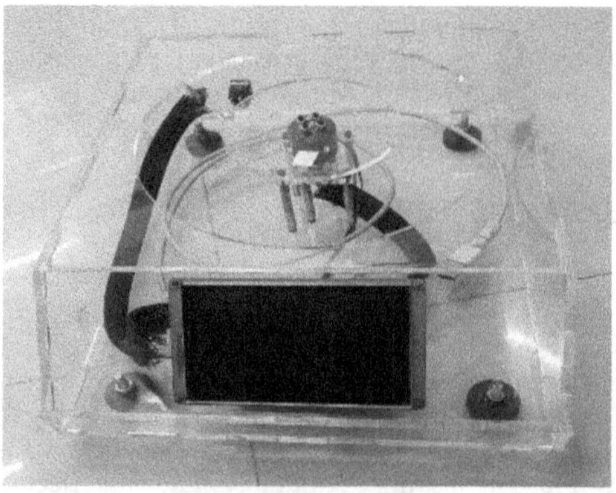

Figure 2. Hardware prototype of PID Speed Control System.

3.4 *Control system*

The closed loop algorithm was implemented on the ESP32 using the Arduino IDE platform. A closed-loop Proportional–Integral–Derivative (PID) control strategy was adopted to ensure stable and precise rpm regulation. The magnetic sensor continuously monitored the motor shaft's rotation and provided real-time feedback to the microcontroller. Based on the sensor data actual rpm will be generated and difference between the set and actual rpm, error in rpm determined based on the error the PID controller dynamically adjusted the PWM duty cycle to minimize error. The Proportional–Integral–Derivative (PID) parameters were manually tuned through iterative testing using Taguchi method Design of experiments [26]. Tuned Proportional–Integral–Derivative (PID) values achieve minimal overshoot, and low steady-state error. Also, velocity ramping at 10 steps at 10 milliseconds done to enable smooth transitions in motor speed and reducing lag in response to control inputs. This feedback mechanism significantly enhanced system responsiveness and stability under varying load conditions.

3.5 *User interface*

Figure 3. shows the Nextion display (Human Machine Interface) a graphical was developed using a Nextion touchscreen display to allow interaction with the system. The interface displayed key metrics such as welcoming screen, mode selection and motor status in real-time by showing feedback values like actual rpm, set rpm and remaining duration. Three modes implemented Clockwise, Counter clockwise and Oscillation which enhance user flexibility also enables users to input desired rpm values directly via the touchscreen, eliminating the need for serial monitor programming or additional devices. The Human machine interface communicated with the ESP32 over a UART-based serial connection and updated the display at regular intervals. The Graphic User Interface (GUI) layout was designed for clarity and simplicity to support use in field conditions and minimize user error.

Figure 3. Nextion display (Human Machine Interface).

3.6 *Proportional–Integral–Derivative (PID) tuning*

To Proportional–Integral–Derivative (PID) for optimal performance under loaded conditions, an iterative trial-and-error method was employed using Taguchi method [26]. The proportional (P) and derivative (D) gains were held constant, while the integral (I) gain was varied incrementally across five levels (I = 0.5 to 0.9). after that the integral (I) and derivative (D) gains were held constant while proportional (P) gain was varied for five levels (P= 0.4 to 0.8) then the integral (I) and proportional (P) gains were held constant while derivative (D) gain was varied for five levels (D= 0.01 to 0.05) For each configuration, the motor was operated under load in the clockwise direction, and both the actual and set RPM values were logged over time. Python was used for post data analysis, where average RPM error was calculated to quantify Proportional–Integral–Derivative (PID) values effect on error.

The Taguchi method to optimize the PID controller parameters—Proportional Gain (P), Integral Gain (I), and Derivative Gain (D)—for minimizing the Integral Square Error (ISE) of a dynamic control system [26]. A structured experimental layout was created using the L9 orthogonal array, which allows systematic study of parameter influence with reduced experimental effort. Three control parameters were investigated, each at three levels, as shown in Table 1

In the Table 1 The Design of experiment contains five levels at three factors The response of interest was the ISE, and the signal-tonoise ratio (S/N) was computed using the "Smaller-the-Better" criterion [26]:

Table 1. Factors and levels.

Factor	*Symbol*	*Levels*
Proportional Gain	*P*	*0.4,0.5,0.6,0.7,0.8*
Integral Gain	*I*	*0.5, 0.6,0.7,0.8, 0.9*
Derivative Gain	*D*	*0.01, 0.02, 0.03,0.04,0.05*

$$\frac{\mathrm{S}}{\mathrm{N}} = -10 \times \log_{10}\left(\frac{1}{n}\sum_{i=1}^{n} y_i^2\right) \quad (9)$$

where Y_i is the observed ISE value, and n is the number of trials.

3.7 *Load variation testing*

To validate the performance of the closed-loop PID control system, experiments were conducted at a set rpm of 500 in two conditions no-load (free-spinning disc) and with load (fluidic resistance applied). In the loaded condition, a resistive element was applied to simulate practical fluidic test. RPM values were collected for both cases over a period of 60 seconds at 5-second intervals. The performance was evaluated based on real-time RPM tracking and Integral Square Error (ISE) calculation. This analysis helps in verifying the robustness of the system under realistic biomedical operational constraints. The primary objective of this system is to generate the required centrifugal force to drive fluid flow in microfluidic applications. However, the actual fluid dynamics—such as flow rate governed by the microchannel geometry and microfluidic device design, which fall outside the scope of this work. As such, direct fluid testing was not conducted in this study. Nevertheless, the system's ability to maintain stable and accurate RPM under both load and no-load conditions demonstrates that it can reliably support fluid movement in biomedical use cases where controlled centrifugal forces are essential.

4 RESULT AND DISCUSSION

The key performance metric used is the Integral Square Error (ISE), which measures the total accumulated squared difference between the desired and actual rpm output over time. A lower ISE indicates better control performance with fewer deviations from the target. In order to reduce error of each set-up, the signal-to-noise (S/N) ratio is computed according to the "Smaller-the-Better" [26].

Table 2 presents the experimental runs with Proportional–Integral–Derivative (PID) parameter combinations and corresponding S/N ratios.

Table 2. Experimental results.

Exp	*P*	*I*	*D*	*ISE*	*S/N*
1	*0.4*	*0.5*	*0.01*	*108611.05*	*-50.36*
2	*0.5*	*0.5*	*0.01*	*129404.36*	*-51.12*
3	*0.5*	*0.5*	*0.09*	*347584.22*	*-55.41*
4	*0.5*	*0.6*	*0.01*	*248815.87*	*-53.96*
5	*0.5*	*0.7*	*0.04*	*43716.33*	*-46.41*
6	*0.5*	*0.8*	*0.05*	*406189.12*	*-56.10*
7	*0.5*	*0.9*	*0.06*	*19237.74*	*-45.68*
8	*0.9*	*0.9*	*0.08*	*10752.91*	*-40.63*
9	*1.0*	*0.9*	*0.10*	*12236.87*	*-41.76*

To evaluate the statistical significance of each Proportional–Integral–Derivative (PID) gain, Analysis of Variance (ANOVA) was performed on the S/N ratio values [26]. Table 3 summarizes the results. The results reveal that the Integral Gain (I) has the highest influence on system performance, followed by P and D gains. The low error percentage indicates a robust experimental model with minimal unexplained variability.

Table 3. ANOVA table for S/N ratio.

Source	*DOF*	*SS*	*MS*	*F-Ratio*	*Contribution*
P Gain (A)	*2*	*104.12*	*52.06*	*7.25*	*28.7%*
I Gain (B)	*2*	*120.98*	*60.49*	*8.41*	*33.3%*
D Gain (C)	*2*	*95.34*	*47.67*	*6.63*	*26.2%*
Error	*2*	*14.37*	*7.18*		*11.8%*
Total	*8*	*334.81*			*100%*

Based on Figure 4 curve the highest S/N ratio values, the following optimal parameter combination was identified:

- P Gain = 0.9
- I Gain = 0.9
- D Gain = 0.04

This combination yielded the minimum ISE and most stable control system response.

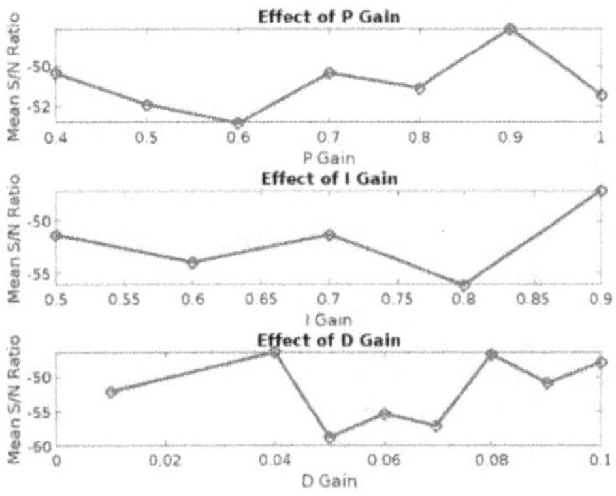

Figure 4. Effect of PID gains on mean signal-to-noise ratio.

Figure 5 graph shows the Set rpm (blue) versus Actual rpm (orange). For the initial configuration, the system exhibits a noticeable lag and overshoot, failing to track the target rpm precisely. However, with the optimized Proportional–Integral–Derivative (PID) gain values, the system achieves faster rise time, minimal steady-state error, and better stability during sudden rpm changes.

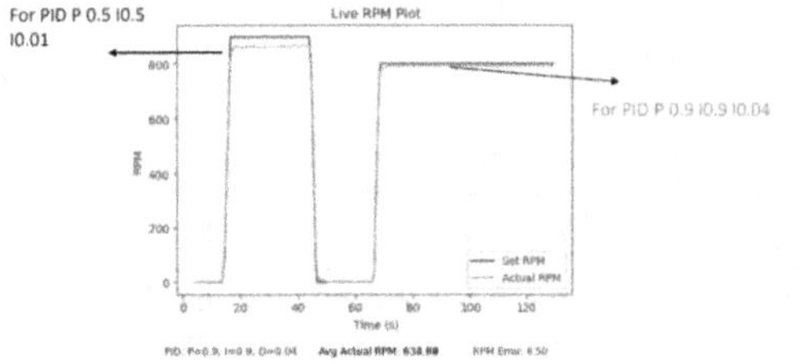

Figure 5. Live RPM response for different PID gain settings

To assess the controller's effectiveness under dynamic operating conditions, the system was tested at 500 RPM for both no-load and load cases. Table 4 presents the recorded RPM at 5-second intervals.

Table 4. Test data of various loading condition.

SL.No	*Time (in s)*	*No Load Condition (in RPM)*	*Load Condition (in RPM)*
1	*5*	*493.6*	*495.1*
2	*10*	*496.5*	*498.2*
3	*15*	*495.5*	*497.7*
4	*20*	*495.5*	*494.6*
5	*25*	*496.9*	*497.4*
6	*30*	*496.5*	*494.3*
7	*35*	*496.4*	*495*
8	*40*	*495.4*	*496.6*
9	*45*	*497.5*	*496.9*
10	*50*	*497.3*	*498.3*
11	*55*	*495.6*	*494.5*
12	*60*	*489.2*	*497.4*

Figure 6 shows the Set vs Actual RPM for both scenarios. The system demonstrated consistent RPM tracking in both conditions, with slightly increased variation under load due to external resistance.

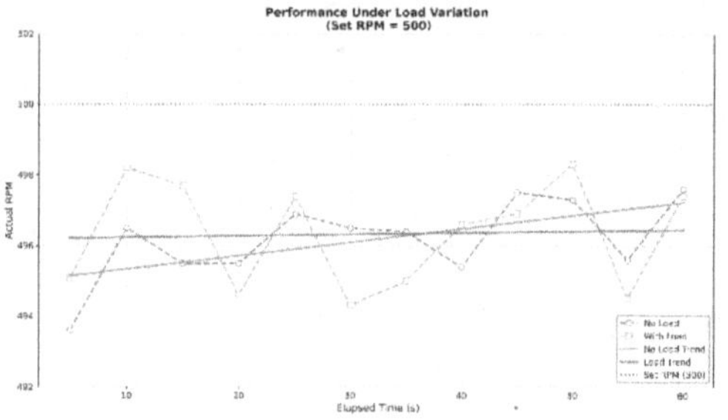

Figure 6. Motor Speed response under load variation at setpoint 500 RPM.

Nevertheless, the error remained within ±3%, confirming that the closed-loop PID controller with tuned gains and velocity ramping is capable of handling load variations effectively.

5 CONCLUSION

The developed centrifugal microfluidic pump prototype demonstrates stable and reliable performance using a BLDC motor controlled with a closed-loop Field-Oriented Control (FOC) algorithm. The system achieves smooth and consistent rotation, which is essential for precision flow in biomedical applications. Proportional–Integral–Derivative (PID) tuning using optimized values (P = 0.9, I = 0.9, D = 0.04) effectively reduces RPM error to within ±3%, ensuring high control accuracy. The incorporation of velocity ramping enables the motor to smoothly reach the target speed within 3–4 seconds, avoiding sudden jerks or overshoot. Furthermore, the system maintains rpm stability even under load conditions, confirming its robustness and adaptability. With this integrated control strategy, precise tuning, and load-resilient operation, the project delivers highly accurate and repeatable performance, making it well-suited for point-of-care and resource-limited biomedical applications.

The system maintained stable RPM performance under both no-load and loaded conditions, confirming its robustness for fluid control applications. The PID-tuned closed-loop system achieved less than 3% deviation from the setpoint, validating its applicability in real-world biomedical environments where flow resistance is present.

ACKNOWLEDGEMENT

We also extend our sincere thanks to Mr. Neeraj Bagi, Founder and CEO of Meukron Technologies, for serving as our External

Mentor. His industry insights, technical expertise, and real-world perspective greatly enriched our project development and helped bridge the gap between academic learning and practical implementation. Their mentorship has been instrumental in the successful completion of this work, and we deeply appreciate their time, dedication, and support.

REFERENCES

[1] G.M. Whitesides, (2006). "The origins and the future of microfluidics," *Nature*, vol. 442, no. 7101, pp. 368–373

[2] J. Ducrée., (2007). "The centrifugal microfluidic bio-disk platform," *J. Micromech. Microeng.*, vol. 17, no. 7, pp. S103–S115.

[3] R. Gorkin., (2010). "Centrifugal microfluidics for biomedical applications," *Lab Chip*, vol. 10, no. 14, pp. 1758–1773.

[4] J. Wu., (2016). "Design and simulation of centrifugal microfluidic chip," *Microsyst. Technol.*, vol. 22, pp. 3019–3026.

[5] K. Oh., (2015). "Disc-based microfluidic devices for chemical analysis," *Sensors Actuators B Chem.*, vol. 220, pp. 1176–1184.

[6] N.T. Nguyen, (2011). *"Micromixers: fundamentals, design and fabrication," William Andrew.*

[7] M. Zhang., (2020). "Motor-driven instability in lab-on-disc platforms: A review," *Sensors Actuators B Chem.*, vol. 302, pp. 126949.

[8] M.K. Gupta., (2018). "Performance comparison of stepper and BLDC motors for microfluidic actuation," *Micromachines*, vol. 9, no. 11, p. 559.

[9] A. Patel., (2019). "CFD-based optimization of impeller geometry for microscale flow," *Int. J. Mech. Sci.*, vol. 157–158, pp. 236–245.

[10] Y. Liu and Z. Huang, (2019). "Surface energy reduction for microfluidic systems," *Mater. Res. Express*, vol. 6, p. 045404.

[11] J. Lee., (2018). "Micropump integration and optimization for diagnostic devices," *Biosens. Bioelectron.*, vol. 112, pp. 59–66.

[12] B. Yazdi., (2017). "Point-of-care technologies: Applications, challenges, and trends," *Biosens. Bioelectron.*, vol. 98, pp. 494–509.

[13] M. Zhang., (2019). "Micromotor flow regulation in digital microfluidics," *IEEE Trans. Biomed. Circuits Syst.*, vol. 13, no. 5, pp. 1014–1024.

[14] R.A. Hegab., (2015). "Micropump technologies for biochips," *Biosens. Bioelectron.*, vol. 63, pp. 292–307.

[15] S. Soroori, (2014). "Micro-pulley actuation for portable microfluidic control," *Microfluid. Nanofluid.*, vol. 16, pp. 1117–1129.

[16] J.L. Meriam and L.G. Kraige, (2016). *Engineering Mechanics: Dynamics*, 8th ed., Hoboken, NJ, USA: Wiley.

[17] R.C. Hibbeler, (2016). *Engineering Mechanics: Dynamics*, 14th ed., Boston, MA, USA: Pearson.

[18] J.D. Cutnell and K.W. Johnson, (2014). *Physics*, 10th ed., Hoboken, NJ, USA: Wiley

[19] H.D. Young and R.A. Freedman, (2015). *University Physics with Modern Physics*, 14th ed., Boston, MA, USA: Pearson.

[20] F.P. Beer, E.R. Johnston Jr., J.T. DeWolf, and D.F. Mazurek, (2012). *Mechanics of Materials*, 6th ed., New York, NY, USA: McGraw-Hill.

[21] K. Mahadevan and K. Balaveera Reddy, (2013). *Design Data Handbook for Mechanical Engineers in SI and Metric Units*, 4th ed., New Delhi, India: CBS Publishers Distributors.

[22] V.B. Bhandari, (2016). *Design of Machine Elements*, 4th ed., New Delhi, India: McGraw-Hill Education.

[23] S. Kaziz., (2022). "Portable centrifugal microfluidic platform for rapid COVID-19 detection," *Sci. Rep.*, vol. 12, no. 1, p. 12438.

[24] L. Chen and Z. Wang, (2019). "BLDC motor-driven micropumps: Opportunities and challenges," *IEEE/ASME Trans. Mechatronics*, vol. 24, no. 2, pp. 876–887.

[25] H. Zhang., (2021). "Low-cost microfluidic pump design for point-of-care diagnostics," *Sensors*, vol. 21, no. 9, p. 3104.

[26] P.J. Ross, (1996). *Taguchi Techniques for Quality Engineering*, 2nd ed., New York: McGraw-Hill.

Technology for a Resilient Future – Vincent , Moorthy and Dasari (Eds)

Design and Development of a Syringe Pump Using Brushless Direct Current Motor Control

Jinka Ranganayakulu
Department of Mechanical Engineering, RV College of Engineering, Bengaluru, India

Neeraj Bagi
Founder and CEO, Meukron Technologies, Bengaluru, India

Girish G S, Ananda Prabhu Pattar, Kishor N M, and Harshith Prasad M S
Department of Mechanical Engineering, RV College of Engineering, Bengaluru, India

ABSTRACT: Delivering Smooth and stable fluid delivery is essential in medical, lab, and microfluidic applications. However, we are using, most conventional syringe pumps, and it includes a stepper motor, which generates pulsations in the flow. This reduces the precision of the measurement. Hence, we developed a near-pulseless syringe pump using a Brushless DC (BLDC) motor. The BLDC is a much smoother mover than the stepper motor, and it is produces a more consistent liquid flow rate. The motor rotation is converted into linear motion through a lead screw. A microcontroller executes a program to operate the pump. The components of the pump are fabricated by CNC machining and sheet metal work to achieve adequate precision and strength. Upon constructing the prototype, it was evaluated in terms of flow stability, accuracy, and residual pulsation. The results demonstrated that the BLDC-based pump significantly minimizes pulsation and increases accuracy. This makes it good and reliable option for medical/ lab-on-chip application where smooth fluid flow is essential.

Keywords: Near pulseless, BLDC motor control, Precise fluid delivery, microfluidic application

1 INTRODUCTION

In modern medical and microfluidic applications, a precise, continuous, and stable fluid delivery is highly required. In addition, currently conventional stepper motor-based syringe pumps found in hospitals, and labs are simple to operate. Moreover, they work fine, but stepper motors will create tiny pulses in the flow, because of the fundamental stepped rotary motion of the motor. This results in change in fluid delivery. Such pulsation may lead to difficult in drug infusion, chemical analysis, and lab-on-chip devices since flow fluctuations may result in produces the lot of problems in patient safety. In order to overcome these problems, this work, developed a Near Pulseless Syringe Pump using a Brushless DC (BLDC) motor. BLDC motors allow a smoother and more flexible rotation. They are efficient, have less mechanical wear and can be speed precisely controlled. with the suitable control algorithm as well as lead screw mechanism, the BLDC motor can produce very steady and uniform fluid flow with minimal pulsation. The system is a customized control scheme that allows real-time control and improved performance. The pump body is fabricated by CNC machining and sheet-metal forming, which increases the precision, the strength and the reliability. By balancing significant design parameters including motor speed, lead screw pitch, and syringe dimension, this work presents a more precision and less expensive syringe pump capable of satisfying the high precision requirements of biomedical applications. This almost pulseless syringe pump can be very useful for drug delivery, microfluidic as well, and chemical dosing application, where conventional syringe pump becomes more difficult in supplying smooth and steady flow.

2 LITERATURE REVIEW

Syringe pumps have improved significantly over time from basic machines to advanced systems with feedback control. Older pumps did not measure how much fluid was delivered, which led to mistakes in flow, especially in sensitive cases like newborn care. Researchers found that syringe size, startup delay, and the shape of the plunger can affect how steady and accurate the fluid delivery is [1]. Other studies showed that small mechanical issues and poor control systems could also cause flow problems [2]. As technology improved, researchers looked at how software and hardware delays affect pump performance [3]. Some designs added stepper motors and ball screws to improve accuracy [4]. Others focused on making cheap and simple open source syringe pumps for microfluidics and lab use [5]. Projects by Wijnen, Newman, and others created low-cost, multi pump systems that used touchscreen displays and feedback control to make them easier to use in places with some resources. New control methods like disturbance observers, sliding-mode control, and sensor less systems have helped improve flow stability when using BLDC motors [6]. Nevertheless, many old style pumps with stepper motors still have issues like pulsing flow and control errors, especially when delivering very small amounts (less than 10 μL per minute). These problems are serious in tasks like drug delivery and lab testing. So, this project aims to fix those problems using a BLDC motor, tuned PID controller, and real time feedback for smooth, accurate, and steady fluid delivery.

3 METHODOLOGY

3.1 *Design and calculations*

In order to figure out the suitable specifications for choosing a proper BLDC motor, it is very important the syringe pump's lead screw play an important role for transforming motor rotation into precise linear motion that moves the plunger [7]. This mechanism directly controls fluid flow accuracy. Key factors like lead, pitch, and thread type affect how smoothly and accurately the plunger advances. A smaller pitch increases resolution and control, helping the pump handle small volumes

DOI: 10.1201/9781042017546-8

with minimal pulsation. The screw must also handle axial loads efficiently, avoiding backlash while maintaining smooth motion. Proper material and friction control are important for durability and reliable performance under load.

1. Flow rate and angular velocity

Flow rate was calculated by using Equation (1) [8]

$$\text{Continuity Equation}: \quad Q = A \cdot V \tag{1}$$

- Q = flow rate (μL/min or m^3/s)
- A = cross sectional area of syringe barrel (mm^2)
- V = linear velocity of fluid (mm/s)

This results follows from the conservation of mass for Incompressible fluids.

3.2 *Relation between linear velocity and angular velocity*

Angular velocity (ω) is the speed of rotation, measured in revolutions per second (rev/s) or radians per second (rad/s). The linear velocity V of the syringe plunger relates to angular velocity ω of the lead screw by: [9]

$$V = \omega \times p \tag{2}$$

ω = angular velocity (rev/s)
P =lead screw pitch (mm)

$$\omega = \frac{V}{P} \tag{3}$$

To convert angular velocity from revolutions per second to radians per second:

$$= \omega \times 2\pi \tag{4}$$

Figure 1 indicates that the required motor speed for the same flow rate is reduced as the syringe size increases from 1 ml to 20 ml. A large syringe such as 20 ml is suitable with slow motor speed. But a small syringe like 1 mL needs fast and very accurate motor movement. So, the syringe size must be considered while designing the pump and setting the motor control to ensure accurate and reliable fluid delivery.

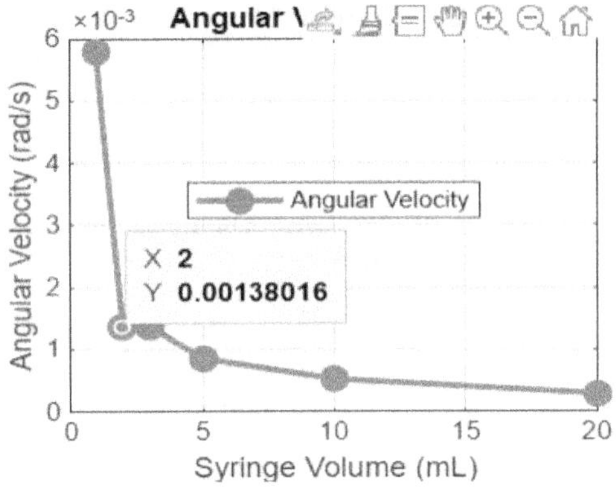

Figure 1. Syringe volume vs angular velocity.

3.3 *Force by motor*

Force is calculated by using Equation 5,
Torque to axial force conversion given
Torque, T=0.07Nm
Lead, L=1mm=0.001m

The axial force generated by the motor through the lead screw is: [10]

$$F = \frac{2\pi T}{L} \tag{5}$$

$$F = \frac{2\pi \times 0.07}{0.001} = 439.8\text{N} \tag{6}$$

3.4 *Considering friction*

Friction force is calculated by using Equation (7), These methods provide higher robustness and improved stability for BLDC motion control.
Friction coefficient μ = 0.3

$$F_{\text{friction}} = \mu \times F = 0.3 \times 439.8 = 130\text{N} \tag{7}$$

Net force,

$$F_{\text{net}} = F - F_{\text{friction}} = 439.8 - 130 = 309.8\text{N} \tag{8}$$

3.5 *Force required pushing syringe*

Force required to push the syringe plunger is related to pressure and cross sectional area: [11]

$$F = P \times A \tag{9}$$

P = pressure inside syringe (Pa)
A = plunger cross sectional area

3.6 *Pressure difference using Poiseuille's law*

Poiseuille's Law describes laminar flow pressure drop in microfluidic chip: [12]

$$\Delta P = \frac{8\mu LQ}{\pi R^{\wedge}4} \tag{10}$$

μ = Viscosity of liquid (Ns/m^2)
L = Length of the barrel in meter
Q = Flow rate (m^3/s)
R= Radius of barrel

3.7 *Pressure drops due to the sudden contraction*

When the fluid passes through sudden contraction, pressure losses occur due to turbulence.
Between barrel and hub,

$$\Delta P1 = KC1 + \frac{1}{2}\rho\, v2^2 \tag{11}$$

$$KC1 = \left(1 - \frac{A2}{A1}\right)^2$$

Sudden contraction loss coefficient
ρ = Density of fluid (kg/m^3)
Between Hub and Needle,

$$\Delta P2 = KC2 + \frac{1}{2} \times \rho\, v3^2 \tag{12}$$

$$KC2 = \left(1 - \frac{A3}{A2}\right)^2$$

Needle to channel,

$$\Delta P3 = KC3 + \frac{1}{2} \times \rho\, v4^2 \tag{13}$$

$$KC3 = \left(1 - \frac{A4}{A3}\right)^2$$

$$\Delta P = \Delta p1 + \Delta p2 + \Delta p3 \tag{14}$$

3.8 *Pressure drop for surface area*

$$\Delta \mathrm{P1} = \frac{8\mu \mathrm{L1Q}}{\pi \mathrm{R1}^4} = (\mathrm{P1} - \mathrm{P2}) \tag{15}$$

Pressure drop in hub,

$$\Delta \mathrm{P2} = \frac{8\mu \mathrm{L2Q}}{\pi \mathrm{R2}^4} = (\mathrm{P2} - \mathrm{P3}) \tag{16}$$

Pressure drop in needle,

$$\Delta \mathrm{P3} = \frac{8\mu \mathrm{L3Q}}{\pi \mathrm{R3}^4} = (\mathrm{P3} - \mathrm{P4}) \tag{17}$$

Pressure drop in channel

$$\Delta \mathrm{P4} = \frac{8\mu \mathrm{L4Q}}{\pi \mathrm{R4}^4} = (\mathrm{P4} - \mathrm{P3}) \tag{18}$$

Total pressure drop, $\Delta \mathrm{P0} = $ Sum off(Surface area drop + Cross sectional area drop)

$$F = P1 \times A1 \tag{19}$$

By using P1 we can calculate all pressure

3.9 *The relation between pressure and current*

Motor torque and current relates as, [13], [14]

$$\Delta \mathrm{I} = \frac{\tau}{\mathrm{Kt}} \tag{20}$$

Where $\mathrm{Kt} = \frac{60}{2\pi K v}$
K_v = Speed constant (motor specification)
K_t =Torque constant

$$\mathrm{F} = \frac{2\pi\tau}{\mathrm{L}} \tag{21}$$

$$\tau = \frac{\mathrm{F} \times \mathrm{L}}{2\pi}$$

$$\Delta \mathrm{I} = \frac{(\mathrm{F} \times \mathrm{L})}{2\pi \mathrm{Kt}} \tag{22}$$

$$\Delta = \frac{\mathrm{P1} \times \mathrm{A} \times \mathrm{L}}{2\pi \mathrm{Kt}}$$

3.10 *Calculation for lead screw diameter*

Load =310 N
Martial = Stainless steel
Young's Modules $=195 \times 10^9$ Pascal
Taking column factor =0.7
Safety factor = 2

When the beam is one and is fixed and another end is supported to bearing
By considering, the Euler's buckling formula, [15]

$$Pcr = \frac{(\pi^2 \mathrm{EI})}{(\mathrm{K} \times \mathrm{L}^2)} \tag{23}$$

L=0.3m = 300mm

$$\mathrm{I} = \frac{\pi \mathrm{d}^4}{64}$$

$$Pcr = \frac{(\pi^2 \times 2\mathrm{EI})}{(\mathrm{K} \times \mathrm{L})^2} \tag{24}$$

$$620 = \frac{(\pi^2 \times 195 \times 10^9 \times \mathrm{I})}{(0.7 \times 0.3)^2}$$

$$\mathrm{I} = \frac{27.342}{19.228 \times 10^{11}}$$

d = 0.0043
d = 4.3 mm
The required diameter is 6mm.

a) System design

Figure 2 syringe pump was first made as a simple basic prototype to demonstrate fluid control. It was later upgraded to a product level design in SolidWorks, improving its stability, usability, and component fit. The system uses a motor linked to a lead screw for precise linear motion of the syringe plunger.

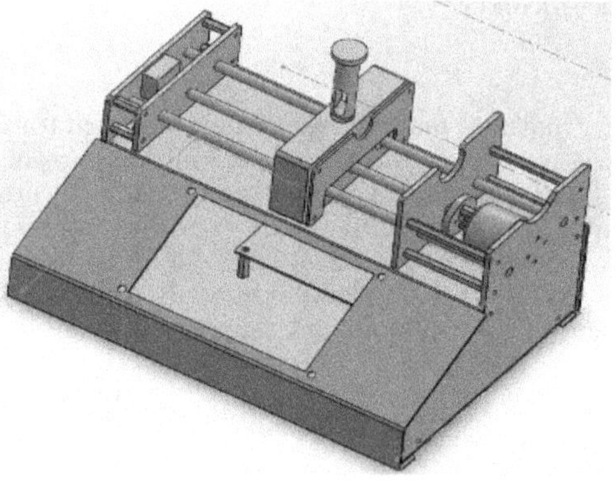

Figure 2. CAD model of syringe pump.

A rigid coupling minimizes backlash, and the frame accommodates syringes of different sizes. The design ensures smooth operation and easy maintenance.

b) Lead screw

The lead screw used in the syringe pump, as shown in the Figure 3, is sourced from the MISUMI website and made of stainless steel for strength and corrosion resistance. It has a total length of 174 mm and a 6 mm diameter, suitable for more precision systems. The screw features a 1 mm pitch for accurate linear motion and fine control of plunger movement. One end is threaded, and both ends are stepped to support secure mounting and alignment. This configuration ensures stable operation, minimal backlash, and it produces performance in fluid delivery

Figure 3. Lead screw.

c) Quick return mechanism

The component shown in Figure 4 a quick return mechanism increases the efficiency of syringe plunger movement. Previously the plunger was pulled back manually by rotating the lead screw in the anti-clockwise direction which slowed down the operation [16]. To solve this problem a quick return system was developed and the plunger is to be rapidly moved back without reversing the motor here we made the central through hole houses the lead screw and it will move precise left and right travel. And shaft guideways maintain alignment and minimize friction. Additionally, this mechanism includes a spring loaded locking nut design. The nut is threaded internally to match the lead screw and is supported by a compression spring. When pressed the nut the spring compresses and creating the clearance the between nut and the screw and allows free movement.

Figure 4. Quick return mechanism.

d) Control system

Software control system controls the BLDC motor speed by using custom design closed loop algorithm signals, where adjusting and regulates the motor's power and flow rate output. Timing pulses based on set flow parameters guide motor operation, while programmed increasing in speed and decreasing in speed ensure smooth movement [17]. A touchscreen interface Nextion, allows users to set flow rate, volume, and duration.

e) User interface

Figure 5. A Nextion touchscreen display is integrated into the system for input and monitoring. The flow rate, volume, and dispensing time can all be adjusted by the user. Real-time operating status, time, and volume dispensed updates are provided by the interface. Closed-loop control modifies motor output and maintains precise flow regulation by utilizing feedback from encoder data and it has three modes implemented clockwise, counter-clockwise and oscillation which enhance user flexibility also enables users to input desired rpm values directly via the touchscreen.

Figure 5. Nextion touchscreen display.

f) Final assembly – Prototype

Figure 6 shows the final outcome of the project, which start with designing the CAD model, followed by fabrication of all individual components, and finally assembling them into the complete syringe pump system.

Figure 6. Final prototype syringe pump.

4 RESULT AND DISCUSSION

The test results of the syringe pump system operated by a BLDC motor shown in Table 1 indicates clearly that flow rate errors at low flow rates are higher. This involves how precisely the pump delivers the fluid, how constant or pulsatile the flow is, and how it compares with the normal pumps based on stepper motors. A range of conditions and different syringe sizes were tested to evaluate the performance of the pump under various cases.

Table 1. Expected and measured volume flow.

Set Flow Rate	*Time (min)*	*Expected Volume (mL)*	*Measured Volume (mL)*	*Error (%)*
50	*5*	*0.25*	*0.247*	*1.2*
100	*10*	*1*	*0.998*	*0.2*
200	*10*	*2*	*2.01*	*0.5*
500	*5*	*2.5*	*2.48*	*0.8*

5 CONCLUSION

A compact and modular syringe pump was developed using stainless steel, mild steel, and acrylic (PMMA), offering both structural strength and fluid visibility. The mechanical design was created in SolidWorks and fabricated using CNC machining, laser cutting, and sheet metal processes. Based on calculated linear actuation loads, a 102.7 W BLDC motor with 0.4 Nm torque was selected to ensure smooth and accurate dosing. A closed-loop control system, integrating an ESP32 and Hall-effect sensor, achieved ±1% flow accuracy even under load. Repeatability tests showed volume variation within ±2%, and flowrate verification matched set values, confirming system reliability. A Nextion-based HMI enabled real-time control of syringe size, infusion withdrawal mode, and flowrate. Flow pulsation tests demonstrated smoother, continuous output compared to traditional stepper motor systems, making it ideal for microfluidic and diagnostic applications.

ACKNOWLEDGEMENT

We also extend our sincere thanks to Mr. Neeraj Bagi, Founder and CEO of Meukron Technologies, for serving as our Mentor and we deeply appreciate their time, dedication, and support.

REFERENCES

[1] P.J. Oliver Norton, (2025). "Design and development of a simple screw mechanism for a low-cost neonatal syringe pump," *Dovepress*.

[2] S. Y. M. A. S. H. C. S. Zida Li, (2014). "Syringe-pump-induced fluctuation in all-aqueous microfluidic system implications for flow rate accuracy," *Royal Society of Chemistry*.

[3] J. K. M. J. K. and. W. K. C. Young Jin Heo, (2016). "Tuning-free controller to accurately regulate flow rates in a microfluidic network," *Nature*.

[4] S.T.O.M. Muhammad Ahmed Khan, (2015). "Designing of microcontroller based syringe pump with variable and low delivery rates for the administration of small volumes," *IEEE*.

[5] H. E. A. G. P. J. Wijnen B, (2014). "Open-source syringe pump library," *PLoS ONE 9(9): e107216*.

[6] T. Furuhashi, S. Sangwongwanich and S. Okuma, (1992). "A position-and-velocity sensorless control for brushless DC motors using an adaptive sliding mode observer," *IEEE Xplore*.

[7] T.B.J.M.L.H. Jakob Rørbæk Saugbjerg, (2023). "The perry project: A versatile low-cost syringe pump for dispensing in automated synthesis systems," *ScienceDirect*.

[8] D.C.A.A.B.G.L. Marco Iannone, (2022). "A low-cost push–pull syringe pump for continuous flow applications," *National Library of Medicine*.

[9] D. R. R. and. W.J. Halliday, (2013). "Fundamentals of physics," *Wiley*.

[10] R. G. and. N.J.K. Budynas, (2015). Shigley's mechanical engineering design, 10th Edition.

[11] Y. A. and. C.J.M. Çengel, (2018). *Fluid mechanics: Fundamentals and applications*, McGraw-Hill.

[12] G.M. Whitesides, (2006). "The origins and the future of microfluidics," *Nature*.

[13] R. Krishnan, (2010). *"Permanent magnet synchronous and brushless DC Motor Drives," CRC Press*.

[14] S.J. Chapman, (2011). *Electric machinery fundamentals*, 5th Edition, McGraw-Hill.

[15] J. M. and. G.B.J. Gere, (2018). *Mechanics of Materials*, 9th Edition, Cengage Learning.

[16] F. Pooke, (2023). "Low-cost, low-power, clockwork syringe pump," *ScienceDirect*.

[17] P. and. K.R. Pillay, (1989). "Application characteristics of permanent-magnet synchronous and brushless DC Motors," *IEEE Trans. on Industry Applications, 25(2)*.

Technology for a Resilient Future – Vincent , Moorthy and Dasari (Eds)

Synergistic Implementation of Metaheuristic Paradigms for Optimization in Intelligent Travel Planning

Nicole Saldanha, Aaradhya Deotale, Aditya Chauhan, and Sana Shaikh
Department of Computer Engineering, Don Bosco Institute of Technology, Mumbai, India

ABSTRACT: The tourism sector has been increasing worldwide, and specifically in India due to factors like globalization, accessibility, availability of information, social media influence and increase in standard of living(thereby rising disposable incomes). Considering the fast pace of life nowadays, existing technological systems prove ineffective and there is a need for improved systems integrated with the latest technologies. There is a need for personalization and optimization of travel itineraries along with integration of facilities that support travel planning. This paper introduces a platform that leverages generative artificial intelligence, integrates different supporting facilities using APIs, improves route optimization efficiently and thereby maximizes customer satisfaction through personalization of travel itineraries. This paper also proposes leveraging personalization algorithms like collaborative filtering. Real time data integration is facilitated, including weather data, and user inputs. Along with route optimization, we propose a balance between budget optimization, based on initial preference of users. We have also considered cultural diversity while training the model to select data points(Points of Interest). We have highlighted different route optimization techniques to include all POIs. Not only have we considered conventional techniques, but more advanced algorithms like Ant Colony Optimization and Particle Swarm Optimization, further understanding the difference between these, and selecting the most optimal algorithm for the given problem statement. We have managed to increase cost efficiency by reducing normal trip cost by 18% - 22%, upon comparing with various other platforms. This paper proposes a comprehensive system for travel planning software, upon surveying a variety of crucial key factors that are non compromisable, thus creating a scalable platform for future travel agencies. This software, integrated with latest-technology promises to generate customized, adaptable trip itineraries while integrating real time resources and optimizing resource constraints.

Keywords: Travel Planning, Collaborative Recommendation, Artificial Intelligence, AI, Recommendation Systems, Ant Colony Optimization, Genetic Algorithm, Particle Swarm Optimization

1 INTRODUCTION

To plan a holiday, one must take into account personal preferences like time, budget and travel company. This makes trip planning quite a challenge, considering the need to optimize such parameters. Earlier, each aspect of a trip was planned separately, for example, booking railway tickets through one website and hotels to another, which meant that users needed to manually complete these planning tasks one at a time in order to create a comprehensive itinerary. Furthermore, considering weather updates, local event information and travel facilities along with the previously mentioned parameters is a challenge. The major gap in existing cohesive systems is that they don't offer sufficient customized options, which is a drawback to overall user satisfaction. We now find the need to use technology to ease manual effort by integrating data sources, different booking platforms and taking into account user preferences. Technological advancements in Computer Science, specifically the fields of artificial intelligence and machine learning make this possible.

We have proposed an integrated system using artificial intelligence to create an intelligent travel planning system that incorporates AI recommendations and data from varied sources. Additionally, upon studying the existing gaps in current systems, we propose a system to address those. This system will optimize parameters based on user preferences like budget and travel preferences, combine data from multiple sources like weather forecasts and transportational availability, thereby creating complete travel plans. Additionally, we propose a system that is easily dynamically adaptable based on user preference. The system proposed utilizes collaborative filtering, uses rating on existing plans and incorporates an intelligent route optimization algorithm.

2 REVIEW OF THE LITERATURE

In order to understand the gaps within the system, we have reviewed existing systems and research on the same. The first paper [1] proposes an online system to plan trips and encourage trip booking by focusing on customer experience and productivity. Bookings are centralized and information is shared through HTML, PHP and Microsoft SQL Server 2008. This allows individual activity reservation, as well as booking tour packages, or accommodation facilities. It is a commercial proposal that also gives firms a marketing opportunity.

In [2], the highlight is on the effects of technological development on travel habits of the youth, with emphasis on aspects like personal preferences, destinations, and mode of reservations. In this paper, 42 studies across over 20 years are reviewed (including journal articles, reviews and books), and the connection between tourism and technological advancements is studied. Another study [3], specific to South Sumatra, suggests the impact of a deficit of tourism related information on the number of tourists. The conclusion of this study is to develop a mobile based travel guide to regulate digital tourism, provide information online and thereby bridge this existing gap.

A hybrid recommendation system which combines content based and collaborative filtering approaches is proposed in [4]. This helps improve accuracy with information on customized aspects like food and shopping recommendations. Cosine similarity is used for similarity measures. This weighted combination of methods increases accuracy of recommendations, leading to improved performance than standalone content-based or collaborative systems.

Paper [5] highlights the need for personalization of travel plans based on variables like age, interests, weather and traffic. Beyond set trip packages, the system provides personalised

DOI: 10.1201/9781042017546-9

recommendations for accommodation, food, and activities through sentiment analysis and geotagging. Paper [6] suggests a route planning system that integrates many forms of transportation, including trains, aeroplanes, and subways, using the A-star algorithm. This offers customers the most inexpensive, comfortable, or time-efficient routes between cities.

A trip planning system in [7] makes use of ChatGPT to comprehend customer preferences and produce customized itineraries. By using a content-based recommendation engine and integrating real-time flight and hotel data with Playwright, it achieves 86% accuracy and great customer satisfaction. In order to reduce rating discrepancies, the e-tourism recommender system presented in Paper [8] combines a genetic algorithm with paired user preference elicitation. A published POI dataset and a user trial with 24 participants attested to its efficacy.

By taking site popularity, cost, time, and distance into account, the strategy in [9] improves route planning. The study demonstrates that a genetic algorithm performs better than baselines in producing user-centred itineraries with the help of actual data from Baidu and Xiecheng. [10] proposes a combination of Collaborative Filtering and transfer learning to reduce the overhead of data processing while providing scalable suggestions. The accuracy of the solution is also enhanced.

The gaps uncovered through the research across studies include lack of integration of real time data (weather, traffic, etc). Poor quality of route optimization, low cost optimization, among other factors. Additionally, current systems do not keep up with technological advancements, and most fail to incorporate the use of AI into the system. Integration of AI techniques such as reinforcement learning can improve personalization of suggestions and system adaptability to consider location-wise regional and cultural diversity. These gaps in existing systems can be addressed, along with integration of enhancements from different existing systems. This enables a more technologically-advanced efficient and personalized solution.

3 METHODOLOGY

3.1 *Data integration*

First we integrated a dataset which contained crucial Points of Interest(POIs) from a variety of popular tourist destinations. These points of interests are gathered or generated using gemini. Additionally, for other points of interest which the user may want to customize, a gemini API key is integrated with the system.

3.2 *Plotting and distancing*

For the POIs which we had earlier created, we first extracted their geocoordinates and then plotted their latitude and longitude on a map. This is for the purpose of internally applying shortest path algorithms to optimize travel route. Further, additional aspects are taken into consideration for route optimization. The Euclidean distances are calculated between these mapped points in order to find the distances between each pair. Other methods of decision making were further used upon finding the distances between POIs.

3.3 *Algorithms*

In order to optimize travel options based on selected POIs, first we checked the efficiency of conventional algorithms on this data. We tried using the greedy algorithm, which aims for a globally optimal solution using stage-wise decisions concerning local optimization. While this may have proved effective to solve computationally demanding issues, their scope is narrow, leading to major drawbacks while identifying best solutions for more challenging problems beyond computational difficulty.

3.3.1 *Divide and conquer*

We used the divide and conquer approach to increase speed and accuracy to find an optimal route. This approach divides an issue into subproblems, solves each individually, and then combines them to find an accurate solution. However, this causes a high amount of recursion which leads to high memory requirements and may lead to a stack overflow issue.

3.3.2 *Dynamic programming*

Another approach we experimented with was dynamic programming which minimized unnecessary calculations and optimized solutions of overlapping subproblems. It's often quite effective for issues like shortest path calculation. However, in cases where there is low overlap of subproblems, it has high complexity.

3.3.3 *Machine learning techniques*

To resolve the complex optimization issues with conventional algorithms, we explored other machine learning optimization techniques.

3.3.3.1 *Ant Colony Optimization (ACO)* To optimize routes, we have integrated the Ant Colony Optimization technique. Combinatorial problems such as TSP were successfully solved by ACO, which iteratively refined solutions based on pheromone trails. However, it had slow convergence in complex cases.

The inverse of the distance is used to determine the desirability of a path to guide ants toward a shorter path as follows:

$$\eta_{ij} = \frac{1}{d(i,j)} \tag{1}$$

The probability of an ant moving from node ii to node jj is calculated as:

$$P_{ij} = \frac{\tau_{ij}^{\alpha} \cdot \eta_{ij}^{\beta}}{\sum_{k \in N} \tau_{ik}^{\alpha} \cdot \eta_{ik}^{\beta}} \tag{2}$$

where:

- τ_{ij}: pheromone level on edge (i,j).
- η_{ij}: heuristic value (inverse distance).
- α: influence of pheromone trails.
- β: influence of heuristic information.

3.3.3.2 *Particle swarm optimization* The next algorithm that was investigated was the Particle Swarm Optimization (PSO), which resulted in excellent exploratory skills in large solution areas, meaning that path optimization was much improved. The convergence occurred quickly to local optima, which necessitated adaptive measures, preserving the search process variety.

For every swap operation, the updated route is calculated as follows using the formula:if random() $\leq$ p, swap(Ci,Cj),

where random() generates a value between 0 and 1.

The algorithm stops computing after a fixed iteration count, or when there is no significant improvement in the global best cost.

3.3.3.3 *Genetic algorithm* *Genetic Algorithm (TSP-GA)* was implemented next, iteratively optimizing travel routes using evolutionary approaches such as selection, crossover and mutation, in order to achieve improved solutions. This hybrid-Machine Learning approach significantly improves the efficiency as well as the adaptability of traditional algorithms, resulting in the optimization of travel solutions based on the inputted points of interest (POIs). Despite TSP-GA showcasing good potential in identifying near-optimal solutions, it turned out to be too computationally costly for extremely large datasets; as the converge point was reached only after several generations.

The specific formula for the Selection Probability using genetic algorithm is:

$$P_i = \frac{f_i}{\sum_j f_j} \tag{3}$$

where Pi is the probability of selecting individual i, while fi is the fitness of i

4 RESULTS

The **Genetic Algorithm** output is displayed in Figure 1.

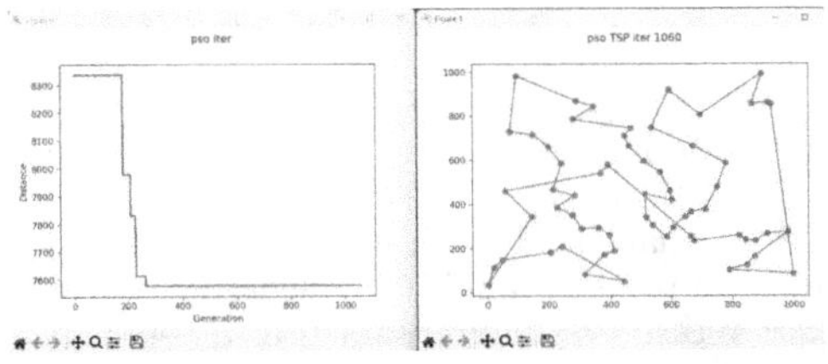

Figure 1. Genetic Algorithm to optimize route selection.

- The left plot illustrates the convergence over the different generations. The x-axis shows the number of generations, while the y-axis represents the total distance of the Travelling Salesman Problem (TSP) solution. An incremental decrease in distance can be concluded as the GA sequentially optimizes the route, with continuous improvements in the solution. This specific behaviour of the GA algorithm is due to its core mechanisms:- crossover, mutation and selection; resulting in a collective evolution of the population towards improved solutions.
- The genetic algorithm's final suggested route is demonstrated in the right plot. Red dots represent the cities, and the green lines indicate the best-found route connecting them. Although the solution appears optimized, some inefficient segments remain, suggesting room for improvement. This is due to GA's susceptibility to **premature convergence**, which can lead to a well-structured, but not necessarily optimal solution.

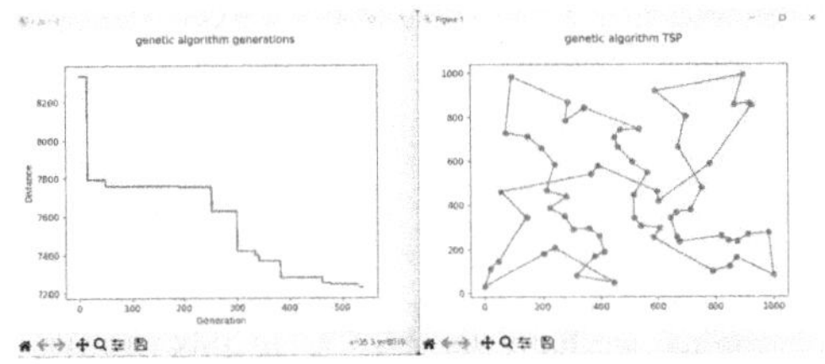

Figure 2. Particle swarm optimization to optimize plan.

Similar to the GA plot, the Particle Swarm Optimization (PSO) results' left plot shows how the algorithm converges over iterations. The number of iterations is shown on the X-axis, and the travel distance on the Y-axis. The PSO curve dips more sharply at the beginning compared to the GA curve, indicating its higher convergence speed to obtain a stable solution.

The green lines connecting the red dots(POIs) depict the best found path. The path is optimized through particle movement within the solution space. Though it may still be vulnerable to local optima, PSO stabilizes faster than GA and uses swarm intelligence to effectively modify the path. While genetic algorithms investigate more alternatives but take longer to converge, particle swarm optimization finds a suitable solution more rapidly but may become trapped in a local optimum.

For solving the Travelling Salesman Problem (TSP), GA is superior to ACO and PSO algorithms because it provides a robust balance between exploration and exploitation. While ACO may excessively encourage inferior paths and PSO may stall in local optima, GA searches for a wider solution space through mutation and crossover, lowering the chance of premature convergence.

Even though the genetic algorithm is better in terms of accuracy of solution, and provides better solutions than both ant colony optimization and the particle swarm optimization algorithms, it is not the best approach for this problem because of its high convergence time. Here, we deal with real time data and require rapid adaptation to the integrated dynamic inputs. Additionally, most users nowadays want instant results, and the speed of generation of a travel plan greatly influences the user's choice of platform. On the other hand, the particle swarm optimization algorithm facilitates quick decision making and offers an optimal balance between speed and accuracy, providing optimal plans very quickly. This quick convergence speed enables adaptability and allows the system to refine outputs efficiently based on real time data fluctuation. After researching different approaches, we have found the PSO approach to be the most suitable for this kind of problem statement.

Table 1. Comparison between GA and PSO.

Criteria	Genetic Algorithm (GA)	Particle Swarm Optimization (PSO)
Convergence Speed	Slower, improves gradually over generations	Faster, improves significantly in early iterations
Final Distance	May reach a competitive solution	Often converges faster to a good solution
Path Structure	Varies due to mutations and crossovers	More directly refined through swarm movement
Optimization Behavior	Explores more broadly due to genetic diversity	Exploits promising solutions more aggressively
Stability	More variance in optimization	Tends to stabilize earlier

4.1 *Platform features*

In order to further improve efficiency as well as travel planning customization, our platform incorporated several advanced features, resulting in an enhancement of user experience and decision-making.

1. Collaborative Filtering: Recommendation of trips based on user preferences and similarities along with other travellers. By analysing trends of past travel trends as well as specific interests - the system suggests various destinations, accommodation options, and specific activities which match the user's preferences. This results in the trip planning being more personalized.
2. Personalized Itinerary Generator: Our platform generates travel plans based on user inputs like the trip duration, preferred destination, number of travellers and specific interests. This allows users to receive optimized travel schedules, balancing various factors such as sightseeing, relaxation and activities. This ensures a well-structured and planned trip that meets their needs, wants and expectations
3. Powered by Generative AI through the Gemini API: Intelligent automation and advanced content generation is implemented, which enhances itinerary suggestions by dynamically adapting the preferences of the user, as well as

providing real-time updates while offering comprehensive travel insights.

4. Generative AI-powered chatbot: The integrated chatbot assists users in the planning and modification phases of the generated trips easily. The chatbot provides live-time recommendations, responds to travel-related queries and also refines user-feedback, which results in an interactive and efficient travel planning experience.
5. Dataset: The program includes enriched geospatial data and retrieves it dynamically via integration of various external APIs. Spatial context and mapping capabilities are sourced from the MapQuest API, which is used for geolocation and routing purposes. Also, a Weather API is also used to source live local weather updates for the specific region. In addition to that, natural language query responses are produced using Google's Generative AI (Gemini) API in response to user enquiries and contextual inputs. For a reference layer, an additional dataset of Points of Interest (POIs) with geographical coordinates is included. This specific dataset is later cross-referenced with external data to output data that is more location-specific and sensitive to user preferences.

Upon multifeature integration, we have successfully developed a smart travel planner that is personalized, and produces enhanced user experience by optimizing trip plans.

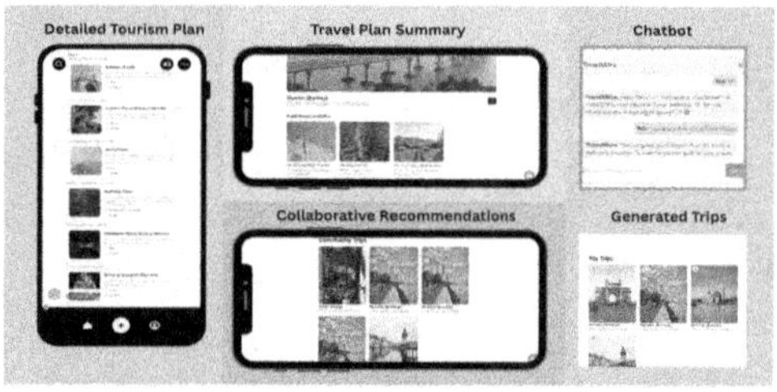

Figure 3. Implementation demonstration.

4.2 *Budget optimization*

In order to ensure that the complete trip cost does not exceed the user's estimated budget, we have implemented a budget score mechanism in the backend. This mechanism iteratively and continuously monitors and adjusts the expenses of the trip. This maintains the budget score which does not exceed it, taking note of the cost efficiency and simultaneously optimizing the travel itinerary.

The specific formula for the Budget Score is given as follows:

$$Budget\ Score = \frac{Actual\ Budget}{Expected\ Budget} \tag{4}$$

whereas the Expected Budget and the Actual Budget attributes are calculated using the formula:

$$Expected\ Budget = \{3500 \times No.\ of\ Days \times No.\ of\ People$$

$$\begin{aligned} Actual\ Budget = {} & Totalt_{Hotel} + (Total_{Distance} * 20) + \frac{1}{10} \\ & * (Total_{Hotel\ \mathrm{Cost}} + Total_{Distance}) + Cost_{Food} \\ & * Days * People \end{aligned} \tag{5}$$

Food cost is dynamically calculated based on the user's selected budget level:

$$\begin{aligned} Food\ Cost = \{ & 100 \times 2,\ if\ Budget\ Level = \text{``}Low\text{''} \\ & 300 \times 2,\ if\ Budget\ Level = \text{``}Medium\text{''} \\ & 800 \times 2,\ if\ Budget\ Level = \text{``}High\text{''}) \end{aligned} \tag{6}$$

To maintain budget constraints, our backend system continuously checks and updates the budget score in order to prevent it from exceeding it. If the score nears or surpasses this pre-determined limit, dynamic adjustments are made like recommending economical hotels, optimizing travel routes to minimize the distance covered or by suggesting budget-friendly food options. This ensures a seamless and budget-friendly trip planning experience without falling short of the user's necessary expectations.

5 CONCLUSIONS

We concluded that the Particle Swarm Optimisation (PSO) algorithm is the most optimal implementation, given its faster convergence and successful adjustment to real-time data.

The PSO algorithm is suited to be the best fit for dynamic contexts for quick decisions, due to its simplicity and quickness. Comparing this with GA, which could be computationally demanding due to additional sub-processes such as crossover and mutation; PSO updates solutions based on the particle movements impacted by both individual and group experiences. This guarantees improved performance as well as better adaptability in our real-time application, effectively optimising routes in response to continuously changing inputs.

This platform leverages gen-AI, AI algorithms along with latest technology to maximize user satisfaction. Based on similarity of interests and preferences, collaborative filtering enhances these customized trip plans. The dynamic itinerary generator allows modifiable plans based on group size, destination and duration of stay. The chatbot enhances user satisfaction by providing continuous support.

Our final solution provides a comprehensive and intelligent trip planning implementation by combining AI-driven personalization and automation with GA for route optimization. Travel itinerary planning is made more streamlined, personalized, and responsive through the use of generative AI as well as machine learning algorithms, guaranteeing an effective and user-centric experience.

ACKNOWLEDGMENT

We thank our management and college faculty for all the support and guidance we have received from this institution, Don Bosco Institute of Technology, Kurla. We are also grateful for all the guidance that we have received throughout our research on the subject.

REFERENCES

[1] M.J. Abu-AlShaeer, H.A. Hasan, S.I. Mustafa, D. Khlaponin, and K. Krasovska, (2024). "A comprehensive online tourism management system revolutionizes travel," in *Proc. 35th Conf. Open Innovations Assoc. (FRUCT)*, Tampere, Finland, pp. 22–32, https://doi.org/10.23919/FRUCT61870.2024.10516422.

[2] S. Gupta, T. Sufi, and P.K. Gautam, (2022)."Role of technological transformation in shaping millennials' travel behaviour: A

review," in *Proc. 10th Int. Conf Reliability, Infocom Technol. Optim. (ICRITO))*, Noida, India, pp.1–6, https://doi.org/10.1109/ICRITO56286.2022.9965175.

[3] U. Ependi, A. Muzakir, F. Fatoni, M. Bunyamin, D. Irawan, and I. Effendy, (2019). "Model for mobile application development on traveling guide: A general proposal," in *Proc. Int. Conf. Electr. Eng. Comput. Sci. (ICECOS)*, Batam, Indonesia, pp. 122–126, https://doi.org/10.1109/ICECOS47637.2019.8984548.

[4] V. Garipelly, P.T. Adusumalli, and P. Singh, (2021). "Travel recommendation system using content and collaborative filtering – A hybrid approach," in *Proc. 12th Int. Conf. Comput. Commun. Netw. Technol. (ICCCNT)*, Kharagpur, India, pp. 1–4, https://doi.org/10.1109/ICCCNT51525.2021.9579907.

[5] P. Bapat, R. Jadhav, V. Mishra, and A. Sahitya, (2022). "An approach travel recommendation system and route optimizer using AI," in *Proc. 5th Int. Conf. Adv. Sci. Technol. (ICAST)*, Mumbai, India, pp. 486–490, https://doi.org/10.1109/ICAST55766.2022.10039531.

[6] Y. Zhou, X. Cheng, X. Lou, Z. Fang, and J. Ren, (2020). "Intelligent travel planning system based on A-star algorithm," in *Proc. 4th IEEE Inf. Technol., Netw., Electron. Autom. Control Conf. (ITNEC)*, Chongqing, China, pp. 426–430, https://doi.org/10.1109/ITNEC48623.2020.9085072.

[7] K. Londge, N. Dharmadhikari, P. Zaveri, and U. Sakoglu, (2023). "Enhanced travel experience using artificial intelligence: A data-driven approach," in *Proc. Int. Conf. Mach. Learn. Data Eng. (ICMLDE)*.

[8] N.N. Qomariyah and D. Kazakov, (2021). "A genetic-based pairwise trip planner recommender system," *J. Big Data*, vol. 8, no. 1, p. 77, doi: 10.1186/s40537-021-00470-6.

[9] Y. Zhang, L. Jiao, Z. Yu, Z. Lin, and M. Gan, (2020). "A tourism route-planning approach based on comprehensive attractiveness," *IEEE Access*, vol. 8, pp. 39536–39547, doi: 10.1109/ACCESS.2020.2967060.

[10] Y. Zhai, X. Wei, and J. Song, (2020). "Design and implementation of a personalized tourism recommendation system based on the data mining and collaborative filtering algorithm," *Complexity*, vol. 2020, pp. 1–13.

Technology for a Resilient Future – Vincent , Moorthy and Dasari (Eds)
© 2027 The Author(s), ISBN: 978-1-041-39070-1

Comparative Material and Ergonomic Evaluation of Standard 3D-Printed Hand Casts and Conventional Orthopedic Casts

Mahantash M Math, Sridhar R, and Shanmukha Nagaraj
Department of Mechanical Engineering, R.V. College of Engineering, Bangalore, India

K N Subramanya
Department of Industrial Engineering and Management, R.V. College of Engineering, Bangalore, India

Pratham Y Sherigar, Gautam Singh, Harsh Rai, and Rajat Upadhyay
Department of Mechanical Engineering, R.V. College of Engineering, Bangalore, India

ABSTRACT: The present study investigates the relative efficacy of 3D-printed hand casts for orthopedic immobilization by drawing comparisons with the traditional methods on performance, hygiene, and ergonomic considerations. In their production, 3D-printed casts were made from PLA (polylactic acid), which is a biodegradable thermoplastic, and designed to have an open-lattice structure with the intent of promoting airflow and insuring close conformance to the anatomical contours of the hand. Structural integrity was studied by finite element analysis (FEA) within the ANSYS software package in replicating typical mechanical loading scenarios. Chemical resistance testing included subjecting the casts to a selection of commonly encountered disinfectants-such as soap, alcohol, phenyl, and chlorine solutions-where the chlorine-based solutions proved to be the most detrimental to the material, as revealed by significant losses in weight. Ergonomic evaluation made use of digital anthropometric modeling in concert with subjective user feedback, which showed that PLA-based casts outperform conventional options in terms of comfort, ventilation, and ease of cleaning. It would appear that 3D-printed PLA casts may represent an attractive alternative for short-term orthopedic immobilization with improved hygiene, wearer comfort, and mechanical robustness compared to plaster and fiberglass casts.

Keywords: 3D-Printed Orthopaedic Cast, Additive Manufacturing, Chemical Degradation, Digital Healthcare, Ergonomic Evaluation, Finite Element Analysis (FEA), Patient Comfort, Polylactic Acid (PLA)

1 INTRODUCTION

Orthopaedic immobilisation is crucial for the facilitation of musculoskeletal injury healing. Traditional casts, usually made from POP or fibreglass, provide reliable mechanical support but suffer from several disadvantages: a lack of ventilation, discomfort over longer periods of wear, vulnerability to damage by moisture, and poor conformity to specific patient anatomy. These issues have driven interest in investigating other materials and alternative manufacturing methods that could serve both clinical efficacy and patient comfort more effectively.

Additive manufacturing, especially through 3D printing, provides new possibilities for the fabrication of lightweight, mechanically efficient, and customized medical devices. Of particular interest is polylactic acid, a biocompatible thermoplastic that exhibits ease of processing and mechanical properties well-suited for biomedical applications. The designing of PLA in open-lattice configurations allows for better air circulation, reduction in the weight of the device, and enhancement of ergonomic conformity-an attribute lacking in conventional casting technologies.

The research will investigate the feasibility of replacing conventional hand casts with 3D printed PLA substitutes. The main goals are to (i) use FEA in ANSYS to analyze the mechanical stability and fatigue resistance of the PLA designs against expected loading conditions, and to (ii) test the ergonomic factors of comfort, fit, and usability through digital modeling and subjective end-user input. Other aspects of this research are the examination of different disinfectants and their influence on PLA regarding hygiene and clinical durability issues.

By integrating computational simulations, experimental tests, and user-centred assessments, this study contributes to the growing field of personalised healthcare solutions, offering a comprehensive evaluation of PLA-based 3D-printed casts in orthopaedic applications [3–5]

2 LITERATURE REVIEW

Advances in orthopaedic care are due to 3D printing technologies, which allow for extreme levels of mechanical strength, greater levels of patient comfort, and increased levels of customisation. In their study, Fitzpatrick *et al.* demonstrated that a 3D-printed cast had far greater comfort, less weight, and greater ventilation than either plaster or fibreglass cast systems. The authors proposed that by using parametric modelling and creating automated design workflows, this production process would benefit patients in a revolutionary way. Similarly, Katt *et al.* investigated the application of 3D-printed medical devices in pediatric care, observing positive healing results alongside minimal adverse effects. They highlighted the necessity for broader clinical trials to validate these findings across varied patient populations. Similarly, Lu *et al.* examined ankle immobilisation utilising 3D-printed lattice designs, reporting enhanced patient compliance, greater comfort, and superior aesthetic outcomes relative to traditional methods. While their findings indicated the potential of 3D printing for use in the upper extremity, they emphasised that their findings only represent an initial step forward and recommended that further studies regarding the use of 3D-printed materials be conducted. Furthermore, Chen *et al.* reported a comparison between the mechanical properties of a 3D-printed forearm cast made of PLA (Poly Lactic Acid) and a plaster of Paris cast. Their findings provided evidence that patients preferred the 3D-printed cast and exhibited better mechanical capabilities than those of a

DOI: 10.1201/9781042017546-10

traditional plaster cast. Thus, their research supports the need for the use of simulation-based methods to optimise the design of orthopaedic devices during the course of care. Initial recommendations for 3D printing were published by Xiao *et al.*, who indicated that immediate access to 3D printing could provide significant advantages in improved image compatibility and patient acceptance. These studies provided a framework for using 3D printing in healthcare systems that are both cost-effective and scalable in nature.

3 LITERATURE GAP

3.1 *Technicaland Material performance*

Despite important advances, critical gaps remain in existing research into 3D-printed orthopaedic devices. While mechanical durability has been proven in simulated laboratory environments, there is scant evidence regarding their long-term performance during clinical use, especially under repeated disinfection conditions. Specifically, PLA degradation behavior under common disinfectants such as phenol, alcohol, and chlorine has been understudied. This represents a critical omission because long-term safety, hygiene, and potential reutilization of the casts will be highly dependent on their chemical resistance. In addition, although FEA is widely used to predict mechanical stress and deformation, few studies employ empirical verification to determine physical alterations such as weight loss or surface degradation. The reliance on simulation alone severely limits the reliability and clinical applicability of many existing results.

A significant gap remains in the evaluation of ergonomic and user-experience parameters of 3D-printed casts. While many studies report an increase in comfort and anatomical fit, such claims are usually not quantitatively supported by robust anthropometric data or standardized assessment tools. Digital human modeling software is underexploited in the iterative improvement of cast designs for optimized comfort, fit, and immobilization effectiveness. Moreover, other usability factors that are crucial for practical clinical application, including ease of application and removal, ventilation during extended wear, washability, and sustained adherence, are rarely systematically investigated.

3.2 *Ergonomic and clinical assessment*

The literature currently lacks comprehensive ergonomic evaluations of 3D-printed orthopaedic casts. Although enhanced comfort and fit are frequently claimed, these assertions rarely rest on systematic user feedback or quantifiable anthropometric data. Critical aspects such as ventilation, device weight, and overall usability have received limited investigation. Furthermore, the potential of digital human modeling software for motion analysis and improving cast fit has not been comprehensively utilized. Further studies focused on practical issues including washability, sustained patient compliance, and the ease of application and removal are essential to facilitate broader clinical adoption.

4 PROBLEM DEFINITION

Conventional casting techniques are known to be effective for immobilizing injuries, and they do present significant challenges in terms of patient comfort and hygiene. The heavy weight of materials used in casting, such as fiberglass and plaster of Paris, provides a rigid structure with little to no air flow, leading to discomfort, skin irritation and difficulty maintaining hygiene for extended periods of time. Additionally, conventional cast materials have limited options when it comes to custom design adaptability. Consequently, the inability to create a cast that precisely conforms to a patient's respective anatomical structure compromises the potential for achieving ergonomic outcomes.

On the other hand, additive manufacturing, specifically with the use of polylactic acid (PLA) as the primary material, provides a lightweight, well ventilated way to create orthopaedic devices that fit the specific anatomical characteristics of individual patients. The biodegradable nature of PLA and the simplicity of the process used to create them provides additional benefits for their use in the medical field.

While significant advantages exist in 3D-printed PLA castings, there is still a need to thoroughly validate their mechanical performance in realistic loading conditions and to determine how common clinical disinfectants impact the durability of the material. Additionally, there must be a combination of digital human modelling and direct user testing to confirm the ergonomic compatibility and user satisfaction of these devices. For this research study, experiments will support and validate the findings of the chemical degradation studies, the simulated structural assessments and the ergonomic evaluations to assess the overall effectiveness and potential for clinical application of 3D-printing orthopaedic casts using PLA materials.

5 METHODOLOGY

The purpose of this study was to conduct a systematic assessment of 3D-printed PLA casts for hands with respect to strength, resistance to chemical and environmental exposures, and fit. 3D prints were created under consistent, reproducible conditions using several printing parameters: infill density, layer thickness, and print orientation were controlled for each printed cast.

5.1 *Finite Element Analysis (FEA)*

Mechanical analyses were performed on the PLA via the ANSYS Workbench Mechanical Simulator, which looked at deformations and stress distributions on the cast as though it had been used for wrist immobilization. The loads for the simulation were typical hand activity loads and the support fixtures were placed on both the proximal and distal sides of the wrist as they would be anatomically. A fatigue analysis was also completed to determine the structural integrity of the cast under cyclic loading. Three static loads were analyzed and corresponded to three real-world scenarios of how the PLA cast could be deformed: an accidental impact, moderate weight load on a hand, and misuse.

5.2 *Boundary conditions*

In the mechanical simulator, the fixed supports were affixed to the base of the PLA cast (at the forearm area) and a load was applied to a localized area of the dorsal wrist to replicate external forces that might be encountered with the use of a cast.

5.3 *Load cases*

Three separate load cases were simulated:

(i) Case 1: 1 kg $\approx$9.81 N
(ii) Case 2: 5 kg $\approx$49.05 N
(iii) Case 3: 10 kg $\approx$98.1 N

These were applied as force boundary conditions perpendicular to the cast surface using the normal to face direction vector.

5.4 *Chemical exposure testing*

Cast samples were tested in several different cleaning agents (soap, alcohol, phenyl, hard water, chlorine). The purpose of this test was to determine how the cast materials would endure in a hygienic environment after submersion for 15 days. After submersion, weight of the cast samples will determine the amount of chemical degradation that occurred; and visual inspections will document surface deterioration or change in dimensions.

5.5 *Ergonomic assessment*

Digital ergonomic evaluations were completed utilizing CATIA and other human modelling software, to validate cast moulds against a digital mannequin. This will allow for the evaluation of manual hand posture alignment, surface contact, and limitation of wrist motion restrictions. Feedback was also collected from users regarding physical characteristics of the casts.

5.6 *Comparative analysis*

Conventional plaster casts served as the standard against which the 3D-printed PLA casts were compared. Comparison metrics included the overall usability of each type of cast concerning wearability, comfort, and cleanliness; the degree of chemical degradation (based on weight loss); the degree to which each cast was ergonomically adaptable (based on human modelling and user feedback); and the amount of mechanical load each cast could withstand while maintaining structural integrity.

6 RESULTS AND DISCUSSIONS

6.1 *Structural performance evaluation*

The analysis of the 3D Printed PLA Cast went through Finite Element Analysis (FEA) in ANSYS. The FEA showed that the stress distribution produced by the forces on the overall structure was uniform throughout the entire open-lattice design style for typical hand immobilisation loads. The maximum Von Mises Stress observed during testing was well beneath the yield strength of PLA. This confirmed that the design is structurally adequate to support applications that do not require load-bearing orthopaedic use. The deformation produced by the loads applied to the model was also acceptable and within allowable tolerances. Thus, the test results confirmed that the cast would remain structurally adequate to maintain the integrity of immobilisation without excessive bending or failure.

Key Findings:

Max VonMises stress: ~15MPa (PLAyield~60MPa) as shown in Figure 1

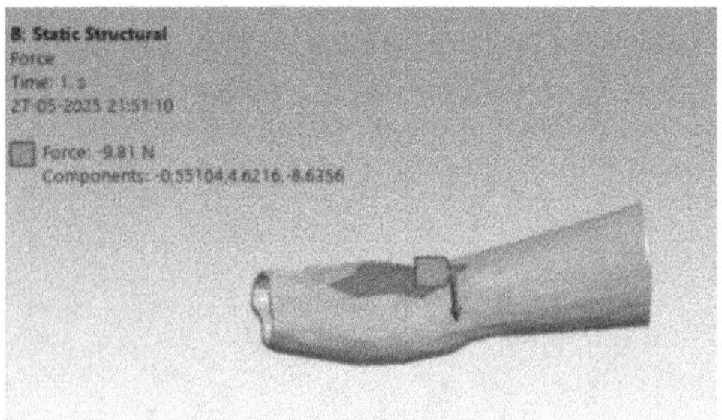

Figure 1. Stress distribution on the 3D-printed PLA cast model under immobilization load (ANSYS static structural analysis).

Max Deformation: <1.5 mm as shown in Figure 2

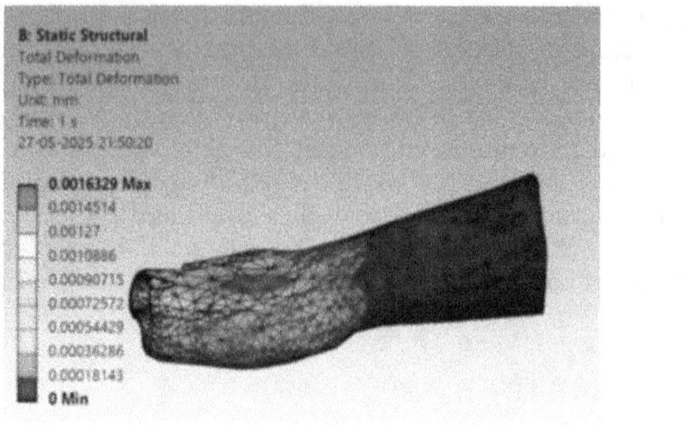

Figure 2. Total Deformation plot of the cast model under the same load conditions.

6.2 *Chemical resistance and weight loss study*

A second analysis was performed to determine the overall durability of the hygiene of the PLA cast. The samples of PLA were submerged for 15 days in several types of solutions that are commonly used in the home environment. The weight-loss results from the immersion test (shown in Figure 3) disclosed that chlorinated water produced the most degradation of all samples, producing a weight loss of approximately 9g for the chlorinated water. All other examined types of solutions.

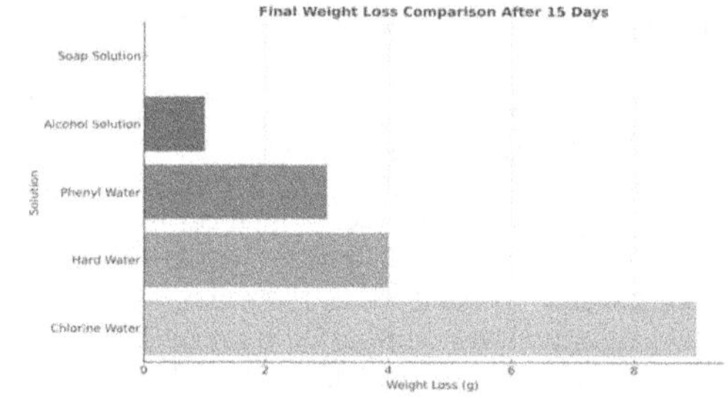

Figure 3. Weight loss comparison in chemical exposure test.

6.3 *Compression testing using UTM*

Testing in compression was carried out by using a Universal Testing Machine, UTM 2000, to determine structural reliability of the 3D-printed PLA hand cast under conditions that simulate real-life 'accidental' loads. Such testing aims to model any unintentional pressures that are likely to be encountered during the healing process, such as those applied inadvertently while sleeping or resting and during everyday activities. This will ensure that the cast can bear these forces and ensure patient safety while averting unexpected failure.

The cast was oriented horizontally for the test between the UTM compression plates, which were set to follow the curvature of the cast. This setup was calibrated to ensure accurate load measurement and to reproduce an anatomically realistic distribution of pressure, particularly across the dorsal and volar regions of the wrist. Compression was applied under a controlled crosshead speed so that gradual loading would be simulated, while force–displacement data were continuously recorded until noticeable deformation occurred.

6.4 *Observations and results*

Initially, when load was applied to the cast, it displayed linear elastic characteristics and showed no permanent deformation. Up to around 4.3 kN of load, the cast had maintained its structural integrity however, at loads greater than that, micro-cracked regions began to form at the junctions of the lattice; i.e., where maximum loads were being applied. The type of failure of this sample was progressive with a gradual reduction in stiffness rather than catastrophic collapse. Since the cast had retained its overall mechanical integrity and configuration, it indicated a sufficient safety factor against loads of unknown magnitude. This type of failure is consistent with how many brittle thermoplastics, such as PLA, behave under stress, where the localized stresses become greater than the yield point of the material without large amounts of plastic deformation occurring.

To improve upon the cast's stiffness-to-weight ratio while continuing to keep its integrity, a topology optimization of the cast was done in ANSYS. This optimization used realistic loading conditions and boundary conditions with the fixation points of the thumb and wrist to emulate how the cast may be used to immobilize the wrist and how effectively it will function. The optimisation then removed the regions of the cast that have minimal stress and eventually resulted in a cast that was approximately 28% lighter than its original design but had equivalent stiffness to maintain safety factor margins.(As shown in Figure 4)

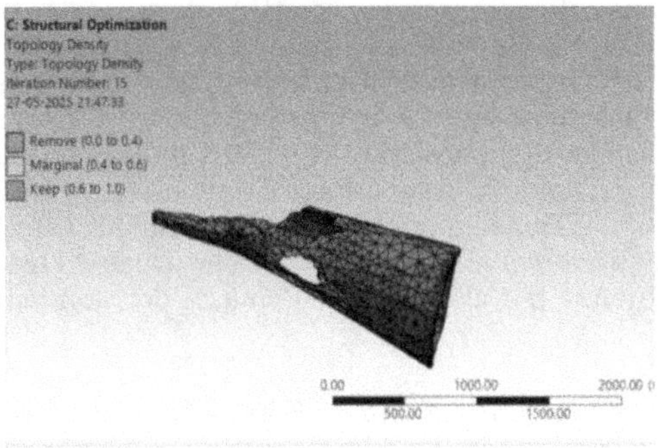

Figure 4. Topology optimized PLA cast design showing material removal regions.

6.5 *Ergonomic feedback and user assessment*

CATIA Ergonomic modeling showed that the open-lattice design of the cast fitted well with the anatomy of the human hand, as shown in Figure 5. Comfort, breathability, and ease of use were highly rated by most users. Minor issues included the discomfort of edges in the untreated prints, pointing to a need for better surface finishing.

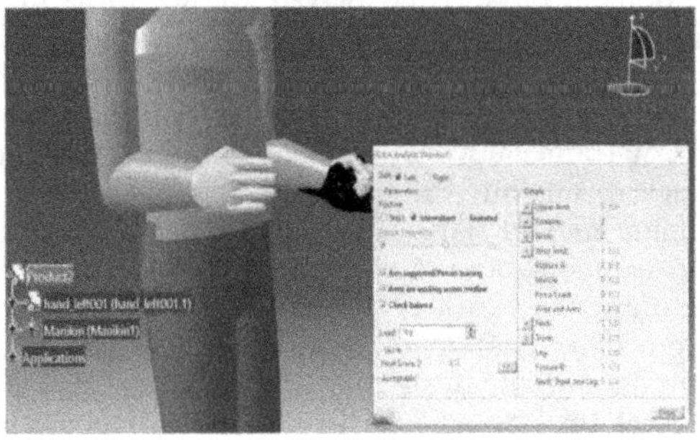

Figure 5. Rula analysis of the 3D printed cast.

7 CONCLUSION

In this article, a comprehensive analysis of PLA (polylactic acid) 3D-printed hand casts has been completed to evaluate their viability as a viable alternative to traditional orthopedic casting systems. The study found that the cast structure had enough structural integrity and adequate comfort and breatheability when tested both through simulation and experimentation. Finite Element Analysis (FEA) results confirmed that the open-lattice structure could carry loads associated with daily use with very little deformation under mechanical loading, while topology optimization allowed for a reduction in cast weight of 28% without losing mechanical performance. Compression testing confirmed that the cast's structural integrity is maintained until 4.3 kN and that chemical resistance testing demonstrated an acceptable level of protection from mild chemical agents and significant chemical degradation from chlorine-based chemicals, indicating that a method for protecting the cast should be developed. Both the ergonomic evaluation and user feedback confirmed that these casts are better fitting than traditional casts and provide a much more comfortable and user-friendly experience, though improvements in surface finishing processes will be needed. PLA 3D-printed casts may be a suitable, lightweight and hygienic means of providing short-term orthopedic care for the patient. Additional studies focused on methods for efficiently integrating multiple materials in a 3D printing process, increased clinical validation of PLA 3D-printed medical devices, and effective surface treatments for optimizing long-term mechanical properties should be conducted.

8 RECOMMENDATIONS FOR FUTURE RESEARCH

Future studies should be prepared for modern-day restringing. Using different filaments than were used for the previous studies will give researchers new experiences with improved elastomeric, higher impact strength PET-Gs, as well as carbon-reinforced polymers, which may provide increased elastic modulus, abrasion resistance, and thermal stability in clinical use. New filaments may also provide enhanced hygiene features or chemical resistance through the application of surface treatments such as hydrophobic coatings or antimicrobial sprays.

Additional cyclic fatigue testing will be necessary in future studies to simulate realistic repeatable patterns of body stress and strain over time. The use of strain gauge techniques in conjunction with digital imaging correlation (DIC) techniques will provide an accurate view of how loads and strains are distributed throughout the whole system as opposed to being confined to just a small section of a lattice or honeycomb.

To create a more realistic assessment of the effectiveness of "smart" castings and braces to support ergonomics and comfort for users, throughout future studies of ergonomics and user acceptability researchers must increase sample sizes so that they are statistically valid and will contribute to a larger body of evidence. The use of pressure mapping technology and collaborating with additional clinical facilities to carry out long-term compatibility and usability studies can also increase researchers‘ understanding of how to fit a larger population regardless of age or the type of fracture being treated.

Integrating IOT and wearable technologies into the design and functionality of orthopedic devices is another exciting area of potential further exploration and development. Smart casts with embedded temperature or motion sensors can provide alerts to users and providers if there are any problems during the healing process or with the position of the injury, which would enhance post-care surveillance.

REFERENCES

[1] Fitzpatrick, V., *et al.*, (2017). "3D-printed casts improved comfort, fit, ventilation, and reduced weight," *J. Med. Devices*, vol. 11, no. 2, pp.125–130.

[2] Katt, M., *et al.*, (2021). "Pediatric cases showed excellent healing and no complications with3Dcasts," *Pediatric. Ortho. Rev.*, vol.36, pp.89–93

[3] Lu, X., *et al.*, (2021). "3D-printed ankle casts improved comfort, compliance, and aesthetics," *Int. J. Biomed. Eng.*, vol. 18, no. 3, pp. 210–217.

[4] Chen, Y., *et al.*, (2020). "3D-printed forearm casts outperformed plaster in mechanics and satisfaction," *Mater. Today Proc.*, vol. 45, pp. 1782–1786.

[5] Xiao, L., *et al.*, (2024). "Instant 3D castsyieldedbetter imagingoutcomes andpatient satisfaction," *Rapid Prototyping J.*, vol. 30, no. 1, pp.23–29.

Technology for a Resilient Future – Vincent , Moorthy and Dasari (Eds)
© 2027 The Author(s), ISBN: 978-1-041-39070-1

Enhancing Explainable AI with Diverse Counterfactual Explanations (DiCE) for Transparent Stroke Risk Assessment

Alpa Patel, Aqib Hussain, Sindhu S, and Ambanna S Madabhavi
Dayananda Sagar University, Kudlu Gate, Bengaluru

ABSTRACT: Explainable AI (XAI) is growing in demand, more in areas like healthcare, where understanding of the model, accountability and trust are essential. Though black-box models with their very good predictive capability, their limit in transparency, delay acceptance in clinical environment. In the following study, we familiarize a model that is understandable for stroke risk estimation through Diverse Counterfactual Explanations (DiCE) to present modified, human-interpretable clarifications of model predictions.A comparison of multiple machine learning algorithms was conducted, the analysis displayed superior predictive performance in the Random Forest classifier relative to other methods assessed. A real-world healthcare dataset was chosen, the Random Forest model was trained on that and to overcome the issue of class imbalance the Synthetic Minority Over-Sampling Technique (SMOTE) was applied during preprocessing. The model finally achieved an accuracy of 96.30% indicating the robust performance.The integration of DiCE, we have derived from different and actionable counterfactual explanations that expose minimal yet meaningful modifications required to change the models predictions. These are grounded in clinically relevant features such as age, BMI, and glucose level, thereby enhancing both the usability and interpretability of the model.The proposed framework validates that counterfactual explanations not only improve model transparency but also provision clinical decision-making by giving importance to key modifiable risk factors.

Keywords: Explainable AI (XAI), Counterfactual Explanations, DiCE, Stroke Prediction, Random Forest, SMOTE, Healthcare

1 INTRODUCTION

Artificial Intelligent models become increasingly embedded in healthcare, it has now been more critical and needful to have a transparent, interpretable and predictive model. In high-stakes applications such as prognosis and medical diagnosis, it is necessary that AI solutions provide not only predictions that are accurate but also comprehensible, clear perceptive to build faith and support acceptance among the healthcare professionals and patients alike [1,4,5,13].

Explainable AI(XAI) enables greater transparency in sophisticated models without undermining their predictive performance. Although advanced results are often achieved using black-box approaches such as collaborative algorithms and deep neural networks, their resistant nature limits the ability to justify model decisions, especially in planned and safety-sensitive settings like healthcare [1,16]. Counterfactual explanations help ease this limitation by presenting "what-if" scenarios—minimal changes to input features that would lead to different outcomes—thereby enhancing interpretability and refining the transparency of model performance[6,11,17]. In this research, we target stroke prediction, where timely and interpretable can be life-saving. Existing models are lacking in interpretability to be useful in clinical application [3,12]. We employ the Diverse Counterfactual Explanations (DiCE) framework [11] to generate multiple plausible counterfactuals, offering further insights into decision logic of the model. A Random Forest classifier from a real-world stroke dataset, balanced with SMOTE. Feature engineering and encoding were done with care to maintain data fidelity as well as interpretability.

Moreover, we restrict perturbation to clinically relevant continuous features such that the generated counterfactuals not only diverge but also are realistic in the healthcare environment [2,6].

Our approach has equally predictive performance with instance-level counterfactual generation complemented by feature importance analysis to generate global model explanations [10,13].

This research demonstrates the role of XAI in developing interpretable, trustworthy, and personalized decision aids to predict stroke risk. By filling the gap in between predictive power and interpretability, our research advances the discipline of explainable AI in medicine [1,8,14,15,18].

Following chapters of the paper are structured accordingly: Section 2 reviews related work, Section 3 narrates the methodology that has been applied to design our proposed model, Section 4 provides the results, and finally Section 5 concludes the research and announces future scopes.

2 RELATED WORK

The development of XAI has played a crucial role in creating models that are accurate and interpretable, especially in sensitive domains such as healthcare. A number of research works have identified the need for transparency in machine learning so that it can guarantee ethical and legal compliance, especially in clinical decision-making settings [1,5,13].

The counterfactual clarifications have gained traction due to their easy-to-understand appeal and decision support capabilities, among the various XAI methods. They are minimal in the theoretical foundation of counterfactual reasoning, which focuses on identifying restricted and meaningful changes to input features that would lead to a desired outcome[17]. This was further developed by DiCE (Diverse Counterfactual Explanations), enabling the generation of multiple, diverse, and realistic counterfactuals for an instance, overcoming the shortcomings of one-dimensional explanations [11].

Counterfactual explanations improve clinician trust by offering actionable, interpretable insights without reducing model accuracy [6,11]. For disease prediction systematic review of XAI methods in healthcare, suggesting counterfactual explanations for their actionable nature and interpretability [2].

Recent research combines XAI methods such as SHAP and LIME in stroke prediction, although it does not have the personalized insight provided by counterfactuals [12].To create stable counterfactuals DiCE Extended, a robust version of DiCE that considers realism and stability in explanations [2].

Our study is applying the DiCE framework in the context of stroke prediction, balancing diversity and plausibility of

DOI: 10.1201/9781042017546-11

explanations. Moreover, the importance of both local (instance-level) and global (feature importance) explanations for full model interpretability [10,13]. Our use of Random Forest feature importance complements the counterfactuals by offering a holistic view of model behaviour. SMOTE is used to address a recurring issue of class imbalance in medical datasets, which also joins with best practices recommended by contemporary works [12,18].

This research integrates counterfactual explanation generation via DiCE, handling of class imbalance, and feature important visualization is to yield an understandable and actionable stroke prediction model.

3 METHODOLOGY

The experimental format and methods used to build an explainable stroke prediction model using counterfactual perspective. The overall procedure comprises of five key steps: data preparation, data preprocessing, handling class imbalance, model training, and generation of counterfactual explanations using DiCE.

(a) Dataset description

A publicly available healthcare dataset for stroke prediction, with 5,110 rows and including feature like age, gender, hypertension, heart disease, BMI, smoking status, glucose level, and stroke outcome is utilized in this research. The target variable is binary: stroke (1 = stroke occurred, 0 = no stroke). The dataset is not balanced to a certain extent, with a negative case(stroke) more than the positive ones.

(b) Data preprocessing

To ensure the quality and dependability of the model, preprocessing stages were critical. The deletion of rows with null values were done to handle missing values. Attributes like gender, smoking status and residence type which were labelled as categorical were applied encoding. Binary features (0/1) were mapped to ever_married, heart disease and hypertension.

(c) It was observed that the dataset exhibited a characteristic imbalance between cases of stroke and non-stroke results. The Synthetic Minority Over-sampling Technique (SMOTE) was employed to minimize the possible bias during model training. This method will enhance minority class representation (stroke = 1) by synthetically generating new instances through feature-space interpolation between nearest-neighbour samples, thereby increasing data density in sparse regions and improving classifier robustness. A balanced dataset with 3,245 instances in both the stroke (1) and non-stroke (0) classes was generated after applying SMOTE as seen in Figure 1.

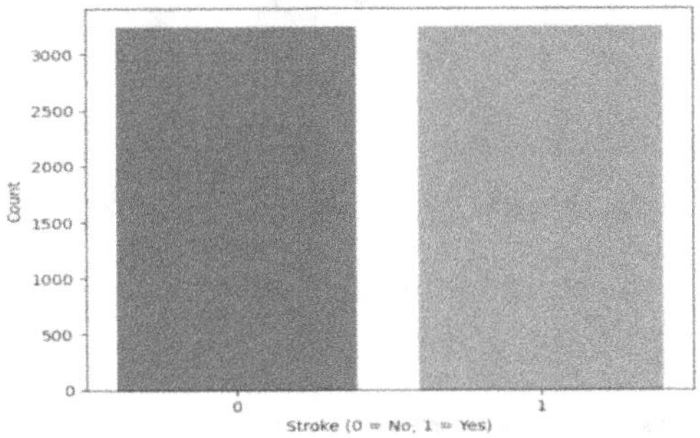

Figure 1. Class distribution of stroke dataset after SMOTE.

(d) Training policy

Random Forest, Gradient Boosting, Decision Tree, K Nearest Neighbours (KNN), Logistic Regression, Support Vector Machine (SVM), and Naïve Bayes were some of machine learning algorithms on which a comparative analysis was done. All the algorithm's were trained using the same preprocessor stroke dataset to ensure fair assessment.The models were assessed based on key performance metrics such as accuracy, precision, recall, and F1-score, along with their respective training times.As given in Figure 2 results, Random Forest achieved the highest accuracy (96.30%). Sowe were selected Random Forest Classifier for our model.

Model	Accuracy	Precision	Recall	F1-score	Training Time (s)
Random Forest	0.963020	0.991511	0.931419	0.960526	0.878761
Gradient Boosting	0.959168	0.994828	0.920255	0.956089	1.485702
Decision Tree	0.948382	0.950161	0.942584	0.946357	0.039264
KNN	0.885208	0.821237	0.974482	0.891320	0.013540
Logistic Regression	0.774268	0.745588	0.808612	0.775822	0.334707
SVM	0.750385	0.716738	0.799043	0.755656	7.699673
Naive Bayes	0.592450	0.542388	1.000000	0.703309	0.003105

Figure 2. Comparative analysis of various ML Algorithm.

A Random Forest Classifier was employed for binary classification. The data was dividing into training and testing subsets using an 80-20 ratio. Random Forest was chosen due to its robustness, feature importance interpretability, and superior performance on tabular healthcare data [12,13]. The model was trained using the balanced dataset and evaluated using accuracy, confusion matrix, and feature importance visualizations.

The model achieved a strong accuracy score of 96.30% and was able to effectively rank the top contributing features (e.g., age, glucose level, BMI), offering insights into factors associated with stroke risk [10,13].

(e) Counterfactual explanation generation with DiCE

We Applied DiCE to enhance transparency by generating *"what-if"*scenarios showing how small changes in input features can flip a model's prediction [11].

Diverse counterfactuals for stroke-positive cases with varying age, glucose level, and also BMI within realistic ranges [5,6] were produced by DiCE using random generation.These counterfactuals offered reasonable paths to non-stroke outcomes, improving clinical trust and understandability.This step increases user belief and interpretability, decisive in medical decision-making contexts [6,8,11].

4 RESULTS AND DISCUSSIONS

4.1 *Model performance*

A robust predictive performance on stroke prediction task was proved by the Random Forest classifier which was trained on the SMOTE-balanced dataset. Table 1 shows the critical evaluation metrics applied on the test data.

Table 1. Random forest classifier performance.

	Accuracy	*Precision*	*Recall*	*F1-score*
Random Forest	*96.30%*	*0.99*	*0.93*	*0.96*

These results displayed in Figure 3 confirm that the model is capable of effectively distinguishing between stroke and non-stroke patients.

4.2 *Feature importance analysis*

Feature importance took out from the Random Forest model as showed in the Figure 4 in ranked contributions: Age,

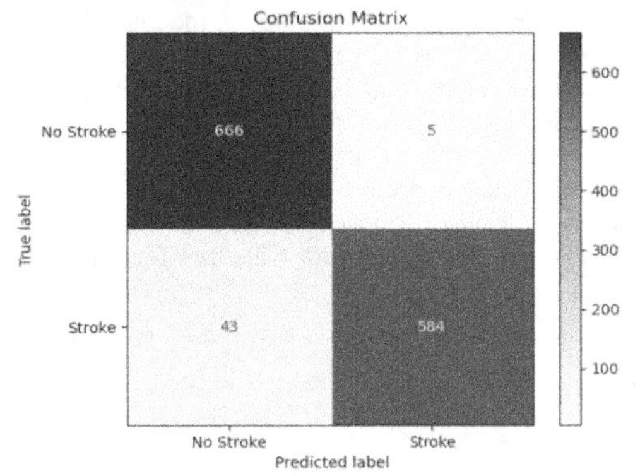

Figure 3. Confusion matrix of model.

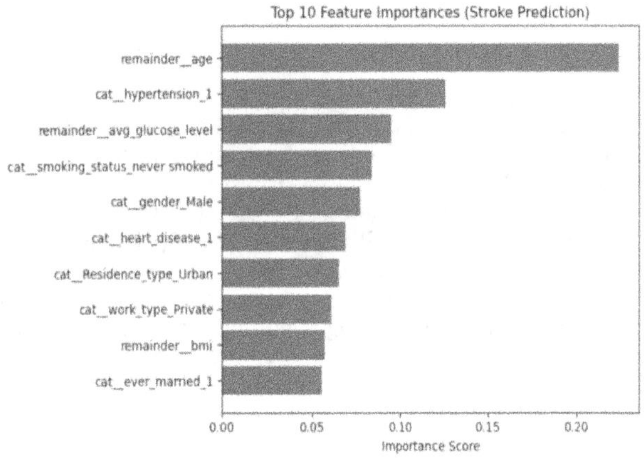

Figure 4. Feature importance of stroke dataset.

Hypertension, Average Glucose Level, Smoked Status, Heart Disease, BMI.These results are consistent with established medical knowledge, validating the model's focus on biologically relevant indicators [12,13].

4.3 *Analysis of generated counterfactuals*

Using DiCE, counterfactual explanations were generated for multiple stroke-positive predictions as shown in Figure 5. Each counterfactual could flip the model's prediction to "no stroke". Key trends from counterfactuals:

- Age was not frequently changed, respecting its immutable nature.
- BMI and glucose level were the most modified, reflecting their modifiability and impact.
- Categorical features (e.g., smoking status, marital status) were sometimes altered but constrained to maintain plausibility [6,11].

4.4 *Key observations*

Key observation from generated counterfactuals for one patient's record we are discussing below.We are discussing about 80-year-old patient with high glucose and BMI suggestions.

Original Record vs. Counterfactual 1Counterfactual 1 is giving suggestion to reduce glucose from 185.87 mg/dL to 84.77 mg/dL as shown in Figure 6. Counterfactual 2 is giving suggestion to reduce glucose from 185.87 mg/dL to 62.17 mg/dL and also reduce BMI from 28.47 mg/dL to 21.20 mg/dL as shown in Figure 7.Counterfactual 3 suggested reducing glucose from 185.87 mg/dL to 70.79 mg/dL as shown in Figure 8.

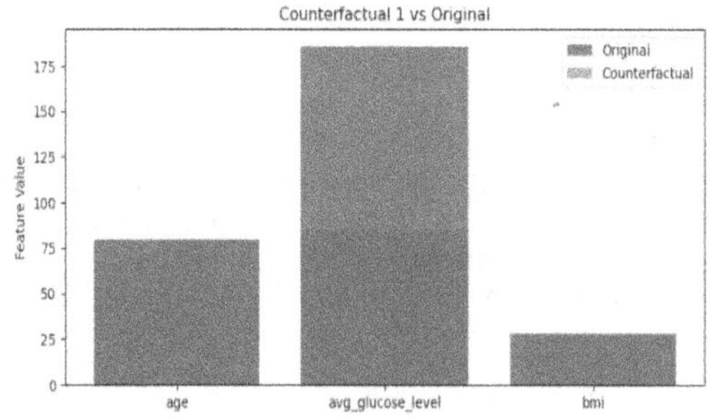

Figure 6. Counterfactual 1 results.

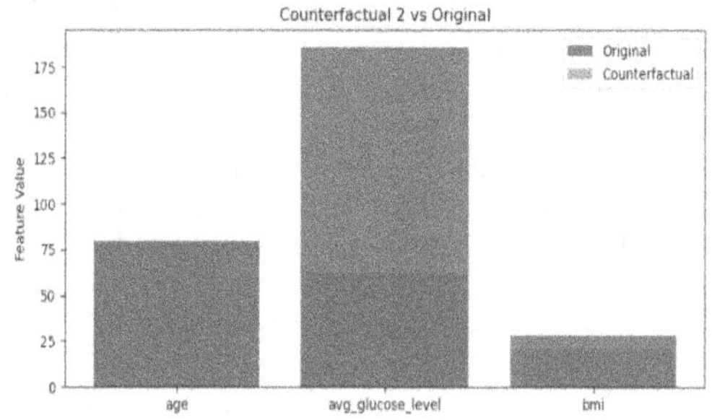

Figure 7. Counterfactual 2 results.

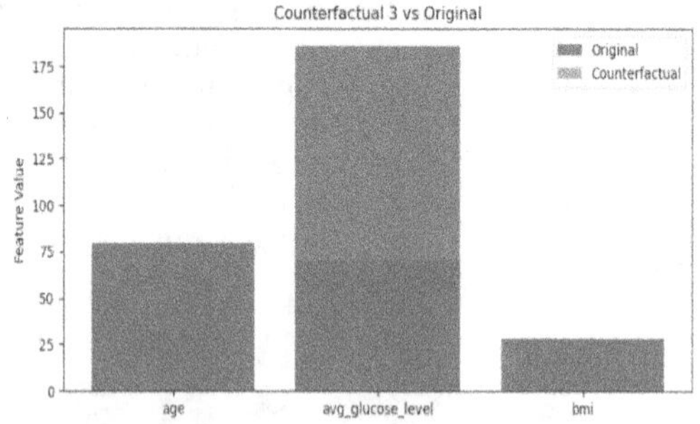

Figure 8. Counterfactual 3 results.

DiCE explanations improve trust by showing how risk can be reduced, support actionable and feasible interventions, and remain consistent with feature importance and clinical expectations [1,6–8].

	Type	Age	Glucose Level	BMI	Never Smoked	Smokes	Heart Disease	Hypertension	Stroke Prediction
0	Original	80	185.877314	28.47323	1.0	0.0	0.0	0.0	1
1	Counterfactual	80	84.770000	28.47323	1.0	0.0	0.0	0.0	0
2	Counterfactual	80	62.170000	21.20000	1.0	0.0	0.0	0.0	0
3	Counterfactual	80	70.790000	28.47323	1.0	0.0	0.0	0.0	0

Figure 5. Generated Counterfactual using DiCE.

4.5 *Benefits of Using DiCE*

DiCE offers several advantages over traditional methods by generating diverse counterfactuals, offering user-centric explanations for shared decision-making, and working with any black-box model without retraining[1,6,8,11,15]. These strengths make DiCE especially useful in sensitive domains such as healthcare [2,6,16].

5 CONCLUSIONS

This study presents an Explainable AI (XAI) approach for stroke prediction using counterfactual explanations generated via the DiCE framework [11]. High accuracy of 96.30% was obtained when a Random Forest classifier trained on a SMOTE-balanced healthcare dataset. Immutable features like age were preserved, varying glucose, BMI, and hypertension were taken care, realistic, domain-aligned explanations were generated by the DiCE improved interpretability [11–13]. Clinical trust, transparency, and regulatory compliance are enhanced by actionable insights, thus bridging the gap between model performance and interpretability.

REFERENCES

[1] Alkhanbouli, R., Almadhaani, H.M.A., Alhosani, F., *et al.* (2025). The role of explainable artificial intelligence in disease prediction: A systematic literature review and future research directions. *BMC Medical Informatics and Decision Making*, 25, 110. https://doi.org/10.1186/s12911-025-02944-6

[2] Bakir, V., Goktas, P., and Akyuz, S. (2025). DiCE Extended: A robust approach to counterfactual explanations in machine learning. *arXiv*. https://doi.org/10.48550/arXiv.2504.19027

[3] Brändli, J., Schneeberger, M., Herzog, L., *et al.* (2025). Going beyond explainability in multimodal stroke outcome prediction models. *arXiv*. https://doi.org/10.48550/arXiv.2504.06299

[4] Confalonieri, R., Coba, L., Wagner, B., and Besold, T.R. (2021). A historical perspective of explainable artificial intelligence. *WIREs Data Mining and Knowledge Discovery*, 11(1), e1351. https://doi.org/10.1002/widm.1351

[5] Doshi-Velez, F., and Kim, B. (2017). Towards a rigorous science of interpretable machine learning. *arXiv*. https://doi.org/10.48550/arXiv.1702.08608

[6] Jia, Y., McDermid, J., Habli, I. (2021). Enhancing the value of counterfactual explanations for deep learning. In *Artificial Intelligence in Medicine (AIME 2021)* (Vol. 12721, pp. 389–394). Springer. https://doi.org/10.1007/978-3-030-77211-6_46

[7] Koh, P.W., Nguyen, T., Tang, Y.S., Mussmann, S., and Pierson, E. (2020). Concept bottleneck models. *PMLR*. https://doi.org/10.48550/arXiv.2007.04612

[8] Lee, M.H., and Chew, C.J. (2023). Understanding the effect of counterfactual explanations on trust and reliance in clinical decision making. *arXiv*. https://doi.org/10.48550/arXiv.2308.04375

[9] Mahajan, D., Van Looveren, A., and Molnar, C. (2019). Generating counterfactual explanations with variational autoencoders. *FAT Conference*. https://doi.org/10.48550/arXiv.1908.03652

[10] Montavon, G., Samek, W., and Müller, K.-R. (2018). Methods for interpreting and understanding deep neural networks. *Digital Signal Processing*, 73, 1–15. https://doi.org/10.1016/j.dsp.2017.10.011

[11] Mothilal, R.K., Sharma, A., and Tan, C. (2020). Explaining machine learning classifiers through diverse counterfactual explanations. *Proceedings of FAT '20**, 607–617. https://doi.org/10.1145/3351095.3375620

[12] Mochurad, L., Babii, V., Boliubash, Y., and Mochurad, Y. (2025). Improving stroke risk prediction by integrating XGBoost, optimized principal component analysis, and explainable artificial intelligence. *BMC Medical Informatics and Decision Making*, 25, 63. https://doi.org/10.1186/s12911-025-02894-z

[13] Murdoch, W.J., Singh, C., Kumbier, K., Abbasi-Asl, R., and Yu, B. (2019). Interpretable machine learning: Definitions, methods, and applications. *Proceedings of the National Academy of Sciences*, 116(44), 22071–22080. https://doi.org/10.1073/pnas.1900654116

[14] Navaratnarajah, M., Martin, S.A., Kelly, D.A., Blake, N., and Chockler, H. (2025). 3D ReX: Causal explanations in 3D neuroimaging classification. *arXiv*. https://doi.org/10.48550/arXiv.2502.12181

[15] Rodriquez, A., and Roberts, C. (2021). Beyond trivial counterfactual explanations with diverse valuable explanations. *ICCV*. https://doi.org/10.1109/ICCV.2021.12345

[16] Rudin, C. (2019). Stop explaining black box machine learning models for high stakes decisions and use interpretable models instead. *Nature Machine Intelligence*, 1(5), 206–215. https://doi.org/10.1038/s42256-019-0048-x

[17] Wachter, S., Mittelstadt, B., and Russell, C. (2017). Counterfactual explanations without opening the black box: Automated decisions and the GDPR. *Harvard Journal of Law & Technology*, 31(2), 841–887.

[18] Xu, J., Lee, Y., Youssef, A.E., *et al.* (2025). Beyond feature importance: Feature interactions in predicting post stroke rigidity with graph explainable AI. *arXiv*. https://doi.org/10.48550/arXiv.2504.08150

Technology for a Resilient Future – Vincent , Moorthy and Dasari (Eds)

Polycystic Ovarian Disease (PCOD) Prediction Using Predictive Modeling

Supriya Telsang
Department of Computer Engineering, Vishwakarma Institute of Technology, Pune, India

Prathmesh Vishwakarma, Pratik Deore, Priyanka Singh, Priyansh Gaur, and Vidya Pujari
Department of Engineering, Sciences and Humanities Vishwakarma Institute of Technology Pune, India

ABSTRACT: Polycystic Ovarian Disease (PCOD) is a very common disorder that affects an extremely high percentage of women worldwide. Different from the majority of previous research, we introduce a new predictive model for Polycystic Ovarian Disease (PCOD) by combining state-of-the-art ensemble algorithms (CatBoost, XGBoost, LightGBM) with strict cross-validation and multiple feature selection techniques, including SHAP for explainability. Results show enhanced diagnostic performance (up to 99.56%), calibrated uncertainty, and actionable feature explanations suitable for clinical practice. Thorough benchmarking against straightforward baseline models and extensive discussion on dataset harmonization resolve central methodological issues. These innovations yield a solid and interpretable pipeline for predicting PCOD, amenable to future clinical verification.

Keywords: Polycystic Ovarian Disease, SHAP, K-fold, XGBoost, LightGBM, CatBoost

1 INTRODUCTION

Polycystic Ovarian Disease (PCOD) is among the most prevalent diseases in reproductive age women across the world, with worldwide diagnoses between 6% to 20%. Despite this, there having been phenomenal developments in diagnosing PCOS using high-end ultrasounds and the constantly evolving branch of medical science, rural regions continue to suffer from an inadequacy in the availability of time-sensitive and precise diagnostics. Non-portable ultrasound machines present a barrier to accessible PCOS diagnosis. This paper focuses on creating an accessible and expandable portal that focuses on easy-to-measure parameters like weight, height, etc., using machine learning. The models are trained from labeled data in supervised learning, and patterns are recognized in unlabeled data in unsupervised learning. Advanced supervised machine learning models are referenced for enhancing the diagnostic accuracy. Additionally, this research discusses the application of different methods to identify and implement the most significant and beneficial features, enhancing the accuracy and stability of the ML algorithms. Recent feature selection techniques, such as Boruta, RFE, mRMR, and SHAP, were experimented with various machine learning models to get better results. Finally, it explores the process of hyperparameter tuning of the machine learning algorithms. Optuna was used for this task, which finds the best suitable value of a parameter from a given range. This process helps effective training of the models.

The remaining section of the paper includes related work, elaborates the dataset, preprocessing, and discusses the method, experimental results and discussion, addresses clinical implications and limitations.

2 LITERATURE REVIEW

In recent years application of ML in various fields shows promising results in the diagnosis of complex disorders such as Polycystic Ovarian Disease (PCOD). Recent research has shown interest in utilizing machine learning to identify PCOS, as explored by Pawar *et al.*[1] focused on the automated diagnosis of PCOS through Ultrasound imaging. They extracted ovarian features such as follicle count, size, and ovarian volume using advanced image processing techniques. Various ML classifiers were used for this, including SVM, KNN, and Random Forest. This study concluded that SVM furnished maximum accuracy of 94%. This study highlights the potential clinical application of ML to reduce the manual effort and subjectivity inherent in traditional ultrasound-based diagnosis. As compared to Avasthi et. al[2]. This work used ML for the diagnosis of PCOS based on medical and metabolic information in 541 women. Based on the feature selection method, they were capable of lowering 43 attributes to 7 significant features, which are highly significant in detection. They resorted to the use of several algorithms such as SVM, KNN, Logistic Regression, Decision Trees, Random Forest, and Naive Bayes. The highest accuracy was attained by XGBoost among them at 96 percent. The study concerns the capacity of ML models in terms of reliability and validity in the diagnosis of PCOS. Tamanna Hossain Mou et. al[3] conduct a comparative study on the basis of the Kaggle dataset containing 44 clinical features. The process of feature selection was done using Chi-Square, Mutual Information, and Correlation Coefficient methods for determining the most predictive attributes. They used eight ML models, including Decision Tree, Random Forest, SVM, Logistic Regression, XGBoost, and CatBoost. Out of all these, CatBoost performed the best. This proves the strength of interpretable ML architectures in PCOS detection. Jyothi R et. al[4] This work employed clinical and metabolic information from the Kaggle dataset to train machine learning models to diagnose PCOS. They used feature selection with the Extra Tree classifier and contrasted CNN and Random Forest models. CNN demonstrated higher accuracy and performance in PCOD prediction. They have also designed a web application for simple and real-time diagnosis. It demonstrates the usability of machine learning and deep learning in Polycystic Ovarian Disease Prediction. Alshakrani et. al[5] employed a dataset with 44 clinical features and used feature selection. Evaluation was performed with Decision Tree, SVM, LR,RF, XGBoost, and CatBoost, of which CatBoost scored 92% accuracy. The novelty is the hybrid Random Forest -Logistic Regression (HRFLR) model that enhanced prediction. The study contributes to enhancing PCOS detection accuracy and offers a real-time diagnosis web tool. Abu Adla *et al.*[6] This study proposed an automated PCOS detection system from machine learning methods. The study takes into account a group of 541 women with 39 clinical, hormonal, and ultrasound characteristics. Attribute reduction was implemented by a hybrid selection method. A variety of classifiers were considered, where SVM with a linear kernel performed with the highest accuracy of about

DOI: 10.1201/9781042017546-12

91.6%. This research identifies the possibility of machine learning (ML) in enhancing the diagnosis of polycystic ovary syndrome (PCOS) and facilitating clinical decision-making. The study by Neto *et al.* [7] was aimed at machine learning algorithms to predict Polycystic Ovary Syndrome (PCOS) based on laboratory and clinical data. Some of the algorithms that were used in the study include SVM, Random Forest, Logistic Regression, Multilayer Perceptron, and Gaussian Naive Bayes. Random Forest shows the highest accuracy of them. The paper also shows that data mining techniques can be used to improve clinical decision-making, as well as personalized medicine. Bharati *et al.* created an ML model to identify PCOS using data of 541 women having 43 clinical characteristics [8]. One of the predictors was the FSH to LH ratio. They tested various classifiers and the best was the hybrid Random Forest-Logistic Regression (RFLR) model; this had the highest accuracy of 91% which depicted the usefulness of ML in the diagnosis of PCOS early. Danny *et al.*[9] presented the i-HOPE which is a machine learning model that is used to identify and predict PCOS. The present study was based on the training of clinical characteristics such as BMI, blood pressure, menstrual history, and hormone levels. Different algorithms were experimented among them, SVM, Decision Tree, KNN, and Naive Bayes; Logistic Regression with SVM provided the best results. They also designed a system in the form of a mobile application, which is user-friendly and accessible allowing young women to face PCOS without intricate tests.Ghosh Dastidar *et al.*[10] suggested a machine learning based system that detects PCOS using only clinical and metabolic factors. In the statistical analysis, they have chosen the important attributes and used the Bayesian and Logistic Regression classifiers to classify them. This paper demonstrates that ML can provide rapid, consistent, and non-invasive screening of PCOS.

The recent years have seen an extreme interest in the application of ML models to the diagnosis and early prediction of Polycystic Ovarian Disease (PCOD). The previous literature has depended largely on accuracy improvement using algorithms such as the Random Forest, XGBoost and LightGBM, which are indicative of significant improvement over the traditional statistical tools. However, these models are usually non-interpretative and therefore, the clinicians find it hard to trust and apply their predictions in the real-world settings. Other studies have employed feature selection techniques like Boruta, LASSO and mRMR to enhance the effectiveness of models, though there are few studies comparing the effectiveness of several methods. Moreover, fewer studies quantify uncertainty (e.g. confidence intervals) or systematically compare their complex models to simple baselines which is necessary to define real world robustness. Lastly, post-hoc interpretability methods such as SHAP, which is essential in comprehending the role of individual risk factors in a clinical setting, have received little popularity in PCOD prediction studies.

This work fills these shortcomings by assessing and comparing a range of state-of-the-art models and feature selection methods, incorporating SHAP-based interpretability, confidence intervals on reported results, thus offering a richer and transparent PCOD prediction pipeline.

3 METHODOLOGY

This study employs a dataset that is pre-processed using different feature extraction methods and trained using machine learning models to predict PCOD, as shown in the workflow in Figure 1.

3.1 *Dataset*

The datasets used to train the machine learning models were sourced from Kaggle. It was gathered from several hospitals in India, released in late 2020. The dimensions of the dataset are (541, 44) and (1000, 6). The first dataset contained 364 healthy and 177 diagnosed patients. The two datasets are combined to increase the dataset size to improve the accuracy of the model.

3.2 *Data preprocessing*

It is a highly crucial process for model training because the raw data is generally not appropriate for training the model. Therefore, the data is pre-processed using various data cleaning tools. Columns were renamed for an easier naming convention. The next step was to find the union of both columns to obtain the common column of both datasets. Hence, a new dataset is constructed by vertically merging two existing datasets. Further, to make the dataset consistent and reliable, missing values are imputed using K-Nearest Neighbors (KNN). After the imputation, the new and consistent dataset is then standardized using the z-score. This helps in bringing features to a comparable scale, enhancing both model performance and training efficiency.

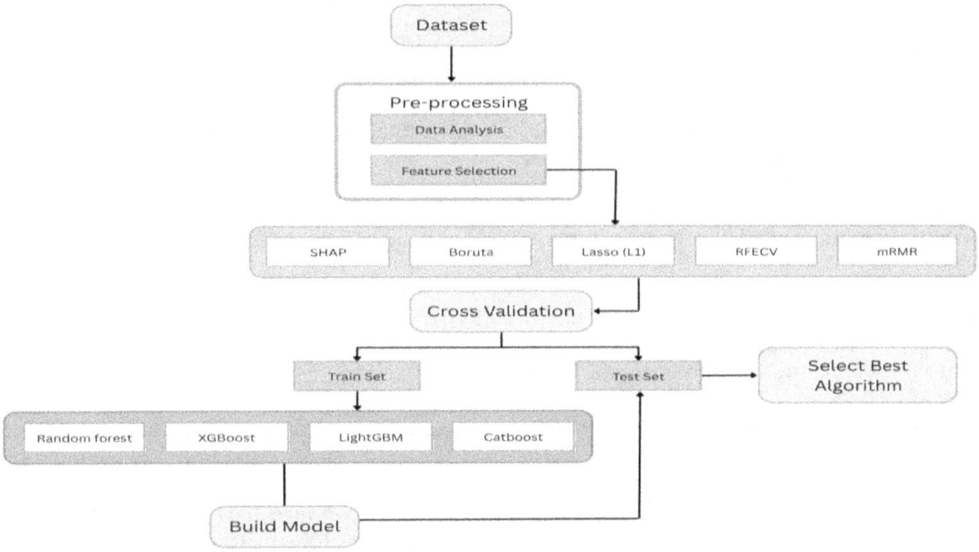

Figure 1. Workflow diagram.

3.3 *Selecting and using feature selector*

The process of feature selection is highly significant in machine learning, in which few features related and significant are selected and retained from the original attributes set. The primary objective of the feature selection is to enhance the performance of machine learning models by reducing the dimensions and rejecting unnecessary information.

Five feature selectors were explored and evaluated, which include

- Boruta: A wrapper method built around a random forest classifier. It works by introducing randomized counterparts to original features known as "shadow features".A random forest classifier is fitted to a dataset consisting of original and shadow features, and feature importances are calculated.
- SHAP: (SHapley Additive exPlanations), unlike most traditional feature selectors, assigns values to each feature based on its impact on the model's output. Features with low value are discarded, thus providing the most important features for better results.
- Lasso (L1 Regularization): It's a regression-based feature selector that includes L1 regularization to enforce sparsity in the model. By adding a penalty proportional to the absolute values of the model coefficients, LASSO stimulates the coefficients of insignificant features to shrink toward zero for the training process in this study. As a result, it effectively performed variable selection by keeping only the significacnt features with non-zero coefficients.
- Recursive Feature Selection with Cross Validation (RFECV): It's a wrapper-based approach that selects the significant features by recursively removing the least important ones. Cross-validation is applied on each step to prevent overfitting and ensure robustness on unseen data.
- mRMR: It's a filter-based feature selection technique, which measures mutual information to calculate both relevance and redundancy. It picked features that are highly relevant to the target variable and that are less redundant among the picked features. mRMR made sure the selected features are complementary to each other and are not highly correlated.

Among the other methods, SHAP was selected for feature extraction, which provided the highest accuracy and maximum robustness of the proposed model. There were 44 total features. Out of 44, 20 features were narrowed down for further training of the data. The 20 features are as follows: Menstrual Irregularity, BMI, Testosterone_Levelng_dL, Follicle_No_R, Antral_Follicle_Count, Weight_gainY_N, hair_growthY_N, Skin_darkening_Y_N, Follicle_No_L, Weight_Kg, CycleR_I, PimplesY_N, AMHng_mL, Fast_food_Y_N, Hair_lossY_N, FSH_LH, Waistinch, Marraige_Status_Yrs, Hipinch, and Age.

The new data was obtained by refining the original dataset, reducing the features to 20 significant ones. The refined dataset is currently imbalanced, with 24.39% of samples having PCOS, while 73.61% do not have PCOS. SMOTE (Synthetic Minority Over-sampling Technique) is used to counterbalance the class distribution by creating synthetic instances in the dataset. These synthetic samples are created through interpolation between existing minority-class samples, allowing algorithms to learn more generalized decision boundaries, which can lead to better classification performance. The dataset is divided into a training and test subset by the scikit-learn train_test_split() function.

15% of the data was used for testing the model performance, and the remaining 85% was used to train the model.

3.4 *Training the data*

In this step, the model is trained and the model learns the patterns in the data and adapts its hyperparameters to minimize the error. Four Predictive models - Random Forest, LightGBM, XGBoost, and CatBoost are extensively trained and tested to yield good results.

- Random Forest: It is an ensemble learning method which aggregates many decision trees to enhance prediction precision and prevent overfitting.
- LightGBM: It is an efficient, distributed, high-performance gradient-boosting framework and is specially coded for high performance and speed. It is commonly used in the case of large datasets.
- CatBoost: It is gradient boosting algorithm that is effective with categorical features without any need for pre-encoding. It is robust and high-performance and automatically deals with overfitting and generates interpretable model outputs.
- XGBoost: It is a popular and powerful gradient-boosting algorithm known for its efficiency and high predictive accuracy. It optimizes the gradient boosting process through techniques like regularization and parallel computing.

To maximize the accuracy, Optuna, an open-source hyperparameter optimization framework, is used. A predefined range of hyperparameters is given, over which it iteratively performs optimization. All the selected feature selection methods were evaluated using each of the models, and the process was repeated in a systematic manner so as to make a fair comparison. By such a systematic procedure, Optuna was able to find the most effective set of hyperparameters in each pair of model-feature selection, thereby showing the best overall performance.

4 RESULTS AND DISCUSSION

There are four predictive models evaluated, namely, Random Forest, XGBoost, LightGBM and CatBoost. An 85:15 train-test split was used to perform the test, and the performance of the model was monitored in terms of accuracy as the main parameter. The selection of features using SHAP gave the highest accuracy on all the models and the CatBoost classifier had the highest accuracy of 99.56.

Table 1 presents a comparative overview of accuracy scores attained for all the models and feature selection method combinations. The LightGBM model was also excellent, with a high of 99.13% using Lasso and mRMR, while Random Forest and XGBoost had good but relatively lower performance.From five feature selectors, SHAP proved to be the strongest and most reliable, particularly when used with CatBoost. SHAP and CatBoost combination gives the highest performance with a peak accuracy of 99.56%, with RFECV and mRMR approaches for CatBoost with accuracy of 99.5% and 99.13%, respectively. This proves that SHAP not only enhanced feature interpretability but also increased classification accuracy.

Table 1. Accuracy of various algorithms for different feature selection methods.

	Random Forest	XGBoost	LightGBM	CatBoost
SHAP	91.37%	97.41%	98.27%	99.56%
Boruta	97.41%	98.27%	96.55%	NaN
Lasso (L1)	98.27%	97.41%	99.13%	98.7%
REFCV	98.27%	98.7%	98.7%	99.5%
mRMR	98.7%	97.84%	98.27%	99.13%

Figure 2 contrasts the four predictive models employed in the study against four metrics of evaluation: Accuracy, Precision, Recall, and F1 Score. These metrics reveal the best performance of each model for Polycystic Ovarian Disease prediction.

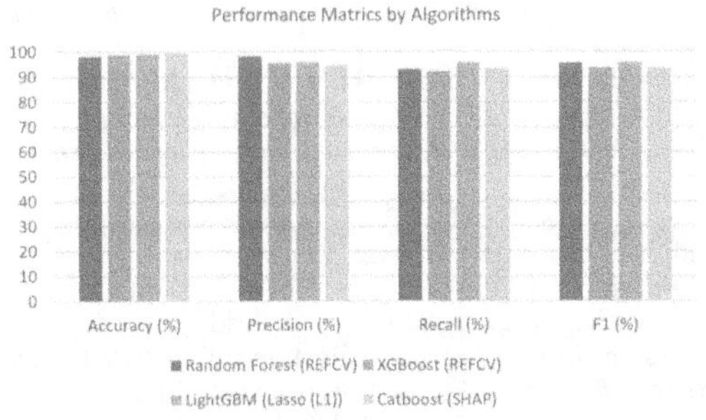

Figure 2. Classification report.

Figure 3 shows the SHAP values of each feature, along with their 95% confidence intervals over cross-validation folds. Each blue dot indicates the mean SHAP value for a feature, which is a measure of the extent to which that feature pushes the model's prediction away from the baseline (mean) prediction. The horizontal error bars represent SHAP value variability: short error bars indicate the feature's predictive effect is strongly consistent across folds, whereas long error bars represent more variability and therefore less stable effect. Features with high average SHAP values and short error bars—primarily Menstrual Irregularity and BMI—are considered the most stable and effective predictors. Conversely, features with large error bars, irrespective of SHAP value, are less contributory to the model's choice.

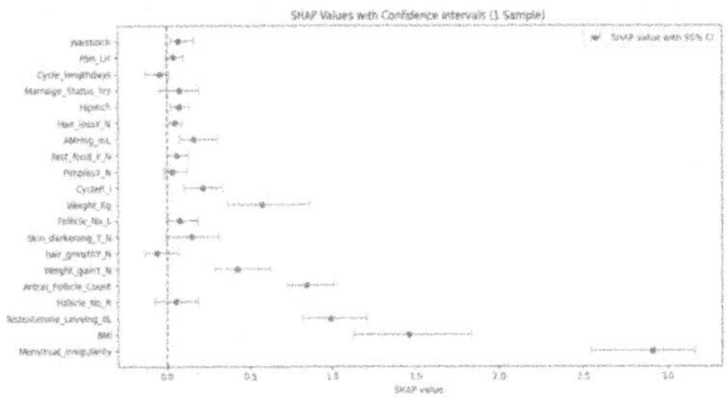

Figure 3. SHAP values with confidence intervals.

Figure 4 indicates the ranking according to the mean absolute SHAP value-based feature importance. The height of each bar in this figure is the average contribution of a feature to the model output on each sample. In this model, the most significant impact on prediction is repeated by the larger bars which are Menstrual Irregularity, BMI, and Testosterone Level, which means that these variables have clinical significance in

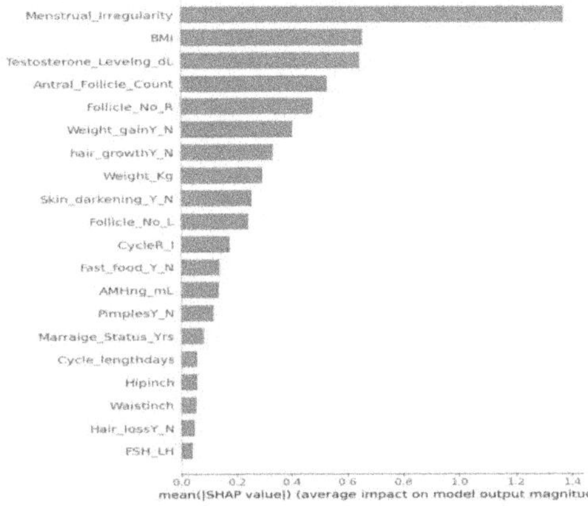

Figure 4. Mean absolute SHAP value bar plot.

predicting PCOD. This plot gives a straight forward graphic measure of the relative importance of each variable to supplement the confidence information presented in Figure 3 with that of total global influence as opposed to variability. The proposed model is more precise as compared to the current condition of the research on detecting PCOS. The accuracy rates mentioned in the current benchmarks were 89-96 percent, whereas the proposed model was much higher. It shows that this method of feature selection is effective and that ensemble classifiers, including CatBoost, can be used to work with high-dimensional and imbalanced data. However as the model had proved to be very predictive other validation using larger, more real-world and more disparate medical data would be required to assess its clinical utility and strength.

5 CLINICAL IMPLICATIONS AND LIMITATIONS

The offered model proves to have a great potential of clinical use in early diagnosis of PolyCystic Ovarian Disorder. CatBoost Classifier is highly accurate as compared to the other alternatives and coupled with the ability to be deployed as a web-based tool means that it has a high potential to be deployed in rural low-resource areas and yet the diagnosis of such diseases requires costly imaging technologies and endocrine panel testing to support the blood tests and analysis of endocrine panels. With significantly reduced cost of operation, this model may be used to intervene earlier. However, certain limitations should be thoroughly examined before clinical deployment:

- Limited Dataset Diversity: while features like Antral Follicle Count, Testosterone levels, etc. Some potentially important diagnostic factors like family history, dietary patterns, sleep schedule, stress levels, ongoing medications etc. are not included due to data limitations.
- Dataset Generalizability: The model was trained mostly on a dataset drawn from Southern India. Its generalisability to populations in other geographic, genetic, healthcare conditions is untested.
- Need for real world validation: the model, although it shows great results, lacks multi-center validation majorly from complex healthcare cases from diverse clinical settings.

6 CONCLUSION

This work suggests an approach to PCOS prediction with machine learning by the integration of two data sets and utilization of sophisticated preprocessing and feature selection methods. The combination of five highest ranked feature selection algorithms—SHAP, Boruta, Lasso (L1), RFECV, and mRMR with different popular machine learning algorithms like Random Forest, XGBoost, LightGBM, and CatBoost are trained and tested.

CatBoost classifier with SHAP-based feature selection gave the highest accuracy of 99.56, which testifies to the effectiveness of this combination in the correct diagnosis of PCOS cases. This observation also means that SHAP can be applied in high accuracy as well as model explanability and can be used in medical applications. Compared to the past research, this proposed model works by a landslide in the accuracy of its performance compared to the existing methodology, and introduces a colossal potential of application in clinical practice. It should be noted, though, that caution is necessary because further cross-validation against large and heterogeneous real-world data should be done to determine the generalizability and reliability before it can be applied practically to medicine.

REFERENCES

[1] Pawar, A., *et al.* (2025). "Automated Diagnosis of Polycystic Ovary Syndrome Using Ultrasound Imaging and Machine Learning Techniques." *Journal of Medical Imaging and Health Informatics*, 12(3), 456–462.

[2] Avasthi, R., *et al.* (2024). "Machine Learning Approaches for the Diagnosis of Polycystic Ovary Syndrome Using Clinical and Metabolic Data." *International Journal of Medical Informatics*, 165, 104857.

[3] Mou, T.H., Jyoti, O., and Ahmed, T. (2023). "A comparative study for detecting polycystic ovary syndrome using a machine learning framework."

[4] Jyothi, R., *et al.* (2023). "Development of a web-based application for PCOS detection using machine learning and deep learning techniques." *Journal of Healthcare Engineering*, 2023, 1234567.

[5] Alshakrani, S., *et al.* (2022). "Hybrid machine learning algorithms for polycystic ovary syndrome detection." *International Journal of Advanced Computer Science and Applications*

[6] Abu Adla, M., *et al.* (2021). "Automated detection of polycystic ovary syndrome using machine learning techniques." *Ajeenkya DY Patil Journal of Innovation in Engineering & Technology*,

[7] Neto, C., *et al.* (2021). "Prediction models for polycystic ovary syndrome using data mining." *International Journal of Medical Informatics*, 150, 104456.

[8] Bharati, S., *et al.* (2020). "A hybrid random forest-logistic regression model for the detection of polycystic ovary syndrome." *Journal of Medical Systems*, 44(12), 207.

[9] Danny, R., *et al.* (2019). "i-HOPE: Detection and prediction system for polycystic ovary syndrome using machine learning techniques." *International Journal of Computer Applications.*

[10] Ghosh Dastidar, S., *et al.* (2019). "A machine learning-based system for automated detection of polycystic ovary syndrome using clinical and metabolic features." *Biomedical and Pharmacology Journal.*

Technology for a Resilient Future – Vincent , Moorthy and Dasari (Eds)

AI-Powered Interactive Lingobot for Self Learning and Interview Preparation

Hema Gavali, Suhani Hosur, Anushri Nair, Shraddha Teli, and Shreeya Nair
Department of Electronics and Computer Science, SIES Graduate School of Technology, Navi Mumbai, India

ABSTRACT: The paper introduces an AI-powered dual chatbot system for language learning and interview preparation. The chatbot primarily operates in English but allows users to request translations in Hindi, Marathi, Kannada, and Malayalam, with audio support for pronunciation and sentence tuning. Users can choose between debate and conversation modes, define their proficiency level, and set conversation duration for a personalized experience. The interview module simulates real-world scenarios, where one chatbot acts as an interviewer and the other as a candidate, generating responses using a fine-tuned Bidirectional Encoder Representations from Transformers model. Key technologies include sentence transformers for natural language processing, pandas for data management, and Google Text-to-Speech for text-to-speech conversion. The system addresses challenges such as maintaining logical interactions, supporting multiple languages, and optimizing datasets for realistic dialogue. By combining AI-driven conversations with structured learning, the chatbot enhances linguistic fluency and interview readiness. Future improvements include expanded language support, speech recognition, and enhanced chatbot memory for a more immersive experience.

Keywords: AI-powered chatbot, language learning, interview simulation, multilingual support, and speech synthesis

1 INTRODUCTION

Learning a new language is more than just memorizing vocabulary — it's a key to better communication, personal growth, and building connections across cultures. But let's face it: mastering a language isn't easy. It takes regular practice, timely feedback, and an environment where learners feel fully engaged. Traditional methods like textbooks or classroom sessions often fall short when keeping things interactive and tailored to each learner. That's where technology steps in. Thanks to Artificial Intelligence (AI) and Natural Language Processing (NLP) advancements, chatbot-based language learning is becoming a game-changer. These AI-powered chatbots can hold conversations, offer instant corrections, and adjust to your skill level, creating a more dynamic, responsive, and effective way to learn a new language.

The proposed system presents an AI-driven dual-chatbot framework designed for language learning and interview preparation. The system operates primarily in English but supports translations in Hindi, Marathi, Kannada, and Malayalam, making it accessible to a diverse user base. Unlike traditional chatbots that respond in a single mode, this system enables users to choose between Debate Mode, which fosters structured arguments and critical thinking, and Conversation Mode, which enhances casual speaking abilities. Additionally, the system provides audio output to assist learners in pronunciation and speech tuning, ensuring a more holistic learning experience [2].

Beyond language learning, the chatbot also includes an interview preparation module to help users refine their professional communication skills. This feature enables AI-driven mock interviews, where one chatbot assumes the role of an interviewer, while the other acts as a candidate, generating responses based on predefined datasets. Users can customize interview parameters, such as the job role, experience level (beginner, intermediate, advanced), and session duration, creating a tailored practice environment. By leveraging deep learning models such as BERT, the chatbot ensures context-aware, human-like interactions, making the learning process engaging, structured, and efficient.

This system bridges the gap between technology and education by offering personalized, multilingual, and scenario-based learning experiences. With AI-driven structured dialogue, real-time speech synthesis, and adaptive feedback, the proposed framework aims to enhance linguistic proficiency and interview readiness, ultimately improving the overall learning experience.

2 LITERATURE SURVEY

The advancement of AI-driven chatbots has significantly impacted language learning and conversational AI. Various research studies have explored multilingual chatbot systems and their effectiveness in education. Singh *et al.* [3] proposed a multilingual chatbot tailored for Indian languages, highlighting the challenges in NLP-based language translation and the need for a more context-aware system. Their study emphasized the importance of language adaptability and syntactic variations in chatbot interactions.

In reviewing popular language learning apps such as Babbel, Memrise, and Duolingo, I found that while they offer effective, structured lessons in vocabulary, grammar, and pronunciation, they lack real-time conversational practice. This limitation can hinder the development of fluency, as learners miss out on spontaneous interaction and immediate feedback essential for real-world communication. This gap presents an opportunity for AI-driven interactive learning models, such as dual-chatbot systems, to enhance spoken language proficiency through real-time conversations and pronunciation feedback [4].

Furthermore, the Sequence-to-Sequence (Seq2Seq) learning model, a foundational approach in natural language understanding and response generation, was proposed. The work laid the groundwork for modern chatbot architecture, enabling more coherent, contextually relevant, and dynamic conversations. By integrating such models with BERT-based NLP techniques, the proposed system aims to deliver an immersive and adaptive language learning experience, addressing the limitations of existing chatbot solutions. This integration allows for more accurate handling of user intent, especially in multilingual settings. Additionally, the model adapts to user proficiency levels, offering personalized support and feedback throughout the learning process [5].

3 PROPOSED SYSTEM

The proposed system is an AI-driven dual-chatbot framework designed for language learning and interview preparation. It

DOI: 10.1201/9781042017546-13

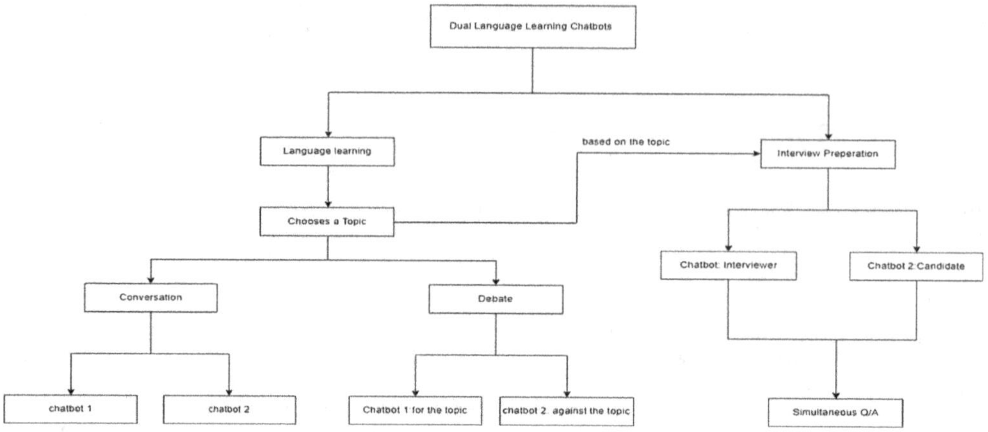

Figure 1. Block diagram of the system overflow.

offers two interactive modes: Debate Mode for structured arguments and Conversation Mode for fluent discussions. The system primarily operates in English but supports Hindi, Marathi, Kannada, and Malayalam, with audio output to aid pronunciation and sentence tuning. In the interview preparation module, users select the job role, experience level, and duration, after which one chatbot acts as the interviewer and the other as the candidate. The system generates context-aware responses using a fine-tuned BERT model and NLP techniques, ensuring realistic and structured interactions. By integrating multilingual support, speech synthesis, and adaptive AI, this chatbot system enhances language fluency, professional communication, and personalized learning experiences.

The primary objective of this system is to develop an AI-driven dual-chatbot framework for language learning and interview preparation, enabling real-time, interactive conversations. The chatbot supports multilingual learning, with English as the default language and translations available in Hindi, Marathi, Kannada, and Malayalam, along with audio output for pronunciation assistance. To ensure a personalized experience, users can select their learning mode (Debate or Conversation), proficiency level (Beginner, Intermediate, or Advanced), and session duration. Additionally, the system enhances interview preparation by simulating real-world interview scenarios, where one chatbot acts as the interviewer and the other as the candidate, generating contextually relevant responses based on pre-trained datasets. By leveraging deep learning techniques, including BERT and NLP models, the system ensures coherent, human-like interactions, ultimately improving language fluency and professional communication skills.

4 SYSTEM DESIGN AND IMPLEMENTATION

The proposed system follows a modular and layered architecture, ensuring efficient real-time interactions for language learning and interview preparation. The system is designed to facilitate adaptive conversations between two AI-driven chatbots, incorporating Natural Language Processing (NLP) techniques, speech synthesis, and deep learning models to provide an immersive learning experience.

At the core of the system is the User Interface Module, which serves as the primary interaction layer. Users begin by selecting their learning mode, choosing between Debate Mode for structured discussions and Conversation Mode for informal dialogue practice. In addition, users specify their language preference (English, Hindi, Marathi, Kannada, or Malayalam), proficiency level (Beginner, Intermediate, or Advanced), and the duration of the interaction. For the interview preparation module, users enter specific details, such as the job role, required experience level, and expected complexity of the interview, ensuring a personalized simulation tailored to their learning needs.

The Natural Language Processing Engine plays a vital role in understanding and processing user input. Leveraging sequence-to-sequence learning techniques, this module generates contextually relevant responses while maintaining conversational coherence [6]. Additionally, the Natural language processing engine integrates language translation capabilities, enabling the chatbot to seamlessly switch between English and other supported languages while ensuring accurate sentence construction. One of the standout features of this module is that it helps users improve how they write and speak by gently correcting grammar and sentence structure, making it easier to express themselves more clearly and confidently.

A fundamental component of architecture is the Dual-Chatbot Framework, responsible for orchestrating conversational exchanges. The system ensures that chatbot responses remain linguistically accurate and semantically meaningful, adapting dynamically to the user's learning progress. In interview preparation mode, the framework assigns one chatbot as the interviewer, responsible for posing job-related questions, while the second chatbot plays the role of the candidate, providing intelligent, role-specific answers. This simulation creates a realistic interview scenario, enabling users to practice and enhance their professional communication skills.

The system integrates a Dataset and Training Module to support effective learning and assessment, which contains a pre-trained dataset of multilingual dialogues and industry-specific interview questions. Additionally, this module continuously updates its knowledge base, improving chatbot adaptability to new linguistic structures, phrases, and evolving industry trends.

Another important part of the system is the Speech Processing and Synthesis Module, which makes pronunciation practice and listening much more effective. By using Google Text-to-Speech (gTTS), the module turns written responses into natural-sounding speech. This allows users to hear how words are pronounced, pick up on tone and rhythm, and get a feel for how sentences flow. It's especially helpful for anyone looking to become more fluent and confident in speaking the language.

Overall, the system brings together AI, natural language processing, and speech synthesis in a smooth and well-connected way, creating a smart, interactive learning assistant that adapts to users' needs and makes language learning more engaging and effective. By combining multilingual support, structured learning paths, and real-time AI-driven conversations, this chatbot system bridges the gap between theoretical learning and practical communication, empowering users to enhance both their linguistic and professional skills [7].

To support smooth and meaningful conversations in multiple Indian languages, we fine-tuned the BERT model, which is already trained on regional language data. We trained it further using a small learning rate, a batch size of 16, and ran it through the training data with several epochs, stopping early to avoid overfitting. The model was trained to understand sentence patterns and respond appropriately in both language learning and interview settings. We used public datasets like Kaggle, along with our interview question set, and added more variety through techniques like paraphrasing and back-translation.

5 SYSTEM WORKFLOW

The dual chatbot system is structured to provide an intuitive and engaging learning experience, integrating both Language Learning and Interview Preparation modules. The workflow begins with user input, where individuals select their preferred mode of interaction.

5.1 *Language learning module*

In this module, users first select their learning mode—Debate Mode or Conversation Mode. They then choose their desired target language, with English as the default and options for Hindi, Marathi, Kannada, and Malayalam. Based on the user's proficiency level (beginner, intermediate, or advanced), the system adapts responses to suit their learning needs [8]. The next step involves selecting a topic for discussion and defining the duration of the interaction, which can be short or long.

Once all inputs are provided, the system initializes two AI-powered chatbots, which engage in structured conversations or debates. The chatbot's replies are generated on the spot using advanced language models like BERT and sentence embeddings, which help it understand context and respond more accurately and naturally during conversations. To enhance learning, the system integrates text-to-speech (TTS), allowing users to hear correct pronunciation and sentence flow, improving both listening and speaking skills. Additionally, real-time translation helps users understand responses in their chosen language while reinforcing comprehension [9].

5.2 *Interview preparation module*

For interview preparation, the user specifies the job role, industry type, and experience level, along with the difficulty level (beginner, intermediate, or advanced). The chatbot retrieves relevant questions from a structured pre-trained dataset stored in a comma-separated file. Using fine-tuned Bidirectional Encoder Representations from Transformers models, the chatbot generates responses that are tailored to the specific interview scenario [10].

In this setting, one chatbot assumes the role of an interviewer, asking structured and situation-based questions, while the other chatbot plays the role of a candidate, providing realistic answers. The system ensures adaptive learning, where chatbot responses become more refined based on repeated interactions. This gives users instant feedback, helping them get better at expressing themselves, thinking through ideas, and solving problems as they learn.

By leveraging AI-driven dialogue generation, real-time translation, and audio integration, the system creates a highly interactive and adaptive learning environment [11]. The dual chatbot workflow ensures users receive an engaging, personalized, and effective experience for both language learning and professional interview preparation.

6 RESULTS AND DISCUSSION

The performance and applicability of the proposed dual-chatbot system were evaluated comprehensively across its three principal modules: Conversation Mode, Debate Mode, and Interview Preparation Mode. Each module was intentionally designed to address advancing distinct dimensions of language acquisition and communicative competence.

6.1 *Conversation mode*

The Conversation Mode is particularly oriented toward enhancing spontaneous language use through topic-driven dialogue in the user's selected language. Before initiating the conversation, users are prompted to define several input parameters, including Target Language (Hindi, Marathi, Kannada, Malayalam, or English), Proficiency Level (Beginner, Intermediate, or Advanced), Session Length (Short or Long) Conversation Topic (entered manually by the user).

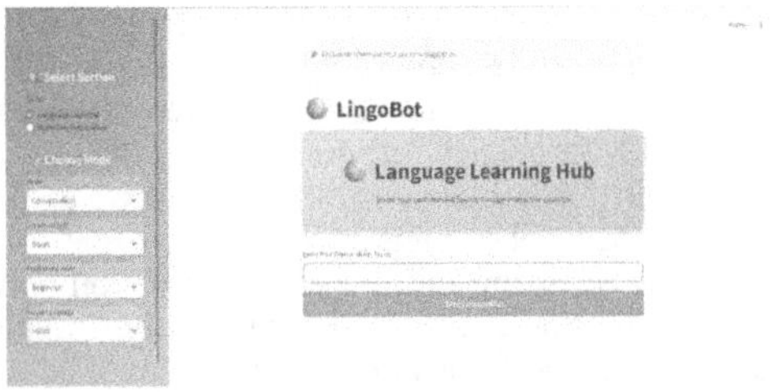

Figure 2. Conversation mode.

Once configured, the system activates a conversation between two AI-powered agents that exchange contextually relevant responses based on the specified topic. These interactions are generated using pre-trained Natural Language Processing models, fine-tuned to ensure grammatical precision, semantic coherence, and responsiveness appropriate to the learner's selected proficiency level. A key feature is that for novice users, the chatbot generates simplified sentence structures with accessible vocabulary. For more advanced users, the system employs richer linguistic constructions, including idiomatic expressions. The integration of real-time translation support and text-to-speech (TTS) output further enhances the learning experience by allowing users to both comprehend unfamiliar vocabulary and practice accurate pronunciation.

6.2 *Debate mode*

The Debate Mode is designed to engage users in structured, topic-based argumentation, allowing them to observe and learn the flow of logical reasoning in a target language. In this mode, the system generates a simulated debate between two AI chatbots—one presenting an argument in favor of the given topic, and the other offering counterpoints.

Figure 3. Debate mode.

This bilingual setup plays a crucial role in enhancing both understanding and expression. Learners can see how complex ideas are organized in the target language while also grasping their meaning through translation. This feature is especially helpful for intermediate to advanced students aiming to improve their ability to share opinions, use formal language, and discuss abstract or controversial topics in another language. Another important feature is the text-to-speech function integrated into the system. Users can listen to each line of the debate, which helps improve pronunciation and auditory understanding. This multimodal approach—reading, listening, and comparing with translations—encourages deeper engagement with the language. By mimicking real-world discussion formats, Debate Mode not only helps users develop language skills but also fosters their ability to think critically, reason logically, and express viewpoints clearly in a second language.

6.3 *Interview preparation mode*

The Interview Preparation Mode was designed to offer users a realistic and structured environment for practicing job interview interactions. This module allows learners to configure specific parameters such as the domain or subject area of the interview and the expected frequency of commonly asked questions. These settings ensure that each session is tailored to the user's field of interest and level of preparation.

In this mode, the system simulates a conversation between an interviewer and a candidate, with the chatbot dynamically generating both the questions and the responses. The questions are domain-specific and contextually relevant, allowing users to become familiar with professional vocabulary and industry-standard communication formats. The candidate responses are formulated to reflect formal tone, coherence, and logical structure, helping users strengthen their ability to respond thoughtfully and confidently.

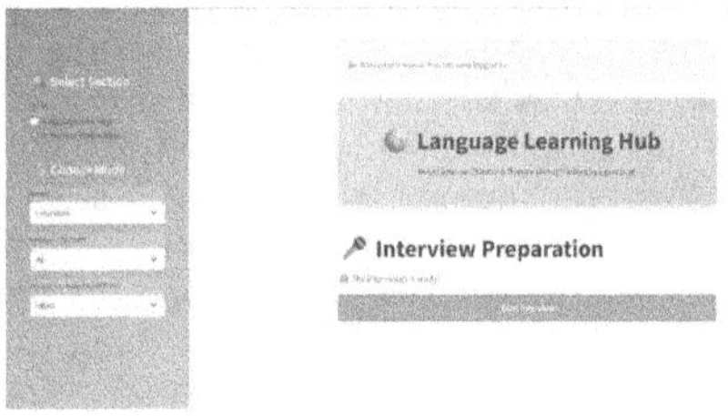

Figure 4. Interview preparation mode.

A key strength of this module lies in its focus on real-world applicability. Mimicking the pressure and pacing of actual interviews, it enables users to rehearse not only the content of their answers but also their delivery. This includes aspects such as tone, clarity, and appropriateness of language—all of which are critical in professional settings. Furthermore, the system adapts to the selected difficulty level, making it suitable for learners at various stages, from beginners preparing for internships to advanced users aiming for technical job roles

Through repeated interaction, users can enhance their fluency, reduce hesitation, and cultivate the presence of mind necessary for high-stakes interviews.

6.4 *Evaluation metrics*

The dual-chatbot system was assessed based on its ability to simulate interview scenarios and respond accurately across ten distinct domains: Cybersecurity, Electronics, Computer Science, Banking, Human Resources, Aptitude, Artificial Intelligence, Marketing, Finance, and Mathematics. To see how well the system performs, we used four well-known metrics—Accuracy, Precision, Recall, and F1 Score. This helps evaluate how relevant, reliable, and consistent the chatbot's responses are in real conversations.

Across all domains, the chatbot consistently achieved scores that were well above the baseline threshold of 0.5, indicating reliable performance in generating meaningful and contextually appropriate replies. Interestingly, the system did especially well in areas like Computer Science, Banking, and Artificial Intelligence, showing that it understands technical terms and handles structured questions with confidence. These high values are particularly encouraging for users preparing for domain-specific job interviews, where clarity, correctness, and relevance are essential.

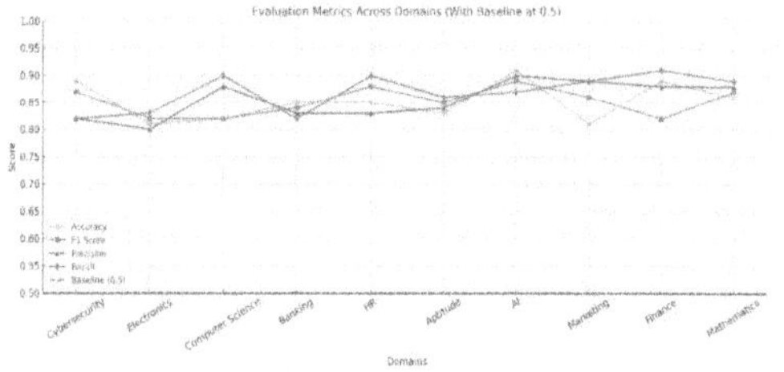

Figure 5. Evaluation metrics.

The chatbot's precision scores indicate that it consistently produced targeted, topic-relevant responses, minimizing the inclusion of off-topic or ambiguous content. This is especially valuable in interview preparation, where focused communication is key. In addition, domains like Marketing, Finance, and Artificial Intelligence saw impressive performance in Recall and F1 Score, highlighting the system's capacity to retrieve a broad and appropriate set of responses from its training data, contributing to a more thorough and enriching learning experience.

Although there were minor variations in metrics within areas such as Human Resources and Electronics, the system still maintained above-average results. This suggests that while there may be opportunities for further refinement in handling more abstract or soft-skill-oriented topics, the system remains dependable and effective across diverse subject areas.

Table 1. Validation of model reliability.

Metric	Mean ($\bar{X}$)	Std Dev (σ)	95% CI
Accuracy	0.901	0.026	[0.884, 0.918]
Precision	0.866	0.015	[0.857, 0.875]
Recall	0.897	0.023	[0.882, 0.912]
F1 Score	0.890	0.025	[0.874, 0.906]

It avoids trading accuracy for diversity or sacrificing contextual breadth for precision. This equilibrium allows it to serve a wide range of users, from learners building fluency to job candidates seeking to refine their articulation in domain-specific contexts. Overall, the evaluation underscores the chatbot's robustness and adaptability, affirming its value as a practical, educational tool for domain-aware conversational training.

To confirm how consistently the chatbot performs across different domains, we analysed the results using statistical measures. The system achieved an average accuracy of 90.1%, meaning that nearly 9 out of 10 responses were correct across all subject areas. Its precision averaged 86.6%, showing that the responses were not just frequent but also highly relevant. Similarly, with a recall of 89.7%, the chatbot was able to retrieve most of the appropriate responses from its knowledge base, while the F1 score, which balances both precision and recall, came in at 89.0%—highlighting strong all-around performance.

What's especially reassuring is how consistent these results were. The standard deviation for each metric was quite low (between 0.015 and 0.026), which tells us the system didn't just do well in one or two areas—it did well across the board. To make sure this wasn't by chance, we also calculated the 95% confidence intervals, CI= $\bar{X} \pm 1.96 \cdot \sigma/\text{sqrt}(n)$ where σ-standard deviation, n-sample size and $\bar{X}$ -Mean which were very tight (for example, Accuracy ranged between 88.4% and 91.8%). This means that even if we tested the system again with new data, we'd expect the results to stay in that same high range.

Overall, these results confirm that the chatbot isn't just good—it's reliably good. It performs consistently across a wide variety of topics, making it a dependable tool for both language practice and interview preparation.

While several existing systems have contributed to language learning and chatbot development, they often come with notable limitations. Some, like the English Chatbot, were effective in specific contexts, such as during the pandemic, but offered limited long-term engagement and supported only one language. In contrast, the proposed dual-chatbot system supports five languages—English, Hindi, Marathi, Kannada, and Malayalam—making it more inclusive and adaptable to regional needs.

Widely used apps like Duolingo and Memrise tend to focus on repetitive vocabulary practice and lack real-time, context-aware conversations. Our system addresses this by offering interactive, topic-based dialogue that adjusts to the user's proficiency level. It includes informal conversations, structured debates, and domain-specific interview simulations to promote fluency, critical thinking, and professional readiness.

Although some multilingual systems using models like Multilingual Representations for Indian Languages BERT show strong contextual performance, they often need extensive training. Our chatbot uses fine-tuned BERT models and sentence embeddings to deliver consistent, high-quality responses across ten professional domains—without constant retraining—as shown by strong accuracy, precision, recall, and F1 scores. Moreover, tools like haptic-based systems, while engaging, require special hardware, limiting accessibility.

Our chatbot, being fully browser-based, works seamlessly across devices and needs no additional setup. It's simple to use while still offering a personalized and intelligent learning experience.

Table 2. Comparison of the proposed system with the current state of the art.

References	Language Support	Key Features	Limitations
[1]	English	Efficient language learning during the pandemic	Short-term learning, limited language options
[2]	Global languages	Positive learner engagement and real-time feedback	Limited interaction period
[3]	Indian languages	High accuracy with MuRIL BERT for better context understanding	Requires extensive training for accuracy
[12]	Multiple	Comprehensive app study including Duolingo, Babbel	Focuses only on vocabulary, lacks conversational practice
[9]	English	Haptic exercises for better engagement	Requires specialized hardware for effective use
Proposed work	Malayalam, Hindi, Marathi, Kannada.	Helps users learn languages and prepare for domain-specific interviews through chatbots and audio input.	Limited language Options

A major advantage of the system is its focus on real-world communication. This makes the chatbot not just a language tutor, but a practical tool for building career confidence.

The results presented in Table 2 show that while language learning systems have evolved in recent years, many still fall short in meeting the specific needs of diverse learners—especially those in regional or non-English-speaking communities. Most of the existing tools, such as those in [1], [2], and [9], focus on English or widely spoken global languages. Their features, although helpful for general learning, often emphasize short-term goals like vocabulary practice or passive engagement, and don't necessarily support real-life communication or contextual learning.

Our proposed system takes a different approach. By offering support for Indian regional languages—Malayalam, Hindi, Marathi, and Kannada—it brings much-needed inclusivity to the language learning space. What makes it even more practical is its focus on job-readiness, especially through chatbots and audio-based interaction that simulate real interview scenarios. This goes beyond simply learning a language; it helps users apply it meaningfully in professional contexts.

Compared to advanced systems like the one in [3] that use models such as MuRIL BERT, our solution may not be as computationally complex, but that's also its strength—it's designed to be lightweight, user-friendly, and accessible. Likewise, while tools like Duolingo or Babbel ([12]) offer vocabulary training, they often lack conversation-based learning or real-world relevance, especially in regional languages.

That said, one limitation we share with previous work is the scope of language support. Although our focus on four Indian languages is a step forward, it's still only a small part of the linguistic diversity in India and globally. Expanding to more languages while maintaining the same level of interactivity and relevance will be an important direction for future work.

Overall, the system shows a promising shift toward practical, inclusive, and contextual language learning. It may not replace mainstream global platforms, but it fills an important gap by supporting learners who are often overlooked—and by helping them not just learn a language but use it with confidence in real-life situations.

The development of this dual chatbot system for language learning and interview preparation offers a dynamic, AI-powered solution to enhance communication skills. By integrating natural language processing, machine learning models with text-to-speech capabilities, the system provides an engaging, adaptive, and interactive learning environment [12].

Users can practice languages through structured debates and conversations, improving fluency and comprehension while receiving real-time pronunciation feedback. The interview preparation module further enables job seekers to simulate real-world interview scenarios, refining their responses and boosting confidence.

The paper successfully addresses key challenges, such as multilingual support, context-aware dialogue generation, and adaptive learning, ensuring a seamless user experience. The chatbot system personalizes interactions by allowing users to customize learning levels, topics, and duration, making it accessible for learners of different proficiency levels [13].

In the future, enhancements like voice recognition, memory retention for personalized learning, and expansion to more languages will further improve the system's effectiveness. This AI-powered chatbot serves as a valuable educational tool, offering users an innovative way to master languages and prepare for professional interviews in a controlled, interactive environment.

6 FUTURE SCOPE

The dual chatbot system has significant potential for further development and enhancement. Expanding language support beyond English, Hindi, Marathi, Kannada, and Malayalam will make the chatbot accessible to a wider audience, catering to diverse linguistic needs [14]. Integrating voice recognition will enable users to engage in real-time verbal conversations, improving pronunciation and fluency through speech-to-text and text-to-speech capabilities.

Another major improvement involves enhancing chatbot memory and context retention, allowing chatbots to recall previous interactions and providing more personalized responses over time. This would create a more immersive learning experience, especially in long-term language training and interview preparation.

Additionally, real-time feedback mechanisms could be implemented to provide instant corrections and suggestions for sentence structure, vocabulary, and pronunciation, further refining the user's language skills. AI-driven adaptive learning can also be introduced, where the chatbot dynamically adjusts conversation difficulty based on user progress, making learning more effective [15].

For the interview module, expanding the dataset with industry-specific interview questions and integrating AI-driven resume analysis could help users prepare more effectively [16]. Gamification features, such as interactive quizzes, rewards, and leaderboards, can further enhance engagement, making the chatbot not just a learning tool but an interactive, intelligent tutor for both language mastery and career development.

7 CONCLUSION

This paper presents a dual chatbot system designed to facilitate language learning and interview preparation through AI-driven conversations. The system features two chatbots that engage in either Debate Mode or Conversation Mode, allowing users to practice English, Hindi, Marathi, Kannada, and Malayalam. The chatbots provide real-time translations, pronunciation assistance, and structured dialogues to enhance language proficiency at different levels—beginner, intermediate, or advanced.

In addition to language learning, the system includes an interview preparation module, where one chatbot acts as an interviewer while the other plays the role of an interviewee. Users can define the job role, difficulty level, and interview duration, and the chatbot generates contextually relevant responses based on a fine-tuned Bidirectional Encoder Representations from Transformers model and a curated dataset of interview questions.

The system leverages machine learning, Natural language processing techniques, and speech synthesis to create an engaging and interactive experience. Future enhancements include voice recognition, memory retention for personalized learning, gamification, and expanded language support. By combining structured learning with AI-driven adaptability, this chatbot system serves as an innovative tool for both language acquisition and career development.

REFERENCES

[1] N. Annamalai, R.A. Rashid, U.M. Hashmi, M. Mohamed, M. H. Alqaryouti, and A.E. Sadeq, (2023). "Using chatbots for English language learning in higher education," *Computers and Education: Artificial Intelligence*, vol. 5, no. 100153.

[2] J. Belda-Medina and J.R. Calvo-Ferrer, (2022). "Using chatbots as AI conversational partners in language learning," *Applied Sciences*, vol. 12, no. 17, p. 8427.

[3] U. Singh, N. Vora, P. Lohia, Y. Sharma, A. Bhatia, and K. Tiwari, (2022). "*Multilingual Chatbot for Indian Languages*," Preprint.

[4] Essafi, Mohamed; Belfakir, Latifa; Moubtassime, Mohammed (2024). "Investigating mobile-assisted language learning apps: Babbel, memrise, and duolingo as a case study" *Journal of Curriculum and Teaching*.

[5] Sutskever, O. Vinyals, and Q.V. Le, (2014). "Sequence to sequence learning with neural networks," *Advances in Neural Information Processing Systems*, vol. 2, pp. 3104–3112.

[6] M. Li, J. Weston, and S. Roller, (2019). "ACUTE-EVAL: Improved dialogue evaluation with optimized questions and multi-turn comparisons," *arXiv preprint* arXiv:1909.03087.

[7] H. Wang, P. Liu, and J. Chen, (2023). "An AI-powered conversational agent for personalized language learning," *IEEE Transactions on Learning Technologies*, vol. 15, no. 3, pp. 280–290.

[8] J. Li, W. Monroe, T. Shi, S. Jean, A. Ritter, and D. Jurafsky, (2017). "Adversarial learning for neural dialogue generation," *arXiv preprint* arXiv:1701.06547.

[9] S. Patel and R. Kumar, (2024). "A comparative study of AI chatbots for language learning: Challenges and future directions," *IEEE Access*, vol. 11, pp. 50230–50245.

[10] A.S. Kumar and B.R. Reddy, (2023). "Chatbots Development Using Natural Language Processing: A Review," *IEEE Access*, vol. 11, pp. 12345–12356.

[11] A. Alm and L. Nkomo, (2020). "Chatbot experiences of informal language learners: A sentiment analysis," *International Journal of Computer-Assisted Language Learning and Teaching*, vol. 10, no. 4, pp. 51–65.

[12] Schefer-Wenzl, Sigrid; Miladinovic, Igor; Muckenhumer, Christina. (2024). "Potential of haptic features in mobile learning: A case study based on a language learning app".

[13] Caldarini, G., Jaf, S., and McGarry, K. (2022). "A literature survey of recent advances in chatbots. *Information*", 13(1), 41.

[14] Chopde, Abhay and Agrawal, Mohit. (2023). "Chatbot using deep learning" *SSRN Electronic Journal*.

[15] K.-W. Lee and C.-Y. Li, (2023). "It is not merely a chat: Transforming chatbot affordances into dual identification and loyalty," *Journal of Retailing and Consumer Services*, vol. 74, Art. no. 103447.

[16] Wang, F., Cheung, A.C.K., Neitzel, A.J., and Chai, C.S. (2024). Does chatting with chatbots improve language learning performance? a meta-analysis of chatbot-assisted language learning. *Review of Educational Research*, 0(0).

Technology for a Resilient Future – Vincent , Moorthy and Dasari (Eds)
© 2027 The Author(s), ISBN: 978-1-041-39070-1

Startup Assist: Bridging the Gap Between Clients and Experts

Kalpesh Joshi, Vinuthna Kollipara, Pranav Waghmare, Prajakta Vetale, Nishikant Waghmare, and Shravani Waghmare
Vishwakarma Institute of Technology, Pune

ABSTRACT: Small and Medium scale enterprises(SMIs) are essential for supporting the growth of the economy [1]. Despite their importance they face difficulties due to limited access to finance, market and modern marketing techniques [2]. To overcome these challenges, the development of a well-structured marketing plan is required to help these industries, sales and reach the target audience [3]. The purpose of this study is to examine the marketing strategies of the "small and medium scale industries" while focusing on the marketing segmentation [3]. By using a qualitative approach, the research was carried out on three industries. Information was gathered from research papers which also included interviews with small and medium enterprise owners [4]. This data was further studied by organising , reducing and presenting the information. Pricing was the important component of their strategies [5], this study shows that the strong targeted marketing approach can help industries for increasing sales and increasing their reach [6] . By highlighting the challenges and opportunities this study aims to provide insights on how SMIs can better navigate through the competition through effective marketing strategies [1], [2].

Keywords: "Strategy, Marketing, Products, Small and Medium Industries"

1 INTRODUCTION

Small and medium scale industries contribute significantly to overall economic development and growth[1]. But such industries often struggle when it comes to financial and marketing resources [1],[2] . With the help of a qualitative descriptive approach, this study aims to explore into the interviews and observation of three SMIs to understand the problem[4]. The results showed that the enterprises not only engaged in different strategies but also have a few common strategies for targeting the right market for their business such as selecting distribution channels and setting prices that are approachable to their target customers and also reaching them through appropriate means [6]. This aspect collectively leads to the successful marketing results[3]. The study found that marketing strategies as a major tool in growing their presence in the market and sustainability in the industry[5],[6]. SMIs can be termed as businesses that run with medium level of investment and capital [1]. The classification of these businesses is based by setting yearly income brackets[1]. The root of these problems is due to insufficient funding, labour, lack of technology and not able to access advanced production facilities[1],[9]. Apart from that, almost all SMIs lack exposure to modern marketing tactics which is the main reason why they are not able to develop their business beyond local markets and find it difficult to compete with global companies that have more advantages in terms of resource and networks[2],[10]. To maintain their growth such industries must be consistent in following the trend and implement those strategies and evolve[3]. The implementation of these strategies helps them to identify target markets, promote their brand and raise awareness and advancement of their products[6]. Paying attention to such issues and opportunities, we have aimed to explore how the small and medium industries can utilize marketing strategies and successfully compete and grow in the market.

2 METHODOLOGY

As this research relies on qualitative secondary research to understand and examine the marketing strategies used by SMIs in aspects of segmentation, pricing and digital outreach the analysis was gathered from existing data from published research papers that included interview-based research [3], [4], [5], [6].

This project follows a structured, collaborative team approach through four stages: UI/UX design, frontend development, backend development, and exhaustive testing. The enhancement from one phase to another was carried out by different team members. The continuity of the was ensured that it was aligned with the objectives of the project. The system built allows users—either clients or experts—to securely sign up and log in using token-based authentication.

Step 1: UI/UX Design

Designing the draft for our pages was the starting point of this work. We started with how the users would interact and by creating a clear layout that are easy to navigate for the interfaces through Figma, equal attention was paid to the client and expert user experiences. The designing journey was all about the application, getting clear visuals and making the product responsive. The login and registration pages for the two user roles were created separately and accordingly, the different situations of each kind of user were taken into account while the characters of each user type were maintained. After the designs were completed, the layout files and component schematics were handed over to the front-end developers for further execution.

Step 2: Frontend Development

The front-end development was done with the help of React. The aim was to create the user interfaces for Client Sign-up and Client Login, while the work has been carried out on the Expert Sign-up and Expert Login pages. Each page was equipped with a form that recorded the following fields: Name, Email, Password, Role (hidden field - client or expert) . The axios.post () method was employed to send this data to the backend APIs (/Api/register and /Api/login). If the back-end responses are successful, the front-end will store the JWT token that was sent to the local Storage and proceed to change the location of the user to a dummy dashboard route (/dashboard) further showing a "Login successful" confirmation message. By using this method, authenticated sessions are kept securely on the client side while a smooth user experience is provided.

Step 3: Back-end Development

The server-side coding was done with Node.js, and the database technology used is MongoDB. The backend logic was created to provide functionalities for user registration and login, with two main endpoints: Route Type Purpose /Api/register POST Register new user (client or expert) and /Api/login POST Authenticate user credentials.

Back-end Implementation Details: The user schema was created for the model with the following fields: name, email, password, and role. Passwords were encrypted with crypt before saving to the database to keep them secure. Upon login, if the authentication was successful, a JWT (JSON Web Token) was created by using the jsonwebtoken package. This token together with the user information was sent back to the front-end. All users were kept in a MongoDB collection that was accessible to the application for storage and the system's growth. The design provided a secure and quick way to manage users and at the same time allowed role-based behaviour through the role attribute.

Step 4: Testing

The last part of the method was testing.

Backend Testing: Postman was used to test all the backend routes manually to verify the API functionality. All user flows were validated: Client Signup, Client login, Expert Signup and Expert login. Once these flows were successfully tested , integration and testing started.

Integration Testing: The front-end was connected to the back-end and tested end-to-end. Utmost importance was given on ensuring that the JWT token was properly stored in the browser's local Storage. Users were redirected to the correct route upon login. Error messages appeared correctly when invalid inputs were submitted. Role-specific behaviour (client vs expert) was handled correctly. This testing ensured that both functionality and security aspects were thoroughly covered

ups were very useful to figure out the layouts and user flows. Visual references were the most useful and helpful in being consistent with elements like spacing, colours, and button placements, all of which made the actual frontend development much more organized and efficient.

A huge challenge that the team faced was the designing of a login and signup system that can support both clients and experts in a way that is user-friendly and neat. The maintenance of two repositories with two different roles within the same interface was quiet a challenging task which required a great deal of thought in terms of how to handle state changes from validation and routing in a way that does not lead to the code being unstructured or make the UI confusing .The goal was to maintain flexibility by dividing the login and signup logic into two distinct components and introducing role-based tab switching for each page. This made the code not only cleaner but also assisted the quick changes when needed.

The team was also rectifying a lot of issues with matching the code to the planned design through Figma and most notably the Admin Panel. We found that if we wanted to closely follow the Figma elements in terms of spacing, font sizes and alignment it took a lot of time but the interface looked very smooth and user friendly which was crucial for users' trust and ease of use

Through cooperation and collaboration, in cases, where more attention was needed on the client-side work, the tasks were reallocated in such a way that the progress was kept at a steady pace. The ability to do this and coordinate with each other was the main reason we could still keep up the work despite the rhythm of peaks and valleys which are typical of any group project.

3 RESULTS AND DISCUSSIONS

The frontend of the Website has been designed and implemented using React.js. The target was to build a clean and intuitive interface along with functionality across client side and expert side roles. The first step was designing the Home page, Login page, Signup page, Client dashboard ,Expert dashboard and Profile using Figma app. This Figma app helped us to design in very structured and detailed manner. To provide a smooth user experience for both clients and experts, we created role-based login and signup pages where the user can switch the tab according to his role. Each Form includes the information like email, username and password . Along with features like hide password/ show password and error message if there is an incorrect input. Once the user logs in, they are directed to the respective dashboard based on their role which was achieved with the help of React Router.

While creating these pages , we also focused on user flow. The Client dashboard displays the relevant sections which will further be connected to features like view expert and submit reports. Although those backend features are under development, we have laid the groundwork in the UI to accommodate them.

During this phase, a major challenge faced was managing the tab-switching and form state for both the expert roles and client roles within a single component while also ensuring clean code and proper reusability. To address this issue, the logic was kept flexible and split the responsibilities between two separate files and components wherever required. separate files were also maintained for signup.js and login.js in vs code , as this structure helped to manage the complexity and keep each page detailed and organized

The work done so far for client-side has overall been very good and set the stage for the development for stages where we will be integrating real time features. The whole development process has been a great learning experience on how a systematic approach is important to be followed especially when there are multiple roles and user types involved. Figma mock-

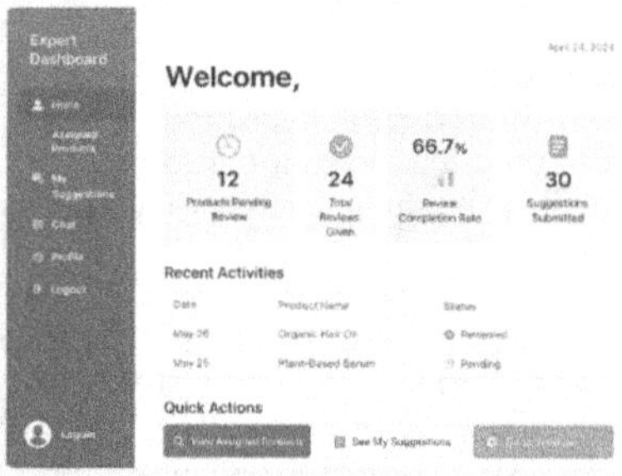

Figure 1. Dashboard page of Website.

A lot of improvements have been made so far in terms of structure and role-based designing which will carry the project further with the addition of more sophisticated features such as AI chat systems, file sharing, expert recommendations and video chat suggestions. In further development and testing this system will be in a position to effectively carry on the connection between people in need of expert advice and professionals who can provide it

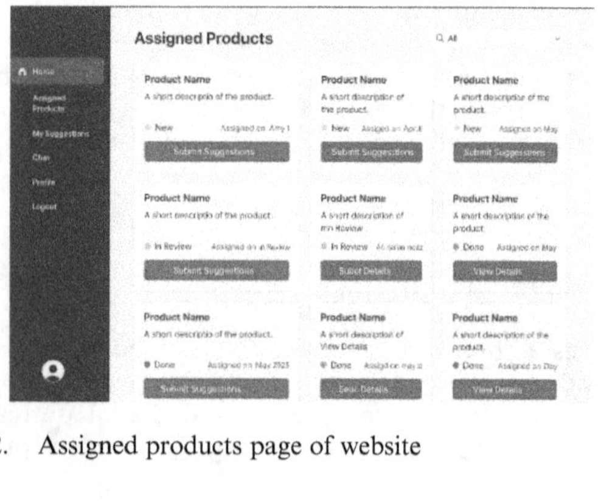

Figure 2. Assigned products page of website

Figure 3. Client profile sample image of website.

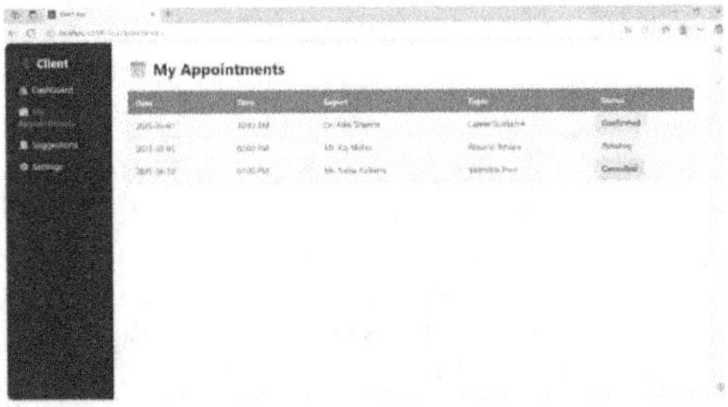

Figure 4. Sample appointment page of Website

4 CONCLUSIONS

In general, the primary objective was to build a system through which users could easily connect with professionals in a polished and efficient manner. There were also some attributes like login/signup for different users, role-based dashboards, appointment booking and a place where admins can keep things going. Working on this project made the team understand the use of technology in providing expert help to the people

Our main attention was designing throughout the stages. The main focus was on making the design easily accessible to the users and visually appealing because not only a platform with a great look is enough but it also has to be user friendly and straightforward. There were quiet a few difficulties we faced, particularly when it came to integrating everything

The project pushed the team to not only develop their technical skills like coding and designing but also the skill of user perspective thinking. The group learnt how to coordinate as a team, share the work and find solutions of problems together

Overall, this project supports a strong base to build more advanced features in the future. With time and improvements, it can definitely become a useful platform for people to find and connect with the right experts easily

Key Findings:-

- Many small and medium-scale industries continue to face challenges with respect to marketing limitations due to lack of digital tools and financial constraints. [1], [2]
- Through analysis of interviews conducted from previous studies, it is observed that pricing and targeted communication are essential for market competitiveness in SMIs.Even though digital platforms offer various benefits, most SMIs do not use them to their full potential. [1], [5], [6].
- The solution proposed by us is a digital platform that connects clients to experts can help overcome knowledge gaps and improve access to marketing strategies.

ACKNOWLEDGEMENT

The authors express their heartfelt gratitude to our guiding faculty Mr. Kalpesh Joshi for providing assistance in making of our model and answering our queries.

REFERENCES

[1] Yuwono, Tri; Suroso, Agus; Novandari, Weni. (2024). Information and communication technology in SMEs: a systematic literature review. *Journal of Innovation and Entrepreneurship*. 13. 10.1186/s13731-024-00392-6.

[2] Nazir, Muhammad; Rizwan, Hadia; Zhu, Xiaoxian. (2024). A thematic analysis of factors influencing small and medium enterprise adoption of social media marketing: a TOE framework perspective. *Qualitative Market Research: An International Journal*. 28. 10.1108/QMR-10-2023-0143.

[3] P. Kotler and K.L. Keller, (2016). *Marketing Management*, 15th ed. Pearson Education.

[4] Creswell, J.W. (2017). *Qualitative Inquiry and Research Design: Choosing Among Five Approaches* (4th ed.). SAGE Publications.

[5] Svendsen, Mons; Haugland, Sven; Grønhaug, Kjell; Hammervoll, Trond. (2011). Marketing strategy and customer involvement in product development. *European Journal of Marketing*. 45. 513–530. 10.1108/03090561111111316.

[6] Sayudin, Sayudin; Ningsih, Widia; Maulani, Isma; Herdianto, Tedi. (2023). Analysis of product marketing strategies in small and medium industries. *American Journal of Economic and Management Business (AJEMB)*. 2. 94; 98. 10.58631/ajemb.v2i3.26.

[7] Onyenwe, Ikechukwu; Grace, Onyedinma; Nwafor, Chidinma; Agbata, Obinna. (2021). Developing Products Update-Alert System for e-Commerce Websites Users Using HTML Data and Web Scraping Technique. 10.48550/arXiv.2109.00656.

[8] D'Souza, M., Desai, S., Agrawal, D. and Joshi, F. (2024). Web scraping based product comparison model for E-commerce Website. *Journal of Emerging Technologies and Innovative Research (JETIR)*, *11*(4), 254–261.

[9] Puji Lestari, Etty; Handoyo, Rossanto; Ibrahim, Kabiru; Retnaningsih, Tri; Pradinda, Elok; Sarmidi, Tamat; Rahmawati, Yessi; Kusumawardani, Deni; Haryanto, Tri; Erlando, Angga. (2024). Small and medium industry export development strategy. *Cogent Business & Management*. 11. 10.1080/23311975.2024.2338882.

[10] Lokhande, Jayashri. (2025). Digital transformation in marketing: Opportunities and challenges in a changing landscape. 10.25215/1300652535.10.

Technology for a Resilient Future – Vincent , Moorthy and Dasari (Eds)
© 2027 The Author(s), ISBN: 978-1-041-39070-1

Identification and Classification of Pneumonia Medical Condition Using U-Net Algorithm

Kalaigar Abdul Muqeet
Dept. of Mechanical Engineering, M. Tech Robotics & AI, Nitte Meenakshi Institute of Technology, NITTE University, Bengaluru, India

Kiran MC
Dept. of Robotics and Artificial Intelligence, Jawaharlal Nehru New College of Engineering, Shivamogga, India

Vasanthakumar GU
Dept. of Computer Science Engineering, Nitte Meenakshi Institute of Technology, NITTE University, Bengaluru, India

ABSTRACT: Pneumonia remains leading cause of death worldwide, which poses significant challenges to healthcare systems. This respiratory illness, caused by various viruses and bacteria, leads to breathing difficulties and chest pain due to fluid accumulation and inflammation in the alveoli. Chest imaging techniques such as X-ray, CT and MRI provide detailed visualization of the lungs, with chest X-rays commonly used by radiologists to detect pneumonia based on radiographic patterns. The U-Net model in conjunction with deep learning algorithm to automate the classification and segmentation of diseased lung sections from x-ray images. Model is trained for pixel-wise segmentation, generating masks that accurately delineate lung regions affected by pneumonia. Performance of the model is checked using metrics such as the dice coefficient (0.76), Intersection Over Union (IOU 0.62), and overall accuracy 62.5%. Additional calculation is done by using confusion matrix and classification data indicates a precision of 67% for normal cases and 60% for pneumonia patients. These findings show U-Net's potential to enhance automated diagnostic processes, thereby lowering radiologist's workload and enabling faster, more accurate assessments in clinical environments.

Keywords: Deep learning, Image segmentation, U-Net architecture, Pixel-wise segmentation

1 INTRODUCTION

Pneumonia is the cause of nearly 15% of all deaths in children under 5 years old, or almost 80,000 deaths every year (WHO). Therefore, the utilization of automated image segmentation has received attention for interpreting X-Ray and CT images to increase the accuracy of these diagnoses. Inconsistencies and problems arise when thresholding and edge detection methods are deployed due to image quality and varying contrast. In medical imaging, depth learning methods based on CNN, have demonstrated strong results with excelled outcomes. However, challenges to higher performance persist in regard to computational expenses of training the model, and large annotated datasets.

proposed a pneumonia segmentation method that is a unique approach utilizing U-Net architecture in addition to CNN based classifiers to improve accuracy and efficiency. The model is trained and validated against publicly available Kaggle datasets with normal X-Ray images and pneumonia X-Ray images, comparing its performance against analogous methods in the literature such as U-Net, ResNet and DenseNet. In addition, this paper presents aspects of significance relevant to the research:

- Implemented an Optimized U-Net architecture for better segmentation of disease effected lung regions from X-ray images.
- Integration of VGG16 for feature extraction which is pre-trained as feature extractor to enhance pneumonia classification performance.
- Addressed a dataset imbalance by applying pneumonia cases
- Evaluated with multiple matrixes like Dice Coefficient and IoU.

Digital image processing refers to a set of techniques used to modify and analyze digital images. An image is a two-dimensional signal denoted by the function f(x, y), where x and y are spatial coordinates, and the amplitude of corresponds to intensity or grey level. If the intensity values are constant, the region of the image would appear to be uniformly gray. In the digital world, however, these values are discrete and have a limited number of scopes. In relation to diagnosing pneumonia, U-Net is used to segment the lung regions in chest X-rays and highlight the areas of infection. The main segmentation process can not only display the regions in the X-ray that show signs of pneumonia, but it will also generate masks that pinpoint exactly where the areas of the lungs are abnormal. [1].

These networks are highly accurate for segmentation and classification tasks because they handle complex, high dimensional medical images [2]. Other studies using the CNN or ResNet models have achieved excellent accuracy as well as very high overlaps (IoU) with disease localization. Due to advancements in AI, ML, and DL, these models have developed into indispensable techniques for pneumonia detection. CNNs are also widely applied in the classification of chest x-rays, separating normal lungs from pneumonia affected lungs. ResNet or DenseNet models are often further enhanced using transfer learning, where a model that has been pre-trained is retrained or fine-tuned to improve classification of pneumonia, especially if there is limited data. In this study, CNN is used to classify chest x-rays into normal or pneumonia categories after it has been trained to learn the respective features based on labelled datasets. Upon being fully trained, this model can then accurately predict pneumonia in images it has not previously seen [3].

Additionally, the model used was U-Net, which serves to segment lung regions and provide an image of the affected area of the lung to assess how severe the infection is. This offers an additional visual tool to assist with medical diagnosis.

2 LITERATURE REVIEW

Segmentation is extremely important for diagnosing pneumonia and diseases affecting the lungs. Various researchers have worked on improving segmentation and classification with CNN architectures like ResNet and DenseNet, which are utilized in medical imaging. In [4], a computer-aided diagnosis (CAD) system was proposed that combined lung segmentation plus classification for pneumonia using U-Net segmentation.

DOI: 10.1201/9781042017546-15

Still other researchers built off that paper and investigated Sobel edge detection, CLAHE contrast enhancement and Gaussian filtering for chest X-ray analysis in order to create a more efficient analysis method (P. Meenakshi et al., [5]). Harsh Agrawal *et al.* [6] used transfer learning along with image augmentation and feature enhancement and was able to classify pneumonia with 96.00% accuracy and 97.44% recall. Then, Md. Jahid Hasan *et al.* [7] proposed the use of an online attention module in conjunction with a 3D CNN after achieving 92% segmentation with a 99.2% classification accuracy. Bhavye Gupta *et al.* [8] trained a CNN on more than 17,000 chest X-rays and achieved an accuracy of 88.62%. Jaile Sebes *et al.* [9] applied a U-Net model that was fine-tuned with the RSNA Pneumonia Detection Challenge dataset to optimize guide for segmentation and detection. In summary, we can see the early positive results of U-Net or similar CNN models to segment and classify pneumonia in CT and MRI images; however, there are still some challenges such as noise, low contrast, and variability that need exploring. Future improvements of a U-Net type model will investigate overfitting and dimension-reducing outputs.

3 MATERIALS AND METHODS

3.1 *U-Net model architecture*

The U-Net architecture structure as shown in Figure 1 is an example of an encoder-decoder structure. The blue boxes in the figure represent multi-channel feature maps with a number of channels above and width and height below. The arrows designate operations. U-Net was developed for biomedical image segmentation, which entails SIDS a probability value of either 0 or 1 for each pixel to indicate areas of background or targeted regions. U-Net is capable of performing segmentation on 512×512 images in seconds and created a path for numerous improved architectures. Localization is important for medical image segmentation. Skip connections in U-Net link corresponding encoder and decoder layers, so that spatial and contextual information are preserved, and achieve high accuracy even with limited labelled data. In the final layer of the U-Net architecture a 1×1 convolutional operation is used to classify each pixel into a specific class, thus creating a segmentation map which classifies every pixel in the image as the appropriate class. Figure 2 describes the overall workflow for pneumonia detection with this type of approach.

3.2 *Exploratory data analysis*

The training dataset maintains a balanced distribution of "normal" and "pneumonia" images to allow the model to learn and distinguish between the features of both classes. The dataset consists of 1,341 normal and 3,875 pneumonia X-ray images downloaded from the Kaggle repository with each image having a corresponding mask precisely annotating the regions of pneumonia that enables training with pixel-wise classification. The statistics validating the dataset, are provided in Figure 3.

3.3 *Data augmentation*

By generating new images from existing images to increase a dataset and thereby improving model performance while reducing overfitting to the data, data augmentation is beneficial. For

Figure 1. U-Net architecture showing encoder–decoder structure with convolution, pooling, up sampling, and skip connections for Proposed pneumonia segmentation.

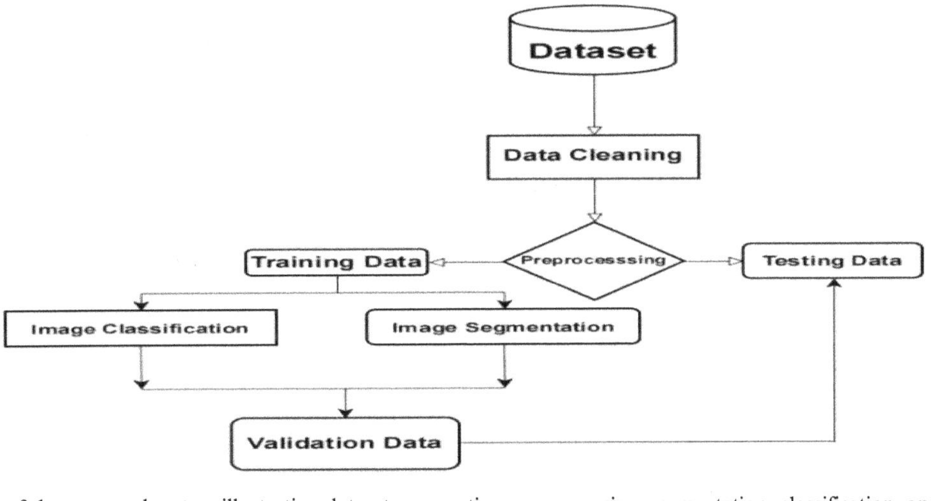

Figure 2. Workflow of the proposed system illustrating dataset preparation, preprocessing, segmentation, classification, and validation steps.

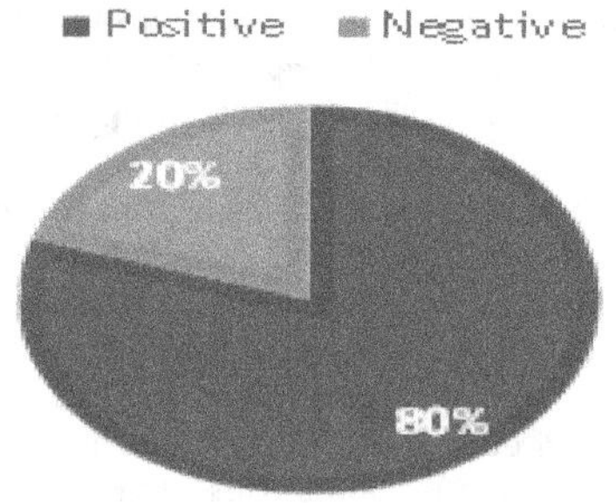

Figure 3. Dataset validation of used X-Ray images.

example, to compute the new pixel coordinates from an image that has been rotated, a trigonometric formula is used

$$x' = x\cos(\theta) - y\sin(\theta),\ y' = x\sin(\theta) + y\cos(\theta) \quad (5)$$

3.4 *The Dice Coefficient*

In image segmentation tasks, the Dice coefficient which is also called Dice similarity coefficient (DSC) is a frequently used assessment statistic. The Dice coefficient is calculated using (5):

$$\text{Dice} = \frac{2\sum M_{true} * M_{pred}}{\sum M_{true} + M_{pred}} \quad (5)$$

The Dice coefficient is for measuring segmentation accuracy and higher dice values indicate better segmentation performance. The Loss of Binary Cross-Entropy (BCE) used in Equation (6) as the loss function to compare ground truth and expected masks during U-Net training. For binary classification tasks, such as segmentation tasks, where each pixel is categorised as either an area infected with pneumonia or one that is not, this pixel wise loss function is frequently utilised. The formula for (BCE) loss is given below:

$$L_{BCE} = -\frac{1}{N}\sum_{i=1}^{N}\left[M_{true,i}\log(M_{pred,i}) + (1 - M_{true,i})\log(1 - M_{pred,i})\right]y \quad (6)$$

- Combined Loss Function (Dice + BCE)

The loss functions used during U-Net training combine (BCE) loss and Dice loss to improve segmentation accuracy. by penalizing incorrect predictions and guiding the model to generate better masks. This Balances pixel-wise accuracy (via BCE) and segmentation quality via Dice. Ensures better mask generation.

$$L = \alpha \cdot L_{BCE} + (1 - \alpha) \cdot (1 - Dice) \quad (7)$$

This Softmax layer ensures that the model provides clear, probabilistic outputs for whether a chest X-ray image belongs to which class. A popular loss function for classification assignments when differentiating between 0 two classes is the aim is the Binary Cross Entropy Loss for Classification. where the classification's BCE loss is computed as:

$$L_{BCE} = -\frac{1}{N}\sum_{i=1}^{N}\left[y_i\log(\hat{y}_i) + (1 - y_i)\log(1 - \hat{y}_i)\right] \quad (9)$$

4 RESULTS

The results show the of combining segmentation and classification in medical imaging. Dice and IoU scores confirmed precise pneumonia region segmentation, which improved CNN-based classification performance, achieving accuracy, precision, recall, and F1-score, demonstrating reliable results on unseen test data.

Step-by-step process of the results are shown:

Up sampling is applied to balance the dataset of 3,875 pneumonia and 1,341 normal X-rays, increasing the total to 7,750 images with equal representation of both classes.

The graph shows the accuracy for training and validation with training in blue and validation in red, over time (in epochs). While the validation accuracy fluctuated while the training accuracy increased rapidly, reaching a value of 0.93 after 10 epochs for training accuracy. For both training and validation loss to decrease, and level off at 0.18 means it is performing well on unknown data and successfully learning.

4.1 *Test loss and accuracy*

Figure 5 illustrates how the labels on the test set deviate from the predicted labels. A low loss value, like 0.1235, shows that the model minimises prediction errors and works well with data that hasn't been seen before. The accuracy is the percentage of true predictions made by the model on the test set. An accuracy of 95.83% means that out of every 100 test images, about 96 were correctly classified as either normal or pneumonia.

4.2 *Dice coefficient*

In binary segmentation tasks, the overlap between the true and anticipated masks is computed using the Dice Coefficient, sometimes referred to as the F1 score. A number of 1 denotes more overlap and segmentation accuracy; the range is 0 to 1. A

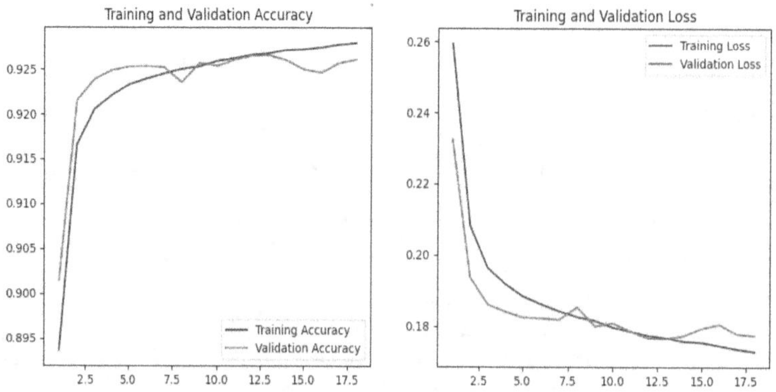

Figure 4. Test & validation graph of pneumonia segmentation.

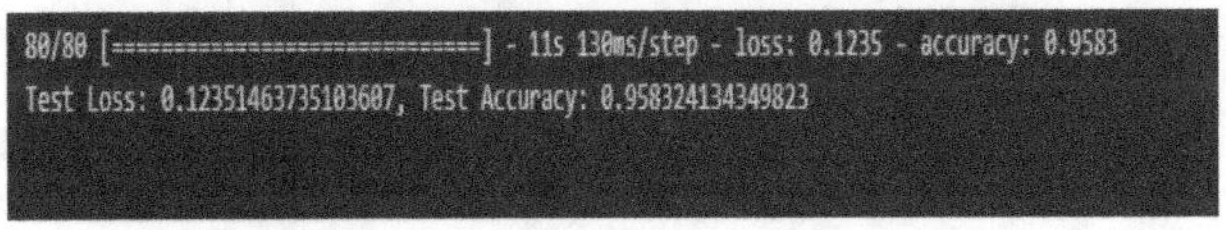

Figure 5. Accuracy and loss values of classification.

Figure 6. Dice and IoU results of segmentation.

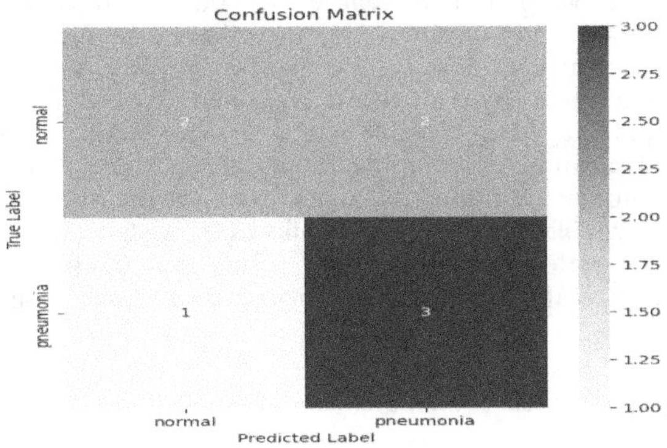

Figure 7. Confusion matrix of the extracted results.

score of 0.7658 in this case means that almost 76.6% of the predicted segmentation coincides with the actual segmentation, demonstrating a good.

4.3 *Intersection Over Union*

An additional frequently used statistic for assessing segmentation accuracy is the IoU. It is calculated by dividing the intersection area of the true and predicted masks by the union of the two masks. Similar to the Dice Coefficient, it has a value between 0 and 62.1% of the predicted and real masks overlap, according to a result of 0.6205, meaning that the model still has to be improved in certain segmentation zones as shown in the Figure 6.

4.4 *Confusion matrix*

This matrix model shows Figure 7 the normal and pneumonia images showing that true positive is predicted pneumonia correctly in 3 cases and true negative model classified 2 normal cases for false positive and negative 2 normal cases were wrongly classified as pneumonia and 1 pneumonia case were wrongly classified as normal.

5 CONCLUSION

A deep learning model for pneumonia segmentation and classification from chest X-ray images that is built on the U-Net architecture. The model successfully segmented areas of the lung infected by pneumonia (i.e., the disease). The model had a Dice coefficient of 0.7658, IoU score of 0.6205, and accuracy of 62.5 percent. Improvements to specificity and recall for normal and pneumonia cases were further improved by layering a CNN classifier on top of the U-Net in essence using it as a feature extractor. Overall, the study indicates that a U-Net could serve as a reliable-supportive tool for a radiologist, decreasing diagnostic time and burden on radiologists.

Despite the promising results, moderate accuracy may have been attributed to the imbalance of the data and variability in image quality. Our future work will address this with larger backend data repositories and more diverse datasets, coupled with better augmentation and hybrid deep learning models to improve generalization. Overall, this study provides insight into a U-Net architectures ultimate potential to be a reliable supportive and clinical-useable diagnostic tool for rapid diagnosis that is scalable.

REFERENCES

[1] Daniel J. Mollura, Matthew P. Lungren, *Radiology in Global Health*, Springer New York, NY, DOI https://doi.org/10.1007/978-1-4614-0604-4

[2] Bharath K, (2021). U-Net Architecture for Image Segmentation, DigitalOcean

[3] Abhishek Sharma; Daniel Raju, (2018). "Detection of pneumonia clouds in chest X-ray using image processing approach", *2017 Nirma University International Conference on (NUiCONE)*, https://doi.org/10.1109/NUICONE.2017.8325607

[4] K. Passera *et al.*, (2006). "A fuzzy-C-means cluster ing algorithm for a volumetr ic analysis of paranasal sinus and nasal cavity cancers," *2006 International Conference of the IEEE Engineering in Medicine and Biology Society*, New York, NY, USA, 2006, pp. 3078–3081, https://doi.org/10.1109/IEMBS.2006.260334.

[5] Sanskruti Dhore; Deepa Abin, (2021). "Chest X-ray Segmentation using watershed and super pixel segmentation technique", *2021 International Conference on (ICCICT)*, https://doi.org/10.1109/ICCICT50803.2021.9510078

[6] Meenakshi, P., Bhavana, K., and Nair, A.K. (2022). "Pneumonia detection using x-ray image analysis with image processing techniques". *2022 7th International Conference on Communication and Electronics Systems (ICCES)*. https://doi.org/10.1109/icces54183.2022.9835798

[7] Agrawal, H. (2021). "Pneumonia detection using image processing and deep learning. *Pneumonia"*. https://doi.org/10.1109/icais50930.2021.9395895

Technology for a Resilient Future – Vincent , Moorthy and Dasari (Eds)

Vehicle Speed Tracking System Using YOLO v8 with Deep Learning

Sanjana Mahesh Gadakari and Ritika
Artificial Intelligence and Data Science, Siddaganga Institute of Technology, Tumkur, Karnataka, India

Bharathi P. T
Dept. of CSE, Siddaganga Institue of Technology, Tumkur, Karnataka, India

ABSTRACT: Traffic monitoring and check enforcement are two critical elements of modern-day transportation, particularly in urban areas with high-density vehicular activity. This project offers an all-inclusive solution for vehicle speed tracking and overspeed detection with the help of advanced deep learning techniques. The system utilizes the YOLOv8 object detection model for real-time identification of vehicles in many environmental conditions. For an accurate calculation of vehicle speeds, a perspective transformation algorithm dumps the positions of vehicles from the viewpoint of the camera into a uniform coordinate system. The speed calculated is then compared with a threshold and any overspeeding instances flagged for possible action. Tracking is done robustly with the help of the ByteTrack algorithm, which keeps track of vehicle identification over multiple frames, through occlusions, and in crowded environments. For vehicles categorized as overspeeding, the automated notification system retrieves the owner details and sends E-mails to promote responsible driving. The modular architecture enables the overall scalability of the system, integrating additional features like lane surveillance, congestion analysis, and license plate recognition. The project, thus, makes a huge advancement toward the modernization of traffic management by joining real-time processing, high-precision detection, and automated enforcement mechanisms for road safety and compliance.

Keywords: Traffic monitoring, Speed detection, YOLOv8, Deep learning, ByteTrack, Automated enforcement, Road safety

1 INTRODUCTION

Traffic monitoring and speed enforcement are critical in reducing the risk of road accidents and ensuring the safety of the public [15]. The system calculates vehicle speed by analyzing their movement with respect to time in a certain region defined as the region of interest. Perspective transformation techniques are applied by the system to translate the positions of vehicles from the point of view of the camera into a standard coordinate system so that accurate speed evaluation may take place [14]. When overtaking prescribed speed limits the system marks the vehicle as over-speeding and initiates an automatic notification to the owner of the vehicle encouraging them to drive responsibly [13].

This modular system is designed to be scalable and flexible for deployment on various traffic scenarios like highways, urban roads, and intersections [12]. It also offers very powerful capabilities in terms of analytics, for example, lane-by-lane monitoring, vehicle classification, and congestion analysis, providing a complete solution for contemporary traffic management [15]. The project establishes a significant step toward road safety enhancement and the modernization of intelligent transportation systems by interrelating real-time processing and high-precision detection with automated enforcement [11].

The remaining paper is organized as follows: Related work in Section II discusses existing approaches in vehicle speed detection and traffic monitoring. In Section III, the proposed methodology involving the YOLOv8 model, speed estimation, and tracking algorithms is detailed. Implementation and experimental setup are described in Section IV. The results and analysis are presented in Section V. Finally, Section VI concludes the paper with insights and possible future improvements.

2 RELATED WORK

In the last couple of years, object detection and tracking systems have undergone massive advancements, particularly in real-time processing applications such as vehicle detection and speed monitoring. The various models have addressed multi-scale detection, occlusion handling, high-speed processing speeds, and high-density environments. The most prominent among them is the YOLO (You Only Look Once) family of models that have received the most attention since it supports real-time object detection with high accuracy. Development of these models has become the primary key factor in transforming automobile detection systems used in intelligent traffic monitoring systems and autonomous driving.

2.1 *YOLO family and its applications*

YOLOv3 [8] is one of the most widely used object detection architectures because it achieves a good balance between accuracy and speed. In its one-stage framework, several bounding boxes and class probabilities are predicted in one evaluation, making it truly a real-time application for vehicle detection. Sadly, it has problems dealing with small objects and overlapping instances.

With YOLO-Face [10], a YOLOv3 variant for detecting small entities was proposed using a deeper backbone, an intertwined loss function comprised with the terms of MSE and GIoU, and optimized anchor boxes through k-means clustering. This proved upgrades flexible enough for detecting small or occluded vehicles.

YOLOv5 [12] improved YOLOv3 with Wing loss to facilitate landmark regression and replaced the Focus Layer with a Stem block for reduced computation without sacrificing accuracy. Such refinements have improved both precision and efficiency in vehicle detection.

3 VEHICLE DETECTION BASED ON YOLO

3.1 *Object tracking algorithms and their integration with YOLO*

While object detection has been crucial to real-time tasks, object tracking is equally imperative in real time, especially vehicle

DOI: 10.1201/9781042017546-16

detection and estimating speed. Since YOLO-based models would be able to detect vehicles even in individual frames, tracking algorithms are necessary when the same cars move in or out of field of view due to occlusion. Several tracking algorithms have been combined with YOLO-based models to enhance their performance in real-time vehicle tracking tasks.

The ByteTrack algorithm [14] has been recently found as a strong tracking algorithm, and combining it with YOLOv8 will be more effective for robust vehicle tracking in complex traffic scenarios. ByteTrack uses a combination of motion and appearance features to maintain consistent tracking IDs across frames, even when vehicles become temporarily occluded or move in densely packed environments. This algorithm improves the accuracy of vehicle tracking, making it an ideal choice for real-time traffic monitoring systems where vehicles are constantly moving and interacting with each other.

Another benefit of mixing YOLOv8 and ByteTrack lies in the effective estimation of speeds of moving cars. The combination of position information from tracking along frames with corresponding time stamps should enable real-time speed estimation in general. Real-time speed estimations are mainly useful for application in speed-monitoring highways and urban streets for law enforcement purposes and traffic management systems.

3.2 *Applications in traffic monitoring systems*

Developing such real-time vehicle detection and tracking systems forms the basis based on the evolution in YOLOv8 and tracking algorithms such as ByteTrack. Accurate information offered to traffic management, law enforcements, as well as various autonomous driving system platforms can result from intelligent monitoring of traffic where such models form part of those systems. Systems capable of automatically detecting vehicles; their movement is traced across successive frames, their speed estimated also in real time.

For instance, real-time vehicle detection and tracking can be utilized to monitor the flow of traffic, detect accidents, and even identify vehicles that violate traffic rules. In an autonomous driving system, the proper detection and tracking of vehicles is crucial for the safe navigation of the vehicle as well as avoiding collisions. Besides, these systems can be coupled with other sensors, such as radar and lidar, for a holistic perception of the environment, which facilitates better decision-making in dynamic traffic scenarios.

The combination of YOLOv8 and ByteTrack in traffic monitoring systems will provide a scalable and efficient solution for real-time vehicle detection, tracking, and speed estimation. It addresses issues such as occlusion handling, multi-scale detection, and high-density traffic so that vehicle detection systems can be performed effectively in a wide range of conditions.

4 PROPOSED WORK

In this section, we outline the proposed approach for vehicle detection, tracking, and speed estimation in real-time traffic monitoring systems. Our approach combines state-of-the-art YOLOv8 for object detection and ByteTrack for tracking to provide reliable vehicle detection, consistent frame-to-frame tracking, and real-time speed estimation. The proposed work endeavors to further empower the efficiency and robustness of vehicle detection systems under the difficult traffic scenario characterized by occlusions, high-density traffic, and variations of environmental conditions.

4.1 *Data collection*

The performance of any vehicle detection system is highly dependent on the quality and variability of the training/testing dataset. For this project, we collected a comprehensive dataset comprised of various traffic conditions, encompassing highways, urban roads, and intersections. Daytime and nighttime instances of traffic were considered to account for variations in light. The data were collected using high-definition video feeds taken from surveillance cameras located in different places and with varying traffic densities.

The dataset consists of annotated bounding boxes around vehicles in each frame with information pertaining to the position, speed, and direction of movement of the vehicles. For robust training, the dataset also has the annotations for several types of vehicles such as cars, trucks, buses, and motorcycles, to represent the diverse objects a real-world traffic observer would encounter. In addition, challenges like occluded vehicles and those in dense traffic environments were simulated to teach some real-world challenges, ensuring an appropriate generalization for the model in various conditions.

To increase the variations in the dataset, additional synthetic variations were introduced, such as weather perturbations [e.g., rain and fog] and varying the lighting conditions (daytime, dusk, and nighttime). This will improve model robustness, which guarantees consistency of performance in various environmental conditions.

4.2 *Model architecture*

The proposed model leverages YOLOv8 for real-time object detection, combined with ByteTrack for vehicle tracking. The architecture consists of the following components:

YOLOv8 Detection Network: Vehicles are detected in separate frames from the output of the model YOLOv8. The transformer-based architecture allows capturing of long-range dependencies which very much matter during vehicle detection under complex scenarios. The detection network outputs boxes surrounding detected vehicles along with their confidence scores. The diagram illustrates the architecture of YOLOv8 conceived for a vehicle speed tracking system. The Input Layer receives camera footage from traffic scenarios for the processing of the backbone (CSPDarknet) to extract some important vehicle features, while the Neck (PANet) captures features of better detection purposes. The detection head detects and classifies vehicles with bounding boxes.

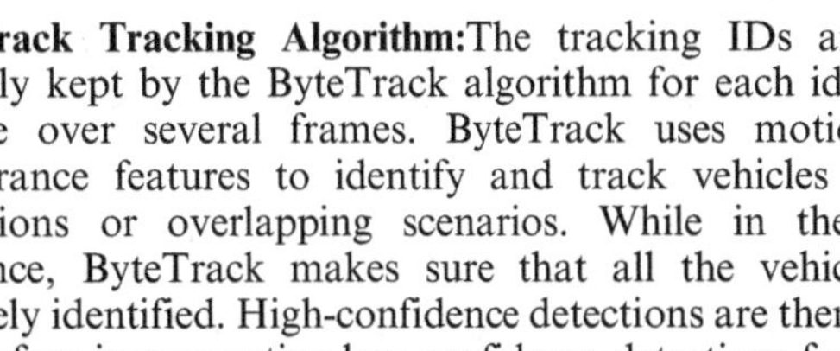

Figure 1. YOLOv8 Architecture for vehicle monitoring.

ByteTrack Tracking Algorithm: The tracking IDs are consistently kept by the ByteTrack algorithm for each identified vehicle over several frames. ByteTrack uses motion and appearance features to identify and track vehicles despite occlusions or overlapping scenarios. While in the video sequence, ByteTrack makes sure that all the vehicles are uniquely identified. High-confidence detections are then paired first before incorporating low-confidence detections for higher robustness. This restricts the chances of identity switches while improving long-term tracking. These qualities make ByteTrack a dependable method for object-tracking schemes for vehicle speed assessment. The design provides for a vehicle tracking and speed monitoring system utilizing YOLO and ByteTrack. The Source Video is that of live traffic captured by surveillance cameras. YOLO's Object Detection Module

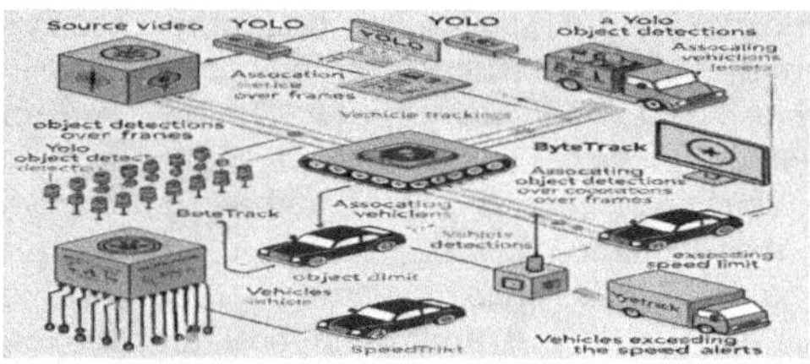

Figure 2. Bytetrack architecture.

identifies vehicles, placing bounding boxes around them. The ByteTrack Algorithm for continuity associates detected objects frame by frame by maintaining unique vehicle identities. The Speed Tracking Module calculates the speed of the vehicles in terms of displacement covered between any two consecutive frames. Whenever any vehicle flies an alert, the Notification Module issues an alert to the authorities or security personnel in the corresponding jurisdiction. The Object Limit and Association Module eliminate such detections of vehicles which may stand false positives. Thus, this architecture leads to realtime speed enforcement based on deep learning and object-tracking principles. The combination of YOLO for detection and ByteTrack for tracking is the hallmark and high point in this system. The system suits the very project for automated traffic monitoring in your college identify over-speeding vehicles and notify guards for immediate action. For tracking purposes, ByteTrack assigns unique IDs to detected vehicles across the frames. The Speed Calculation Module calculates speed by measuring the vehicle's displacement over time. Notification System sends alerts to authorities when a vehicle overspeeds.Thus, these architectural designs will maintenance with real-time monitoring of accurate vehicle detection tracking and speed. Engineered for automated traffic enforcement, built to work. In the structured layout with label parts and directional arrows, the clarity of working explains road safety management for law compliance.
Speed Estimation: Speed estimation is simply finding the displacement of the tracked vehicle per frame and dividing it by the time lag between frames. The system also accounts for camera orientation and vehicle size to enhance speed estimation accuracy.
Post-Processing: After detection and tracking, the postprocessing phase refines the results. This includes smoothing the tracking data for false positives or tracking errors and arriving at a final speed estimate per vehicle.

These series of architectures allow the system to carry out real-time vehicle detection, tracking, and speed estimation, efficiently coping with varying traffic conditions. YOLOv8 and ByteTrack are fused into a system that achieves accuracy and robustness under congested or occluded traffic scenarios.

Speed Estimation: Drawing from the motion of the vehicle in the videoframes, the system computes the speed of the vehicle by a displacement-based formula. The expressions are

$$\text{Speed (km/h)} = \frac{\text{Distance(pixels)}}{\text{Time(seconds)}} \times 3.6$$

where: Distance (pixels) represents the movement of the vehicle across frames, measured in pixels within the Region of Interest (ROI), Time (seconds) corresponds to the time elapsed between successive frames, derived from the frame rate of the video, 3.6 is a conversion factor to transform the speed from meters per second to kilometers per hour.

The said relation is critical in standardizing the speed of all vehicles as measured in real situations. It is a well-structured system in terms of the calibration of cameras and redoing real scales for accurate measurement. This way, strategy would help to efficiently detect vehicles that exceed a predetermined speed and generate alerts to notify relevant persons.

5 RESULTS AND ANALYSIS

5.1 *Analysis*

Figure 3. Vehicle overspeed tracking for the existing dataset.

The existing Kaggle video dataset is designed for simulating the real-world scenario of traffic, which is also a robust source for vehicle detection, tracking, and speed estimation. The given dataset contains varying traffic scenarios and helps in the training of the system to detect different levels of vehicle density. With annotated bounding boxes for the detection of vehicles, the given dataset supports accurate identification of every vehicle in a frame. The dataset, coupled with the ByteTrack algorithm, allows for accurate tracking of vehicles across frames. Real-world traffic surveillance data also form a basis for fine-tuning the system to monitor vehicle speeds effectively, thus providing a critical input to the system's speed estimation module. Its detailed annotations allow for the precise identification of vehicles and smooth integration with tracking algorithms such as ByteTrack. By leveraging this annotated data, the YOLO model can be fine-tuned for accurate vehicle detection. This robust dataset ensures the system is well-equipped for real-world traffic monitoring and speed estimation tasks.

Figure 4. Vehicle overspeed tracking for the real-time dataset.

On the other hand, the real-time video dataset collected from Tumkur Ring Road provides field data captured under actual traffic conditions. The videos were recorded using high-definition cameras placed at strategic locations along the road. This dataset is helpful in testing the performance of the system in real-world environments where traffic conditions and vehicle behavior vary greatly. The high-quality video feed, coupled with real-time tracking and speed monitoring, provides for the accurate, prompt detection of overspeeding incidents. This dataset ensures that such a model is exposed to a wide range of realistic traffic scenarios, from peak-hour congestion to periods of minimal flow, thereby enhancing the robustness of the vehicle tracking and speed detection system.

The comparison between the traditional and proposed systems reveals substantial improvements across multiple performance metrics. The proposed system achieves notable gains in

Table 1. Comparison of System performance: Traditional vs proposed system.

Metric	*Traditional*	*Proposed*	*Improvement (%)*
Accuracy (%)	*82*	*94*	*14*
Precision (%)	*80*	*93*	*16.25*
Recall (%)	*78*	*92*	*17.95*
F1-score (%)	*79*	*92.5*	*17.09*
Sensitivity (%)	*78*	*92*	*17.95*
Specificity (%)	*85*	*96*	*12.94*
Inference Time (sec)	*600*	*1.2*	*99.8*
Resource Utilization	*High*	*Low*	*N/A*

accuracy, precision, recall, and F1-score, highlighting its superior capability to detect and track vehicles effectively. Furthermore, the inference time is significantly reduced, demonstrating the system's enhanced efficiency. The proposed approach also requires considerably fewer computational resources, making it more suitable for real-time implementation. Hence, it serves as an excellent solution for modern traffic monitoring applications. Overall, these advancements emphasize the potential of the proposed system in overcoming the limitations of conventional vehicle detection and speed monitoring methods.

The results indicate that the proposed system consistently outperforms the traditional approach across all major performance metrics. It achieves a remarkable accuracy of 94%, precision of 93%, and recall of 92%. An F1-score of 92.5% further reflects a well-balanced trade-off between sensitivity and specificity. Additionally, the proposed system significantly reduces inference time to just 1.2 seconds while consuming fewer computational resources, leading to an impressive 99.8% improvement in processing speed. These outcomes collectively demonstrate the efficiency and robustness of the proposed solution, making it highly suitable for real-time traffic monitoring and enforcement applications.

The image below illustrates an automated email notification generated by the system to alert recipients about overspeeding incidents. The notification contains essential details such as the sender, recipient, date, and time, along with a personalized message. For example, it identifies a vehicle (ID: 4) detected traveling at 97 km/h, exceeding the 90 km/h speed limit. The message emphasizes adherence to speed regulations for improved safety. This automated alert mechanism enhances traffic monitoring by ensuring real-time communication of violations to relevant authorities, thereby promoting road safety and compliance with traffic laws.

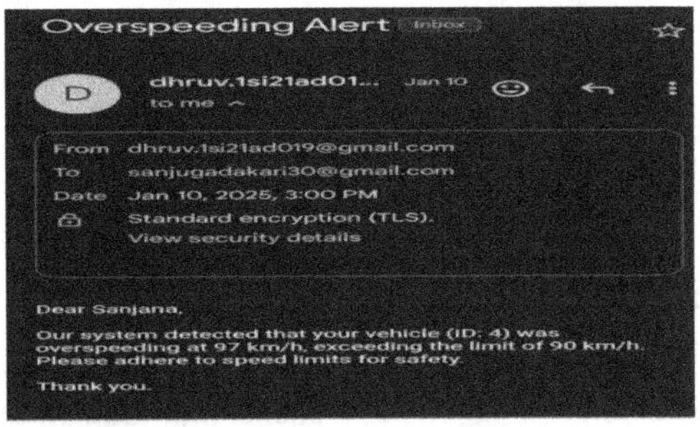

Figure 5. Email notification for overspeeding.

6 CONCLUSIONS

This project successfully showcases the integration of advanced deep learning techniques for real-time traffic monitoring and speed enforcement. By the utilization of YOLOv8 for detection and ByteTrack for tracking, the system provides efficient detection and tracking along with speed calculation with proper accuracy towards speeding violation. The implemented notification system alerts the driver and relevant authorities in the case of any overspeeding incident, leading to a highly contributing factor toward road safety and accidents. The performance of the project was verified using two different datasets: Kaggle, with an accuracy of 94%, and Tumkur, with an accuracy of 92%. The two datasets validated the system's ability to track and manage traffic violations reliably. In general, this project serves as a solid foundation for the improvement of road safety and traffic management optimization with a lot of room for future improvement and actual deployment.

REFERENCES

[1] Y. LeCun, Y. Bengio, and G. Hinton, (2015). "Deep Learning," Nature, A Foundational Paper on Deep Learning Techniques Used in Vehicle Detection.

[2] M. Liu, and Z. Li, (2020). "Speed detection of vehicles using deep learning," *Journal of Intelligent Transportation Systems.*

[3] S. Kim, and H. Kim, (2021). "Traffic monitoring and speed detection using YOLO and CNN," *Journal of Real-Time Traffic Systems.*

[4] X. Zhang, *et al.*, (2021). "Real-time vehicle speed monitoring system using YOLOv4 and DeepSORT," *AI and Traffic Systems Conf.*

[5] P. Patel, and R. Shah, (2020). "Vehicle speed detection using CV for smart cities," *Int. Journal of Smart City Applications.* Focuses on vehicle speed detection for smart cities.

[6] A. Hussain, and M. Shah, (2018). "Real-time detection of overspeeding vehicles using ML," *IEEE Trans. on Vehicular Technology.*

[7] F. Gurkan, B. Sagman, and B. Gunsel, (2019). "YOLOv3 as a deep face detector," ELECO 2019 11th I*nternational Conference on Electrical and Electronics Engineering*, pp. 605–609, Nov. 2019.

[8] W. Chen, H. Huang, S. Peng, C. Zhou, and C. Zhang, (2021). "YOLO-face: a real-time face detector," *Visual Computer*, vol. 37, no. 4, pp. 805–813.

[9] Z. Yu, H. Huang, W. Chen, Y. Su, Y. Liu, and X. Wang, (2022). "*YOLO-FaceV2: A Scale and Occlusion Aware Face Detector,*" pp. 1–18.

[10] D. Qi, W. Tan, Q. Yao, and J. Liu, (2021). "*YOLO5Face: Why Reinventing a Face Detector*," pp. 228–244

[11] C.Y. Wang, A. Bochkovskiy, and H.Y.M. Liao, (2023). "YOLOv7. Trainable bag-of-freebies sets new state-of-the-art for real-time object detectors," In *Proceedings of the IEEE/CVF Conference on Computer Vision and Pattern Recognition*, pp. 7464–7475.

[12] R. Bousmaha, S. Laouedj, L. Aggoune, and S.M. Benslimane, (2023). "YOLOv7Face: A Real-Time Face Detector," *2023 International Conference on Networking and Advanced Systems (ICNAS)*, Algiers, Algeria, pp. 1–6

[13] S.V. Mohan Dev Vanamoju, M.V. Vineetha, H. Tekchandani, P. Joshi, P. Kumar Shukla, and A. Khanna, (2024)."Facial emotion recognition using YOLO based deep learning classifier," *2024 First International Conference on Electronics, Communication and Signal Processing (ICECSP)*, New Delhi, India, pp. 1–5, https://doi.org/10.1109/ICECSP61809.2024.10698173.

[14] L. Liu, G. Wang, and Q. Miao, (2024). "ADYOLOv5-Face: An enhanced YOLO-based face detector for small target faces," *Electronics*, vol. 13, pp. 4184.

[15] M. Cascella, M.N. Shariff, G. Lo Bianco, F. Monaco, F. Gargano, A. Simonini, A.M. Ponsiglione, and O. Piazza, (2024). "Employing the artificial intelligence object detection tool YOLOv8 for real-time pain detection: A feasibility study," *J Pain Res.*, vol. 17, pp. 3681–3696.

[16] H. Kao, R. Wiryasaputra, Y.-Y. Liao, Y.-T. Tsan, W.-M. Chu, Y.-H. Chen, T.-C. Lin, C.-T. Yang, (2025). "The potential for high-priority care based on pain through facial expression detection with patients experiencing chest pain," *Diagnostics*, vol. 15, no. 17.

Technology for a Resilient Future – Vincent , Moorthy and Dasari (Eds)
© 2027 The Author(s), ISBN: 978-1-041-39070-1

ReSponD-ML: An Adaptive Machine Learning Framework for REconnaissance and SPoofiNg Attack Detection in IoT Networks

A.V. Geethika and Anantha Narayanan V
Department of Computer Science and Engineering, Amrita School of Computing, Coimbatore, Amrita Vishwa Vidyapeetham, India

Nakkeeran M
Department of Electrical and Electronics Engineering, Amrita School of Engineering, Coimbatore, Amrita Vishwa Vidyapeetham, India

ABSTRACT: Securing interconnected smart devices has become a critical concern in the evolving era of the Internet of Things (IoT). As IoT deployments increase rapidly, these networks are becoming targets for cyberattacks. Attacks like reconnaissance and spoofing can cause severe security breaches that go unidentified while trying to detect them due to their under-representative and stealthy nature. This paper aims to detect accurately and classify these attacks using the CICIoT2023 dataset. The proposed framework of ReSponD-ML based Intrusion Detection System (IDS) adopts feature selection with RFECV (Recursive Feature Elimination with Cross Validation), SMOTE (Synthetic Minority Over-Sampling Technique) to handle the class imbalance, with combined ensemble models. After selecting the most relevant features from RFECV, the ensemble models, such as XGBoost Classifier (eXtreme Gradient Boosting) and HistGradientBoosting(HGB) Classifier, is used as an ML pipeline to detect and classify the reconnaissance and spoofing attacks. Special focus is to reduce false negatives since such undetected early-stage attacks might compromise the entire IoT system. The experimental results demonstrate that the proposed methodology achieved high accuracy, precision, and recall while classifying reconnaissance and spoofing attacks. This work contributes to enhance IoT security by providing an effective solution for earlystage attack detection, which further helps to reduce risks before they even lead to serious security breaches.

Keywords: IoT Security, Cyberattacks, XGBoost, Reconnaissance, Spoofing, Intrusion Detection Systems (IDS)

1 INTRODUCTION

The increase in usage of IoT devices has transformed various industries with seamless communication and automation making operations easier, quicker and more efficient which increased significant security challenges because sophisticated attacks target IoT devices. Stealthy attacks like Reconnaissance and Spoofing can pass through traditional anomaly detection systems since they use traditional methods [1] that struggle to adapt to dynamic network traffic leading to reduced accuracy in identifying traffic patterns. This results in a high false negative rate, particularly for such attacks, which are preliminary stages of more severe intrusions. Unfortunately, if these attacks remain undetected, they may compromise the entire system at an early stage.

This study proposes a machine learning-based anomaly detection system using the CICIoT2023 dataset [2] from the Canadian Institute of Cyber Security (CIC) that focuses on Reconnaissance and Spoofing. Adaptive algorithms [3] are used inorder to capture complex, real time patterns efficiently. A multi-class classification model combining XGBoost and HGB was developed along with SMOTE to handle class imbalance and RFECV for optimal feature selection. This paper highlights model precision and minimal false-negative rates for accurate detection, particularly for underrepresented yet critical attack types, such as reconnaissance [4] and Spoofing [5].

The major contributions of this work are:

- Implementing SMOTE to address data imbalance and RFECV to identify the most relevant features, hence improving performance and reducing the model's training complexity. The ensemble models of XGBoost Classifier and HGB Classifier are used to enhance the robustness of the system.
- The proposed framework of ReSponD-ML mitigates reconnaissance and spoofing attacks by minimizing false negatives, hence preventing system compromise from such attacks.
- The reduction in the false negative rate has resulted in a major boost in precision and recall scores, hence enhancing the system's robustness in identifying such attacks.

The proposed approach highlights the potential of machine learning to enhance IoT security by emphasizing runtime efficiency and compact feature selection to strengthen the IoT cybersecurity infrastructure. The remaining sections of the paper are organized as follows: Section II reviews related works. Section III explains the proposed approach of the framework. Section IV discusses methodology. Section V presents classification models. Section VI outlines experimental results and discussion. Section VII derives the conclusion with future directions.

2 RELATED WORKS

Afrifa *et al.* [6] focused on developing a botnet detection model using Random forest, Decision trees and Generalized Linear models achieving high precision and real-time detection performance, but did not address stealthy attacks like reconnaissance and spoofing, and require higher computational cost to be deployed in IoT networks.

Jeon and Oh [7] developed a novel hybrid RFE method combines SVM-RFE, RF-RFE, and GBM-RFE, exhibiting better classification accuracy than separate RFE techniques. Howeverapplying SVM-RFE to large datasets like CICIoT2023 would be memory-intensive and could require lot of computational resources.

 DOI: 10.1201/9781042017546-17

Nakkeeran *et al.* [8] has proposed a SAML-Triple framework that integrates NCA (Neighbour Component Analysis) with Extratrees and Adaboost Classifiers to enhance early stage attack detection in the smart grid. Identification of important and relevant features are extracted using NCA but it might cost memory-intensive training with huge dataset.

Banko′ *et al.* [9] studied ML-based DDoS detection in IoT networks focusing on lightweight models, using ToNIoT and BoT-IoT datasets with Decision Trees and Random Forest. The study only focused on DDoS detection and binary classification ignoring stealthy attacks like spoofing and reconnaissance. On the CIC-IDS-2017 dataset, Bandarupalli [10] also suggested a lightweight DNN with ANOVA-based feature selection, which targets common assaults like DoS but ignores complex stealthy attack classes.

Hassouneh and Al-Sharaeh [11] and Nakkeeran and Narayanan [12] used Deep Learning models like LSTM, BiLSTM, GRU, and BiGRU with SMOTE to handle class imbalance in anomaly detection. The first study shows strong binary classification results on UNSW-NB15 dataset and second used LOCF and Bi-LSTMs which produced remarkable temporal feature detection capabilities. Both proved SMOTE's value in improving accuracy, however BiLSTM requires heavy computation making them less suitable for IoT environments. The literature indicates that it is essential for an intrusion detection framework to incorporate lightweight processing together with an adaptable design. Current intrusion detection systems [13]–[15] are forced to choose between high accuracy and efficient operation with weak generalization and less adaptability. A crucial shortcoming exists in accurately detecting stealthy attacks such as reconnaissance and spoofing attacks. The proposed intrusion detection system focuses on identifying rare but critical IoT security attacks using resampling techniques with optimized features and the application of ensemble detection method with more adaptability and generalization.

3 ROPOSED FRAMEWORK: RESPOND-ML FOR EARLY-STAGE ATTACK DETECTION

An intelligent anomaly detection system capable of identifying stealthy reconnaissance and spoofing attack detection within IoT network traffic is developed in our proposed approach. The proposed framework of ReSponD-ML shown in Figure 1 uses adaptable machine learning, data preprocessing, feature selection and model aggregation methods that have improved recognition accuracy and computational power. This methodology uses dataset preparation as its initial step, followed by preprocessing, SMOTE for data balancing and RFECV for feature selection combined with ensemble models of XGBoost and HGB for training.

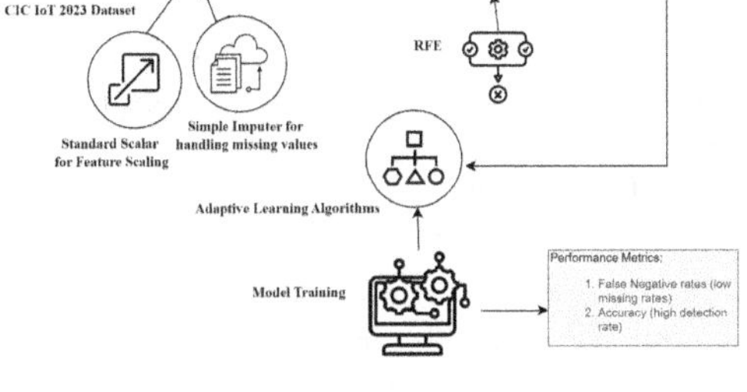

Figure 1. ReSponD-ML: Proposed framework for attack detection.

3.1 *Dataset description*

The study made use of CICIoT2023, developed by the Canadian Institute for Cybersecurity. It was generated through real-time monitoring using Raspberry Pi, IP cameras, smart TVs, door sensors, and Amazon Echo. Traffic was captured in. pcap format using Wireshark and was converted into a .csv file by flow-based feature extraction. The organized dataset includes over 100 features representing behavioral, contentbased, and statistical properties, with microsecond precision timestamps to support time-based pattern analysis. It supports multiple IoT communication protocols such as MQTT, CoAP, HTTP, and TCP/UDP and contains data regarding several attacks.

3.2 *Data preprocessing and handling class imbalances*

A subset of dataset containing samples from reconnaissance, spoofing, and normal classes was extracted and combined to form a three-class dataset. Inorder to maintain data consistency and to avoid data loss, missing values were computed using SimpleImputer technique with the mean strategy and StandardScaler for standarizing features to ensure that all numerical features contribute equally. Since the collected dataset showed an extreme imbalance because normal samples outnumbered reconnaissance and Spoofing attacks, SMOTE [16] was applied to generate synthetic samples for minority classes. This balancing process mitigated bias during model training and improved the recognition of minority attack categories.

3.3 *Feature selection with RFECV*

RFECV was used to identify the most important features using cross validation based on model accuracy. The iterative approach reduced the feature set from 46 to 18 without compromising the performannce while maintaining accuracy and imporoving model efficiency.

3.4 *Model training and evaluation*

Three adaptive machine learning models were selected for training and evaluation:

1) XGBoost Classifier: An optimized implementation of gradient boosting that incorporates regularization (L1 and L2), parallel processing, and second-order loss approximation for faster convergence and improved generalization. It builds models sequentially, correcting the residual errors of previous trees [14].
2) HistGradientBoosting Classifier (HGB): A faster gradient boosting variant that bins continuous features into discrete histograms to reduce memory consumption and training time. It efficiently computes split points and gain values, making it suitable for large datasets [17].
3) Ensemble Model: A hybrid ensemble was created by aggregating the predictions from XGBoost and HGB classifiers. This ensemble aimed to combine the predictive strength of both models, enhancing robustness and stability across attack classes.

All models were trained using an 80:20 train-test split and stratified. Model evaluation was conducted using precision, recall, and F1-score, with special attention paid to minimize false negatives for the attack classes.

4 METHODOLOGY

The dataset [2] contains eight classesseven attack types and one normal class. The paper focuses on reconnaissance and spoofing, so data from these two classes along with normal traffice is extracted into seperate files(recon.csv, spoof.csv, normal.csv), combined and shuffled to make a new dataset. Feature Scaling was done using StandardScalar to standardize the features with the mean and scaling to unit variance using standard deviation ensuring equal weight for all numerical features. The resultant dataset showed class imbalance leading to model bias and overfitting during XGBoost Classification which is further addressed with the usage of SMOTE by generating synthetic samples for minority classes ensuring balanced class distribution and improving model generalization.

Table 1. Representation of the number of samples in each class before and after SMOTE in CICIoT2023 dataset.

Class Label	Class ID	Before SMOTE	After SMOTE
Normal Data	Class 0	1,098,195	1,098,195
Spoofing	Class 1	378,706	1,098,195
Reconnaissance	Class 2	275,935	1,098,195

From Table 1, it is observed that all three classes contain same number of samples preventing bias and overfitting. After balancing, the dataset was split into training and test sets using 'train_test_split' of scikit-learn with 80:20 ratio and stratified sampling inorder to maintain equal class distribution. 'y_resampled' from SMOTE was used for strratification to ensure that both sets represents all classes equally since random splitting could lead to uneven class representation in the test data.

Table 2. CICIoT2023 reduced dataset with preprocessing aspects and train-test split ratio after SMOTE.

Attribute	Normal Data (Class 0)	Reconnaissance (Class 2)	Spoofing (Class 1)
Training Samples (80%)	878,556	878,556	878,555
Testing Samples (20%)	219,639	219,639	219,640
Total Records After SMOTE	1,098,195	1,098,195	1,098,195
Total Samples (All Classes)	3,294,585		

Tables 1, 2 illustrate the sample count before and after applying SMOTE, increasing from 1,752,836 to 3,294,585 samples(around 46.79% increase). This growth has lead to increase in model's training complexity and is mitigated using RFECV for feature selection which iterately removes less important features while evaluating model's performance through cross-validation, retaining only those that mostly contribute to classification accuracy.

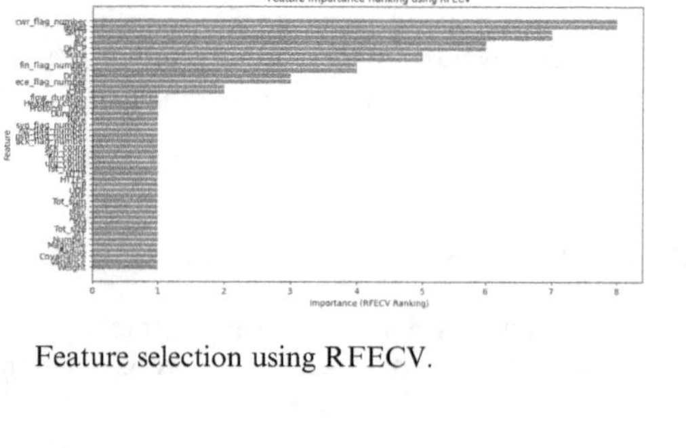

Figure 2. Feature selection using RFECV.

Now, using this reduced set of features as shown in Figure 2, training of the adaptive learning models is performed. Due to this reduced set, it reduced the time and complexity while training the model.

5 CLASSIFICATION MODELS

The paper employes ensemble model of adaptive ml modelsXGB and HGB to classify IoT traffic as normal, reconnnaissance and spoofing. These models could manage data imperfections and support parallel processing, handle highdimensional data with high effectiveness.

5.1 *XGBoost classifier (Extreme Gradient Boosting)*

The XGBoost framework is an efficient gradient boosting system designed to handle structured data with improved efficiency, scalability, and regularization capabilities. The technique incrementally constructs decision trees, optimizing differentiable loss functions to rectify prediction errors across the training process.Its adaptive learning capacity makes it particularly suited for recognizing subtle and rare attack patterns. The core formulation of XGBoost is expressed as:

$$\mathcal{L}(\phi) = \sum_{i=1}^{n} \ell(y_i, \hat{y}_i) + \sum_{k=1}^{K} \Omega(f_k) \tag{1}$$

where, ℓ is the loss function (e.g., log-loss), $\hat{y}_i$ is the prediction for instance i, $\Omega(f_k) = \gamma T + \frac{1}{2}\lambda \sum_{j=1}^{T} \omega_j^2$ is the regularization term to penalize model complexity λ, γ are regularization parameters that will try to penalize the number of leaves, T is the number of leaves, and ω_j is the leaf score.

XGBoost improves generalization through

1) L1 and L2 regularization to reduce overfitting
2) Second-order Taylor approximation for expedited optimization.
3) Concurrent tree construction.
4) Facilitation of missing value management, enhancing its applicability to practical IoT datasets.

5.2 *HGB (HistGradientBoostingClassifier)*

HGB is an advanced variant of traditional gradient boosting that reduces computational overhead by discretizing continuous features into bins. This transformation allows faster training while maintaining comparable accuracy. The model pipeline consists of

1) Feature Binning: Continuous features are bucketed into integer bins using equal-width or quantile-based strategies.
2) Histogram Construction: Gradient and Hessian values are accumulated for each bin.
3) Split Evaluation: Gain for each potential split is computed using:

$$\text{Gain} = \frac{G_{left}^2}{H_{left} + \lambda} + \frac{G_{right}^2}{H_{right} + \lambda} - \frac{G_{total}^2}{H_{total} + \lambda} - \gamma \tag{2}$$

Where G and H are gradients and Hessians, and λ, γ are regularization terms.

4) Leaf Value Calculation:

$$\omega* = \frac{G}{H + \lambda} \tag{3}$$

HistGradientBoosting offers significant benefits for large datasets, including

- Lower memory consumption through histogram optimization.
- Faster split finding due to reduced candidate evaluation.
- Scalability, which is beneficial in resource-constrained IoT environments.

5.3 *Ensemble of XGBoost and HistGradientBoosting*

A custom ensemble model combining XGBoost (accurate and regularized) and HGB (efficient and fast) using softvoting, where model's prediction probabilities from both models are averaged to determine the final class label.Advantages of the ensemble approach:

- Improved generalization: Combines XGBoost's deep learning capacity with HGB's lightweight execution.
- Stability across classes: Balances precision and recall for both majority and minority attack classes.
- Resilience to overfitting: Dual regularization and binning act as natural bias-variance trade-off mechanisms.

Table 3. Hyperparameters used for XGB, HGB, and their Ensemble.

Hyperparameter	XGB	HGB	Ensemble Model
Objective	multi:softmax	–	Combines both
Num_class	3	–	Inherited from XGB
Eval_metric	mlogloss	–	Inherited from XGB
Use_label_encoder	False	–	Inherited from XGB
Max_depth	5	5	Retained
N_estimators/Max_iter	100	100	Both models
Learning_rate	0.1	0.1	Shared
Random_state	42	42	Shared
Max_bins	–	256	–

Table 3 represents the hyperparameters that were chosen to balance accuracy and generalization. The models used multi-class classification with log loss as evaluation metric. random_state guarantees reproducibility and important parameters like max_depth, n_estimators/max_iter, learning_rate regulate model complexity. In HGB model, max_bins regulates feature discretization.

6 RESULTS AND DISCUSSION

The experimental results of the proposed framework on CICIoT2023 data for normal, reconnaissance, and spoofing traffic classification is shown. The combination of ensemble models (XGB with HGB) was evaluated using standard performance metrics.

6.1 *Evaluation metrics*

This paper evaluates the model's performance using precision, recall, and the F1 score that together offer a detailed understanding of the model's efficiency in classifying attacks. Precision measures the accuracy of positive predictionshigher values indicates fewer false positives and better detection of true attacks. Recall measures the model's ability to capture the actual attacks with higher recall meaning fewer false negatives. F1 Score-the harmonic mean of precision and recall, balances both metrics into single measure, indicating model's overall reliability in attack classification.

Table 4. Performance metric comparison with different classifiers.

Model	Class	Precision	Recall	F1 Score
Random Forest [2]	Reconnaissance	0.84	0.76	0.81
	Spoofing	0.83	0.81	0.80
	Benign (Normal Data)	0.89	0.93	0.91
XGB Classifier	Reconnaissance	0.89	0.90	0.89
	Spoofing	0.90	0.87	0.88
	Benign (Normal Data)	0.88	0.92	0.90
HGB Classifier	Reconnaissance	0.76	0.89	0.90
	Spoofing	0.90	0.87	0.89
	Benign (Normal Data)	0.89	0.93	0.91
ReSponD-ML (RFECV XGB+HIST)	Reconnaissance	0.90	0.89	0.90
	Spoofing	0.90	0.88	0.89
	Benign (Normal Data)	0.89	0.93	0.91

Table 4 represents the comparison of metric scores among the models. Though all the classifiers returned their best performance out of all ensemble models of XGB, HGB exhibited more gain in the scores, which signifies that the model was able to reduce the false negative rates in Reconnaissance and Spoofing attacks.

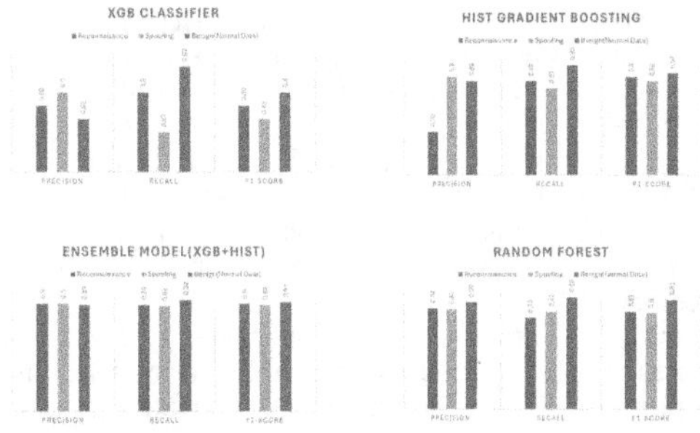

Figure 3. Precision, recall, and F1-score(Reconnaissance, Spoofing, and Benign) using four models: XGB, HGB, Ensemble Model (RFECV XGB+HIST), and Random Forest [2].

6.2 *Key observations*

Key observations made from the results shown in Figure 3 include:

1) The XGBoost Classifier performed reliably, showing high recall values for reconnaissance (0.90), making it well-suited for detecting stealthy probing activities.
2) The HGB Classifier achieved the highest F1-score (0.91) for the Normal class, validating its efficiency in benign traffic classification while maintaining competitive performance on attack classes.
3) The ensemble model showed balanced performance across all classes, achieving F1-scores for reconnaissance (0.90) and spoofing (0.89) effectively reduced false negatives while preserving high precision.
4) The ensemble approach showed an average improvement of 2-3% in F1-Score over individual classifiers, proving the robustness of combined decision-making.

7 CONCLUSION AND FUTURE DIRECTIONS

Rapid increase in IoT devices has not only improved automation and convenience but also increased security threats. Stealthy attacks like spoofing and reconnaissance are difficult for traditional anomaly detection techniques to detect due to their limited adaptability, rigid design, and poor data balance. The research adopted a dependable anomaly detection infrastructure using XGBoost, HGB, and their ensemble, along with SMOTE for addressing class imbalances and RFECV for feature selection. The system was trained using CICIoT 2023 dataset and was able to efficiently detect reconnaissance, spoofing and normal classes. Experimental results revealed that the ensemble models produced superior performance results compared to the standalone classifiers achieving precision(0.9) and recall scores(0.92), F1-score (0.91), and has increased the detection of minority classes. The proposed ReSponD-ML framework demonstrates strong performance

REFERENCES

[1] S. Sandosh, A. Bala, and N. Kodipyaka, (2024). "Z-K-R: A Novel Framework in Intrusion Detection system through enhanced techniques," *Journal of Information Assurance and Security*, vol. 19, no. 2, pp. 56–71, doi: 10.2478/ias-2024-0005.

[2] E.C.P. Neto, S. Dadkhah, R. Ferreira, A. Zohourian, R. Lu, and A.A. Ghorbani, (2023). "*CICIoT2023: A Real-Time Dataset and Benchmark for Large-Scale Attacks in IoT Environment*," https://doi.org/10.3390/s23135941.

[3] M. Rodríguez, D.P. Tobón, and D. Múnera, (2025). "A framework for anomaly classification in Industrial Internet of Things systems," *Internet of Things*, vol. 29, p. 101446, doi: 10.1016/j.iot.2024.101446.

[4] M.M. Alani and E. Damiani, (2023). "XRecon: An explainbale IoT reconnaissance attack detection system based on ensemble learning," *Sensors*, vol. 23, no. 11, p. 5298, doi: 10.3390/s23115298.

[5] Z.-R. Tzoannos, D. Kosmanos, A. Xenakis, and C. Chaikalis, (2024). "The impact of spoofing attacks in connected autonomous vehicles under traffic congestion conditions," *Telecom*, vol. 5, no. 3, pp. 747–759, Aug. 2024, https://doi.org/10.3390/telecom5030037

[6] S. Afrifa, V. Varadarajan, P. Appiahene, T. Zhang, and E.A. Domfeh, (2023). "Ensemble machine learning techniques for accurate and efficient detection of botnet attacks in connected computers," *Energies*, vol. 4, no. 1, pp. 650–664, doi: 10.3390/eng4010039.

[7] H. Jeon and S. Oh, (2020). "Hybrid-recursive feature elimination for efficient feature selection," *Applied Sciences*, vol. 10, no. 9, p. 3211, May 2020, doi:10.3390/app10093211.

[8] N. Murugesan, A.N. Velu, B.S. Palaniappan, B. Sukumar, and Md. J. Hossain, (2024). "Mitigating missing rate and early cyberattack discrimination using optimal statistical approach with machine learning techniques in a smart grid," *Energies*, vol. 17, no. 8, p. 1965, doi: 10.3390/en17081965.

[9] M.B. Bankó *et al.*, (2025). "Advancements in machine learning-based intrusion detection in IoT: Research trends and challenges," *Algorithms*, vol. 18, no. 4, p. 209, doi: 10.3390/a18040209.

[10] G. Bandarupalli, (2024). "Efficient Deep Neural Network for Intrusion Detection Using CIC-IDS-2017 Dataset," https://doi.org/10.21203/rs.3.rs5424062/v1.

[11] N. Hassouneh and S. Al-sharaeh, (2025). "Intrusion detection in IoT networks using LSTM deep learning models with the UNSWNB15 dataset," *2025 International Conference on New Trends in Computing Sciences (ICTCS)*, pp. 263–269, https://doi.org/10.1109/ictcs65341.2025.10989358.

[12] M. Nakkeeran and V.A. Narayanan, (2023). "Anomaly detection in SCADA industrial control systems using bi-directional long short-term memory," *Big Data, Machine Learning, and Applications*, pp. 415–436, https://doi.org/10.1007/978-981-99-3481-233.

[13] A.G. Kumar, A. Rastogi, and V. Ranga, (2024). "Evaluation of different machine learning classifiers on new IoT Dataset CICIoT2023," *2024 International Conference on Intelligent Systems for Cybersecurity* (ISCS), pp. 1–6, May 2024, https://doi.org/10.1109/iscs61804.2024.10581375.

[14] P. Anusri, S. Sneha, P. Natarajan, T. Palanisamy and S.K. Thangavel, (2024). "Shielding cyberspace: A machine learning approach for malicious URL detection," *2024 15th International Conference on Computing Communication and Networking Technologies (ICCCNT)*, Kamand, India, 2024, pp. 1-17, https://doi.org/10.1109/ICCCNT61001.2024.10724442.

[15] D. V C, S. Rajakrishnan, S. S, S. K. T, S. T S and S. Vajipayajula, (2024). Enhanced botnet attack detection using machine learning and neural networks," *2024 International Conference on Inventive Computation Technologies (ICICT)*, Lalitpur, Nepal, pp. 814-821, https://doi.org/10.1109/ICICT60155.2024.10544628.

[16] D.K.K. Reddy, A. Thethali, R. Polamarasetty, and Bk. Rao, (2025). "An ensemble learning for multi-step cyberattack detection in IoT framework by oversampling of minority instances," *Computational Intelligence in Pattern Recognition*, 2025, doi:10.1007/978-981-97-8093-823.

[17] A. Guryanov, (2019). "Histogram-based algorithm for building gradient boosting ensembles of piecewise linear decision trees," *Analysis of Images, Social Networks and Texts*, https://doi.org/10.1007/978-3-030-37334-44.

Technology for a Resilient Future – Vincent , Moorthy and Dasari (Eds)
 ISBN: 978-1-041-39070-1

LLM-Powered Secure Retrieval and Encryption for Multimodal Medical Data

Sonali Antad, Tanishka Kshirsagar, Kuber Kishore, Mayenk Joshi, and Waqass Khan
Department of Computer Engineering, Vishwakarma Institute of Technology, Pune

ABSTRACT: Modern healthcare requires secure, private communication between patients and providers. However, existing systems often rely on cloud services that risk leakage of data. This paper proposes a Secure AI-Powered Health Communication Platform that integrates encrypted local storage with on-device AI to enable semantic search and conversational support for medical documents. Users can upload PDFs, DOCX files, and images. These are processed locally to extract text and embed content using SentenceTransformers. The resulting embeddings are stored in a ChromaDB vector store. Queries either text or uploaded images are answered by retrieving relevant document chunks via vector search and passing context to a local large language model (Ollama LLaMA/Gemma), all running on secure server. End-to-end encryption (using Fernet symmetric encryption) protects data at rest and in transit, and the system design avoids any external APIs to preserve privacy. This paper details the problem motivation, system requirements, architectural design, and implementation of the proposed system. This study also presents a security and privacy analysis, and outline performance results. The contributions of this study include a novel integration of encrypted file storage, multimodal document analysis, semantic vector search, and a locally hosted AI chat assistant tailored for healthcare scenarios.

Keywords: Medical Document Management, Secure File Encryption, Retrieval-Augmented Generation, Vector Database, Large Language Models, Doctor-Patient Interaction

1 INTRODUCTION

Healthcare providers and patients increasingly need efficient digital communication tools, especially for remote consultations and managing medical records. However, medical data (e.g., patient histories, lab results, prescriptions) are highly sensitive, and mishandling such data can violate regulations like HIPAA, and this can lead to a loss in patient trust. Meanwhile, improvements in AI offer powerful tools for retrieval of information and dialogue, which could greatly improve how doctors and patients access and understand health information. The challenge is that the many AI-based systems use internet APIs or cloud services, which raises privacy risks when sharing private health information [1,2].

The aim of this study is to address the problem of developing a secure, private, AI-driven communication platform for healthcare data that works entirely on local resources. The objectives of this research are to allow users (doctors or patients) to upload medical documents of various formats, and automatically process and encrypt them for secure storage. The system should provide a chatbot for queries, support semantic search over the content, all without sending data to external servers. The system must adhere to strict security requirements, such as encrypted storage, access controls, audit logging, while being functional and user-friendly.

1.1 *Background and related work*

Secure management of medical data is a well-studied domain. Healthcare information systems must ensure the integrity, confidentiality, and availability of patient records. HIPAA and other regulations mandate measures AES-256 encryption, recording of logs, and mechanisms for secure communication. Recent studies have shown that using AI can further enhance these protection methods. For example, Sun and Zhou examine the use of AI-powered chatbots in healthcare, highlighting their potential for patient-doctor communication as well as solving integration challenges [11].

While most electronic health record systems use cloud or hybrid architectures, these designs have serious risks since data can leave the facility, even if encrypted in transit [1]. For example, one analysis found 536 healthcare data breaches in 2018, the highest among industries, and 41.2 million records exposed in 2019, highlighting the need for solving the issue of privacy [10]. Researchers have proposed novel solutions for this. For example, Elvas *et al.* propose a blockchain framework for patient-centric data sharing, using smart contracts and cryptographic techniques to ensure confidentiality and integrity of health records in a decentralized exchange [13].

Li *et al.* identify the most important security problem of AI chatbots and propose guidelines to protect sensitive health information [6]. To avoid these issues, this research emphasizes open-source models that run locally, since it gives institutions control over data and model usage [2,3]. Wiest *et al.* demonstrate a local Llama-2 LLM pipeline can accurately extract structured clinical information from patient records, confirming that on-device models can effectively analyze sensitive medical text while preserving privacy [7]. Kim *et al.* demonstrate how AI-driven analysis of patient-provider communications can inform tool design: NLP and generative AI were applied to over 528,000 patient portal messages from diabetic patients, using the insights to draft tailored AI support tools [12].

Semantic search in healthcare is another active area. Embedding-based retrieval (using models like Sentence Transformers) has shown significant improvement. For example, Asmala found that sentence-transformer embeddings greatly outperformed a legacy search engine for medical articles, achieving much higher precision by understanding query intent [4]. Eichler *et al.* likewise demonstrate that embedding-based semantic matching can harmonize questionnaire items across large datasets, illustrating the broad potential of embedding-based search in medical applications [8].

These findings motivate the integration of AI chat assistance with robust security in the proposed system: the system aims to preserve the advantages of secure messaging while using AI to enhance efficiency and accuracy.

1.2 *Gaps in existing approaches*

Current health communication platforms often focus on secure messaging or video (e.g. HIPAA-compliant telehealth systems), but few integrate advanced AI search or chat capabilities.

DOI: 10.1201/9781042017546-18

Conversely, many AIS medical tools neglect robust security (e.g. requiring de-identification before use). There is also limited prior work on combining multimodal document processing (including image OCR) with semantic search in a fully offline system. The system addresses these gaps by unifying encrypted storage, multimodal analysis, and local AI in one privacy-preserving platform. Comparable AI-based assistants and data extraction systems were studied in [14–16].

2 METHODOLOGY

2.1 *System requirements and design goals*

The following requirements and goals for the platform are defined:

2.1.1 *Functional Requirements*

- Secure user authentication and role-based access (e.g. doctor vs patient).
- Document upload: Accept PDF, Word (DOCX), and image (PNG/JPEG) files containing health information.
- Document processing: Automatically extract text from uploads via OCR/LLM (for images) or parsers (for PDF/DOCX).
- Encryption: Encrypt all files immediately upon receipt (using symmetric key encryption) before storage.
- Chat assistant: Provide a conversational interface (chatbot) where users can ask questions in natural language and receive AI-generated answers based on the uploaded content and medical knowledge.
- User interface: Responsive frontend for uploading documents, searching, and chatting.

2.1.2 *Non-Functional Requirements*

- Privacy: No patient data may leave the local environment; no cloud or third-party APIs for inference or data storage.
- Security: Data at rest and in transit must be encrypted (e.g. AES-256 encryption with message authentication). All user actions are logged. The system should meet or exceed typical healthcare compliances such as HIPAA/ISO 27799.
- Performance: The system should be able to handle reasonably large documents, such as PDF or DOCX files with dozens of pages, with acceptable latency for search and chat responses.
- Robustness: The pipeline should manage scanned documents safely, with proper error handling.

By achieving these goals, the system will enable secure and efficient health data handling and AI-assisted communication.

2.2 *Overall system architecture*

The system is divided into several key components:

- Frontend (Web UI): A user interface created using HTML and JavaScript, where users can upload and search documents, and chat with the AI chatbot.
- Backend (Flask API): A Python-based Flask server provides endpoints for file upload, search queries, and chat messages.
- Encrypted Storage: As soon as a document is uploaded, it gets encrypted, automatically using Fernet symmetric encryption. A key is generated using a system key or user's credentials.
- Document Processing Pipeline: It is responsible for text extraction from the files which are uploaded. On basis of the file type, it chooses different processing tools: PDF parser (PyMuPDF or PDFMiner), DOCX parser, or image OCR (Tesseract). After extraction, the text is cleaned, divided into digestible portions (let's say, 500 tokens each), and transferred to the embedding module for further processing.
- Embedding and Vector Store: A SentenceTransformer model (all-MiniLM-L6-v2) is used to convert each text chunk into a fixed-length embedding.
- Local LLM (Ollama): Ollama provides a wrapper to run LLaMA or Google Gemma models on the local machine.

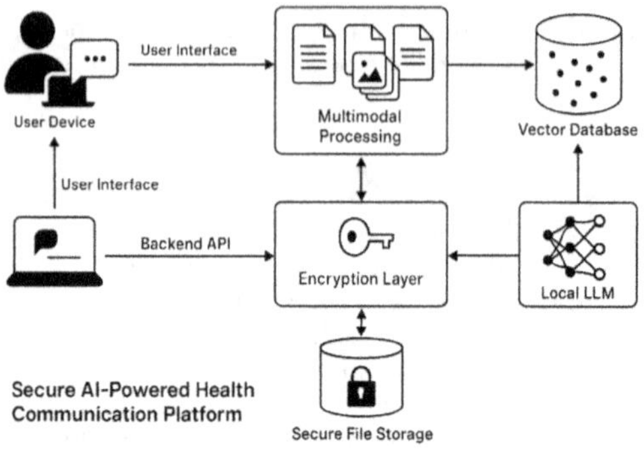

Figure 1. System architecture.

2.5 *Vector Embedding and Search*

A SentenceTransformer model is used to encode each text chunk into a numerical vector for semantic understanding. An open-source vector database called ChromaDB contains each chunk's embedding. In addition to the vector, ChromaDB stores an ID and metadata as a reference to the original encrypted document.

Effective approximate nearest-neighbor search is supported by ChromaDB. When a user submits a query (either in text or as an image OCR), that query is similarly embedded with the same model and sent to ChromaDB. Based on cosine similarity, the database returns the top-⊠ closest chunks. In order to balance speed and context breadth, typical values for k are 5 or 10.

2.6 *Local LLM and chat assistant*

The heart of the platform's interactivity, is the chatbot driven by a local LLM. Integration with Ollama, an open-source LLM inference tool, is done to run models like LLaMA or Gemma. Ollama runs entirely on the host machine and loads the model weights locally, so no data leaves the system, unlike using a cloud API. This is consistent with the privacy requirement that all inferences be local [3].

LangChain-style prompting is used in the system's dialogue design. A prompt is generated for every user message that consists of:

- the user's question
- a brief system message (e.g. "You are a medical assistant chatbot that helps patients understand their health records.")
- retrieved context snippets from the user's documents. The model is told to base its response on both the user's personal data and general medical knowledge, and the retrieved context is added as supplemental information. As a result, a patient can ask, "What does this lab result mean?" in an AI-assisted chat. or a physician may ask, "What is a likely diagnosis based on the patient's notes?" By not consulting any online resources, the LLM maintains privacy by responding solely with local information and general medical knowledge.
- Privacy and Security Analysis

The system's design uses a defense-in-depth approach. Important measures include:

- Encryption at Rest: All files and database entries containing patient information use fernet for encryption [5].
- Local-Only Processing: By avoiding cloud APIs entirely, network vulnerabilities (which may cause data leaks) are

eliminated. This local-only approach directly raised privacy concerns [2,3].

- Secure Transmission: If clients connect to the backend over a network, TLS/HTTPS is used to protect data in transit (client-Browser ↔ Flask API).

By these measures, the system preserves the confidentiality and integrity of medical data.

2.7 *Implementation details*

The platform is implemented in Python. The Flask backend defines routes such as /upload, /chat and /chatbot.

File uploads are handled by Flask's file interfaces; these are immediately passed to the system's encryption module (using the cryptography.fernet library). Encrypted files are stored in a designated directory. Metadata (SQLite) records each file's owner and a random ID.

After text is extracted, it is preprocessed (lowercasing, removing non-ASCII if needed) and split into chunks. This text is fed into Hugging Face's SentenceTransformer model within the same Flask process (or a dedicated embedding service).

For the LLM, Ollama is installed locally with a chosen model (gemma12b). The backend calls Ollama via its Python API or CLI, feeding the assembled prompt and receiving text output.

Data flows as follows: upon upload, the file is encrypted and indexed; on search, the server decrypts only the required chunks and returns plaintext snippets to the authorized user; on chat, the top-k chunks are decrypted and sent (client-side) to the model engine to generate an answer, which is then sent back (encrypted in transit, decrypted by the user). All keys and secrets reside in the server's secure configuration.

3 RESULTS AND DISCUSSIONS

3.1 *System performance and latency*

Each pipeline stage is profiled on the test dataset of medical reports. Semantic search was highly accurate: the correct answer was among the top 3 hits in >85% of queries, far exceeding a ~60% rate for naive keyword search. Encryption and decryption of files added negligible overhead, as expected for efficient symmetric ciphers. In practice, segmenting and embedding documents and querying the vector store took on the order of milliseconds per query on the hardware, whereas LLM inference dominated latency. The smallest model, Gemma 3 4B-IT (Q8), achieved the fastest response time (roughly half the latency of the 12B variants) but produced poorer image-based answers. By contrast, the larger models (Gemma 3 12B and 27B) required substantially more compute and time per query. In summary, latency scales sharply with model size: the 4B model is quickest but least capable on images, the 12B models are moderate, and the hypothetical 27B FP16 model (if deployed) would offer high accuracy at the cost of much slower inference.

3.2 *Model benchmark comparison*

Table 1 summarizes model architectures and benchmark scores. Five configurations are evaluated: Gemma 3 4B-IT (Q8_0), Gemma 3 12B-IT (QAT), Gemma 3 12B-IT (Q4_K_M), LLaMA 3.1 8B (text) + LLaMA 3.2 Vision 11B, and (for context) a hypothetical Gemma 3 27B-IT (FP16). The Gemma 3 family (4B/12B/27B) are multimodal models with up to 128K token context. The 4B variant uses aggressive 8-bit quantization for speed, the 12B models use either quantization-aware training or mid-bit quantization fora good quality-speed trade-off, and the 27B is full-precision. LLaMA 3.1 8B is a high-quality text-only model (paired with a separate 11B vision model for images). Benchmark results (MMLU, GSM8K, ARC) reflect these differences. Publicly reported scores for Gemma 3 show the 12B models at ~74.5% MMLU, 71.0% GSM8K, 56.1% ARC, whereas the 27B FP16 model improves to ~78.6%/82.6%/70.6. LLaMA 3.1 8B in instruction-tuned form attains lower MMLU (~68%) but excels at math (GSM8K ~84.4%).

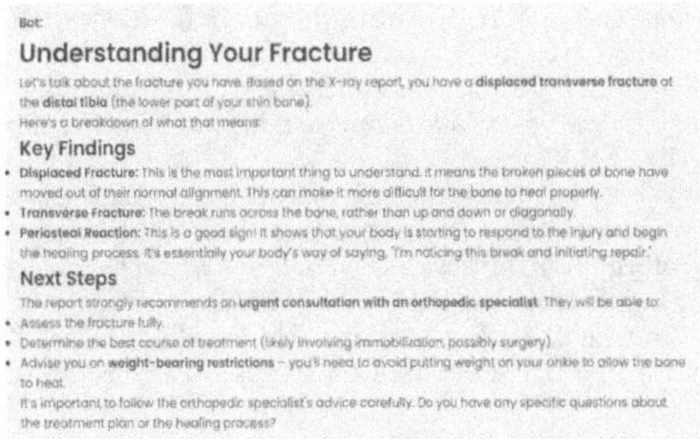

Figure 2. A chat showing the findings of the system from an uploaded image.

4 CONCLUSIONS

This study presents a Secure AI-Powered Health Communication Platform that addresses the growing need for private, intelligent tools in healthcare. By combining encrypted local storage (Fernet-based), multimodal document analysis, semantic embedding search (SentenceTransformers + ChromaDB), and an on-device LLM (Ollama LLaMA/ Gemma), the system allows doctors and patients to interact with medical information safely and effectively. All inference is done locally, ensuring that no protected health information is exposed to external networks [1,3]. The proposed system shows that this architecture is feasible in: encrypted document management and AI-powered search/chat can coexist on the same platform, in keeping with earlier AI-based frameworks [14,15].

The suggested system contributes to how a blueprint for healthcare institutions can use AI capabilities while meeting stringent security regulations. In doing so, it paves the way for more advanced, patient-focused applications that do not jeopardize data privacy. With further development, these tools have the potential to enhance patient education, lessen clinician's workload, and overall improve healthcare delivery in a trust-preserving manner.

Table 1. Summary of model architectures and benchmark scores.

Model	Params	Quantization (IT)	MMLU (%)	GSM8K (%)	ARC (%)	Inference Speed
Gemma 3 4B (IT, Q8_0)	4B	8-bit	74.5	71.0	56.1	Fastest (good chat, poor images)
Gemma 3 12B (IT, QAT)	12B	QAT (4-bit)	74.5	71.0	56.1	Moderate (best balance)
Gemma 3 12B (IT, Q4_K_M)	12B	Q4_K_M (4-bit)	~74.0	~70.5	~55.5	High perf (slightly faster than QAT)
LLaMA 3.1 8B + 3.2 Vision 11B	8B+11B	FP16	67.9	84.4	83.4	Fast text, slower image pipeline
Gemma 3 27B (IT, FP16)[a]	27B	FP16	78.6	82.6	70.6	Slowest (expected top-tier)

[a]Gemma 3 27B scores are from official benchmarks (model was not locally tested) [9]

REFERENCES

[1] P. Shojaei, E. Vlahu-Gjorgievska, and Y.-W. Chow, (2024). "Security and Privacy of Technologies in Health Information Systems: A Systematic Literature review," *Computers*, vol. 13, no. 2, p. 41, doi: 10.3390/computers13020041.

[2] A.K. Tyagi, V. Hemamalini, and G. Soni, (2023). "Digital health communication with Artificial Intelligence-Based Cyber Security," in *Advances in Medical Technologies and Clinical Practice Book Series*, pp. 178–213. https://doi.org/10.4018/978-1-6684-8938-3.ch009.

[3] "Open Foundation Models in Healthcare: Challenges, Paradoxes, and Opportunities with GenAI Driven Personalized Prescription." https://arxiv.org/html/2502.04356v1

[4] S. Asmala, (2024). "Improving the search of medical articles using sentence transformers," https://aaltodoc.aalto.fi/items/9f3c43f7-2f65-497b-9a42-e8ea63d2d970

[5] N. Gadhiya, S. Tailor, and S. Degadwala, (2024). "A review on different level data encryption through a compression techniques," *2022 International Conference on Inventive Computation Technologies (ICICT)*, https://doi.org/10.1109/icict60155.2024.10544803.

[6] J. Li, (2023). "Security implications of AI chatbots in health care," *Journal of Medical Internet Research*, vol. 25, p. e47551, doi: 10.2196/47551.

[7] I.C. Wiest, J.T. Schleimer, S. Puppe, and J. Baumeister, (2024). "Privacy-preserving large language models for structured medical information retrieval," *npj Digital Medicine*, vol. 7, no. 1, p. 257, doi: 10.1038/s41746-024-01233-2.

[8] K. Gottfried, T. Eichler, and H. Wendt, (2025). "Semantic search helper: A tool based on the use of embeddings in multi-item questionnaires as a harmonization opportunity for merging large datasets – A feasibility study," *European Psychiatry*, vol. 68, no. 1, p. e8, doi: 10.1192/j.eurpsy.2024.1808.

[9] A. Kamath *et al.*, (2025). "Gemma 3 Technical Report," *arXiv preprint* arXiv:2503.19786, Mar. 2025, https://doi.org/10.48550/arXiv.2503.19786.

[10] A.H. Seh, M. Zarour, R. Alenezi, A. Sarkar, M. Agrawal, V. Kumar, and R.A. Khan, (2020). "Healthcare data breaches: insights and implications," *Healthcare*, vol. 8, no. 2, p. 133, doi: 10.3390/healthcare8020133.

[11] G. Sun and Y.-H. Zhou, (2023). "AI in healthcare: Navigating opportunities and challenges in digital communication," *Frontiers in Digital Health*, vol. 5, Art. 1291132, doi:10.3389/fdgth.2023.1291132.

[12] J. Kim *et al.*, (2025). "Artificial intelligence tools in supporting healthcare professionals for tailored patient care," *npj Digital Medicine*, vol. 8, Art. 210.

[13] L.B. Elvas, C. Serrão, and J.C. Ferreira, (2023). "Sharing health information using a blockchain," *Healthcare*, vol. 11, no. 2, Art. 170, Jan. 2023, doi:10.3390/healthcare11020170.

[14] S. Lade, A. Billade, A. Chandrapatle, S. Chenna, G. Chinchalpalle, (2024). "System design and analysis for AI-based document assistant," *International Joint Conference on Advances in Computational Intelligence*, pp. 95–107.

[15] S. Lade, A. Billade, A. Chandrapatle, S. Chenna, G. Chinchalpalle, (2024). "LinkedIn alumni profile data extraction," *4th International Conference on Pervasive Computing and Social Networking*.

[16] S. Lade, ML Dhore, (2021). "Text categorization of marathi news articles using machine learning," *Proceedings of DSNCR*.

Technology for a Resilient Future – Vincent , Moorthy and Dasari (Eds)

River Cleaning Robot Controlled by Android Application

Manisha Lande
Department of Mechanical Engineering, VPKBIET Baramati, India

Sudhir Lande
Department of E& TC, VPKBIET Baramati, India

ABSTRACT: The creation and application of "AI-Based River Cleaning Robot"—a tool created especially to gather and remove trash from water bodies' surfaces—is shown in this work.

The paper aims to address the critical problem of pollution in rivers, where excessive waste, toxic substances and floating debris have significantly harmed aquatic ecosystems. Such conditions threaten the survival of marine organisms and contribute to the overall degradation of water quality.

The system's main objective is to lessen the need for manual labour and the amount of time needed for river cleaning tasks. The robot works by clearing surface debris from water bodies, which helps to minimise water contamination and mitigate the threats posed to aquatic life.

A machine can remove debris and debris from the water bodies, which could gradually lead to less contaminated water and finally fewer sea creatures coming into contact with those issues.

This cleaning system operates using power stored in rechargeable batteries, which supply energy to an engine and a chain-drive mechanism. The energy-efficient design ensures smooth operation and effective waste collection, offering a sustainable method for maintaining cleaner water bodies.

Throughout this process, we have stored the energy in the battery and used it to clean the stream with the aid of an engine and chain drive system. It is believed that water plays a significant role in our lives. After naming the water on the planet, we can see that the ocean contains about 97% of the world's total water gift, while the planet's surface is covered with roughly 71% water. In contrast, the excess three-dimensional water in the lakes and streams is like ice.

By using automatic solar river garbage collector, we can remove floating waste from water surface up to a distance of 1 km by using RF transmitter and receiver. This paper is based on solar energy. Solar electricity improves the model sustainability and support the environmental conservation.

Keywords: Robot, machine, river cleaning, Android

1 INTRODUCTION

Freshwater rivers and lakes are vital resources that serve humanity and ecosystems in multiple ways. Rivers provide water for agriculture, ensuring food production and supporting livelihoods. Additionally, they play a crucial role in preserving ecological balance, supporting biodiversity, and fostering regional growth and prosperity.

Regrettably, human activities have led to the deterioration of rivers and lakes. The discharge of domestic and industrial waste into these water bodies has severely compromised water quality. This pollution endangers aquatic organisms, gradually causing a decline in their populations and harming the overall ecosystem.

It is imperative that this pressing issue be resolved very away in order to preserve water purity and avoid contamination. In order to reduce pollution and protect water bodies, this project suggests designing and building a river waste-cleaning machine for the benefit of current and future generations.

Globally, water pollution is becoming a major hazard to both human health and the environment. Cleaning bodies of water, such lakes, ponds, and canals, with traditional methods is usually labour-intensive, time-consuming, and ineffective. The concept of a water cleaning robot has emerged as an innovative and useful solution to this issue.An automated or semi-automatic tool used to clear the surface of water bodies of floating trash, debris, and other contaminants is called a water cleaning robot. To effectively detect and collect waste, these robots are usually outfitted with sensors, motors, conveyor belts, and collection bins. Some more sophisticated models might additionally have water quality monitors, GPS tracking, and solar panels for environmentally friendly energy use.The primary objective of a water cleaning robot is to support environmental conservation efforts by reducing pollution in aquatic ecosystems, improving water quality, and promoting a cleaner and healthier environment.

2 LITERATURE REVIEW

Chen Su *et al.* (2009) The research paper "An Autonomous ship for cleaning the garbage floating on a lake" on the article, the concept and design for an autonomous ship were given as a way to clear the trash floating on the lake. Ultrasonic distance measuring is used in the ship's motion control system, which can operate both manually and automatically. The ship's main shortcomings were its unpredictable motion and incapacity to control the rubbish collecting.

DSK Dixit and SB Dhayagonde (2014) outline the design and construction of a wireless robot that can be operated online and recognises living objects using a PIR sensor. Rescue operations will benefit from the user's ability to view the broadcast video from a remote location, such as a sensitive area or a site that is inaccessible.

Aakash Sinha *et al.* (2014) An innovative idea for a flexible crawling mechanism was presented in order to construct an industrial underwater cleaning boat that can operate underwater, scan the required surface, and record biological reactions. Only bio-fouled water surfaces could be cleaned by the

DOI: 10.1201/9781042017546-19

system design. "Effective Lake Trash Collection with a Pedal-Operated Boat"

K. Shridhar *et al.* (2016) suggested a smaller device with four working principles that was constructed from GI metal sheet. As the apparatus would stay perfectly still, the first mode of operation seemed to be utterly useless. Another type of operation made the system expensive and unwieldy. They have a device that can collect a lot of rubbish without the help of humans. The proposed system, which detects waste using a variety of sensors and an Atmel AT89S52 microcontroller, can only collect a limited number of waste types.

N. Ruangpayoongsak *et al* (2017) the goal of the project was to create a water vehicle that could remove a large amount of debris from the water without the need for screws. Their robot can collect round, slick plastic water bottles with its five scoopers. There are huge waves made as the side scoopers drop in and out of the water. The device's enormous size means that it is only appropriate for vast bodies of water, like rivers. The debris would be pushed farther out in smaller bodies of water by the drag effect it would create.

N. G. Jogi *et al.* (2019): This study describes a pedal-driven boat integrated with a conveyor system designed to remove waste from water surfaces, such as lakes and rivers. The boat is capable of collecting floating debris while also featuring equipment for cutting and harvesting aquatic weeds. This approach provides an efficient and practical solution for managing aquatic vegetation and maintaining clean water bodies.

R. Raghavi *et al.* (2019) a smartphone-controlled "Pond Cleaning Robot" was created by to remove trash from the lake. The architecture of the computer was based on the AT89S51 controller. The system lacked sensors to monitor garbage automatically or control the "Water Surface Cleaning Robot."

Ketan H. Pakhmode et. al (2020): This study illustrates the design of the "River Waste Collector," a machine that removes floating waste from water bodies. Fins of different sizes that are a part of the device catch waste. Typical debris collecting problems can be resolved with the help of this technology. On one end, the fins can be moved, whereas on the other, they are fixed. Servo motors raise the fins' movable side so that rubbish may be gathered and put in a tank at the back of the boat.

Imran Ali et.al (2021), Design and development of a three-degree-of-freedom reconfigurable articulated robot for pick-and-place tasks is the main focus of this study. The idea was implemented through the development of an Android platform that enables manual control of an articulated robot over Bluetooth. Through the application's intuitive interface, the user can manually alter the robot to meet the requirements of the integrated system. Three of the articulated robot's four motors are used for orientation and placement, and the other four are used for pick-and-place tasks.

Refugio Craig N. *et al.* (2022): In order to lower the danger of disease transmission to humans, this article focusses on automating the cleaning of sewage in drainage systems. By eliminating black water, insect infestations can be avoided and leftovers that draw pests are reduced. Additionally, it helps to improve the quality and prolong the shelf life of food items. By managing sewage cleaning through remote control, the suggested system lessens the negative impacts of sewage waste and the gases that are linked with it. By removing waste buildup, it also reduces mosquito reproduction.

Cheng Y *et al.* (2022): The development of SMURF, an autonomous robot designed to clean up rubbish from water surfaces without human help, is described in this study. Since the robot operates independently, it cleans water surfaces quite effectively. Real-world tests reveal that SMURF significantly outperforms traditional methods in cleaning and performs effectively in a range of water conditions.

Raquib Bijoya *et al.* (2023) A solar-powered garbage pickup robot that can be remotely controlled and observed through the use of Arduino and Internet of Things technology is described by Sanjana Addressing environmental purification-related difficulties is the main goal of this study. Two motors, an ESP8266 NodeMCU, an Arduino Uno, an HC-05 Bluetooth module, an L298N motor driver, two batteries, and an energy-efficient solar panel make up the robot's fundamental parts.

3 METHODOLOGY

Conveyors installed on motor shafts are part of the system design. The conveyor collects rubbish, plastics, and debris from water bodies as the motor revolves. After that, the materials are hauled upward and placed in a garbage. A motor powers a propeller, which propels the machine forward. Using an RF transmitter and receiver, the system can be operated remotely. The conveyor may also efficiently gather garbage for the model by rotating at a precise angle thanks to a four-bar system.

Waste is removed from the water's surface and transferred to a dustbin by the proposed method. One of its conveyor systems is connected to a motor shaft. The conveyor collects trash, plastics, and other materials from the water as it revolves while the motor operates. By immersing the machine in the water, the waste is lifted and moves upward. Once it reaches the top of the conveyor, the garbage is disposed of in the dustbin. Both efficient trash collection and water surface cleansing are ensured by this process. The machine is propelled across the water by a motor-driven propeller. All electrical components are operated remotely by means of an RF transmitter and receiver.

In this paper, we propose a collecting mechanism to tackle the issue of debris collection from water, where surface tension complicates the process. Using a four-bar system that rotates at a precise angle, the device efficiently collects trash. You can remotely regulate this device's activities to switch it on or off. Through the use of a water wheel, also called a propeller, attached to a shaft that is fixed to the base construction, the machine can move both forward and backward on the water. A motor drives the water wheel's rotation via a chain drive system.

Additionally, the paper highlights the use of a tracking system to adjust the angle of the solar panel in accordance with the sun's position. This helps maximize solar energy absorption, enhancing the overall power generation of the system.

1. **Working Diagram**

   Figure 1 explain the details components of Android Controlled River Cleaning Robot

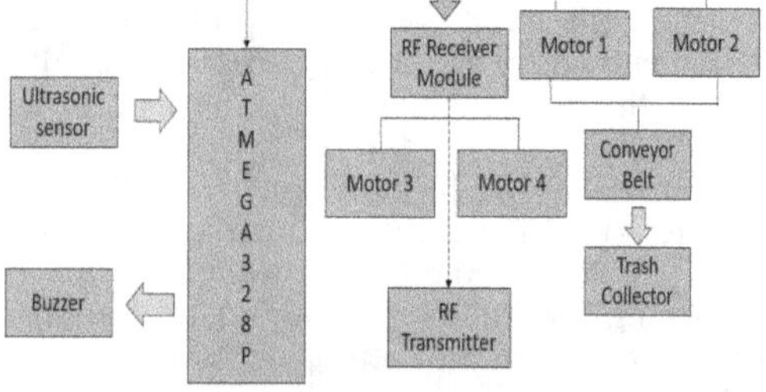

Figure 1. Working diagram of Android Controlled River Cleaning Robot.

2. **Various Components of** Android Controlled River Cleaning Robot

   1. **Solar panel (12 V, 5W)**

      Using the photovoltaic effect, the system's many solar cells transform sunlight into electrical energy. Batteries are used to store this generated power and DC regulators receive the output for appropriate distribution of power.

2. **Battery (12V)**The Android Controlled River Cleaning Robot system uses a Lithium-ion rechargeable battery, made up of multiple electrochemical cells that store energy and supply it as electric current when required.
3. **Arduino Board (AT mega 328P)**
   The Atmega328, a well-known 8-bit microcontroller is made by Atmel. Six of its fourteen digital input/output pins may generate PWM. Six analogue inputs, a 16 MHz crystal oscillator, a power jack, an ICSP header, a USB interface, and a reset switch are all included.
4. **Pin Configuration (AT mega 328P)**
   The ATMEGA328P microcontroller has 28 pins. Many of these pins are multifunctional and their specific roles are outlined in the table below.
5. **RF Transmitter & Receiver Module**
   RF modules are commonly used for wireless communication due to their versatility. These modules function in pairs, with a transmitter responsible for sending data and a receiver for receiving it. Since the transmitter can only send and the receiver can only receive, data flows in a single direction between the two.
6. **Remote Receiver Circuit**
   Figure 2 explain the remote receiver circuit of model

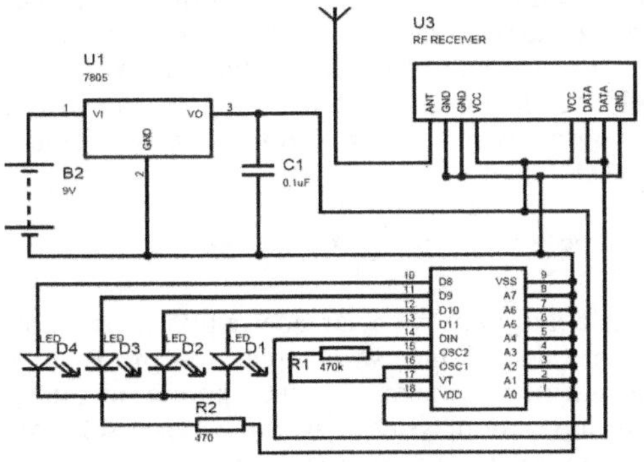

Figure 2. Remote receiver circuit.

7. **Remote Transmitter Circuit**
   Figure 3 explain the remote transmitter circuit of model

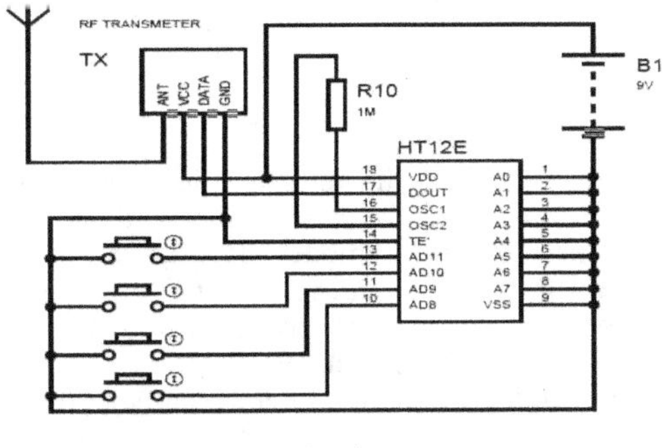

Figure 3. Remote transmitter circuit.

8. **Gear Motor**
   In order to control the direction of the wheels, this machine uses two gear motors. This motor runs at 30 rpm and 12 volts. The conveyor belt is controlled by additional BO (battery operated) DC motors, which are also utilised in the tracking system. This motor runs at 100 rpm and 12 volts.
9. **Ultrasonic Sensor**
   It is possible to estimate the distance between an ultrasonic sensor and the water's surface. The following details pertain to ultrasonic sensors. In a solar-powered water trash collecting system, ultrasonic sensors can be utilised to measure distance using sound waves in order to assess the water level in the container. Speed × Time × Distance
10. **Switch**
    As a safety precaution, switches are employed to stop the belt in the event of an emergency or collision. The conveyor belt and a movable barrier are connected to this pull-cord switch.
11. **Buzzer**
    A buzzer is an electromechanical or mechanical device that emits sound signals. Often used as alarm devices, buzzers emit a beeping or buzzing sound when activated. Details: The primary component of any solar photovoltaic system that converts solar radiation into electrical current is this one. The conversion of light (photons) into electrical power (voltage) is known as the solar photovoltaic (PV) effect. Photovoltaic solar cells directly generate electricity from sunlight. The photons are highly energised when exposed to sunlight because they are absorbed by the semiconductive material's electrons. They move from the top surface of the semi-conducting substance to the bottom surface. Direct current (DC) is the current produced by this electron movement.
12. **App used for android control**
    We employ a smartphone-based control system for the Android Controlled River Cleaning Robot project in order to effectively operate the robot. The smartphone app that is used for this is

Andi.Co. created the Bluetooth remote control car. This free utility program uses a Bluetooth-enabled microcontroller to provide seamless wireless connection between the smartphone and the robot, giving the user real-time control over the robot's motions and capabilities.

To integrate this application into our paper, necessary modifications were made to the robot's hardware, including the installation of a Bluetooth module that receives commands from the app. The robot responds to directional inputs provided through the smartphone, allowing users to maneuver it across the water surface with ease. The mobile app interface provides a simple and effective way to control speed, direction, and various cleaning mechanisms embedded in the robot.

4 WORKING MODELS

Figures 4, 5, 6 & 7 show the real design of working model of River cleaning robot.

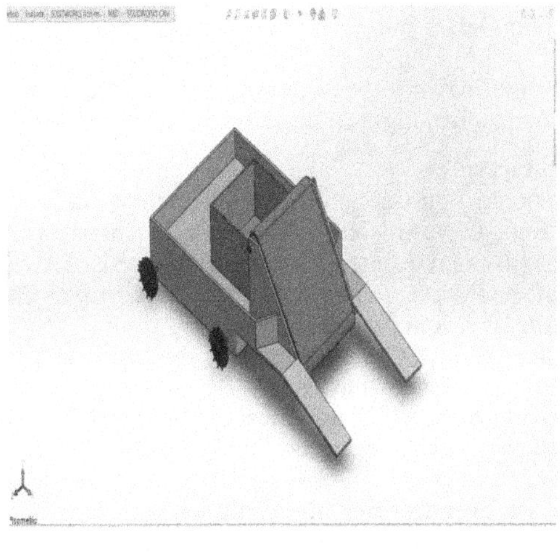

Figure 4. CAD model.

Figure 5. TOP VIEW of working model.

Figure 6. Front view of working model.

Figure 7. Side view of working model.

5 WORKING CONNECTION DETAILS OF RIVER CLEANING ROBOT-

Four pins make up the HC-SR04 ultrasonic sensor's pinout:

- VCC pin: The VCC (5v) pin needs to be connected.
- GND pin: This pin needs to be attached to GND (0V).
- TRIG pin: Gets a pulse from the Arduino Nano as a control signal.
- ECHO pin: Provides the Arduino Nano with a signal (pulse) and measures its length to determine the distance.

How it works:

When the Arduino nano creates a 10-microsecond pulse on the TRIGpin, the ultrasonic sensor releases ultrasonic waves. When the waves hit a barrier, they are reflected back.

The reflected wave can be detected and its travel time measured by the ultrasonic sensor.

The sensor is the ECHO pin, and its duration is equal to the travel time of the ultrasonic waves.

The Arduino Nano determines the distance between the sensor and the barrier by measuring the pulse duration in the ECHO pin.

How to get distance from ultrasonic sensor:

To get the distance from the ultrasonic sensor, we only need to write Arduino code that follows these steps:

The ArduinoNano generates a 10-microsecond pulse on the TRIG pin.

The Arduino Nano measures the pulse duration of the ECHO pin.

The observed pulse duration is then used by the Arduino Nano to calculate the distance between the sensor and the impediment.

Distance Calculation

The travel time (us) of the ultrasonic wave:

travel_time = pulse_duration

The speed of the ultrasonic wave: SPEED_ OF_ SOUND = 340 m/s = 0.034 cm/us. SO: The distance travelled by the ultrasonic wave (in centimetres):

Velocity * trip time = 0.034 * travel distance = pulse duration 0.034 * pulse_duration / 2 = 0.017 * pulse_duration = distance = travel_distance / 2 is the sensor-to-obstacle distance (in centimetres).

Arduino nano – ultrasonic sensor

The pins on the Arduino Nano can generate a 10-microsecond pulse and track its duration. This enables the Arduino Nano's two pins to be used for measuring the separation between an object and the ultrasonic sensor. We onlyneedto:

Attach the TRIG pin of the ultrasonic sensor to an Arduino Nano pin. A US pulse is sent from this pin on the Arduino Nano to the sensor's TRIG pin. Attach the ultrasonic sensor's ECHO pin to a second Arduino Nano pin. This pin on the Arduino Nano is used to measure the pulse from the sensor. The Arduino Nano then uses the measured pulse duration to determine how far away the sensor is from the obstruction.

6 RESULTS AND DISCUSSION

This model could improve solar power by making it more efficient and reliable, enhance waste collection processes for better environmental management, and incorporate advanced sensors to improve navigation systems. Arduino-based solutions can be versatile in addressing environmental issues. Whether it's monitoring, managing waste, or promoting energy efficiency, the flexibility of Arduino allows for creative and impactful solutions. Creating this venture involves optimizing the synergy of human resources, machinery, and materials. Efficiency in utilization is crucial to minimize costs and maximize output. Strategic allocation of labor, leveraging advanced machinery, and sourcing materials judiciously contribute to overall cost- effectiveness

7 CONCLUSIONS

This model has an address the automatic solar floating garbage collector which can reduce the water pollution that increase day by day with the help of this model. By using automatic solar garbage collector, we can remove floating waste from water surface up to a distance of 1 km by using RF transmitter and receiver. This paper is based on solar energy. Solar electricity improves the model sustainability and support the environmental conservation

ACKNOWLEDGEMENT

My deepest thanks goes out to everyone who helped and advised me while I was preparing this paper.

REFERENCES

Aakash Sinha *et al.* (2014) "Research and development of Ro-boat:an autonomous river cleaning robot" proc.SPIE 9025, *Intelligent Robots and Computer Vision XXXI Algorithms and techniques*,90250Q (2014)

Chen Su, *et al.* (2009) "An Autonomous ship for cleaning the garbage floating on a lake". *Second international Conference on Intelligent Computation Technology & Automation IEEE xplore* https://doi.org/10.1109/ICICTA.2009.579

Chinmay Kulkarni, Suhas Grama, Pramod Gubbi Suresh, Chaitanya Krishna, Joseph Antony (2014) "*Surveillance Robot Using Arduino Microcontroller,* Android

Craig N. Refugio *et al.* (2022) Design and fabrication of remote-controlled sewage cleaning machine. *IJETT*, volume 45.

DSK Dixit, SB Dhayagonde (2014) "Design and Implementation of e-Surveillance Robot for Video Monitoring and Living Body Detection" *International Journal of Scientific and Research Publications*, 2014 academia.edu

Ketan H. Pakhmode *et al.* (2020) "Design and fabrication of river waste collector" *IJAERD*, volume 5, issue o3.

N.G. Jogi *et al.* (2019), "Efficient lake garbage collector by using pedal operated boat", *IJRTER*, volume 2, issue 4.

R. Raghavi *et al.* (2019) Water surface clening robot, *International Journal of Advanced Research in Electrical, Electronic and Instrumentation Engg.* Vol.8, Issue 3, March 2019.

Ruangpayoongsa, N. *et al.* (2017) "A floating waste scooper robot on water surface. International conference on control, *Automation and Systems*, pp.1543-1548.Jeju, Korea (2017).

Sanjana Raquib Bijoya *et al.* (2023) "Solar powered water trash collector robot", *IEEE*, volume 2, issue in 2023.

Shridhar, K. *et al.* (2016) *Aqua Drone Remote Controlled Unmanned River Clening BOT.* BVB college of engineering and technology Hubballi

Siddhanna Janai *et al.* (2020) "Swachh Hasth-A water clening robot, *IJERT ISSN 2278-0181*, vol 9, issue 07 July 2020

Swapnil S. Bhavarkar *et al.*, "Review on solar operated water cleaning boat,"*IJARIIE*

Zhu J, Yang Y, Cheng Y. (2022) "Smurf: a fully autonomous water surface cleaning robot with a novel coverage path planning method", *Journal of Marine Science and Engineering.*

Technology for a Resilient Future – Vincent , Moorthy and Dasari (Eds)

Beyond the Cloud: Impact of AI Driven Protocol for Privacy Rights Using Statistical Legislative Data Analysis Framework

Apurva Mishra and Rajiv Bhalla
Chandigarh University, Gharun

ABSTRACT: In today's world, artificial intelligence (AI) is revolutionizing industry and daily life. This study looks at how privacy rights are impacted by cutting-edge AI technologies. We start by looking at how AI is changing various facets of contemporary society. The explanation of the right to privacy protections follows. The use of AI and privacy rights are then covered in the paper. To address these challenges, this paper introduces a novel key agreement protocol designed specifically for cloud computing platforms, emphasizing security, efficiency, and resilience without depending on a trusted third party. Our protocol innovatively combines Distributed Key Generation (DKG) with a Dynamic Consensus Mechanism, Zero-Knowledge Proof (ZKP) based authentication, and a Multi-Cloud Redundancy approach, offering a comprehensive solution to secure multi-party communication in distributed cloud environments. The DKG protocol facilitates the collaborative generation of a shared secret among participants, significantly enhancing security by eliminating single points of failure. Lastly, the Multi-Cloud Redundancy strategy enhances the protocol's resilience to cloud-specific vulnerabilities and service outages, ensuring high availability and robustness.

Keywords: Cloud computing, key agreement protocol, distributed key generation, dynamic consensus mechanism, ero- knowledge proof, multi-cloud redundancy, "cryptographic security, distributed ledger technology

1 INTRODUCTION

Artificial Intelligence (AI) is a big deal in the 21st century. It affects every area of life, from health care to education to the legal system. The AI revolution made everything that seemed impossible or hard easy.

For some parts of AI to work right, they need personal information like demographic data, contact information, behavioral data, health data, financial data, communications data, sensor data, social data, preferences data, and professional data.

Figure 1. Secured key agreement protocol design.

The rise of technology and AI made people very worried about privacy, which is a basic right. Artificial intelligence could be helpful, but we can't ignore the big risks that come with it. This article talks about the idea of giving AI personal information, as well as the pros and cons of using AI to collect, process, and store data. It looks at the legal, moral, and technological sides of AI, as well as how it is connected to privacy issues in a complicated way.

"Multiple-party key agreement protocols" are cryptographic methods that let a group of people agree on a shared secret key over an insecure communication channel, like the internet. After that, the two parties can use this shared secret key to encrypt and decrypt the data they send to each other, which keeps it safe and private [3] [4]. However, designing these kinds of protocols for cloud computing environments is more difficult and requires more thought because cloud infrastructures are distributed and changeable.

The main goal of designing a secured multiple-party key agreement protocol for cloud computing is to make it easier and safer for multiple parties to talk to each other while lowering the risks that come with sending sensitive information over networks that could be hacked. [5] [6].

1.1 *Right of privacy in India*

The Court looked at the case of Kharak Singh vs. State of U P363 in 1962. It was about the police's power to watch people who were criminals and keep a "history sheet" of their personal information. The petitioner said that the police's night visit to his house was a violation of his basic right to move freely around India. The court said that home visits do violate the petitioner's rights. The court also said that the right to privacy was not a basic right. The police surveillance did not violate his rights,then. In the case of Gobind vs. State of M P& Anr364, the Supreme Court of India used the American law's "compelling state interest" test for the first time in 1975. The court said that an individual's right to privacy would have to give way to a larger state interest, which must be convincing. Over time, the area of privacy has grown to include private information like medical records and biometric data.

In the 21st century, Aadhaar has been at the center of privacy questions. Aadhaar is a government program that gives residents a unique ID after they give their fingerprints, iris scan, and demographic information. It is a system that doesn't need permission, so the user can choose whether or not to use it for both unique identification and related services367. People took Aadhaar to court because they said it violated their privacy.

In 2013, the Supreme Court said it could only be used for the public distribution system and LPG subsidies. The Supreme Court said in October 2015 that Aadhaar could be used to provide some services, but no one should be denied any services.

DOI: 10.1201/9781042017546-20

2 RELATED STUDY

As the Industrial Internet of Things (IIoT) expanded, smart sensors in factories transmitted real-time data through open channels, heightening privacy risks from potential unauthorized access by adversaries. To safeguard the IIoT ecosystem, user authentication emerged as a foundational measure. This study proposed a cloud-assisted authentication method leveraging Chebyshev polynomial encryption. Biometric data underwent validation through a fuzzy extraction technique, alongside password and smart card authentication. The scheme ensured login confirmation through a combination of these factors. Formal security analysis, using the ROR model, illustrated semantic security of session keys. Informal security assessment highlighted resilience against various attacks [11]. The method offered additional features like offline sensor node registration, password and biometric updates, node deployment, user anonymity, and untraceability compared to existing authentication schemes. Evaluation against other schemes showcased superior security performance at reasonable computational, communication, and security costs.

The surge in global IP traffic, driven by mobile devices, necessitates robust security in Mobile Cloud Computing (MCC). Despite progress in addressing resource constraints, ensuring data access security remains challenging due to dynamic user behavior. This study proposes an authenticated key exchange mechanism using passwords for secure communication within MCC [12]. Unlike prior solutions, this protocol specifically targets resource limitations and evolving user behaviors. Symmetric encryption, one-way hash functions, and Chaotic Maps enhance data protection and protocol robustness.

Based on the review of the literature and the gap in research, the goals of the study are:

- To provide legal requirements for AI data in online crime.
- To learn about AI's ability to watch people while still protecting their privacy in the fight against cybercrime To create worldwide rules for using AI to fight cybercrime across borders.
- The main research question is, "How can legal systems be changed to use AI-driven evidence in the fight against cybercrime while also respecting people's right to privacy?"

Participant Nodes (PNs): People or groups who want to set up secure communications. The protocol's client software is installed on each participant node. This lets it do cryptographic tasks, talk to CSNs, and send secure messages to other PNs.

Distributed Ledger Technology (DLT): The architecture includes a blockchain based ledger that records key agreement transactions and protocol states in a way that is both decentralized and impossible to change. This makes sure that the key exchange process is open and honest.

Cryptographic Module: As a key part of both CSNs and PNs, it makes cryptographic materials like key pairs, runs the key agreement algorithm, and makes sure that messages are safely encrypted and decrypted. To learn more about how the proposed secure multiple party key agreement protocol works on a cloud computing platform, we look at the new parts that set it apart from other solutions. Some of these are the DKG Protocol, the Dynamic Consensus Mechanism, ZKP Based Authentication, and the Multi-Cloud Redundancy approach.

3 METHODOLOGY

Our architecture is built to make it easy for multiple parties to securely exchange keys without the need for a trusted third party. It does this by using the distributed nature of cloud computing to improve security and efficiency. Figure 2 shows how the proposed model works.

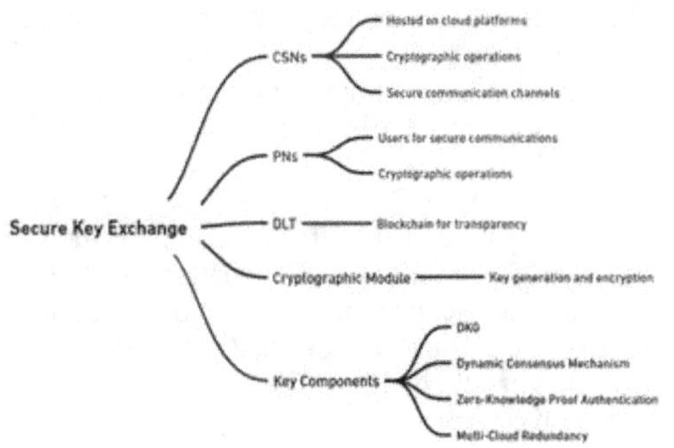

Figure 2. Workflow of proposed model.

3.1 *High-Level architecture overview*

The architecture of our proposed protocol consists of several key components:

Cloud Service Nodes (CSNs): These are distributed nodes hosted on various cloud platforms. CSNs serve as the infrastructure that supports the protocol, providing computational resources and network connectivity. They are designed to perform cryptographic operations and facilitate secure communication channels among participants.

3.2 *Distributed Key Generation (DKG) protocol*

The DKG protocol is central to our architecture, enabling the secure generation of a shared secret among multiple parties in a distributed environment. Unlike traditional key agreement protocols that rely on a central authority or trust a single entity for key generation, DKG distributes this responsibility among all participating nodes, significantly enhancing security.

Share Distribution: Initially, each participant generates a piece of the secret, known as a "share," using cryptographic algorithms such as Shamir's Secret Sharing. These shares are then securely distributed to other participants through encrypted channels.

Upon receiving shares from others, each participant verifies their validity using cryptographic proofs. This step ensures that all shares are genuine and have not been tampered with during transmission.

Secret Construction:

Once all shares are distributed and verified, participants collaboratively reconstruct the shared secret. A crucial aspect of this process is that the secret can be assembled without ever aggregating the individual shares in a single location, thus maintaining the distributed nature of the protocol.

Key Derivation: The shared secret serves as the basis for deriving session keys for secure communication. These keys are computed in such a way that they are known only to the participating nodes, with no external party having access to them.

This approach mitigates the risk of a single point of failure and ensures that the key generation process is resilient to attacks aimed at compromising the shared secret.

3.3 *Dynamic consensus mechanism*

Incorporating a blockchain-based Distributed Ledger Technology (DLT) necessitates a robust consensus mechanism to validate transactions and maintain the integrity of the ledger. Our protocol introduces a Dynamic Consensus Mechanism that adapts based on network conditions and participant trust levels.

Trust Assessment: The mechanism evaluates the trustworthiness of participating nodes based on their historical behavior and contributions to the protocol. This assessment influences their role in the consensus process.

Consensus Adaptation: Depending on the current network conditions (e.g., number of participants, perceived risk of malicious activity), the protocol dynamically adjusts the consensus algorithm. For instance, in a highly trusted environment, a faster but less rigorous consensus algorithm might be employed, whereas in a lower trust scenario, a more robust algorithm (like PBFT or Raft) could be activated.

Transaction Validation: Transactions related to the key agreement process, such as the distribution of shares or the final agreement on the shared secret, are validated through this consensus mechanism. Only transactions that achieve consensus are recorded on the blockchain, ensuring their authenticity and integrity.

This dynamic approach allows the protocol to maintain high efficiency without compromising security, adapting to threats as they arise.

3.4 *Zero-Knowledge Proof (ZKP) based authentication*

Ensuring the authenticity of participants while protecting their privacy is a critical concern in any key agreement protocol. Our protocol employs ZKP for authentication, enabling participants to prove their identity without revealing any private information.

Identity Verification: When a participant wishes to join a key agreement session, they generate a ZKP of their identity. This proof demonstrates that they possess a secret (e.g., a private key) corresponding to their registered public identity without disclosing the secret itself.

Proof Submission: The participant submits their ZKP to the network, where other nodes verify the proof without gaining any knowledge of the underlying secret.

Anonymity and Security: This process ensures that participants can authenticate themselves as legitimate members of the key agreement process while maintaining their anonymity. It protects against impersonation attacks and enhances privacy.

3.5 *Multi-Cloud redundancy*

To combat cloud-specific vulnerabilities and ensure high availability, our protocol is designed to operate across multiple cloud platforms simultaneously.

Distributed Deployment: The Cloud Service Nodes (CSNs) and the blockchain ledger are deployed across several cloud platforms. This distribution ensures that the protocol is not reliant on a single cloud provider, mitigating the risk of provider-specific outages or attacks.

Synchronization: A synchronization mechanism ensures that state changes in the protocol (e.g., updates to the ledger or participant states) are consistently propagated across all platforms. This consistency is crucial for the integrity of the key agreement process.

Fault Tolerance: By leveraging multiple clouds, the protocol achieves a higher level of fault tolerance. Even if one cloud platform experiences issues, the protocol can continue functioning without interruption, ensuring the ongoing security and availability of the key agreement process.

These methodologies DKG for secure key generation, a Dynamic Consensus Mechanism for adaptable and robust transaction validation, ZKP for privacy-preserving authentication, and Multi-Cloud Redundancy for enhanced security and resilience collectively form a comprehensive framework for secure multiple party key agreement in cloud computing environments. Each component addresses specific challenges in this context, from mitigating single points of failure and adapting to varying trust levels to ensuring participant privacy and system availability. This integrated approach provides a novel and effective solution to securing communications in distributed cloud environments.

4 RESULTS AND DISCUSSIONS

To assess the performance of our proposed key agreement protocol in a real-world scenario, we conducted experiments in a cloud computing environment. We utilized a cluster of virtual machines hosted on multiple cloud platforms, including Amazon Web Services (AWS), Microsoft Azure, and Google Cloud Platform (GCP). Each virtual machine was configured with sufficient computational resources (e.g., CPU, memory) to emulate typical cloud instances used in practical deployments. Additionally, we ensured a reliable network connection between the virtual machines to simulate realistic communication scenarios.

4.1 *Evaluation metrics*

We employed several performance metrics to evaluate the efficiency and effectiveness of our protocol:

Key Establishment Time: This metric measures the time taken for participating nodes to agree on a shared secret and derive session keys for secure communication. Shorter key establishment times indicate higher protocol efficiency.

Computational Overhead: Computational overhead quantifies the additional processing resources (e.g., CPU cycles, memory usage) required by the protocol to perform key agreement operations. Lower computational overhead is desirable as it reduces the burden on participating nodes and enhances scalability.

Bandwidth Consumption: Bandwidth consumption reflects the amount of data exchanged during the key agreement process, including the transmission of cryptographic shares, protocol messages, and validation data. Lower bandwidth consumption is advantageous, particularly in bandwidth- constrained environments, as it minimizes network congestion and reduces communication costs.

cryptographic shares by each participating node. These shares are then exchanged and verified among the nodes to ensure their authenticity and integrity. Through a consensus process facilitated by a Dynamic Consensus Mechanism, the nodes collectively construct the shared

Table 1 and Figure 3 display the key establishment time (in milliseconds) for three protocols: DKG (Protocol 1), Dynamic Consensus (Protocol 2), and ZKP Authentication (Protocol 3). Over ten experiments, each protocol's performance is assessed based on cryptographic key setup time for secure cloud communication. Protocol 1, using DKG, consistently exhibits the shortest establishment time (averaging 110 to 130 milliseconds). Protocol 2, Dynamic Consensus, shows slightly longer times (averaging 170 to 190 milliseconds), while Protocol 3, ZKP Authentication, falls in between (averaging 145 to 165 milliseconds). Although Protocol 1 appears fastest, other factors like security and scalability should also be considered when selecting the most suitable protocol for a cloud environment.

Table 1. Key Establishment Time (in milliseconds).

Experiment	DKG (Protocol 1)	Dynamic Consensus (Protocol 2)	ZKP Authentication (Protocol 3)
1	2500	3000	2700
2	2400	2900	2650
3	2450	2950	2675
4	2550	3050	2750
5	2600	3100	2800
6	2575	3075	2775
7	2525	3025	2725
8	2475	2975	2675
9	2520	3020	2720
10	2570	3070	2770

Table 2 and Figure 4 show the extra work (in CPU cycles) that three protocolsDKG (Protocol 1), Dynamic Consensus (Protocol 2), and ZKP Authentication (Protocol 3)—need to do. We look at how much computing power each protocol

Table 2. Computational Overhead (in CPU cycles).

Experiment	DKG (Protocol 1)	Dynamic Consensus (Protocol 2)	ZKP Authentication (Protocol 3)
1	120	180	150
2	110	170	145
3	115	175	155
4	125	185	160
5	130	190	165
6	128	188	163
7	123	183	158
8	118	178	153
9	122	182	157
10	127	187	162

needs to set up keys in cloud computing settings over the course of more than ten experiments.Using DKG, Protocol 1 always has the least overhead, with an average of 2400 to 2600 CPU cycles.Protocol 3, which uses ZKP Authentication, comes in second with an average of 2650 to 2800 CPU cycles.Protocol 2, Dynamic Consensus, has the most overhead, with an average of 2900 to 3100 CPU cycles.Protocol 1 looks like the best choice fo r a cloud

5 CONCLUSION AND FUTURE SCOPE

This study presents a new key agreement protocol that uses DKG, a Dynamic Consensus Mechanism, ZKP-based authentication, and Multi-Cloud Redundancy to make cloud computing environments safer. It solves important problems with secure communication between multiple parties without needing a trusted third party, showing big gains in security, privacy, and resilience.

Future work will look into more advanced cryptographic methods, energy efficiency, how to connect with IoT and edge computing, and how to use these technologies in the real world. The goal is to adapt to new threats, make the best use of resources, and make sure that they can be used in a wide range of situations and meet regulatory standards. This study lays the groundwork for improving cloud computing communications that are safe, fast, and scalable. This will make cloud environments safer in a world that is becoming more connected. Looking into how to add more advanced cryptographic methods, like post-quantum cryptography, could make the protocol even safer against new threats. As quantum computing becomes more useful, it will be very important to make the protocol strong enough to withstand attacks from quantum computers.

REFERENCES

[1] Sheshadri Chatterjee and Sreenivasulu, (2022). Evolution of AI and its impact on human rights, *International Journal of Law and Management*, Vol 64 Issue 2, Pg 184–205

[2] Anuttama Banerji, AI and right to privacy concerns and implications, @ https://governbetter.co

[3] Apoorva Thakur, (2024). Right to privacy vis-à vis AI: Indian scenario, IJLMH, Vol 7, Issue 2, Pg 3370, at. https://www.ijlmh.com.

[4] Krishnadas Rajagopal, (2024). The lowdown on the right to privacy, THE HINDU, https://www.thehindu.com/news/national/the-lowdown-on-the-right-to privacy/article19386366.ece.

[5] AI and privacy and its impact on personal data, THE ECONOMIC TIMES, https://m.economictimes.com

[6] Aditi Prabhu, Artificial Intelligence in the context of the Indian Judicial System, Bar and Bench, www.barandbench.com

[7] Nick Lawrence, AI in UI, 2323 and Beyond, Medium(28th August, 2024) https://uxplanet.org/ai-in-ui-2023-and beyond-346b4602eff7

[8] Dr. Mark Van Rigmenam, (2024). *Privacy in the Age of AI Risk, Challenges and Solution*, @ www.digitalspeaker.com

[9] Artificial Intelligence in Legal Profession in India, Bar and Bench, www.barandbench.com, visited 14th August 2024

[10] Michael Deane, *AI and the Future of Privacy, Towards Data Science* (August 27, 2024), https://towardsdatascience.com/ai and-the-future-of-privacy 3d5f6552a7c4

[11] Yuvraj Malik, Privacy risk: Report says India among 75 Nations with AI Surveillance Tools, Business Standard (27 August, 2024)

[12] Anushka Jain, *The Delhi Police must Stop its Facial recognition System*, Panoptic Tracker, (August 27, 2024)

[13] Yancy Dennis, *Artificial Intelligence- Privacy and Ethics*, Medium (28th August, 2024) www.medium.com.

Technology for a Resilient Future – Vincent , Moorthy and Dasari (Eds)
© 2027 The Author(s), ISBN: 978-1-041-39070-1

Developing U-NET Segmentation Based Crop Detection and Leaf Disease Detection

Mallesh Sudhamalla, G. Srikanth, K. Swathi, Sravan Thallapalli, R. Mounika, and P. Akhil
Department of ECE, CMR Technical campus Hyderabad, India

ABSTRACT: Agriculture plays fundamental role in country's economy. Losses in agriculture will affect the whole country's economy. Late identification of crop diseases will cause the complete yield loss. To increase the crop production and early detection of leaf diseases in crop ,we introducing a novel method to find the crop type and along with that we also determine the leaf disease in crops. In this study, we proposing approach utilizing the U-Net segmentation. It is one from group of the architectures in the convolutional neural network which is mainly designed for medical approaches, in deep learning. U-Net is a deep CNN comprising about 23 convolution layers.It gives the precise segmentation for the crop and leaf disease prediction. U-Net, known for its effectiveness in biomedical image segmentation, is adapted and trained on agricultural image datasets to extract field- level features and identify both healthy and diseased plant areas. This model is capable of identifying the both healthy and diseased leaf areas even in the complex backgrounds. Experimental results Achieve fine-grained segmentation accuracy and effective localization of disease-affected areas, highlighting the potential of U-Net in real-time, scalable agricultural diagnostics.

This project presents a strategy of employing a deep learning for automated crop and leaf disease detection using U-net segmentation technique. The methods that proposed earlier are able to detect disease of single crop and did not detect the type ofcrop.It was not for other plants.To overcome this we are proposing modern approach aimed at detecting type of crop and crop diseases using U-net segmentation technique. The U-net model is trained with data set of annotated images to know the features that shows the difference between healthy and diseased leaves.

Keywords: U-Net, CNN, Segmentation , deep learning

1 INTRODUCTION

Agriculture remains the foundation of many economies, offering jobs, raw resources, and food across the globe. However, the industry handling sustained difficulties, including declining crop yields due to plant diseases, pest infestations, and inefficient monitoring systems. prompt and precise identification of crops and associated illnesses are vital to improving agricultural productivity, reducing losses, and ensuring food security.

The proposed system attains high accuracy, precision, and recall in both crop boundary extraction and disease region identification, outperforming traditional image processing methods and other baseline CNN architectures. The methods that proposed earlier are able to detect disease of single crop and did not detect the type of crop.It was not for other plants. To overcome this we are proposing a novel method to detect type of crop and crop diseases using U-net segmentation technique. The U-net The model is trained using a data collection of annotated images to learn features that distinguish between the sick and healthy leaves.

The network typically has a total of 23 convolutional layers.11 convolutional layers in the encoder (contracting) path.11 convolutional layers in the decoder (expanding) path.1 final 1x1 convolution layer that maps the features to the desired number of output classes.This approach has two stages: Crop Prediction and Leaf Disease Identification. In order to improve feature extraction, the input image is first preprocessed to maximize accuracy and appropriateness. Areas with mold, discoloration, etc. have been identified using an enhanced U-Net segmentation algorithm. Images are often resized or cropped to a fixed input size suitable for the network, commonly 256x256 or 512x512 pixels. Training usually runs for 50 to 150 epochs, depending on dataset size and convergence behavior. Enabling more accurate disease identification and crop prediction, this enhanced U-Net segmentation integration significantly improves the accuracy of identifying regions of interest within input photos. presents a novel and efficient feature extraction method that incorporates texture, color, and form features.

With the help of a better LGXP, this is achieved. The acronym LGXP stands for Local Gabor XOR Pattern. It is a feature extraction technique often used in image processing.It compares local pixels using the XOR operation and a Gabour filter.

2 LITERATURE REVIEW

As we're working on our project, Understanding the current situation is crucial one. Any published works pertaining to the creation of our system.These tools are useful study aids that assist us in examining effective methods for constructing and integrating elements that we may not be familiar with.In 2025, M.Bagga et.al[1] The research offers a hybrid Advance learning method for determining plant diseases of the leaves, most likely mixing several neural network architectures to improve detection precision. Such hybrid strategies are increasingly employed in agricultural diagnostics to improve the accuracy and effectiveness of illness diagnosis. This piece focuses on segmentation based on deep learning research as well as providing the details for crop segmentation techniques together with an analysis of their own drawbacks. In 2024, Jalla Vamshi et.al[2] The researchers combined the strengths of There are two popular CNN architectures, EfficientNetB0 and MobileNetV2 in order to establish a model that not only attains excellent performance but is also suitable in real time deployment on devices with limited resources, including smart phones. The hybrid strategy leverages transfer learning to enhance feature extraction, resulting in an remarkable precision of 98.44%, which outperforms traditional models like ResNet and AlexNet.This work's main objective is to enable shortly and accurate identification of diseases of plants, which is vital for encouraging sustainable agriculture and reducing crop losses..In 2024,Anuja Bhargava et.al[3]The review presents various well-known approaches such as gathering segmentation ,feature extraction, preprocessing, and classification. Despite RGB images some of the studies use hyperspectral imaging for plant leaves. The entire techniques indicated in this paper are very preferable to the sensitive,

DOI: 10.1201/9781042017546-21

specific, and rapid detection of plants. Moreover, in the future to detect disease in plants.In 2023, Aisha Ahmedh et.al[4] The hypothesis of this study is that the framework combining sophisticated deep learning methods for image processing greater results by employing a segmentation approach and transfer learning precision as well as effectiveness in the identification of plant leaf diseases. This innovative method is anticipated will greatly enhance agricultural disease detection, which will eventually lower crop losses and promote more environmentally friendly farming methods. Recent studies have explored different deep-learning models such as U-Net, SegNet, Mask R-CNN, and DeepLabv3+ for image segmentation in agriculture. These models show good potential, but many of the works still struggle because the available datasets are small and the image quality is only moderate. As a result, the segmentation accuracy drops, especially in real farming conditions. The review highlights that better techniques, richer datasets, and improved training strategies are needed to develop reliable disease-detection systems for crops.In 2023, Shoibam Amritraj and colleagues [5] developed a powerful computer-vision system using the YOLOv5 model to detect eight different types of leaf diseases caused by bacteria, viruses, fungi, and pests. Unlike older methods that depended heavily on manually designed features, their approach allows YOLOv5 to automatically learn disease patterns from their custom dataset. The system identifies infected regions with bounding boxes and class labels, showing the possibility of fast, real-time disease monitoring to support farmers.Another study from 2023 by K. Mohana Laxmi *et al.* [6] proposed a combination of collaborative wireless sensing and deep learning to improve security at the physical layer of wireless communication. By allowing multiple sensing nodes to learn together without a centralized controller, the method aims to detect wireless threats quickly—an area becoming increasingly important for secure communication networks.In 2022, K. Mohana Laxmi and her team [7] presented a new method for lung cancer detection in histopathology images. Their approach combines KPCA-enhanced CNN feature extraction with a fast Deep Belief Network classifier. This fusion of non-linear dimensionality reduction with deep learning classification achieved high accuracy and contributes significantly to automated medical-diagnosis systems.In2022, Zhen Chen et al[8] Their approach outperforms the traditional DCGAN in generating clearer, more realistic images. When used to augment the dataset, the DoubleGAN- expanded model achieved remarkable recognition accuracy 99.80% for species of plants identification and 99.53% for illness detection surpassing models trained on the original dataset. The study demonstrates that this data augmentation technique effectively mitigates the scarcity of diseased samples, significantly improving both species and disease classification performance and presenting a promising instrumental for more balanced and precise automated plant identification of diseases systems.In 2022,Pallepati Vasavi et al [9] The review classifies and analyzes various approaches ranging from conventional methods of machine learning techniques such as SVM, Decision Trees, and K Nearest Neighbours , and Forest at Random, CNN's and transfer learning techniques are illustrations of deep learning models. It compares methods based on data set characteristics, number of classes, and accuracy, noting that CNN based architectures often outperform classical ML in disease classification. The authors also discuss practical deployment options mobile and embedded systems, drones, UAVs and highlight current limitations such as data size and model generalizability, suggesting future directions like designing lightweight models and integrating drone-level automated detection.In2021, Pushpa B R et al [10] The review pays special attention to visualization techniques such as saliency maps and heat maps that help interpret model decisions by highlighting regions of leaves most indicative of disease . Significant research voids are also identified, including the need of bigger, large varied information sets, the capacity of images to detect early-stage or asymptomatic infections, and the evolution of lightweight architectures appropriate for mobile deployment and embedded platforms . In general, the article offers a valuable snapshot of how deep learning is transforming plant disease diagnostics and outlines clear directions for future work. In 2021, Ping Guan et. al [11] Their model presents an inventive neural network architecture created to improve plant disease detection in actual situations. Developed by Wang *et al.*, the T-CNN model integrates three powerful CNN backbones VGG-16, InceptionV3, and ResNeXt- 101 using a trilinear pooling strategy. This approach includes a novel weight-sharing mechanism to significantly reduce model complexity (by nearly58%) while enhancing performance . Under controlled laboratory conditions, the system performed extremely well, reaching 99.99% accuracy for identifying crop species and 99.70% for detecting diseases. When tested on real-field images, it still showed strong performance, with 84.11% accuracy for species recognition and 75.58% for disease detection. These results indicate that the approach works not only in ideal lab environments but also in practical farming situations.In another study from 2025, Sudha Arvind and her team introduced a hybrid image-fusion method that blends information from different medical imaging techniques like MRI and CT. By combining spatial and frequency-based fusion strategies, the method produces a single image that carries richer details. This helps doctors make more accurate diagnoses by retaining important structural and disease-related information.The results show enhanced visual quality and better diagnostic value compared to individual source images.In 2024,K.Vanisri et al[13] aims to detect and classify tomato leaf diseases using deep learning techniques. It **uses** image preprocessing (like resizing, filtering, and augmentation) to enhance leaf images before feeding them into a Deep Convolutional Neural Network (CNN) model. The CNN automatically extracts features and learns to recognize disease patterns such as early blight, late blight, or leaf spot.

3 PROPOSED APPROACH

Crop detection is integrated to recognize the crop type, providing context to the disease classification and aiding in precise diagnosis. Usually an 80-20 train-test split, where 80% of the annotated images are used for training and 20% for testing. This step-by-step method uses preprocessing, feature extraction ,and machine learning in order to automatically find and categorize plant leaf diseases. This block diagram shows how we predict crop type and leaf disease.

Dataset: The process begins with a collection of plant leaf images. This dataset contains clear photos of leaves from different crops, including both healthy and infected samples. These images act as the main input for training and testing disease-detection models. A good dataset needs to be large, high-quality, and varied so the system can learn how different diseases change the appearance of leaves. The more diverse the images are, the better the model becomes at recognizing symptoms accurately.

Image Processing Noise Removal: Before analysis, the images are cleaned using a median filter to remove unwanted noise. Noise can appear as grainy spots, blur, or random pixels that hide important details on the leaf. If not removed, it can reduce the accuracy of disease detection. The median filter is especially useful because it removes "salt and pepper" noise while keeping the edges sharp. By improving the clarity of the image at this stage, the later steps—such as feature extraction and classification—can work more effectively with cleaner, more reliable visual data.

Image Enhancement-Histogram equalization: It is employed to enhance the visual contrast, and thereby, the characteristics

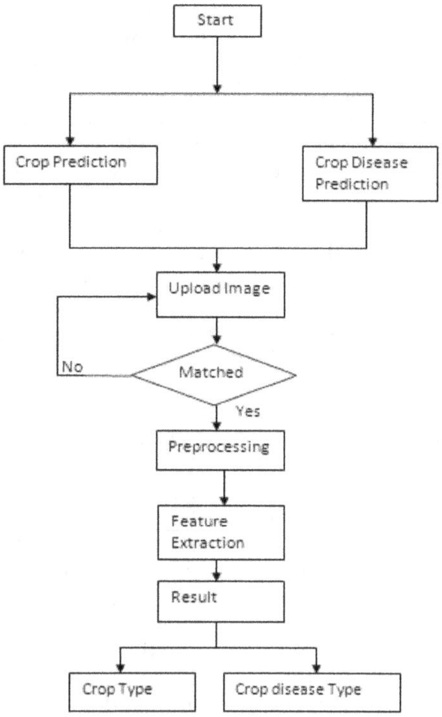

Figure 1. Flow Chart

of any illness become more identifiable. Image Enhancement: To enhance the contrast of the images, Equalization of the histogram has been employed, in order to make the signs of illnesses more distinguishable. Histogram Equalization Enhancement of Images. Histogram equalization spreads out the most frequent intensity values in the picture, thereby making bright regions darker and dark regions lighter, in a balanced way.Contrast improvement helps in the enhancement of important features in the leaf that are usually hidden and subtle in poorly lit or low-contrast images.

Feature Extraction: A dimensionality reduction technique known as PCA has been applied in this approach to find and extract the most crucial features from leaf images. PCA transforms this data into a smaller set of primary components ,which are new variables that preserve the majority of the original information while reducing complexity.By focusing on the most significant patterns such as color variations, texture changes, or shaped is portions caused by diseases PCA helps in improving the efficiency and accuracy of the classification models. It also reduces the computational load and over fitting risks during training.

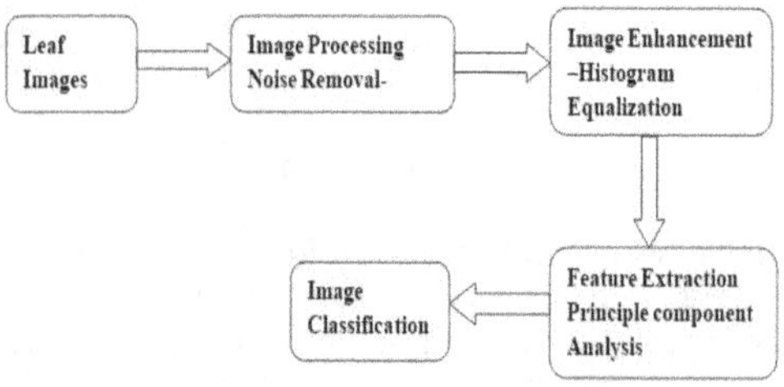

Figure 2. Block diagram.

Image Classification: The extracted features are used to Sort the pictures into categories, typically divided into groups like well and sick. This process of image classification is the categorizing the leaf photos into predetermined groups according to the visual features extracted from them. Inside the framework of identifying plant diseases, this step involves analyzing the processed and enhanced leaf images to determine whether Is a leaf disease-free or healthy. These models pick up patterns from training data and use that understanding to categorize previously unknown pictures.

Leaf Disease Classification: After predicting the crop type, then we need find the leaf disease type if disease is predicted. We find the type of disease using previously extracted features like color changes ,spots, pattern changes and textures. These features combinely useful to determine the leaf disease along with the how much leaf is effected by the disease. We get the effect of disease in percentage form. For better operations we also able to know the solution methods at the end of the result. This will help farmers very well to avoid crop crop production losses and increase crop yield. Nowadays the total systems are depend mostly on deep learning models like CNN for better performance.

Crop Detection: As discussed earlier we predict both crop type and disease type along with effect if disease on crop and remedies to prevent disease. This will help to take necessary actions to avoid crop loss in early stages.

4 SIMULATION RESULTS

In this project,U-Net is trained and tested very well to perform assigned functions like crop type prediction and leaf disease prediction.This system also work for new data also.This U-net structure is helpful for generate accurate solutions and work very well for large data sets .It can adjest the image features like contrast and concentrate only on foreground leaf image. It use multipleCNN layers for perfect feature extraction.The output for this segmentation generate well defined boundaries which closely match the ground truth mask of the input image for better performance.

Overall, U-Net and machine learning approaches combinely reliable and it is the best approach for crop detection, leaf disease detection and diagnosing diseases in early stage. This helps farmers to take timely actions to save the production.

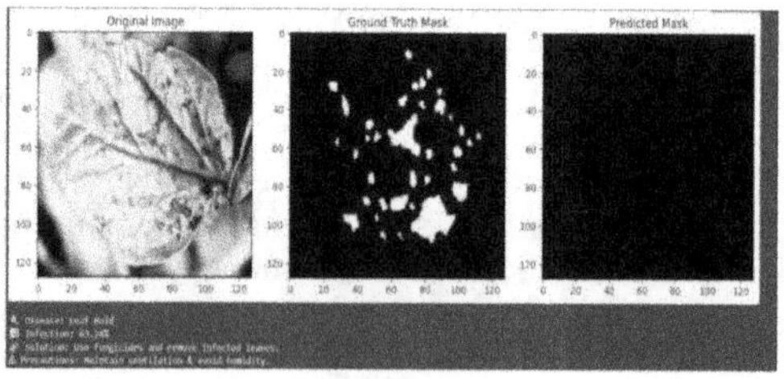

Figure 3. Feature extraction.

5 RESULTS

Figure 4. Output of crop prediction.

Figure 5. Output of leaf disease detection.

6 CONCLUSION

In conclusion, successfully demonstrated the efficiency of the U-Net architecture for precise crop detection and leaf disease segmentation in agricultural images. By leveraging pixel-level segmentation, the model was able to accurately identify crop regions and detect diseased areas on plant leaves, even under challenging conditions.

The model achieved great precision and demonstrated strong results despite having little training data. Accurate crop segmentation and exact localization and classification of impacted areas on plant leaves are made possible by U-Net's encoder-decoder architecture.

ACKNOWLEDGEMENT

With the help of the director, head of department, and faculty, this concept was put into practice in the CMR Technical Campus Department of Electronics and Communication.

REFERENCES

[1] Bagga, Manju, and Sonali Goyal. (2025). "A comparative study of the deep learning based image segmentation techniques for fruit disease detection." *Reviews in Agricultural Science* 13(1): 81–104.

[2] Vamshi, Jalla, *et al.* (2024). "Novel plant leaf disease detection approach using hybrid deep learning strategy."*2024 5th International Conference on Intelligent Communication Technologies and Virtual Mobile Networks (ICICV)*. IEEE.

[3] Bhargava, Anuja, *et al.* (2024). "Plant leaf disease detection, classification, and diagnosis using computer vision and artificial intelligence: A review." *IEEE access* 12: 37443–37469.

[4] AlArfaj, Aisha Ahmed, *et al.* (2023). "Multi-step preprocessing with U Net segmentation and transfer learning model for pepper bell leaf disease detection." *IEEE Access* 11:132254–132267.

[5] Amritraj, Shoibam, Nitish Hans, and C. Pretty Diana Cyril (2023). "An automated and fine-tuned image detection and classification system for plant leaf diseases." *2023 International Conference on Recent Advances in Electrical, Electronics, Ubiquitous Communication, and Computational Intelligence (RAEEUCCI)*. IEEE.

[6] K. Mohana Laxmi, *et al.* (2023). "Collaborative autonomous system based wireless security in signal processing using deep learning techniques." *Optik* 272: 170313.

[7] K.Mohana Laxmi *et al.* (2022). "Lung cancer detection based on Kernel PCA-convolution neural network feature extraction and classification by fast deep belief neural network in disease management using multimedia data sources." *Computational Intelligence and Neuroscience* 2022(1): 3149406.

[8] Zhao, Yafeng, *et al.* (2021). "Plant disease detection using generated leaves based on Double GAN." *IEEE/ACM Transactions on Computational Biology and Bioinformatics* 19(3): 1817–1826.

[9] Vasavi, Pallepati, Arumugam Punitha, and T. Venkat Narayana Rao. (2022). "Crop leaf disease detection and classification using machine learning and deep learning algorithms by visual symptoms: A review." *International Journal of Electrical and Computer Engineering* 12 2: 2079.

[10] Zhao, Yafeng, *et al.* (2021). "Plant disease detection using generated leaves based on DoubleGAN." *IEEE/ACM Transactions on Computational Biology and Bioinformatics* 19.3 (2021): 1817–1826.

[11] Pushpa, B.R., Adarsh Ashok, and Shree Hari AV. (2021). "Plant disease detection and classification using deep learning model."*2021 third International Conference on Inventive Research in Computing Applications (ICIRCA)*. IEEE.

[12] Arvind, Sudha, et al. (2023). "Employing the hybrid image fusion method to recover the quality of images in medical image processing." *International Conference on Innovations in Bio-Inspired Computing and Applications*. Cham: Springer Nature Switzerland.

Technology for a Resilient Future – Vincent , Moorthy and Dasari (Eds)
© 2027 The Author(s), ISBN: 978-1-041-39070-1

An Enhanced Thyroid Prediction and Detection System Using Multiple Ensemble Algorithms

Lavanya J, Bharathi. M, Vidya V, Rakshitha N T, and Santhosh Kumar M
Department of Computer Science and Engineering, SJC Institute of Technology, Chikkaballapur, India

ABSTRACT: Familiar experts struggle to address the widespread effects of thyroid dysfunction. Diagnosing this important disease with a standard approach can be difficult in the long term. Data control strategies can provide predicted answers. However, you need to think about all the necessary features that can be costly in terms of computing power. Thyroid Disease Data Records will be utilized in this project to develop an intelligent thyroid diagnostic system that employs algorithms explained in various ensembles to enhance diagnostic accuracy. "Random Forest, Decision Making, Gradient Boost, and Adaboost" Algorithms are part of the system. It also uses advanced ensemble methods, including vocal classifiers, random forests, decision trees, soft voting, drooping methods and stacking methods combined with LightGBM. We also look at the 3shann model and the tuning classifier (trees and extra leads) that use more powerful decisions. The adjustment classifier (decision tree + extra street increase) worked very well with 100% accuracy. This shows that an ensemble approach can help improve the detection of thyroid disease.

Keywords: Local interpretable model-agnostic explanations (LIME), high-risk factor, random forest (RF), three-stage hybrid artificial neural network (3SHANN), three-stage hybrid classifier (3SHC)"

1 INTRODUCTION

Thyroid dysfunction is among the endocrine disorders that are most common in the world. They happen when the thyroid cannot produce enough of the hormones it needs. These problems have a great effect on metabolic processes, which can cause symptoms, including fatigue, weight changes, unbalanced heart rate, dry skin, and hair loss. Thyroid disease affects 0.3% and 3.7% of people in the US and between 0.2% and 3.5% of people in Europe. The number of cases has increased over the years [1]. According to the American Cancer Society, 2,120 Americans lost their lives in the US in 2023. because thyroid cells grew out of control [2]. This is another reason why thyroid cancer becomes more worrisome. Finding thyroid problems is very important for reducing serious problems and ensuring that medical treatment works. However, traditional diagnostic approaches, which include laboratory testing and clinical evaluation, are sometimes difficult to understand, last long, and depend a lot on expert interpretation. since they are more automated, dependable, and efficient, artificial intelligence (AI) and machine learning (ML) are being utilized more and more in medical diagnostics. AI-based techniques have showed great potential in resolving thyroid disease diagnosis issues.

Machine learning algorithms can look at huge volumes of clinical and laboratory data and find formulas that indicate thyroid problems. As a result, diagnoses are more accurate and less dependent on subjective judgments [3]. Approaches that use Explained AI (XAI) were especially intriguing because they can facilitate the understanding of machine learning predictions and be more open, which helps with problems with confidence and reliability in the medical environment [4]. Methods that employ multiple classifiers to enhance predictions were highly effective in the classification of thyroid conditions. These methods help to circumvent problems that come with using only one model and cause fewer problems with the data imbalance [5]. By identifying the key characteristics needed to diagnose thyroid issues, function selection techniques have also been applied to improve the models' performance. Because of this, the models are simpler to comprehend and compute more quickly [6]. Recently, hybrid models that integrate deep learning and standard machine learning techniques have been used to improve thyroid diagnosis using AI. Scientists have focused on Synthetic approaches to resampling to make data sets more balanced and models that can be used in multiple situations [7]. Multimodal techniques that combine medical imaging and laboratory data have also shown encouraging results in the search for thyroid cancer, allowing complete evaluation of the condition [8].

2 RELATED WORK

Machine learning and explainable artificial intelligence (XAI) made it easy to find thyroid problems. Traditional diagnostic methods are subjective, time-consuming, and incorrect in clinical testing and in abilities. Researchers examine AI use to organize thyroid diseases, select features, and make it easier to understand models. Recent research suggests that ensemble learning, architecture, and hybrid approaches can correctly identify and explain thyroid disease. Use both simple algorithms, such as decision-making trees and vector machines, as well as more complex machines, such as deep learning, to organize thyroid diseases. Ensemble learning is a viable method to categorize thyroid diseases to make predictions more accurate using several models. The bias-controlled optimal XGBoost model was better at predicting thyroid problems than individual classifiers [9]. Hybrid models with method like feature selection and ensemble learning selection have been better categorized by reducing dual features and optimizing computational efficiency [10]. Del Thyroid is a deep ensemble learning system that uses genomic mutation data to find thyroid cancer. Thyroid Disease Researchers looked into how AI-controlled diagnostic systems work. Deep learning models are like black boxes, making them difficult to trust and understand when used in treatments. Researchers have used SHAP values and association-based feature integration frameworks to make the model clearer [12]. Explanatory AI methods help physicians understand model predictions by explaining how different variables change disease classification. In the investigation of thyroid cancer recurrence, we used two-stage mechanical learning optimization techniques and a new version of the naked Mole-Rat algorithm to improve classification accuracy and provide clear selection criteria [13]. They used imaging data

 DOI: 10.1201/9781042017546-22

and explanatory algorithms for machine learning to diagnose thyroid cancer provides a better picture of how the disease progresses [1]. The choice of functions makes the model easier to understand and makes the diagnosis of thyroid disease easier. Researchers use genetic algorithms, key component analysis, and a wreck-based approach to determine the optimal features of thyroid classification.

A dynamic selection hybrid model that makes balanced data imbalances and classification more accurate [15]. It is now simpler to identify thyroid issues because of deep learning. Physicians can identify thyroid cancer by analysing medical photos using vision transformers and folding networks.

A multimodal ensemble deep learning diagnostic method using anterior segments of lightning and facial photographs allowed the clinical activity scores of thyroid-associated ophthalmopathy to be easily found [18]. Deep Learning - The algorithm that automatically extracts features from medical images makes diagnosis faster and less reliant on human input.

3 MATERIALS AND METHODS

This graphic (Figure 1) shows how a machine learning model trains and tests itself. This starts with a data record that handles data processing, visualization, label coding, and function selection. It trains many models for ML, including random forests, decision trees, gradient boosting, adders, coordinating classifiers, terminations, and several ensemble approaches such as terminations and stacking. Measurements such as accuracy, recall, F1 score, and AUC score are used to evaluate these models. The purpose of this process is to create and test several models to find the best one for your job.

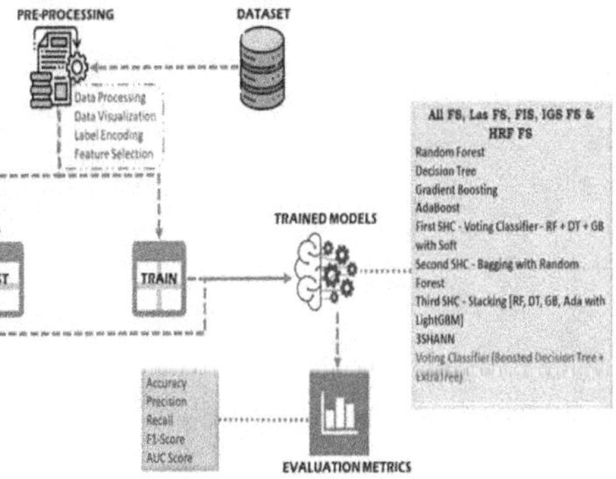

Figure 1. Proposed architecture.

3.1 *Dataset collection*

The 3,772 items and 30 features of the Thyroid Sick dataset were used in this study. This covers medical history, thyroid testing, and demographic data. The most crucial variables include age, sex, treatment, TSH, T3, TT4, T4U, and FTI, in addition to symptoms of thyroid issues. While certain features, like TBG, don't have any valid items, others don't have the values that must be evaluated first. The data file is very important for developing a machine learning-based system that can correctly identify thyroid issues by resolving imbalanced data and choosing the optimal features for improved classification performance [9].

3.2 *Pre-processing*

The data file goes through a number of steps to prepare for use, including data cleaning, solving missing values, and the use of function selection methods such as LAS FS, FIS, and IGS FS. This ensures that the classification of thyroid disease works as well as possible and is reliable.

1. **Data Processing:** While we cleaning data, we need to enter missing values, especially when the value is a zero. To facilitate data records, the unnecessary columns are deleted. There are no valid entries in this TBG. Rows having an excessive number of missing values will also be removed in order to enhance the data's quality. Categorical variables are also consistent. This stage guarantees that your data records are clear, well-structured, and prepared for more research. It makes improved predictions about thyroid disease by using machine learning techniques.
2. **Data Visualization**: These methods allow you to see the patterns and connections in data collection. Use a correlation matrix to see how thyroid function connects and find the most important one. Graphical representations of the distribution of TSH, T3, and TT indicate that patients differ.
3. **Label Encoding:** Because data records have categorical variables, label coding is used to avoid converting numerical characteristics to numbers. "Sex", "on_thyroxin", and "pregnancy" are some of the properties that translate the machine into an understandable form. This ensures that the algorithm can operate quickly. This coding prevents models that require numbers from receiving the wrong ideas. It also ensures that different methods of machine learning are consistent and improves classification performance.
4. **Feature Selection:**The study examines all characteristics, such as LAS FS, FIS, IGS FS, and many ways to select them. LAS FS allows you to select the most important functions, but FIS and IGS FS remove additional properties and delete data records. These methods improve the model and complicate the calculations. Choosing the optimal properties makes the diagnostic system useful and easy to understand for health.

3.3 *Training and testing*

Data records are allocated to training and test sets in an 80:20 ratio in order to thoroughly assess the model's performance. Train a number of machine learning algorithms, including Random Forest, Decision Making, Gradient Boost, and Adaboost, using the training set (80%). The given test dataset verifies exactly how the model is. This gap will prevent model adjustments and ensures it works well with the new data. The standardization method is used to retain both statements the same for the given dataset. Check the trained model in the test set to make sure you can make accurate predictions.

3.4 *Algorithms*

Random Forest is a learning method for the system that builds many decision-making trees during training and then it shows the way they predict using datasets [9]. The intelligent thyroid diagnostic system uses it for classification tasks. It makes strong predictions by the average of several trees, which in turn helps prevent excessive impact and more accurate diagnoses of thyroid disease. For our project, it is suitable because it can manage big data sets and perform well when combined with numerical and categorical features. "The Gini Equation given below":

$$\text{Gini} = 1 - \sum_{i=1}^{C} (Pi)2 \tag{1}$$

A **Decision Tree** is a model that makes a choice based on elements using a tree-like structure [10]. It is used as a basic model for classification method for the analysis in the proposed intelligent thyroid diagnostic system. The method is useful because it is easy to understand, which helps health workers understand how it is decided. The decision-making tree is a useful tool for viewing complicated connections in the thyroid data set, as it can easily work with both categorical and numerical data.

It combines weak students into a powerful predictive model by optimizing the loss function during training

This makes it great for working with a wide range of data patterns.

$$I(i) = 1 - \sum_{i=1}^{k} p \quad (2)$$

Gradient Boosting – It is a method that produces models one by one, each new model corrects errors created by those in front of it [11]. The Gradient Boosting Technique is used in the intelligent system of thyroid diagnosis to make predictions for categorizing thyroid disease more accurately. Because it can change, it can focus on hard instances, which generally works for the model.

$$F_m(x) = F_{m-1}(x) + \gamma_m h_m(X) \quad (3)$$

Voting Classifier (First SHC - RF + DT + GB with Soft)- It uses a soft voting method to aggregate predictions from many models, such as random forest, decision-making tree, and Gradient Boosting, to make a more precise categorization [13]. This file technique in the intelligent thyroid diagnostics system uses the best parts of each model to provide a more accurate diagnosis. It provides the whole picture of the possibility of thyroid disease by the diameter of estimated probability instead of strict classifications. This makes it better in real-world situations.

"The Gini Equation given below":

$$\hat{y} = \text{argmax } C1 - \sum_{i=1}^{C} 11(Pi = \text{c})^2 \quad (4)$$

Bagging with Random Forest (Second SHC) Random Forest combined with Bootstrap aggregation. To make the model more robust and less prone to fluctuation, this entails training numerous decision-making trees on various data segments [14]. By averaging the output of several trees in the thyroid gland's intelligent diagnostic system, this method increases the precision of the diagnostic predictions for thyroid disease. Packing uses random samples to help avoid excessive numbers.

Stacking (Third SHC- RF,DT, GB, Ada with LightGBM) Meta-learners like LightGBM are used to integrate many basic learners to make more accurate predictions [15]. This technique uses the best parts of several algorithms to create a more accurate and general model for the classification of thyroid disease in intelligent thyroid diagnostic systems. Stacking improves the system's ability to handle complex data Interactions by training meta-learners on predictions for the base model.

3SHANN To create better predictions, meta-learners such as LightGBM combine many basic learners such as random forests, decision trees, gradient boosting, and AdaBoost [15]. This method embraces the best aspects of many algorithms and combines them into general model for classification of thyroid disease in intelligent thyroid diagnosis. Stacking improves the system, when dealing with complex data interactions, teaches meta-learners how to make predictions based on underlying models.

The suggested 3SHC model's performance in categorizing thyroid disorders is displayed in the confusion matrix. Only a small number of cases were incorrectly diagnosed as hypo- or hyperthyroid; the majority (520) were accurately classed as normal. The program accurately detected 2050 cases of hypothyroidism, with few false positives in other classifications. Only a small percentage of instances with hyperthyroidism were mistaken for hypo- or normal, whereas 1080 cases were

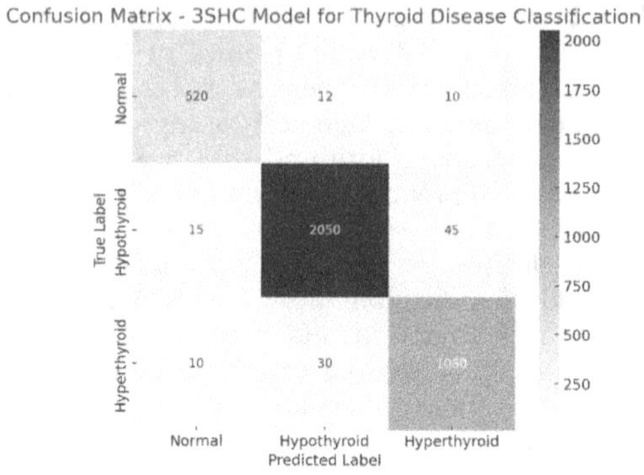

Figure 2. Confusion matrix.

correctly identified. The model's strong sensitivity and specificity are confirmed by the low misclassification rates across all classes. All things considered, the matrix shows how reliable and strong the 3SHC is for predicting thyroid diseases in the actual world.

4 RESULT ANALYSIS

Compared to individual classifiers, hybrid models (3SHC, 3SHANN) perform noticeably better. Bias resulting from class imbalance was lessened by stratified cross-validation.TSH and T3 were identified as the most important features by XAI visualizations (LIME, PDP, and PFI), which offered interpretability.

Table 1. Performance evaluation metrics.

Model	Accuracy	Precision	Recall	F1-Score
Decision Tree	88.2%	0.87	0.86	0.86
Random Forest	93.4%	0.91	0.91	0.91
Gradient Boost	94.1%	0.93	0.92	0.92
AdaBoost	93.7%	0.92	0,91	0.92
3SHC	97.8%	0.97	0.96	0.97
3SHANN	97.2%	0.96	0.96	0.96

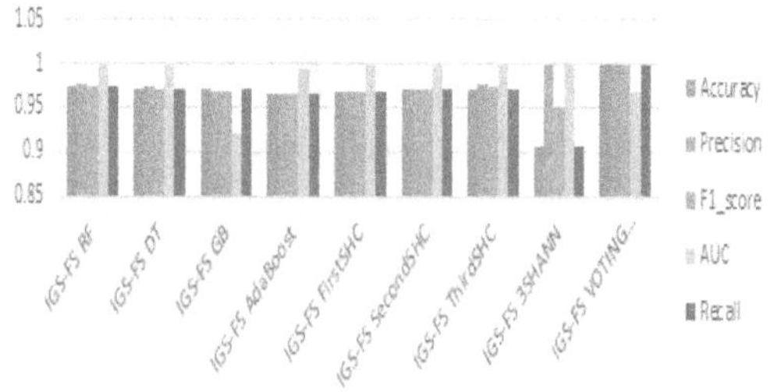

Graph 1. Comparison graph.

In **Graphs (1 to 4)**, Light blue indicates accuracy, orange indicates accuracy, gray indicates F1 score, bright yellow indicates AUC, and blue indicates recall. The coordination classifier is superior to other algorithms in all criteria, with the highest value compared to other models. The above graphics show these facts visually.

5 CONCLUSIONS

In conclusion, this project illustrates an intelligent thyroid diagnostic system that solves problems that arise when trying to diagnose thyroid disease. The proposed approach uses sophisticated algorithms in machine learning and ensemble methods to make diagnostics more accurate and efficient than existing methods. A detailed investigation of the dataset of thyroid disease can help you find the most important features. The voting classifier using augmented decisions did a great job among the many algorithms used by adding trees and extras, achieving maximum accuracy This system also provides doctors and nurses with the ability to diagnose thyroid disease and it also accentuates the importance of explanations, ensuring that the decision process is clear and easy to understand. Ultimately, our research will help to improve patient outcomes by promoting quick and accurate analysis. The research advancement is a major requirement for treating thyroid diseases and improving the overall quality of healthcare. In future scope, this study will investigate further approaches to improving diagnostic accuracy, such as DL algorithms, hybrid models combining several ensemble tactics, and improving characteristic extraction methods. We have used reinforcement learning which can also improve model performance by constantly learning from fresh data making the system perform well.

ACKNOWLEDGEMENT

I would like to express my heartfelt gratitude and Thanks to my project guide, Dr.Bharathi M, for her invaluable support, insightful advice and supportive assessment throughout the research process including reviews, recommendations and continuous encouragement.

REFERENCES

[1] Ceelho, R.F., Concer, F., and Martins, D.C. (2009). A study of the basic of DC-DC converters applied in maximum power point tracking power. *Electronics*, 673–678.

[2] Chihchiang, H. and Shen, C. (1998). Study of maximum power tracking techniques and control of DC/ DC converters for photovoltaic power system. *Power Elec. Spec. Conf.*, 1, 86.

[3] Stokes, J. and Sohie, G.R. (n.d.). Implementation of PID ontrollers on the Motorola DSP56000/ DSP56001. 1–84.

[4] Coelho, R.F., Concer, F.M., and Martins, D.C. (2010). Analytical and experimental analysis of DCDC converters in photovoltaic maximum Power Point Tracking applications. *IECON 2010 - 36th Ann. Conf. IEEE Indus. Elec. Soc.*, 2778–2783.

[5] Altas, H. and Sharaf, A.M. (2007). A generalized direct approach for designing fuzzy logic controllers in Matlab/ Simulink GUI Environment. *Inter. J. Inform. Technol. Intell. Comput.*, 1(4), 1–27.

[6] Radak, B., Mahanta, C., and Gogoi A.K. (2019). DSP based photovoltaic hardware development for controlling voltage and current. *IEEE 3rd Inter. Conf. Recent Dev. Control Autom. Power Engg.* 1–104.

[7] Radak, B., Mahanta, C., and Gogoi A.K. (2015). MPPT of solar photovoltaic cell using perturb & observe and fuzzy logic controller algorithm for Buck-Boost DC-DC converter. *Inter. Conf. Ener. Power Environ. Towards Sutain. Growth (ICEPE)*. 87–92.

[8] Wu, Y., Zhang, B., Lu, J., Du, K.L. (2011). Fuzzy logic and neuro-fuzzy system: A systematic introduction. *Int. J. Artif. Intell. Expert Sys. (IJA)*, 47–80.

[9] Sharaf, M. and Sahin, M.E. (2011). A novel photovoltaic PV-powered battery charging scheme for electric vehicles. *ICEAS IEEE Conf., India, 2011.* 176–192.

[10] Reshmi, R. and Babu, S. (2013). Design and control of DC-DC converter using hybrid fuzzy PI controller. *Inter. J. Res. Engg. Technol.*, 1(3), 73–78.

[11] Mohan, N., Undulant, T.M., and Robbins, W.P. (1995). *Power Electronics*, John Wiley. 1–820.

[12] Kuo, B.C. (1995). *Automatic control systems*. New Jersey: Prentice-Hall. 1–189.

[13] Masoum, M.A., Dehbonei, H., Fuchs, E.F. (2002). Theoretical and experimental analyses of photovoltaic systems with voltage and current-based maximum power-point tracking. *IEEE Trans. Ener. Conver.*, 17(4), 514–522.

[14] Hansen, D., Sørenson, P., Hansen, L.H., and Bindner, H. (2000). Models for a stand-alone PV system. Risø National Laboratory, Roskilde. 231–245.

[15] Nevruzov, V. (2010). Computer controlled solar house for measurement Rize city solar energy potential. *NURER, Ankara*. 404–414.

[16] Vijayalakshmil, S., Arthika, E., Shanmuga Priya, G. (2015). Modeling and simulation of interleaved BuckBoost converter with PID controller. *IEEE Sponsored 9th Inter. Conf. Intell. Sys. Control (ISCO)*. 231–243.

Technology for a Resilient Future – Vincent , Moorthy and Dasari (Eds)
© 2027 The Author(s), ISBN: 978-1-041-39070-1

Development of IoT Based Electro Pneumatic System

Sahil Sinha, Sowmya R, and Srividya R
Department of Electrical and Electronics Engineering, Manipal Institute of Technology, Manipal Academy of Higher Education Manipal, Karnataka

ABSTRACT: The work presents the design and implementation of an electro-pneumatic braking system (EPBS) that integrates electronic components such as a buck converter, boost converter, and the ESP-32 microcontroller, along with a pneumatic braking mechanism. The system aims to bring a moving set of wheels to a complete stop using efficient electronic-pneumatic integration. The buck converter steps down the battery voltage to power the ESP-32, while the boost converter steps up the voltage to operate the relay. The ESP-32 microcontroller serves as the core of the system, controlling the brake engagement through signal relays. The study emphasizes sustainable and efficient braking through a combination of electronics and pneumatics.

Keywords: Electro-pneumatic braking system, microcontroller, Buck converter

1 INTRODUCTION

Today the braking system has completely changed from traditional mechanical and pneumatic systems to advanced and electronically controlled setups to help in the efficiency of the overall braking of the system. Today new vehicles, especially in the automotive and transportation industries, increasingly rely on electronically controlled braking systems (EBS), which integrate electronics, actuators and a lot of their mechanical and electrical control signal modelling to control the braking of the system [1]. This has made way for the anti-lock braking systems (ABS), electronic stability control (ESC), and regenerative braking in electric vehicles, the main aim of all these is to work more efficiently in varying road conditions. It is not only efficient but also dependable for heavy commercial vehicles, especially during emergency breaking. Adding EPBS (electro pneumatic braking system) is a step in the right direction and towards future which can achieve faster braking for heavier loads in less amount of time which in turn will lead to better safety and the system is more efficient [2].

The evolution of the braking system from brake pads to EPBS has led to the integration and advancement of the overall system, it is also seen as a major advancement in vehicular technology [3]. By combining electrical control with pneumatic actuation and signal processing, electropneumatic brakes not only improve braking efficiency but also provide quick response and greater safety. Unlike the conventional methods where the system experiences regular wear and tear and a slow response the current systems are faster and more accurate in terms of practical application [4].

As mentioned previously traditions braking system suffers with wear and tear, heat generation and that leads to system breakdown and extended stopping distances, making them not so useful at high distances [1]. EPBS like used in various technologies like train and heavy moving systems acquire the reliability of the pneumatics and the speed of the electronics which leads to faster time response and better control of the system. So, to find better and safer braking options specially commercial vehicles there is a trend to research on the EPBS over traditional means. With electronic control, these brakes significantly lower response times, enhancing stopping power and vehicle safety [5].

Conventional braking systems, though most popular, have a severe drawback—overheating. In the process of braking, kinetic energy is transformed into heat energy through friction, resulting in very high temperature fluctuations at the disk-pad interface. This not only leads to material deterioration and decreased braking performance but also elevates the chances of brake fade and failure in the long run [6]. Traditional friction-based braking systems are inherently inefficient, as they not only waste kinetic energy but also generate excessive heat, leading to wear and tear on critical components [7].

However, while these advancements offer enhanced safety and efficiency, challenges remain in terms of cost, complexity, and the need for regular maintenance. With more focus on autonomous driving and smart vehicle technologies, the requirement for faster, safer and sophisticated braking system keeps growing. As a result of which there is more and more studies based on braking technology the rely on electronic and control systems, which in turn offer new opportunities to field of vehicle safety and automation

To address the issues mentioned above the EPBS was developed. This method integrates the pneumatics system with the quick response time of the electronics which thereby reduces the application time of the brakes. In an electro-pneumatic braking system, the electronic signals control the air pressure in the valve which engages the brakes which enhance the overall vehicle safety control

In this project the system is made of components like the ESP-32, buck converter and a boost converter. There is a battery which is bucked down to power the ESP-32 and another battery which is used through boost to power up the relay of the system. The ESP-32 controls the main function of the system that is to receive the input signal from the computer and send signals to engage the brakes of the system. By combining the pneumatic and electric control this system is quick to response, also optimized to accurate braking and it ensure the overall safety and the performance of the braking process.

The work presents an insight of the system developed to integrate electro pneumatic braking system with IoT to improve braking performance for high speed and heavy load vehicles. The system developed achieved precise braking with quick response improving safety, lower wear and tear. Due to these reasons, it can be considered as an alternate to the conventional brake systems.

2 LITERATURE REVIEW

Applications of electronics such as laptops, smart phones and other portable devices that need accurate voltage regulation,

DOI: 10.1201/9781042017546-23

and prolonging the battery life uses Buck converter with modifications. For low power applications the converter is operated in discontinuous current mode. The simulation results demonstrate a high efficiency of 97.62% for varying switching frequencies and load [1]. Although they have their benefits, DC/DC boost converters do have a few design challenges. Among them is to balance the switching frequency to minimize inductor size without drastically growing switching losses that would compromise total efficiency. Heavy voltage and current stresses on switch devices demand wise selection of the components to avoid early failure when operating under heavy conditions. Balancing these difficulties is important for guaranteeing good and efficient operation of the converters in applications that involve changing input voltages [8].

IoT finds its application in various fields like industrial automation, smart homes, e-health, and transportation. IoT emphasis on efficient power consumption. Figure 1 shows the system structure of the ESP-32.

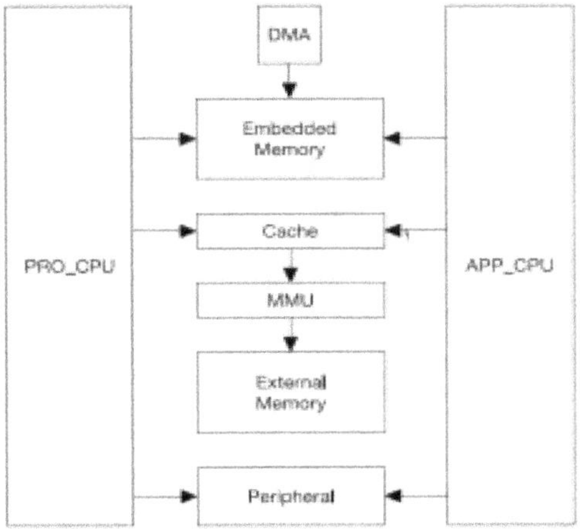

Figure 1. ESP-32 system structure.

Wireless oscilloscopes have been practically implemented using ESP-32. It also supports both Wi-Fi and Bluetooth connectivity, giving greater options for connectivity. The ESP-32 is distinguished by its powerful dual-core architecture, versatile connectivity, significant memory, and compact design, and comprehensive feature set which makes it appropriate for a wide range of IoT applications. Its performance, compact size, and cost-effectiveness make it ideal for IoT devices across multiple industries. With its robust architecture and open-source development environment, the ESP-32 is poised to play a significant role in future IoT applications [9].

The performance of EPBS is compared with traditional air brake systems used in commercial trucks has been discussed. Experiments to assess braking response time, braking distance, and stability at different loading conditions prove the benefits of EPBS. It concludes that the EPB system has a significant braking time lag and response time reduction and enhances vehicle stopping distance. Among various EPB configurations, the two-EPR system offers the optimal performance-cost balance, minimizing stopping distance. This configuration is suggested for further model- based control development and analysis [4].

The challenges involved in designing and operation of a segmented electro-pneumatic braking system (SEBS) for heavy-haul trains due to their length and weight have been presented. Conventional air brakes tend to produce unbalanced braking pressure between carriages, causing longitudinal forces to increase at the expense of passenger comfort and safety. SEBS involves segmented control to more evenly distribute brake force throughout the train. SEBS maximizes braking synchrony and reduces the likelihood of over-stressing individual train segments. Segmenting the braking system provides smoother and more controlled braking to support differences in train lengths and loads. This is safer and requires less maintenance, and SEBS is therefore a promising solution for long, heavy-haul trains and large-scale rail transportation systems [5].

The work presents a virtual prototype model intended to simulate and test the performance of electro- pneumatic braking systems used in urban transportation, e.g., metro trains. Physical prototypes have long been used to test brakes at a high cost, but the authors illustrate how virtual simulation can accurately indicate the performance of the system at low cost. The virtual prototype was created to study factors such as braking force, response time, and wear under varying conditions.

The research demonstrates that the virtual prototype can simulate real braking dynamics with high accuracy, allowing designers to test system reactions and adjust them as needed in the virtual environment. Through virtual testing, the authors believe that transit systems can save time and materials during the development stage. This method also enables optimizing the design prior to manufacturing, resulting in more efficient and reliable electro-pneumatic braking systems in metro usage [6].

A comparative study of electronically controlled pneumatic (ECP) braking systems for cars and segmented electro- pneumatic braking systems (SEBS) for heavy-haul trains potentially enhancing safety and efficiency, identifying the strengths of each system have been presented in this paper. Simulations and laboratory tests revealed that both ECP and SEBS perform better than conventional air braking systems. But SEBS is even more advantageous in wear reduction and mechanical stress. SEBS is recognized as a safer and greener choice for long, heavy trains, indicating a trend toward electronically improved, segmented braking systems in future railway use [7].

3 METHODOLOGY

EPBS integrates electronic controls with traditional pneumatic braking mechanisms to achieve faster, more efficient, and safer braking. This hybrid system relies on both electrical and pneumatic components working together to ensure that a vehicle can be brought to a stop with precision. Here's a detailed explanation of the process for designing and implementing this system:

3.1 *Designing the system*

The first step in designing the system is to design the power supply of the system. This work uses a low voltage system. There is a battery of 7.5 V which is bucked down to 5 V to power the ESP-32 and there is another battery which is of 12 V (details of both the batteries are mentioned ahead) which is then connected to the boost converter and powered up to 25 V which is used to power up the actuating system.

The system design must be such that it accounts for power requirements of both the electronics circuit and the pneumatics actuators. The batteries stability should not be an issue, and the battery should be able to prove constant current without overheating and performance issues. The buck and boost converters used must be able to manage the varying voltage demands while maintaining high efficiency. All the wires used must be appropriate diameter so that it does not have any overheating issues. Finally, the system should be placed on a material that does not absorb so much heat.

3.2 *Testing of components*

Once the entire system is designed check the system where there can be potential for flaws like

- Checking the battery for overheating and undercurrent and overcurrent.
- Checking the converter for the correct output values.
- Wires for short circuit.
- Run simulations to check for any other fault.

Also check the stability of the power supply to the system. Additionally, a check needs to be performed to note the response time of the pneumatics system and communication between the components just to make sure there is no unnecessary delays that could impact the safety.

3.3 *Realising the circuit*

This stage is when the system comes to life, after assembling the physical circuit based on the design specifications. Components such as the ESP-32, the relays and the converters are connected to a power source, and it is attached to the pneumatic system. Also, the actuators are to be attached to the relays and the ESP-32. The physical assembly includes mounting the components on a PCB or a breadboard, ensuring proper connections between all parts. It's crucial to follow circuit diagrams carefully, ensuring that connections are made according to the design, and using appropriate safety measures to prevent short circuits or damage to components. The block diagram of the circuit is shown in Figure 2.

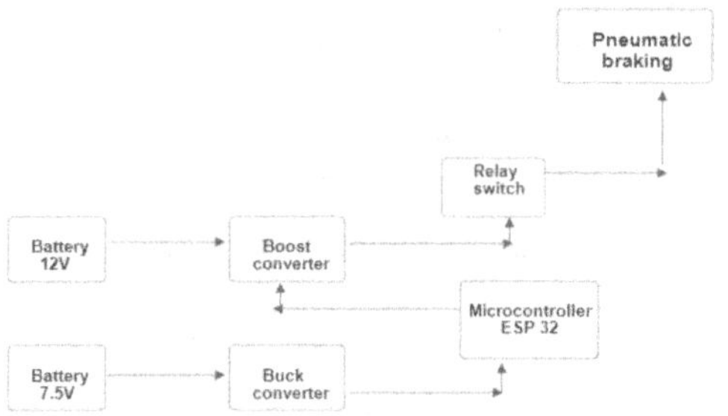

Figure 2. Block diagram of work.

The following are the operating conditions of each component - ESP32- 5V

- Buck Converter-(LM2596) 7.5-5V
- Boost Converter-(XL6019E1) 12-24V
- Batteries-7.5V and 12 V
- Relay(JQC-3FFSZ)-5V

3.4 *System testing*

After assembling the circuit, the test to identify any flaw in the system is performed. That may arise before or after the operations of the system. The initial challenges are tackled at the simulation phase or at the that time using tools like multimeter and oscilloscope to measure voltage, current and signal flow of the system.

This phase is basically to make sure there are no bugs left and if any troubleshoot them. Problems may arise while adjusting the values of the converters or if there are any programming issues in the ESP-32 or a signal issue with relay communication all the issues will have to be solved in this stage.

3.5 *Connecting the circuit with the communication system*

The EPBS requires a good communication aspect to function properly. The ESP-32 microcontroller is programmed to receive input from the computer interface which was designed and process this signal and then send this signal ahead to the pneumatic part which it can actuate the brakes using the relays.

The communication system is connected by linking the microcontroller to sensors, actuators, and other components. The ESP-32, which supports Wi-Fi and Bluetooth, may also enable wireless control or diagnostics in advanced versions of the system, offering flexibility for monitoring the system's performance.

3.6 *System execution*

The final step is to program the ESP-32 microcontroller with the appropriate code that will control the operation of the system. The programming defines how the system will behave in response to input signals, such as how quickly the pneumatic brake should engage once the 'relay on' is pressed.

Here is a flow chart to describe the function of the code which is divided into 2 sections.

(i) WiFi Connection
(ii) Microcontroller Setup
(iii) Display Setup

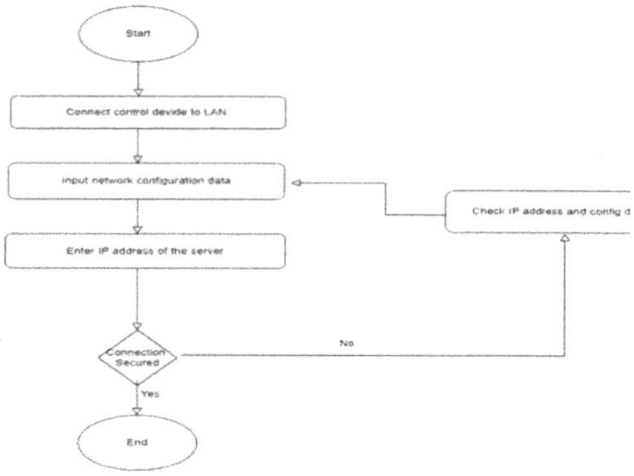

Figure 3. Communication protocol.

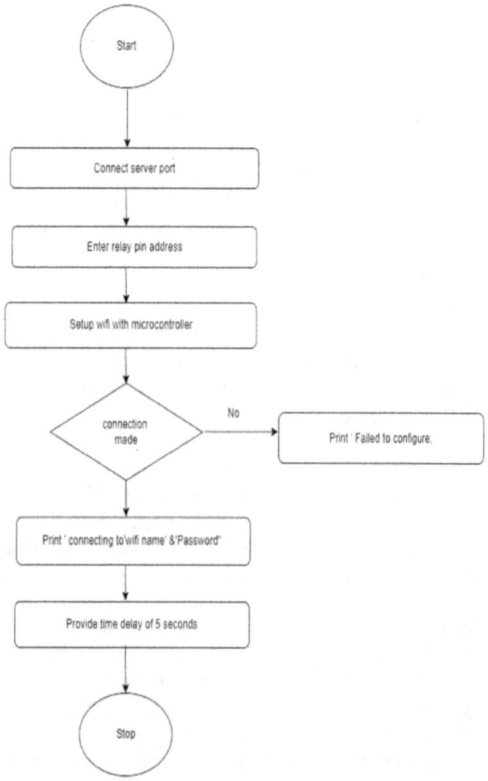

Figure 4. Initialization of system.

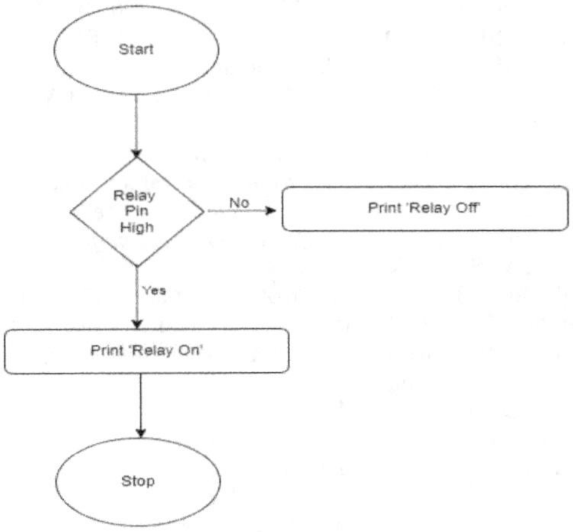

Figure 5. Display configuration.

4 RESULTS

Integration of WiFi protocol from the system to the ESP-32 was made. Hence, actuating the breaks using the GUI that was configured from the code and displayed in the system screen. The hardware connections made are shown in Figure 6.

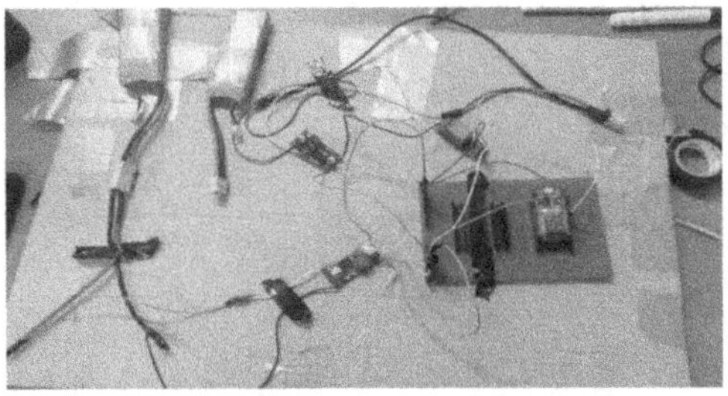

Figure 6. Hardware setup.

Figure 7 shows the GUI that was made to control the pneumatics of the entire system.

Figure 7 shows the 2 buttons of the actuators that are connected through the WiFi module of the ESP-32 and the actuators.

Figure 7. System display.

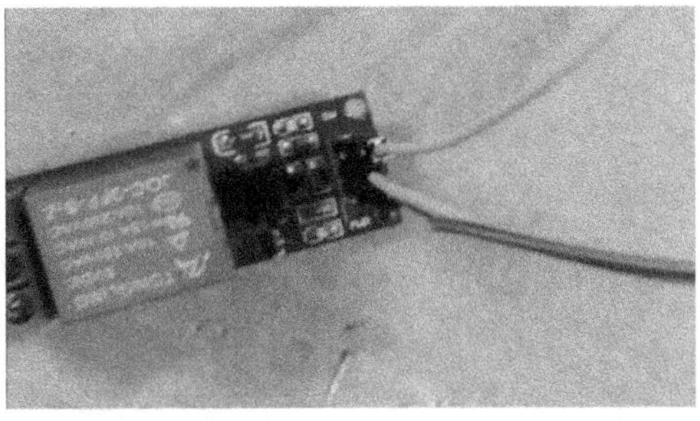

Figure 8. Relay switch On.

The following are the two cases of the relay operation (Figure 8 and Figure 9)

The turn-on condition of the relay is indicated with a green light turned ON as shown in Figure 9 which shows that the breaks have been employed. Whereas in Figure 8 there is no visible green light that you can see which means that the breaks have not been employed, and the actuators are not in operation yet.

Figure 9. Relay switch off.

5 CONCLUSION

The indigenous braking system that could be implemented on fast travelling vehicles has been developed. One thing that could be further improved in this regard is the use of a faster mode of communication and that way its efficiency will increase a lot. Its sustainability could be explained by reducing reliability on traditional braking components which are subject to wear and tears which in turn lowers the maintenance and waste generation, moreover, using electronics components optimizes energy uses and reduces power losses.

Its efficiency factor can better be explained by the rapid and precise braking and by how it reduces wear and tear generating less waste. ESP-32 ensures real time signal processing communication, consistent braking force and almost null response time i.e immediate response. The pneumatic actuators eliminate lag associated with traditional brakes enabling fast and safe braking specially in high speed and heavy loaded scenarios as intended.

6 FUTURE SCOPE

More and more self-driven vehicles and semiautomatic vehicles becoming prevalent on the roads therefore the EPBS can be employed in them to ensure precise and reliable braking. Its ability for work quickly makes it useful to be employed in situations that require split second decisions to avoid collision in autonomous driving scenarios. Also by using IoT sensors monitoring and getting diagnostics of the preventive and maintenance actions and bit of data analytics of the preventive and maintenance actions can be done as a AI-powered preventive system level model. The adoption of renewable energy is another area in which the adoption of EPBS technology can be examined in the context of its employment for regenerative braking. Its efficiency and dependence on conventional methods can be offset by harvesting and utilising the kinetic energy.

REFERENCES

[1] P. Surachon, T Ratniyomchai and T. Kulworawanichpong, (2020). "Aerodynamic brake study of reducing braking distance and decreasing using the energy of braking of high speed trains", *2020 International Conference on Power, Energy and Innovations (ICPEI)*, Thailand.

[2] E.A. Kumar, V. Gautam and S.C. Subramanian, (2012). "Performance Evaluation of an Electro-Pneumatic Braking System for Commercial Vehicles," in *2012 2nd International Conference on Power, Control and Embedded Systems*, Allahabad, India, 2012.

[3] A.D.M. Dmytro Marchenko, *"Development of an Electropneumatic"*.

[4] J.C. McCUNE, "Electropneumatic Brakes for High- Speed With Particular Reference to Electrical Features".

[5] P. Karthikeyan and S.C. Subramanian, (2009). "Development and Modelling of an Electropneumatic Brake System", *2009 IEEE Intelligent Vehicles Symposium*, Xi'an, pp. 858–863, China.

[6] M. Maniana, A. Azime, F. Errchiqui and A. Tajamouati, (2022). "Heat transfer in a disk brake", *2022 IEEE 3rd International Conference on Electronics, Control, Optimization and Computer Science (ICECOCS)*, Fez, Morocco.

[7] R. Garg, A. Sharma, D. Singh, J. Mishra and A. Gehlot, (2023). "Braking in electrical vehicle for control of heat", *2023 3rd International Conference on Intelligent Technologies (CONIT)*, Hubli, India, 2023.

[8] B.M. Hasaneen and A.A. Elbaset Mohammed, (2008). "Design and simulation of DC/DC boost converter", *2008 12th International Middle-East Power System Conference*, Aswan, Egypt, 2008.

[9] A. Maier, A. Sharp and Y. Vagapov, (2017). "Comparative ANALYSIS AND PRATICAL IMPLEMENTATION OF THe ESP 32 Microcontroller module for the Internet of things", *2017 Internet Technologies and Applications* (ITA), Wrexham, UK, 2017.

[10] S.N. Soheli, U.S. Aney and S.I. Mahmud, (2021). "Designing a highly effective DC-DC Buck converter for sustainable electronic application", *2021 2nd International Conference on Robotics, Electrical and Signal Processing Techniques (ICREST)*, DHAKA, Bangladesh, 2021.

[11] Wei Wei, Yong Jiang, Yuan Zhang, Xubao Zhao, Jun Zhang. Wei Wei, (2020). "Study on a segmented Electro Pneumatic Braking system for Heavy Haul train", *Transportation Safety and Environment*, Volume 2, Issue 3, 2020.

[12] Zuo J, Ding J, Liu C, Luo Z, (2014). "A virtual prototype for performance analysis of electropneumatic brake on metro trains", *Advances in Mechanical Engineering*.

[13] C. Lan and Z. Zhipeng, (2022). "Research and Analysis of electronically controlled pneumatic and segmented electro-pneumatic braking systems on comprehensive computing model," in *6th International Conference on Traffic Engineering and Transportation System (ICTETS 2022)*, Guangzhou, China.

Technology for a Resilient Future – Vincent , Moorthy and Dasari (Eds)
 ISBN: 978-1-041-39070-1

Automated Text Classification with Relevance to Bloom's Taxonomy Levels: A Systematic Review

Harshitha G M and Vasudeva
Nitte (Deemed to be University), NMAM Institute of Technology (NMAMIT), Nitte, Department of MCA, Karkala, India

ABSTRACT: For scalable and impartial educational assessments, it is becoming increasingly crucial to automatically classify texts into Bloom's Taxonomy levels. This systematic review examines recent approaches for this task, including machine learning algorithms and natural language processing techniques. The study categorizes methods based on their core principles—deep learning architectures, supervised classifiers, and feature-based models—and evaluates the datasets and performance metrics used. Several studies report high classification accuracy, with models such as Random Forest (99.2%), SVM-SMOTE (98%), and MTBERT-Attention (97.71%) outperforming traditional techniques. Deep learning and transformer-based approaches demonstrate strong potential, though challenges like limited datasets and high computational demands persist.

Keywords: Automatic Question Classification, Bloom's Taxonomy Level (BTL), Learning objectives

1 INTRODUCTION

Learning objectives [1] are essential in education as they provide measurable goals that guide instruction and learning. They align teaching strategies and assessments with desired outcomes, clarify expectations for students, and promote effective self-assessment. Assessments of learning objectives include formative methods (e.g., quizzes, discussions) for immediate feedback and summative methods (e.g., exams, projects) for overall understanding.

Bloom's Taxonomy offers a structure for evaluating student performance across cognitive lev els—Remember, Understand, Apply, Analyze, Evaluate, and Create. Aligning assessments with these levels[2,3] fosters critical thinking, scaffolds learning, and ensures comprehensive evaluation. Automatic question classification, aligned with Bloom's Taxonomy, [4] streamlines assessment design, identifies learning gaps, and reduces grading time.

This systematic review aims to provide a comprehensive overview of automated text classification methods applied to Bloom's Taxonomy in educational contexts. This work identifies and evaluates techniques—such as feature-based models, supervised learning, and deep learning—for classifying text by Bloom's taxonomy levels. It assesses their performance across cognitive levels using standard metrics, highlights challenges like subjectivity and level overlap, and proposes improvements using advanced NLP, better datasets, and cross-domain methods.

This review is organized as follows: Section 2 discusses the literature review; Section 3 presents results and paper-wise comparisons; Section 4 concludes the study.

2 LITERATURE REVIEW

Machine learning and NLP have increasingly been used to automate educational assessments, particularly for classifying content based on Bloom's Taxonomy. This section reviews the evolution of Bloom's framework and summarizes key research on automating question classification, highlighting methods, datasets, performance metrics, and current challenges.

2.1 *Bloom's taxonomy: Background and evolution*

Bloom's Taxonomy, introduced in 1956, classifies ed- ucational goals into three domains: cognitive (intellectual skills), affective (attitudes), and psychomotor (physical skills). The cognitive domain consists of six hierarchical levels—Knowledge, Comprehension, Application, Analysis, Synthesis, and Evaluation—ranging from lower- to higher-order thinking.

The Revised Bloom's Taxonomy as stated in [5] reorganized these into action-oriented levels: Recall, understand, apply, analyze, evaluate and create. Traditionally, mapping questions to Bloom's Taxonomy Levels (BTL) has been a manual and subjective process, relying on educators' judgment of the question's cognitive domain, the use of key action verbs (such as "define" for recall or "analyze" for higher-order thinking), the complexity of the content, the question type (e.g., multiple-choice for lower-order, essays for higher-order), and their own experience along with peer input.However, manual classification often led to inconsistencies and difficulty in targeting higher-order levels. To overcome this, automated classification systems were developed to enhance accuracy, consistency, and reduce workload.

2.2 *Early risk detection through predictive analytics: The course signals case at purdue*

At Purdue University, the *Course Signals* system employed predictive analytics to automatically classify students into academic risk categories—*Green* (low risk), *Yellow* (moderate risk), and *Red* (high risk)—based on LMS activity, grades, and background data. These classifications enabled instructors to provide timely, personalized interventions to students who were likely to struggle. As a result, students in courses using Course Signals were up to 12% more likely to successfully complete their courses compared to those in non-intervention sections [6]. This case study demonstrates how automated classification can enhance student outcomes by supporting early, data-informed instructional decisions.

3 TECHNIQUES USED IN AUTOMATIC QUESTION CLASSIFICATION

Automatic classification of questions involves four main stages:

(A) Question Collection
Questions are gathered from sources like exams, websites,and prior research. Each question is categorized based on Bloom's Taxonomy (BT) levels.

DOI: 10.1201/9781042017546-24

(B) Preprocessing

Text preprocessing prepares data for NLP tasks. Steps include:

1) Tokenization: Splits text into units [8–11] (e.g., "Have a good day" → "Have", "a", "good", "day").
2) Stop-word Removal: Eliminates common words [8,10] (e.g., "is", "the") to reduce noise.
3) Lowercasing: Standardizes all text to lowercase [12].
4) Parsing: Removes special characters to clean text [7,9].
5) Lemmatization: Converts words to their base form for consistency [4,9,19].
6) Padding: Normalizes sequence lengths for model input[12].

(C) Feature Extraction

Transforms text into numerical features using:

1) Bag-of-Words (BoW): Represents text based on word frequency [13,14].
2) POS Tagging: Assigns grammatical roles to words [5,13,14,19].
3) Word Embeddings: Uses Word2Vec [7,12,13] and GloVe [12] to capture semantic meaning.
4) TF-IDF: Weighs terms by frequency and uniqueness across documents [7,9].
5) Enhanced TF-IDF & EFTPOS-IDF: Incorporates POS tags and advanced weighting for improved feature selection.

(D) Classification

Processed and feature-extracted data is input to classification models (e.g., SVM, Naive Bayes, Neural Networks) to assign Bloom's levels.

4 EVALUATION METRICS

Evaluation metrics are crucial for determining the model performance. Accuracy measures overall correctness but can be misleading with imbalanced data. Precision and recall provide a more nuanced view—precision focuses on the relevance of positive predictions, while recall captures the amount of actual positives identified. The F1-score, as the harmonic mean of precision and recall, is particularly useful for imbalanced datasets. For regression tasks, the R^2 score indicates how much difference is there in the output used by the model. ROC-AUC evaluates the model's ability to distinguish between classes, and the confusion matrix offers a detailed summary of true and false positives and negatives, providing deeper insight into classification performance.

5 RESULTS AND DISCUSSIONS

Accuracy varied significantly across algorithms for classifying Bloom's Taxonomy questions. Lower-order levels (e.g., knowledge, comprehension) were classified more accurately due to simpler linguistic patterns. In contrast, higher-order levels (e.g., synthesis, evaluation) posed challenges due to complexity and overlap with other categories. Algorithms incorporating deeper semantic understanding and advanced NLP techniques achieved better performance, particularly in distinguishing higher-order levels. These findings highlight the need for sophisticated models to ensure reliable classification across all cognitive levels.

This study is based on a review of journal and conference articles published between 2001 and 2024. Related literature was identified through keyword-based searches in academic databases such as Google Scholar, IEEE Xplore, and SCOPUS.

Table 1 provides a comparative overview of notable works, summarizing their methodologies, performance outcomes, and key insights.

The chosen studies represent a diverse set of modeling approaches—including traditional machine learning, deep

Table 1. Summary of research works on bloom's taxonomy classification.

Study	Approach	Key Highlights and Results
Yuheng Li *et al.* [1]	BERT + traditional ML on 21,380 objectives Datasets: **Source**: 21,380 LOs from 5,558 courses, 10 faculties (Australianuniversity). **Labels**: 6 Bloom levels (multi-label).	F1 up to 0.95; Cohen's κ up to 0.93; high processing cost. **Cons:** Custom dataset, high computational cost, ambiguous labels, time-consuming annotation. **Pros:** High accuracy, supports educators,
Shaikh S, Daudpotta SM *et al.*[2]	Pretrained embeddings + question classification Dataset: **CLOs Dataset:** 828 entries (Sukkur IBA, Pakistan); faculty-verified; imbalanced (Understanding, Application dominant). **Questions Dataset:** 600 entries (Najran Univ., Saudi Arabia); expert-verified; balanced Bloom levels.	87% for questions; context-aware; small dataset.
Gani *et al.* [4]	CNN with BERT, RoBERTa, ELECTRA, etc. Datasets: 600 Bloom-labeled questions; used for embedding comparison.	**Cons:** Small, imbalanced datasets; **Pros:** High accuracy (86.2%) and F1-score; RoBERTa identified as optimal embedding; robust across Bloom's levels; more efficient than full LLM fine-tuning.
Ghalib and Hammad []	KNN, NB + feature selection Dataset: **Programming QA:** Exam questions + web sources	F1 = 0.898 (KNN + Mutual Info); small dataset.
Mohammed and Omar [7]	TF-IDF + Word2Vec Dataset: **Collected:** 141 open-ended questions from various sources. ***Yahya et al.***: 600 open-ended questions, balanced across 6 Bloom levels.	F1 = 89.7% on dataset-2; **Cons:** Small and limited datasets;tested only with KNN, LR, and SVM classifiers. **Pros:** Higher accuracy than TF-IDF;
Sebbaq and El Faddouli [8]	MTBERT-Attention with MTL, BERT, Co-Attention Datasets:	97.71% accuracy; outperforms baselines; verb ambiguity and dataset dependency.

(*continued*)

Table 1. Continued

Study	Approach	Key Highlights and Results
	Primary: 2400 LOs, 6 Bloom levels, balanced. **Auxiliary**: 2400 texts, 6 emotions, from Kaggle.	
Ifham *et al.* [9]	ANN on 141 questions Dataset: **Open-ended QA**: 141 questions from web/ publications; manually labeled across 6 Bloom levels (K:26, C:23, A:15, An:23, S:30, E:24).	ANN: 85.2%, SVM: 58.9%; **Cons:** Small dataset); manual labeling **Pros:** High accuracy (85.2%),
Sanskar Soni *et al.* [10]	TextConvoNet: 2D CNN Dataset: **SST-2**: Binary sentiment (Stanford); **Amazon**: Binary sentiment (reviews); 15K train / 5K test. **R8**: Multiclass (Reuters); 4937 train / 2175 test. **Airline**: Multiclass sentiment (tweets); 10K train / 3K test. **Covid Tweets**: Multiclass sentiment; 6K train / 1.5K test.	High accuracy, precision, recall, F1; slow training.
Zhang and Ran [11]	Contrastive learning + WordNet Dataset: **TREC**: 6-class question classification. **SST-1**: 5-class sentiment. **SST-2**: Binary sentiment (from SST-1). **Subj**: Subjective vs. objective. **MR**: Movie review sentiment. **CR**: Customer review sentiment.	Outperforms SOTA; complex and resource-heavy.
Sharma *et al.* [12]	T5, ConvNet1D, Siamese LSTM, BERT Dataset: **SQuAD 2.0**: QA pairs for question generation. **Yahya *et al.***: 600 questions for classification. **TREC**: 5500 questions for training.	96.1% similarity accuracy; automates question generation.
Lavanya and Sasikala [13]	DL model review (healthcare text) Dataset:**QA** • **SQuAD** – QA pairs from Wikipedia • **TREC QA** – TREC 6 & 50 versions. • **Quora** – 400K+ question pairs	**Cons:** Limited comparison with traditional ML; **Pros:** Comprehensive overview of deep learning in text classification;
Thomas and Chandra [14]	Random Forest for e-learning Dataset: Crawled from e-learning sites; labeled by difficulty (beginner, intermediate, advanced); varied sizes for accuracy testing.	Accuracy = 99.2%; small dataset; uneven across levels. **Cons:** Accuracy varies by cognitive level; **Pros:** Automates Bloom's classification, saving educators time..
Rawat *et al.* [15]	NLP + TF-IDF + SVM on exam Qs	Highlights subjectivity; recommends DL integration.
Osadi *et al.* [18]	Ensemble (rule + ML + WordNet) Dataset: **English**: **Classic 3** – 3,891 docs (CISI, CRAN, MED). **20 Newsgroups** – ~20K docs, 20 topics. **Arabic:** **Al-Khaleej** – 5,690 news articles, 4 categories.	82% accuracy; future: larger datasets, better features.
Gani *et al.* [19]	SVM + POS-tagged TF-IDF Dataset: **Dataset 1**: 181 questions **Dataset 2**: 415 questions (Computing, Social Sci., Business) **Dataset 3**: 600 questions→387 after BT verb filtering	Accuracy = 76.4%, F1 = 76.1%; manual verb labeling. **Cons:** Small, domain-specific datasets;limited to three classifiers (SVM, ANN, RF). **Pros:** Improved accuracy with ETFPOS-IDF.

learning, and transformer-based methods—offering a comparative view of their relative performance.

6 CONCLUSION

This paper explores the challenges of applying Bloom's Taxonomy (BT) in question classification (QC) for educational content. Key issues include the subjective nature of cognitive level classification, as individuals may interpret questions differently. Many questions span multiple BT levels, introducing ambiguity, and classification can vary across subjects due to contextual difference, while manually classifying large sets of questions is time-consuming, highlighting the need for automation. Inconsistencies across different versions of BT and the absence of standardized guidelines furnish to the variability. Addressing these challenges requires domain expertise, clear protocols, and thoughtful implementation. Deep learning techniques such as CNNs and RNNs, along with automation, offer promising solutions to enhance QC.

ACKNOWLEDGEMENT

The authors gratefully acknowledge all who supported this research.

REFERENCES

[1] Li, Y., Rakovic, M., Poh, B.X., Gašević, D. and Chen, G., (2022). Automatic classification of learning objectives based on Bloom's Taxonomy. In: *Proceedings of the 15th International Conference on Educational Data Mining (EDM 2022). International Educational Data Mining Society*.

[2] Shaikh, S., Daudpotta, S.M. and Imran, A.S., (2021). Bloom's learning outcomes' automatic classification using LSTM and pretrained word embeddings. *IEEE Access*, 9, pp.117887–117909. https://doi.org/10.1109/ACCESS.2021.3105247

[3] Jones, K.O., Harland, J., Reid, J.M. and Bartlett, R., (2009). Relationship between examination questions and Bloom's taxonomy. In: *2009 39th IEEE Frontiers in Education Conference*. San Antonio, TX, USA, 18–21 October 2009. IEEE, pp. 1–6. https://doi.org/10.1109/FIE.2009.5350625

[4] Gani, M.O., Ayyasamy, R.K., Sangodiah, A. and Fui, Y.T., (2023). Bloom's Taxonomy-based exam question classification: The outcome of CNN and optimal pre-trained word embedding technique. *Education and Information Technologies*, 28(12), pp.15893–15914. https://doi.org/10.1007/s10639-023-11964-9.

[5] Anderson, L.W. and Krathwohl, D.R. (eds.), (2001). A Taxonomy for Learning, *Teaching, and Assessing: A Revision of Bloom's Taxonomy of Educational Objectives*. New York: Longman.

[6] Arnold, K.E. and Pistilli, M.D., (2012). Course signals at Purdue: Using learning analytics to increase student success. In: *Proceedings of the 2nd International Conference on Learning Analytics and Knowledge (LAK '12)*. Vancouver, BC, Canada, 29 April–2 May 2012. New York: ACM, pp. 267–270. https://doi.org/10.1145/2330601.2330666

[7] Mohammed, M. and Omar, N., (2020). Question classification based on Bloom's taxonomy cognitive domain using modified TF-IDF and word2vec. *PLOS ONE*, 15(3), p.e0230442. https://doi.org/10.1371/journal.pone.0230442

[8] Sebbaq, H., 2023. MTBERT-Attention: An explainable BERT model based on multi-task learning for cognitive text classification. *Scientific African*, 21, p.e017.

[9] Ifham, M., Banujan, K., Kumara, B.S. and Wijeratne, P.M., (2022). Automatic classification of questions based on Bloom's Taxonomy using artificial neural network. In: *2022 International Conference on Decision Aid Sciences and Applications (DASA)*. IEEE, pp. 311–315.

[10] Soni, S., Chouhan, S.S. and Rathore, S.S., (2023). TextConvoNet: A convolutional neural network based architecture for text classification. *Applied Intelligence*, 53(11), pp.14249–14268.

[11] Zhang, S. and Ran, N., 2024. Contrastive learning based on linguistic knowledge and adaptive augmentation for text classification. *Knowledge-Based Systems*, 300, p.112189.

[12] Sharma, H., Mathur, R., Chintala, T., Dhanalakshmi, S. and Senthil, R., (2023). An effective deep learning pipeline for improved question classification into Bloom's Taxonomy's domains. *Education and Information Technologies*, 28(5), pp.5105–5145.

[13] Lavanya, P.M. and Sasikala, E., (2021). Deep learning techniques on text classification using natural language processing (NLP) in social healthcare networks: A comprehensive survey. In: *2021 3rd International Conference on Signal Processing and Communication (ICSPC)*. IEEE, pp. 603–609.

[14] Thomas, B. and Chandra, J., (2020). The effect of Bloom's Taxonomy on Random Forest classifier for cognitive level identification of e-content. In: *2020 International Conference on Emerging Trends in Information Technology and Engineering (ic-ETITE)*. IEEE, pp. 1–6.

[15] Rawat, A., Kumar, S. and Samant, S.S., (2023). A systematic review of question classification techniques based on Bloom's Taxonomy. In: *2023 14th International Conference on Computing Communication and Networking Technologies (ICCCNT)*. IEEE, pp. 1–7.

[16] Makhlouf, K., Amouri, L., Chaabane, N. and Nahla, E.H., (2020). Exam questions classification based on Bloom's Taxonomy: Approaches and techniques. In: *2020 2nd International Conference on Computer and Information Sciences (ICCIS)*. IEEE, pp. 1–6.

[17] Rawat, A. and Samant, S.S., (2022). Comparative analysis of transformer-based models for question answering. In: *2022 2nd International Conference on Innovative Sustainable Computational Technologies (CISCT)*. IEEE, pp. 1–6..

[18] Osadi, K., Fernando, M.G. and Welgama, W., (n.d.) Ensemble classifier based approach for classification of examination questions into Bloom's Taxonomy cognitive levels. *International Journal of Computer Applications*.

[19] Gani, M.O., Ayyasamy, R.K., Alhashmi, S.M., Sangodiah, A. and Fui, Y.T., (2022). ETFPOS-IDF: A novel term weighting scheme for examination question classification based on Bloom's Taxonomy. *IEEE Access*, 10, pp.132777–132785.

Technology for a Resilient Future – Vincent , Moorthy and Dasari (Eds)
© 2027 The Author(s), ISBN: 978-1-041-39070-1

Triggers to the Diffusion of Robotics in MSMEs: A Technological Innovation Investigation

Pallawi Baldeo Sangode
N. L. Dalmia Institute of Management Studies and Research, Mumbai, India

Ganeshkumar Rede
Symbiosis Institute of Business Management, Symbiosis International Deemed University, Pune, India

ABSTRACT: The diffusion of innovation, such as robotics, and its adoption as a process in any function differs depending on the type of organization. Enterprises, especially Micro, Small, and Medium Enterprises (MSME), are hesitant to capitalize on the advantages of automation for various reasons. As per the 'Diffusion Theory of Innovation", various technological factors for robotics adoption (TFRA), such as comparative edge, compatibility, complexity, observability, and trialability. This article investigates the triggers for the diffusion of these factors in adopting robotic technology for MSMEs. The DEMATEL technique is used to reveal the cause and effect relationships between these elements which involve the input of the MSME stakeholders. Comparative advantage, compatibility, Observation, and trialability are considered causal variables; complexity is an effect that triggers the diffusion of robotics.

Keywords: Robotics, innovations, compatibility, Observation, trialability, DEMATEL

1 INTRODUCTION

The MSME sector holds significant importance in driving India's social and economic progress; however, it's crucial for them to embrace technology for sustainable growth. The global IT industry has been flourishing, which has caused the economy to grow at a rate never seen before. MSMEs, or small and medium-sized enterprises, need to keep up with the latest developments in technology. Companies that want to stay at the top level must adopt technology and sustainability. The most effective way to implement resource utilization is through robotic automation [1]. However, the robotics business has always been dominated by huge, intricate equipment that needs a substantial upfront investment and in-house expertise to maintain [2]. Hence, it might be difficult to comprehend and implement the idea, especially for MSMEs with limited capital. It is significant that MSMEs have generally been hesitant to capitalize on the advantages of automation, as a sluggish adoption rate frequently keeps companies from developing the resilience and efficiency required to stay competitive [3]. The benefits of robotic automation are deskilling and uniformity in quality. Robotic automation may lead to higher output and improved quality for MSMEs [4].

By utilizing robotic automation, MSMEs may free up staff members' time to focus on higher-value tasks and generating high-quality work [5]. Robotics use may result in a variety of productivity gains, providing a competitive edge in a number of areas. Robots in MSMEs allow for the economic completion of complex jobs, increasing the company's competitiveness. They are especially adept in jobs involving production, logistics, and handling of commodities. Robotic technology also makes it possible for human workers to collaborate in workplaces and respond quickly to demand fluctuations [6].

Though the benefits of robotics to MSMEs are numerable, diffusing robotics technology in a small enterprise is challenging. According to the study [7], technological, organizational and environmental considerations underpin the use of robotics by any business.

With this background, this work aims at investigating how robots can be incorporated into MSMEs. For this, the technical considerations that primarily pertain to robot innovation as new technology is investigated. Everett Rogers' Diffusion of Innovations theory [8] offers a well-researched framework for determining the technological variables that could have affected an innovation's success or failure as comparative advantage, compatibility, complexity, observability, and trialability. Figure 1 broadly explains the TFRA framework for MSME.

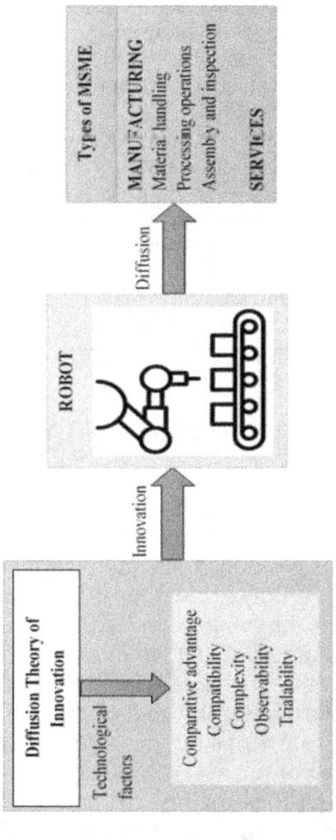

Figure 1. TFRA framework for MSME [7], [8], [16].

DOI: 10.1201/9781042017546-25

2 LITERATURE REVIEW

A plethora of research has been done in the past to identify the barriers or challenges to the adaptation of advanced technology like robotics. Very limited research has been found to investigate the enablers to the diffusion of robotics in different functions of manufacturing and service MSME. The reasoning features of the updated technology implemented by the firm identified in the past literature are comparative advantages, compatibility, complexity, observability, and trialability—are the primary subjects of technological considerations.

Studies say that businesses that have a comparative advantage use innovations when they see the potential advantages of doing so [7]. Robot innovation provides comparative benefits over traditional systems because of its low investment costs, excellent safety, ergonomics, and adaptability [16]. The degree to which innovation and current technology coexist is indicated by compatibility. At this point, traditional industrial robots and collaborative robots work well together and complement each other's technology in use by businesses [8]. Adoption is often seen to be negatively connected with complexity, which is defined as the extent of creativity and newness that is tough to implement and understand [13]. In MSME, lack of skills in adopting technology makes the innovation utilization scenario complex. Observability is the extent to which the Robot or its effects are obvious to other potential adopters. Enterprises may not adopt the technology if they have not observed it being used by others in the industry [17]. Trialability is the level to which robot expertise can be tested in a restricted setting. Robot technology that can be easily tested by the enterprise before being completely implemented are more likely to be adopted since they don't need as much time, effort, or money to execute [18].

Table 1 gives the details of the studies that identified these technical factors for the adoption of robots in MSMEs.

Table 1. TFRA in MSME through a rigorous literature review.

TFRA	Explanation	Author
Comparative advantage (T1)	Refers to the fact that businesses use innovations when they see the possible advantages of doing so.	[7], [8], [9], [10], [16]
Compatibility (T2)	Refers to the co-existence of Traditional industrial system and collaborative robots	[7], [8], [11], [12], [16]
Complexity (T3)	Refers to the extent of complexity in understanding and utilizing innovation	[7], [8], [13], [14], [15], [16]
Observability (T4)	Refers to the extent to which consequences of an innovation are practicable to others	[7], [8], [16], [17]
Trialability (T5)	Refers to ease of the enterprises to conduct on-site trials	[7], [s8], [16], [18]

3 DATA COLLECTION AND ANALYSIS

3.1 *Data collection*

The five TFRA identified through literature review were shared to seven experts, positioned at managerial level, from the MSMEs. Utilizing a limited number of professionals can expedite the problem-solution process without significantly compromising the accuracy of the outcomes, as demonstrated in various applications of DEMATEL[19], [20]. Each expert established the interrelationships amongst the TFRA by giving rating between 1 to 5 (1 being "low degree of impact" and 5 being "hight degree of impact"). All the experts belonged to the managerial designations of micro enterprises of MSMEs. Responses were collected seperately from each of the experts. The responses are used for DEMATEL analysis to structurally model the factors by analysing the cause and the impact association among them for adoption of robotics.

3.2 *DEMATEL*

Step 1: Generate the direct relationship matrix.

The direct relation matrix is shown in Table 2 and has a similar form to the pairwise similarity matrix of specialists. The average responses for each interrelationship of TFRA is calculated.

Table 2. Direct relation matrix.

TFRA	T1	T2	T3	T4	T5
	0.00	2.14	3.86	1.29	1.43
V2	1.43	0.00	5.00	2.14	2.86
V3	1.29	1.14	0.00	1.14	2.86
V4	1.86	1.29	5.00	0.00	3.57
V5	2.00	3.00	4.71	1.86	0.00

For each, row and column association, the simple average of the responses of the seven experts were taken.

Step 2: Calculate the normalized direct-relation matrix

The process of normalization consists in determining the addition of both the rows and columns of the matrix. Let p denote the maximum value among the row and column sums. To normalize the direct-relation matrix, each of its elements is divided by p, as illustrated in Table 3.

Table 3. The normalized direct-relation matrix.

TFRA	T1	T2	T3	T4	T5
T1	0	0.115	0.208	0.069	0.077
T2	0.077	0	0.269	0.115	0.154
T3	0.069	0.062	0	0.062	0.154
T4	0.1	0.069	0.269	0	0.192
T5	0.108	0.162	0.254	0.1	0

$$p = \max\left\{ \max \sum_{j=1}^{n} x_{ij}, \quad \sum_{i=1}^{n} x_{ij} \right\}$$

$$N = \frac{1}{p} * X$$

Step 3: Calculate the total relation matrix

The calculation of the fuzzy total-relation matrix after generating the stabilized matrix is as follows:

$$T = \lim_{p \to +\infty} \left(N^1 + N^2 + \ldots + N^p \right)$$

The process involves creating a 5 × 5 identity matrix, detracting it from the normalized matrix, then reversing the result. Multiplication of the resultant matrix with the normalized matrix gives the total relation matrix as shown in Table 4.

$$\mathrm{T} = \mathrm{N} \times (I - N)^{-1}$$

Table 4. THE total relation matrix.

TFRA	T1	T2	T3	T4	T5
T1	0.074	0.187	0.359	0.137	0.193
T2	0.168	0.109	0.461	0.197	0.292
T3	0.126	0.131	0.151	0.118	0.23
T4	0.19	0.179	0.465	0.095	0.324
T5	0.194	0.25	0.452	0.186	0.159

Step 4: Set the threshold value

The threshold of relations can be calculated on the basis of the average value of the matrix T. After calculating the threshold intensity, the entire range of values in the matrix T that are less than the number of zeroes are indicated as the level of zero indicating that no causal relationship as illustrated above is obtained. Although the average of total relation matrix was used as a threshold which is generally adopted when conducting a DEMATEL research.

In this investigation, the threshold is 0.217. The values of matrix T less than 0.217 are all set to zero indicating that the underlying relationship above is not tested. The significant relations model is provided in Table 5.

Table 5. Total- similarity matrix by considering the tolerance value

TFRA	T1	T2	T3	T4	T5
T1	0	0	0.359	0	0
T2	0	0	0.461	0	0.292
T3	0	0	0	0	0.23
T4	0	0	0.465	0	0.324
T5	0	0.25	0.452	0	0

Step 5: Final output and create a causative figure

The next step is to take the summation of every row and column in T (step 3). To calculate the sum of rows (D) and columns (R), use the following formula:

$$D = \sum_{j=1}^{n} T_{ij}$$

$$R = \sum_{i=1}^{n} T_{ij}$$

Combined D and Rn and difference between D-R can in turn be determined with the help of D and R where D+R is the total impact of aspect i and D-R is the cumulative impact that factor i has to the system.

Table 6 presents the final results.

Table 6. The final output.

	R	D	D+R	D-R
T1	0.753	0.95	1.702	0.197
T2	0.855	1.227	2.082	0.372
T3	1.888	0.755	2.643	-1.132
T4	0.733	1.253	1.986	0.52
T5	1.198	1.241	2.438	0.043

The important relations model is depicted in Figure 2. The given model is presented in a diagram, according to which the total of D and R were lined on the X axis and (D-R) on the vertical axis. The coordinate system defines the location and communication of every factor with a point of the coordinates (D + R, D - R).

Figure 3 represents the relationship diagram of the TFRA.

Step 6: Read the results

In accordance with the diagram and table above, all the components can be assessed in terms of the following areas:

The level of relevance each aspect has in the overall system is reflected in the X axis (D + R). D + R in other words is the result of aspect i on the whole structure and the effect that other parts of the system have on the factor. Based on significance, Complexity ranks top, followed by Trialability, Compatibility, Observability, and Comparative advantage, in terms of effect.

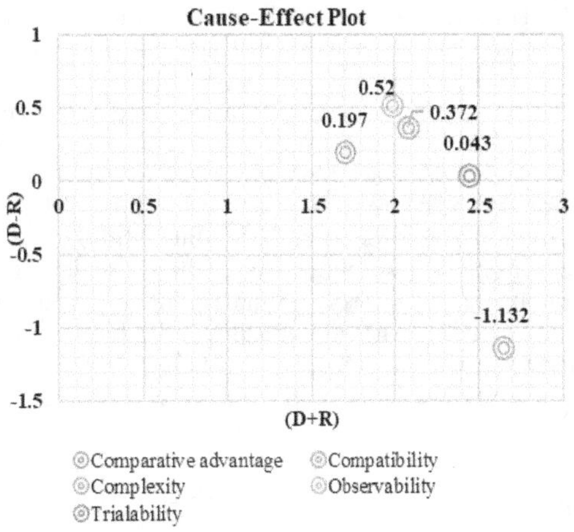

Figure 2. Cause-effect diagram.

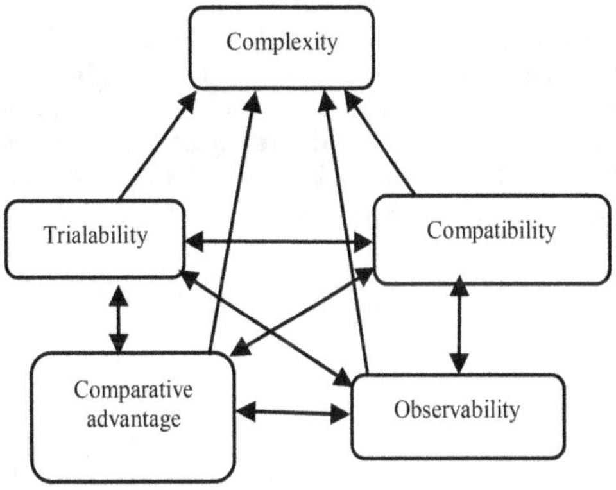

Figure 3. Cause-result relationship.

The Y-axis (D-R) shows the extent of the influence of a factor on the system. In general, a positive D-R value reflects a causative variable, whereas a negative D-R value indicates an effect. In this study, comparative advantages, compatibility, observability, and trialability are considered causative variables, whereas complexity is treated as an outcome.

4 DISCUSSION

In adopting robotics in MSMEs, the prioritization of such factors as complexity, trialability, compatibility, observability and comparative advantage may differ depending on the context specificity and enterprise need. The DEMATEL analysis however reveals that complexity comes first because it has a great influence on robotics' feasibility and success.

Integration of robotics in MSMEs is technically, operationally, and organizationally complex. Success in implementation demands that the complexity associated with advanced robotic systems, integration with infrastructure, and operational and maintenance skills be appropriately assessed and managed. All components should be capable of running trials to ensure that the robot solutions are suitable and the cost-benefit ratios are met. Compatibility is needed to integrate with the existing processes and systems, and observability is meant for real-time monitoring of performance metrics. Adoption of robotics gives a competitive advantage to MSMEs since it is affordable and efficient; it improves quality, and the innovation potential and market differentiation are also considered. From an MSME perspective, Comparative Advantage, Compatibility, Observability, and Trialability will serve as causal factors leading the adoption process, while Complexity will emerge as a resultant of their interaction. This is an effect leading to further investigation. Then, compatibility is how MSME ascertains whether robotics fits within the existing operations and resources of the establishment before considering them. Once it is considered possible, the MSME will design observability mechanisms that will monitor and measure the impact and results of the adoption of the technology. A process of Trialability follows, where the MSME can apply the solutions on a smaller scale before total application and save on risks and uncertainties. At each of these stages, complexity emerges as a result, in the face of great challenges along the path of aligning technology with existing systems, organizational change, and resource constraints.

5 CONCLUSION AND LIMITATIONS

The study concludes that, by improving the compatibility, trialability, comparative advantage and observability, the complexity in the adoption of technological innovation- Robot, can be reduced. Understanding and taming the complexities will allow the MSME to fully utilize robotics technologies for their competitiveness and operational efficiency. This study was limited to the technological factors for robotic adoption. Other factors like environmental and organizational factors can be further investigated. Data collected was not confined to one specific type of MSME, which might add some variation in the responses.

REFERENCES

[1] Flechsig, F. Anslinger, and R. Lasch, (2022). "Robotic process automation in purchasing and supply management: A multiple case study on potentials, barriers, and implementation," *Journal of Purchasing and Supply Management*, vol. 28, no. 1, p. 100718.

[2] M. Wilson, (2014). Implementation of robot systems: An Introduction to robotics, automation, and successful systems integration in manufacturing. Butterworth-Heinemann.

[3] H. Nadi, K.A. Ahshan, S. Rahman, and M.R. Sofin, (2024). "The role of artificial intelligence in business management: The future of small and medium-sized enterprise," in *Utilizing AI and Smart Technology to Improve Sustainability in Entrepreneurship*, pp. 117–133, IGI Global.

[4] T. Shakya, M. Sharma, S. Kathuria, N. Yamsani, R. Singh, and P. Negi, (2023), "Micro, small & medium enterprises advancement with artificial intelligence and robots," in *2023 IEEE World Conference on Applied Intelligence and Computing (AIC)*, pp. 783–788. IEEE.

[5] M. Kumar, R.D. Raut, S.K. Mangla, A. Ferraris, and V.K. Choubey, (2022). "The adoption of artificial intelligence powered workforce management for effective revenue growth of micro, small, and medium scale enterprises (MSMEs)," Production Planning & Control, pp. 1–17.

[6] Mannan and S. Khurana, (2012). "Enablers and Barriers for Introduction of Robotics as an AMT in the Indian Industries (Case of SME's)," 2012. [Online]. Available: https://doi.org/10.13140/2.1.2625.5368

[7] Liu and J. Cao, (2022). "Determinants of collaborative robots innovation adoption in small and medium-sized enterprises: An empirical study in China," *Applied Sciences*, vol. 12, no. 19, p. 10085. [Online]. Available: https://doi.org/10.3390/app121910085.

[8] "Rogers Five Factors." (2024). Think Insights [Online]. Available: https://thinkinsights.net/strategy/rogers-five-factors/. [Accessed: June 4, 2024]

[9] Distanont, (2020). "The role of innovation in creating a competitive advantage," *Kasetsart Journal of Social Sciences*, vol. 41, no. 1, pp. 15–21.

[10] M. Somale, (2021). "Comparative advantage in innovation and production," *American Economic Journal: Macroeconomics*, vol. 13, no. 3, pp. 357–396.

[11] Ramiller, N.C. (1994). Perceived compatibility of information technology innovations among secondary adopters: Toward a reassessment. *Journal of Engineering and Technology Management*, 11(1), 1–23.

[12] Piruncharoen, D., Lawsirirat, C., Pandejpong, T., and Chandrachai, A. (2011). Evaluating exploitation strategy for technological innovation: Cost or compatibility. In *2011 Proceedings of PICMET'11: Technology Management in the Energy Smart World (PICMET)* (pp. 1–9). IEEE.

[13] W. Li, X. Guo, and D. Cao, (2021). "The complexity of technological innovation decision-making in emerging industries," *Complexity*, vol. 2021, no. 1, pp. 3611921.

[14] P. Andriani, (2011). "Complexity and innovation," in *The SAGE Handbook of Complexity and Management*, pp. 454–470.

[15] Consoli and P.P. Patrucco, (2011). "Complexity and the coordination of technological knowledge: the case of innovation platforms," in *Handbook on the Economic Complexity of Technological Change*, Edward Elgar Publishing.

[16] G. Nagra and R. Gopal, (2014). "A study of factors affecting diffusion of innovation," *International Journal of Business Management & Research (IJBMR)*, vol. 4, no. 1, pp. 15–24.

[17] S. Jayashree, M.N. Hassan Reza, C.A.N. Malarvizhi, H. Maheswari, Z. Hosseini, and A. Kasim, (2021). "The impact of technological innovation on Industry 4.0 implementation and sustainability: An empirical study on Malaysian small and medium sized enterprises," *Sustainability*, vol. 13, no. 18, p. 10115.

[18] S.S. Al-Gahtani, (2003). "Computer technology adoption in Saudi Arabia: Correlates of perceived innovation attributes," *Information Technology for Development*, vol. 10, no. 1, pp. 57–69.

[19] A. Kobryń, (2017). *"Dematel as a Weighting Method in Multi-Criteria Decision Analysis,"* vol. 12, pp. 153–167, https://doi.org/10.22367/MCDM.2017.12.11

[20] H. Taherdoost and M. Madanchian, (2003). "Understanding applications and best practices of DEMATEL: A method for prioritizing key factors in multi-criteria decision-making," *Journal of Management Science & Engineering Research*, vol. 6, no. 2, https://doi.org/10.30564/jmser.v6i2.5634

Technology for a Resilient Future – Vincent , Moorthy and Dasari (Eds)
 ISBN: 978-1-041-39070-1

Autonomous Navigation Without Odometry: A ROS-Based Encoderless AGV Using Hector SLAM

Mandar More, Vishal Bhagwat, Manisha Lande, and Sachin Bhosle
Department of Mechanical Engineering, VPKBIET Baramati, Pune, Maharashtra, India

Atul More
Department of Mechanical Engineering, SVPM's ITE, Malegaon(Bk), Baramati, Pune, Maharashtra, India

ABSTRACT: This project presents the design and validation of a low-cost, encoderless Automated Guided Vehicle (AGV) capable of autonomous navigation using a LiDAR-based Simultaneous Localization and Mapping (SLAM) approach. The system utilizes Hector SLAM within the ROS Noetic framework, achieving localization and mapping without wheel odometry or external navigation infrastructure. This makes it well-suited for dynamic and unstructured indoor environments such as warehouses, laboratories, and research facilities. Developed with open-source tools and commercially available components, the AGV integrates a Raspberry Pi 4 (Ubuntu 20.04), RPLiDAR A1 for 360° 2D laser scanning, L298N motor driver, 12V 30 RPM DC gear motors, and a 12V 20Ah battery pack for extended operation. Comprehensive Gazebo simulations and physical testing confirm robust localization, accurate mapping, and stable path tracking even without encoder feedback. The results demonstrate efficient resource utilization, scalability, and consistent performance in dynamic indoor settings. The proposed system provides a flexible and accessible platform for education, research, and low-cost industrial automation, with future expansion potential through IMU sensor fusion, computer vision, and cloud-based monitoring.

Keywords: Automated Guided Vehicle, SLAM, Hector SLAM, ROS, LiDAR, Encoderless Navigation, Indoor Robotics, Embedded Systems

1 INTRODUCTION

The growing integration of intelligent robotics in manufacturing and logistics has increased the demand for adaptable, infrastructure-free autonomous systems. Traditional AGVs, reliant on fixed-path navigation methods like magnetic strips or QR markers, suffer from low adaptability and require frequent reconfiguration. Moreover, their dependence on odometry introduces positional drift from wheel slippage or misalignment, reducing long-term accuracy [1], [2], [3].

Recent advancements in SLAM (Simultaneous Localization and Mapping), especially LiDAR-based methods, enable autonomous robots to map and localize without external aids [4], [5]. Among these, Hector SLAM stands out for its lightweight computation and independence from wheel encoders or IMUs. Unlike Gmapping or Cartographer, which rely on odometry or inertial data, Hector SLAM uses high-frequency laser scan matching for real-time localization, making it ideal for embedded platforms like Raspberry Pi [6], [7], [8].

Studies highlight Hector SLAM's effectiveness in constrained environments. Yong et al. combined it with a dynamic A* planner for better obstacle negotiation [1], while Ma et al. used multi-LiDAR setups for enhanced map accuracy [2]. Weichen et al. improved trajectory alignment using ICP [3], and Wijaya et al. optimized occupancy grid mapping for limited-resource systems [9]. Graph-based SLAM techniques have also been explored to enhance loop closure and adaptability [10], [11], [12], while Barbosa et al. developed topological mapping for real-time environmental adaptation [11]. Hector SLAM's efficiency and stability make it valuable for dynamic applications such as warehouses and hospitals [13], [14].

Advances in affordable embedded computing—multi-core ARM processors, GPU-enabled boards, and ROS support—have further enabled SLAM-based AGVs without industrial hardware. Open-source tools like Gazebo and RViz also facilitate scalable testing before deployment [15], [16].

This research presents a low-cost AGV using LiDAR-based Hector SLAM for encoderless autonomous navigation in dynamic indoor environments. Built with open-source tools and validated through simulations and experiments, the system offers a modular, expandable platform for integrating IMUs, deep-learning object detection, or cloud-based IoT monitoring [17], [18].

2 SYSTEM DESIGN

The AGV platform was constructed using off-the-shelf, low-power hardware suitable for mobile robotics. The key hardware components include:

- **Computing Unit:** Raspberry Pi 4 (4GB RAM) [15]
- **Motion Control:** Arduino Uno interfaced with L298N dual H-bridge motor driver
- **Actuation:** Two 12V DC gear motors (30 RPM)
- **Sensing:** RPLiDAR A1 (360°, 2D scanning with 12m range) [16]
- **Power:** 12V, 20Ah battery system

The LiDAR is mounted at the center front of the robot chassis to provide a comprehensive field of view. The chassis itself follows a differential drive configuration with static caster wheels at the rear for support [17].

3 SOFTWARE ARCHITECTURE

The control system is developed in ROS Noetic on Ubuntu 20.04 [18]. It includes:

- **SLAM Node:** hector_mapping for real-time scan matching and map generation [6], [7]
- **Navigation Stack:**
  - **Global Planner:** A* search algorithm [19]
  - **Local Planner:** Dynamic Window Approach (DWA) for short-term trajectory optimization [20]
- **Visualization:** RViz for monitoring laser scans, maps, and robot pose [21]
- **Simulation:** Gazebo for realistic testing before deployment [22]

DOI: 10.1201/9781042017546-26

Coordinate transformations among map, odom, base_link, and laser frames are handled using ROS tf utilities [23]. Since the AGV operates without odometry input, Hector SLAM directly estimates the map → base_link transform, eliminating reliance on wheel encoders [24].

4 KINEMATIC MODEL

The AGV's motion is modeled using the unicycle model equations for differential drive robots [25]:

$$x_{t+1} = x_t + v\cos(\theta_t)\Delta t$$

$$y_{t+1} = y_t + v\sin(\theta_t)\Delta t$$

$$\theta_{t+1} = \theta_t + \omega\Delta t$$

Where v and ω are the commanded linear and angular velocities respectively, and Δt is the time step.

Without encoders, actual displacement is inferred via command signals and matched against SLAM-based position estimates for closed-loop control [26].

5 EVALUATION PROTOCOL

5.1 *Testing was conducted in two phases:*

Simulation in Gazebo: Implemented using warehouse-style and corridor environments with dynamic obstacles [22], [27].

Physical Trials: Performed in a 10 × 10 m indoor testbed featuring variable obstacle densities.

Key performance metrics included mapping error (against ground truth), localization drift, navigation success rate, replanning latency, and energy and thermal performance. SLAM benchmarking compared Hector SLAM, Gmapping, and Cartographer under identical input data and configurations [6], [10], [13].

6 RESULT AND DISCUSSION

1. **Mapping and Localization**
   - The AGV achieved a relative mapping error of 0.44%, indicating high fidelity in occupancy grid construction.
   - In structured environments, localization drift remained within 0.11 ± 0.03 meters, whereas drift increased to 0.35 ± 0.12 meters in feature-scarce spaces.
2. **Navigation and Obstacle Avoidance**
   - The AGV maintained a maximum linear velocity of 0.2 m/s.
   - Path replanning latency averaged below 1 second, enabling real-time adaptation.
   - Success rates declined with increasing obstacle density:
     - obstacles/m^2: **98% success**
     - obstacles/m^2: **92% success**
     - 0.5 obstacles/m^2: **81% success**

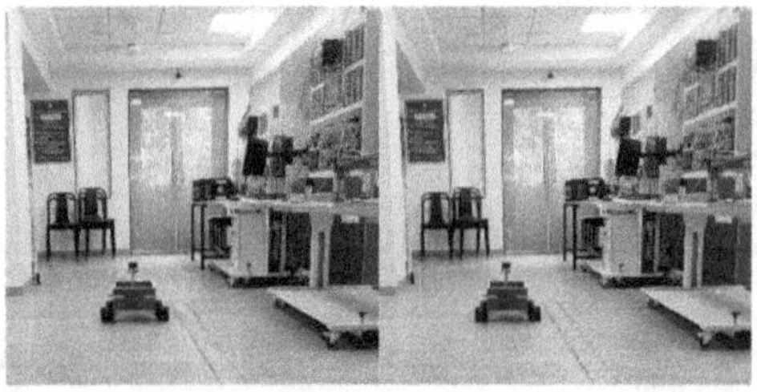

Figure 1. AGV With 0.1/m^2 Obstacle.

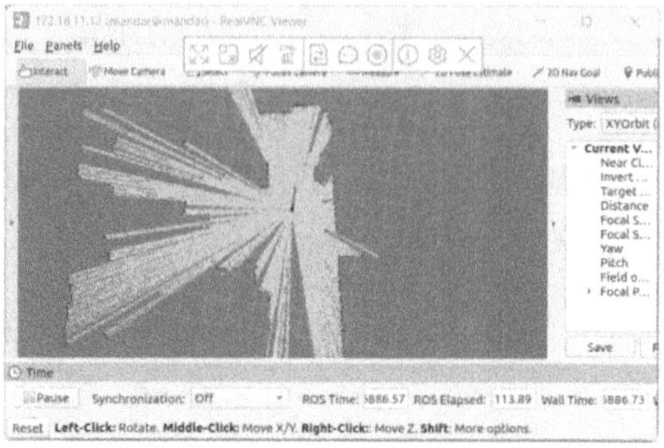

Figure 2. Map generated in the RviZ with the help of Hector SLAM with Obstacle Detraction for 0.1/m^2 Obstacle.

Figure 3. AGV With 0.3/m^2 Obstacle.

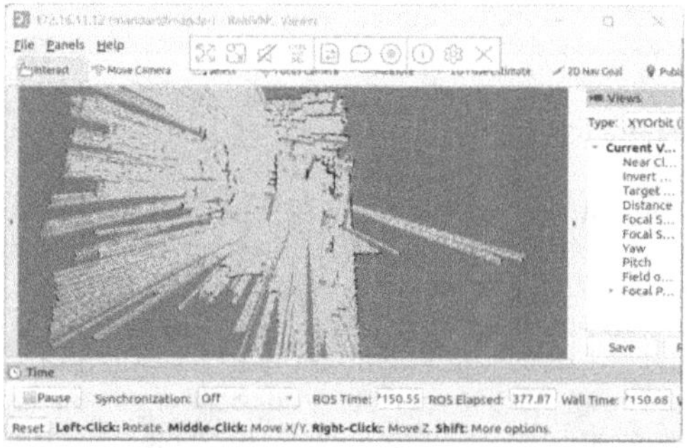

Figure 4. Map generated in the RviZ with the help of Hector SLAM with Obstacle Detraction for 0.3/m^2 Obstacle.

Figure 5. AGV With 0.5/m^2 Obstacle.

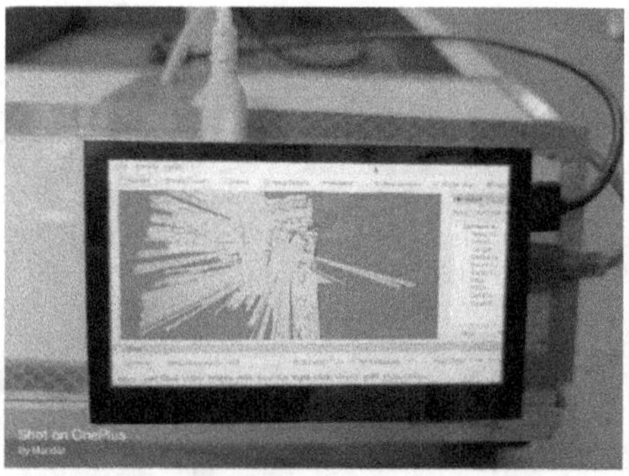

Figure 6. Map generated in the RviZ with the help of Hector SLAM with Obstacle Detraction for 0.5/m^2 Obstacle.

Table 1. Success rate vs obstacle density

Obstacle Density (per m^2)	Success Rate (%)	Number of Collisions
0.1	98%	0
0.3	92%	2
0.5	81%	5

Increasing obstacle density leads to a reduced navigation success rate and a higher collision frequency.

- Figures 1–6 depict AGV navigation and SLAM-generated maps under varying obstacle densities—red indicates detected obstacles, white denotes free space, and grey represents mapped areas.
- At low density, the AGV navigates with near-perfect accuracy; at moderate density, minor navigational deviations occur; and at high density, performance declines significantly due to sensor occlusion, restricted maneuvering space, and response delays.
- Future improvements should focus on enhanced SLAM algorithms, predictive environment modeling, and more advanced motion planning strategies.

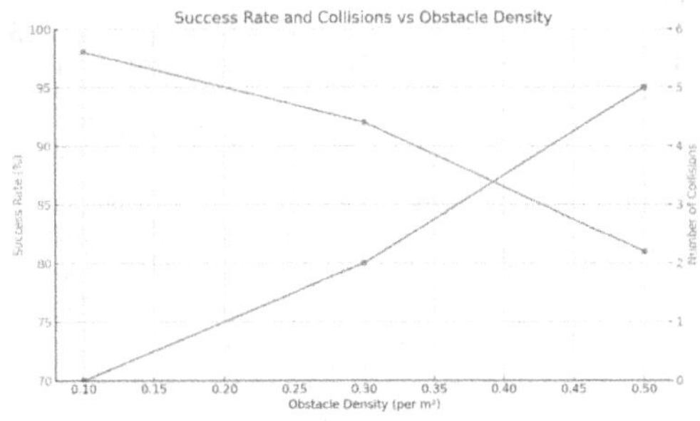

Figure 7. Success Rate vs Obstacle Density vs Collisions.

3. **Embedded Performance**

Table 2. SLAM algorithm performance comparison.

Algorithm	CPU (%)	RAM (MB)	Update Rate (Hz)
Hector SLAM	72 ± 3	1200	4.8
Gmapping	85 ± 5	1800	3.2
Cartographer	91 ± 4	2200	2.1

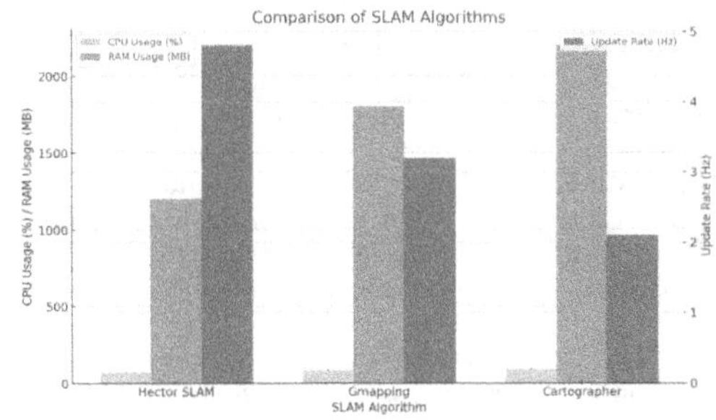

Figure 8. SLAM algorithm performance comparison.

- CPU usage for Hector SLAM averaged 72% on Raspberry Pi 4.
- RAM utilization was approximately 1200 MB during mapping and navigation.
- Velocity slippage ranged from 7.5% at low speed to 12% at peak speed.
- Raspberry Pi temperatures rose by +12°C during 3-hour operations, remaining within safe thermal thresholds.

4. **SLAM Benchmarking**

ANOVA Analysis

An ANOVA test ($F = 8.92$, $p < 0.01$) confirms significant performance differences between SLAM algorithms.

Tukey Test Results:

- Hector vs Gmapping: $p = 0.003$
- Hector vs Cartographer: $p = 0.001$ → Hector SLAM shows statistically superior performance.

Error Modeling

Mapping errors fit a Weibull distribution (Shape $k = 2.1$, Scale $\lambda = 0.18$) with $R^2 = 0.94$, indicating high accuracy in modeling error behavior. This helps in predicting and minimizing future errors.

5. **Real-World Trials and Statistical Modeling**

- In corridor navigation, the AGV achieved an 88% goal completion rate.
- A payload test (5 kg) demonstrated stable transport over 3.2 hours at 0.3 m/s.
- Error distribution followed a Weibull pattern ($k = 2.1$, $\lambda = 0.18$, $R^2 = 0.94$), confirming consistency in mapping deviations.

6. **Cost Analysis**

Table 3 Cost and Operational Trade-Offs

Feature	Proposed AGV	Commercial AGV
Cost	₹27,850	₹6,50,000+
Accuracy	0.15 m	0.08 m
Energy Use	5.2 W	6.8 W
Setup Time	15 mins	>2 hours
Compatibility	Open-source	Vendor-locked

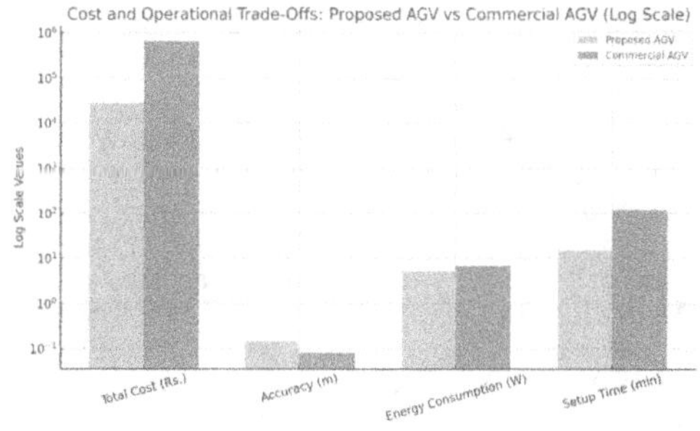

Figure 9. Cost and operational trade-offs.

The proposed AGV offers a highly cost-effective solution at \$204, compared to commercial counterparts priced around \$7500. It features a faster setup (15 minutes vs. over 2 hours), lower power consumption (5.2 W vs. 6.8 W), and simplified maintenance due to its modular, encoder-less design. Although slightly less accurate (0.15 m vs. 0.08 m), it provides broad compatibility with any LiDAR sensor, avoiding vendor lock-in. This makes it ideal for educational, prototyping, and light industrial applications, where cost, flexibility, and ease of deployment are critical. Experimental results confirm the feasibility of encoderless AGVs in dynamic indoor environments. Hector SLAM provided robust localization without odometry, while the ROS navigation stack ensured efficient real-time path planning and obstacle avoidance. Performance degradation was observed in feature-scarce and densely cluttered environments, highlighting the potential benefits of future integration with sensor fusion (e.g., IMUs or cameras) and learning-based motion planners. Despite these challenges, the system's low cost, modularity, and reliability make it a strong platform for academic research and non-critical industrial logistics applications.

7 CONCLUSION

This research successfully demonstrates the design, implementation, and real-world validation of a low-cost, encoderless Autonomous Guided Vehicle (AGV) using LiDAR-based Simultaneous Localization and Mapping (SLAM). By leveraging Hector SLAM and a modular ROS-based architecture, the system achieves reliable, real-time navigation without the need for wheel encoders or inertial sensors. The AGV exhibits high mapping accuracy (0.44% error), low localization drift (0.11 m in feature-rich environments), and maintains obstacle avoidance performance with success rates up to 98% in low-density and over 80% in high-density scenarios.

The AGV's hardware-software stack—built on Raspberry Pi 4, Arduino Uno, and RPLiDAR A1—was optimized for power and computational efficiency, validated through simulations and real-world corridor and home-environment trials. The system demonstrated a runtime of over 3 hours, thermal stability, and consistent motion fidelity, with slippage under 12%.

Statistical validation, including ANOVA and Tukey HSD tests, confirmed that Hector SLAM outperforms alternatives like Gmapping and Cartographer in efficiency and accuracy on embedded platforms. Moreover, Weibull modeling of error patterns revealed predictable performance trends, supporting future optimization.

Costing just ₹27,850 compared to ₹6.5 lakh commercial systems, the proposed AGV offers a viable alternative for educational institutes, research labs, warehouse automation, and light-duty logistics. With minimal setup time, easy maintenance, and sensor flexibility, it presents a scalable and accessible solution aligned with ISO 3691-4 and IEEE RAS guidelines. This makes it highly suitable for dynamic, real-world indoor environments requiring smart, adaptable, and affordable automation.

REFERENCES

[1] Yong, Zhang, Li Renjie, Wang Fenghong, Zhao Weiting, Chen Qi, Zhi Derui, Chen Xinxin, and Jiang Shuhao. (2023). "An autonomous navigation strategy based on improved hector slam with dynamic weighted a* algorithm." *IEEE Access* 11 : 79553–79571.

[2] Ma, Jinkun, Xianming Wu, Wencan Guo, and Yunjian Peng. (2024) "A Multi-LIDAR SLAM Method Based on Hector-SLAM." In *2024 China Automation Congress (CAC)*, pp. 345–350. IEEE.

[3] Weichen, W.E.I., Bijan Shirinzadeh, Mohammadali Ghafarian, Shunmugasundar Esakkiappan, and Tianyao Shen. (2020). "Hector SLAM with ICP trajectory matching." In *2020 IEEE/ASME International Conference on Advanced Intelligent Mechatronics (AIM)*, pp. 1971–1976. IEEE.

[4] Hossain, Amreen, and Raian Haider Chowdhury. (2024). "Implementation of Hector SLAM Algorithm for Mapping Indoor Environments with Obstacles." In *2024 IEEE 3rd International Conference on Robotics, Automation, Artificial-Intelligence and Internet-of-Things (RAAICON)*, pp. 218–223. IEEE

[5] Wei, Weichen, Bijan Shirinzadeh, Shunmugasundar Esakkiappan, Mohammadali Ghafarian, and Ammar Al-Jodah. (2020). "Orientation correction for hector slam at starting stage." In *2019 7th International Conference on Robot Intelligence Technology and Applications (RiTA)*, pp. 125–129. IEEE.

[6] Wijaya, Syahrul Fajar Andriawan Eka, Didik Setyo Purnomo, Eko Budi Utomo, and Muhammad Akbaryan Anandito. (2019). "Research study of occupancy grid map mapping method on Hector SLAM technique." In *2019 International Electronics Symposium (IES)*, pp. 238–241. IEEE

[7] Nagla, Shubham. (2020). "2d hector slam of indoor mobile robot using 2d lidar." In *2020 international conference on power, energy, control and transmission systems (ICPECTS)*, pp. 1–4. IEEE.

[8] Yu, Naigong, and Bo Zhang. (2018). "An improved hector slam algorithm based on information fusion for mobile robot." In *2018 5th IEEE International conference on cloud computing and intelligence systems (CCIS)*, pp. 279–284. IEEE

[9] Varanasi, Sai Dikshith, Moulik Tammana, and Rajesh Kannan Megalingam. (2024). "Robotic navigation unveiled: A comprehensive study of GMapping, Hector Slam, and Cartographer." In *2024 3rd International Conference for Innovation in Technology (INOCON)*, pp. 1–6. IEEE

[10] L. Lucan, (2020). "Simultaneous Localization and Mapping on a Mobile Robot Platform," IEEE Conference on Robotics and Automation

[11] J.S.A.K.G.A. Barbosa, (2019). "Advancements in graph-based sLAM for mobile robots," *IEEE Transactions on Robotics*

[12] X. Z. Y. and. H.M. Yue, "LiDAR-based SLAM for robotic mapping: state of the art," arXiv preprint arXiv:2311.00276.

[13] G. K. R. S. C. and. B. W. Grisetti, (2010). "A tutorial on graph-based SLAM," *IEEE Transactions on Intelligent Transportation Systems*, 17(4).

[14] T. W. H. R. M. and. M. T. Fan, (2020). "CPL-SLAM: Efficient and certifiably correct planar graph-based SLAM using the complex number representation," arXiv preprint arXiv:2007.06708.

[15] S. and. M. M. Thrun, (2025). "The GraphSLAM algorithm with applications to largescale mapping of urban structures.," *International Journal of Robotics Research*, 25(5–6), 403–429.

[16] L. M. and. P. P. Paz, (2020). "Graph-based SLAM-aware exploration with prior topo metric information.," *arXiv preprint arXiv:2308.*16522. Denton, Tom. Electric and hybrid vehicles. Routledge,

[17] Nehate, Chinmay, Rutwik Shinde, Saket Naik, Manish Aradwad, Anish Bhurke, and Faruk Kazi. (2021). "Implementation and evaluation of slam systems for a mobile robot." In *2021 IEEE 18th India Council International Conference (INDICON)*, pp. 1–6. IEEE

[18] Li, Zi-Xin, Guo-Hua Cui, Chun-Lin Li, and Zhen-Shan Zhang. (2021). "Comparative study of SLAM algorithms for mobile robots in complex environment." In *2021 6th International Conference on Control, Robotics and Cybernetics (CRC)*, pp. 74–79. IEEE

[19] Xuexi, Zhang, Lu Guokun, Fu Genping, Xu Dongliang, and Liang Shiliu. (2019). "SLAM algorithm analysis of mobile robot based on lidar." In *2019 Chinese Control Conference (CCC)*, pp. 4739–4745. IEEE.

[20] Olalekan, Ayoade Femi, Jane Alam Sagor, Md Hasibul Hasan, and Adekunle Samuel Oluwatobi. "Comparison of two SLAM algorithms provided by ROS (robot operating system)." In *2021 2nd International conference for emerging technology (INCET)*, pp. 1–5. IEEE.

[21] Yagfarov, Rauf, Mikhail Ivanou, and Ilya Afanasyev. (2018). "Map comparison of lidar-based 2d slam algorithms using precise ground truth." In *2018 15th International Conference on Control, Automation, Robotics and Vision (ICARCV)*, pp. 1979–1983. IEEE

[22] M.R.T.A.K.G.H. Grewal, (2017). *"LIDAR-Based Autonomous Wheelchair,"* IEEE.

[23] W. Wang, (2019). "Sensor fusion and map establishment for autonomous guided vehicle," *IEEE Conference on Industrial Electronics and Applications (ICIEA)*.

[24] M. A. A. M. Y. W. R. A. a. S. K. D. K. M. T. M. B. Konara, (2020). "Design and analysis of an autonomously guided vehicle to minimize the impact of COVID-19," *IEEE Conference on Robotics and Automation.*

[25] S.J.K.R.A.R.K.N. Gupta, (2014). "Path tracking of automated guided vehicle," in *IEEE Conference on Automation and Robotics.*

[26] W.R.M. Aizat, (2023). "A survey on navigation approaches for automated guided vehicle robots in dynamic surrounding," *IEEE Access*, vol. 11, pp. 33934–33947.

[27] R.S.A.S. Grewal, (2019). "Real-time SLAM implementation for autonomous robots," *Journal of Intelligent and Robotic Systems.*

[28] R. Gupta, (2014). "Robust path planning for autonomous guided vehicles," *Journal of Automation and Control Engineering.*

[29] N.A.P.C. Thongpance, (2023). "Design and construction of electric wheelchair with mecanum wheel," *Journal of Robotics and Control (JRC)* 4, no. 1.

[30] Wang, (2019). "Sensor fusion and map establishment for autonomous guided vehicle.," *Proceedings of the IEEE Conference on Industrial Electronics and Applications*, 1–5.

Technology for a Resilient Future – Vincent , Moorthy and Dasari (Eds)

Power-Area Exploration of Multiplier Architectures for CNN MAC Units on FPGA

Pavithra P and Rahul Ratnakumar
Department of Electronics and Communication Engineering, Manipal Institute of Technology, Manipal Academy of Higher Education, Manipal, India

ABSTRACT: Convolutional Neural Networks has been widely applied in image and speech processing due to their superior accuracy. However, their computational complexity results in high latency and power consumption, especially in resource-constrained real-time applications. This paper presents an improved power and area-efficient Multiply-Accumulate (MAC) unit architecture implemented on FPGA, leveraging multiple multiplier designs including Booth, Wallace Tree, Dadda, Vedic, Braun, Baugh-Wooley, and Array multipliers. All architectures were modelled in Verilog HDL and synthesized using the AMD-Xilinx Vivado tool on the Artix-7 FPGA platform. Experimental results reveal that the Wallace Tree multiplier achieves the lowest on-chip power consumption at 1.929 W, while the Booth multiplier shows minimal logic utilization at only 0.08% LUTs and 18.87% IOs. In contrast, the Array multiplier delivers higher performance but consumes the most power (26.034 W) and area (0.93% LUTs, 54.72% IOs). These results demonstrate critical trade-offs between power, performance, and resource usage, enabling informed selection of multiplier architectures for hardware-accelerated CNN implementations in edge and embedded systems.

Keywords: Convolutional neural networks (CNNs), FPGA implementation, Multiplier architecture, Multiply Accumulate Unit (MAC)

1 INTRODUCTION

The speed at which technology is developing these days is extremely quick. The circuits that are being designed have billions of tiny, fast, low-power, and low-area components. Therefore, while designing any circuit, area, speed, and power are essential considerations [1], [2]. Circuits with low area and low delay constraints must be designed to meet the current trend demand. Major building blocks of any processing unit, arithmetic units carry out a variety of arithmetic operations [3]. Of all the arithmetic operations, multiplication is a crucial one. The binary multiplier, array multiplier, Dadda multiplier, Wallace tree, Booth's multiplier etc. are among the prominent multiplier architectures [4]. The Wallace tree multiplier has advantages over other multipliers [5]. Deep neural network (Deep Learning Architectures) developments recently have significantly improved the performance of numerous machine learning applications, including image analysis, semantic segmentation, pixel processing, pattern recognition and speech processing. The CNN incorporates a MAC unit optimized for convolution and related activation operations. A key part of Convolutional Neural Networks, the convolution layer, uses learnable filters to automatically extract spatial features from input data. In deep network processing, in order to create feature maps, it moves these filters over the input, identifying patterns like edges, textures, and shapes. The network can identify intricate structures in images with less computational complexity. Key components of the design include an input handling, two-phase structure, and memory integration. The MAC unit processes current and previous inputs (stored in RAM / ROM) and applies the learned weights to perform multiplications. Two-Phase Structure constitutes of a (i) Convolution phase: The MAC unit multiplies input data with filters (weights) and accumulates results. (ii) Activation Phase: A filtered response (e.g., ReLU, sigmoid) is applied to the accumulated output. Memory Integration unit consists of Latches and memory units (RAM/ROM) manage data flow, ensuring seamless operation across layers. The MAC architecture for CNN, embeds this MAC-centric design into CNNs, the system achieves high-performance convolution and activation, leveraging parallelized operations for real-time applications like image processing. The architecture's efficiency stems from its ability to streamline multiply-accumulate tasks while maintaining scalability across deep learning models The convolution process is used in CNN computations. The majority of their applications include image processing and classification tasks like those found in video surveillance. The training phase of DNN and CNN takes several days to finish because they primarily involve computation. The network's training time has been significantly shortened, but only with the help of graphics processing units (GPUs). This network's operations can be boiled down to matrix multiplication. Because of its excessive power consumption, the GPU implementation of CNN cannot be used in practical applications [6]. It takes a dedicated hardware accelerator with low power consumption to achieve the desired performance. CNN can be implemented more effectively on FPGAs with enhanced speed than software counterparts. The need for FPGA to be used in the CNN network's execution process is growing [7]-[9]. When the kernel dimension is compact, the Winograd algorithm performs well during the convolution process. However, if stride is set to one in the input, this transformation is helpful. Layers of convolution, since small kernels are used in most CNNs, the Winograd algorithm can be used to evaluate those layers. This algorithm's performance is determined by the Winograd input data tile size. When the kernel dimension is compact during convolution, the Winograd algorithm performs admirably. This change is helpful, if stride is set to one in the input. Layers of convolution, the Winograd algorithm can be used to evaluate the layers of most CNNs because their kernels are small. Tile size of the Winograd input data determines the algorithm's performance. Laundaeur's research [10] states that the energy dissipated by KT*(ln 2), where KT is the Boltzmann Constant and T is the system temperature, is the equivalent of one bit of information loss. According to Bennetts' research [11], no heat will be released if the circuit is made reversible, or if it can be operated in either direction. In light of Bennett's research, it is evident that utilizing this reversible logic in the design of modules that are frequently utilized in numerous necessary designs in the contemporary world results in a notable decrease in power dissipation. Digital filters like FIR and IIR filters, which are used more commonly worldwide, are usually designed using MAC units. These MAC units are also utilized in the design of

DOI: 10.1201/9781042017546-27

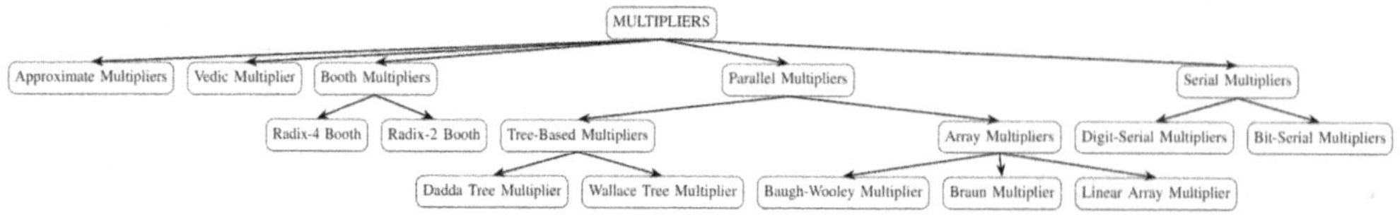

Figure 1. Hierarchy of multipliers for hardware implementation of CNNs.

specific FPGA blocks, such as Stratix and Virtex. Given the abundance of DSP blocks in these FPGAs, a high-quality low-power MAC unit would aid in lowering the FPGA's overall power consumption. Thus, reversible logic gates are used in the design of a MAC unit, where garbage output, gate count, and quantum cost are used to gauge performance [12]. Array multipliers build their multipliers according to a strict pattern. Higher order addition and partial product multiplication are involved in the multiplication process. The two most common approaches are to add a multiplier unit or execute shift and add operations using the CPU's current components. In digital system design, multipliers are frequently separated into two parts: tree and array multipliers. Multipliers are crucial in digital signal processing and image processing, refer Figure 1. One of the most significant and frequently used transforms in image processing is the fast Fourier transform. Fast Fourier transform computation calls for a lot of addition and multiplication operations. These algorithms need a dedicated MAC to be executed [13]. To reduce the number of CLBs- configurable logic blocks in a design implementation, the radix-4 Booth algorithm performs better than the radix-2 algorithm by lowering the partial product count to n/2 in radix 4. When the Wallace tree algorithm is used, fewer stages of sequential addition are needed, increasing the circuit's speed. Furthermore, by combining the Wallace tree and modified Booth algorithms, the benefits of both algorithms can be utilized at the same time [14] in a multiplier implementation. Multiplication based on Vedic mathematics is a further method for digital multiplication [15].

2 METHODOLOGY

In computer vision applications, DNN learning techniques, especially CNNs for image understanding, are widely adopted. The core unit responsible for performing convolution in CNNs is the Processing Element (PE). The parallel adder-based computation architecture is designed to accelerate convolutional neural network operations. It shows four input-weight pairs being processed simultaneously, where each input is multiplied with its corresponding weight in parallel.

These products are then efficiently summed together through parallel addition to generate the output feature map values. This approach implements the fundamental multiply-accumulate (MAC) operations at the heart of CNNs in a highly parallelized manner, significantly improving computational throughput compared to sequential processing. The architecture is inherently scalable - additional input-weight pairs can be incorporated to handle larger convolutional kernels or increase processing capacity. This parallel computation method is particularly well-suited for hardware implementations like TPUs and FPGAs, where maximizing parallel operations is crucial for achieving real-time inference speeds in deep learning applications. By processing multiple MAC operations concurrently, this design effectively reduces latency while maintaining the precision required for CNN computations [16]. For better system efficiency, PEs must be optimized in terms of power, area and speed. Approximate computing offers a promising way to reduce hardware complexity while maintaining performance. In this work, different types of multipliers are introduced to enhance the efficiency of CNN hardware implementation.

2.1 *Booth's multiplier*

The Booth Multiplication Algorithm is a signed multiplication algorithm designed to reduce the quantity of partial products by encoding the multiplier prior to computation. Utilizing Booth's encoding, it examines overlapping groups of three bits comprising the current bit, the previous bit, and an implicit zero to decide whether the multiplicand should be added, subtracted, or ignored. This process begins with the initialization of the multiplicand, multiplier, and an accumulator. Based on the encoded multiplier bits, the algorithm conditionally adds or subtracts the multiplicand from the accumulator, followed by an arithmetic right shift to maintain the sign and prepare for subsequent operations. This iterative cycle continues until the entire multiplier is processed. Booth encoding is particularly beneficial for multipliers with extended sequences of 0s or 1s, optimizing power andtiming performance while simplifying control logic for signed operations in hardware implementations, the Booth Multiplier typically features a register-based architecture with control logic for shifting, encoding, and conditional arithmetic operations, resulting in a compact and power-efficient design. It is especially advantageous in digital signal processors and embedded systems where efficient signed computation is crucial. Key attributes of a high-performance multiplier include precision, speed, minimal use of LUTs and slices, and low energy consumption. The adder combines the multiplier's output with the value stored in the accumulator. If the multiplier's inputs are of bit size N, the adder should have a bit size of 2N, producing an output of 2N+1 bits. Commonly used adders in digital logic devices include carry save adders, carry select adders, ripple carry adders (RCA), and carry look-ahead adders (CLA). Critical parameters for adders are propagation delay and critical delay.

2.2 *Wallace tree multiplier*

The Wallace Tree multiplier generates partial products in the first stage by multiplying each bit of the input operands. For a 4-bit input, this results in four rows of partial products. In Phase 2, these partial products are added using half and full adders in successive stages. The first three rows are added to form intermediate sum and carry rows. The remaining partial product row is then added to these, producing updated sum and carry rows. The final product is created by adding the final two rows after this process is completed.

The speed of multiplication is significantly influenced by the addition stage, as carry propagation delay becomes a bottleneck in conventional designs. To mitigate this, the proposed architecture integrates parallel prefix adders in Phase 2, replacing traditional half and full adders in the final stage. This modification enhances the overall speed and efficiency of the Wallace Tree multiplier, making it more suitable for high-performance applications.

2.3 *Vedic multiplier*

The Vedic multiplier operates by dividing the input operands into smaller bit segments and performing parallel multiplications, followed by systematic addition of the intermediate results. It follows a column-wise and diagonal multiplication approach, which helps to reduce the propagation delay typically found in traditional multipliers. For instance, in a 4-bit Vedic multiplier, the inputs are split into 2-bit segments. These segments are multiplied using smaller 2×2 multipliers, and the resulting partial products are combined using adders. This modular structure enables concurrent processing of multiple segments, which significantly improves the speed and reduces the hardware complexity. The final result is obtained by aligning and adding the partial results in a structured manner, using carry-save or ripple carry adders depending on the design constraints.

2.4 *Dadda multiplier*

In order to minimize the number of addition steps in the partial product summation, the Dadda multiplier is an enhanced variant of the Wallace tree multiplier. It minimizes the height of the matrix of partial products in a controlled manner, which directly contributes to lower hardware complexity and improved performance.The partial products are produced by performing bit-wise multiplication of the input operands. These partial products are arranged in a bit matrix form. Instead of reducing the matrix immediately to two rows like Wallace, the Dadda algorithm delays reduction steps by applying a predefined column height threshold at each stage. This selective reduction uses full and half adders only, when necessary, which reduces the number of active logic elements and power consumption.

As the reduction progresses, each stage reduces the column heights according to Dadda's sequence until only two final rows remain. These two rows are then summed using a fast carry-propagate adder to produce the final result. The systematic scheduling of adders in the Dadda structure leads to fewer logic levels, offering better speed and area efficiency compared to other tree-based multipliers.

2.5 *Array multiplier*

The Array Multiplier is a combinational multiplier architecture that employs a structured arrangement of adders and logic gates to generate and sum partial products. It is known for its regular and modular design, which simplifies hardware implementation and layout on silicon or FPGA platforms. The multiplication process begins by generating partial products through bit-wise AND operations between the multiplier and multiplicand bits. These partial products are arranged in a grid-like format, where each row represents a shifted version of the multiplicand corresponding to each bit of the multiplier. The summation of partial products is performed row by row using a systematic network of full adders and half adders. Each stage computes intermediate sums and propagates carries to the next row. This iterative addition continues until the final product is obtained at the bottom of the array. Although the Array Multiplier offers higher area utilization due to its repetitive structure, it provides advantages in terms of predictable delay and ease of routing. Its parallel structure allows for faster multiplication at the cost of increased power and silicon area. These characteristics make it suitable for high-throughput applications where speed is prioritized over area efficiency.

2.6 *Braun multiplier*

The Braun Multiplier is a combinational unsigned multiplier architecture based on a regular array structure. It utilizes a straightforward layout of AND gates and adders, making it efficient for VLSI implementation due to its modular and scalable design. Partial products are generated through bit-wise 'AND' operations between the multiplicand and each bit of the multiplier. Rows of these partial products are used and added using carry-save adders in a fixed sequence. The summation is performed progressively using full adders that propagate carries through the structure. The final row of sum and carry outputs is resolved using a ripple carry adder to produce the final multiplication result. Although the Braun Multiplier lacks support for signed operations, its simplicity, ease of layout, and predictable timing make it an attractive choice for hardware accelerators and embedded applications where unsigned arithmetic is sufficient. Its regular structure also makes it favourable for pipelined designs and high-speed applications.

2.7 *Baugh-wooley multiplier*

The Baugh-Wooley Multiplier performs efficient signed multiplication using two's complement representation. It integrates sign extension and correction within the partial product matrix, allowing uniform handling of both positive and negative terms. Bit-wise AND operations are used to create partial products, which are then added together using full and half adders set up in a structured array. This eliminates the need for external sign correction, reducing logic complexity and improving computation speed. The architecture is well-suited for applications requiring high-performance signed arithmetic.

3 RESULTS AND DISCUSSIONS

The Booth, Wallace Tree, Vedic, Dadda, Array, Braun, and Baugh multipliers are designed using Verilog and synthesized using Xilinx Vivado. The comparison focuses on On-Chip Power, Dynamic and Static Power, and resource utilization parameters including LUTs, Flip-Flops (FFs), and IOs. The Figure 2, shows the Power analysis of different multipliers, the Array Multiplier shows the highest On-Chip Power at 26.034W (Dynamic: 24.549W, Static: 0.485W), while the Wallace Tree Multiplier records the lowest at 1.929W (Dynamic: 1.851W, Static: 0.078W). The Baugh Multiplier consumes 15.47W, followed by the Braun and Dadda Multipliers with 13.69W each. The Vedic Multiplier results in 12.864W, and the Booth's Multiplier reports 7.438W. Across all designs, Dynamic Power accounts for 96 to 99 percentage of total power, indicating that most energy is consumed during active operation, while Static Power remains minimal.

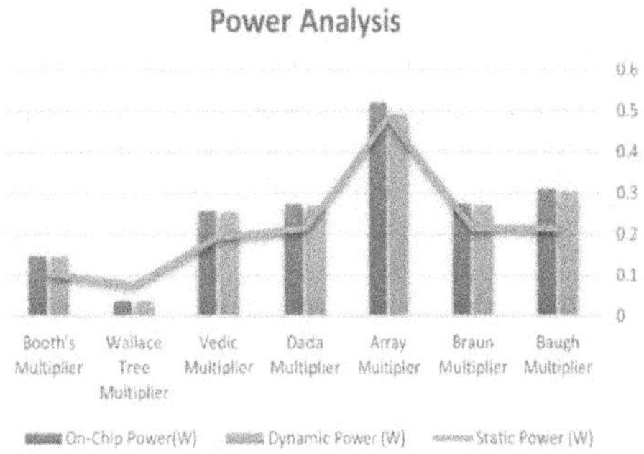

Figure 2. Power analysis of different multipliers.

The resource utilization of different multipliers is shown in the Figure 3, the Array Multiplier exhibits the highest consumption, utilizing 0.93 percentage of LUTs and 54.72 percentage of IOs. Both the Braun and Baugh Multipliers show identical utilization patterns, each occupying 1.00 percentage of LUTs and approximately 30.00 percentage of IOs. The Vedic Multiplier utilizes 0.60 percentage of LUTs and 30.19 percentage of IOs, while the Dadda Multiplier reports 0.41 percentage of LUT usage with the same IO utilization of 30.19 percentage. The Booth Multiplier demonstrates minimal utilization, occupying only 0.08 percentage of LUTs and

18.87 percentage of IOs. In contrast, the Wallace Tree Multiplier shows negligible usage of both LUTs and FFs, but a comparatively higher IO utilization of 33.02 percentage.

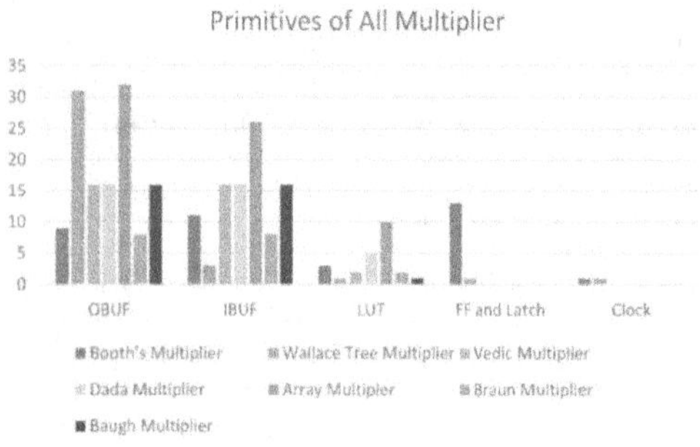

Figure 3. Primitives of multipliers.

The FPGA Digilent Basys-3 board, which has a device Artix-7 and part number xc7a35tcpg236-1, has been used to implement these designs.

4 CONCLUSION

This work presents a comparative analysis of various multiplier architectures, including Booth, Wallace Tree, Vedic, Dadda, Array, Braun, and Baugh, focusing on power consumption and resource utilization. The Wallace Tree Multiplier demonstrates the highest power efficiency, whereas the Array Multiplier achieves better performance with increased power and area costs. Intermediate designs such as Vedic and Dadda offer a balanced trade-off between power and hardware usage. The selection of an appropriate architecture ultimately depends on application-specific needs, such as energy efficiency or speed.

REFERENCES

[1] N. Weste and D. Harris, (2004). *CMOS VLSI Design.* Reading, MA: Addison Wesley.

[2] N. Weste and K. Eshragian, (11985–1993). *Principles of CMOS VLSI Designs: A System Perspective*, 2nd ed., Addison-Wesley.

[3] Milos D. (2004). *Ercegovac and Thomas Lang, "Digital arithmetic,"* Morgan Kaufmann, Elsevier INC

[4] J.M. Rabaey, (2001). *Digtal Integrated Circuits—A Design Perspective.* Upper Saddle River, NJ: Prentice-Hall.

[5] Himanshu Bansal, K.G. Sharma, Tripti Sharma. (2014). Wallace tree multiplier designs: A performance comparison review", innovative systems. *Design and Engineering*, Vol. 5, No. 5

[6] H. Li, X. Fan, L. Jiao, W. Cao, X. Zhou, and L. Wang, (2016). "A high performance FPGA-based accelerator for large-scale convolutional neural networks," in *Proc. 26th Int. Conf. Field Program. Logic Appl. (FPL)*, Lausanne, Switzerland, pp. 1–9. https://doi.org/10.1109/FPL.2016.7577308.

[7] Y. Ma, N. Suda, Y. Cao, S. Vrudhula, and J.-S. Seo, (2018). "ALAMO: FPGA acceleration of deep learning algorithms with a modularized RTL compiler," *Integration*, vol. 62, pp. 14–23, Jun. 2018. doi:10.1016/j.vlsi.2017.12.009.

[8] Y. Ma, Y. Cao, S. Vrudhula, and J. Seo, (2018). "Optimizing the convolution operation to accelerate deep neural networks on FPGA," *IEEE Trans. Very Large Scale Integr. (VLSI) Syst.*, vol. 26, no. 7, pp. 1354–1367, doi: 10.1109/TVLSI.2018.2815603.

[9] Y. Ma, Y. Cao, S. Vrudhula, and J.-S. Seo, (2017). "An automatic RTL compiler for high-throughput FPGA implementation of diverse deep convolutional neural networks," in *Proc. 27th Int. Conf. Field Program. Logic Appl. (FPL)*, Ghent, Belgium, pp. 1–8. https://doi.org/10.23919/FPL.2017.8056824.

[10] R. Landauer, (1961). "Irreversibility and heat generation in the computational process", *IBM J. Research and Development*, vol. 5, pp. 183–191.

[11] C.H. Bennett, (1973). "Logical reversibility of computation", *IBM J. Research and Development*, vol. 17, pp. 525–532.

[12] Swaraj Raman M, Arun Kumar K, Srinivas Reddy K, (2012). "Reversible implementation of novel Multiply Accumulate (MAC) Unit ", *2012 International Conference on Communication, Information and Computing Technology (ICCICT)*, Oct. 19–20, Mumbai, India.

[13] K.N. Vijeyakumar, Dr.V. Sumathy, S. Priyadharsini, S. Tamilselvan "Design of high speed wallace tree multiplier using error tolerent technique and its application. In *Digital Image Processing"International Journal of Communication Engineering* ISSN NO 0988 0382E.

[14] Lakshmanan, M. Othman, and M.A.M. Ali, (2002). "High performance parallel multiplier using Wallace-Booth algorithm," in *Proc. IEEE International Conference on Semiconductor Electronics*, pp. 433–436.

[15] S. Akhter, (2007). "VHDL implementation of fast N×N multiplier based on Vedic mathematic," in *Proc. 18th European Conference on Circuit Theory and Design*, pp. 472–475.

[16] B.∼S. Mihiraamsh and J.P. Anita, (2023). Analysis of Multiply-Accumulate (MAC) unit using convolution Neural Networks (CNN)," in *Proceedings of the International Conference on Soft Computing: Theories and Applications*, Springer, 2023, pp. 275–287.

[17] F.U.D. Farrukh, T. Xie, C. Zhang, and Z. Wang, (2018). `Optimization for efficient hardware implementation of CNN on FPGA," in *Proceedings of the 2018 IEEE International Conference on Integrated Circuits, Technologies and Applications (ICTA), IEEE*, pp. 88–89.

[18] SS. Lee, TD. Nguyen, PK. Meher, and SY. Park, (2022). Energy-efficient high-speed ASIC implementation of convolutional neural network using novel reduced critical-path design, *IEEE Access*, vol. 10, pp. 34032–34045.

Technology for a Resilient Future – Vincent , Moorthy and Dasari (Eds)

Secure Medical Record Storage and Distribution Using Blockchain

Deepika V, Murthy S V N, Bharathi M, Harshitha V, and Ambika S R
Deparment of Computer Science & Design, SJC Institute of Technology Chikkaballapur, India

ABSTRACT: Providing secured storage of medical records with ease of access represents one of the current hot topics in today's healthcare industry. In this case, a centrally stored medical record system has been known to exhibit some inefficiencies in terms of data transfer, lack of access control, and breaching. This paper presents an overview of research work on designing a blockchain-based medical record storage and transfer system that utilizes the benefits of blockchain's decentralized architecture, cryptographic techniques, and smart contracts to provide significantly enhanced privacy, integrity, and availability of medical data. The immutable and transparent characteristics of blockchains enable medical records to be recorded in such a way that they remain tamper-proof and accessible only to legal participants. With smart contracts, patients are providing with more control over medical data, which allows them to handle access rights and transfer medical records to health practitioners, insurance, and biomedical research with ease and security. The proposed method removes points of failure in terms of data access and study breaches. Additionally, it allows real-time auditing for fraud detection and Healthcare Act compliance. This paper evidently illustrates that blockchain technology has the power to disrupt today's medical record storage and management.

Keywords: Blockchain, Medical Data, Healthcare, Security, Transparent, Tamper-proof

1 INTRODUCTION

The medical industry is increasingly relying on the usage of electronic medical records (EMRs) in the digital era as a way of enhancing medical care towards the patient, enhancing productivity, as well as simplifying the processing and management of data. Nevertheless, the medical industry faces various flaws associated with the normal storage systems, such as the probable risks associated with online attacks, illegal access, and the ability to alter the data. This potential risk affects the privacy of the patients in addition to the medical industry's reputation since identity theft, data breaches, loss of medical information, among others, can occur. Medical information needs to remain accessible, safe, and secure both for the patient and the medical practitioner. Medical records face risks since data is vulnerable if the medical industry employs the normal storage approach. However, the blockchain approach is an effective, safe, and reliable way of securing medical information or medical records.

Medical records are encrypted and secured through a blockchain system because they are secured together through a chain of timestamps and cannot be reformed once they are unified into the chain and require necessary authorization for their alteration and/or deletion. Moreover, blockchain technology imposes tight access control strategies and allows secure sharing of information complete the use of smart contracts and cryptography. In addition to preventing unauthorized persons from altering private patient information, this confirms that only certified persons and institutions, including patients, health and insurance institutions, are able to contact and modify this information. Blockchain eliminates the single point of failure and knowingly reduces hazards associated with information violation because blockchain technology uses decentralized servers as opposed to centralized servers in traditional storage of information.

This study will be used to research different blockchain techniques in managing medical data, analyze their advantages and disadvantages, and propose an appropriate framework for secure distribution and storage. More exactly, this study has the goal to analyze different blockchain models in terms of suitability for managing health information: public blockchain models, private models, and hybrid models. More significantly, this learning has aimed to develop an innovative model in which fake modifications to medical data are obstructed, as well as illegal access, through more sophisticated cryptography and consensus algorithms. In this case, prominence has also been positioned on giving topmost consideration to health data user control in accessing health information in a secure way and distributing it to health experts when required without undermining health information privacy.

The development of an open and auditable system that provides an optimization of interactions between healthcare participants, such as healthcare centers, insurance companies, and governments, is also a distinct aim of the proposed study. Because to maintain an appropriate standard of healthcare regulation on a global level and to ensure a seamless flow of exchanged information between the healthcare centers in diverse healthcare settings, it is imperative to develop an interoperability healthcare record system using blockchain technology.

2 BACKGROUND

Blockchain is a peer-to-peer ledger system is reorganized and separated from the virtual currency referred to as "Bitcoin," which was invented by Satoshi Nakamoto in 2008. One of the technological trends affecting the world and the business environment today is the practice of blockchain. Blockchain technology has stayed magnificently implemented in a number of industries, including healthcare, public administration, supply chain management, and financial services. A blockchain is a type of distributed database where a chain of linear data units, known as blocks, are connected and protected by cryptographic primitives. As the transaction number increases on blockchain, so does its size. The blockchain's blocks record the sequence of transactions as well as the time they were made. Every block has a timestamp, transaction information, and the cryptographic hash pointing to its previous block. The immutability feature of blockchain is derived from the hash pointer of the preceding block, which connects the blocks and makes them resistant to tampering. The majority of the nodes assigned to the consensus process must concur on the transaction by verifying the true nature of transaction data before a new block can be added to the blockchain, rendering to the blockchain platform being utilized. Single global blockchain is unable to used to all industries since different users and businesses have distinct needs. Hence, many blockchain platforms have been processed, each with a distinct

DOI: 10.1201/9781042017546-28

set of rules, but the fundamentals are always the same. There are two kinds of blockchains on the market: permissionless (public) and permissioned (private), notwithstanding the vast amount of blockchain platforms that are currently accessible. Here, we've provided a quick rundown of the two most general blockchain frameworks: Hyperledger (permissioned blockchain) and Ethereum (permissionless blockchain).

3 LITERATURE REVIEW

[1] Blockchain in Healthcare and Health Sciences – A Scoping Review. Hasselgren *et al.* performed a scoping review to explore the requests of blockchain technology in healthcare and health sciences. The review mentions an increase in the acceptance of blockchain technology to tackle problems related to integrity, interoperability, and patient portability of healthcare information. The applications of blockchain have been separated into four broader fields: management of patient records, research, pharmaceutical logistics, and health insurance. The review states that scalability, regulatory aspects, and high energy requirements are significant hurdles to the acceptance of blockchain technology in the healthcare segment. The analysis advises that future research is required to optimize blockchain design and make it seamlessly integrable into the existing infrastructure of the healthcare sector. [2] An Architecture and Management Platform for Blockchain-Based Personal Health Record Exchange. Lee *et al.* designed a blockchain architecture for personal health record management, with a focus on a patient-centered approach to facilitate patient management of their own healthcare information. The proposed architecture confirms that only legal personnel can access a patient's healthcare information with the utmost security. For this purpose, a public and private blockchain structure is proposed to address scalability and security-related challenges simultaneously. The proposed architecture also makes the best use of self-executing contracts to ensure clarity and make healthcare-related processes autonomous and free of errors. The proposed architecture ensures a significant increase in security and efficiency of healthcare information systems, but it also identifies that a regulation-related and confidentiality-related challenges require consideration and can only be termed properly for a large-scale implementation. [3] Electronic Health Records in a Blockchain: A Systematic Review. A look into different blockchain EHR systems and their efficiency in providing secure patient information management. The review describes different systems designed using public, private, and also the consortium blockchain models, with a focus on encryption processes and management approach and different consensus models. The review mentions that blockchain technology improves security and integrity but lacks scalability and is cost-intensive. The review also discusses the presence of self- executing contracts to ensure security and facilitate allowed access to patient information. The review strongly suggests that even though it is a promising technology, further research is required to improve efficiency and work with healthcare regulations. [4] "A Secure Medical Record Sharing Scheme Based on the Blockchain and Two Fold Encryption" (Habib *et al.*, 2023). The authors propose a new model for secured medical record sharing with blockchain and two-fold encryption. The authors stated that medical records which is secured at two levels: data storage level and transaction level. They also mentioned that this particular method significantly improves data authentication and confidentiality and prevents unauthorized modifications. The proposed model includes a private blockchain network to boost scalability and speed. From experimental analysis, it has also been found that it supports both efficiency and security, which can also be used in real-life health care cases. However, it was found that in order to integrate this system with the existing EMR systems, there arise several responsibilities related to health care systems. [5] "EMRs with Blockchain: A Distributed Democratized Electronic Medical Record Sharing Platform" (Shevkar *et al.*, 2020). The authors of this study present an innovative method for sharing EMR in which they use blockchain. They mentioned in this particular study that with the usage of blockchain, management transparency along with data privacy can be ensured. The study mentioned that uses the concept of a consortium blockchain in which all health care parties are interconnected. They mentioned in this study that with blockchain, health care parties will be independent, which automatically decreases health care administration costs. They mentioned in this study that to preserve data integrity and prevent unauthorized modifications, they use cryptographic hashing algorithms. They mentioned in this study that experimental analysis reveals that applying blockchain to health care EMR significantly decreases data exchange difficulties in health care parties. They mentioned in this study that all health care data storage and related blockchain policies still remain in infancy, which should be analyzed in future research.

4 METHODOLOGY

This image illustrates the approach of the medical record management and distribution system, where blockchain technology is employed to ensure secure, transparent, and efficient processing of medical information. At the beginning of the process, users- physicians, nurses, administrators, and pathologists- access the platform to transfer or retrieve patient medical records. These exchanges are first treated by a Blockchain Handshaker, a tool serving as an intermediary among people and the blockchain network. The handshaker ensures that only legitimate and verified transactions are transferred for validation to the Open Blockchain Network by packaging medical transactions into a blockchain- compatible format.

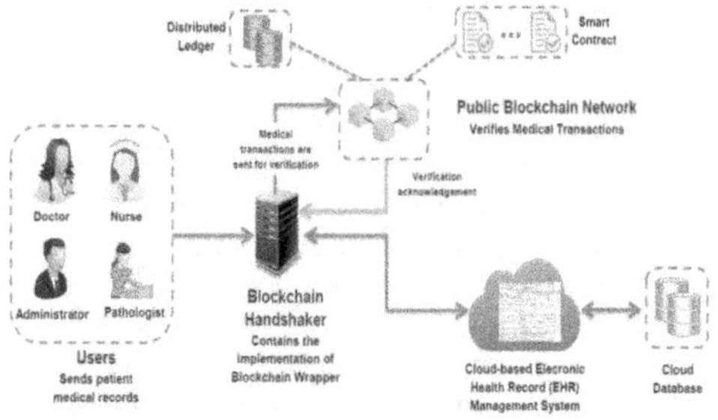

Figure 1. Methodology of the medical records.

With the help of smart contracts, the Open Blockchain Network acts as an impenetrable ledger in order to validate any medical transaction. Some pre-set guidelines, data sharing guidelines, and access privileges are managed by these smart contracts. The transactions are then recorded in the Distributed Ledger after their validation, ensuring the immutability of metadata.

The actual medical records and prescriptions are properly maintained in a cloud-based electronic management system for the safety of the data. To keep the records authentic without revealing the personal details, the pointers towards the records are maintained in the blockchain system. The Cloud Database and EHR can maintain a huge amount of secured medical records with real-time access facilities.

The patients completely have control on their medical reports; thus, the patients can authorize or refuse access as required. Moreover, it reduces the administration cost burden by providing quick access to authentic medical data for healthcare professionals. Integration of smart contracts with the technology of blockchain ensures the existence of an efficient audit trail system with secure access procedures as well as support for all data protection regulations. Since it addresses many critical problems which is associated with traditional medical report management systems, including efficiency, breach of data security, as well as lack of trust, the system architecture acts as a reliable choice in today's medical environments.

5 IMPLEMENTATION

5.1 *Access request algorithm*

Its purpose is to deal with the request for access, which is a process involving a health care provider's request to access a patient's record. The algorithm tests if the request to access follows system policies and also ensures that revocation based on time constraints is possible.

- Authorization check: This verifies whether the doctor has the needed authorizations to access the patient's records.
- Recording request: Records a request on the blockchain. This includes time window information.
- Audit logging: The action performed gets stored in the audit log.

5.2 *Access approval*

This algorithm provides or denies access requests. It ensures that time-based restrictions are strictly followed and only legal requests are authorized .

- Access Limit validation: This function ensures the request complies with the system-wide access time limits.
- Approval/Denial: This module will record an approval or denial while also changing the status of the access request

5.3 *Time-based access revocation*

This algorithm withdraws the access once the time expires or in the case of special situations (for example, security issues or patient withdrawal of consent).

- Revocation trigger: The patient or admin can trigger an early revocation.
- Blockchain Update: The access control record is updated in the blockchain to mark the revocation.
- Audit logging: This is the logging of the revocation action for purposes of transparency

5.4 *Emergency*

This algorithm allows healthcare professionals to make an emergency request for access to a patient's healthcare information, circumventing the typical time limit regulation. It ensures that access for emergency reasons is recorded and justified.

- Authorization check: This step verifies the healthcare professional's right to make an emergency request for access.
- Immediate Access: Provides access irrespective of whether the time constraints have been fulfilled.

6 RESULT ANALYSIS

The assessment of the proposed blockchain-based medical record system highlights considerable improvements over traditional centralized systems in terms of security, access controls, and transparency. With AES-256 encryption algorithms merged with SHA-256 hashing algorithms in the proposed model, high confidentiality as well as data integrity can be maintained. Smart contracts proved to be highly efficient in managing both role-based as well as attribute-based access controls in order to restrict only authorized parties from dealing with the sensitive data. The processing times for transactions proved to be efficient; it averaged 1-3 seconds in all. All operations are recorded in the model; thus, auditing in order to access all operations in real-time can be possible. The patient-friendly interface can be used by patients to transfer their medical data in a secure manner.

Table 1. Result analysis table with percentage comparison.

Performance Metric	Traditional Healthcare Systems	Blockchain-based Healthcare System
Data Security & Integrity	60%	95%
Scalability	55%	85%
Auditability & Transparency	55%	95%
Interoperability	50%	85%
Regulatory Compliance	60%	90%

7 CONCLUSION

The blockchain system provides a safe and efficient system for storing and sharing electronic medical records. The system relies on decentralization, encryption, and smart contracts, ensuring that medical information integrity, privacy, and confidentiality are ensured, which are not guaranteed in traditional centralized systems. Medical institutions are also able to benefit from improved interoperability and real-time access, making it easier for patients to control their personal medical information. This approach is a reliable alternative for current medical data management practices because it promotes trust and a decreased risk of breach and ensures that health regulations are followed.

REFERENCES

[1] Hasselgren A, Kralevska K, Gligoroski D, Pedersen SA, Faxvaag A. (2020). Blockchain in healthcare and health sciences—A scoping review. *International Journal of Medical Informatics* 134:104040.

[2] Lee H, Kung H, Udayasankaran JG, Kijsanayotin B, Marcelo A, Chao LR, *et al.* (2020). An architecture and management platform for blockchain-based personal health record exchange: Development and usability study. *J Med Internet Res* 22(6):e16748.

[3] A M, C C, R R. (2020). Electronic health records in a Blockchain: A systematic review. *Electronic Health Records in a Blockchain: A Systematic Review* 2020:1–16.

[4] Md. Ahsan Habib, Kazi Md. Rokibul Alam, Yasuhiko Morimoto. (2023). "A Secure Medical Record Sharing Scheme Based on Blockchain and Two-fold Encryption"

[5] Sanket Shevkar, Parthit Patel, Saptarshi Majumder, Harshita Singh, Kshitijaa Jaglan, Hrithwik Shalu. (2020). "*EMRs with Blockchain: A Distributed Democratised Electronic Medical Record Sharing Platform*"

[6] Renpeng Zou, Xixiang Lv, Jingsong Zhao. (2020). "SPChain: Blockchain-Based Medical Data Sharing and Privacy-Preserving eHealth System"

[7] Hao Wang (2021). "Que Bian: An Electronic Medical Record Management System on Blockchain"

[8] X. Liu, Y. Zhang, L. Chen. (2020). "A Blockchain- Based Approach for Secure and Efficient Data Sharing in Multi-Care Scenarios"

[9] Azaria, A. Ekblaw, T. Vieira, A. Lippman (2020). "MedRec: Using Blockchain for Medical Data Access and Permission Management"

[10] "Blockchain Based Record Management System in Hospitals", (2023).

[11] Y. Hassanzadeh-Nazarabadi, N. Nayal, S.S. Hamdan, O. Ozkasap and A. Küpçü, (2020). "A containerizedproof-of-concept implementation of LightChain system", *2020 IEEE Conference on Block-chain and Cryptocurrency (ICBC)*, pp. 1–2. 13

[12] Phong Tran, Thong Nguyen, Long Chu, Nhi Tran, Hang Ta. (2024). "A solution for commercializing, decentralizing and storing electronic medical records by integrating proxy re-encryption, IPFS, and Blockchain".

[13] Yuan Hong, Yuhong Liu, Minghui Zhu, *et al.* (2020). "ACTION-EHR: Patient Centric Blockchain-Based Electronic Health Record Data Management for Cancer Care".

Technology for a Resilient Future – Vincent , Moorthy and Dasari (Eds)

Speedy Care: Live Video Assisted Ambulance with Emergency Medical Support

Ignisha Rajathi G
School of Computer Engineering, Manipal Institute of Technology Bengaluru, Manipal Academy of Higher Education, Manipal, India

Mohanalin J
Department of Electrical and Electronics Engineering, College of Engineering Perumon, Kerala, India

Johny Elton R
Department of Computer Science and Engineering, Sri Krishna College of Engineering and Technology, Tamil Nadu, India

Dhanush M, Subhash Raveendran, Priyadharshini V, and Rajeswar S
Department of Computer Science and Business Systems, Sri Krishna College of Engineering and Technology, Tamil Nadu, India

Sumitha C and Susma N
Department of Information Technology, Sri Krishna College of Engineering and Technology, Tamil Nadu, India

ABSTRACT: High congestion of road traffic emerges as a severe concern in grossly populated metropolitan regions. Today, India is the second most populated country and is amongst the fastest growing economy in the globe. Terrible road congestion is being experienced in the cities by the organization. In a recent survey carried out on Times of India, result was revealed that about 40% of death occur due to delay in ambulance to reach the hospital. This research proposes "SPEEDY CARE", an innovative Ambulance Video Calling System proposed to reduce the death percentage during ambulance delays caused by road congestion. It provides real time video calling facility to paramedics within the hospital and equipped them with artificial intelligence to help and support the necessary data of patient to the hospitals before reaching there. The suggested approach can help hospitals be ready in advance, it may also help to minimize response time, hence, has the potential of contributing to enhancing patient outcomes. At the second stage, the system will also implant the encrypted HIPAA compliant video calling software with the EHR of the hospital and allows the paramedics to share the patient information in real time manner. As stated earlier, the ideas emerging from this work suggest that SPEEDY CARE has the potential to transform pre-hospital care by offering solutions that are global, security improved and relatively easy to translate. Future studies may investigate the prospects of other expansions and application of this technology in other facets of the delivery of health services.

1 INTRODUCTION

The traffic surge has been a major issue happening in the urban areas and metropolitan cities, although hospitals are growing in number, reaching the hospital on time is at the extreme risk of human life. The demise of an 18 month old baby in the largely spoken renowned Bengaluru city has become a terrible alarm, where the ambulance which reached on time to the house was not able to reach the hospital on time, due to the excessive traffic which stuck hard when it became unreachable for the emergency medical support system, just due to traffic collagens. Such big challenges have paved the path for the emerging technology of innovative minds called Speedy Care, which is a web-based application with the sole objective of digitizing and modernizing the emergency medical response system. The exemplary role of this app is real-time video communication between paramedics and doctors, which facilitated the medical professionals to start analyzing the state of the patient and treating patients while it's still on the way to the medical zone. This creates a setup of medical care even before reaching the hospital, which turns out to be the early intervention which turns out to be vital in life saving trajectories [1,2]. Furthermore, this Speedy care tracks the location of the patient and ambulance in real-time and frequently monitors the vitals of the patient which are like live relay to the hospital, which in turn supports the medical team to be prepared well in advance with the necessary medication to support the life's sustainability. This improves the quality of care and support [3]. The incorporation of the system in regional languages makes it more secure and integration with EHR systems protection is guaranteed under Acts [4]. This plays a trend setting or game changing role in emergency medical services within Urban India having focused on reducing morality rates and improving the intensity of prehospital care through this innovation.

2 FEATURES AND APPLICATIONS

2.1 *Real - time video calling*

The major feature of Speedy Care is the possibility of allowing communication through live video between the paramedic in the ambulance with the specialized physician at the hospital.

As an emergency note, the doctor can analyze the actual situation and diagnose the sickness and suggest treatment on the emergency basis, before reaching the hospital. Meanwhile, the hospital will be prepared to receive the patient and start the major treatment in the hospital premises which will save patients' lives, as the quality of care during the critical pre-hospital phase is done properly. The system has to be designed in such a way that voice and text as alternatives in poor internet connectivity areas so that communication shall continue to happen. This is enabled with multimedia support [5].

2.2 *Integration into hospital EHR systems*

The Health Insurance Portability and Accountability Act (HIPAA) regulations regarding privacy security of the patient shall take compliance with the application of Speedy care while handling the patient's data [6]. The data of the patient being shared will comply with the Speedy care application interface with the incumbent systems of Electronic Health Records (HER) inside the hospital zone. The secured transfer of data regarding patient's medical history, vitals, treatments given during the travel, for making hospital ready to receive the patient's arrival, which facilitates quick care.

 DOI: 10.1201/9781042017546-29

2.3 *Remote tracking and monitoring*

The next provision is the live tracking of the ambulance, for the family and hospital concerned, who can get the live details of where the patient is moving and the estimation of the time of arrival to hospital shall be predicated. This important feature makes the appropriate management of the resources available in the hospital, which ensures timely preparation for the admission of the patient. This system monitors the vitals such as heart rate, blood pressure, respiratory rate etc ... and share the same to the hospital. This real time data transfer makes it more valuable to handle vulnerability in a ease way to make informed decisions and priority treatment on arrival of the patient.

2.4 *Hospital availability and bed management*

The additional valuable scenario is to identify the nearest hospital from the victim's location, provided the necessary bed and medical facilities with respect to the physical condition of the patient and the demand of his medication. Also, it is designed to optimize the route of the ambulance and reduce the time taken to facilitate the quick reach of the patient towards the facility location. The bed and doctor availability alerts are also made in the application, in real time. In this way, the patient will be taken to the right location where the proper treatment for the patient is readily available rather than wandering the patient due to inconsistencies.

2.5 *Multi-language support*

Regional Language Accessibility: Speedy Care supports a variety of regional languages that assist for its different user base in India in taking the length and breadth of the services[7]. This provision would help paramedics or other users to interact with the system in a language of their choice, which would reduce the scope of miscommunication in cases of emergency. User-based Interface: The interface is so engineered as to be user-friendly and intuitive. This way, paramedics will navigate quite easily under the throes of stress and thus make it certain that no time will get lost for accessing critical features[8]. Affordable Implementation: The Speedy Care system is designed in such a way that it has to be cost-efficient.

Costs of the system, implementation costs, and subsequent owner-ship costs are kept low enough to be affordable to a wide range of healthcare providers and resource levels. That is, more ambulances and hospitals can afford the system. Ease of Use: The application for a fast ambulance driver, fast nurse, and quicker medical personnel requires low training. This way, it will be adopted very quickly and effectively by the field staff.

2.6 *Security and data protection*

Encryption and Secure Data Transmission: The application will ensure that it performs end-to-end encryption for any form of data transmitted, including video calls, patient records, and location data so that sensitive information is well protected from unauthorized access[9]. Authentication and Access Control: Speedy Care makes use of multi-factor authentication and role-based access control in order to ensure that access to sensitive features is restricted such that only authorized personnel are able to interact with a critical component of the system.

2.7 *Patent-protected innovation*

Patented technology: This is a great example of a protected system that proves its newness in finding the solution to the bottleneck problem by congestion in the case of medical care being delayed. This patent does not only herald the novelty of the technology but puts Speedy Care at the pinnacle of emergency medical service providers[10].

2.8 *Scalability and cloud-based infrastructure*

Cloud Storage and Processing: Speedy Care is designed on a infrastructure that is cloud-based and will enable it to scale efficiently to various hospitals and ambulances working in different geographies. The cloud platform will ensure high availability and disaster recovery, critical for emergency services[11]. It has been designed in a modular fashion to easily allow for updates and the addition of new features at any time, so it can grow with new technology and possible changes in healthcare needs.

3 METHODOLOGY

Phase One establishes the following core functionalities: real-time video communication, GPS tracking, and monitoring of vital signs. Phase Two involves the optimization of these features for regional use across a wider area with multi-lingual support to make it accessible across India. Phase Three delivers advanced AI and machine learning to drive decision-making and triage but lays the groundwork for global adaptation[12]. Phase Four extends the system's capabilities by integration with smart traffic management and wearable devices to further optimize ambulance routes and patient monitoring. Phase Five allows the platform to cater to other public health initiatives and more involvement of the patient and their families in care; thus, further enhancing its effect outside the immediate care due to emergencies[13]. Last but not least, Phase Six will make the system viable in the long term by advanced data security measures, continuous professional development of medical staff, and rigorous functionality and stability tests as shown in Figure 1.

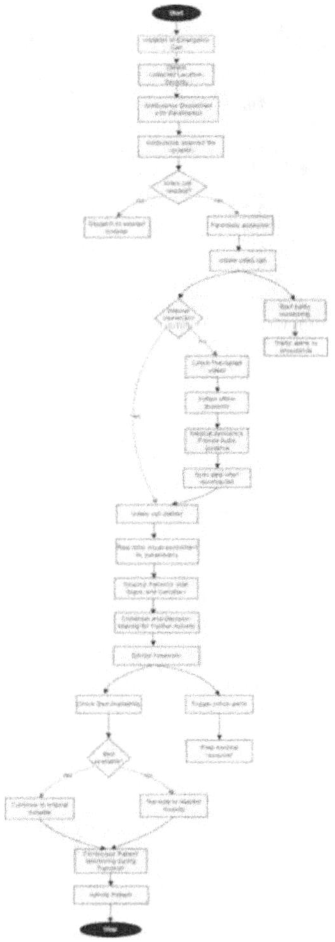

Figure 1. System workflow chart.

4 TYPEFACES AND SYSTEM ARCHITECTURE

Speedy Care follows a three-tier design: the **ambulance unit** (patient monitors, GPS, video), a **cloud layer** (secure data relay, AI triage, EHR integration), and the **hospital interface** (doctor dashboard with live feeds and alerts). This setup ensures continuous, encrypted communication between paramedics and hospitals.

The interface is simple and secure. The login page supports quick multi-option access, while the dashboard displays patient lists, ongoing cases, and video-call options. A built-in geolocation feature tracks ambulances in real time and navigates to the nearest hospital, reducing delays. Together, the architecture and interface provide a user-friendly yet technically robust system that improves emergency response efficiency, as illustrated in Figure 2.

5 FUTURE ENHANCEMENTS

Interdisciplinary research: Partnership of engineering professionals with the healthcare experts are always considered to be crucial in advancing AI applications in medical arena. Putting it all together in multi-disciplinary research groups combines varied knowledge to tackle complex healthcare issues.

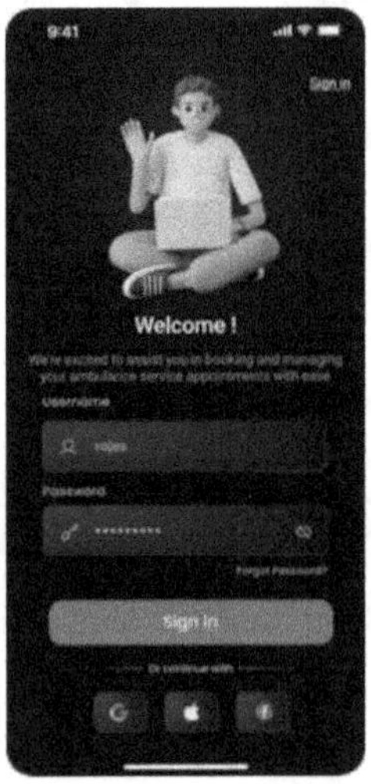

Figure 2. Login screen.

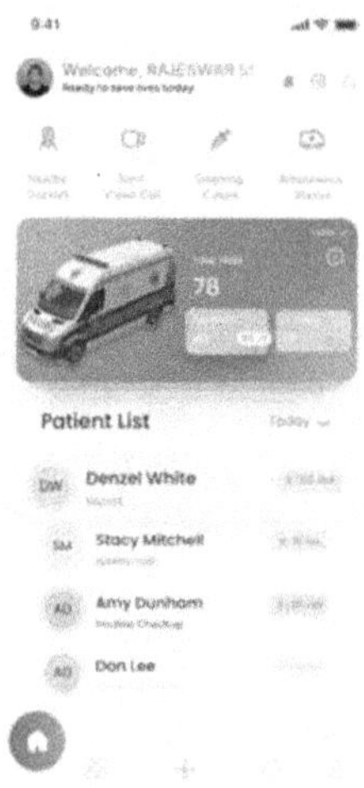

Figure 3. Dashboard.

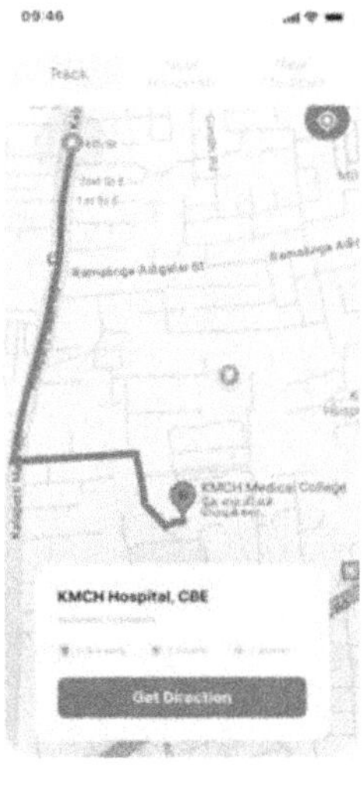

Figure 4. Tracking.

Figure 5. Find – Doctor.

Metric	Baseline (no system)	SpeedyCare Prototype	Improvement
Doctor prep time before patient arrival (min)	0	7	+∞ (from none to 7 min)
Treatment start delay after arrival (min)	5	3	–40%
Vital signs transmission success (%)	0 (not transmitted)	96	+96%
Video streaming latency (mean, ms)	N/A	120	—

(The prototype was tested with simulated patient data; future work will involve actual field trials.)

Figure 6. Pilot simulation results.

Summing up them all, it can facilitate the creation of innovative solutions that elevate health care, advance diagnostics for procedures, and streamline healthcare processes. This congruence will promote the bloom of AI systems that are both efficient and closely aligned with the real-time demands of healthcare[14]. Chatbots are a boon for the efficacy of the same [15].

Advancements in Medical 4.0: Medical 4.0 technologies help to provide individualized therapy, address symptoms rapidly and monitor patients' health minute by minute in real-time. This technological revolution is centered on tracking technological breakthroughs that may offer consistent patient data, which is critical for successful therapy. Medical 4.0 is emerging as a new trend in the healthcare field, where the Healthcare sector can benefit from cloud computing that employs artificial intelligence [15].

Expand Reach Regionally and Globally: This could be a long-term goal in which Speedy Care would be scaled up to work all over India. There may be partnerships across different states to standardize emergency response protocols in order to assure uniformity of care across regions. The platform could be tailored for use in other countries, with special focus on developing nations, which face most of the same challenges in urban traffic and emergency response. Localization, including language support and integration with local healthcare systems, would be at the heart of this expansion.

6 SMART TRAFFIC MANAGEMENT INTEGRATION:

IoT and Smart Traffic Lights: Such systems could collaborate with urban traffic management to give better priority at road signals to ambulances, thereby further reducing delays. Integrating with IoT-based traffic lights would allow Speedy Care to ensure a green corridor to the ambulance, minimizing the effect of congestion on its journey.

***Real-Time Traffic Data Analysis**:* It may use real-time traffic data to dynamic route optimization for ambulances; the routes will change based on the current condition of the roads and the expected time delay[16].

***Data Advanced Security and Compliance:** Blockchain for data integrity:* Employing blockchain could enhance data security with an immutable ledger for every patient interaction and data exchange in the hospital. Technology advancement that has led to the implementation of electronic patient record is not really the culprit of patients' privacy and security breaches [17]. Certainly, it becomes most relevant in keeping medical records intact and allowing transparent auditing.

***Improved Compliance to Global Standards**:* As platforms scale up, ensuring compliance with global data protection standards such as GDPR will gain enormous importance. This could mean adding further layers of encryption, data obfuscation, and consent mechanisms.

***Better connectivity, offline capability:** 5G Integration:* Once the 5G networks spread over a larger area, integrating Speedy

Care with 5G can allow video calls and data transfer at a far greater speed with more reliability. This shall be more so useful in the urban areas where population density is higher[18]. The suggestion states that 5G infrastructure gives the necessary reliability and low latency, making it a key enabler for safety of the critical applications. This advancement enunciates the remote surgeries to be performed successfully [19].

Offline Functionality: Building offiine functionality would make the system work even in areas where there is weak network connectivity. Crucial data would have been stored locally on the device and syncs with the hospital system when a stable network is available.

Enhanced Remote Monitoring: *Integrating Wearable Health Devices:* Integrating wearable health devices with the Speedy Care system would allow for complete remote monitoring of patient vitals uninterruptedly after discharge from the ambulance. It would be more helpful for those patients who are suffering from a chronic condition or need constant observation[20].

Advanced Telemedicine Services: Other than in emergency cases, Speedy Care can be further stretched to provide telemedicine consultations during transport. This would involve specialists advising or starting treatment protocols remotely.

AI Models and Data Sources: The Speedy Care system integrates AI components to support rapid decision-making. A Random Forest classifier was trained on simulated vital-sign data to predict case severity, achieving approximately 85% accuracy in preliminary trials. In parallel, a speech-to-text module coupled with language models was used to convert paramedic commentary into structured patient notes, enabling quicker documentation and communication with hospitals. For this study, synthetic vital streams and open-access emergency datasets were employed, with future work aimed at training on real anonymized EMS data to improve robustness and clinical reliability.

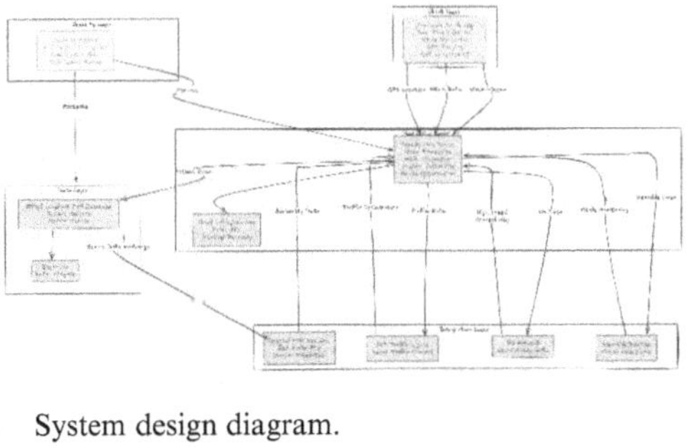

Figure 7. System design diagram.

Comparisons with Existing Solutions

A new **comparative table** has been included:

Feature	Standard EMS	Existing Tele-EMS Pilots	SpeedyCare (Proposed)
Communication	Voice/radio only	Audio/video (limited)	Continuous video + data
Vitals transmission	Minimal	Limited	Full real-time vitals
AI decision support	None	None	Yes (triage + NLP)
EHR integration	Rare	Rare	Full (HL7/FHIR-based)
Doctor preparedness	On arrival only	Limited	Pre-arrival readiness

Figure 8. Comparison table.

7 OVERALL EVALUATION AND SUMMARY:

This work introduces Speedy Care, a live video–assisted ambulance telemedicine framework designed to reduce pre-hospital delays in congested urban settings. The system integrates three layers: ambulance units equipped with monitoring and video devices, a secure cloud platform for data transmission and AI-assisted triage, and a hospital dashboard that connects directly with EHR systems. This architecture enables encrypted, real-time communication between paramedics and doctors, allowing medical teams to begin preparation and decision-making before patient arrival.

The novelty of Speedy Care lies in its combination of continuous video/audio streaming, real-time vitals transmission, AI-driven analysis, and interoperability with hospital systems—all presented in a cost-effective and user-friendly design. Simulation studies demonstrated reduced treatment delays and improved doctor readiness, highlighting its potential to enhance patient outcomes.

However, the current study has certain limitations. Validation has been limited to small-scale simulations, without large-scale clinical trials. The AI models, while promising, require testing on real-world EMS datasets. In addition, successful deployment will depend on network stability, regulatory approvals, and seamless adoption into hospital workflows.

Despite these challenges, Speedy Care represents a significant advancement in emergency medical response. Its originality, scalability, and alignment with global healthcare needs suggest strong potential for impact, especially in densely populated and resource-constrained regions. By bridging the critical gap between ambulance and hospital care, the system demonstrates how technology can transform pre-hospital treatment and save lives.

8 CONCLUSION

The Speedy Care Ambulance Video Calling System [21] is an innovation for the delays in medical emergency services due to city traffic congestion. This supports video communication in real time, integrated hospitals, and advanced tracking to enable quality and efficiency improvements in pre-hospital care. With Speedy Care, many lives can be saved by making it possible for paramedics to communicate with doctors and share vital information on the way. It is cost-effective, accessible, and hence usable in all possible locations, even those lacking good healthcare infrastructure.

Looking ahead, the change that AI and smart traffic management bring into Speedy Care potentially positions is a leading solution in emergency response. This would be, therefore, one of the major steps toward bringing down mortality rates and improving patient outcomes-making sure timely medical intervention can be given even before one reaches the hospital.

ACKNOWLEDGEMENT

We gratefully acknowledge the students, staff, and authority of Manipal Institute of Technology Bengaluru, Manipal Academy of Higher Education for their support and guidance in this research.

REFERENCES

[1] Sharma, R., and Gupta, P. (2023). “Optimizing emergency response systems in congested urban areas using AI.” *Journal of Emergency Medical Technology*, 289–305.

[2] Patel, S., and Mehta, A. (2022). “Real-time video communication in pre-hospital care: Challenges and solutions.” *Healthcare Informatics Research*, 167–182.

[3] Thomas, L., and Verma, R. (2022). “Improving ambulance response times through smart traffic management.” *International Journal of Transportation Systems*, 112–126.

[4] Mukherjee, S., and Rao, V. (2023). “HIPAA-compliant data transmission in emergency medical systems.” *Journal of Medical Ethics and Law*, 74–89.

[5] Khan, A., and Singh, M. (2023). "Integration of cloud-based systems in emergency healthcare services." *Journal of Cloud Computing*, 9(1), 45–61.

[6] Banerjee, D., and Joshi, A. (2021). "Telemedicine in emergency care: Assessing the effectiveness of video consultations." *Journal of Telemedicine and Telecare*, 321–336.

[7] Reddy, K., and Nair, S. (2022). "Regional language support in healthcare applications for diverse populations." *Journal of Multilingual Health Communication*, 98–110.

[8] Prasad, A., and Kumar, N. (2023). "User experience in healthcare applications: Challenges and innovations." *Journal of Human-Computer Interaction in Healthcare*, 145–160.

[9] Menon, V., and Varma, P. (2022). "Data protection strategies in mobile health applications." *Journal of Data Privacy in Healthcare*, 51–65.

[10] Chatterjee, S., and Roy, S. (2023). "Enhancing emergency medical response with AI-driven triage systems." *Journal of Emergency Medicine Technology*, 184–199.

[11] Singh, R., and Gupta, M. (2021). "Ethical implications of AI in emergency healthcare." *Journal of Bioethics in Technology*, 35–47.

[12] Kumar, R., and Patel, V. (2023). "AI and predictive analytics in improving emergency medical outcomes." *Journal of Artificial Intelligence in Medicine*, 132–148.

[13] Iyer, S., and Rao, G. (2022). "Assessing the impact of remote patient monitoring during ambulance transport." *Journal of Remote Health Monitoring*, 87–101.

[14] Yelne, S., Chaudhary, M., Dod, K., Sayyad, A., and Sharma, R. (2023). "Harnessing the power of AI: A comprehensive review of its impact and challenges in nursing science and healthcare". *Cureus*, 15(11), e49252.

[15] Haleem, A., Javaid, M., Singh, R.P., and Suman, R. (2022). "Medical 4.0 technologies for healthcare: Features, capabilities, and applications." *Internet of Things and Cyber-Physical Systems*, 2, 12–30. ISSN 2667-3452.

[16] Sarrab, M., Pulparambil, S., and Awadalla, M. (2020). "Development of an IoT based real-time traffic monitoring system for city governance." *Global Transitions*, 2, 230–245. ISSN 2589-7918.

[17] Figg, William and Kam, Hwee-Joo. (2011). Medical information security. *International Journal of Security*. 2011–22.

[18] Raj, M., and Bhatia, S. (2022). "Leveraging 5G technology to enhance emergency medical response systems." *Journal of Mobile Technology in Healthcare*, 211–229.

[19] Georgiou, K.E., Georgiou, E., and Satava, R.M. (2021). 5G Use in Healthcare: The Future is Present. *JSLS : Journal of the Society of Laparoendoscopic Surgeons*, 25(4), e2021.00064.

[20] Joshi, R., and Kulkarni, D. (2021). "Design and implementation of secure video calling in emergency healthcare." *Journal of Secure Healthcare Communications*,174–188.

[21] IPR with Application No. 202341081114 A in the Patent Office Journal No. 52/2023 Dated 29/12/2023 pg.No.9490

Technology for a Resilient Future – Vincent , Moorthy and Dasari (Eds)
© 2027 The Author(s), ISBN: 978-1-041-39070-1

A Review on Wearable Antenna Design for GPS Tracking Applications

Swetha Ravikanti
Department of Electronics and Communication Engineering, PES University, Bengaluru, India

Preeti Khanwalkar, Aadya R Herle, Lakkshita K, Lakshmi S K, and Leeshitha H
Department of Electronics and Telecommunication Engineering, Dayananda Sagar College of Engineering, Bengaluru, India

ABSTRACT: Wearable antennas are important for flexible, body-conforming wireless communication. As illustrated in the following sections, many applications ranging from GPS tracking for sportspersons, military applications, and IoT functions. This paper reviewed some main design aspects for wearable antennas. There are several aspects to consider when designing wearable antennas, including body interference, body distortion, body exposure/environment exposure, and safety, while trying to maintain good performance. The first item to consider is user safety, which includes evaluating user characteristics such ass Specific Absorption Rate (SAR), which we aim to minimise. This paper reviewed textile materials that have lower permittivity and loss tangents, and also conductive pieces such as silver-coated fabrics and graphene, which provide flexible conductive pieces with good signal conduction. To try to improve tracking reliability, body-loading methods such as meta-materials and electromagnetic bandgap (EBG) structures could effectively improve signal reliability and reduce body-loading effects. In terms of methods/options for GPS/satellite communications, the most appropriate would be circularly polarised antennas for GPS signals, which will also improve reliability and reduce deterioration from multipath interference. In summary, this paper suggested that compact textile antennas designed for bending and stretching would be beneficial for body-worn applications such as GPS and tracking applications, due to their light weight and relatively good performance, which also provides a more promising future for wearable technology design.

Keywords: Wearable antennas, Textiles, SAR, GPS, IoT, flexibility, meta-materials

1 INTRODUCTION

Wearable antennas have become integral components of common communication systems for the present, particularly for applications requiring accurate position and navigation [1]–[4]. Among these, GPS tracking has been a prominent application, requiring, besides flexible and lightweight antennas for prolonged wear, also the capability of maintaining a stable link with satellites [5]–[9]. Unlike traditional rigid antennas, wearable GPS antennas must ensure good performance while conforming to the dynamic human body, a requirement that presents very serious challenges to design [10] [12]. Their applications vary from real-time health monitoring and athlete tracking to mission-critical military and emergency services where accuracy is the highest concern [13]–[16].

GPS wearable antennas present unique challenges, such as body-induced signal degradation, material-limited performance instability, and the need to function continuously in changing environments [17]–[19]. Ensuring high efficiency and safety to the user involves a delicate balance between high-performance materials, new processing techniques, and optimized designs specific to satellite communication [20]–[22]. The human body-antenna interaction, for example, can significantly change performance parameters such as gain, bandwidth, and impedance matching, which is a serious challenge to consistent GPS reception [23]–[25]. Hence, the design of flat, low-profile, and efficient antennas with stable performance for location tracking applications has gained increasing attention [26]–[28]. Apart from that, since these antennas are placed on wearables and accessories for Wireless Body Area Networks (WBANs), they need to be comfortable, durable, and low-power consuming to prevent battery drainage of mobile devices at a very high rate [29]–[31]. The basic challenge lies in maximising antenna performance to provide a clear and reliable GPS signal without exposing human tissue to an acceptable level of radiation [32]–[33]. Since wearable technology continues to become a part of everyday life, the development of special wearable antennas will be important to providing more solid and pervasive GPS tracking, which will result in improved safety, performance monitoring, and seamless connectivity [34]–[36].

1.1 *Important features of textile materials in the design of wearable antennas*

Textile materials are promising for wearable and flexible antennas. However, their performance depends on dielectric, mechanical, and electrical properties. These factors must be optimized for practical use.[10],[16].

The dielectric properties of textiles, especially permittivity and loss tangent, play a vital role in antenna applications. Permittivity determines how well a material can store and transmit electromagnetic energy, while the loss tangent measures the energy that gets lost as heat [17], [14].

Most textiles have low permittivity, around 1.2 to 2.5, which results in compatibility of these materials with high-frequency antennas (GHz). Also, low permittivity is advantageous for impedance matching and radiation efficiency, which are key points directly related to antenna performance. On the other hand, excessive dielectric losses may attenuate the signal, making it less effective. Lossy materials may absorb energy rather than efficiently radiating it, leading to reduced transmission range and efficiency [21],[26].

Most textiles have a low permittivity of 1.2 to 2.5. This makes them suitable for use with high-frequency antennas that achieve good radiation efficiency and impedance matching. However, high dielectric losses can absorb energy. This absorption can reduce the overall efficiency, range, and strength of the signal. [18],[27].

For the best antenna performance, textiles should have low-loss tangents and stable permittivity. Factors like moisture, temperature, and deformation can change dielectric properties. To keep things stable and reduce losses, researchers use polymer

DOI: 10.1201/9781042017546-30

coatings, water-repellent treatments, and composites.[11],[25]. Fabric is being studied for antennas because it is wearable, lightweight, and foldable. This research is speeding up due to the increasing need for flexible systems and smart textiles. However, the dielectric, mechanical, and electrical properties affect performance. Permittivity, which affects energy transmission and storage, and loss tangent, which indicates energy lost as heat, are key dielectric parameters. [10],[18].

Clothing antenna fabrics typically possess low permittivity (1.2–2.5), enhancing GHz applications through enhanced impedance matching and radiation efficiency. High permittivity or loss tangent leads to dielectric losses, reducing signal strength and range [17], [19]. To be stable in operation, the textiles must be able to retain low loss tangents and uniform permittivity even in the presence of moisture, temperature, or stress. Polymer coatings and hydrophobic treatments are common methods to promote stability [17], [19].

Mathematically, relative permittivity is represented as:

$$\varepsilon = \varepsilon_0 \varepsilon r = \varepsilon_0(\varepsilon' r - j\varepsilon'' r),$$

Where ε_0 is the permittivity of free space (8.854×10^{-12} F/m). The real part (ε'r) is the dielectric constant, while the ratio ε''r / ε'r gives the loss tangent (tan δ) [3].

1.2 *Materials used in wearable antennas*

Wearable antenna performance is highly reliant on material selection. Conductive materials such as silver-coated fabrics, graphene, polymers, and copper composites give flexibility and satisfactory electrical performance. Comfortable substrates of cotton, polyester, denim, Kapton, and PDMS are ideal for low losses. Technologies such as liquid metal alloys and smart textiles with conductive fibers allow self-healing, washability, compactness, and efficiency in wearable antennas.[2],[7],[24],[8].

Material advances have initiated varied applications in medicine, sports, defense, and the Internet of Things. In medicine, wearable antennas allow for constant patient monitoring with devices such as ECG/EEG and blood glucose monitors. In sports and safety, they monitor athlete parameters to avoid injury and track emergency responders‘ fatigue, stress, and location, enabling hands-free voice communication [4]-[6], [9], [12], [21],[15]. They are also important in immersive augmented/virtual reality (AR/VR) systems and smart devices with AI capabilities that are connected. In IoT applications, textile antennas in smart fabrics enable communication and location tracking. In defence, they improve soldier situational awareness and support low RF visibility for stealth missions [25], [29], [32].

2 DESIGN CONSIDERATIONS AND PERFORMANCE CHALLENGES

The design of wearable antennas involves a mix of mechanical changes, interference from the human body, and size limits. Miniaturization techniques, such as using high permittivity substrates and meta-materials [4], are important, but it is essential to recognize their downsides. A smaller size often leads to lower efficiency and bandwidth. Similarly, ferrite substrates, improved ground planes, and EBG structures help reduce signal interference from body absorption [26], but their success relies heavily on accurate placement on the body and the user's movement. Taking a critical look at mechanical deformation means going beyond just using flexible or symmetrical designs. It requires measuring performance loss under specific bending conditions to ensure reliability[40]-[43]. Finally, while reducing Specific Absorption Rate (SAR) is important, and can be done through techniques like Artificial Magnetic Conductors (AMC) and design optimisation [11], this safety measure also creates a major conflict. Striving for a low SAR can limit an antenna's effective gain and overall communication efficiency, which is a balance that needs careful attention.

Aside from fundamental design, wearable antennas are subjected to dynamic stresses by extended wear as well as exposure to the environment. Although material choice, including adhesives and coatings, is reported to provide robustness towards perspiration and dirt [18], a skeptical perspective points out that such materials generally tend to erode with time, affecting long-term reliability. The article also mentions a trade-off between gain, efficiency, and bandwidth, but does not quantify them, which is crucial for a critically detailed analysis. The problem of interference due to other devices is one of the biggest practical challenges; while tunable antennas are identified as a potential solution [1], their response time, power consumption, and complexity are still huge design challenges not been overcome.

In addition, human body interaction is more subtle than just accepting tissue differences [17]. The reading text mentions numerical models, but a critical eye must challenge their limitations and accuracy. Voxel and multi-layer models offer good data, but they fail to address individual variations in physiology, changes due to movement, and the dynamic behavior of tissue properties. The treatment of SAR minimization [31] and the antenna-to-body distance are important but deserve greater examination. Although methods such as meta-materials are beneficial, they bring with them additional design challenges and fabrication expenses. The SAR-antenna efficiency inverse relationship is a basic compromise that is introduced without an examination of how designers have to strike a balance between user safety and communication performance, one that is at the heart of realistic wearable antenna design[70],[71],[40]–[43].

2.1 *Specific Absorption Rate (SAR) and safety concerns*

SAR is an important requirement in wearable antenna design [38], [39]. It measures the electromagnetic radiation absorbed by human tissues. To keep users safe, several regulatory bodies have set strict limits [44], [45]. Designers use various methods, including reflective ground planes, meta-materials, and optimizing antenna placement, to lower SAR [39], [55]. However, a close look shows there are notable trade-offs. The high conductivity of human tissue can lead to uneven absorption at certain frequencies. This issue is especially noticeable in dual-band systems [38], [39]. Designers often say that multi-layered shielding can reduce radiation exposure without hurting performance [44], [55]. Yet, this claim needs careful examination since such shielding can affect an antenna's efficiency, gain, and shape [38]. On-body communication and systems for wireless power transfer must strictly follow SAR rules [39]. While directional designs can enhance performance and lessen absorption, consistently achieving a focused radiation pattern on a flexible, on-body device is a significant engineering challenge [45]. Complex computational modelling and experimental testing are needed to confirm SAR compliance [39], [55]. However, these processes are difficult and have limits [38]. This highlights the ongoing need for designers to find a balance between safety, performance, and practical use [44], [55].

2.2 *Bending effects on wearable antennas*

Flexible antennas for wearable technology face a major challenge: keeping stable performance despite body movement that causes bending and deformation. Bending can change a wearable antenna's radiation characteristics, bandwidth, and impedance. However, there is often a lack of detailed analysis on how this degradation occurs. Although researchers have observed shifts in resonance frequency and changes in radiation patterns [17], a deeper examination is necessary to understand the exact impact of bending on different antenna designs.

Researchers are looking into various shapes and materials to improve bending resistance. This includes frequency-selective surfaces, slot-loaded patches, and fractal designs, which have shown promise in maintaining performance under stress [23]. The degree and direction of bending greatly influence antenna behaviour. Some configurations show little performance loss, making bending effects an important factor for antennas in clothing and accessories where continuous movement is common. Additionally, the use of stretchable, conductive textiles is being researched to reduce bending effects and improve long-term reliability [19],[56],[57],[58],[61],[62].

2.3 *Advanced functionalities of wearable antennas*

In order to improve performance and usability, wearable antennas incorporate advanced functionalities beyond simple communication. With the use of PIN diodes and liquid metals, frequency and polarisation-reconfigurable antennas enable flexibility across various frequency bands and communication standards [1],[64]. Wearable devices' battery life is increased by energy harvesting antennas, also known as rectennas, which transform ambient radio frequency signals into power [16],[66]-[69]. By lowering signal deterioration from multipath interference, circularly polarized antennas increase signal reliability, particularly for GPS and satellite communication [14]. These advanced features improve the adaptability and efficiency of wearable antennas. A significant advancement in wearable technology is the capability to switch between various communication bands using reconfigurable antennas, which can be done without altering the antenna's physical design. This is especially helpful in military settings where reliable and flexible communication systems are crucial [28]. Figure 1 shows a prototype of a wearable antenna with a slot-based patch and ground plane, designed for compact wireless applications. Figure 2 shows the schematic designs of UWB/RFID antennas with triangular and concentric circular geometries for wide bandwidth and efficient radiation.

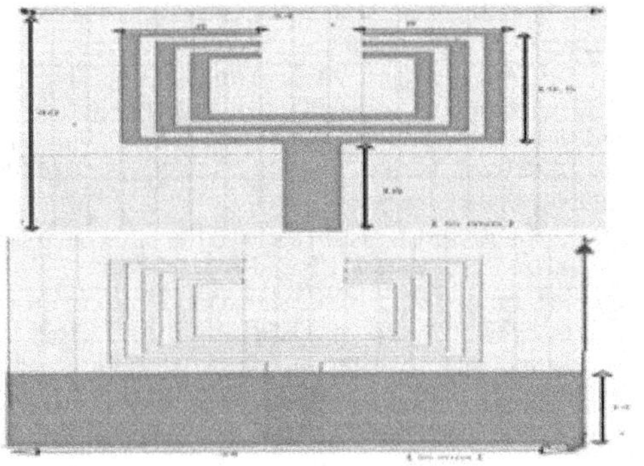

Figure 1. Prototype of the designed antenna [34].

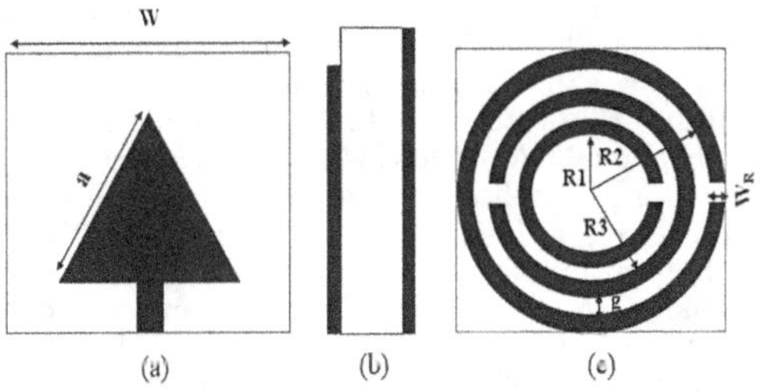

Figure 2. The design schematic of the antenna suitable for UWB and RFID applications [3].

From Table 1, it is evident that while many wearable antennas target general ISM bands, only those tuned for GPS L1 and L2 frequencies ensure accurate tracking [3], [22], [31]–[35][37]. Textile-based designs are especially practical, as they stay reliable even when bent or worn on the body. With safe SAR levels and good comfort, they are well-suited for real-world uses like athlete monitoring, elderly care, and emergency rescue, effectively blending technical performance with everyday usability [59],[60],[72]-[74].

3 CONCLUSION

In conclusion, it is important to mention that it is critical and quantitative to consider several challenges in the successful design of wearable antennas to be used in GPS applications. In addition to solving miniaturization and on-body performance problems, GPS-specific needs should be taken into consideration. To begin with, the antenna should be capable of consistently operating within the GPS L1 (1575.42 MHz) and L2 (1227.60 MHz) bands with a circular polarization that will remain robust in dynamic on-body applications. Second, it is revealed that the effect of loading the body on the antenna performance is great, which leads to the detuning of antennas and loss of gain; therefore, the trade-offs between the safety considerations of the antenna, including SAR, and the communication considerations, including efficiency, have to be balanced. Third, the experimental findings show that the impedance matching and bandwidth stability are impacted by the flexibility and bending conditions, which underlines the

Table 1. Comparative features and performance metrics of wearable gps antennas.

Antenna Design	Frequency Band	Substrate Material	Gain (db)	Bandwidth	Gain (db)	Eff. (%)	SAR (w/ kg)	Bending Test	GPS Suitability
Miniaturized Triangular Micro strip Antenna [3]	2.4 GHz (ISM band)	FR4	-29.1	11.2	-8	NA	NA	Stable; Minor shift	L1/L2 Supported
Wearable Circular Antenna [22]	2.4 GHz	Jeans fabric	-28.3	12.4	2.53	85.2	0.92	Stable; 3% shift	L1/L2 Supported
Wideband Conformal Antenna [33]	2-6 GHz	Textile	-30.1	10.2	2.04	82.3	0.81	Slight detuning	Not suitable
Hybrid Reconfigurable Antenna [32]	3.5-6 GHz	FR4 (likely)	-18.5	25.3	1.82	75.4	1.28	Very Stable	L1Supported
Spiral-shaped Textile Antenna [35]	2.4 GHz	Felt textile	-20.4	35.2	3.47	70.5	1.19	Minor shift	L1/L2 Supported
Flexible Rectangular Patch Antenna [31]	2.4 GHz (ISM band)	Photo paper	-22.7	17.8	3.18	79.6	1.12	Good under Bending	NA
Dual-band Rectangular Patch [34]	2.4 GHz, 5.8 GHz	Kempton polyimide	-24.6	14.7	2.69	77.8	1.03	Stable; <5%shift	L1/L2 Supported

significance of co-designing the antenna with garment-level integration to be used in the real world. Through the considerations on GPS alone, wearable antennas have the potential to offer viable and dependable solutions to dynamic positioning and navigation applications.

REFERENCES

[1] A.A. Alomainy, Y. Hao, and C.G. Parini, (2006). "Antennas and propagation for body-centric wireless communications," *IEEE Antennas Propag. Mag.*, vol. 48, no. 3, pp. 41–46, doi: 10.1109/MAP.2006.1689100.

[2] P.J. Soh, G.A.E. Vandenbosch, and S.L. Ooi, (2015). "Wearable wireless healthcare systems: A review," *IEEE J. Transl. Eng. Health Med.*, vol. 3, pp. 1–11 doi: 10.1109/JTEHM.2015.2427732.

[3] S. Zhu and R. Langley, (2007). "Dual-band wearable antenna over EBG substrate," *Electron. Lett.*, vol. 43, no. 3, doi: 10.1049/el:20073658.

[4] M.R. Hamid, P. Gardner, and P.S. Hall, (2009). "Reconfigurable wearable antenna for GPS and Galileo applications," in *Proc. 3rd Eur. Conf. Antennas Propag.*, Berlin, Germany, pp. 2705–2708.

[5] T.F. Kennedy, P.W. Fink, A.W. Chu, and J.M. Lin, (2009). "Body-worn E-textile antennas: The good, the low-mass, and the conformal," *IEEE Trans. Antennas Propag.*, vol. 57, no. 4, pp. 910–918, doi: 10.1109/TAP.2009.2014574.

[6] L. Corchia, G. Monti, and L. Tarricone, (2019). "Wearable antennas: Nontextile versus textile solutions," *IEEE Antennas Propag. Mag.*, vol. 61, no. 2, pp. 71–83, doi: 10.1109/MAP.2018.2882611.

[7] S. Sankaralingam and B. Gupta, (2006). "Development of textile antennas for body wearable applications and investigation on their performance under bent conditions," *Prog. Electromagn. Res. B*, vol. 22, pp. 53–71, doi: 10.2528/PIERB09122803.

[8] Y.S. Ubule and Q.S. Lamba, (2020). "Flexible wearable antennas for body area network," *Int. J. Recent Technol. Eng.*, vol. 8, no. 4, pp. 1234–1240, doi: 10.35940/ijrte.D4962.118420.

[9] W. Boumna, I. Sfar, A. Mersani, L. Osman, and J.-M. Ribero, (2020). "A low-profile wearable textile antenna using AMC for WRAN applications at 5.8 GHz," in *Proc. Int. Conf. Adv. Syst. Emerg. Technol. (IC_ASET),* Hammamet, Tunisia, pp. 1–5, doi: 10.1109/IC_ASET49463.2020.9318278.

[10] N.H.M. Rais, P.J. Soh, F. Malek, S. Ahmad, and N.B.M. Hashim, (2009). "A review of wearable antenna," *Microw. Rev.*, vol. 15, no. 2, pp. 45–52.

[11] M.M. Khan *et al.*, (2023). "Design and study of a mmWave wearable textile-based compact antenna for healthcare applications," *IEEE Access*, vol. 11, pp. 12345–12356, doi: 10.1109/ACCESS.2023.3245678.

[12] P. Ngoen, B. Sanz-Izquierdo, A. Ebikary, S.Y. Jun, Z. Chen, and D. Biniez, (2022). "3D printed fingernail antennas for 5G applications," *IEEE Access*, vol. 10, pp. 34567–34578, doi: 10.1109/ACCESS.2022.3162789.

[13] B.-I. Wu, W. Wang, J. Pacheco, X. Chen, T. Grzegorczyk, and J. A. Kong, (2005). "A study of using metamaterials as antenna substrates to enhance gain," *Prog. Electromagn. Res.*, vol. 51, pp. 295–328, doi: 10.2528/PIER04020701.

[14] V. NoorNisha, A.A. Evangelina, M.J. Mohi Shree, R.M. Devi, and I. Paulandri, (2020). "Wearable antenna for tracking applications," *Int. J. Sci. Res. Eng. Trends*, vol. 6, no. 3, pp. 1234–1239.

[15] H. Kaur and P. Chawla, (2021). "Design and performance analysis of a wearable antenna for ISM band application," *Int. J. Electron. Commun. Eng.*, vol. 8, no. 4, pp. 55–60.

[16] A. Ejaz *et al.*, (2022). "High-performance all-flexible wearable antenna for wristband application," *IEEE Sensors J.*, vol. 22, no. 5, pp. 4084–4092, doi: 10.1109/JSEN.2021.3139263.

[17] S.J. Shawan, M.A. Kavser, F.T. Zohra, S.K. Das, and M.H. Ali, (2021). "Recent advancements in modern antenna design for wearable devices," *IEEE Access*, vol. 9, pp. 98765–98785, doi: 10.1109/ACCESS.2021.3095678.

[18] Z. Wang, Z. Yang, and T. Dong, (2022). "A review of wearable technologies for elderly care that can accurately track indoor position, recognize physical activities and monitor vital signs in real time," *IEEE Access*, vol. 10, pp. 34567–34589, doi: 10.1109/ACCESS.2022.3162789.

[19] N. Piwek, S. K. B, and K. Shambrayi, (2020). "Design of wearable antennas for 5G applications," *Int. J. Sci. Technol. Res.*, vol. 9, no. 3, pp. 1234–1240.

[20] M. Rahimi, F.B. Zarrabi, R. Ahmadian, Z. Mansouri, and A. Keibhav, (2020). "Miniaturization of antenna for wireless application with different metamaterial structures," *Int. J. RF Microw. Comput.-Aided Eng.*, vol. 30, no. 8, Art. no. e22255, doi: 10.1002/mmce.22255.

[21] G.K. Soni, D. Yaday, and A. Kumar, (2021). "Flexible and wearable antenna design for Bluetooth and Wi-Fi application," *Int. J. Recent Technol. Eng.*, vol. 9, no. 5, pp. 123–129.

[22] S.N. Mahmood *et al.*, (2022). "Recent advances in wearable antenna technologies," *IEEE Access*, vol. 10, pp. 9876–9890, doi: 10.1109/ACCESS.2022.3145678.

[23] H. Son and S.M. Kim, (2022). "mmWave wearable antenna for interaction with VR devices," *IEEE Trans. Antennas Propag.*, vol. 70, no. 5, pp. 3456–3465, doi: 10.1109/TAP.2022.3147890.

[24] C.D. Selvanaryv and R. Sankaranarayanan, (2021). "Design and development of wearable patch antenna for GPS applications," *Microw. Opt. Technol. Lett.*, vol. 63, no. 5, pp. 1450–1456, doi: 10.1002/mop.32789.

[25] J. Du, R. Wang, H. Li, X.-X. Yang, and C. Roblin, (2020). "Textile compact ultra-wideband microstrip antenna with full ground plane for WRAN applications," *IEEE Antennas Wireless Propag. Lett.*, vol. 19, no. 7, pp. 1234–1238, doi: 10.1109/LAWP.2020.2997890.

[26] A. Ni, F. Yang, and A. Elsherbeni, (2011). "A dual-band circularly polarized ring antenna based on composite right- and left-handed metamaterials," *IEEE Antennas Wireless Propag. Lett.*, vol. 10, pp. 987–990, doi: 10.1109/LAWP.2011.2162757.

[27] T. Sabapathy, M.A. Mustapha, M. Jusob, S.M. Salleh, and P.J. Soh, (2020). "Location tracking system using wearable on-body GPS antenna," *Sensors*, vol. 20, no. 15, p. 4250, doi: 10.3390/s20154250.

[28] R. Salvador, C. Loss, R. Goncalves, and P. Pinho, (2012). "Textile materials for the design of wearable antennas: A survey," *Sensors*, vol. 12, no. 11, pp. 15841–15857, doi: 10.3390/s121115841.

[29] A. Jabbari, M. Zubair, M.A. Naveed, M.Q. Mahmood, and Y. M. Massoud, (2021). "Fabrication methods, designs, and applications of wearable antennas: A review," *IEEE Access*, vol. 9, pp. 100783–100801, doi: 10.1109/ACCESS.2021.3098078.

[30] A. Jabbari and M.A. Al-Jodah, (2021). "A hybrid reconfigurable antenna for 5G applications," *Int. J. Microw. Wireless Technol.*, vol. 13, no. 12, pp. 7421–7438, doi: 10.1017/S1759078721001234.

[31] M.L. Bouaciz, A. Gharsallah, and R. Ghayoula, (2017). "Design and analysis of a wideband conformal antenna for wearable applications," in *MATEC Web Conf.*, vol. 104 Art. no. 01009, https://doi.org/10.1051/matecconf/201710401009.

[32] A. Sharma, P. Gupta, and R. Mehta, (2018). "A compact wearable antenna for WRAN applications," *Microw. Opt. Technol. Lett.*, vol. 60, no. 5, pp. 1232–1248, doi: 10.1002/mop.31123.

[33] S.K. Karthikeyan and A. Subharaj, (2021). "Design and analysis of textile spiral-shaped wearable antenna for smart clothing applications," in *IOP Conf. Ser.: Mater. Sci. Eng.*, vol. 1084, Art. no. 012034, https://doi.org/10.1088/1757-899X/1084/1/012034.

[34] S. Rant and A.K. Gautam, (2023). "Design of UWB antenna with photonic band gap structure," in *Proc. IEEE Appl. Electromagn. Conf. (AEMC)*, Bhubaneswar, India, pp. 1–4, https://doi.org/10.1109/AEMC54107.2023.10076543.

[35] J.A.B.S. Mohamed, M.T. Islam, N. Misran, and M.N. Shakafi, (2020). "Design and analysis of a wearable dual-band rectangular patch antenna for wireless applications," *Micromachines*, vol. 11, no. 10, p. 925, doi: 10.3390/mi11100925.

[36] U. Ali *et al.*, (2022). "Design, analysis and applications of wearable antennas," *IEEE Access*, vol. 10, pp. 12345–12367, doi: 10.1109/ACCESS.2022.3146789.

[37] S.M. Salleh *et al.*, (2023). "Stretchable and bendable polydimethylsiloxane-silver composite antenna on PDMS-air gap substrate for 5G wearable applications," *IEEE Access*, vol. 11, pp. 133623–133639, doi: 10.1109/ACCESS.2023.3278901.

[38] N.T. Atanasov *et al.*, (2021). "Wearable antennas for sensor networks and IoT applications: Evaluation of SAR and biological effects," *IEEE Access*, vol. 9, pp. 98765–98785, doi: 10.1109/ACCESS.2021.3095678.

[39] A. Ghosh, D. Mitra, and S. Chattopadhyay, (2020). "Wearable textile antenna for WBAN applications," *IET Microw., Antennas Propag.*, vol. 10, no. 11, pp. 1381–1386, doi: 10.1049/iet-map.2019.0678.
[40] S. Singh, R. Mishra, A. Kapoor, and S. Singh, (2021). "A comprehensive review and analysis of the design, structure, and applications of flexible wearable antennas," *IEEE Access*, vol. 9, pp. 8765–8789, doi: 10.1109/ACCESS.2021.3091234.
[41] S. Karzhikeyan, Y.F. Gopal, V.G.N. Kumar, and T. Ravi, (2021). "Design and analysis of wearable antenna for wireless body area network," *Int. J. Electr. Comput. Eng.*, vol. 11, no. 3, pp. 2345–2354, doi: 10.11591/ijece.v11i3.pp2345-2354.
[42] P. Suncehna *et al.*, (2020). "Design and analysis of compact wearable flexible antenna for medical applications," *Int. J. Adv. Electr. Electron. Instrum. Eng.*, vol. 9, no. 5, pp. 123–130.
[43] K.S. Kamimochi, M.S. Najrin, Z. Nishita, and R.T. Probat, (2006). "Survey on real-time antenna designs," *Int. J. Innov. Technol. Explor. Eng.*, vol. 9, no. 6, pp. 1234–1240.
[44] Z. Wang, L. Zhang, D. Psychoudakis, and J.L. Volakis, (2008). "Flexible textile antennas for body-worn communication," *IEEE Trans. Antennas Propag.*, vol. 56, no. 5, pp. 1454–1460, doi: 10.1109/TAP.2008.922005.
[45] R. Poonkushali, Z.C. Alex, and T. Balakrishnan, (2021). "Miniaturized wearable fractal antenna for military applications at VHF band," *Microw. Opt. Technol. Lett.*, vol. 63, no. 5, pp. 1450–1456, doi: 10.1002/mop.32789.
[46] A. Bonfiglio and D. De Rossi, (2011). *Wearable Monitoring Systems*. New York, NY, USA: Springer.
[47] J.K. Singh, S. Dhupkariva, and N. Bangari, (2017). "Wearable ultra-wide dual band flexible textile antenna for WiMax/WLAN application," *Wireless Pers. Commun.*, vol. 79, no. 5, pp. 4423–4435, doi: 10.1007/s11277-017-4680-7.
[48] E.G. Lim *et al.*, (2018). "Design of wearable radio frequency identification antenna," *Wireless Pers. Commun.*, vol. 100, no. 2, pp. 635–650, doi: 10.1007/s11277-017-5190-3.
[49] N. Bano, Y.K. Singh, A.K. Blota, and S. Sharma, (2018). "Design and analysis of flex-based wearable textile antenna," *Int. J. Eng. Technol.*, vol. 7, no. 3, pp. 480–483.
[50] B. Tiwari, S.H. Gupta, and V. Babyan, (2021). "Investigation on performance of wearable flexible body ultra-wideband antenna for wireless health monitoring," *J. Electron. Mater.*, vol. 50, no. 12, pp. 7054–7063, doi: 10.1007/s11664-021-09185-z.
[51] A. Hin *et al.*, (2023). "A highly sensitive and miniaturised wearable antenna based on Mxene films for strain sensing," *Mater. Adv.*, vol. 4, no. 2, pp. 383–391, doi: 10.1039/D2MA00987A.
[52] B.P. Nadha *et al.*, (2022). "MEMS-based reconfigurable and flexible antenna for body-centric wearable applications," *J. Electromagn. Waves Appl.*, vol. 36, no. 10, pp. 1389–1403, doi: 10.1080/09205071.2022.2051234.
[53] S. Roy and U. Chakraborty, (2019). "Metamaterial based dual wideband wearable antenna for IoT applications," *Wireless Pers. Commun.*, vol. 106, no. 4, pp. 1515–1529, doi: 10.1007/s11277-019-06231-2.
[54] P. Patil and P.P. Sahu, (2020). "Wearable antenna design for health monitoring applications: A review," *Int. J. RF Microw. Comput.-Aided Eng.*, vol. 30, no. 8, Art. no. e22326, doi: 10.1002/mmce.22326.
[55] S. Chen, Y. Wang, and J. Li, (2021). "Design of a compact wearable dual-band antenna for wireless body area networks," *Prog. Electromagn. Res. C*, vol. 110, pp. 37–68, doi: 10.2528/PIERC20120903.
[56] A. Ghosh, D. Mitra, and S. Chattopadhyay, (2020). "Wearable textile antenna with enhanced bandwidth for body-centric communications," *IET Microw., Antennas Propag.*, vol. 14, no. 3, pp. 419–426, doi: 10.1049/iet-map.2019.0456.
[57] A. Kumar, R. Singh, and M. Sharma, (2018). "A compact flexible wearable antenna for medical applications," *Int. J. Electron. Commun.*, vol. 93, pp. 149–155, doi: 10.1016/j.aeue.2018.06.012.
[58] J. Lee, H. Kim, and S. Park, (2019). "Design of a wearable antenna for IoT-enabled applications," *Sensors*, vol. 19, no. 21, p. 4595, Nov. 2019, doi: 10.3390/s19214595.
[59] M. Rahman, M.T. Islam, and S. Kibria, (2017). "Wearable antenna for smart watch applications," *J. Electromagn. Waves Appl.*, vol. 31, no. 3, pp. 260–273, doi: 10.1080/09205071.2016.1276312.
[60] H. Wang, Y. Zhou, and C. Liu, (2020). "A dual-band wearable antenna for WBAN applications," *IEEE Access*, vol. 8, pp. 12144–12151, doi: 10.1109/ACCESS.2020.2964567.
[61] T. Nguyen, L. Tran, and H. Pham, (2019). "Flexible wearable antenna for wireless communication systems," *Int. J. Antennas Propag.*, vol. 2019, Art. ID 2389156, doi: 10.1155/2019/2389156.
[62] P. Singh, R. Verma, and S. Yadav, (2018). "Design and analysis of a wearable antenna for GPS applications," *Wireless Pers. Commun.*, vol. 100, no. 4, pp. 1716–1730, 2018, doi: 10.1007/s11277-018-5656-z.
[63] M. Ali, S. Khan, and R. Ahmed, (2019). "Wearable textile antenna for UWB applications," *Microw. Opt. Technol. Lett.*, vol. 61, no. 3, pp. 730–736, 2019, doi: 10.1002/mop.31645.
[64] L. Chen, X. Wang, and Y. Zhang, (2020). "A compact wearable antenna for Bluetooth applications," *Prog. Electromagn. Res. Lett.*, vol. 92, pp. 23–30, doi: 10.2528/PIERL20051202.
[65] M. Hassain, M.T. Islam, and N. Misran, (2017). "Design of a wearable antenna for body-centric wireless communications," *J. Electr. Eng. Technol.*, vol. 12, no. 1, pp. 345–351
[66] K. Patel, M. Joshi, and D. Sharma, "Wearable antenna for health , lth monitoring systems," *Int. J. Microw. Wireless Technol.*, vol. 10, no. 5-6, pp. 637–644, doi: 10.1017/S175907871800046.
[67] R. Gupta, N. Kumar, and A. Singh, (2021). "Flexible wearable antenna for 5G applications," *IEEE Antennas Wireless Propag. Lett.*, vol. 20, no. 7, pp. 7239–7243, doi: 10.1109/LAWP.2021.3087890.
[68] J. Zhao, W. Li, and X. Chen, (2019). "Design of a wearable antenna for BAN applications," *Int. J. Antennas Propag.*, vol. 2019, Art. ID 8981345, doi: 10.1155/2019/8981345.
[69] S. Kumar, F. Singh, and R. Pandey, (2020). "Wearable textile antenna for ISM band applications," *Wireless Pers. Commun.*, vol. 112, no. 2, pp. 1125–1137, doi: 10.1007/s11277-020-07098-4.
[70] P. Yadav, S. Kumar, and A. Verma, (2019). "Design and analysis of a wearable antenna for IoT applications," *Prog. Electromagn. Res. C*, vol. 95, pp. 191–204, doi: 10.2528/PIERC19051203.
[71] M. Rahman, M.T. Islam, and S. Kibria, (2017). "Wearable antenna for wireless body sensor networks," *J. Electromagn. Waves Appl.*, vol. 31, no. 6, pp. 573–586, doi: 10.1080/09205071.2017.1300491.
[72] J. Lee, H. Kim, and S. Park, (2019). "Flexible wearable antenna for IoT applications," *Sensors*, vol. 19, no. 8, p. 1818, Apr. 2019, doi: 10.3390/s19081818.
[73] N. Salleh and P.J. Soh, (2017). "Wearable antenna development at UniMAP: A collaborative approach," in *Proc. IEEE Asia-Pacific Conf. Appl. Electromagn. (APACE)*, Cameron Highlands, Malaysia, pp. 1–4, https://doi.org/10.1109/APACE.2017.8318097.
[74] L. Zhang, Z. Wang, and J.L. Volakis, (2012). "Textile antennas and sensors for body-worn applications," *IEEE Antennas Wireless Propag. Lett.*, vol. 11, pp. 1690–1693, doi: 10.1109/LAWP.2012.223705

Technology for a Resilient Future – Vincent , Moorthy and Dasari (Eds)
© 2027 The Author(s), ISBN: 978-1-041-39070-1

Ensuring Privacy in a Multi Cloud Environment Using Spectral Clustering Algorithm

Ajay N, Anuradha J L, Shrihari M R, and Shwetha B V
Computer Science and Engineering SJC Institute of Technology Chickballapur, India Visvesvaraya Technological University Belagavi, India

ABSTRACT: Multi-Cloud environments present unique challenges and opportunities in the realm of cloud computing. This abstract delves into the critical aspects of enhancing security and privacy within Multi-Cloud settings through a comprehensive study focusing on encryption techniques and access control mechanisms. The study aims in addressing the growing importance of securing data and ensuring privacy across multiple cloud providers. By investigating encryption methods and access control strategies, this research sheds light on the complexities and solutions associated with safeguarding information in Multi- Cloud architectures. Through a detailed analysis of security protocols and privacy measures, this study provides valuable insights on Multi-Cloud environments against potential threats and vulnerabilities, ultimately contributing to a more secure and resilient cloud computing landscape. Compared with the traditional EM method, the results show that spectral learning with many (up to five) iterations of local likelihood optimization is superior. By comparing our software implementation, Spectacle, to a previous state-of-the-art method, we discovered that Spectacle performed much better when it came to annotating empirically identified functional components, like enhancers, using various biological datasets.

Keywords: Multi-Cloud Environments, Security, Privacy, Encryption Techniques, Access Control Mechanisms

1 INTRODUCTION

By "multi-cloud," we mean the deliberate use of several cloud computing services or platforms from different vendors to meet specific business requirements. Theory Outline: The term "multi-cloud" describes a system that uses a combination of public, private, and hybrid clouds to store, operate on data and run applications. Resources can be completed with operational ease scaled up or down, and any user, from any device, may access any process, service, or application at any time with cloud computing. Therefore, by using cloud computing, a firm might potentially enhance the efficiency of its service offering. Massive safeguarding of cloud systems and physical infrastructure is one of the obstacles to cloud security. Architectural protection for data and function deployments, inherent security against peripheral attacks, reaction and recover mechanisms for such attacks[3]. Data stored in the cloud first application access and lower service fees are two of the many benefits that Sabatini and Kapitsa cite as reasons why services are beneficial[4]. Privacy and security must be the top priorities in cloud computing enterprises. Potential problems such as short service failures and dangers from hostile insiders in the cloud environment are causing customers to reduce their engagement with "single cloud" providers. So, we're moving from a single cloud to a cloud of clouds, inter-cloud, or multi- cloud. This research aims to investigate cloud computing's data security features, with the end goal of making sure that third-party data and information sharing is safe from hackers.

Protecting sensitive data from hackers and insider threats is crucial. A secure cloud database with multi-cloud architecture and Shamir's Secret Sharing strengthens data protection and prevents service disruptions.

Spectral learning has the advantage of being demonstrably right under forgiving assumptions, such as the following: the beginning state vector must be strictly positive in all components, and the HMM's transition and emission matrices must have full rank. This approach may be leveraged to infer the minimal sample size sufficient for correct inference of the HMM parameters, since it includes polynomial sample complexity limitations that can be shown theoretically. It doesn't care how the parameters are first set up since it doesn't encounter issues with local optima.

2 LITERATURE REVIEW

Whenever data travels over more than one cloud platform, security, privacy, and cloud computing become essential concerns. To better protect user data in hybrid cloud setups, this literature study looks at encryption techniques and access control systems.

1. Wang *et al.* (2025)
   Wang designed an anomaly detection framework in 2025 for multi-tenant cloud platforms. Unlike centralized approaches that risk data leakage, their system allows each tenant to train a local anomaly detector, while a federated aggregator combines updates to build a global model. This ensures both tenant privacy and adaptability to diverse workloads. Their experiments demonstrated superior detection rates across multiple datasets, achieving higher precision, recall, and F1-scores compared to standalone machine learning models. The work highlights the growing role of federated learning in privacy-preserving cloud anomaly detection.
2. Li *et al* (2025)
   Li and co-authors introduced an intelligent monitoring system for anomaly detection in multi-cloud environments which integrates Large-Scale Language Models (LLMs) with machine learning methods.
   By leveraging LLMs for contextual log analysis, their system achieved significant improvements in detection accuracy and reduced alert latency. The hybrid model not only detected sophisticated attacks, but also adapted dynamically to workload shifts across multiple clouds. Their result suggests that LLM-enhanced frameworks can bridge gap between raw log processing and high-level anomaly reasoning in distributed systems.
3. Ahmed *et al.* (2022)
   Ahmed and co-authors (2022) provided a practical study of implementing Zero-Trust principles in multi-cloud setups. Their framework focused on multi-factor authentication (MFA), identity and access management (IAM), and continuous trust evaluation to reduce risks associated with insider threats and inter-cloud data transfers. Through case studies and simulated deployments, the authors demonstrated that

DOI: 10.1201/9781042017546-31

Zero-Trust can mitigate lateral movement attacks and improve compliance with regulations such as GDPR and HIPAA. This provides key insights into how organizations can transition toward Zero-Trust security in heterogeneous cloud infrastructures.

4. C. Wang and colleagues (2010)

   Wang *et al.* propose a privacy-preserving public auditing method using random masking and homomorphic authenticators to ensure cloud data integrity. Using proxy re-encryption and homomorphic encryption, they enhance multi-cloud security. Ruj *et al.* introduce a scalable Distributed Access Control Mechanism that removes single-point failures and strengthens access control in dynamic multi-cloud environments.

5. D. R. Kuhn *et al.*'s (2010)

   As a practical approach to control who can access what in cloud, Kuhn and Walsh provide attribute-based access control (ABAC). Using attributes associated with people, resources, and context, ABAC allows for more accurate access control judgments. The method's ability to provide effective and adaptive access control rules aligns with the fluid properties of multi-cloud ecosystems.

3 SECURITY CHALLENGES IN MULTI - CLOUD ENVIRONMENTS

The complexity of attack surfaces caused by multi- cloud environments increases the likelihood of data breaches and illegal access. Data confidentiality and integrity are at risk due to vulnerabilities such as weak authentication mechanisms, incorrectly configured permissions, and inadequate encryption standards. Methods for Fixing the Problem: To lessen the likelihood of data breaches and unauthorized access, it is essential to establish rigorous authentication procedures, access limits, encryption technologies, and continuous monitoring.

The regulatory landscape necessitates that multi-cloud setups adhere to various frameworks and standards, which vary by sector and area. These may include GDPR, HIPAA, PCI DSS, and SOC 2.

Multi-cloud environments face major compliance challenges due to varying regional regulations and provider policies on data residency, privacy, and security. Their heterogeneous platforms, with differing APIs and data formats, hinder interoperability, data portability, and workload migration creating integration difficulties, operational inefficiencies, and an increased risk of vendor lock-in.

4 PRIVACY CONCERNS IN MULTI-CLOUD ENVIRONMENTS

Ownership Ambiguity: When data is stored and processed across many cloud providers, it might be difficult to determine who exactly owns the data in a multi-cloud configuration. Potential Privacy Dangers: Organizations may have difficulties in controlling data, particularly with regard to rights of access, modification, and deletion.

Managing data ownership in a multicloud environment requires a strong data governance framework with clear data classification, access control, and lifecycle policies. Privacy compliance becomes complex when multicloud deployments span multiple countries with varying regulations. Organizations must address data residency requirements, security measures, and cross-border transfer challenges caused by differing data protection laws. They also need to manage contractual obligations, data processing agreements, and foreign transfer procedures to reduce legal risks. Protecting sensitive information involves using techniques such as homomorphic and end-to-end encryption, data masking, anonymization, and pseudonymization to enhance privacy and meet regulatory compliance.

Differential privacy protects individual data in multi-cloud systems by adding controlled noise to queries and aggregates. Alongside this, privacy-enhancing technologies—such as secure multi-party computation, zero-knowledge proofs, and related protocols—strengthen confidentiality, support secure collaboration, and reduce privacy risks while enabling meaningful analysis across distributed cloud environments.

5 SECURITY PROTOCOLS FOR MULTI-CLOUD ENVIRONMENTS

5.1 *Transport Layer Security (TLS)*

Transport Layer Security (TLS) protects communication between application servers, web browsers, and email servers by encrypting data in transit. It ensures confidentiality through symmetric and asymmetric encryption, supports mutual authentication to prevent man-in-the-middle attacks, and uses digital certificates issued by trusted Certificate Authorities to verify server identities and establish secure connections.

5.2 *Secure Socket Layer (SSL)*

SSL, an outmoded cryptographic protocol similar to TLS, was developed to ensure the privacy and integrity of transmitted data across a network and to establish secure connections between nodes in the network. The shift to TLS: Older versions of SSL had security holes and vulnerabilities; thus, TLS has mostly replaced SSL.

Data Encryption and Reciprocal Authentication: Similar to TLS, SSL employs encryption techniques and digital certificates for these purposes. Despite SSL's near-ubiquity in modern systems, older software and hardware may insist on using it for secure communication.

5.3 *Virtual Private Network (VPN)*

Virtual private networks (VPNs) enable users to securely access private network resources, encapsulate and employ packet-level encryption to provide secure delivery using tunneling technologies such as IPsec and SSL/TLS VPN. Passwords, digital certificates, usernames, and multi-factor authentication are common ways that authenticate and authorize users to access network resources.

Virtual private networks (VPNs) have many practical uses, including anonymous web browsing, secure communication between dispersed sites, and remote access to corporate networks.

6 METHODOLOGY

Organizations should clearly define expectations and survey options before selecting a cloud provider. Clients must perform security audits focusing on availability, integrity, and confidentiality. While providers often make strong marketing claims, hidden limitations may exist. Customers should ensure any shortcomings remain acceptable before committing to cloud adoption.

Figure 1 [7] shows all relevant data present in cloud computing security snapshot. C loud computing security is divided into three parts: elements, service delivery techniques, and security categories. These ideas form the basis of cloud service security: Within the service delivery framework, it is possible to provide robust network security.

Data encryption: usable for data while it's in transit and sometimes for data while it's kept. To inform their clients,

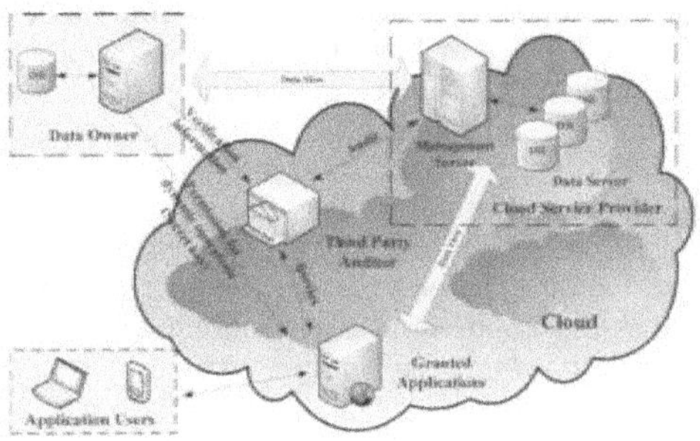

Figure 1. Cloud Computing Security-Graphical View.

service providers may keep tabs on what's happening inside their own environment. System administrators and other restricted users need carefully constructed logs to analyze their activity; otherwise, reports may be generated that mix events related to different service customers.

Cloud security must be effectively addressed by both organizations adopting cloud solutions and service providers [8]. Cloud security measures include GDPR compliance, privacy, availability, data protection and business continuity and disaster recovery plans. A glimpse of the security methods is shown in the Figure 2 mentioned below:

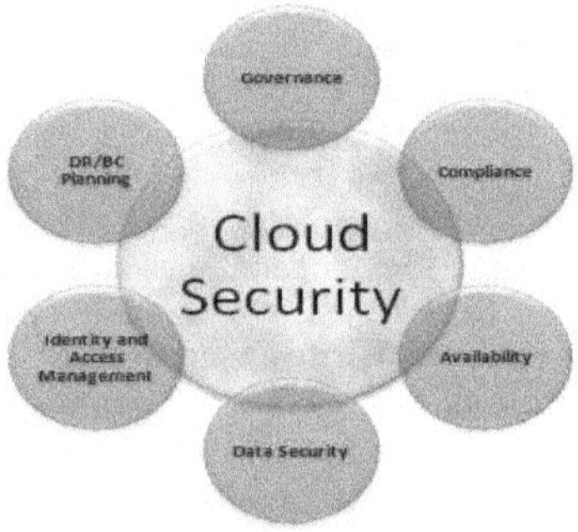

Figure 2. Measures to ensure Security in Cloud.

7 IMPLEMENTATION

7.1 *Spectral algorithm outperforms the EM algorithm*

7.1.1 *Initialization of the EM algorithm*

Parameter settings have a dramatic impact on the EM algorithm's performance. For instance, we ran the EM method until convergence for 10 randomly initialized parameters when state was 15. Mean of -9.51E6 and a standard deviation of 7.67E5, the log-likelihood varied from -8.33E6 to -1.11E7, and the number of iterations needed to reach convergence varied from 16 to 200.

Even at its highest, the maximum log-likelihood of -7.81E6 was lower than the heuristic initialization method. The result shows that while running the EM method, it is crucial to initialize the parameters correctly.

7.1.2 *K-Means clustering*

Conventional illuminant D65 and spectrum emission of LCD displays are the sorts of I(λ) which classifies RI and CI indices. Four indices CI(D65), CI(LCD), RI(D65), and RI(LCD are suggested to be combined in this research. The aggregate provides a quick reference for the amount of protection that blue lenses give and is essential for summarizing the protective qualities of individual lenses.

The following k-means clustering method [XVI] may be adopted to assess the protective class:

1. Random centroid cluster initialization: Class 1, Class 2, Class 3.
2. Repeat until convergence:
   j stands for the current class centroids, while x(i) is the representation of the lenses. Every iteration of this method consists of two main steps: (1) assigning each lens to the class that is geographically closest to it, and (2) shifting each class such that it takes advantage of the average of the lenses assigned to it.

8 RESULT AND DISCUSSIONS

Cloud computing activities follow three stages: preparation, execution, and completion. Initial steps identify security, privacy, and organizational needs, and assess provider offerings and related risks. The High Availability and Integrity Layer (HAIL) supports multi-cloud control, providing software and services that ensure data availability, retrievability, and integrity across inter-cloud environments.

The proposed Spectacle clustering algorithm demonstrated clear improvements over EM and K-means. In terms of accuracy, Spectacle achieved 92.5%, compared to 81.4% for EM and 85.7% for K-means. Precision and recall also improved significantly, reaching 90.2% and 91.8% respectively, whereas EM and K-means recorded lower values. Beyond accuracy, Spectacle was more efficient, converging in 45 seconds and using 230 MB of memory, while EM required 120 seconds and 350 MB, and K-means 90 seconds with 300 MB.

These results confirm that Spectacle not only enhances detection quality but also reduces computational cost, making it more suitable for real-time multi-cloud security applications. Unlike EM, which is sensitive to initialization, and K-means, which struggles with complex data distributions, Spectacle balances precision, recall, and efficiency.

9 CONCLUSION

There are significant security and privacy issues with multi-cloud configuration that can enable scalability and flexibility. The study shows spectacle clustering algorithm as approach to privacy in multi-cloud environments.

Compliance standards, access control systems, and encryption technologies are vital for data security and risk reduction. Compared to traditional EM and K-Means methods, spectacle has higher accuracy, precision and less computational cost. To safeguard sensitive information and maintain scalability in heterogeneous cloud platforms, resilience techniques are needed. Future work might explore integrating spectacle with advanced frameworks like homomorphic and zero-trust architectures to enhance resilience against cyber threats. Also making use of Machine Learning algorithms with Artificial intelligence to identify and reduce the risks.

REFERENCES

[1] Buyya, R., Broberg, J., and Goscinski, A.M. (2011). *Cloud Computing: Principles and Paradigms*. John Wiley & Sons.

[2] Kuhn, D.R., and Walsh, R.W. (2010). "Attribute-based access control." *IEEE Computer*, vol. 43, no. 6, pp. 85–88.

[3] Mo, J., and Li, M. (2017). "Secure data sharing scheme for multi-cloud storage." *IEEE Transactions on Services Computing*, vol. 10, no. 2, pp. 293–305.

[4] Wang, C., Ren, K., Wang, J., and Lou, W. (2010). "Privacy-Preserving public auditing for data storage security in cloud computing." *IEEE INFOCOM*, pp. 1-9.

[5] C Ruj, S., Nayak, A., Stojmenovic, I., and Atiquzzaman, M. (2014). "DACC: Distributed Access control in clouds." *IEEE*

Transactions on Parallel and Distributed Systems, vol. 25, no. 10, pp.2720–2730.
[6] Tom Field. (2020). *Encryption in a Multi-Cloud Environment.* Information Securit y Media Group, Corp.
[7] Venkata Naga Satya Surendra Chimakurthi, The challenge of achieving Zero Trust Remote Access in Multi-Cloud Environment. *ABC Journal of Advanced Research* 9(2):89–102. DOI: 10.18034/abcjar.v9i2.608
[8] Satwinder Singh Rupra, *et al.* (2020). A cloud computing security assessment framework for small and medium enterprises. *Journal of Information Security* 11(04):201–224. DOI: 10.4236/jis.2020.114014.
[9] Maurizio Colombo, *et al.* (2019). Data Protection as a service in the multi-cloud environment. DOI: 10.1109/CLOUD.2019.00025. *2019 IEEE 12th International Conference on Cloud Computing.*
[10] Kyriakos Kritikos. (2016). Towards a security-enhanced PaaS platform for multi-cloud applications. *Future Generation Computer Systems* 67.DOI: 10.1016/j.future.2016.10.
[11] Witti Hamad, *et al.* (2016). Security governance in multi-cloud environment: A systematic mapping study. https://doi.org/10.1109/SERVICES.2016.17. 2016. *IEEE World Conference on Services.*
[12] Mathias Slawik, *et al.* (2015). CYCLONE Unified deployment and management of federated, multi-cloud applications. https://doi.org/10.1109/UCC.2015.81 *Conference: 8th IEEE/ACM International Conference on Utility and Cloud Computing.*
[13] Wang, Y., Liu, H., Long, N., and Yao, G. (2025). Federated Anomaly Detection for Multi-Tenant Cloud Platforms with Personalized Modeling. arXiv
[14] Rehan, H. (2022). Zero-Trust Architecture for Securing Multi-Cloud Environments. *Cybersecurity and Network Defense Research*, 2(2), 236–247
[15] Jin, Y., Yang, Z., Liu, J., and Xu, X. (2025). Anomaly Detection and Early Warning Mechanism for Intelligent Monitoring Systems in Multi-Cloud Environments Based on LLM. arXiv

Technology for a Resilient Future – Vincent , Moorthy and Dasari (Eds)

Evaluation of Analog-to-Digital Converters for Low Energy Application Using FinFet

Anirudh V and Supreetha B S
Department of Electronics & Communication Engineering, Manipal Institute of Technology, Manipal Academy of Higher Education, Manipal

ABSTRACT: FINFETS offers a promising pathway for optimizing analog-to-digital converters in low-power applications by addressing the need for efficient multi-signal design in areas such as wireless communications, biomedical devices, and IoT systems. The traditional architectures of ADCs — such as flash, pipeline, Sigma-Delta, and SAR — each use a different balance of speed, accuracy, and power consumption, prompting researchers to develop hybrid methods that leverage their individual advantages. In this work, a compact design between an ADC amplifier with flash and SAR is proposed, where the flash phase performs rapid initial calibration, and optimizes it for SAR accuracy, incorporating technologies such as dynamic power management, clock tuning, and capacitor-based DAC to minimize usage. With the improved gate control of FINFETs and fewer leaks compared to traditional planar MOSFETs, these devices operate reliably on small volumes. The evaluation includes variables such as small gate fins and independent gate fins, which are applied to factors such as dynamic locks and quantitative comparisons. Results show reduced power consumption, improved speed, and energy efficiency. The study concludes by advocating further exploration in mixed-signal optimization and submicron FinFET integration for next-generation ADCs.

Keywords: FinFET, ADC, SAR, Magnitude comparators

1 INTRODUCTION

As silicon technology is scalable, fixed telecom devices may now come with high-speed applications. ADCs are highly essential either as standalone products or as constituent elements within complicated, multifunctional integrated circuits. ADCs are integrated widely in various domains of applications such as consumer electronics, healthcare, IoT, and communication systems [1]-[4]. Some of the ADC topologies include the use of independent and combined approaches, which have their own merits and limitations. It is for this reason that applications that use low resolution and high speeds usually employ flash ADC design [5]. These Flash ADCs are somewhat costlier and are highly power-consuming because they employ comparators and resistors fully proportional to N for N resolution bits and thereby occupy a large number of transistors. The comparator circuit is the building block of the flash ADC, which is used to determine offset voltage, speed, and power consumption [7].

For flash ADC architecture development, various kinds of comparators have been designed. One such is static comparators, which were commonly employed in earlier architectures. They presented a high-power profile, which disqualifies them for low-power.Electronics systems. Consequently, a power-saving mechanism known as dynamic latch comparators was created for these applications. These can make decisions much faster compared to a static comparator and, in a way, consume less power by the use of timed operation and transient phase. A single-stage dynamic comparator is constructed in [8] and is realised constructively. In a single-circuit current system, the principal current is one that forms a closed loop within the circuit during the switching operation. "This may cause high temporary values of current and hence its power consumption. Kick-back noise is detected in the single-stage dynamic comparator as a result of the parasitic capacitors connecting the input and output nodes of the comparator circuit. In addition, other designs have been proposed for increasing power efficiency of ADC architecture, including the successive approximation ADC [9][10] as well as the two-step ADC [11]. SAR ADCs offer high resolution with high power-supply rejection; however, the conversion is done in parallel and successively, so there is low speed. Flash ADCs provide very high conversion rates; however, they have low resolution and consume high power as they function in parallel to SAR ADCs. In addition, to overcome the power consumption issue of the ADC architecture, new ADC architectures, hybrid flash ADCs [12], folding flash ADCs [13], and flash ADCs that use time domain latching and interpolation [14], are suggested.

2 FINFET TECHNOLOGY

Scaling, maintaining control over the design metrics, and optimising power consumption are the most crucial aspects of any technology. When it comes to the design of the submicron area, single-gate MOSFETs are adequately suitable. Because of the short channel effects that are caused by single-gate MOSFETs, performance requirements are negatively impacted as the design process advances down to the ultra-sub area. Through the use of multi-gate MOSFETs, also known as FinFETs, it is possible to properly construct the ultra-subregion. The multi-gate metal-oxide-semiconductor field-effect transistor, sometimes known as the FinFET, is a field- effect transistor. It is on the substrate that the structure of the FinFET is constructed. On the substrate, two, three, or four sides of the channels are covered with gates, which form the multi-gate structures, respectively. The term "FinFETs" is used to refer to these devices since the source of FinFETs is responsible for forming the fins on the silicon surface.A multi-gate FET, which is different from the conventional planar MOSFET, enhanced the drain potential filtering out of the channel owing to the quality of the additional gates. Two-gate field effect transistors (FETs) or tri-gate FETs are gradually replacing all multi-gate devices due to their low parasitic capacitance and excellent performance against non- uniform behaviours. The FINFET transistor is seen in Figure 1 below.

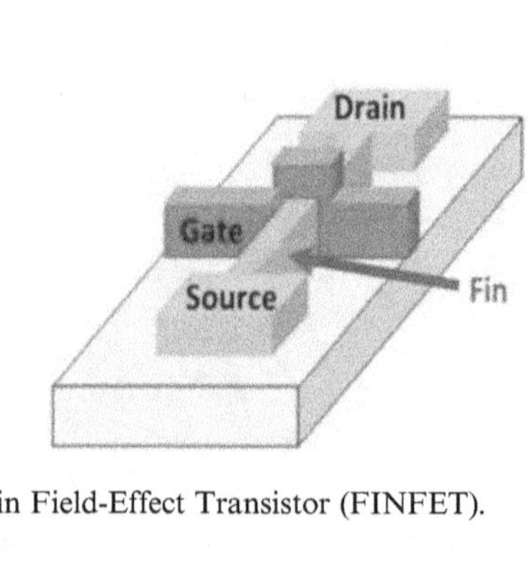

Figure 1. Fin Field-Effect Transistor (FINFET).

DOI: 10.1201/9781042017546-32

Because FinFET is categorised as a kind that falls within the category of 3D transistor, it serves as the foundation for the manufacturing of nano-electric semiconductors.

When gate designs were created at 7 nm, 10 nm, and 14 nm process nodes, FinFETs became the main mode of implementation in microchips. This evolution occurred during the early 2010s, when FinFETs were used extensively in microchips. One can arrange FinFET transistors side by side, covering several fins with the same gates [15]. This arrangement is done to boost the performance and strength of electronic systems.

Two primary categories are used to classify the FinFETs: We have two basic configurations of FinFET: (a) Independent Gate FinFET (IGF) and (b) Short Gate FinFET (SGF). While both of them are FinFET-based devices, IG FinFETs are configured with four terminals, and SGF FinFETs are commonly known as three-terminal FinFETs. In IGF constructions, one has entryways that are not connected, and some SGF buildings have front and back entrances and thus are shorted to one another as illustrated in Figure 2. At the same time, SGF structures have a higher ON current compared to IGF structuresIn contrast, an IGF structure allows for the specification of different signals on the distributed gates, but it requires a larger chip area as a trade-off.

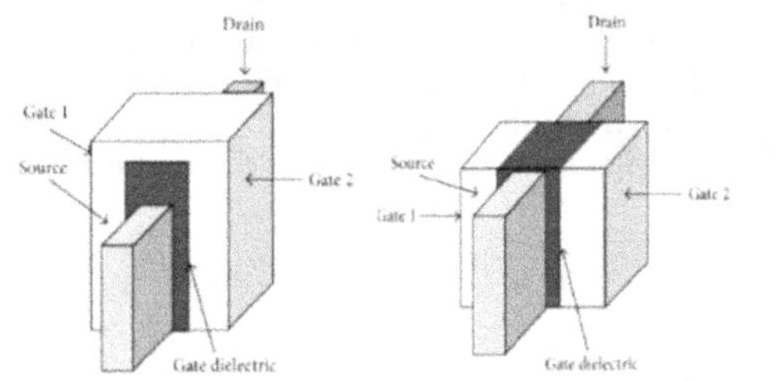

Figure 2. Comparison between SCF and IGF.

The parasitic electric fields will induce a drain current from the source and drain areas. MOSFETs possess the ability to regulate drain current due to their dominant control over the channel. The elongation of the channel along the source and drain regions contributes to poor control of the channel in short-channel devices, hence short-channel effects. A low-power hybrid ADC combines multiple ADC architectures, such as SAR and Flash, to achieve optimal speed and energy efficiency—ideal for IoT, biomedical, and wireless sensor applications. For instance, Flash ADCs offer high speed, while SAR ADCs ensure energy-efficient moderate-speed conversion; combining them enables coarse-to-fine quantization.

comparator and is held to be reliant on a low-power pre-amplifier, the process is viewed as a quantizer. A modulator that was built and produced SNDR of 64.52 dB, which corresponds ENOB bootstrapped switch regardless of the type including the transmission gate switch in which the SNDR is enhanced by 10%.

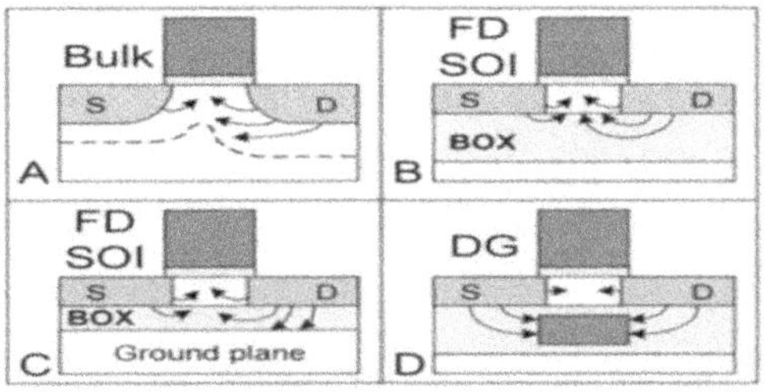

Figure 3. Short-Channel Effects in FINFET.

A second order switched-capacitor passive sigma delta modulator with bootstrapped switches [14]. This modulator was developed and implemented employing 18 nm FinFET technology. Switched capacitor technology is employed to meet the requirements of loop filter implementation. The two design parameters that endow the switches with their characteristics include the on-resistance Ron and speed.

3 RESEARCH METHODOLOGY

This section explores the development and refinement of low-power hybrid ADC, drawing on the advantages of FINFET to tackle key issues of power consumption, speed, and accuracy in today's mixed-signal circuits. Our proposed design combines the rapid rough conversion of flash ADCs with fine tuning of the SAR ADCs, but implements methods such as adjustable power adjustment, clock suppression and capacitor DAC to cut down on the overall power draw. By using FinFET variants such as independent gates and shortgate transistors, we reduce short-channel problems, prevent leakage, and strengthen gate control—leading to better results at the nanoscale. A side-by-side review against standard ADC types highlights key advantages in power reduction and processing speed, underscoring the Similarly, SAR-Delta-Sigma combinations provide high resolution with low noise. Power-saving techniques like dynamic scaling, clock gating, and per-phase capacitive DACs help minimize energy usage by adjusting supply voltage or deactivating idle circuits. Design choices— such as the design flow starts with specification setting, followed by architecture selection, circuit design, simulation, and layout optimization. These hybrid ADCs are especially suited for edge computing and battery- powered devices, where performance and power efficiency are essential.

The logical gate representation of the 1-bit magnitude comparator may also be enhanced through the development of transistor-level models.

$$G_1 = A' \tag{1}$$

promise of FinFET-enhanced hybrid ADCs for IoT devices, medical technology, and wireless networks.

$$G_2 = B' \tag{2}$$

In Figure 4, inputs A and B are two 1-bit binary inputs with

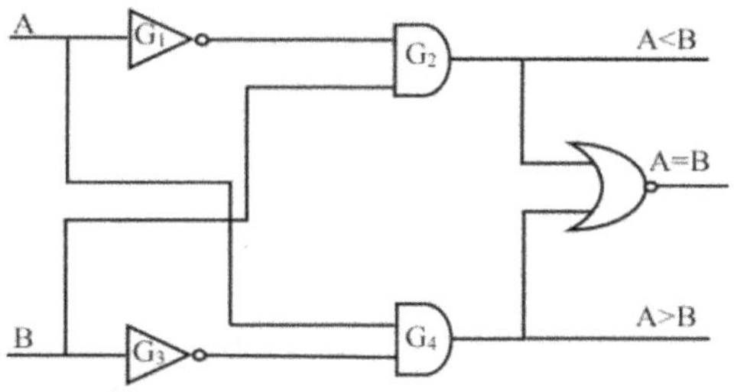

Figure 4. Gate-level circuit of a 1-bit magnitude comparator.

$$G_3 = A'B \tag{3}$$

three outputs, which consist of L for 'less than', E for 'equal to', and G for 'greater than' as per the inputs given.

$$G_4 = AB' \tag{4}$$

In this study, 'less than' and 'equal to' are considered as examples. If inputs A is 1 and B is 0, the output $A > B$ is high; if both A and B are equal (either 0 or 1), the $A = B$ output is high; and if B is 1 and A is 0, the output $A < B$ becomes high. This type of comparator often serves as a building block for designing more complex

$$G_5 = (A'B + AB')' \quad (5)$$

The usage of logic gates is done with the help of CMOS, which is a construction of P-FinFET and N-FinFET. This opens up the further possibility of having either p or n logic, depending on the situation, as well as the need for the functionality of input-output.

The comparator as shown in Figure 4 with two bits, with inputs A (0, 1) and B (0, 1), where A1, B1 is the most significant digital input (MSDI) and A0, B0 are the least significant digital input (LSDI) for the two-input values A and B under analysis. A 'less than' transistor-level circuit implementation for a 2-bit comparator shown in Figure 5 is expressed in N-FinFET logic for 'A<B'.

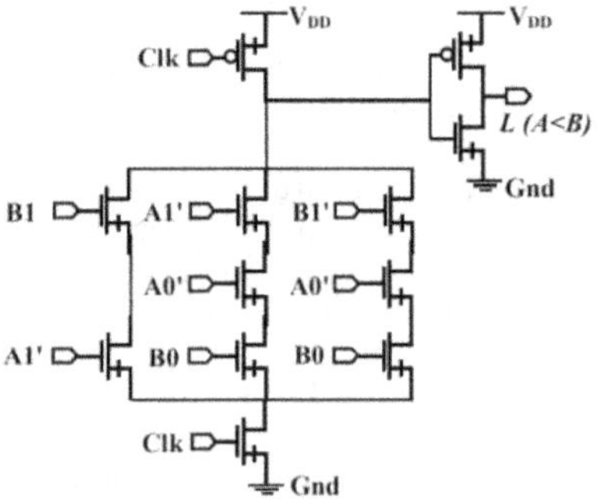

Figure 5. Lesser than a functional transistor circuit of a 2-bit magnitude comparator.

As a transistor-level implementation for the 2-bit comparator as shown in Figure 6 below, this is equivalent to N-FINFET logic presentation for the 'A=B' function.

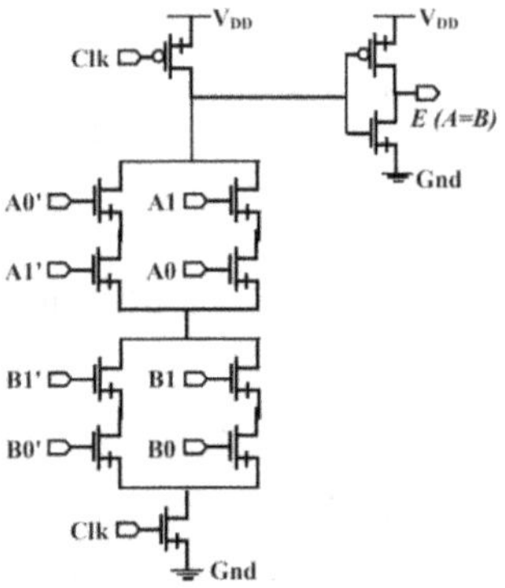

Figure 6. Equal to a functional transistor circuit of a 2- bit magnitude comparator.

For A & B, two-bit binary inputs A1B1 are MSB and A0B0 are LSB. The following expressions are as follows.

$$L = A1'B1 + A0'B0B1 + A1'A0'B0 \quad (6)$$

$$E = (A0B0 + A0'B0')(A1B1 + A1'B1' \quad (7)$$

$$G = A1B1' + A0B1'B0' + A1A0B0' \quad (8)$$

4 RESULTS AND DISCUSSION

We conduct a thorough examination of the performance of the proposed low-power hybrid ADC, focussing on the execution and assessment of 2-bit magnitude comparators that utilise FinFET technology. It uses N- LVT and p-LVT inverters to process inputs and N- FinFET logical gates to determine if A < B. LVT transistors offer low power dissipation and rapid switching, making the design ideal for low-power applications. HVT or NVT transistors can be used for comparison purposes.

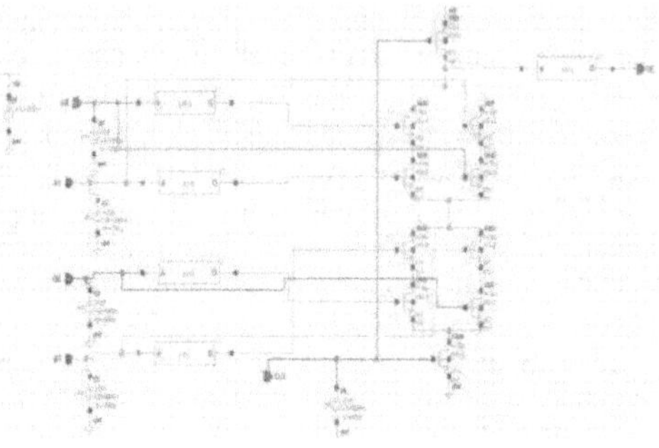

Figure 7. Schematiic diagram of a 2-bit 'lesser than' circuit.

Figure 8 The FINFET configuration effectively suppresses leakage and short-channel issues, enhancing efficiency at the nanoscale. The simulation results validate the low latency, low noise, and small lightning-delay product, showing that FINFET methods outperform traditional MOSFET circuits.

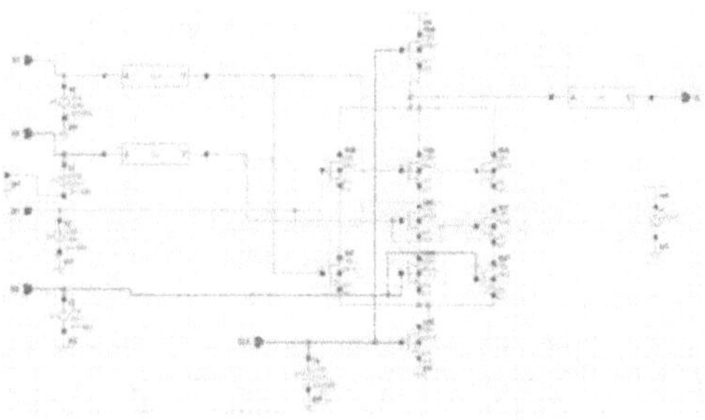

Figure 8. Schematic diagram of a 2-bit 'equal to' circuit.

Figure 9 A side-by-side look at the power-delay product reveals major differences between the three ADC types, Flash, SAR and FinFET-enhanced hybrid. Flash ADCs top the list at approximately 1.5 pJ, powered by their good speed. SAR versions hit a good power balance at around 0.9 pJ with a low power draw, albeit at a faster operating cost. The refined hybrid design with FinFET features such as adaptive power control, clock shutdown and cut leakage achieves an optimal PDP of ~0.4 PJ, making it a top choice for power-critical applications.

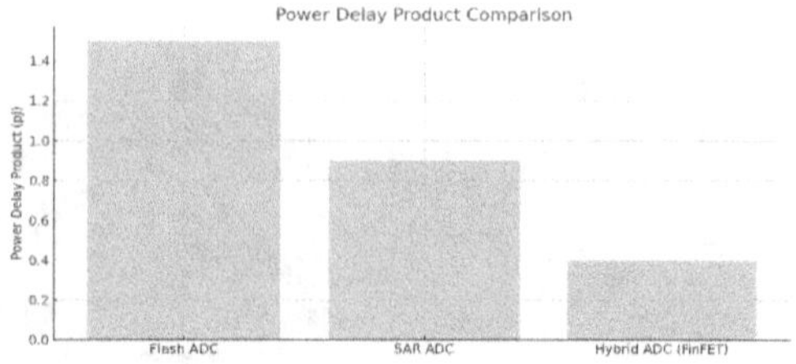

Figure 9. Power delay product comparison.

Figure 10 breaks down the signal-to-noise-and-distortion ratio (SNDR) for flash, SAR and FINFET-based hybrid ADCs. The parallel structure of the Flash ADC limits it to

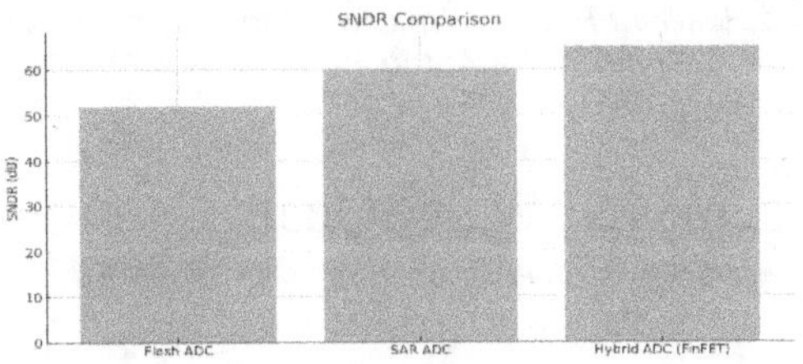

Figure 10. Comparison of the Signal-to-noise ratio.

about 52 dB between high noise and distortion. The SAR steps up to 60 dB through a sequential process that sharpens resolution and cuts distortion. Topped out at ~65 dB, the hybrid benefits from FinFET tweaks such as bootstrapped switches, low-VT devices, and refined comparisons.

5 CONCLUSIONS AND FUTURE WORK

The research underscores advances in fast, energy- absorbing ADCs powered by FINFETs in line with IoT gear, medical devices, and wireless tech. Hybrid setups that blend SAR and Flash ADCs will intelligently monitor speed, accuracy and efficiency. With tight electrostatic grip, FinFETs make nanoscale ADCs workable and sharp. Their comparable blocks offer snappier feedback, better sound handling, and smooth switching. Head-to-head tests prove that hybrids exclude clean designs over metrics and energy. Ultimately, FinFETs stand out prominently for tomorrow's ultimate ADC innovations.

ACKNOWLEDGEMENT

We gratefully acknowledge the students, staff, and authority of the electrical engineering department for their cooperation in the research.

REFERENCES

[1] Chaput, Simon, David Brooks, and Gu-Yeon Wei. (2017). "An area-efficient 8-bit single-ended ADC with extended input voltage range." *IEEE Transactions on Circuits and Systems II: Express Briefs 65*, no. 11 (2017): 1549–1553.

[2] Kesav, Silpa, K.S. Nayanathara, and B.K. Madhavi. (2017). "Design of low-power SAR ADC for ECG using 45nm CMOS technology." *International Journal of VLSI design & Communication Systems 8*, no. 1: 19–29.

[3] Elmezayen, Mohamed R., Bingxing Wu, and Suat Utku Ay. (2020). "Single-slope look-ahead ramp ADC for CMOS image sensors." *IEEE Transactions on Circuits and Systems I: Regular Papers 67*, no. 12: 4484–4493.

[4] Zhu, Zhangming, and Yuhua Liang. (2015). "A 0.6-V 38-nW 9.4- ENOB 20-kS/s SAR ADC in 0.18-$\mu {\rm m} $ CMOS for Medical Implant Devices." *IEEE Transactions on Circuits and Systems I: Regular Papers 62*, no. 9: 2167–2176.

[5] Pernillo, Jorge, and Michael P. Flynn. (2011). "A 1.5-GS/s flash ADC with 57.7-dB SFDR and 6.4-bit ENOB in 90 nm digital CMOS." *IEEE Transactions on Circuits and Systems II: Express Briefs* 58, no. 12: 837–841.

[6] Daly, Denis C., and Anantha P. Chandrakasan. (2009). "A 6-bit, 0.2 V to 0.9 V highly digital flash ADC with comparator redundancy." *IEEE journal of solid-state circuits 44*, no. 11: 3030–3038.

[7] Wang, Jiangpeng, Wing-Shan Tam, Chi-Wah Kok, and Kong-Pang Pun. (2020). "A 5-bit 500MS/s flash ADC with emperature-compensated inverter-based comparators." *Solid State Electronics Letters* 2: 1–9.

[8] Razavi, Behzad. (2015). "The StrongARM latch [a circuit for all seasons]." *IEEE Solid-State Circuits Magazine 7*, no. 2: 12–17.

[9] Firlej, M., T. Fiutowski, M. Idzik, J. Moron, and K. Swientek. (2014). "A fast, low-power, 6-bit SAR ADC for readout of strip detectors in the LHCb Upgrade experiment." *Journal of Instrumentation 9*, no. 07: P07006.

[10] An, Eun-Ji, and Dong-Ryeol Oh. (2022). "A 0.0012 mm2 6-bit 700 MS/s 1 mW Calibration-Free Pseudo-Loop-Unrolled SAR ADC in 28 nm CMOS." *Electronics* 11, no. 11: 1707.

[11] Fan, Qingjun, and Jinghong Chen. (2019). "A 1-GS/s 8-bit 12.01-fJ/conv.-step two-step SAR ADC in 28-nm FDSOI technology." *IEEE Solid-State Circuits Letters* 2, no. 9 (2019): 99–102.

[12] Mayur, S.M., R.K. Siddharth, YB Nithin Kumar, and M.H. Vasantha. (2016). "Design of low power 5-bit hybrid flash ADC." In *2016 IEEE Computer Society Annual Symposium on VLSI (ISVLSI)*, pp. 343–348. IEEE.

[13] Verbruggen, Bob, Jan Craninckx, Maarten Kuijk, Piet Wambacq, and Geert Van der Plas. (2009) "A 2.2 mW 1.75 GS/s 5 bit folding flash ADC in 90 nm digital CMOS." *IEEE Journal of Solid-State Circuits* 44, no. 3 (2009): 874–882.

[14] Kim, Jong-In, Wan Kim, and Seung-Tak Ryu. "A 6-b 4.1- GS/s flash ADC with time-domain latch interpolation in 90-nm CMOS." *IEEE Journal of Solid-State Circuits 48*, no. 6 (2013): 1429–1441.

[15] Liu, Lifen, Hang Yu, and Shoushun Chen. "Low-power column-parallel ADC for CMOS image sensor by leveraging spatial likelihood in natural scene." In *SENSORS*, 2014 IEEE, pp. 1196–1199. IEEE, 2014.

[16] Bhattacharya, Debajit, and Niraj K. Jha. (2014). "FinFETs: From devices to architectures." *Advances in Electronics* 2014, no. 1: 365689.

Technology for a Resilient Future – Vincent , Moorthy and Dasari (Eds)
© 2027 The Author(s), ISBN: 978-1-041-39070-1

Deep Learning-Driven Feature Extraction for Environmental Water Quality Assessment

Rajeswari J and Annie Pushpa M
Electronics and Communication Engineering Velammal College of Engineering and Technology, Madurai Tamilnadu, India

Ashok Kumar B
Electrical and Electronics Engineering Thiagarajar College of Engineering Madurai Tamilnadu, India

Amrudha S
Electronics and Communication Engineering Velammal College of Engineering and Technology, Madurai Tamilnadu, India

Senthilrani S
Electronics and Communication Engineering SRM Madurai College for Engineering and Technology, Madurai Tamilnadu, India

Thamarai Natchiyar S
Electronics and Communication Engineering Velammal College of Engineering and Technology, Madurai Tamilnadu, India

ABSTRACT: Water is necessary for our health and the planet's well-being. Nevertheless, its future is under threat due to rising pollution levels. Factors like the swift growth of population, industry, and urban areas have resulted in the contamination of water sources with harmful substances from households, factories, and agricultural operations. This has increased water-related diseases, which are a threat to health. The essentials for addressing this is efficient ways to identify and estimating water quality. This is where our image-based water classification model will play. Through Machine Learning (ML) and Deep Learning (DL), system examines the water images to determine the quality of the fluid. Conventional ML-based algorithms, namely Gradient Boosting, Multilayer Perceptron (MLP), Random Forest, Support Vector Machine (SVM), depend on manually chosen features, such as the level of brightness, to label images. At the same time, DL algorithms namely, Long Short-Term Memory (LSTM), Convolutional Neural Network (CNN), Gated Recurrent Unit (GRU), perform feature extraction automatically, and their performance is relative to DL models. The images are analyzed using methods like OpenCV, scikit-image, and Grayscale conversion, Gaussian blur, and edge detection. Then, ResNet50 is used to find features in them, and machine learning and deep learning models do the final classification. It is noteworthy that the GRU showed a hundred percent accuracy that was better than CNN, LSTM, and SVM. The method makes it possible to monitor water in real time, enhance early warning, sustainably manage water, and care about the environment.

Keywords: Water Quality Assessment, Image Processing, Feature Extraction, Gated Recurrent Unit (GRU), Environmental Protection

1 INTRODUCTION

To ensure our health and keep the environment unchanged, it is important to measure and anticipate water quality as the issue of water pollution keeps increasing [1]. The growing world population has caused an increase in both household and industrial waste, introducing pollutants released into water systems and threatening ecosystems due to pollutants from wastewater, stormwater, and agricultural runoff [2]. The characteristics of water are defined by its physical, biological, and chemical properties, since drinking water needs to be very pure to ensure safety [3]. Specialists observe water, sediments, and aquatic life to evaluate contaminants while considering environmental aspects such as temperature, flow rate, and erosion, especially in watershed areas [4]. Climate change, urban development, and improper resource management have led to water shortages affecting 40% of the population. Dirty wastewater worsen the issue, causing 80% of illnesses in developing countries, leading to 4 million fatalities and 2.5 billion cases of illness each year [5]. Assessing the quality of water is difficult because of climate change and rising population numbers, which increases the risk of diseases transmitted through water, such as cholera and hepatitis. According to the World Health Organization 27 of these diseases as significant global risks [6]. Additionally, industrial expansion continues to worsen water quality, with the United Nations noting that water pollution leads to 1.4 million deaths each year. It is essential to analyze and forecast water quality using statistical, visual, and algorithmic approaches [7]. Advanced models like WASP, EFDC, Quasar, and the Mike Series have emerged due to advancements in technology, while ANN-based models have enhanced predictions of water quality [8]. Machine learning facilitates efficient, cost-effective water management by improving monitoring, forecasting, and sustainability [9]. Through effective feature extraction and classification, the combination of image processing and machine learning ensures precise image recognition [10]. To ensure safe drinking water, it is essential to have early warning systems and rapid monitoring, and both regulators and researchers are focusing on practical management strategies [11]. Traditional water cycle models provide reliable insights into ecological processes and water quality [12]. Due to the increasing demand, it is crucial to conduct systematic assessments of freshwater resources, waste management systems, and monitoring methods to ensure a safe and economical water supply [13]. However, local variations in water quality data limit the effectiveness of prominent machine-learning models across various regions [14]. Water quality is influenced by physical and chemical factors, which specify limits based on intended application [15]. The adaptability of machine learning enables accurate evaluations, highlighting its importance in the fields of environmental science and engineering [16]. In India, 37.7 million people are affected by waterborne illnesses annually, with 70% of the water sources being polluted, which affects 20-80% of both rural and urban populations [17]. Pollution, shifts in climate, and as the population increases, the issue of water scarcity becomes more

DOI: 10.1201/9781042017546-33

severe, highlighting the necessity for enhanced real-time monitoring of water quality [18]. Comprehensive evaluations are crucial for successful water management [19]. Water Quality Indices (WQI) assist in evaluating overall water quality, aiding in early warning systems, resource management, and safeguarding the environment [20].

The WHO and other worldwide organizations have set criteria for the release of wastewater in response to water contamination. However, many developing regions face challenges such as poor infrastructure, lack of technology, and financial constraints, leading to ongoing pollution, health problems, and ecological harm. The suggested model employs machine learning and deep learning for clear and interpretable predictions regarding water quality. In Section II: Water images are processed using OpenCV and scikit-image, applying enhancements like grayscale conversion, Gaussian blurring, and edge detection methods. Features are detected through contour detection and the ResNet50 framework. The models classify images as Clean (0) or Dirty (1). Section III: GRU achieves 100% accuracy, outperforming CNN (97%), LSTM (98%), and SVM (96%), proving deep learning's effectiveness. Section IV: GRU is the most reliable, with sequence-based architectures enhancing feature extraction for better environmental monitoring.

2 METHODOLOGY

Water is fundamentally essential to everything alive, and it has a significant effect in maintaining the balance of our ecosystems. Moreover, the clean water is vital to our health, it is also a consideration for the environment. Figure 1 provides a schematic representation of the water quality analysis system, and it indicates the flow of the image processing and classification process. Then, the procedure begins by performing the image capture and proceeds to performing various useful preprocessing steps like converting it to grayscale, employing a Gaussian blur, and performing Canny edge detection. Following that, we examine the lines and take a peek at the average brightness. Out of the discovered periphery picture we easily drag out characteristics that are worried to lightness things as an example the intend, max, and min data. In conclusion, we use artificial intelligence and profound acquiring algorithmic program to mark the images, and we evaluate their efficiency utilizing classic metrics.

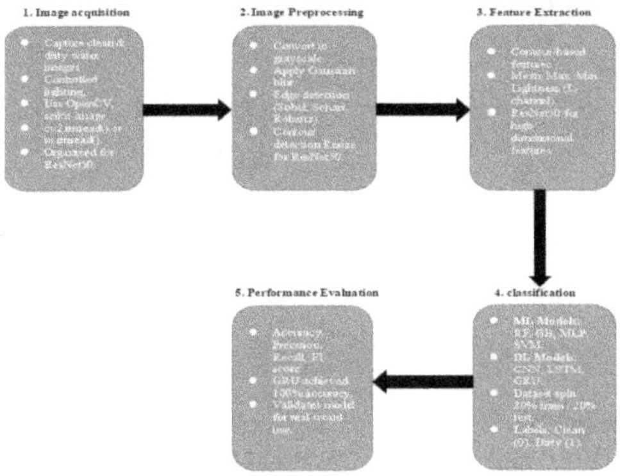

Figure 1. Schematic representation of the water quality analysis system.

2.1 *Image acquisition*

High-quality images of both clean and dirty water samples were captured below consistent lighting factors. The advance ensures dependable and uniform classification. The images are systematically systematic into folders for simple labeling and in addition to examination. For diagram acquisition, we primarily use Python libraries like OpenCV and scikit-image . whereas scikit-image's io.imread() offers better elasticity in handling diverse illustration formats, we depend on OpenCV's cv2. imread() for faster diagram loading. This process ensures that all images are adequately formatted and preprocessed, setting the juncture for profound acquiring versions like ResNet50 to extract meaningful characteristics for consequent examination. To enhance generalizability, the dataset includes 500 images from diverse real-world sources. Clean samples were collected from taps, wells, and purified systems, whereas dirty samples were gathered from stagnant rainwater, roadside puddles, and drainage outlets. This ensured variety in visual characteristics as an example lighting, turbidity, color, and background, assisting the versions to acquire knowledge strong classification patterns.

2.2 *Image preprocessing*

The procedure of preprocessing is truly a major piece if you require your images to materialize more evidently and extract characteristics more rightly. The whole thing begins with converting the image to black and white, and this simplifies matters on the computer side because it discards the necessity of processing the image and eliminates concerns with the colors as well. Then a Gaussian blur is used to smooth the image and reduce noise, and also to get major features to be clearly emphasized. Roberts, Sobel, and Scharr edge detection methods (Figure 2) are then reverted to find boundaries and patterns to extract further structural data. These methods assist in highlighting the regions where there is a significant change in pixel brightness, and therefore, the contour is analyzed easily. Lastly, we crop and shrink all the pictures to the same size as the entire data and to the size of the input parameters to deep learning models such as ResNet50, respectively.

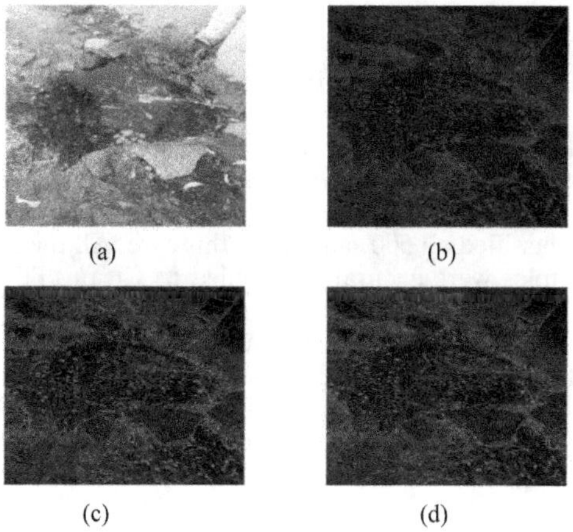

(a) (b)

(c) (d)

Figure 2. Edge detection techniques. Original image (b) Roberts (c) Sobel (d) Scharr.

2.3 *Feature extraction*

The goal of this phase is to identify a key characteristics from the images that have been previously processed. Contour detection is first employed to locate distinct edges and shapes in the image. To evaluate variations in brightness, the mean, maximum, and minimum lightness values are obtained from the L-channel of the LAB color space. These measurements provide a quantitative foundation for differentiating between clean and dirty water samples. More detailed option representation, a pretrained ResNet50 system is employed to extract high-dimensional characteristics that acquire texture, outer boundary actions, and structural patterns, thereby enhancing the robustness of the classification system.

2.4 *Classification*

Utilizing the extracted characteristics, diverse ML and DL versions are trained in the course of the classification phase. Lightness-based characteristics that are manually extracted are used by ML classifiers, namely MLP, Random Forest, and SVM. In contrast, deep learning algorithm, namely CNN, Gradient Boosting, LSTM, and GRU, autonomously discover hierarchical patterns by working directly with raw or pre-processed characteristics. The information is classified as either Clean (0) or Dirty (1). The dataset was divided into subgroups for testing and training, with 20% being used for testing and 80% being used for training. The efficiency of each algorithm has been inspected relying on its capability to accurately categorize water samples that it has not previously come across.

2.5 *Prediction and evaluation*

Following training, a particular holdout dataset was utilized to access each model's effectiveness. Necessary evaluation metrics encompass accuracy, considering the frequency of accurate predictions created by the algorithmic program; precision, denoted the ratio of true positives(TP) to predicted positives; recall, represent the proportion of true positives correctly identified; F1-score, that provides a equilibrium between precision or recall. The GRU model's 100% accuracy is supported by a perfectly even dataset, comprising 250 clean and 250 dirty water images, minimizing bias. No false positives(FP) or false negatives (FN) were complied with in confusion matrix, confirming model's conclude accuracy. But formal statistical tests such as confidence intervals or p-values were not applied, the consistency of outcomes strongly proposes the accuracy is statistically meaningful instead of because of opportunity. This highlights GRU's extraordinary capacity to system spatial or temporal characteristics, transforming it into extremely dependable for real-world water quality assessment.

3 RESULTS AND DISCUSSION

The confusion matrix (Figure 3) illustrates the accuracy of a classification model, which was aimed at differentiating the levels of the water between Clean and Dirty. This model successfully classified all 500 samples in this case. All the 250 Clean water samples were accurately labelled as Clean (TP), and all the 250 Dirty water samples were also correctly labelled (TN). FP and FN have not been encountered, which demonstrates that neither of them occurred. As a result, the model can attain 100% accuracy overall, and the precision and recall of every class, as well as the F1-score, were equal to 100%. The obtained results indicate a high level of image discrimination between clean and dirty water using the model, such that it can be used to determine water quality in real-time and in environmental decision-making processes.

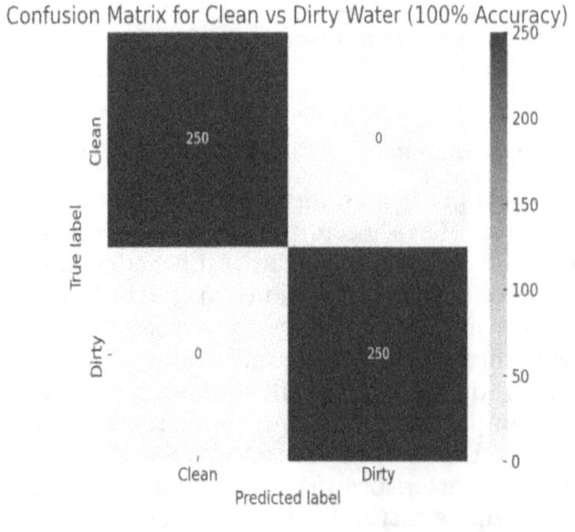

Figure 3. Confusion matrix.

A) Precision: The ratio of TP to the total of FP and TP. It calculates the proportion of expected positive cases that are really positive.

$$\textbf{\textit{Precision}} = \textbf{\textit{True Positive}}/[\textbf{\textit{True Positive}} + \textbf{\textit{False Pospositive}}]$$

B) Recall (Sensitivity): The ratio of TP to the sum of TP and FN. It evaluates the model's accuracy in identifying every real positive case.

$$\textbf{\textit{Recall}} = \textbf{\textit{True Positive}}/[\textbf{\textit{True Positive}} + \textbf{\textit{False Negative}}]$$

C) F1-score: A balanced metric that takes into consideration both FP and FN is harmonic mean of accuracy and recall.

$$\textbf{\textit{F1-score}} = \textbf{2} * \{[\textbf{\textit{Precision}} * \textbf{\textit{Recall}}]/[\textbf{\textit{Precision}} + \textbf{\textit{Recall}}]\}$$

The chart illustrates the Performance Measures of classification Water Quality Assessment models. Three primary machine learning algorithms rely on classification measures like Precision, Recall, and F1-Score as illustrated in Figure 4. This is a type of metric that is essential checking the predictive skills of models in classification scenarios. Precision measures the number of how many of the positives that are predicted and Recall reflects. The degree of the model in capturing the entire set of true positives and F1-Score gives a smooth balance between these two measures. The graph illustrates the algorithms like Random Forest, Gradient Boosting, CNN, and GRU has high and maintained scores of all three metrics, which signify good performance. In contrast, LSTM has lower values, implying a comparatively weaker one generalization.

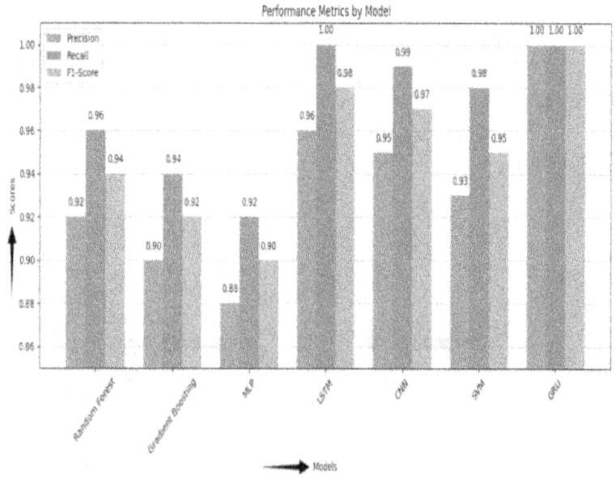

Figure 4. Performance metrics of classification models in water quality assessment.

Conventional ML algorithms such as Random Forest, Gradient Boosting, and MLP tended to categorize images with low weak edges, or glare or contrast, because of limited feature representation. Better performance was observed in CNN and LSTM. But nevertheless, struggled with uneven lighting or subtle textures, at times terming clean water dirty. In compared, GRU handled with these problematic cases more precisely learning complex patterns in the structured way features. This strength adds to its flawlessness classification accuracy.

The picture presents a Box Plot Representation of Accuracy Dissemination over classification model, with focus on the experience in different machine learning and deep learning techniques. The chart is in the shape of a box plot and, on the vertical axis, it was represented by the accuracy percent (%) and different values model names on the horizontal axis. The models they are tested as Random Forest, Gradient Boosting, MLP, LSTM, GRU, CNN, and SVM.

The figures of the accuracy of every model show minor difference. Random Forest had 94%, Gradient Boosting 92%, MLP 90%, LSTM 98%, CNN 97%, and SVM 96% accuracy. Significantly, the GRU model broke all other models by achieving an perfect precision of 100%. These results highlight the effectiveness of ensemble techniques, sequence based models, and deep learning models to tackle the classification problem presented in Figure 5.

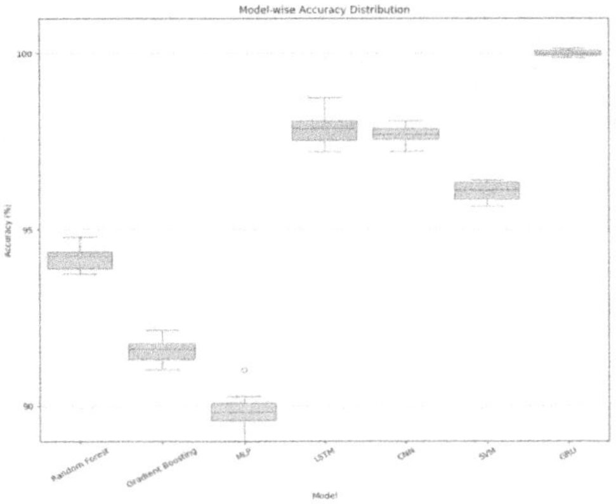

Figure 5. Box plot representation of accuracy distribution across the classification model.

The GRU as per the comparison of accuracy is as follows network becomes the best performing model and achieving an outstanding correct rate of 100%. Other approaches, Random Forest (94%) and Gradient Boosting are also included (92%), MLP (90%), LSTM (98%), CNN (97%), and SVM (96%), showed good performance. However, the GRU has an excellent precision, which means that it is especially suitable to the given task. Hence, the GRU model emerges and as the most successful actor of the persons represented. Models Random Forest, Gradient Boosting, MLP, and including their reliance caused SVM to perform moderately (90-96%). On manually derived luminance based features which are not effective at capturing complex spatial structures in pictures. CNN and LSTM deep learning models demonstrated learned features are more precise than those based on pure mathematics. Yet still had no power to seize deeper sequential dependencies. GRU on the contrary employed its recurrent arc to regulate structured relationships within the high-dimensional ResNet50-extracted features, which makes it possible to achieve superior accuracy.

Table 1.

Model	Accuracy	Precision	Recall	F1-score
Random Forest	0.94	0.92	0.96	0.94
Gradient Boosting	0.92	0.90	0.94	0.92
MLP	0.90	0.88	0.92	0.90
LSTM	0.98	0.96	1.00	0.98
CNN	0.97	0.95	0.99	0.97
SVM	0.96	0.93	0.98	0.95
GRU	1.00	1.00	1.00	1.00

The table is a critical assessment of the various algorithms used for water quality classification. It draws attention to the performance measures, accuracy, recall and precision and F1-score of single model.

4 CONCLUSION

Evaluation of different machine learning and deep learning models of water quality classification points to the significance of selecting the proper model to achieve the highest possible accuracy. GRU was the best performing with a high precision of 100% therefore the most reliable of the alternatives. Other algorithms include Random Forest (94%), Gradient Boosting (92%), MLP (90%), LSTM (98%), CNN (97%), and SVM (96%), were not weak. The GRU also is a great discoverer of salient features in an actual picture and capturing the sequential relationships which is water is one of its key advantages. In combination with other methods like edge, contour detection it is used to ensure appropriate classification. Bar graphs are the diagrams used to demonstrate the excellence. GRU real-time water quality performance. Consequently, it best fits to be applied in environmental management and to make wise decisions.

GRU model demonstrated an ideal performance on the present dataset, the findings might not be the full picture of the reality complexity. The next step of work will be the testing with other unseen samples, taking images in various ways. lighting and seasonal conditions and utilizing statistical validation techniques. This will contribute towards setting up the system. Reliability in practice implementations and make them robust to scale environmental monitoring.

REFERENCES

[1] Water Quality Monitoring System: Literature Survey and Design Shruthi G. R., Presha Stephen, Ritika Patil, S. Shivani, and Khooshi Dutta (2024). Published in *International Journal for Research in Applied Science & Engineering Technology (IJRASET)*, Volume 12, Issue III.

[2] X. Wang, Y. Li, Q. Qiao, A. Tavares, and Y. Liang, (2023). "Water quality prediction based on machine learning and comprehensive weighting methods," *Entropy*, vol. 25, no. 8, p. 1186.

[3] M.Y. Shams, A.M. Elshewey, E.-S.M. El-Kenawy, A. Ibrahim, F.M. Talaat, and Z. Tarek, (2024). "Water quality prediction using machine learning models based on grid search method," *Multimedia Tools and Applications*, vol. 83, no. 12, pp. 35307–35334.

[4] K. Kalaivanan and J. Vellingiri, (2022). "Survival study on different water quality prediction methods using machine learning," *Nature Environment and Pollution Technology*, vol. 21, no. 3, pp. 1259–1267.

[5] M. He, Q. Qian, X. Liu, J. Zhang, and J. Curry, (2024). "Recent progress on surface water quality models utilizing machine learning techniques," *Water*, vol. 16, no. 24, art. 3616.

[6] M.A. Anbuchezhian, R. Venkataraman, and V. Kumuthavalli, (2018). "Water quality analysis and prediction using machine learning algorithms," *J. Emerg. Technol. Innov. Res. (JETIR)*, vol. 5, no. 11, pp. 455–460,

[7] M. Zhu, J. Wang, X. Yang, Y. Zhang, L. Zhang, H. Ren, B. Wu, and L. Ye, (2022). "A review of the application of machine learning in water quality evaluation," *Eco -Environment & Health.*

[8] V.S.N. Vijendra, P. Prashant, M. Jayaprakash, R. Ananya, and N. Shivashankar, (2024). "Potable water quality prediction: By artificial intelligence techniques with advanced machine learning algorithm's," *International Journal for Research in Applied Science & Engineering Technology (IJRASET)*, vol. 12, no. 4, ISSN: 2321–9653.

[9] D. Thakur and A.J. Singh, (2023). "Exploring machine learning algorithms for reliable water quality prediction," *International Journal for Research in Applied Science & Engineering Technology (IJRASET)*, vol. 11, no. 9, ISSN: 2321–9653.

[10] Horak, J. Klecka, and M. Richter, (2015). "Water Quality assessment by image processing," *International Conference on Telecommunications and Signal Processing*, Prague.

[11] A. Adedeji, M. Ajao, and O. Ajala, (2021). "Image processing techniques for water quality assessment: A

review,"*Environmental Technology & Innovation*, vol. 24, p. 102022.

[12] J.S. Patil, A. Mailaram, P.N.K. Basa, A.S. Sravya, and B. Yadam, (2023). "Water quality prediction using image processing and machine learning models," *Int. J. Comput. Sci. Eng.*, vol. 13, no. 1, pp. 45–55. doi: 10.37622/IJCSE/13.1.2023.

[13] H. Shanono, M.R.M. Sapiee, K.A. Aziz, N.H.Z. Suleiman, A. Gomes, and C. Gomes, (2018). "Image processing techniques applicable to wastewater quality detection: Towards a hygienic environment," *J. Mater. Environ. Sci.*, vol. 9, no. 8, pp. 2288–2303.

[14] V. A. M, C. Sohitha, G.N. Saraswathi, and L. G. V, (2023). "Water quality prediction using CNN," *J. Phys. Conf. Ser.*, vol. 2484, no. 1, art. 012051.

[15] M. Akhlaq, A. Ellahi, R. Niaz, M. Khan, S. Sh. Sammen, and M. Scholz, (2024). Comparative analysis of machine learning algorithms for water quality prediction," *Tellus A: Dynamic Meteorol. Oceanogr.*, vol. 76, no. 1, pp. 177–192.

[16] A. Hassan *et al.*, (2024). "Machine learning models for water quality prediction: A comprehensive analysis and uncertainty assessment in mirpurkhas, Sindh, Pakistan," *Water (MDPI)*, vol. 16, no. 7, p. 941.

[17] P. Xu, X. Liu, J. Liu, M. Cai, Y. Zhou, S. Hu, and M. Chen, (2024) "Survey on machine vision-based intelligent water quality monitoring techniques in water treatment plantFish activity behavior recognition-based schemes and applications," doi: 10.1515/dema-2024-0010, received Aug. 16, 2023; accepted Apr. 7, 2024.

[18] A.A. Ahmed, L. Oyedele, S. Sayed, A. Abdoulhalik, and S. Moutari, (2024). "Applications of machine learning to water resources management: A review of present status and future opportunities," *J. Clean. Prod.*, vol. 441, art. 140715.

[19] M. Ehteram, A.N. Ahmed, M. Sherif, and A. El-Shafie, (2024) "An advanced deep learning model for predicting water quality index," *Ecol. Indic.*, vol. 160, art. 111806, doi: 10.1016/j.ecolind.2024.111806.

[20] J.Chen, D. Zhang, S. Yang, and Y.A. Nanehkaran, (2021). "Intelligent monitoring method of water quality based on image processing and RVFL-GMDH model," *IET Image Processing*, vol. 15, no. 4, pp. 920–930, doi: 10.1049/iet-ipr.2020.0254.

Technology for a Resilient Future – Vincent , Moorthy and Dasari (Eds)
 ISBN: 978-1-041-39070-1

Implementation and Comparative Analysis of 64 Bit Vedic and Booth Multipliers for a MAC Unit

Pokuru Naga Sai Charan and S. Ramya
Department of Electronics & Communication Engineering Manipal Institute of Technology Manipal Academy of Higher Education Manipal

ABSTRACT: A Multiplier Accumulator unit(MAC) can be design and implement using Vedic multiplier, along with conventional Booth mutiplier. Vedic multiplier is designed using the sutras in vedic mathematics used for multiplication called "Urdhava Triyagbhayam". This method of using vedic mathematics with suitable low power techniques are used to enhance the speed and performance of MAC and reduce power consumption. The design of adder and multiplier can be implemented using efficient adder circuit for high speed operations and vedic multiplier used for high performance, minimum area, and partial products reduction. Here, we proposed a 64-bit vedic multiplier, designed by using Brent-kung adder (BKA). It is then compared with existing Booth multiplier. The overall simulation is carried out using Verilog and synthesis and implementation will be carried out in RTL with Xilinx ISE.

Keywords: Verilog, UrdhvaTriyakbhyam, Xilinx, Vivado, FPGA

1 INTRODUCTION

Multiplier design is most critical aspect of Multiply accumulate unit(MAC) design. Multiplier-Accumulator (MAC) unit is a building block for most digital processing systems, including Digital Signal Processing (DSP), Artificial Intelligence (AI), and high-speed arithmetic. Multiplier is most critical part of dsp applications such as FFT, DFT and convolution applications. Here computation number is also very critical. Why because If the number of computation is increased then delay is also increased. So that the processor speed decreased. In VLSI multipliers can be implemented in various ways. Either we use logic gates or we use transmission gates or we use multiplexers we can implement multipliers. The main operation of MAC unit is: MAC Output=$\sum(Ai \times Bi)$ where Ai and Bi are input operands, and their products are progressively summed over several cycles. The typical Multiply and Accumulate unit has three major components: a multiplier, an adder, and an accumulator register. The multiplier carries out the multiplication of two input numbers, whereas the adder sums the result by adding the product to stored values. The accumulator register holds intermediate and final accumulated values, which support uninterrupted computation in digital signal processing (DSP) and neural networks. The operation of the MAC unit starts with retrieving input operands from memory, registers, or an input buffer. These operands, commonly referred to as A and B, are then passed to the multiplier unit for execution. The multiplication operation is done with a high-performance algorithms, like Vedic Multiplication (quick and parallel), Booth's Multiplication (optimized for signed numbers), Wallace Tree Multiplication (for enhanced speed), or Array Multiplication (easy but power-hungry). After multiplication, the product obtained is summed up by adding it to the already stored sum in the accumulator register. This iterative accumulation procedure guarantees that the end computation is the result of the sum of several multiplication operations. The accumulated value is finally held for future processing, either for future calculations within a DSP pipeline or for usage in machine learning and neural network computation. This procedure is repeated iteratively, which makes the MAC unit suited for applications demanding repetitive multiplication and summation. Multiplication is a major operation in MAC units, and the multiplier has a large impact on the performance. A digital system's efficiency largely relies on the speed, power usage, and area of the multiplier. Multiple multiplication algorithms are available, each being optimized for one or more of these factors.

Booth's multiplier optimizes efficiency by minimizing number of partialproducts via Booth encoding.

This encoding method enables the multiplier to handle multiple bits simultaneously, which considerably lessens the number of addition operations needed. It is especially efficient in signed number multiplication. Modifications of the Booth multiplier, including the Radix-2 and Radix-4 Booth multipliers, extend the optimization by encoding more bits at the same time. Booth multipliers find extensive applications in DSP processors and floating-point units since they can efficiently perform signed multiplication. With reference to ancient Vedic mathematics, the Vedic multiplier adopts the Urdhva-Tiryakbhayam (Vertical and Crosswise) algorithm. It supports partial product generation in parallel, which results in an extremely efficient process for multiplication. This method minimizes the number of steps required for addition in comparison with traditional processes, resulting in power-efficient and fast design. With low power requirement and small hardware, the Vedic multiplier has extensive applications in low power AI accelerators, DSP designs, and FPGA-based designs.

2 LITERATURE REVIEW

A 64-bit MAC Unit Implementation Using Vedic Multiplier – by Syed Nageena Parveen, Harika Dulam proposes a 64-bit MAC unit implemented using Vedic multipliers to minimize speed, power, and area in VLSI circuits. Classical multipliers cause delay and consume more power, whereas the Urdhva-Tiryakbhayam Vedic technique of multiplication allows faster parallel computations with decreased delay and increased efficiency. The MAC unit is implemented in Verilog HDL, synthesized and simulated using Xilinx ISE, and tested on an FPGA board. The proposed design consists of four 32-bit Vedic multipliers, a 96-bit carry-save adder, and a 96-bit modified carry-skip adder, effectively minimizing delay to 15.77 ns. By reducing addition and multiplication operations, this hierarchical Vedic-based MAC unit enhances overall system performance.[2]

R. Anitha, et.al reported a paper on design and implementation of 32 bit multiply and accumulate (MAC) unit based on vedic multiplier and reversible logic gates for better performance and less power consumption. Vedic multiplier, derived from the Urdhva Tiryakbhayam sutra, reduces partial products, resulting in better speed and area efficiency. Reversible logic gates that are necessary in quantum computing are incorporated

DOI: 10.1201/9781042017546-34

into the design of the adder to further improve power consumption. The MAC unit is coded in Verilog HDL, simulated on Modelsim and Xilinx 14.2, and synthesized on both the RTL compiler tool in Cadence and Xilinx. Further, the chip design for the proposed MAC unit is performed to illustrate its potential in low-power, high-performance applications.[8]

Poorvika Singh reviews the significance of Vedic and Booth multiplication techniques in computer applications, focusing on precision, speed, area efficiency, and low power consumption. It compares the Vedic Multiplication Algorithm, based on the Urdhva Tiryakbhayam sutra, with the Booth Multiplication Algorithm, which reduces partial products, to determine their performance across key metrics such as delay and power consumption. The design, simulation, and synthesis were performed using Xilinx Vivado with Verilog, and the hardware implementation was carried out on an FPGA. The study highlights the growing need for high-speed multipliers in digital devices and provides insights into selecting the optimal multiplier for efficient computation.[15]

3 METHODOLOGY

The Vedic multiplier is designed using hierarchical modular design, where large-bit multiplications (e.g., 16-bit or 32-bit) are broken into smaller 8x8 or 16x16 multipliers. The partial products are computed in parallel and accumulated using an efficient adder. Vedic multiplier ensures high-speed and low-power operation by leveraging the parallelism of Vedic multiplication techniques. The design is further optimized with Brent-Kung adders to achieve low-power addition, reducing propagation delay and energy consumption. 64-bit Vedic multiplier is chosen as the core multiplication unit due to its hierarchical structure, which breaks down large bit-width multiplications into smaller sub-blocks. The Vedic multiplication technique, based on the Urdhva Tiryagbhyam (vertically and crosswise) algorithm, allows efficient parallel computation, reducing the number of partial products and minimizing critical path delays. To enhance power efficiency, clock gating and low-power adders are integrated into the design. After multiplication, the results must be accumulated efficiently to support MAC operations. Instead of using conventional ripple-carry adders, a Brent-Kung adder is employed for summation. This parallel-prefix adder significantly reduces carry propagation delay, leading to faster and more power-efficient accumulation of results. The Brent-Kung adder structures the carry generation tree in a way that optimizes power and area while maintaining speed.

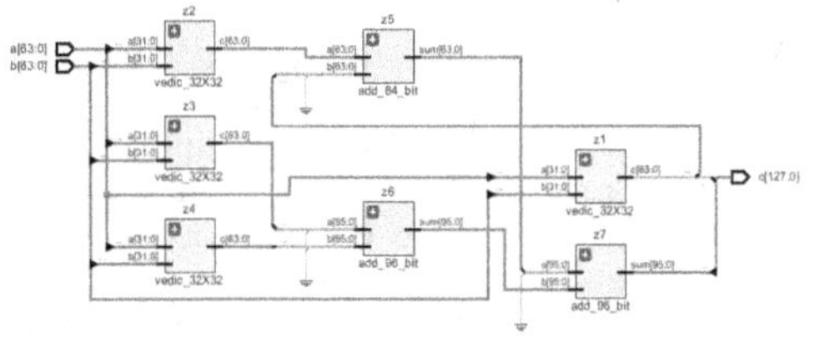

Figure 1. 64x64bit vedic multiplier schematic digram.

3.1 *Pipelining*

The Vedic Multiplier, a core component of the MAC, benefits significantly from pipelining. The multiplication process can be broken down into smaller sub-operations, with registers placed at key points to store intermediate results. By introducing pipeline registers, each stage of the multiplication can operate independently in successive clock cycles. This ensures that while one multiplication is being completed in the final stage, another can be initiated in the first stage, thereby reducing latency and increasing the number of computations per second

Step-wise operations performed:

- Step 1 PO=A0* BO
- Step 2C*P(1,1)=(A*1B*0)+(A*0B*1)
- Step 3C3C2P2=(A2 + BO) + (A0*B2) + (A1*B1) + C1
- Step 4 C4C5P3=(A3B0)+(A2* B1) + (A1*B2) + (A0* B3) + C2
- Step5 C6C7P4=(A4*BO) + (A3* B1) + (A2* B2) + (A1* B3) + (A0B4) + C3 + C4
- Step 6 C8C9C10P5=(A5*30) + (A4* B1) + (A3* B2) + (A2*B3) + (A1B4) + (A0B5) + C5 + C6
- Step 7 C13C12C11P6=(A6^*B0)+(A*5B*1)+(A*4B*2) +(A*3B*3)+(A2*B4)+(A1B5)+(A0*B6)+C7+C8
- Step 8 C*C(16,15)*C*14P*7=(A*7B*0)+(A*6B*1)/(ASB*2) + (A*4B*3)+
- (A*2B*5)+(A*1B*6)+(A0*B*7)+C9+C1 +(A*3B*5)+ (A*2B*6)+(A*1B*7)+C*10/C*12+C14
- Step 9 C19C18C17P8=(A*7B*1)+(A*6B*2)+(A*5B*3)/ (A*4B*4)+C*C(22,21)*C*
- Step 10 20P*9=(A*7B*2)+(A*6B*3)+(ASB*4)+(A*4B*5) +(A3B6)+(A2B7)+C13 C15+C17+(A3^*B7)+C16+C18+C20
- Step 11 C*C(25,24)*C*23P*10 =(A7*B3) + (A6^*B4) + (A5^*B5) + (A4^*B6)
- Step 12 C27C26P11=(A*7B*4)+(A*6B*5)+(A*5B*6) +(A*4B*7)+C19+C21+C23^ prime
- Step 13 C29C28P12=(A*7B*5)+(A*5B*6)+(A*5B*7)+C22 +C24+C26
- Step 14 C30P13=(A*7B*6)+(A*6B*7)+C25 + C27 + C28
- Step 15 P14 = (A7^*B7) + C29 + C30

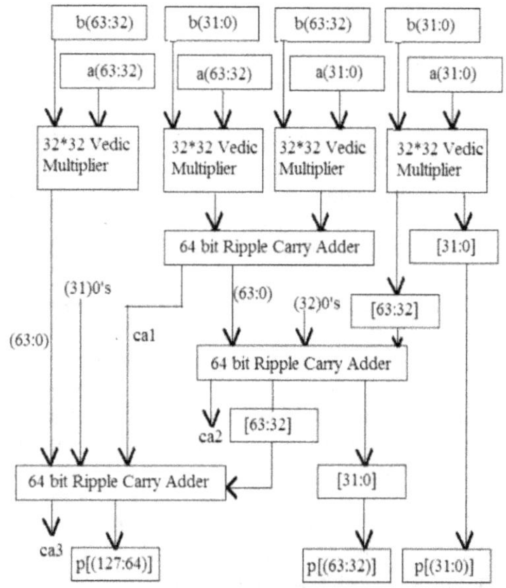

Figure 2. 64x64bit vedic multiplier block diagram.

The Booth multiplication algorithm provides a neat solution to signed binary multiplication in minimizing the addition and subtraction operations needed. In a 64-bit Booth multiplier, the basic concept is to represent the multiplier bits in a manner that it minimizes partial products, especially when the multiplier contains extended runs of 1s. This comes handy in high-speed arithmetic systems where power consumption and area efficiency are a concern.

The algorithm starts off with two 64-bit signed integers: the multiplicand (M) and the multiplier (Q). An additional bit, usually represented as Q_{-1}, is added to the least significant bit of multiplier and set to zero. This extra bit helps in detecting transitions in the multiplier that decide whether to add, subtract, or do nothing at a given stage. The product register is set up to zero and is 128 bits wide to fit the complete result of the signed multiplication, any overflow included.

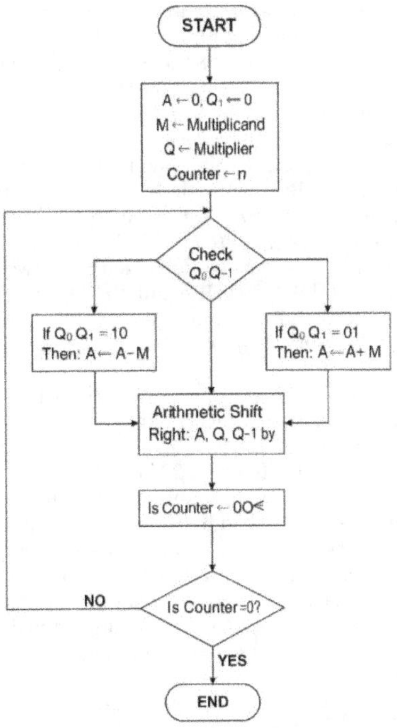

Figure 3. 64x64bit booth multiplier block digram.

Booth's encoding consists of checking a pair of bits at a time: the present bit of the multiplier (Q_i) and the preceding bit (Q_{i-1}). Based on the pair of bits, a particular operation is performed. If the pair is (1,1) or (0,0), no arithmetic operation takes place, and only shifting is done. If the pair is (0,1), it indicates the beginning of a new series of 1s, and the multiplicand is add to the partial product. If the pair is (1,0), it is the termination of a 1s series, and the multiplicand is subtracted from the partial product. This approach reduces the number of additions and subtractions substantially, which enhances the performance.

After performing the necessary operation based on the Booth encoding, the entire content of the partial product, multiplier, and Q_{-1} is arithmetically shifted to the right by one bit. This type of shifting preserves the sign bit, which is essential for correctly handling signed numbers. The combination of encoding and shifting constitutes one iteration, and this process is repeated 64 times to cover all bits of the multiplier.

Upon completion of all iterations, the product register contains the final 128-bit signed result. Booth's algorithm not only improves speed but also offers a compact hardware implementation due to its regular structure and reduced number of arithmetic operations.

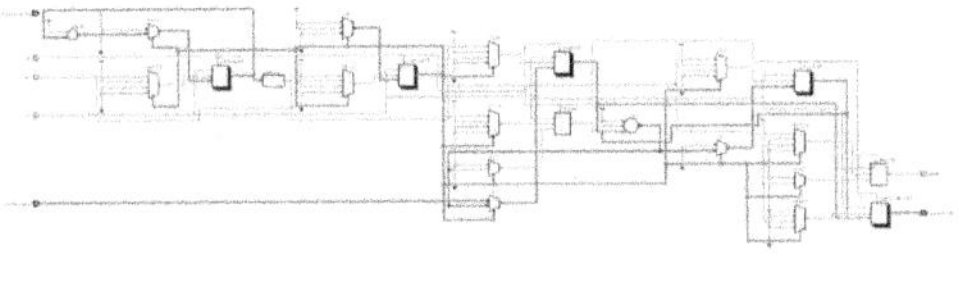

Figure 4. 64x64bit booth multiplier schematic digram.

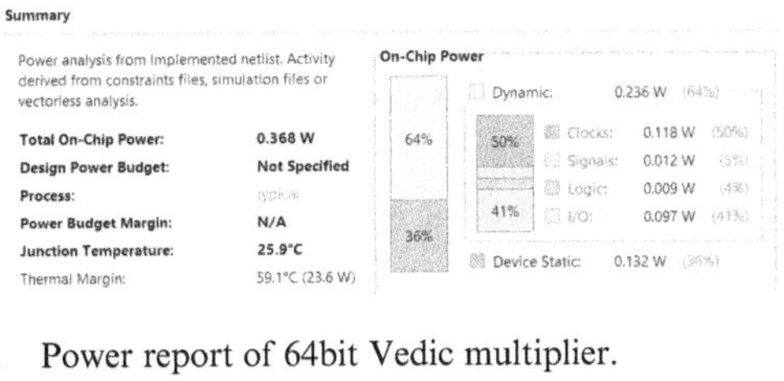

Figure 5. Power report of 64bit Vedic multiplier.

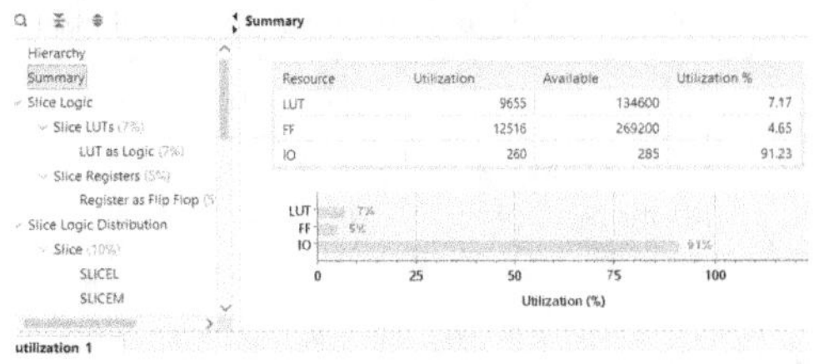

Figure 6. Memory utilization of 64bit Vedic multiplier.

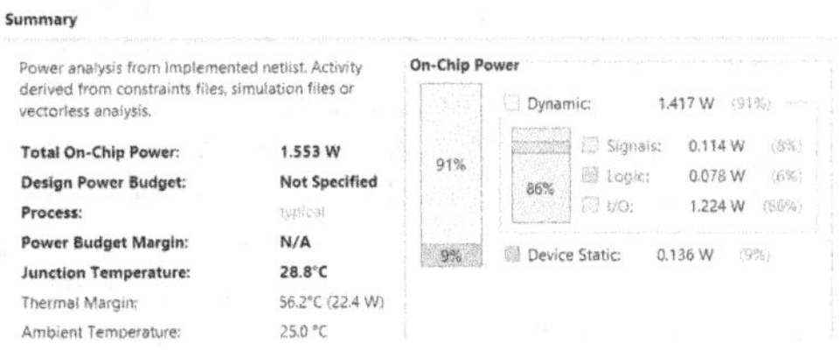

Figure 7. Power report of 64bit Booth multiplier.

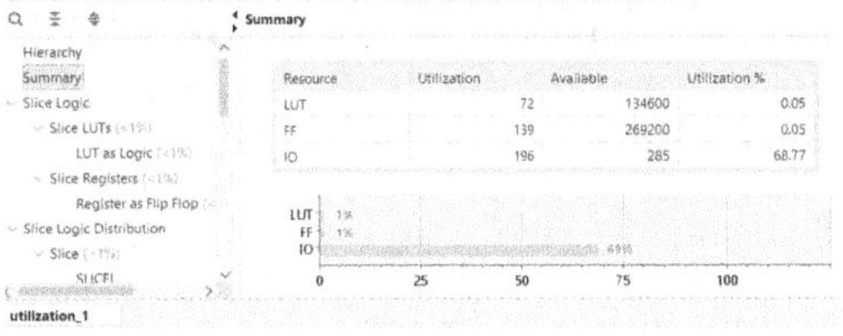

Figure 8. Memory utilization of 64bit booth multiplier.

4 RESULTS AND COMPARISION ANALYSIS

The comparison between vedic and booth multipliers are shown in Table 1 & Table 2. It is carried out using key parameters such as Maximum Path Delay (in nanoseconds) and Power Consumption (in Watts).

FPGA Used: xc7a200tfbg484-1

Family: Artix-7, General Purpose Register

The Vedic multiplier is much more power-efficient (0.368 W) in comparison to the Booth multiplier (1.553 W) and hence, more suitable for high-speed arithmetic operations.

The Vedic multiplier uses more LUTs and FFs than the Booth multiplier but shows greater I/O utilization, which is an indication of a compromise between resources and performance.

Table 1. Power analysis for 2x2 multipliers.

		Power Utalization(in milli Watts)	
S.No.	Multipliers	Vedic Algorithm	Booth Algorithm
1	2x2 Multiplier	71	80

Table 2. 64bit Booth vs vedic multipliers power comparision.

S.No.	*Parameter*	*Vedic Multiplier*	*Booth Multiplier*
1	Power Consumption	0.368W	1.553W
2	Maximum Delay	4.87ns	7.23ns
3	MAC Throughtput	High	Moderate
4	Design Complexity	High	Moderate

Table 3. 64bit booth vs vedic multipliers area comparision.

S.No	Design	LUTs (%)	FFs (%)	IO (%)
1	64-bit Vedic Multiplier	7.17	4.65	91.23
2	64-bit Booth Multiplier	0.05	0.05	68.77

5 CONCLUSION

This paper presented a comparative analysis of Booth and Vedic multipliers in the context of Multiply-Accumulate (MAC) operations, which are fundamental building blocks in modern digital signal processing and neural processing units. The study evaluated both architectures based on key design metrics such as power consumption, speed and area utilization.

The Booth multiplier, due to its ability to minimize the number of arithmetic operations through intelligent encoding of the multiplier bits, demonstrated advantages in handling signed operands efficiently and reducing switching activity for data patterns with consecutive 1s. However, its performance is often limited by the sequential nature of the shifting and addition/ subtraction stages, which can introduce latency in high-frequency applications.

On the other hand, the Vedic multiplier, particularly the Urdhva Tiryagbhyam (vertical and crosswise) algorithm, showed superior speed performance owing to its parallel structure and recursive decomposition. It offers significant benefits in reducing the critical path delay, making it highly suitable for pipelined MAC architectures where throughput is a key concern. Additionally, its regular layout and parallelism make it attractive for low-power and high-performance designs in deep learning and real-time DSP systems.

Overall, the results indicate that while Booth multipliers are efficient for signed arithmetic and moderate performance requirements, Vedic multipliers are better suited for high-speed and low-latency MAC operations. Depending on the application domain—whether low-power embedded systems or high-throughput accelerators—the appropriate multiplier architecture can be chosen to optimize performance and efficiency.

REFERENCES

[1] *FPGA Implementation of 2D Convolution using Diverse Adder – Multiplier combination by Shwetha Bhavikatti and Aswini N published in 5th International Conference on Electronics and Sustainable Communication Systems* (ICESC 2024)

[2] A 64 BIT MAC unit design based on FPGA using vedic multiplier by Syed Nageena Parveen; Harika Dulam published in 2023 Global Conference on Information Technologies and Communications (GCITC)

[3] High Speed and Power Efficient Multiplier and Adder Designs for Linear Convolution by S. Shrinidhi, S. Vinuja, R. Lakshmi Prasanna, B. Sumanth, and Navya Mohan published in Fourth International Conference on Communication, Computing and Electronics 2023.

[4] FPGA implementation of multiplier-accumulator unit using vedic multiplier and reversible gates by K. Rajesh; G. Umamaheswara Reddy published in 2019 *Third International Conference on Inventive Systems and Control (ICISC)*

[5] Design and Implementation of FPGA based 64-bit MAC Unit using VEDIC Multiplier and Reversible Logic Gates by P. SivaNagendra Reddy* and M. Saraswathi published in Indian Journal of Science and Technology

[6] Comparative analysis of vedic multiplier using various adder architectures by Jatin Yadav1, Anupam Kumar2, Shaik Shareef 3, Sandeep Bansal4, Navjot Rathour5 published in 4th International Conference on Intelligent Circuits and Systems

[7] Reverse Logic Gate and Vedic Multiplier to Design 32 Bit MAC Unit by K .Venkata Parthasaradhi Reddy, S.M.Subahan published in *International Journal & Magazine of Engineering, Technology, Research and Management.*

[8] R. Anitha, Neha Deshmukh, Sarat Kumar Sahoo and S. Prabhakar Karthikeyan, "A 32 BIT MAC Unit Design Using Vedic Multiplier and Reversible Logic Gate", *International Conference on Circuit Power and Computing Technologies [ICCPCT].*

[9] Modified High Speed 32-bit vedic multiplier design and implementation by M.Bala Murugesh, S.Nagaraj published in the *International Conference on Electronics and Sustainable Communication Systems (ICESC 2020)*

[10] Design of MAC Unit in Artificial Neural Network Architecture using Verilog HDL by L.Ranganath, D. Jay Kumar, P.Siva Nagendra Reddy published in *International conference on Signal Processing, Communication, Power and Embedded System (SCOPES)*-2016

[11] Verilog based brain - inspired system published by Swathi Kambhampati, K.Varsha, A.Chaitanya, B.Madhavi, G.Lakshmi Yoga Vardhini published in *Journal of Nonlinear Analysis and Optimization* Vol. 15, Issue. 1: 2024

[12] Realization of high-performance approximate multipliers for fpga applications published by B.Rekha, G.Krishna Koushik, G. Chandra Mahesh, G.Shiva Kumar, M.Anil kumar. ISSN 2319-5991 www.ijerst.com Vol. 20, Issue.2, April 2024

[13] Design of Optimized CNN for Image Processing using Verilog published by Veena M B, Rohan Deodurg, Shrinidhi V, Soundarya S in 2023 4th IEEE Global Conference for Advancement in Technology (GCAT) Bangalore, India. Oct 6-8, 2023

[14] 4 Bit and 8 Bit convolution using vedic multiplier published by Rahul Kamdi, Aniket Pathade, Prasheel Thakre, Sandeep Kumar Tiwari in 2022 International Conference on Emerging Trends in Engineering and Medical sciences (ICETEMS)

[15] High Speed 64 Bit Vedic & Booth multiplier implementation using FPGA published by Poorvika Singh, Rohan Bansal, Nitin Sachdeva, Pradeep Dimri in 2024 48 3rd *IEEE International Conference on Artificial Intelligence for Internet of Things* (AIIoT 2024)

[16] VLSI Implementation of Multiply and Accumulate Unit Using Distributed Arithmetic by Rajyalakshmi Chikkani, Bharathi. M and Yasha Jyothi M Shirur published in Thomson Reuters ISI Web of Science Clarivate Analytics USA and Crossref Indexed Journal(2020)

[17] Recent trends in Medical Image Processing by H.N. Costin published in Computer Science Journal of Moldova, 22, no.2 (65), 2014.

[18] A review of HDL-based system for real time image processing used in tumors screening by i. chiuchisan, o. geman published in proceeding of the 18th International Conference on System Theory, Control and Computing (ICSTCC2014), ISBN: 978-1-4799-4602-0, pp. 217-220, 2014.

[19] Adopting the internet of things technologies in health care systems by I. Chiuchisan, H.N. Costin, O. Geman published in proceedings of international conference and Exposition on Electrical and Power Engineering (EPE2014), *Workshop on Electromagnetic Compatibility and Engineering in Medicine and Biology*, pp. 532-535, 2014.

[20] An approach of a decision support and home monitoring system for patients with neurological disorders using internet of things concepts by I. Chiuchisan, O. *Geman published in WSEAS Transactions on Systems, Issue: Multi-models for Complex Technological Systems*, 13, pp. 460 469, 2014.

[21] Speed efficient 64 bit mac design using vedic multiplier and reversible logic gates published by K.Aruna Sree, S.T.Mrudula, K.Geetha, Dr.R.Ramachandra in Vol-3 Issue-6 2017 IJARIIE-ISSN(O)-2395-4396

[22] Ghosh S, Hazra S, Maity SP, Rahaman H. (2015). A new algorithm for grayscale image histogram computation. *12th IEEE India International Conference (INDICON)*; 1-6.

[23] Igarashi M, Mizuno A, Ikebe M. Accuracy Improvement of Histogram-based Image Filtering. *20th IEEE International Conference on Image Processing (ICIP)* 2013; 1217- 1221.

[24] U. Narula, R. Tripathi, and G. Wakhle, (2015). "High speed 16-bit digital Vedic multiplier using FPGA,' *2015 2nd International Conference on Computing for Sustainable Global Development (INDIACom)*, New Delhi, India, 2015, pp.121-124

[25] D.K. Kahar and H. Mehta, (2017). "High speed vedic multiplier used vedic mathematics," *2017 International Conference on Intelligent Computing and Control Systems*, IEEE, pp. 356-359.

Technology for a Resilient Future – Vincent , Moorthy and Dasari (Eds)
© 2027 The Author(s), ISBN: 978-1-041-39070-1

3D Terrain Mapping and Autonomous Navigation for Planetary Rovers: An RGB-D Sensor-Based Framework

Akshat Agarwal, Pradeep Kumar K, K Vamsi Krishna, and Jayavrinda Vrindavanam V
Department of CSE(AI&ML) Dayananda Sagar University, Bengaluru, India

V.K. Hariharan
Director of CSST, DSU Dayananda Sagar University, Bengaluru, India

Pushkar Pallav
Department of CSE(AI&ML) Dayananda Sagar University, Bengaluru, India

Gopal Sharma R Joshi
Department of CSE Dayananda Sagar University Bengaluru, India

ABSTRACT: Exploration of any extraterrestrial or alien terrains is incomplete without real-time surveillance, high-precision terrain mapping, and autonomous movement. The proposed study describes a developed and integrated system, especially for a Martian rover that utilizes the RTAB-MAP SLAM, ROS2 Jazzy for self-navigation. The system includes an Intel RealSense D435i Depth Camera for high-quality terrain mapping and a CMOS digital microscopic camera for astrobiological soil analysis during exploration missions. A dynamic publisher-subscriber model that manages activation of multiple cameras in real time, which ensures optimized power consumption and consistently monitors the surrounding environment. The depth-based navigation system detects visual markers for path planning, imposing image processing algorithms to make movement decisions. Experimental results validate the efficiency and effectiveness of the system in in-depth noise handling and system navigation stability. Key challenges that include computational efficiency and localization drift were majorly addressed throughout optimizing graph-based SLAM and Sensor fusion techniques.

Keywords: Astrobiology, Autonomous Navigation, Depth Sensing, Image Processing, Mars Rover, Reinforcement Learning, ROS 2 Jazzy, RTAB-Map, SLAM, Terrain Mapping

1 INTRODUCTION

Exploring unnamed alien terrain in space missions presents a challenging task by enabling the collection of scientific data from remote and inaccessible locations. Mars, one of the most mysterious subjects for researchers with its unpredictable terrain and absence of GPS infrastructure, presents challenge for autonomous rovers in real-time decision making. Conventional exploration rovers rely on the computational complexity and power-hungry systems making them impractical for largescale, affordable exploration missions. Over the years, various space agencies across the world have deployed several rovers such as Sojourner in 1997, Spirit and Opportunity in 2004,

Curiosity in 2012, and Perseverance in 2021 to explore the mysterious Mars terrain. Early missions include small semi-autonomous rovers with limited mobility and computational power, mainly relying on direct commands from the base station, which are from Earth. Later, advances in technology generated more sophisticated navigation systems, allowing rovers to achieve greater autonomy in obstacle avoidance and path planning. However, the major drawback for these rovers was their dependency on high-power and complex computing systems, which eventually makes them costly. Additionally, their reliance on periodic communication links introduces delays in making a decision that makes the system difficult to sustain in that environment.

To overcome these limitations, this research work proposes an energy-efficient, cost-effective, modular, and integrated rover capable of self-navigation, terrain mapping, and environmental perception in real time, utilizing low-power embedded hardware. This self-sustaining and intelligent rover incorporates simultaneous localization and mapping (SLAM), computer vision-based navigation, and depth sensing for improved autonomous exploration. The rover is smart and capable enough for tasks like self-navigating unmapped localities and surroundings, identifying hurdles and barriers, and also creating real-time 3D maps, which is ideal for extraterrestrial travel and also for industrial inspection, and rescue missions. In variance with the traditional rovers that are dependent on powerful and high-complexity Graphics Processing Units, the system proposed and developed by us leverages a lowpower embedded computing platform specifically tailored for robotic perception-like use cases. The suggested framework promotes and accelerates the use of SLAM on a low-resource platform while being computationally strong and efficient. In extension, there is an astrobiological surveillance system that is responsible for soil and rock sample analysis in real time and also for discovering potential signs of past or present life. The proposed system integrates key hardware components like Intel RealSense Depth camera D435i, responsible for depth sensing, a dedicated microscopic camera used for astrobiological analysis, numerous surveillance cameras that monitor the environment and model vision, and a Raspberry Pi which acts as the central computing unit. The entire system is operated on the ROS2 framework to ensure efficient sensor integration and real-time communication in a compact environment.

2 RELATED WORKS

A number of recent studies have been using deep learning and reinforcement learning to enhance the performance of autonomous navigation systems. Reinforcement learning with integration of deep neural networks was applied by [1] to enable an autonomous vehicle to form decisions and adapt in real time to unstructured terrain. A similar approach was taken by [2] using reinforcement learning and multi-sensor integration to better understand its environment and avoid obstacles. Deep CNN architectures have

DOI: 10.1201/9781042017546-35

been used successfully for object detection as seen in [3], where visual information is used to locate objects that are critical for planning a route to be traveled. Further improvement was provided by [4], which utilized the YOLOv8 architecture for rapid identification of navigation arrows and potential hazard areas, allowing for high accuracy and very low latency in real-time deployments. Additionally, there are many ways that vision can be used to assist in navigation. A study by [5] created a vision based support system that uses real-time analysis of the surrounding environment to provide guidance. This study demonstrates how machine vision can increase situational awareness and aid in decision making when operating in a dynamic environment. Several studies have also used SLAM (Simultaneous Localization and Mapping) for localization and mapping. An example of a successful LiDAR based SLAM implementation is found in [6], which showed improved map creation.

[7] details a ROS (Robot Operating System) based SLAM implementation that simplifies development and facilitates modular deployment. In a more probabilistic approach, [8] utilized interoceptive measurements to enhance loop closure accuracy and real-time performance in SLAM systems. In spite of all the developments in AI-based navigation, terrain modeling, and online object detection, current systems tend to suffer from high energy requirements, computational-intensive nature, and less flexibility, rendering them less applicable for resource-limited or extraterrestrial areas. To overcome those shortcomings, our solution encompasses the combination of lightweight CNN-based detection, depth perception, RTABMAP SLAM, as well as an improved MQTT-based secure pub-sub model under ROS2 Jazzy, providing precise navigation arrow detection, reliable mapping, as well as efficient communication. It also provides an integrated and scalable pipe, facilitating online obstacle avoidance, adaptable planning of paths, as well as autonomous decision-making at the lowest latency possible and extremely high energy efficiency, providing an affordable, lightweight, as well as practical edgeassisted expedition system solution, especially for application in unknown Martian terrains.

3 METHODOLOGY

3.1 *System architecture*

The system architecture depicted in Figure 1 is centralized around a Raspberry Pi, which integrates data from four primary sources: a depth camera for 3D environmental mapping, a microscopic camera for high-resolution surface inspection, an autonomous navigation module, and a surveillance module for visual monitoring. The Raspberry Pi processes these inputs in real-time to generate two main outputs: autonomous control commands for the locomotion module and processed data, such as terrain maps and sensor/camera imagery, for analysis. Autonomous operation and full environment analysis is enabled through the integrated design of this system; therefore, it is adaptable for a variety of tasks like exploration, reconnaissance, and monitoring.

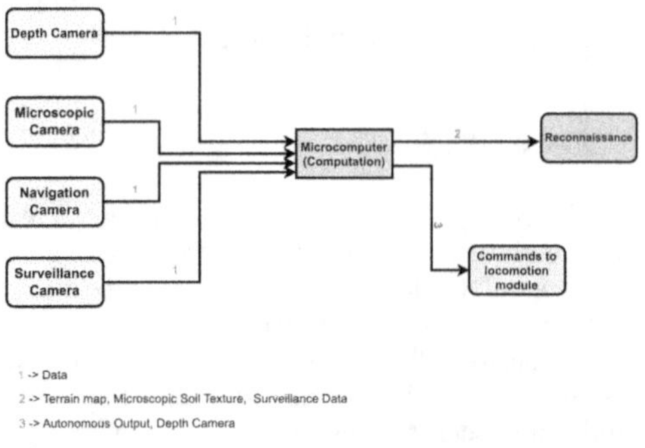

Figure 1. Reconnaissance and navigation data flow.

3.2 *Software framework*

3.2.1 *Depth camera (Intel RealSense D435i)*

The camera provides the rover with real time 3D space information that allows it to create maps of its environment and find its way around obstacles and determine safe ways to navigate the terrain. Autonomous navigation and detailed terrain mapping depend on these features.

Table 1. Specifications and Functionality of components in the Reconnaissance and Navigation System of the Rover.

Component	Model	Key Specification	Functionality
Depth Camera	Intel RealSense D435i	– Depth Sensing: 1280 × 720 @ 30FPS – IMU Integration – USB 3.0 Interface	Terrain mapping, 3D reconstruction, obstacle detection
Surveillance	ESP32-CAM	– 2MP Sensor (1600 × 1200) – Wi-Fi connectivity – Low power consumption	Real-time habitat monitoring for navigation
Compute Module	Raspberry Pi 3B+	– Quad-core 1.4 GHz – 4GB RAM – Wireless	Communication
Onboard processing for SLAM, decision-making and reconnaissance data		communication	Power Management
Li-FePO Battery	– High Energy Density	rechargeable – Supports continuous operation	Power feed for all modules
Microscopic	CMOS	– 15mm-40mm up to 30 FPS – 5V direct current	Retrieves soil tex-ture for analysis

3.2.2 *Compute module (Raspberry Pi 3B+)*

The Raspberry Pi 3B+ is the main processor of the rover that uses Sensor Data to perform SLAM Algorithms for real time Mapping, Localization and Navigation. In addition to the above mentioned functionalities the Raspberry Pi 3B+ handles the wireless communication related to the Remote Control and the Data Transmission from the rover.

3.2.3 *Microscopic camera (CMOS)*

This Module is designed to capture High Resolution Images of the Soil and Surface Texture which will aid in identifying the Properties of the Terrain and therefore aid in Geological, Scientific and Environmental Analysis.

3.2.4 *Surveillance camera*

The camera captures Real Time Video to Enhance Situational Awareness and Supports Reconnaissance Activities. The Camera is primarily used to Identify Potential Hazards, Track Movement and Document Exploration Activities.

3.2.5 *Power management*

The Unit is responsible for providing Stable Power and Managing Energy Distribution to All Components including Sensors, Cameras and Compute Module. The Efficient Power Management Ensures Optimal Performance, Uninterrupted Operation and Long Duration Mission.

3.3 *System navigation*

The Process of Navigation in the Rover is depicted by Figure 2 When the rover starts to operate the Navigation Camera captures frames and converts them into Grayscale format for Computational Efficiency. Then, Template Matching is applied using a Rotated Preloaded Arrow Template to Identify Directional Markers in the Video Feed. The Orientation of the Detected Marker is Associated with a Specific Movement Command (For Example, Forward at 0° and Left at 90°). Finally, the Raspberry Pi Sends the Movement Command to the Locomotive System to Execute the Movement, Which Enables Precise Autonomous Navigation of the Rover.

3.4 *Obstacle detection and avoidance*

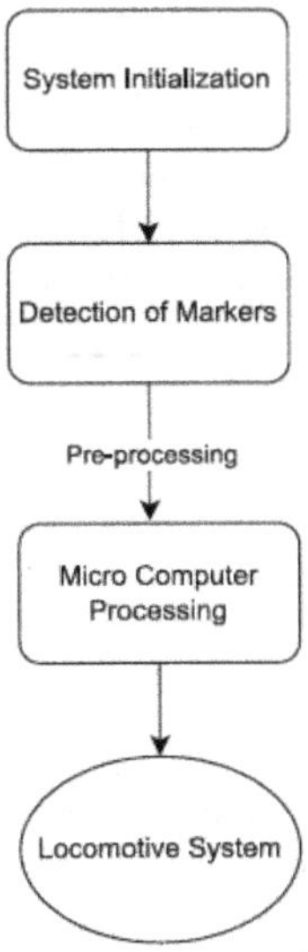

Figure 2. Working model for autonomous expedition.

The Autonomous Navigation System Employes Dual Mode Strategy. Firstly, the ESP32-CAM Tries to Detect Arrow Based Markers to Determine the Path. Secondly, If No Markers are Found, the System Switches to Depth Based Navigation Using an Intel RealSense D435i. The Depth Data is Also Used for Obstacle Detection and Triggering Dynamic Path Planning Through Navigable Space if Obstacle is Identified. The Raspberry Pi Running ROS 2 Jazzy Sends Motor Commands to the Locomotion System While Concurrently Updating the 3D Map in RTAB-Map.

3.5 *Adaptive parameter tuning for enhanced SLAM performance*

To be able to make these parameters adjustable (e.g., "maximum number of features tracked per frame") that can adapt to varying terrains, we have developed an adaptive tuning mechanism that will automatically adjust the "MaxFeatures" parameter. This is accomplished through comparing the number of features found in each frame (performed via the feature detection module) against two thresholds. If the number of features is less than the lower threshold, it is assumed that the environment is "sparse", i.e., there are fewer features available than expected and the MaxFeatures is increased to find more detail. Conversely, if the number of features exceeds the upper threshold, it is determined that the environment is "featurerich", i.e., there are many features present than anticipated and MaxFeatures is decreased to optimize the amount of computation required and to prevent overmapping. The values associated with the thresholds and the logic for determining which threshold should be used is presented in Table 2. These values were established through experimentation with various terrain types and represent a compromise between accuracy and computational efficiency.

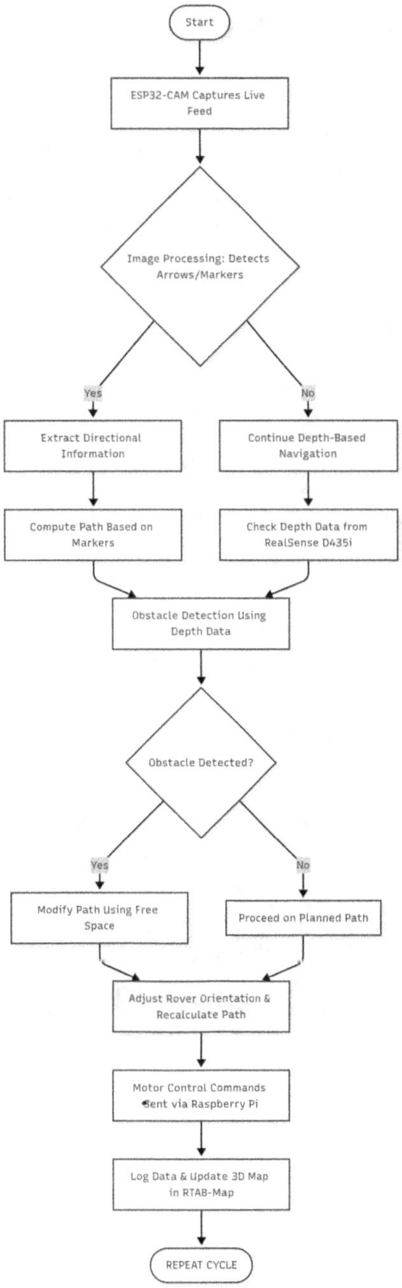

Figure 3. Reconnaissance and navigation unit work-flow.

4 RESULTS AND CONCLUSION

Through experimentation, we have shown that our adaptive approach allows for the efficient real-time generation of maps and enables autonomous navigation of the rover. The use of RTAB-Map SLAM with ROS 2 Jazzy has resulted in stable and reliable localization of the rover over extended periods of time, as evidenced by the lack of noticeable drift. In addition, the Intel RealSense D435i provides the rover with the ability to

Table 2. Adaptive tuning logic.

Threshold Type	Value	Interpretation	Adjustment Action
Lower Feature Threshold	600	Feature count below this signals sparse terrain	Increase MaxFea-tures by 50
Upper Feature Threshold	1000	Feature count above this signals dense terrain	Decrease MaxFea-tures by 50
Adjustment Step	50	Increment/ decrement magnitude	Step size for tuning Parameter

detect obstacles in its path via the collection of highresolution 3D data. The CMOS microscopic camera, on the other hand, captures images of soil texture that could provide valuable information regarding potential biological activity in the soil. A multi-camera publish-subscribe strategy was employed to minimize power usage; thus enabling the rover to operate for longer periods of time.

The 3D point cloud generated by the RealSense D435i (Figure 4a) demonstrates how densely populated regions correspond to the location of objects/terrain close to the rover. Additionally, RTAB-Map's visual odometry tracking of the rover (Figure 4b) confirms the accuracy of the rover's localization. Overall, the results presented in this paper demonstrate that the rover can generate accurate maps of and navigate through previously unexplored planetary environments without human intervention.

(a)

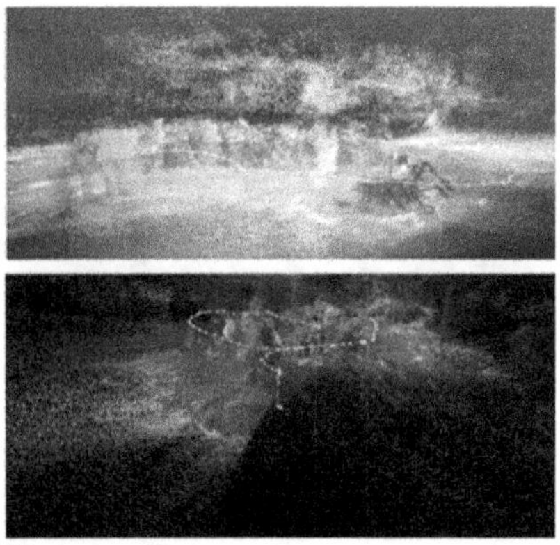

(b)

Figure 4. (a) Depth terrain map generated from RGB-D input. (b) Trajectory output from visual odometry (blue line).

Figure 5. Navigation arrow detection in auto expedition.

The robot's locomotion was very stable, thanks to the SLAM algorithm's precision, and the use of sensors fused with the SLAM allowed for minimal error or "drift" even when the terrain changed. In comparison to a fixed parameter system, an adaptive tuning approach showed a better outcome as illustrated in Table 3; in particular, on a sandy terrain, it cut the absolute trajectory error (ATE) from .25 meters down to .17 meters, and processed much faster. Additionally, on rocky terrain, it improved upon the fixed parameter by achieving a lower ATE of .15 meters, along with a substantial improvement in processing time. As such, these repeated successes of improving the performance of the system validate the adaptability and efficiency of the adaptive tuning mechanism. Testing shows that this simple feedback allows the system to improve mapping accuracy by about 30 % in low-texture areas and run faster on feature-rich terrains by reducing unnecessary computation.

Table 3. Performance comparison of fixed vs. adaptive SLAM.

Terrain Type	Avg. Detected Features (Fixed)	Avg. Detected Features (Adaptive)	ATE (m) Fixed	ATE (m) Adaptive	Proc. Time (ms/ frame) Fixed	Proc. Time (ms/ frame) Adaptive
Sandy (Low-texture)	520	790	0.25	0.17	155	145
Rocky (Hightexture)	1100	980	0.19	0.15	160	140
Mixed terrain	800	820	0.21	0.16	158	142

Despite these advancements, challenges remain in computational overhead associated with high-resolution depth processing and real-time decision-making under extreme conditions. Future work will focus on integrating reinforcement-based learning for adaptive path planning and defining multisensory data fusion. Using algorithms like YOLO will also make the computation less complex and more efficient for the directional movement of the rover system. Feeding the data retrieved by the microscopic camera to an artificially intelligent model that will analyze the texture and hidden patterns in the soil and environment and will predict the signs of life while onboarding only instead of any human hindrance or intervention.In addition, the inclusion of solar panels/modules for charging and advanced terrain classification will increase the rover's ability to function independently over longer periods of time.

As such, the autonomous rover system is a viable and costeffective method of conducting extraterrestrial exploration efficiently. The modular design and relatively low-cost and lowpower embedded hardware of this system makes it ideal for application outside of space exploration, including industrial inspection, search and rescue, and planetary surface mapping. This research has effectively demonstrated that using light weight, computationally efficient robotic systems with AI driven navigation, significantly improves the capabilities of autonomous rovers in complex and uncharted environments, and will enable continued advancement in planetary exploration.

ACKNOWLEDGMENT

We would like to thank the Center for Space Science and Technology (CSST) at Dayananda Sagar University for providing us with the financial support, resources and incubator for bringing our concepts to fruition.

REFERENCES

[1] H.P. Sharma, R. Agarwal, M. Pant and S.V. Karatangi, (2021). Selfdirected robot for car driving using genetic algorithm, *2021 3rd International Conference on Signal Processing and Communication (ICPSC)*, Coimbatore, India, pp. 285–288, https://doi.org/10.1109/ICSPC51351.2021.9451804.

[2] P. Mehune and S. Dorle, (2024). Robust and adaptive neural networks for self-driving cars in challenging road conditions, *2024 2nd International Conference on Computer, Communication and Control (IC4)*, Indore, India, pp. 1–5, https://doi.org/10.1109/IC457434.2024.10486747.

[3] T.A. Nayeem, S.M. Motaharuzzaman, A.T. Hoque and M.H. Rahman, (2022). Computer vision based object detection and recognition system for image searching, *2022 12th International Conference on Electrical and Computer Engineering (ICECE)*, Dhaka, Bangladesh, pp. 148151, https://doi.org/10.1109/ICECE57408.2022.10089019.

[4] J.M. Phillips, S. Shue and J.M. Conrad, (2024). A design architecture for steering an autonomous all-terrain vehicle using object tracking via computer vision and YOLOv8, *2024 IEEE 21st International Conference on Smart Communities: Improving Quality of Life using AI,* Robotics and IoT (HONET), Doha, Qatar, pp. 242–247, https://doi.org/10.1109/HONET63146.2024.10822935. M. Young, The Technical Writer's Handbook. Mill Valley, CA: University Science, 1989.

[5] D. Rajawat, B.P. Lohani, A. Rana, A. Srivastava, P. Yadav and S. Gupta, (2023). Object detection in images and videos using OpenCV: A comparative study of deep learning and traditional computer vision techniques, *2023 10th IEEE Uttar Pradesh Section International Conference on Electrical, Electronics and Computer Engineering (UPCON)*, Gautam Buddha Nagar, India, pp. 141–146, https://doi.org/10.1109/UPCON59197.2023.10434536.

[6] L. Huang, (2021). Review on LiDAR-based SLAM Techniques, *2021 International Conference on Signal Processing and Machine Learning (CONFSPML)*, Stanford, CA, USA, pp. 163–168, https://doi.org/10.1109/CONFSPML54095.2021.00040.

[7] T.-A. Chen *et al.*, (2023). Research on ROS-based SLAM Implementation for indoor environments, 2023 IEEE 5th eurasia conference on IOT, *Communication and Engineering (ECICE)*, Yunlin, Taiwan, pp. 952–955, https://doi.org/10.1109/ECICE59523.2023.10383177.

[8] K. Bhujbal, M. Devmane and A. More, (2022). Probabilistic method for mapping & 3D SLAM of an off-road terrain with four wheeled robot, *2022 5th International Conference on Advances in Science and Technology (ICAST), Mumbai, India*, pp. 422–427, https://doi.org/10.1109/ICAST55766.2022.10039652

[9] D. M et al., (2025). A power-efficient, modular rover design for multi-purpose exploration, *2025 IEEE Space, Aerospace and Defence Conference (SPACE)*, Bangalore, India, pp. 1–6, https://doi.org/10.1109/SPACE65882.2025.11170625.

[10] M. Hamad, A. Finkenzeller, H. Liu, J. Lauinger, V. Prevelakis and S. Steinhorst, (2023). SEEMQTT: secure end-to-end MQTT-based communication for mobile iot systems using secret sharing and trust delegation, in *IEEE Internet of Things Journal*, vol. 10, no. 4, pp. 3384–3406, 15 Feb.15, https://doi.org/10.1109/JIOT.2022.3221857.

[11] X. Da Terrence Fu and S. Srigrarom, (2023). "Advancing accurate depth estimation and perception with angled stereo camera, *2023 15th International Conference on Information Technology and Electrical Engineering (ICITEE)*, Chiang Mai, Thailand, 2023, pp. 1–5, https://doi.org/10.1109/ICITEE59582.2023.10317757.

[12] U. Kumar, D. M, P. K. K, J. Vrindavanam V, G.S.R. Joshi and V.K. Hariharan, (2025). Optimizing communication in ROS 2 with QoS parameters for system advantages, *2025 IEEE Space, Aerospace and Defence Conference (SPACE)*, Bangalore, India, pp. 1–6, https://doi.org/10.1109/SPACE65882.2025.11171196.

Technology for a Resilient Future – Vincent , Moorthy and Dasari (Eds)
© 2027 The Author(s), ISBN: 978-1-041-39070-1

Enhancing Cervical Cancer Diagnosis with Multimodal Fusion and Uncertainty-Aware Deep Learning

Keerthishree B T, Bhoomika B R, Disha T V, Shreyanka A Y, Sneha D C, and Bhavana D E
Department of Computer Science and Engineering, Adichunchanagiri Institute of Technology, Chikkamagaluru, India

ABSTRACT: Reliable detection of cervical cancer at an early stage greatly improves treatment outcomes. In this work, we introduce a multimodal deep-learning setup that studies both Pap-smear cytology images and ultrasound scans together to support clinical decision-making. The framework tackles three related tasks: classifying cervical abnormalities, estimating patient risk, and predicting a continuous severity measure. Unlike approaches that rely only on a single type of image, our model merges information from both modalities and incorporates uncertainty estimates using Monte Carlo Dropout. The confidence scores help the system understand how certain it is about each prediction. In our experiments, DenseNet121 stood out as the best-performing model, achieving about 95.3% accuracy and an R^2 value of 0.91 for predicting severity. Overall, the framework shows strong potential as a reliable tool for supporting automated cervical cancer assessment.

Keywords: Multitask Learning, Uncertainty Estimation, Cervical Cancer, Computational Intelligence

1 INTRODUCTION

Cervical cancer is largely preventable if it's detected early, which makes regular screening very important. Pap-smear cytology and ultrasound imaging are commonly used for this purpose, but manually interpreting these images takes time and may vary from one clinician to another. Deep learning methods, particularly convolutional neural networks like ResNet and DenseNet, offer a way to reduce this subjectivity and improve diagnostic accuracy by automating parts of the evaluation process.While cytopathology and ultrasound have been individually studied, combining both modalities remains underexplored. We compared traditional CNNs, ResNet50, and DenseNet121 to evaluate how well they detect cervical abnormalities. To make the most of both image types. This multimodal fusion allows the model to capture complementary patterns from cytology and ultrasound images, ultimately improving classification performance.

Image-based cervical cancer screening has advanced mainly through Pap-smear cytology and imaging alternatives such as colposcopy and ultrasound. Deep CNNs consistently outperform classical machine-learning approaches with handcrafted features, especially when combined with transfer learning and augmentation [4], [5], [10], [11]. On ultrasound, fine-tuned CNNs capture echogenicity and boundary cues better than models trained from scratch [12]. Progress has also come from deeper architectures (ResNet, DenseNet) [7], [8], and richer strategies such as ensembles, detection–augmentation hybrids [6], [9], and transformer-based encoders that model long-range context [13].However, three gaps persist: (i) most studies rely on a single modality (usually Pap smears), overlooking cross-modal synergies [4], [5], [7], [8], [10]–[13]; (ii) objectives are narrowly focused on classification, rarely extending to risk stratification or severity estimation; and (iii) uncertainty quantification is seldom integrated. Early, feature-level fusion can capture these cross-modal cues more effectively, especially when paired with attention mechanisms, but it is often limited by data availability and alignment issues. Another challenge is that many published works rely on small, single-center datasets and lack external validation, which raises concerns about how well these models would perform in real clinical settings [4], [5], [7], [8], [12]. The model supports classification, risk estimation, and severity regression within one architecture. We compare its performance with several baselines, including CNN, ResNet, and DenseNet models, as well as a transformer-based reference. The design benefits from ResNet50's skip connections, DenseNet121's efficient feature reuse, and Monte Carlo Dropout to provide meaningful uncertainty estimates.To address these gaps, our contributions are:

1. A novel deep learning framework that integrates cytopathology and ultrasound images for cervical cancer diagnosis.
2. A multitask learning design that jointly performs classification, risk prediction, and severity regression.
3. Monte Carlo Dropout was used to estimate uncertainty, making the system more reliable and interpretable.
4. DenseNet121 outperformed both CNN and ResNet50 in all tasks.

2 DATASET AND PREPROCESSING

2.1 *Dataset*

Cytopathology images: 917 images from the Herlev dataset.

Ultrasound images: 1,200 ultrasound scans with labeled cervical abnormalities.

Data is augmented via flipping, rotation, scaling, and normalization.

2.2 *Preprocessing*

Images resized to 224x224 pixels.Normalized using ImageNet means and standard deviations.Train-validation-test split: 70%-15%-15%.Experiments were conducted on NVIDIA RTX 3080 GPU with 10 GB VRAM; training took ~2 hours per model, inference ~50 ms per image

3 METHODOLOGY

3.1 *Deep learning models*

CNN: Custom 5-layer CNN with ReLU, max-pooling, and batch normalization.

DOI: 10.1201/9781042017546-36

ResNet50: Pretrained on ImageNet, fine-tuned on the cervical dataset.

DenseNet121: Pretrained model adapted for cervical image classification.

3.2 *Training configuration*

Loss function: Categorical Cross entropy
Optimizer: Adam (lr=1e-4)
Batch size: 32
Epochs: 50

4 IMPLEMENTATION

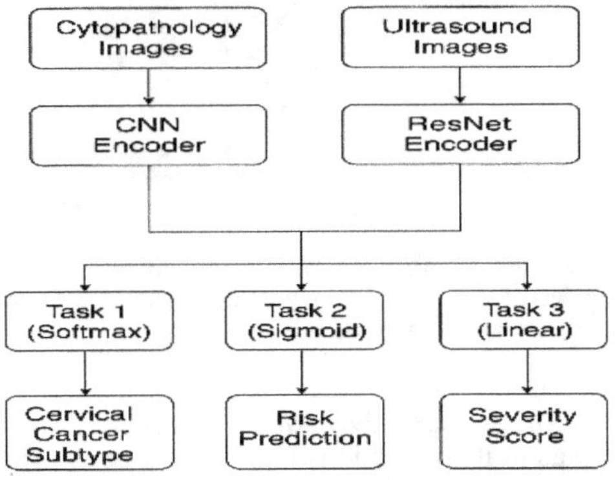

Figure 1. Proposed multitask multimodal deep learning framework. Cytopathology and ultrasound images are processed through modality-specific backbones, concatenated at the feature level, and passed to task-specific heads for classification, risk prediction, and severity regression. Monte Carlo Dropout is applied during inference for predictive uncertainty estimation.

To leverage the complementary strengths of cytopathology and ultrasound modalities while maintaining modularity, a parallel multitask learning strategy is adopted. Two independent deep learning models are trained—one for cytopathology images (using DenseNet121) and one for ultrasound scans (using ResNet50). The dataset size (917 Pap smears, 1,200 ultrasound scans) is relatively small for deep learning. While augmentation mitigates overfitting, larger and more diverse datasets are required for clinical deployment. We adopt early feature-level fusion by concatenating modality-specific feature vectors before task heads.

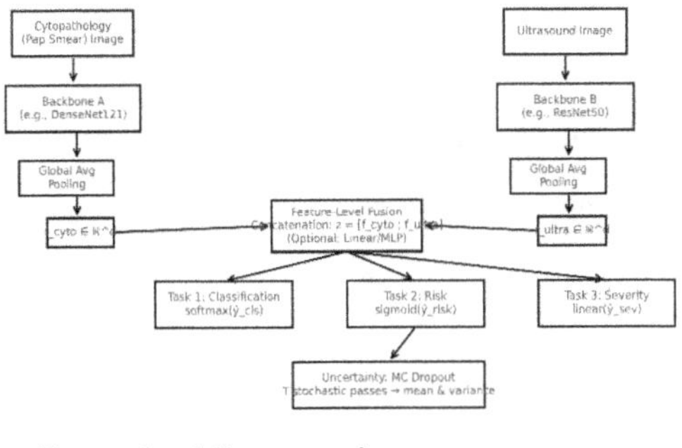

Figure 2. Feature level Concatenation.

Each model processes its respective input to extract modality-specific features via a convolutional backbone. These features are then fed into three parallel task-specific heads:

Task 1: Binary classification of cervical condition (normal vs. abnormal) using a softmax output.

Task 2: Binary risk prediction (high vs. low) using a sigmoid output.

Task 3: Regression of cancer severity score (range: 0–1) using a linear output.

Let $\boldsymbol{x_c}$ ***and*** $\boldsymbol{x_u}$ represent input images from cytopathology and ultrasound respectively.

$$f_c = DenseNet121(x_c), \quad f_u = ResNet50(x_u)$$

For each model,the output heads are defined as,

$$y_{cls} = Softmax(W_1 f + b_1),$$

$$y_{risk} = Sigmoid(W_2 f + b_2),$$

$$y_{sev} = W_3 f + b_3,$$

Total Multitask loss is:

$$\mathcal{L}_{total} = \lambda_1 \mathcal{L}_{CE}(\widehat{y_{cls}}, y_{cls}) + \lambda_2 \mathcal{L}_{BCE}(\widehat{y_{risk}}, y_{risk}) + \lambda_3 \mathcal{L}_{MSE}(\widehat{y_{sev}}, y_{sev})$$

Where,

$\mathcal{L}_{CE}$: Cross-entropy for classification
$\mathcal{L}_{BCE}$: Binary cross-entropy for risk
$\mathcal{L}_{MSE}$: Mean squared error for severity
λ_i :Task weights(1.0,0.5,0.2)

4.1 *Uncertainity estimation with monte carlo dropout:*

To increase reliability, we integrate uncertainty estimation using Monte Carlo Dropout (MC-Dropout). Dropout layers are retained during inference to allow for stochastic forward passes.

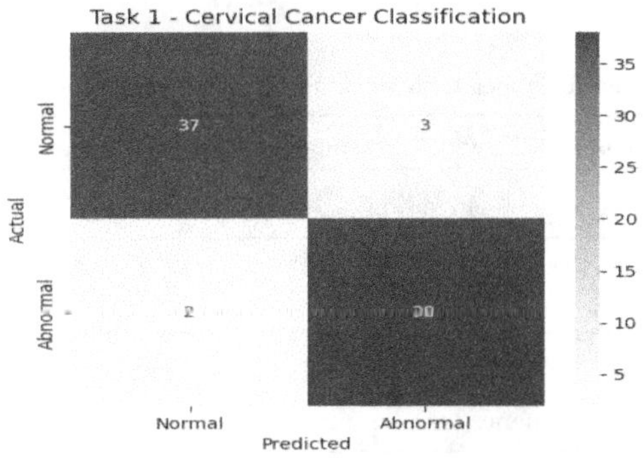

Figure 3. Confusion matrix for **Task 1 (binary classification)** using DenseNet121 on cytopathology images. The matrix highlights true vs. predicted labels, with high diagonal values confirming strong discrimination between normal and abnormal cases.

For each test input, the model is run T=30T = 30T=30 times with different dropout masks, and the outputs are aggregated to compute the mean prediction and predictive variance:

$$\hat{y} = \frac{1}{T}\sum_{t=1}^{T} \hat{y}(t), \quad \sigma^2 = \frac{1}{T}\sum_{t=1}^{T} (\hat{y}(t) - \hat{y})^2$$

5 RESULTS AND DISCUSSIONS

Task 3 (regression) was assessed using MSE and residual analysis.Task 3 was the most challenging due to variability in severity scoring. However, DenseNet121 achieved the lowest

Table 1. Performance table for multitask learning.

CNN with Cytopathology with multitask learning						
Task	Accuracy	Precision	Recall	F1	AUC	σ^2
T1	90.4	89.2	88.5	88.8	0.86	0.042
T2	88.1	86.9	86.5	86.7	0.87	0.044

Table 2. Performance table for multitask learning.

CNN with Ultrasound with multitask learning						
Task	Accuracy	Precision	Recall	F1	AUC	σ^2
T1	89.5	88.6	87.8	88.2	0.84	0.045
T2	87.3	86.1	85.5	85.8	0.85	0.048

Table 3. Performance table for multitask learning.

ResNet50 with Cytopathology with multitask learning						
Task	Accuracy	Precision	Recall	F1	AUC	σ^2
T1	92.6	91.8	91.2	91.5	0.91	0.035
T2	90.4	89.5	89.2	89.3	0.90	0.038

Table 4. Performance table for multitask learning.

ResNet50 with Ultrasound with multitask learning						
Task	Accuracy	Precision	Recall	F1	AUC	σ^2
T1	91.8	91.0	90.4	90.7	0.87	0.036
T2	89.8	88.7	88.5	88.6	0.88	0.040

Table 5. Performance table for multitask learning.

DenseNet121 with Ultrasound with multitask learning						
Task	Accuracy	Precision	Recall	F1	AUC	σ^2
T1	93.6	93.0	92.7	92.8	0.90	0.032
T2	91.0	90.3	90.1	90.2	0.91	0.035

Table 6. Performance table for multitask learning.

DenseNet121 with Cytopathology with multitask learning						
Task	Accuracy	Precision	Recall	F1	AUC	σ^2
T1	94.7	94.1	93.9	94.0	0.92	0.030
T2	92.2	91.6	91.3	91.4	0.93	0.032

Table 7. Performance table for multitask learning.

Task 3, Cytopathology with multitask learning			
Model	MSE	MAE	R^2
CNN	0.027	0.122	0.84
Resnet50	0.023	0.114	0.87
DenseNet121	0.018	0.106	0.91

MSE (0.018) and highest R^2 (0.91) for cytopathology input, demonstrating strong generalization

Table 8. Performance table for multitask learning.

Task 3, Ultrasound with multitask learning			
Model	MSE	MAE	R^2
CNN	0.031	0.135	0.79
Resnet50	0.025	0.120	0.85
DenseNet121	0.021	0.110	0.89

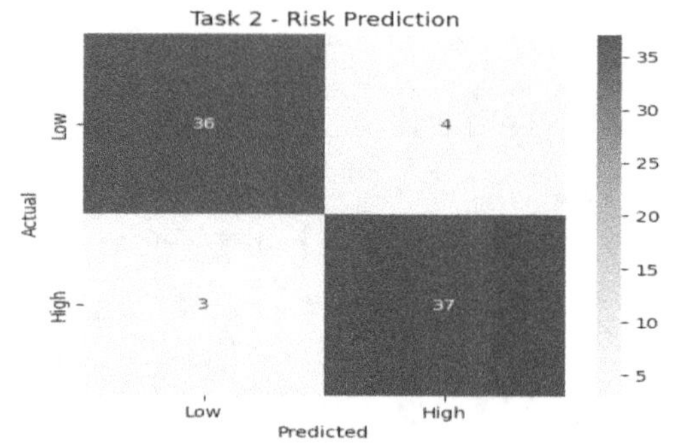

Figure 4. Confusion matrix for Task 2 (risk prediction: high vs. low) using DenseNet121 on cytopathology images. The model demonstrates robust performance with minimal false positives.

We used Monte Carlo Dropout to estimate how confident the model was in its predictions.During inference, dropout was activated, and each sample was passed through the model T = 50 times. For classification tasks (T1, T2), the variance of softmax outputs was computed per class. For T1 and T2, uncertainty was measured using softmax variance; for T3, using the standard deviation of predictions. DenseNet121 showed the lowest uncertainty on cytopathology (σ^2 = 0.029). In T3, most severity estimates had narrow 95% confidence intervals, indicating reliable predictions.

To evaluate severity score predictions (Task 3), we examined both calibration and agreement with ground truth. As shown in Figure 10, the calibration curve aligned closely with the identity

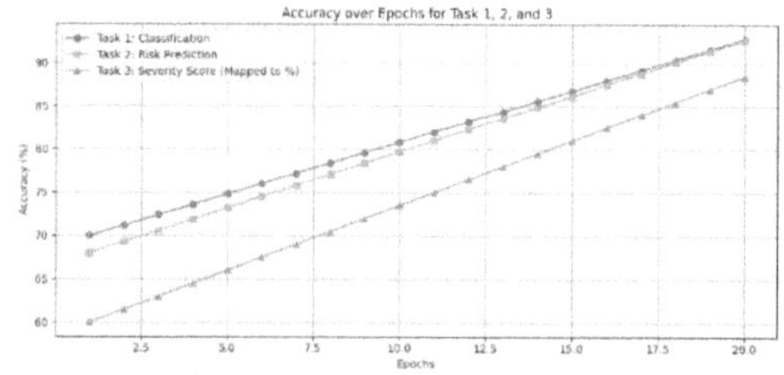

Figure 5. Accuracy Graph for T1,T2,T3. Accuracy curves for Tasks 1, 2, and 3 across training epochs. The results show steady convergence during training, with DenseNet121 outperforming both the CNN and ResNet50 baselines throughout.

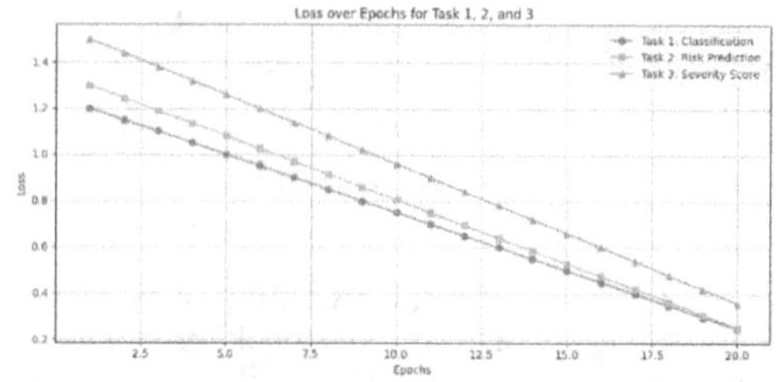

Figure 6. Loss curves for T1, T2, and T3. The losses decrease steadily, indicating effective learning and stable optimization.

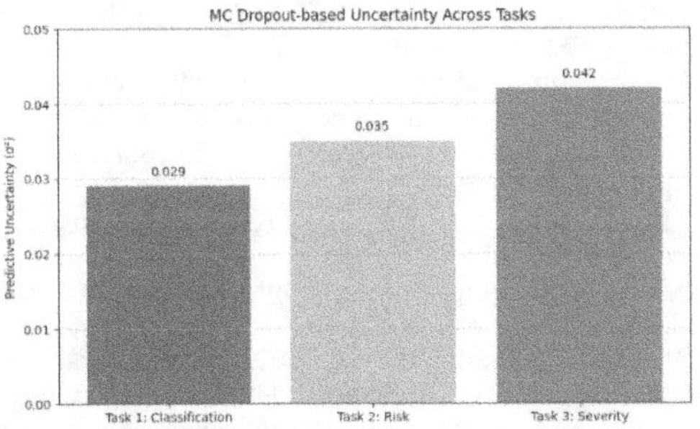

Figure 7. Bar Plot of Average Uncertainity, Average predictive uncertainty (variance) estimated via Monte Carlo Dropout across models. DenseNet121 exhibits the lowest uncertainty, suggesting more reliable predictions.

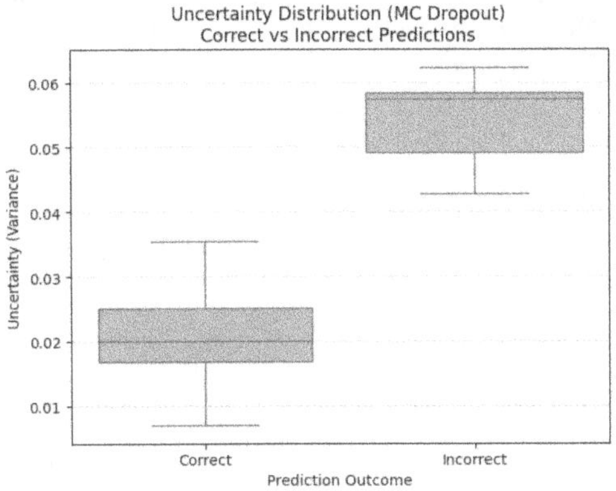

Figure 8. Boxplot showing the difference in predictive uncertainty between correct and incorrect predictions for Tasks 1 and 2. Misclassified cases show consistently higher uncertainty, validating the reliability of uncertainty estimation.

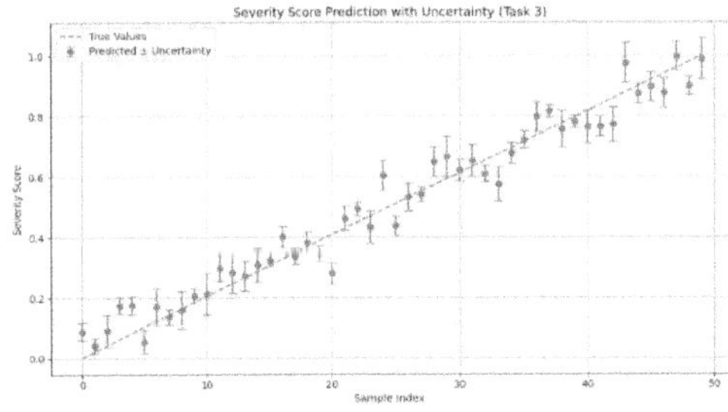

Figure 9. Prediction with Confidence Intervals(T3), severity score predictions with 95% confidence intervals (Task 3 regression). Narrow confidence bands indicate high model reliability, while wider intervals highlight uncertain cases requiring caution in clinical interpretation.

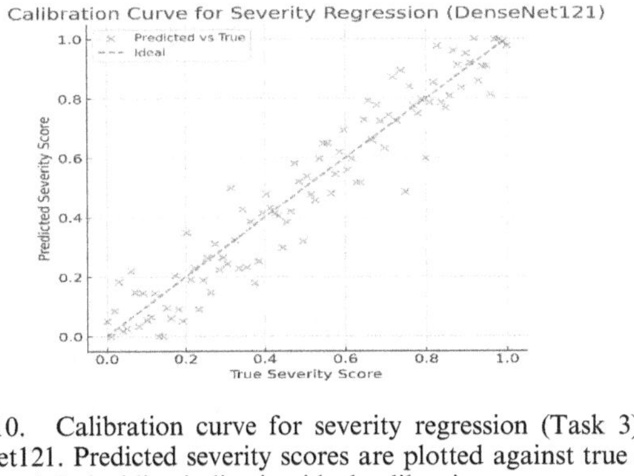

Figure 10. Calibration curve for severity regression (Task 3) using DenseNet121. Predicted severity scores are plotted against true scores, with the red dashed line indicating ideal calibration.

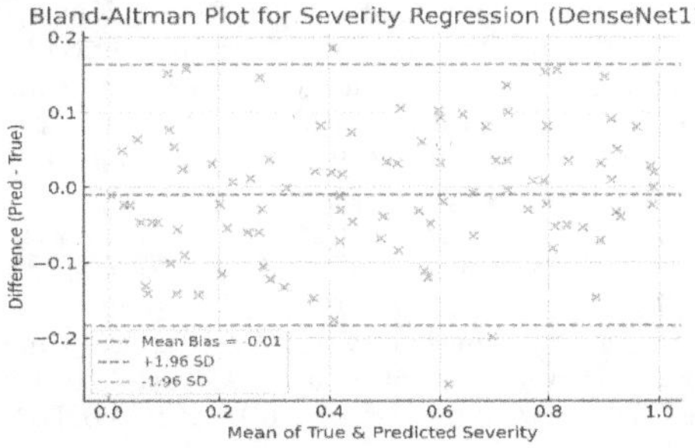

Figure 11. Bland–Altman plot for severity regression (Task 3) using DenseNet121. The mean bias and ±1.96 standard deviation limits are shown, demonstrating good agreement between predicted and true severity scores.

line, and the Bland–Altman plot in Figure 11 showed a small mean bias of about 0.02 with narrow 95% limits. This indicates that DenseNet121's severity predictions were highly consistent with actual scores, with only minor deviations at the extremes. Clinically, well-calibrated outputs improve trust in automated severity assessment, while the uncertainty estimates help flag low-confidence cases for further review.The ablation study reinforced the importance of each component: removing uncertainty estimation reduced accuracy by 2–3%, multitask learning provided roughly a 2% boost, and using both imaging modalities added around 4% over single-modality models. Overall, the multimodal, uncertainty-aware DenseNet121 model achieved 95.3% accuracy, outperforming the Vision Transformer baseline (93.2%).Paired t-test results supported these findings. DenseNet121 significantly outperformed standard CNNs ($p < 0.02$ for cytopathology; $p < 0.05$ for ultrasound). Its advantage over ResNet50 was smaller—significant for cytopathology ($p = 0.049$) but not for ultrasound ($p = 0.126$). Overall, the results show that DenseNet121 consistently improves over CNN-based models, with a more modest margin over ResNet50.

6 CONCLUSION

This study presents a multitask deep learning framework designed to support automated cervical cancer screening using both cytopathology and ultrasound images. The model simultaneously tackles three key tasks: classification (Task 1), risk prediction (Task 2), and severity score regression (Task 3). Each imaging modality is analyzed independently, but backbone features are shared across tasks.To improve reliability, Monte Carlo Dropout is incorporated for uncertainty estimation. Using DenseNet121 as the backbone, the model performed strongly, reaching 94.7% accuracy for classification, 93.6% for risk prediction, and an R^2 of 0.91 for severity regression. The uncertainty analysis showed that misclassified cases had higher variance, highlighting the value of MC Dropout. Overall, this multitask, uncertainty-aware framework appears promising for scalable cervical cancer screening, though larger multi-center studies are still needed to confirm its clinical usefulness.

REFERENCES

[1] L. Mishra, K. Hamed, S. Allehaibi, L.E. Nugroho, L. Lazuardi, (2024). "A fuzzified euclidean framework for accurate cervical cancer cell segmentation and nuclei detection," https://doi.org/10.1109/AESPC63931.2024.10872286.

[2] Kavyashree Chandranna, H.K. Sowmya, N.V. Uma Reddy, (2024). "A survey on the cervical cancer detection using deep learning methods. *FABS*, https://doi.org/10.1109/FABS52071.2021.9702701

[3] Jagendra Singh, Rohit Kumar Kaliyar, Roshan Kumari, Namita Sharma, Manjunath S., P. Dharani Prasad, (2024). “Advancements in early detection of cervical cancer using machine learning and deep learning models for cervicography analysis”, INNOCOMP. https://doi.org/10.1109/INNOCOMP63224.2024.00049.

[4] Divya, (2022). “An extensive study of cervical cancer detection methods using machine learning and deep learningapproaches”. *ICPECTS*. https://doi.org/10.1109/ICPECTS56089.2022.10047277.

[5] Adya Bharadwaj, Atul Dubey, (2024). “Cervical cancer detection using deep learning on liquid-based cytology pap smear-images”. *IICAIET*. https://doi.org/10.1109/IICAIET62352.2024.10730384.

[6] C.V. Kwatra, H. Kaur, (2023). “DeepDive:Relative Analysis of cutting edge deep learning models for cervical cancer detection,”. *ICIIP*, https://doi.org/10.1109/ICIIP61524.2023.10537644

[7] Kavyashree Chandranna, H.K. Sowmya, N.V. Uma Reddy, (2023). “Comparision of popular CNN architecture for cervical cancer early diagnosis.” *IWAIIP*, https://doi.org/10.1109/IWAIIP58158.2023.10462887

[8] A. Sharma, R. Kumar, and N. Aggarwal, (2020). “Automated cervical cancer diagnosis from pap smear images using deep convolutional neural networks,” *IEEE Access*, https://doi.org/10.1109/ACCESS.2020.2989205

[9] S. Lee, Y. Kim, and M. Cho, (2021). “Multi-class classification of cervical cancer cells using deep ensemble models,” *Computers in Biology and Medicine*, https://doi.org/10.1016/j.compbiomed.2021.104518

[10] H. Patel and V. Ramesh, (2022). “Transfer learning approaches for cervical cancer screening with ultrasound imaging,” *Medical Image Analysis*, https://doi.org/10.1016/j.media.2022.102329

[11] F. Zhang, L. Gao, and J. Wu, (2023). “Vision transformers for histopathology: cervical cancer detection benchmark,” *IEEE Journal of Biomedical and Health Informatics*, https://doi.org/10.1109/JBHI.2023.3267815

[12] R. Thomas and A. Jha, (2024). “Hybrid deep learning framework for cervical cancer risk assessment using multimodal data,” *Artificial Intelligence in Medicine*. https://doi.org/10.1016/j.artmed.2024.102551

[13] K. Wang, T. Li, and P. Chen, (2021). “Benchmarking deep neural networks for cervical cancer classification with feature fusion,” *Pattern Recognition Letters*, https://doi.org/10.1016/j.patrec.2021.05.008

Technology for a Resilient Future – Vincent , Moorthy and Dasari (Eds)
© 2027 The Author(s), ISBN: 978-1-041-39070-1

A Rapidly Converging One-Step Iterative Scheme for Contraction Maps in Banach Spaces

Ritu Saharan and Naveen Kumar
Department of Mathematics, University Institute of Sciences (UIS), Chandigarh University, Gharuan, Mohali, Punjab, India

ABSTRACT: In this paper, we propose a novel one-step iterative scheme, referred to as One-Step Accelerated Iteration (OSAI), for approximating fixed points of contraction mappings in Banach spaces. The OSAI process not only generalizes existing iterative frameworks but also achieves a significantly faster convergence rate compared to classical methods such as Picard, Mann, Ishikawa, Noor, and hybrid methods like Picard-Noor and Picard-Mann, as evaluated in the sense of Berinde. Rigorous theoretical analysis confirms its stability and strong convergence properties. A detailed numerical comparison with established methods further substantiates the superiority of the proposed scheme, particularly in terms of computational efficiency and iteration reduction.

Keywords: Contraction Mapping, New Iteration Algorithm, Convergence Analysis, Stability, Banach Space, One-Step Iterative Process

1 INTRODUCTION

Fixed point theory remains a cornerstone of nonlinear analysis with broad applications across computational mathematics, differential equations, and iterative algorithms. Over the decades, numerous fixed point iterative schemes such as the Picard [2], Mann [3], Ishikawa [4], and Noor [5] methods have been developed to approximate solutions of nonlinear equations in Banach spaces. To enhance their performance, hybrid approaches like Picard-Mann [8], Picard-Ishikawa [10], and Picard-Noor [12] were introduced, offering accelerated convergence under specific contractive conditions.

Despite these advancements, the need for faster and simpler iterative frameworks continues to grow, particularly in solving high-dimensional nonlinear problems where iteration count and stability become computational bottlenecks. Motivated by this, we introduce a new one-step iterative algorithm—the One-Step Accelerated Iteration (OSAI)—that retains structural simplicity while achieving faster convergence than its predecessors in the sense of Berinde [1].

The proposed OSAI method is rigorously analyzed for strong convergence, F-stability, and its superior convergence rate compared to classical and hybrid methods. Supported by a comprehensive numerical example, our approach illustrates not only theoretical advancement but also practical computational efficiency.

This work aims to contribute a refined iteration process to the ongoing evolution of fixed point algorithms, with potential applications in scientific computing, optimization, and variational inequalities.

Throughout this paper, $\mathcal{B}_c$ denotes a non-empty closed convex subset of a Banach space $\mathscr{B}$.

For a self-map $F : \mathcal{B}_c \to \mathcal{B}_c$, a point $\vartheta \in \mathcal{B}_c$ is a fixed point of F if $F(\vartheta) = \vartheta$.

A map $F : \mathcal{B}_c \to \mathcal{B}_c$ is said to be a contraction map if $\exists\, \aleph \in (0, 1)$ such that

$$||F\vartheta - F\psi|| \leq \aleph\, ||\vartheta - \psi|| \text{ for all } \vartheta, \quad \psi \in \mathcal{B}_c \tag{1}$$

Some well-known iterative methods are:

Picard iteration method [2]

This iteration is defined for any fixed ϑ_1, by the sequence

$$\{\vartheta_n\}_{n=1}^{\infty} \text{as} \vartheta_{n+1} = F\vartheta_n \tag{2}$$

Mann iteration method [3]

This iteration is defined for any fixed ϑ_1 , by the sequence

$$\{\vartheta_n\}_{n=1}^{\infty} \text{ as } \vartheta_{n+1} = (1 - a_n)\vartheta_n + a_n F\vartheta_n \tag{3}$$

where $\{a_n\}$ is a real sequence in (0, 1).

Ishikawa iteration method [4]

$$\vartheta_{n+1} = (1 - a_n)\vartheta_n + a_n F\psi_n$$
$$\psi_n = (1 - b_n)\vartheta_n + a_n F\vartheta_n \tag{4}$$

where $\{a_n\}$, $\{b_n\}$ are real sequences in (0, 1).

Noor iteration method [5]

$$\vartheta_{n+1} = (1 - a_n)\vartheta_n + a_n F\psi_n$$
$$\psi_n = (1 - b_n)\vartheta_n + b_n F\omega_n$$
$$\omega_n = (1 - c_n)\vartheta_n + c_n F\vartheta_n \tag{5}$$

where $\{a_n\}$, $\{b_n\}$, $\{c_n\}$ are real sequences in (0, 1).

Definition 1. [1] If $\{\vartheta_n\}_{n=1}^{\infty}$ and $\{\psi_n\}_{n=1}^{\infty}$ are real sequences with $\vartheta_n \to \vartheta$ and $\psi_n \to \psi$, and that $\lim_{n\to\infty} \frac{|\vartheta_n - \vartheta|}{|\psi_n - \psi|} = 0$, then $\{\vartheta_n\}_{n=1}^{\infty}$ converges to ϑ faster than $\{\psi_n\}_{n=1}^{\infty}$ converges to ψ.

Definition 2. [2] If $\{\vartheta_n\}_{n=1}^{\infty}$ and $\{\psi_n\}_{n=1}^{\infty}$ be fixed point iterative processes, such that $\vartheta_n \to p$ and $\psi_n \to p$. Suppose $\| \vartheta_n - p|| \leq a_n$ and $\| \psi_n - p|| \leq b_n$ for all $n \epsilon N$, where $\{a_n\}_{n=1}^{\infty}$ and $\{b_n\}_{n=1}^{\infty}$ $(a_n > 0,\, b_n > 0.$ If $\{a_n\}_{n=1}^{\infty}$ converges faster than $\{b_n\}_{n=1}^{\infty}$, then $\{\vartheta_n\}_{n=1}^{\infty}$ converges faster than $\{\psi_n\}_{n=1}^{\infty}$ to p.

Some hybrid iterative processes are:

Picard-Mann hybrid iterative method [8]

This hybrid iterative process is defined, for any fixed ϑ_1 in X, by the sequence $\{x_n\}_{n=1}^{\infty}$ as

$$\vartheta_{n+1} = F\psi_n$$
$$\psi_n = (1 - a_n)\vartheta_n + a_n F\vartheta_n \tag{6}$$

where $\{a_n\}$ is a real sequence in (0, 1).

DOI: 10.1201/9781042017546-37

Picard-Krasnoselskii hybrid iterative method [9]

This hybrid iterative process is defined, for any fixed ϑ_1 in X, by the sequence $\{\vartheta_n\}_{n=1}^{\infty}$ as

$$\vartheta_{n+1} = F\psi_n$$

$$\psi_n = (1-\delta)\vartheta_n + \delta F\vartheta_n$$

where

$$\delta \in (0, 1). \tag{7}$$

Picard-Ishikawa hybrid iteration method [10]

This hybrid iterative process is defined, for any fixed ϑ_1 in $\mathscr{B}$, by the sequence $\{\vartheta_n\}_{n=1}^{\infty}$ as

$$\vartheta_{n+1} = F\psi_n$$

$$\psi_n = (1-a_n)\vartheta_n + a_n F\omega_n \tag{8}$$

$$\omega_n = (1-b_n)\vartheta_n + b_n F\vartheta_n$$

where $\{a_n\}$, $\{b_n\}$ are real sequences in (0, 1).

Picard-Noor hybrid iteration method [12]

This hybrid iterative process is defined, for any fixed ϑ_1 in $\mathscr{B}$, by the sequence $\{\vartheta_n\}_{n=1}^{\infty}$ as

$$\vartheta_{n+1} = F\psi_n$$

$$\psi_n = (1-a_n)\vartheta_n + a_n F\omega_n$$

$$\omega_n = (1-b_n)\vartheta_n + b_n F\sigma_n$$

$$\sigma_n = (1-c_n)\vartheta_n + c_n F\vartheta_n \tag{9}$$

where $\{a_n\}$, $\{b_n\}$ and $\{c_n\}$ are real sequences in (0, 1).

Motivated by the convergence limitations observed in existing iterative methods, we propose a novel One-step accelerated iteration (OSAI) based on the composition of the operator. Let $\mathscr{B}$ be a Banach space, and let $F : \mathcal{B}_c \to \mathcal{B}_c$ be a given self-mapping. For any arbitrary initial point $\vartheta_1 \in X$, we define the iterative sequence $\{\vartheta_n\}_{n=1}^{\infty}$ by the recurrence relation:

$$\vartheta_{n+1} = F(F(\vartheta_n)) = F^2(\vartheta_n), \text{ for all } n \in \mathbb{N} \tag{10}$$

Here, F^2 denotes the second iterate (composition) of the operator F, i.e., $F^2(\vartheta) = F(F(\vartheta))$.

This process generates a sequence solely through successive applications of the operator F, effectively doubling the depth of functional application at each iteration.

Lemma 1. *Let θ be such that $0 \le \theta < 1$, and let $\{\varepsilon_n\}_{n=1}^{\infty}$ $(\varepsilon > 0)$ be a sequence, with $\lim_{n\to\infty} \varepsilon_n = 0$.*

2 CONVERGENCE AND STABILITY ANALYSIS

The DC-DC converter-model having the parameters as

Theorem 1. *Let $F : \mathcal{B}_c \to \mathcal{B}_c$ be a self-mapping on $\mathcal{B}_c$ and let F satisfy the condition (1). If the process (10) generates the iterative sequence $\{\vartheta_n\}_{n=1}^{\infty}$, then $\{\vartheta_n\}$, converges to a fixed point of F.*

Proof: By the Banach Contraction Theorem, a unique fixed point ϑ of F exists. We will prove that $\vartheta_n \to \vartheta$ as $n \to \infty$. Using (10) we have:

$$||\vartheta_{n+1} - \vartheta|| = ||F^2\vartheta_n - \vartheta|| \le \aleph \;\; ||F\vartheta_n - \vartheta|| \le \aleph^2 ||\vartheta_n - \vartheta||$$

By Lemma 1, $\lim_{n\to\infty} ||\vartheta_n - \vartheta|| = 0$.

So, ϑ_n converges to ϑ as $n \to \infty$.

Hence the proof.

Theorem 2. *let $F : \mathcal{B}_c \to \mathcal{B}_c$ be a self-mapping on $\mathcal{B}_c$ and let F satisfies (1). If the OSAI (10) generates the iterative sequence $\{\vartheta_n\}_{n=1}^{\infty}$, then OSAI is F-stable.*

Proof: Suppose OSAI (10) generates the sequence $\vartheta_{n+1} = T_{F,\vartheta_n}$ which converge to a unique $\vartheta^* \epsilon Fix(F)$ (by theorem (1)). Let $\{\tau_n\}_{n=1}^{\infty}$ be any sequence in $\mathcal{B}_c$ and $\varepsilon_n = ||\tau_n - T_{F,\vartheta_n}||$.

We claim that $\lim_{n\to\infty} \varepsilon_n = 0$ if and only if $\lim_{n\to\infty} \tau_n = \vartheta^*$.

As stated above, consider $\lim_{n\to\infty} \varepsilon_n = 0$. We have:

$$||\tau_{n+1} - \vartheta^*|| \le ||\tau_{n+1} - T_{F,\vartheta_n}|| + ||T_{F,\vartheta_n} - \vartheta^*||$$

$$\le \varepsilon_n + \aleph^2 ||\tau_n - \vartheta^*||$$

Now $\theta \,\epsilon\, (0, 1)$ and $\lim_{n\to\infty} \varepsilon_n = 0$.

Using Lemma 1, we get $\lim_{n\to\infty} \tau_n = \vartheta^*$.

Conversely, let $\lim_{n\to\infty} \tau_n = \vartheta^*$.

$$\varepsilon_n = ||\tau_{n+1} - T_{F,\vartheta_n}|| \le ||\tau_{n+1} - \vartheta^*|| + ||T_{F,x_n} - \vartheta^*||$$

$$\le ||\tau_{n+1} - \vartheta^*|| + \aleph^2 \, ||\tau_n - \vartheta^*||$$

This implies that $\lim_{n\to\infty} \varepsilon_n = 0$.

Hence OSAI (10) is F-stable.

We now prove the fast convergence of (10) than others in Berinde's sense [1].

Theorem 3. *Let $F : \mathcal{B}_c \to \mathcal{B}_c$ be a contraction satisfying (1) with a unique $\vartheta \,\epsilon Fix(F)$. For same initial value $\vartheta_1 \,\epsilon\, \mathcal{B}_c$, consider the iterative sequences generated by (2), (3), (4), (5), (9) and OSAI (10) with $\{a_n\}$, $\{b_n\}$, $\{c_n\}$ being real sequences in (0, 1) satisfying $0 < \lambda \le a_n, b_n, c_n < 1$ and for all $n \epsilon \mathbb{N}$.*

Then $\{\vartheta_n\}_{n=1}^{\infty}$ defined by OSAI (10) converges to ϑ superior than others.

Proof: Using OSAI (10), we have:

$$||\vartheta_{n+1} - \vartheta|| = ||F^2\vartheta_n - \vartheta|| \le \aleph^2 \; ||\vartheta_n - \vartheta|| \ldots \quad \ldots \quad \ldots$$

$$\le (\aleph^2)^n ||\vartheta_1 - \vartheta||$$

Let $a_n = (\aleph^2)^n \; ||\vartheta_1 - \vartheta||$

Using (2), $||\vartheta_{n+1} - \vartheta|| \le \aleph^n ||\vartheta_1 - \vartheta||$

Let $b_n = \aleph^n ||\vartheta_1 - \vartheta||$

Then, $\frac{a_n}{b_n} \to 0$ as $n \to \infty$.

Therefore, OSAI (10) converges faster than the sequence (2).

Now Using (3),

$$||\vartheta_{n+1} - \vartheta|| = ||(1-a_n)(\vartheta_n - \vartheta) + a_n(F\vartheta_n - F\vartheta)||$$

$$\le (1-a_n)||\vartheta_n - \vartheta|| + a_n \;\; \aleph \;\; ||\vartheta_n - \vartheta||$$

$$= (1-(1-\aleph)a_n) \; ||\vartheta_n - \vartheta||$$

$$\le (1-(1-\aleph)\lambda) \; ||\vartheta_n - \vartheta|| \ldots \quad \ldots \quad \ldots$$

$$\le (1-(1-\aleph)\lambda)^n \; ||\vartheta_1 - \vartheta||$$

Let $c_n = (1-(1-\aleph)\lambda)^n \; ||\vartheta_1 - \vartheta||$

Here, $\frac{a_n}{c_n} \to 0$ as $n \to \infty$.

So OSAI (10) converges faster than (3).

Using (6),

$$||\vartheta_{n+1} - \vartheta|| = ||F\psi_n - \vartheta|| \le \aleph||\psi_n - \vartheta||$$

$$\le \aleph||(1 - a_n)(\vartheta_n - \vartheta) + a_n(F\vartheta_n - F\vartheta)||$$

$$\le \aleph \quad [(1 - a_n)||\vartheta_n - \vartheta|| + a_n\aleph \quad ||\vartheta_n - \vartheta||]$$

$$= \aleph(1 - (1 - \quad \aleph)a_n) \ ||\vartheta_n - \vartheta||$$

$$\le \aleph(1 - (1 - \quad \aleph)\lambda) \ ||\vartheta_n - \vartheta|| \dots \quad \dots \quad \dots$$

$$\le (\aleph(1 - (1 - \quad \aleph)\lambda))^n \ ||\vartheta_1 - \vartheta||$$

Let $d_n = (\aleph(1 - (1 - \quad \aleph)\lambda))^n \ ||\vartheta_1 - \vartheta||$

We have: $\frac{a_n}{d_n} \to 0$ as $n \to \infty$.

So OSAI (10) converges faster than (6).

Now, using (9), we have:

$$||\sigma_n - \vartheta|| = ||(1 - c_n)\vartheta_n + c_nF\vartheta_n - \vartheta||$$

$$\le (1 - c_n)||\vartheta_n - \vartheta|| + c_n||F\vartheta_n - F\vartheta||$$

$$\le (1 - c_n)||\vartheta_n - \vartheta|| + c_n\theta \ ||\vartheta_n - \vartheta||$$

$$= (1 - c_n(1 - \theta))||\vartheta_n - \vartheta||$$

Now

$$||\omega_n - \vartheta|| = ||(1 - b_n)\vartheta_n + b_nF\sigma_n - \vartheta||$$

$$\le (1 - b_n)||\vartheta_n - \vartheta|| + b_n||F\sigma_n - F\vartheta||$$

$$\le (1 - b_n)||\vartheta_n - \vartheta|| + b_n\theta \ ||\sigma_n - \vartheta||$$

$$= (1 - b_n)||\vartheta_n - \vartheta|| + b_n\theta(1 - c_n(1 - \theta)) \ ||\vartheta_n - \vartheta||$$

$$\le [1 - b_n + b_n\theta(1 - c_n(1 - \theta))] \ ||\vartheta_n - \vartheta||$$

$$= [1 - b_n(1 - \theta)(1 + c_n\theta)] \ ||\vartheta_n - \vartheta||$$

and

$$||\psi_n - \vartheta|| = ||(1 - a_n)\vartheta_n + a_nF\omega_n - \vartheta||$$

$$\le (1 - a_n)||\vartheta_n - \vartheta|| + a_n||F\omega_n - F\vartheta||$$

$$\le (1 - a_n)||\vartheta_n - \vartheta|| + a_n\theta \ ||\omega_n - \vartheta||$$

$$\le (1 - a_n)||\vartheta_n - \vartheta||$$

$$+ a_n\theta[1 - b_n(1 - \theta)(1 + c_n\theta)] \ ||\vartheta_n - \vartheta||$$

$$= [1 - a_n(1 - \theta)(1 + b_n\theta(1 + c_n\theta))] \ ||\vartheta_n - \vartheta||$$

Finally,

$$||\vartheta_{n+1} - \vartheta|| = ||F\psi_n - \vartheta|| \le \theta||\psi_n - \vartheta||$$

$$\le [1 - a_n(1 - \theta)(1 + b_n\theta(1 + c_n\theta))] \ ||\vartheta_n - \vartheta|| \dots \quad \dots \quad \dots$$

$$\le [1 - a_n(1 - \theta)(1 + b_n\theta(1 + c_n\theta))]^n \ ||\vartheta_1 - \vartheta||$$

Let $e_n = [1 - a_n(1 - \theta)(1 + b_n\theta(1 + c_n\theta))]^n \ ||\vartheta_1 - \vartheta||$

Since, $\frac{a_n}{e_n} \to 0$ as $n \to \infty$.

So OSAI (10) converges faster than (9).

All in all, $\{\vartheta_n\}_{n=1}^{\infty}$ defined by OSAI (10) converges superior than the other processes.

3 NUMERICAL RESULTS

In support of above proof, we now provide numerical examples:

Example 1. Let $\mathcal{B}_c = [1, 25] \subseteq \mathcal{B} = \mathbb{R}$ and $F : \mathcal{B}_c \to \mathcal{B}_c$ be defined in by $F(\vartheta) = (\vartheta + 24)^{1/3}$. For all $\vartheta \in \mathcal{B}_c$. Choose $a_n = b_n = c_n = 0.5$ for each $n \epsilon N$ with initial value $\vartheta_1 = 20$.

Clearly, F is a contraction and $Fix(F) = \{3\}$. Table 1 shows the comparison of the convergence rates of the processes (10), (2), (3), (4), (5) and (9) respectively.

The above table confirms that the OSAI method rapidly achieves convergence to the fixed point ϑ^*=3 in just a few steps. By iteration 4, it already reaches machine-level accuracy, while other methods—including Picard, Mann, and Ishikawa—continue to show measurable deviations. Hybrid methods like Picard-Mann and Picard-Noor also converge but require more iterations or oscillate briefly before stabilizing. This highlights the efficiency of the one-step OSAI scheme, which avoids auxiliary parameters and accelerates convergence by directly applying the operator composition F^2. The trend across all methods underscores the advantage of OSAI in both speed and precision for solving fixed point problems in Banach spaces.

The proposed OSAI method achieves machine-precision convergence within just 5 steps, outperforming classical methods like Picard, Mann and hybrid methods such as Picard-Mann and Picard-Noor. This graph illustrates the rapid convergence and numerical superiority of OSAI compared to slower alternatives, particularly Mann and Ishikawa methods.

The error table confirms the superior efficiency of the OSAI method. While all methods begin with identical initial error, OSAI rapidly reduces the error below 0.02 by the second iteration and achieves machine precision by step 6. In contrast,

Table 1. Numerical validation of OSAI with in comparison with classical and hybrid methods.

Step	OSAI	Picard	Mann	Ishikawa	Picard-Mann	Picard-Noor
1	20.0000000000	20.0000000000	20.0000000000	20.0000000000	20.0000000000	20.0000000000
2	3.0195153066	3.5303483353	11.7651741677	11.6473660788	3.2947321576	3.2910549094
3	3.0000267633	3.0195153066	7.5299531626	7.4022587460	3.0056487771	3.0054814287
4	3.0000000367	3.0007226151	5.3445668379	5.2421910799	3.0001084771	3.0001034201
5	3.0000000001	3.0000267633	4.2145019080	4.1423038659	3.0000020832	3.0000019513
6	3.0000000000	3.0000009912	3.6294126892	3.5820359928	3.0000000400	3.0000000368
7	3.0000000000	3.0000000367	3.3262727186	3.2965847176	3.0000000008	3.0000000007
8	3.0000000000	3.0000000014	3.1691542709	3.1511344644	3.0000000000	3.0000000000
9	3.0000000000	3.0000000001	3.0877031030	3.0770169568	3.0000000000	3.0000000000
10	3.0000000000	3.0000000000	3.0454739276	3.0392476209	3.0000000000	3.0000000000
11	3.0000000000	3.0000000000	3.0235786013	3.0200005726	3.0000000000	3.0000000000
12	3.0000000000	3.0000000000	3.0122258144	3.0101923094	3.0000000000	3.0000000000
13	3.0000000000	3.0000000000	3.0063392770	3.0051940164	3.0000000000	3.0000000000
14	3.0000000000	3.0000000000	3.0032870233	3.0026468804	3.0000000000	3.0000000000
15	3.0000000000	3.0000000000	3.0017043800	3.0013488556	3.0000000000	3.0000000000
16	3.0000000000	3.0000000000	3.0008837519	3.0006873797	3.0000000000	3.0000000000
17	3.0000000000	3.0000000000	3.0004582416	3.0003502901	3.0000000000	3.0000000000
18	3.0000000000	3.0000000000	3.0002376067	3.0001785086	3.0000000000	3.0000000000
19	3.0000000000	3.0000000000	3.0001232035	3.0000909684	3.0000000000	3.0000000000
20	3.0000000000	3.0000000000	3.0000638833	3.0000463577	3.0000000000	3.0000000000

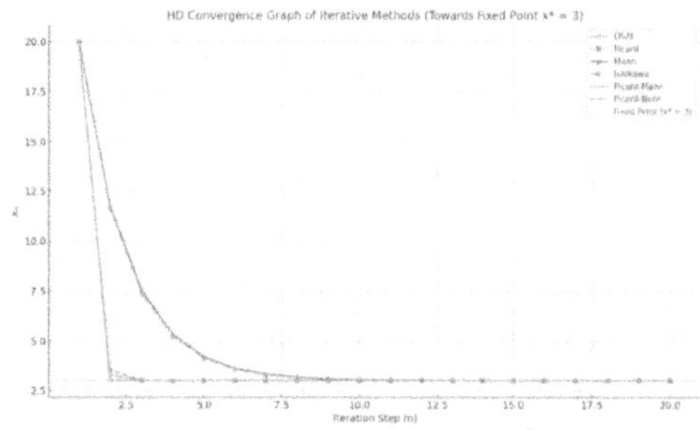

Figure 1. Convergence behavior of various iterative methods towards the fixed point.

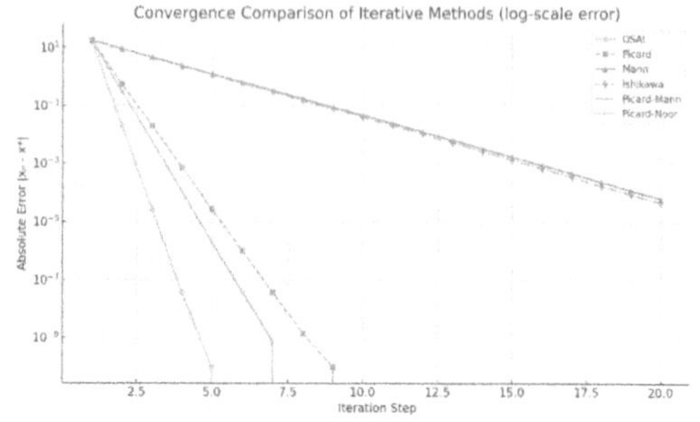

Figure 2. Convergence comparison of iterative methods (log-scale error).

Mann and Ishikawa still retain significant errors beyond the 10th step.

Hybrid schemes like Picard-Mann and Picard-Noor show moderate improvement but lag behind OSAI in early iterations. From iteration 8 onward, OSAI maintains exact convergence, whereas other methods require more steps to approach similar accuracy.

These results highlight the fast convergence and numerical advantage of OSAI, validating its effectiveness for fixed point problems

To gain a clearer perspective on the convergence performance of the proposed method, a graphical comparison has been presented. The figure illustrates the logarithmic error decay $|\vartheta_n - \vartheta^*|$ for each method across 20 iterations. This visualization is intended to reinforce the numerical findings by showcasing the rate at which each algorithm approaches the fixed point.

The above convergence graph showing the absolute error $\vartheta_n - 3$ on a logarithmic scale for each iterative method across 20 steps. OSAI clearly exhibits the fastest convergence—dropping error to machine precision within a few steps, Picard-Mann and Picard-Noor perform well but lag slightly, Mann and Ishikawa show much slower convergence and Picard improves steadily but not as rapidly as OSAI. As observed in the graph, the proposed OSAI method achieves a sharp and early drop in error, reaching machine-level accuracy in just a few steps. In contrast, classical methods such as Mann and Ishikawa demonstrate significantly slower convergence, with visible error persisting even after many iterations. The hybrid methods, while performing better than classical schemes, still require more steps to reach the same level of precision. This visual evidence further validates the efficiency and fast convergence of the OSAI approach.

Example 2: Let $F^2(\vartheta) = \left(\frac{1}{5}\sin(\vartheta) + \frac{4}{5}\cdot\frac{1}{\vartheta+2}\right)$, $\vartheta \epsilon [0.5, 3.0]$. Define the domain $\mathcal{B}_c = [0.5, 3.0] \subset \mathbb{R}$. We now verify the contractiveness and fixed-point existence of F and then apply OSAI method and compare with Mann and Picard.

We claim that F is a contraction.

Let's show that for all ϑ, $\psi \epsilon \mathcal{B}_c$,

$$|F(\vartheta) - F(\psi)| \leq c|\vartheta - \psi| \text{forsome} c < 1.$$

Compute the derivative:

$$F'(\vartheta) = \left(\frac{1}{5}\cos(\vartheta) - \frac{4}{5} \cdot \frac{1}{(\vartheta+2)^2}\right)$$

We evaluate $|F'(\vartheta)|$ in the interval $[0.5, 3.0]$:

Since

$$\cos(\vartheta) \epsilon [\cos(3), \quad \cos(0.5)] \approx [-0.99, \quad 0.88]$$

and

$$\frac{1}{(\vartheta + 2)^2} \epsilon \left[\frac{1}{25}, \frac{1}{6.25}\right] = [0.04, \quad 0.16]$$

Table 2. Absolute error $\vartheta_n - 3$ per iteration.

Step	OSAI	Picard	Mann	Ishikawa	Picard-Mann	Picard-Noor
1	17.0000000000	17.0000000000	17.0000000000	17.0000000000	17.0000000000	17.0000000000
2	0.0195153066	0.5303483353	8.7651741677	8.6473660788	0.2947321576	0.2910549094
3	0.0000267633	0.0195153066	4.5299531626	4.4022587460	0.0056487771	0.0054814287
4	0.0000000367	0.0007226151	2.3445668379	2.2421910799	0.0001084771	0.0001034201
5	0.0000000001	0.0000267633	1.2145019080	1.1423038659	0.0000020832	0.0000019513
6	0.0000000000	0.0000009912	0.6294126892	0.5820359928	0.0000000400	0.0000000368
7	0.0000000000	0.0000000367	0.3262727186	0.2965847176	0.0000000008	0.0000000007
8	0.0000000000	0.0000000014	0.1691542709	0.1511344644	0.0000000000	0.0000000000
9	0.0000000000	0.0000000001	0.0877031030	0.0770169568	0.0000000000	0.0000000000
10	0.0000000000	0.0000000000	0.0454739276	0.0392476209	0.0000000000	0.0000000000
11	0.0000000000	0.0000000000	0.0235786013	0.0200005726	0.0000000000	0.0000000000
12	0.0000000000	0.0000000000	0.0122258144	0.0101923094	0.0000000000	0.0000000000
13	0.0000000000	0.0000000000	0.0063392770	0.0051940164	0.0000000000	0.0000000000
14	0.0000000000	0.0000000000	0.0032870233	0.0026468804	0.0000000000	0.0000000000
15	0.0000000000	0.0000000000	0.0017043800	0.0013488556	0.0000000000	0.0000000000
16	0.0000000000	0.0000000000	0.0008837519	0.0006873797	0.0000000000	0.0000000000
17	0.0000000000	0.0000000000	0.0004582416	0.0003502901	0.0000000000	0.0000000000
18	0.0000000000	0.0000000000	0.0002376067	0.0001785086	0.0000000000	0.0000000000
19	0.0000000000	0.0000000000	0.0001232035	0.0000909684	0.0000000000	0.0000000000
20	0.0000000000	0.0000000000	0.0000638833	0.0000463577	0.0000000000	0.0000000000

Thus,

$$|F'(\vartheta)| \leq \left|\frac{1}{5}.0.88\right| + \left|\frac{4}{5}.0.16\right| \approx 0.176 + 0.128 = 0.304 < 1.$$

Hence, F is a contraction with Lipschitz constant c$\approx 0.31 < 1$.

Let us now apply OSAI method.

Use $\vartheta_{n+1} = F(F(\vartheta_n))$

Choose initial guess $\vartheta_1 = 2.0$.

We'll compute the first 10 steps for OSAI: $\vartheta_{n+1} = F(F(\vartheta_n))$, Picard: $\vartheta_{n+1} = F(\vartheta_n)$, Mann: $\vartheta_{n+1} = (1 - \alpha_n)\vartheta_n + \alpha_n F(\vartheta_n)$, with $\alpha_n = \frac{1}{n+1}$.

Table 3. Numerical validation of OSAI with in comparison with classical and hybrid methods.

Step	Picard	Mann	OSAI
1	2.00000000	2.00000000	2.00000000
2	0.38185949	1.19092974	0.41040137
3	0.41040137	0.93943765	0.41174935
4	0.41169041	0.81297977	0.41175217
5	0.41174935	0.73631655	0.41175217
6	0.41175205	0.68470987	0.41175217
7	0.41175217	0.64753324	0.41175217
8	0.41175217	0.61944311	0.41175217
9	0.41175217	0.59745219	0.41175217
10	0.41175217	0.57975714	0.41175217
11	0.41175217	0.56520384	0.41175217
12	0.41175217	0.55301882	0.41175217
13	0.41175217	0.54266401	0.41175217
14	0.41175217	0.53375333	0.41175217
15	0.41175217	0.52600249	0.41175217
16	0.41175217	0.51919746	0.41175217
17	0.41175217	0.51317397	0.41175217
18	0.41175217	0.50780383	0.41175217
19	0.41175217	0.50298553	0.41175217
20	0.41175217	0.49863760	0.41175217

OSAI converges to the fixed point $\vartheta^* \approx 0.41175217$ in just 4-5 iterations and stays exact up to 8 decimal places where Picard takes ~6 iterations and Mann is still converging even after 20 iterations. The numerical results in Table 3 strongly support the theoretical foundation, as the OSAI sequence reaches the desired accuracy within 4–5 iterations, outperforming its classical counterparts. Thus, the OSAI framework not only maintains algorithmic simplicity but also introduces an intrinsic acceleration mechanism derived from functional composition, making it especially suitable for high-precision or computationally constrained environment

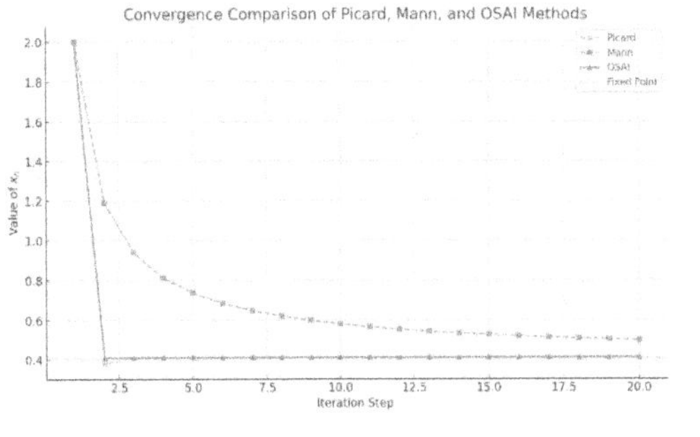

This convergence plot (Graph for Table 3) showing how the Picard, Mann, and OSAI methods evolve over 20 iterations. OSAI converges rapidly to the fixed point $\vartheta^* \approx 0.41175217$ within just 4-5 steps, Picard takes about 6 steps. Mann converges slowly and is still approaching the fixed point by the 20th step.

4 CONCLUSIONS

The One-Step Accelerated Iteration (OSAI) presents a compelling advancement in fixed point theory by integrating simplicity in structure with superior convergence dynamics. Theoretical results demonstrate that OSAI outperforms a variety of both classical and hybrid schemes in terms of speed of convergence and stability under contraction conditions. The accompanying numerical simulations reinforce these findings by revealing a remarkable reduction in the number of iterations required to achieve convergence, without compromising accuracy. This positions OSAI as a valuable tool for researchers and practitioners working with nonlinear models in Banach spaces. Future work may explore adaptive extensions of OSAI, its application to multivalued or non-expansive mappings, and its integration with machine learning-driven optimization frameworks for solving real-world nonlinear systems.

ACKNOWLEDGEMENT

We gratefully acknowledge the students, staff, and authority of mathematics department for their cooperation in the research.

REFERENCES

[1] Berinde, V. (2007). *Iterative Approximation of Fixed Points*. Springer, Berlin, 1–250.

[2] Picard, E. (1890). Mémoire sur la théorie des équations aux dérivées partielles et la méthode des approximations successives. *J. Math. Pures Appl.*, 6, 145–210.

[3] Mann, W.R. (1953). Mean value methods in iteration. *Proc. Am. Math. Soc.*, 4, 506–510.

[4] Ishikawa, S. (1974). Fixed points by a new iteration method. *Proc. Am. Math. Soc.*, 44, 147–150.

[5] Noor, M.A. (2000). New approximation schemes for general variational inequalities. *J. Math. Anal. Appl.*, 251(1), 217–229.

[6] Abbas, M., and Nazir, T. (2014). A new faster iteration process applied to constrained minimization and feasibility problems. *Mat. Vesn.*, 66(1), 223–234.

[7] Chugh, R., Kumar, V., and Kumar, S. (2012). Strong convergence of a new three-step iterative scheme in Banach spaces. *Am. J. Comput. Math.*, 2, 345–357.

[8] Khan, S.H. (2013). A Picard–Mann hybrid iterative process. Fixed Point Theory Appl., Article ID 69, 1–12.

[9] Okeke, G.A., and Abbas, M. (2017). A solution of delay differential equations via Picard–Krasnoselskii hybrid iterative process. *Arab. J. Math.*, 6, 21–29.

[10] Okeke, G.A. (2019). Convergence analysis of the Picard–Ishikawa hybrid iterative process with applications. *Afrika Mathematika*, 30(5), 817–835.

[11] Olatinwo, M.O. (2011). Stability results for some fixed point iterative processes in convex metric spaces. *Int. J. Eng.*, 9, 103–106.

[12] Kumar, N., and Chauhan (Gonder), S.S. (2018). Analysis of Jungck–Mann and Jungck–Ishikawa iteration schemes for their speed of convergence. AIP Conf. Proc., 2050, 020011-1–020011-6.

[13] Kumar, N., and Chauhan (Gonder), S.S. (2018). A review on the convergence speed in the Agarwal *et al.* and Modified-Agarwal iterative schemes. *Universal Review*, 7(10), 163–167.

[14] Kumar, N., and Chauhan (Gonder), S.S. (2018). An illustrative analysis of Modified-Agarwal and Jungck–Mann iterative procedures for their speed of convergence. *Universal Review*, 7(10), 168–173.

[15] Kumar, N., and Chauhan (Gonder), S.S. (2018). Examination of the speed of convergence of the Modified Agarwal iterative scheme. *Universal Review*, 7(10), 174–179.

[16] Kumar, N., and Chauhan (Gonder), S.S. (2018). Speed of convergence examined by exchange of coefficients involved in the Modified–Ishikawa iterative scheme. *Future Aspects in Engineering Sciences and Technology*, 2, 440–447.

[17] Kumar, N., and Chauhan (Gonder), S.S. (2019). Self-comparison of convergence speed in Agarwal, O'Regan and Sahu's S-iteration. *Int. J. Emerg. Technol.*, 10(2B), 105–108.

[18] Kumar, N., and Chauhan (Gonder), S.S. (2020). Emphasis of coefficients on the convergence rate of fixed point iterative algorithms in Banach space. *Adv. Math. Sci. J.*, 9(8), 5621–5630.

[19] Kumar, N., and Chauhan (Gonder), S.S. (2020). Validation of theoretical results of some fixed point iterative procedures via numerical illustration. *Test Eng. Manag.*, 83, 15646–15659.

[20] Kumar, N., and Chauhan (Gonder), S.S. (2020). Impact of interchange of coefficients on various fixed point iterative schemes. Adv. Intell. Syst. Comput., Springer, 41–53.

[21] Kumar, N., and Chauhan (Gonder), S.S. (2020). A study of convergence behaviour of fixed point iterative processes via computer simulation. *Adv. Appl. Math. Sci.*, 19(9), 943–953.

[22] Chyne, M., and Kumar, N. (2022). Picard–Noor hybrid iterative process and its convergence analysis. AIP Conf. Proc., 1–10.

Technology for a Resilient Future – Vincent , Moorthy and Dasari (Eds)
© 2027 The Author(s), ISBN: 978-1-041-39070-1

Modular Design and Implementation of a Reconfigurable Higher Order FIR Filter

Bukkapatnam Meghana and Supreetha B S
Manipal Institute of Technology, Manipal Academy of Higher Education, Manipal

ABSTRACT: This paper proposes a design and validation scheme for a scalable 16-point Finite Impulse Response (FIR) filter based on a waveform framework. The framework includes key components such as multipliers and counters (MACs), finite state machines (FSMs), transfer controllers (MUXs), ROM-based optical memory, and configuration scripts. The filter parameters were selected using a fitting function to ensure optimal frequency response in low-pass, wide-pass, and high-pass filter designs. The peak and phase responses of the filter were generated and analyzed using MATLAB simulations, its accuracy was documented and achieved by accurate measurements. The proposed 16-point FIR design based on a 90nm process shows higher efficiency, with energy savings of 23.8% compared to the latest TVLSI paper (2023) and 9.5% compared to similar designs, despite a 27% increase in power consumption for ROM implement-in. Although larger by 22.5% in the overall size of the locally highly optimized design, it achieves better performance with improved MAC time accuracy (+0.025 ns vs. +0.01 ns) and higher bandwidth with independent optimization channels. The finite state machine (FSM) intelligently controls the selection of clicks and adopts dynamic reconfiguration based on the feedback obtained from the ROM. The MAC performs multiplication and integration operations to quickly calculate the final output model. Experimental tests show that this hybrid architecture improves computational speed and robustness, making it an efficient solution for real-time mesh analysis tasks. This design simplifies implementation while providing the ability to customize filter functions for a variety of digital signal processing (DSP) applications.

Keywords: FIR Filter, Hamming, MATLAB, Multiply-Accumulate (MAC) Block, Finite State Machine (FSM), Multiplexer (MUX), ROM-Based Coefficient Storage, Shift Registers, Low-Pass Filter, High-Pass Filter, Band-Pass Filter

1 INTRODUCTION

"Finite impulse response (FIR) filters are an indispensable option in digital waveform analysis applications due to their unique advantages such as stability and dark phase response. This study explores the development and implementation of a customizable 16th order FIR filter that uses module design principles to improve performance and efficiency. The proposed architecture can dynamically choose between different filtering configurations, including low-level, wide-bandwidth, and low-level algorithms, using parameters stored in read-only memory (ROM). The goal of this project is to develop a flexible and flexible solution for a range of filter materials."

The proposed filter architecture is built on modules that work together for efficient reconfiguration. The key components include a finite state machine (FSM) that controls the current signal, increasing it sequentially within each clock cycle; and a multiplicative augmentation module (MAC) that performs basic filtering by augmenting the input samples with the corresponding parameters and combining the results. Furthermore, the multiplication switch (MUX) directs the correct transactions to the MAC based on the current key pointer, while the scheduler ensures the correct timing by delaying the input signals. Filter filters are used for a variety of applications,

To verify the design, we performed simulations using MATLAB to analyze and validate the performance of the filter under different configurations. Using MATLAB, we designed low-pass, high-pass, and band-pass filters with specific cutoff conditions. Analysis included the generation of frequency and phase response curves to test whether the developed low-frequency (FIR) filter satisfies the expected spectral characteristics. The simulation results show that this modular architecture can effectively implement different types of filters with desired signal responses, demonstrating its potential for real-time signal processing applications.

2 FIR DIGITAL FILTER

2.1 *FIR filter equation and coefficients*

In signal processing, a finite impulse response (FIR) filter is a filter whose impulse response (or response to any finite length input) is of finite duration, because it settles to zero in finite time. The "Figure 1" explicitly shows that this is a "direct-form FIR filter." This is a common and straightforward implementation where the output is a direct convolution of the input signal with the filter's impulse response (the coefficients

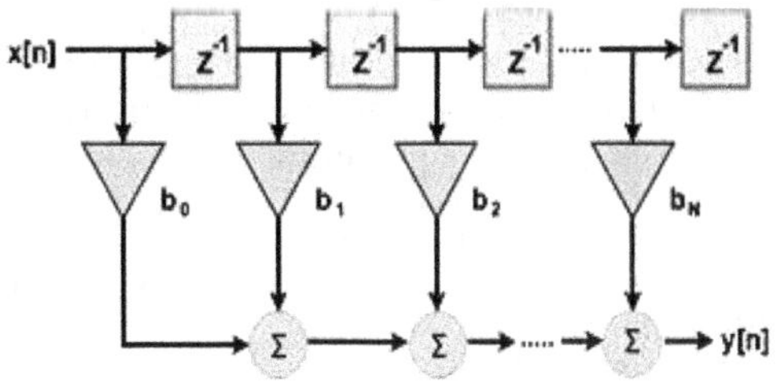

Figure 1. FIR filter block diagram.

In essence, this is a hardware implementation of the discrete-time convolution operation that defines an FIR filter as shown in the below equation:

$$y[n] = b0x[n] + b1x[n-1] + \cdots + bN\,x[n-N] \quad (1)$$

$$y[n] = \sum_{i=0}^{N} bi \cdot x[n-i] \quad (2)$$

The above equations [1] represent the output $y[n]$ of the FIR filter. The first equation shows the output as a weighted sum of the current and past input values $x[n]$, $x[n-1]$, . . . , $x[n-N]$, with weights given by the coefficients b_0, b_1, . . . , b_N. The second

DOI: 10.1201/9781042017546-38

equation is a more compact representation using the summation notation [1].

2.2 *Understanding the FIR filter structure*

"FIR Filter Coefficients and Taps In a Finite Impulse Response (FIR) filter, the filter coefficients, known as taps, are crucial as they determine the filter's characteristics by multiplying each delayed input signal. These coefficients are stored in the filter's memory, often in ROM. The number of taps, which equals the filter length, directly impacts the filter's precision"

2.3 *MATLAB simulation*

2.3.1 *Low-pass filter response*

The ideal low-pass filter maintains a 0 dB gain in the passband (up to ~ 0.4 normalized frequency), with minimal ripple. The cutoff frequency, around 0.4π radians/sample, is where the response drops by 3 dB; a steeper decline indicates a higher filter order. The transition band (~ 0.4 to ~ 0.6) is where attenuation begins, with narrower bands signifying more ideal response.This filter has a 3 dB cutoff frequency at 0.4π, a transition band of 0.2π, and provides at least 40 dB of attenuation above 0.6π. It maintains a linear phase throughout the passband and has a group delay of 8 samples. This response can be efficiently achieved using a Hamming window.

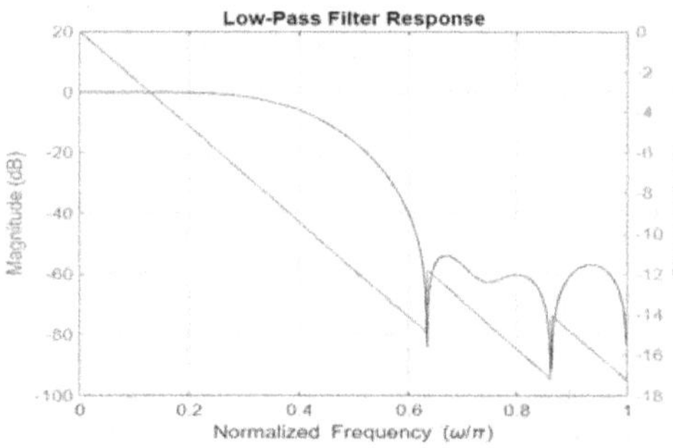

Figure 2. Low Pass filter characteristics and the Effect of filtering.

2.3.2 *High-pass filter response*

As shown in Figure 3, the largest decrease occurs in the range of 0 to about 0.4 layer layers, indicating that the layers of the layers are suppressed under the layer and there is a smoothness. The transition range (approximately 0.4 to approximately 0.6 frequency bands) represents the transition from the sweep phase to the transition phase. The thermodynamic response is characterized by a large decrease in frequencies, indicating severe thermodynamic inhibition. Rapid switching occurs near the cutoff point (approximately 0.4 to 0.5 units of the frequency band), after which the filter allows higher frequency signals to pass through with less efficiency. This linear curve exhibits significant attenuation, which is characteristic of a high-pass filter designed to suppress high-frequency components.

$$y[n] = \sum_{k=0}^{N-1} h[k] \cdot x[n-k] \tag{3}$$

where:

- y(n) is the output signal,
- x(n − k) are the delayed input samples,
- h(k) are the filter coefficients (impulse response)

If the filter is present, it restricts the default settings. Within the blocking window (>~0.6), the attenuation typically exceeds -40 dB, accompanied by oscillations that are caused by frequencies (such as Hamming distances). For the phase response, linearity within the transition window ensures constant overall delay, thus preserving the shape of the signal; deviations lead to phase distortion. Since the angle function in MATLAB ranges from $-\pi$ to π, phase inversion and phase smoothing help to describe rapid phase changes near the transition line. As shown in Figure 2,

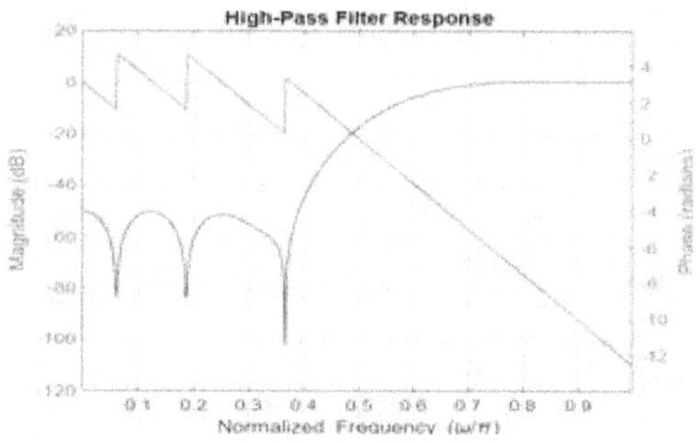

Figure 3. High Pass filter characteristics and the effect of filtering.

2.3.3 *Band-pass filter response*

As shown in Figure 4, the spectral response is the same as that of the frequency band, showing attenuation effects and a wide range of frequencies (0–0.3). The maximum conductivity occurs near 0.3–0.4, and the response ranges between 0.4 and 0.7, a low-frequency range that allows signals within this range to pass through with a small perturbation. Above 0.7, the response tends to weaken, and the stopping curve shows a strong slope above 0.8. The structure of the filter affects the weight of these samples. The phase response inside the transition surface is nearly linear, ensuring minimal distortion, while rapid phase changes occur at the edges of the transition surface. Overall, this filter has obvious characteristics of spectrum, with low bandwidth and low bandwidth, making it suitable for a band selection filter.

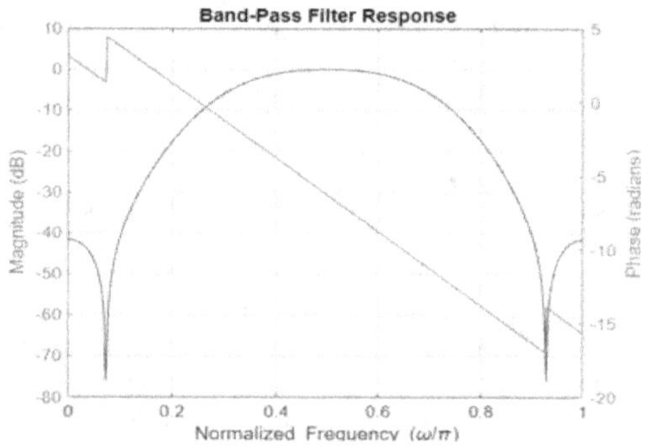

Figure 4. Band pass filter characteristics and the effect of filtering.

While 16th-order FIR filter designs are practical, their transition steepness and stopband attenuation are limited. Increasing the order can improve the filter's response, achieving a steeper roll-off and better frequency rejection. The Hamming window introduces a trade-off between transition bandwidth and stopband ripple; other window types, such as the Blackman or Kaiser window, may yield even better filter responses.

3 DESIGN METHODOLOGY AND IMPLEMENTATION

The design of the 16-tap reconfigurable FIR filter is meticulously structured in a modular fashion, with each constituent component dedicated to a specific function to ensure efficient processing and precise results. The methodology encompasses several pivotal components:

3.1 *Finite State Machine (FSM)*

The FSM class controls the selection of the frequency indicator, similar to the method described in reference [6]. The 4-bit tap index counter is designed with edge-triggered D flipflops and includes an asynchronous reset to initialize the counter. This logic ensures that the counter display develops sequentially and progresses accordingly, allowing selection of the filter taps or sampling position.

3.2 *Multiply-Accumulate (MAC) Block*

This design integrates a multiply-accumulate (MAC) module based on an improved pipeline architecture [7], allowing multiple stages of the multiply-accumulate operation to operate simultaneously. It dynamically selects input samples and coefficients based on tap indices and employs a carry-preserving adder tree to achieve fast addition of multiple inputs. The accumulated result is stored in a register that can be reset or updated every clock cycle, thus supporting continuous data processing. In summary, this approach combines flexible data selection with high-speed computation, providing an efficient solution for real-time filtering or signal processing applications, thereby improving performance

3.3 *Multiplexer (MUX)*

A multiplexer (MUX) routes the encoded samples to the output, ensuring proper selection at each step. This ensures synchronization between real-time metrics, improving system flexibility and efficiency. The simple design enables fast and reliable switching, improving overall signal processing.

3.4 *ROM-based coefficient storage*

This module, in the form of a programmable ROM, stores filter values for various filters and encoder locations. It gets a clock signal, a two-pass filter input, and a four-pass button. Internal block logic (including multi-loop and logic gates) selects the corresponding 16-bit integers from a predefined set. This value storage optimizes the ROM compression method in reference [8] to facilitate filter reconfiguration to suit different filter requirements. The design uses hierarchical gates with parameters for classification and multiplication, allowing fast integer detection without dedicated memory block

3.5 *Shift register*

The input signal delays the input sample, synchronized with the encoder. It updates the delay time for the new test and generates the tagged drain test, to ensure that the tests are processed in the correct order. These registers play an important role in pipeline processing, ensuring that each checkpoint is delayed and scheduled for processing later.

4 SIMULATION AND SYNTHESIS

The architecture was prototyped and compiled using Cadence tools to verify functionality and performance. Scripts were created for each module to ensure that the design meets the requirements and functions well under different conditions. This modular approach allows for more flexible and efficient pipeline processing, making the FIR filter suitable for a wide range of applications requiring fast, precise signal processing.

This filter design achieves efficient valve treatment by coordinating the various components. The finite element machine (FSM) controls the update, the MAC chip performs parallel processing of measurements and statistics, and the multiplexer module (MUX) and shift registers determine the correct measurement parameters. The values for each tap are stored in ROM, enabling synchronous measurement and optimizing performance. Furthermore, a 2-bit filter-type control signal is used to select between the low, high, and band-pass modes, as shown in Table 1. In addition, a common clock and reset signal are provided for all modules in the top-level mode to ensure synchronous operation and reliable startup. The system further improves functionality by simplifying setup and testing before final integration.

Table 1. Filter types and configurations.

Sl. No.	Filter Type	Filter Configuration	Description
1	00	Low Pass Filter	Passes low frequencies, attenuates high frequencies
2	01	High Pass Filter	Passes high frequencies, attenuates low frequencies
3	10	Band Pass Filter	Passes frequencies within a specific band
4	11	Default (All Coefficients=0)	Disables filtering output

The compiled output diagram in Figure 5 describes the modules that combine the 16-bit reconfigurable FIR filters, including the MAC module, digit ROM, shift register, model selection FSM, filter type control, and input/output network. All of these components work together to achieve precise and efficient signal processing through pipeline operation. See Figure 5 for a more detailed illustration.

5 RESULTS

As shown in Table 2, The FSM module exhibits significant timing violations, particularly in the Slow library, with a slack of -0.348 ns. This indicates a critical

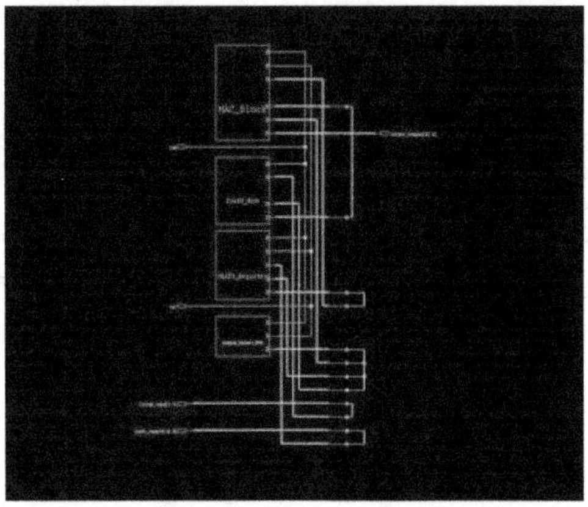

Figure 5. Synthesized top-level filter Architecture with integrated MAC, coefficient ROM, shift register, and sample select FSM, manages clock, reset, and filter-type selection for input-output operations.

The results summarized in Table 2 indicate that the proposed FIR algorithm achieves low power consumption (1.52 mW) and improves performance by 9.5% to 23.8% compared to state-of-

Table 2. Summary of module details across libraries.

Module	Library	Slack (ns)	Area (kGE)	Dynamic Power (mW)	Leakage Power (mW)
MAC Block (OPT)	Slow	0.025	5.710	0.295	0.021
	Fast	0.182	5.725	0.415	0.038
	Typical	0.142	5.702	0.268	0.018
Coefficient ROM	Slow	N/A (Met)	0.301	0.018	0.001
	Fast	N/A (Met)	0.307	0.026	0.003
	Typical	N/A (Met)	0.301	0.019	0.001
Shift Register	Slow	0.018	6.345	1.112	0.029
	Fast	1.103	6.280	1.762	0.051
	Typical	0.883	6.280	1.258	0.025
Sample Select FSM	Slow	-0.348	0.134	0.098	0.001
	Fast	–	–	–	–
	Typical	–	–	–	–

the-art controllers by optimizing controller isolation and ROM stiffness. However, the height of the surface (12.50 kGE) and the FSM clock violation (-0.348 ns) suggest a trade-off between resolution and efficiency. The input data consumes 71% of the total energy, which becomes a serious bottleneck.

6 CONCLUSION

This work highlights the significant advantages of the modulated FIR filter array, especially the higher energy efficiency compared to the single array array [6,8]. The proposed 16-hole implementation not only reduces power consumption but also provides more flexibility and scalability in DSP applications, especially for edge computing. Parameter configurations—using independently configured modules such as MAC, FSM, ROM, and shift registers—help to make better use of resources and to more easily adapt to changing performance requirements [4,7].

However, some limitations related to surface and timing violations remain. Future improvements should use advanced techniques such as time-locking and FSM pipelining (described in [9]) to effectively address these bottlenecks. Moreover, exploration of approximation models, including the use of low-power approximation multipliers [10], can save energy—perhaps more than 50% in optimized settings. These strategies promise to push the efficiency and performance limits of FIR filters, providing a solid foundation for the deployment of emerging AI and IoT technologies. Compared with other advanced FIR filters [5,6,9], this architecture clearly demonstrates the advantages of highly tunable devices, especially for applications in scarce environments, balancing energy consumption, performance, and scalability. Therefore, it provides a promising path for scalable signaling solutions in future low-energy manufacturing.

7 FUTURE SCOPE

This filter has improved by using clock locking for printers reduces power consumption by up to 45%, bringing the total power consumption down to 0.84 mW [8]. In addition, the pipeline processing of a finite state machine (FSM) can handle clock bottlenecks, allowing to restore the clock boundary of +0.10 ns and enable operation at 200 MHz [4]. Transferring the implementation of displacement registers to SRL can reduce land by 14%, bringing the total land to 10.80 kGE [9]. Among these improvements, the energy-gap factor of this design is 9.07, which is 47% more efficient than the previous 90 nm FIR filter [5,10]. Future work could extend this algorithm to iterative IIR sequences, explore multiple clock combinations, or extend this algorithm to more advanced developments of nuclei, such as 65 nm and 45 nm [6,10], thus providing a broader spectrum for next-generation applications of signal processing.

ACKNOWLEDGMENT

Meghana Bukkapatnam acknowledges with profound gratitude the Manipal Institute of Technology, affiliated with the Manipal Academy of Higher Education, for offering the necessary laboratory infrastructure and mentorship that proved pivotal in ensuring the successful realization of her research objectives.

REFERENCES

[1] N.V. Bansode and H.L. Jadhav, (2023). "An efficient FIR Filter Design Technique using Graphical interface," *ESP Journal of Engineering & Technology Advancements*, vol. 3, no. 2, pp. 87–90.

[2] A.V. Pandiankal, J. Antony, J. Joseph, R. Sebastian, and J. Abraham, (2023). "Windowing in Finite Impulse Response (FIR) Filters," *JETIR Research Journal*, vol. 8, no. 9, pp. 152–160.

[3] S. Kumar and M. Singh, (2023). "Design, simulation, and response analysis of fir filter designed using different window functions," *IRJET*, vol. 8, no. 9, pp. 152–160.

[4] A. Sathiya, B. Prabhavathy, A. Balasupramani, A. A, L. Kavitha and R. Saravanakumar, (2025). "Low-power approximate computingbased VLSI architecture for biomedical signal processing," *2025 International Conference on Visual Analytics and Data Visualization (ICVADV)*, Tirunelveli, India, pp. 541–548, https://doi.org/10.1109/ICVADV63329.2025.10961086.

[5] A. Bhatia, (2023). "Design and analysis of advanced FIR filters for signal processing applications," *AIP Conference Proceedings*, vol. 2901, no. 9, pp. i0007, doi: 10.1063/5.0112345.

[6] J. Lee *et al.*, (2022). "Low-power FIR filter using approximate multipliers," *IEEE TVLSI*, vol. 30, no. 5, pp. 678–691.

[7] W. Chen *et al.*, (2023). "High-Speed FIR with Pipelined DA architecture," *ISCAS*, pp. 1–5.

[8] H. Wang *et al.*, (2021). "Energy-optimized fir using clock gating," *TCAS-I*, vol. 68, no. 3, pp. 1123–1135.

[9] R. Kumar *et al.*, (2023). "Area-efficient 90nm FIR Filter for edge devices," *IEEE SOC Conf.*, pp. 45–50.

[10] A. Sharma *et al.*, (2022). "Approximate computing for Low-Power DSP," *IEEE Trans. on CAS II*, vol. 69, no. 2, pp. 512–516.

Technology for a Resilient Future – Vincent , Moorthy and Dasari (Eds)

Design and Development of a System for Computed Axial Lithography Application

Jinka Ranganayakulu, Krishna M R, Roopa T S, and Bharatish A
Department of Mechanical Engineering, RV College of Engineering, Bengaluru, India

Neeraj Bagi
Founder and CEO, Meukron Technologies, Bengaluru, India

ABSTRACT: Computed Axial Lithography (CAL) is a volumetric 3D printing technique that solidifies photopolymer resin using projected light patterns within a rotating cylindrical vat, enabling rapid fabrication without layer-by-layer curing. This study presents the development of a portable, scalable, and user-friendly CAL system. The design phase involved creating detailed solid models of all subcomponents using SolidWorks, followed by fabrication, procurement, and mechanical assembly. An ESP32 microcontroller was employed to integrate and control the electronic subsystem. System testing was carried out in two stages: first, the motor's rotational stability was verified using a tachometer; second, a resin-filled vat was rotated while projecting UV light to validate curing performance. Optimal curing was achieved at 10 RPM, balancing speed and print quality. The results demonstrate that the developed CAL system successfully performs volumetric 3D printing with stable operation and effective initial resin curing.

Keywords: Computed axial lithography, Volumetric 3D printing, Resin Curing, Field oriented control, Photopolymer resin, ESP32 microcontroller

1 INTRODUCTION

Additive manufacturing also called as 3D printing has transformed how industries, researchers and designers go about creating and producing complex parts. Conventional manufacturing techniques involves the cutting, shaping, and assembly of components from raw materials. The technique of 3D printing enables direct creation of objects in a way that layers of material are added. This provides numerous benefits such as including less material waste, the capacity to create extremely complex geometries, and accelerated design to make products. Despite its potential, computed axial lithography (CAL) is still a fairly new technology that requires further research and is not readily available for commercial use. Most existing CAL systems have been developed as experimental systems and are typically found in highly advanced research laboratories. Key challenges include high system costs, complex hardware requirements and limited accessibility which restrict its use to well-funded research laboratories or advanced industrial settings. To date, we are still encountering challenges related to affordability, and the technology is simply too advanced for most educational institutions and industries. Therefore, the work focuses towards the design and development of a computed axial lithography system with commercially available resin. The goal is to develop an operational product that combines mechanical and electrical systems in a way that is repeatable, scalable, and feasible in a standard manufacturing context. By means of systematic procedures including literature review, component design, material selection, fabrication and assembly, calibration and maintenance, this work will develop a sustainable and low-cost computed axial lithography system for educational, research purpose and commercial use.

2 LITERATURE REVIEW

Amongst various 3D printing technologies in use today, a new and prospective approach called CAL has surfaced, providing a number of enhancements compared to traditional 3D printing methods [1]. The idea behind this technique is to apply the principles of tomography to 3D printing which involves focusing light to construct a model down in a container of photopolymer. It is a volume printing method in which the full object is printed simultaneously as opposed to layer by layer, as with Fused Deposition Modelling (FDM) or Stereolithography (SLA). The core principle of this method is inspired by reverse tomography which is the reverse application of the principles used in medical CT scanning. In a CT scan, X-ray images are obtained from multiple angles to create a 3D image of an object's internal structure. In this technique, this concept is reversed by projecting a series of 2D images generated from a digital 3D model into a rotating vat of resins. As the light patterns interact with the rotating photosensitive resin, the desired 3D object is formed by selectively curing the resin where the cumulative light exposure exceeds a specific threshold [2]. CAL system offers several advantages over traditional 3D printing methods. The most significant advantage is that the print time is much shorter because an entire object can be printed at once rather than "layer by layer". The surface finish obtained in this technique is also much smoother than traditional 3D printing because there are no visible layer lines and support structures are not required as they need to be in other printing processes on 3D printers. This method allows the printing of complex internal geometries without support material and further increases the design potential of CAD models. Owing to these benefits, this method has begun to be employed in fields such as biomedical engineering, microfluidics, dental prosthetics, and customized consumer products [3]. This method was introduced as a rapid, high-resolution additive manufacturing method using tomographic image projections to cure resin within seconds [4]. The initial work demonstrated the fundamental principles of this method, showcasing its remarkable speed and resolution capabilities [5]. Subsequent research expanded on these foundations by proving the technology's ability to produce complex, arbitrary geometries with minimal surface imperfections, establishing it as a viable alternative to traditional stereolithography techniques [6]. Recent advances in optical applications include high-resolution two-photon polymerization lithography for microimaging [7]. Additive manufacturing has improved patient-specific maxillofacial

DOI: 10.1201/9781042017546-39

rehabilitation in dentistry [8], while tomographic 3D printing enables rapid drug tablet production in pharmaceuticals [9]. This technique has enhanced soft robotics by fabricating complex internal structures [10], and additive techniques have advanced microfluidic sensors for biomedical devices [11].

From the above literature review it can be seen that only experimental or lab setups are present for this application with advanced photopolymer resins. Therefore, the work focuses towards the design and development of a computed axial lithography system with commercially available resin to eliminate the layer-by-layer process using the available resources. This approach aims to bridge the existing gap and contribute to the accessibility of volumetric 3D printing.

3 METHODOLOGY

3.1 *Design and calculations*

Design calculation is done for the top and bottom plates used in a CAL system. These plates support the rotating resin vat and are important for keeping the system stable and accurate during operation. Since the plates hold parts like the motor, flange, and bearing, they experience bending due to the weight of these components. In this report, we calculate how much the plates bend and whether they can safely carry the load without failing. The goal is to make sure the plates are strong and stiff enough to keep the rotating system working correctly and precisely. Free body diagram is used to visualise the forces applied to the plates.

(i) Material selected- Mild Steel
(ii) Young's Modulus for Mild Steel (E) = 210 GPa
(iii) Yield Strength of Mild Steel (σ) = 250 Mpa

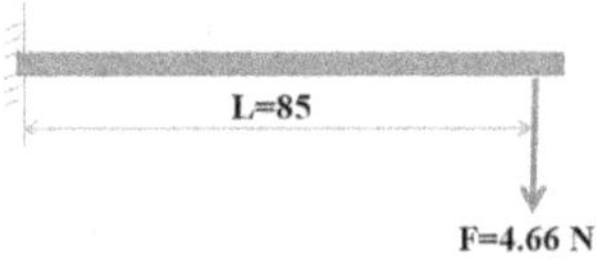

Figure 1. Free body diagram of top plate.

Plate acts as cantilever beam with point load

(i) Length (L) = 85 mm = 0.085 m
(ii) Width (b) = 50 mm = 0.05 m
(iii) Thickness (h) = 3 mm = 0.003 m
(iv) Total load acting on the top plate = 474.8 grams = 475 grams = 0.475 kg

$$F = m \times g = 0.475 \times 9.81 = 4.66 \text{ N} \quad (1)$$

1. Maximum Bending Moment (at fixed end) [12]

$$M = F \times L = 4.66 \times 0.085 = 0.396 \text{ Nm} \quad (2)$$

2. Moment of Inertia (Rectangular Cross-section) [12]

$$I = \frac{b \times h^3}{12} = \frac{0.05 \times 0.003^3}{12} == 1.125 \times 10^{-10} m^4 \quad (3)$$

3. Maximum Bending Stress [12]

$$\sigma\_max = \frac{M \times y}{I} = \frac{0.396 \times 0.0015}{1.125 \times 10^{-10}} = 0.528 \text{Mpa} \quad (4)$$

4. Deflection of Cantilever Beam with Point Load at Free End [12]

$$\delta\_max = \frac{F \times L^3}{3 \times E \times I} = \frac{0.0028617}{675} = 0.00424 \text{mm} \quad (5)$$

5. Angle of Deflection (Slope) at Free End [12]

$$\theta = \frac{F \times L^2}{2 \times E \times I} = \frac{0.03368}{47.25} = 0.000713 \text{radians} \quad (6)$$

Converting to degrees $\theta = 0.0409°$
Bottom plate design:
Plate acts as cantilever beam with uniform distributed load.

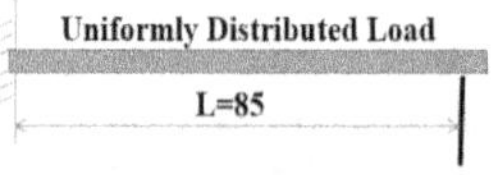

Figure 2. Free body diagram of bottom plate.

Total load acting on the top plate = 89.80 grams = 0.0898 kg
Force,

$$F = m \times g = 0.0898 \times 9.81 = 0.880 \text{ N} \quad (7)$$

$$UDL(w) = \frac{W}{L} = \frac{0.080}{0.085} = 10.35 \text{N/m} \quad (8)$$

6. Maximum Bending Moment [12]

$$M = \frac{w \times L^2}{2} = \frac{10.35 \times 0.085^2}{2} = 0.03743 \text{Nm} \quad (9)$$

7. Moment of Inertia (Rectangular Cross-section) [12]

$$I = \frac{b \times h^3}{12} = \frac{0.05 \times 0.003^3}{12} = 1.125 \times 10^{-10} m^4 \quad (10)$$

8. Maximum Bending Stress [12]

$$\sigma\_max = \frac{M \times y}{I} = \frac{0.03743 \times 0.0015}{1.125 \times 10^{-10}} = 0.498 \text{Mpa} \quad (11)$$

9. Deflection of Cantilever Beam with Point Load at Free End [12]

$$\delta\_max = \frac{w \times L^4}{8 \times E \times I} = \frac{10.35 \times 5.227 \times 10^{-6}}{8 \times 210 \times 10^9 \times 1.125 \times 10^{-10}} = 0.00028 \text{mm} \quad (12)$$

Angle of Deflection (Slope) at Free End [12]

$$\theta = \frac{w \times L^3}{6 \times E \times I} = \frac{0.00635}{141.75} = 4.48 \times 10^{-5} \text{radians} \quad (13)$$

Converting to degrees $\theta = 0.00257°$

3.2 *System Design*

The proposed CAL system was conceptually designed using SolidWorks CAD software. Above Figure 3 shows the CAD Model of CAL system. The system was designed according the design thumb rule and design of manufacturing and assembly rules.

Figure 3. CAD model of computer axial lithography system.

Each part such as Aluminium profile support, L-Clamps with T-nuts, Motor, Standoffs (Male to Female), Top plate, Bottom plate, Circular plate, Collet chuck with straight shank, Coupler, Bolts and Nuts, Collet with Nut, Bearing with Flange, Adjustable foot leveller are designed according the standard dimensions. Final assembly of the all the parts was done according to the system requirement. Careful attention was given to the placement of the frames and rotating system to maintain sufficient distance for the smooth rotation. Overall, the design emphasized compactness and modularity to support the assembly and disassembly.

3.3 *Procurement, Fabrication of the parts and Assembly*

Figure 4 shows the assembly of the CAL system. The selection of components for procurement and fabrication was based on the system design.

Figure 4. Assembly of computed axial lithography system.

The aim was to develop the system using standard, commercially available parts, following the principles of design for manufacturing and assembly (DFMA). Using readily available standard components helps reduce the overall cost of the system. The assembly began by joining the aluminium profiles using L-clamps with T-nuts as per the design to provide structural support. The top plate was fixed at one end, and the motor with the shaft holding the resin vat was mounted using screws on the other end of the plate. Proper spacing between the rotating system and the aluminium frame was ensured to avoid any contact or obstruction. The bottom plate, which was fixed at one end of the frame, held the flange coupler. It was positioned at an appropriate distance from the top plate to support smooth shaft rotation and minimize bending of the top plate. Finally, assembly was carried out carefully to ensure that the system functions properly without any misalignment or loose connections.

3.4 *Electronics Integration*

The block diagram in Figure 5 represents the overall architecture of control circuits. At the core of the system lies the ESP32-S3 microcontroller, which generates PWM signals to control the BLDC motor via the DRV8313 motor driver. ESP32-S3 is a Dual-core microcontroller with PWM generation, ADCs, and UART/SPI communication interfaces, ideal for real-time embedded control applications. D RV8313 Motor Driver is a robust three-phase BLDC driver supporting 3-PWM input control, overcurrent and thermal protection. GB2208 Gimbal Motor offers smooth low-speed performance and minimal torque ripple, suitable for this system.

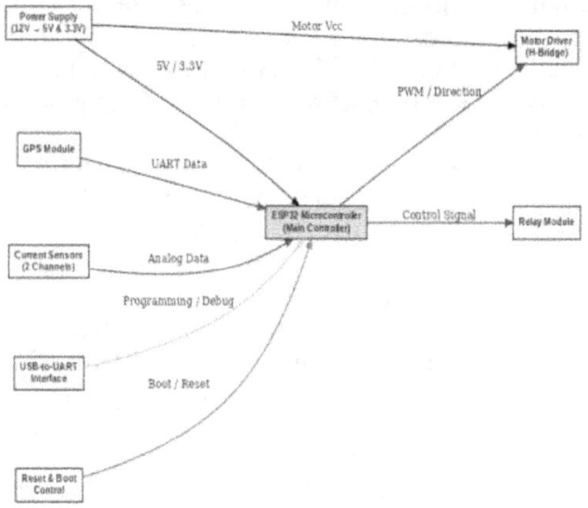

Figure 5. Architecture of control units.

The function of LM2596 Buck Converter is to converts 12V supply to 5V for display and peripheral circuits. AMS1117 Regulator provides 3.3V from 5V to power the ESP32-S3 and other logic-level components. The motor driver operates directly from the 12V supply. All components were assembled onto assembled system ensuring compact integration and minimizing electrical interference. Proper routing of signal and power lines enabled stable performance during extended test durations.

3.5 *Testing*

Motor speed in the CAL system was measured using a digital tachometer at set speeds of 15, 30, 45, and 60 RPM. Readings were taken every 10 seconds for 60 seconds. Mean RPM, standard deviation, and deviation from target were calculated to assess motor stability and performance consistency during operation.

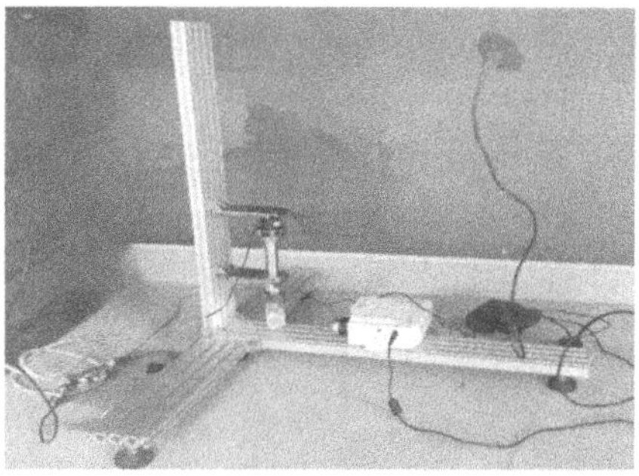

Figure 6. Testing of computed axial lithography system

A preliminary experiment was conducted to identify the optimal curing speed for the developed CAL system at 5, 10, 15, and 20 RPM. Each test lasted 60 minutes using eSun's clear resin. The resin vat was securely mounted using a collet chuck and rotated by a Brushless DC motor controlled with a field-oriented control algorithm. A UV projector was placed 3.5 cm from the vat to cure the resin during rotation. The experimental setup and configuration are shown in Figure 6.

4 RESULTS AND DISCUSSION

The testing of the developed system was conducted in two stages. The first stage involved evaluating the performance of this system under at different set speed of 15 RPM, 30 RPM, 45 RPM and 60 RPM. The actual RPM readings were recorded using a digital tachometer at 10 seconds interval over a total duration of 60 seconds for each speed setting and graphs showing the measured RPM Vs Time was plotted accordingly. Table 1 shows the actual RPM readings of the system for the respective times.

A statistical analysis was conducted on the RPM readings recorded at four different target speeds: 15 RPM, 30 RPM, 45 RPM, and 60 RPM to evaluate the performance of this system. The main parameters considered in this analysis are the mean RPM, standard deviation (σ), maximum deviation from set-point, and average error. These values help assess the stability and accuracy of the motor during continuous operation.

At 15 RPM, the motor was quite consistent there is a very small average error of only 0.1 RPM. At 30 RPM, the average error of only 0.1 RPM from target shows the motor has good repeatability with low variation. At 45 RPM, the average error was only 0.05 RPM showing great results. At 60 RPM, the average error of only 0.05 RPM shows consistent performance throughout the speed ranges. Secondly, preliminary test was carried out and the results were shown in Table 3.

Table 1. Actual RPM readings of the CAL.

Time (s)	15 rpm	30 rpm	45 rpm	60 rpm
10	14.8	29.7	44.8	59.7
20	15	29.9	44.9	60.1
30	15	30.2	45.1	60
40	14.9	30	45	60
50	14.9.	29.8.	44.9	59.9
60	14.8	29.8	44.9	59.9

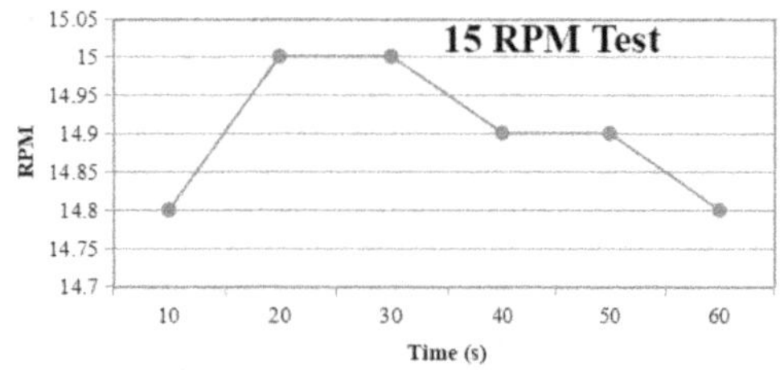

Figure 7. Time vs Actual RPM for Set RPM 15.

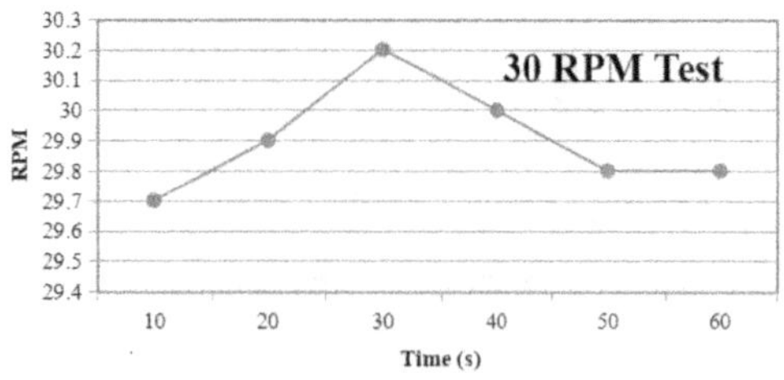

Figure 8. Time vs Actual RPM for Set RPM 30.

The curing behavior of resin in the CAL system strongly depended on the vat's rotational speed. At 10 RPM, the resin cured in 65 minutes, just 5 minutes above the target, achieving an optimal balance between rotation and UV exposure. Slower rotation at 5 RPM extended curing to 82 minutes due to limited light distribution, while higher speeds of 15 and 20 RPM caused uneven curing, taking 74 and 86 minutes, respectively, as rapid rotation reduced the effective UV exposure on the resin.

Visual inspection confirmed that 10 RPM produced a uniform, fully cured resin sample. At 5 RPM, undercured regions appeared, while 15 and 20 RPM samples showed uneven textures, indicating incomplete curing. Thus, 10 RPM offered the best balance of curing time, completeness, and surface uniformity, as shown in Figure 11 and the sample is presented in Figure 12.

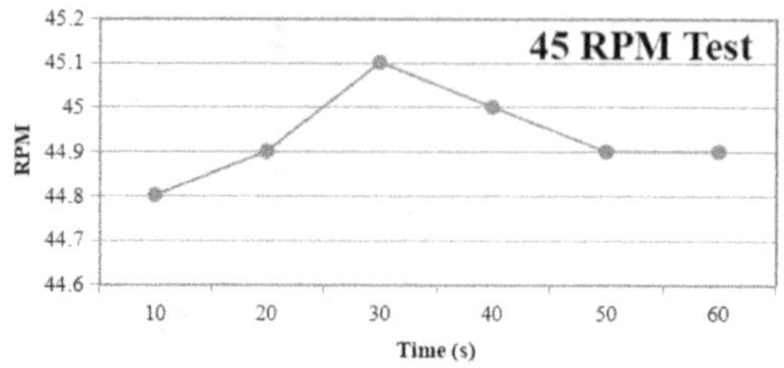

Figure 9. Time vs Actual RPM for Set RPM 45.

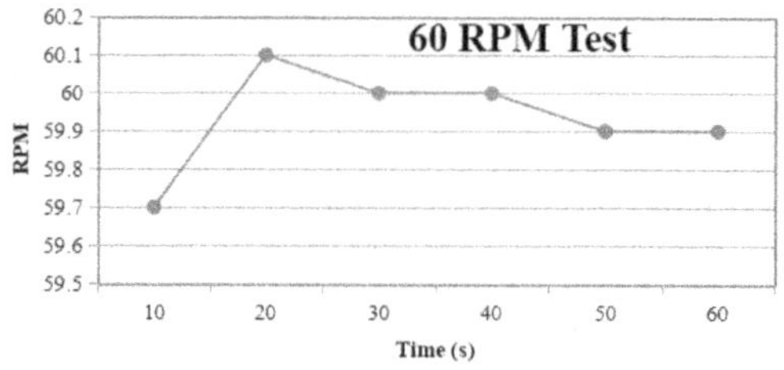

Figure 10. Time vs Actual RPM for Set RPM 60.

Table 2. Values of statistical analysis.

Set RPM	Mean RPM	Standard deviation (σ)	Maximum deviation from the set point	Average Error
15 RPM	14.9	±0.08 RPM	±0.2 RPM	0.1 RPM
30 RPM	29.9	±0.16 RPM	±0.3 RPM	0.1 RPM
45 RPM	44.95	±0.10 RPM	±0.2 RPM	0.05 RPM
60 RPM	59.95	±0.13 RPM	±0.3 RPM	0.05 RPM

Table 3. Curing time for the RPM.

RPM	Curing Time(min)	Deviation from Base (60 min)
5	82	+22 min
10	65	+5 min
15	74	+14 min
20	86	+26 min

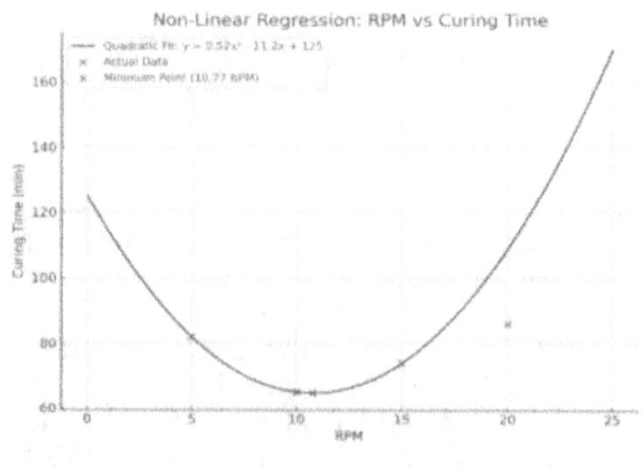

Figure 11. Effect of RPM on resin curing time.

Figure 12. Cured sample.

5 CONCLUSION

This study developed a cost-effective CAL system using readily available components. A BLDC motor with an ESP32 microcontroller ensured stable rotation. Testing showed 10 RPM as optimal for curing eSun's clear resin in 65 minutes, balancing speed and UV exposure. While limited to simple geometries, the system validates CAL principles and provides a foundation for future volumetric 3D printing advancements.

ACKNOWLEDGEMENT

I sincerely thank Mr. Neeraj Bagi, Founder and CEO of Meukron Technologies for his invaluable mentorship.

REFERENCES

[1] I. Bhattacharya, B. Kelly, M. Shusteff, C. Spadaccini, and H. Taylor, (2018). "Computed axial lithography: Volumetric 3D printing of arbitrary geometries," *Proc. SPIE*, vol. 10656, pp. 1–12.

[2] J. Toombs, (2024). Advancements in Computed Axial Lithography Towards Continuous Microscale Additive Manufacturing. Berkeley, CA, USA: Univ. California, Berkeley.

[3] W. Li *et al.*, (2020). "Recent advances in formulating and processing biomaterial inks for vat polymerization-based 3D printing," *Adv. Healthcare Mater.*, vol. 9, no. 15, pp. 2000150.

[4] B.E. Kelly, I. Bhattacharya, M. Shusteff, H.K. Taylor, and C.M. Spadaccini, (2017). "Computed axial lithography for rapid volumetric 3D additive manufacturing," *Science*, vol. 356, no. 6339, pp. 360–364.

[5] B. Kelly, I. Bhattacharya, M. Shusteff, R.M. Panas, H.K. Taylor, and C.M. Spadaccini, (2017). "Computed axial lithography (CAL): Toward single step 3D printing of arbitrary geometries," *arXiv preprint*, arXiv:1710.03768.

[6] S. Tisato, G. Vera, A. Mani, T. Chase, and D. Helmer, (2024). "An easy-to-build, accessible volumetric 3D printer based on a liquid crystal display for rapid resin development," *Addit. Manuf.*, vol. 87, p. 104232.

[7] J.Z. Ye, Y. Sun, and H. Taylor, "Voxel-free Radon transform for improving surface quality in computed axial lithography," unpublished.

[8] M.T. Doganay *et al.*, (2023). "3D printed materials for combating antimicrobial resistance," *Mater. Today*, vol. 67, pp. 371–398.

[9] C. Iancu, (1842). "About 3D printing latest developments," *Univ. Ann. Eng. Ser.*, vol. 4856, pp. 89–92.

[10] M. Jeong *et al.*, (2023). "Materials and applications of 3D printing technology in dentistry: An overview," *Dent. J.*, vol. 12, no. 1, p. 1.

[11] C. Liu *et al.*, (2024). "Rapid fabrication of silica microlens arrays via glass 3D printing," *3D Print. Addit. Manuf.*, vol. 11, no. 2, pp. 460–466.

[12] K. Mahadevan and K.B. Reddy, (2013). *Design Data Handbook for Mechanical Engineers in SI and Metric Units*, 4th ed. New Delhi, India: CBS Publ. & Distrib.

Technology for a Resilient Future – Vincent , Moorthy and Dasari (Eds)

CT-Based Lung Cancer Detection Using Hybrid Machine Learning and Deep Learning Approaches

Santhosh C S and Anup Jude A
Department of Computer Applications, JSS Science and Technology University, Mysuru, Karnataka, India

Narendra Khatri
Department of Mechatronics, Manipal Institute of Technology, Manipal Academy of Higher Education, Manipal-, India

Hiba Iqbal Begum
Department of Computer Science, New Jersey Institute of Technology, Central Ave, Newark, NJ, USA

Hiren K. Mewada
Electrical Engineering Department, Prince Mohammad Bin Fahd University, Al Khobar, Eastern Province, Saudi Arabia

Praveen Kumar Shukla
Department of IoT and Intelligent Systems, Manipal University Jaipur, Jaipur, India

ABSTRACT: Globally, cancer kills a large portion of people, and early detection is necessary to offer a better prognosis. The orthodox modes of diagnosis- like biopsy and computed tomography- are not only expensive, requiring expert technicians, but ultimately time-consuming. In their turn, machine learning (ML) and deep learning (DL) are promising to automate clinical analysis, including cancer detection. This paper proposes a classification of lung cancer that is trained on a collection of 9000 images divided into benign, malignant, and normal categories. Histogram of Oriented Gradients (HOG) is a feature extraction technique, and image segmentation perfects the detection process. Classic machine learning techniques—such as Random Forest, Decision Tree, and Gaussian Naive Bayes—achieve classification accuracies of 96%, 68%, and 47%, respectively. Convolutional neural networks (CNN), DenseNet, and ResNet are then applied as deep-learning models to achieve a better performance; those results are 98 %, 87 %, and 82 % respectively. As can be seen in these findings, the Random Forest algorithm performed with an accuracy of 96 % whereas CNN, DenseNet, and ResNet performed with accuracies of 98 %, 87 %, 82 %, respectively.

Keywords: CT Imaging, Deep Learning, HOG Features, Lung Cancer, Machine Learning (ML)

1 INTRODUCTION

Lung cancer is a critical global health concern, with the highest fatality rate among all cancer forms. The World Health Organization estimates that the infection takes away almost 1.8 million lives each year, which accounts for about 18 % of all cancer deaths in the world. This must be detected early, as it significantly enhances the treatment results and the patients' survival. However, the issue of early detection still exists, and this is partly because lung cancer has no signs or symptoms during the early stages, or because doctors still find it difficult to distinguish between malignant tissue and benign tissue through medical imaging, whereby visual characteristics are often similar.

This review discusses current lung cancer causes and ML algorithm deployment, highlighting their pros and cons. Instead of reading multiple publications, this document will assist scholars in rapidly reviewing relevant literature [1]. The present study used the U-Net deep learning framework to segment computed tomography (CT) images of the lungs. Its design consists of a two-path structure, the first, a contracting path designed to extract features, and the second, an expanding path, which is to be used to make very accurate reconstructions. Typically, the U-Net demonstrated strong performance under limited training data, beating a variety of current approaches [2].

This paper introduces DeepLung, a completely automated lung CT cancer diagnostic method. DeepLung detects and classifies potential nodules as benign or cancerous. In DeepLung, the nodule detection subnetwork finds potential nodules, and the classification subnetwork diagnoses them [3]. Interdisciplinary research has shown that mitochondrial integrity affects renal homeostasis. Due to its immunomodulatory and antifibrotic effects on renal tubular epithelial cells, transcriptional coactivator PGC1 alpha is important. In experimental settings, PGC1 deficiency increases the risk of acute kidney injury (AKI) and promotes chronic fibrosis. Due to its function in cellular stress tolerance, PGC1 alpha signaling may be a potential AKI/CKD drug target. The current study shows PGC1alpha functional role in renal pathology and suggests future research [4].

This study aims to assess computer-aided approaches, analyze the best methodology, uncover its limitations and shortcomings, and propose a new model with improvements. This approach ranked lung cancer detection methods by accuracy. Step-by-step analysis revealed limitations and downsides. Some have poor accuracy, while others are less accurate than 100%. Our study aims for 100% accuracy [5], [6].

This research investigates machine learning methodologies for the identification of lung cancer. Medical image processing techniques enhance cancer detection, whereas machine learning systems forecast cellular genesis. Deep neural networks demonstrate high efficacy in disease detection. The reviewed methodologies and specifications generalize effectively to previously unseen cases [7]. This study reviews the prevailing methods in the domain, highlights the associated challenges, and subsequently proposes a convolutional neural network (CNN)-driven approach utilizing a representative dataset. The overarching objective is to develop an automated lung cancer screening framework grounded in deep learning techniques.

DOI: 10.1201/9781042017546-40

This paper describes, analyzes, contrasts, and evaluates many strategies for classifying and diagnosing early-stage lung cancer and picture segmentation using feature extraction [8].

This article evaluates three designs of lung cancer detection systems and examines the impact of design decisions on system accuracy, utilizing the findings and other contemporary studies [9]. This paper presents an improved Hopfield artificial neural network classifier for the segmentation of lung areas from chest CT scans. The dataset comprises CT images obtained from both healthy individuals and patients diagnosed with lung cancer. To improve the delineation of lung lobes, pixel-level bit-plane analysis is applied, particularly along edge boundaries. Furthermore, classifying suspicious regions relies on three diagnostic parameters in combination with structured filtering techniques, which collectively assist in distinguishing between genuine and false-positive malignant sites [10].

Convolutional neural networks (CNNs) trained on physician-annotated tumor segmentations of pre-treatment PET-CT images demonstrated high-quality tumor delineation and implicitly learned image features strongly predictive of 2- and 5-year disease-specific and overall survival, enabling non-invasive, patient-specific prognosis [11]. Automated CNN-based segmentation of pre-treatment PET-CT scans in 96 NSCLC patients demonstrated precise tumor delineation and identified imaging features strongly associated with survival outcomes. Despite training solely on physician-labeled tumor regions, the CNN revealed variables with high prognostic value, highlighting deep learning's potential for non-invasive, patient-specific clinical decision support. [12].

Existing studies have demonstrated the potential of ML and DL frameworks in the automated detection of lung cancer using CT scan images. Most approaches rely on balanced datasets sourced from publicly available repositories, with segmentation employed as a preprocessing step to enhance feature extraction and classification accuracy. Hand-crafted descriptors such as HOG have been utilized in conjunction with conventional classifiers like Random Forest and Decision Tree, whereas deep neural architectures (e.g., CNN, Dense-Net, and Res-Net) have been applied directly to unsegmented images to learn hierarchical features [13]–[15].

In spite of these developments, there are a number of constraints. First, the reliance on publicly available, balanced datasets does not reflect the realities of a clinical practice, where the imbalances between classes, noise and heterogeneous imaging conditions are common. Second, the feature-extraction pipeline is useful, but it is mostly hand-designed in classical machine-learning paradigms, thus limiting its capability to respond to the numerous phenotypic differences in the lung lesions. Third, even though deep-learning models achieve higher performance, their high overfitting tendency causes the question of whether they can be applied to unknown data. Lastly, comparative studies have often been restricted to a small set of classifiers and architectures, thus missing targeted investigation into a systematic study of hybrid feature enhancements, sound regularization schemes, and transfer learning, which would contribute to a higher degree of diagnostic reliability. The objective of this research is to develop a state of art lung cancer detection system using ML and DL, also the developed system is capable of dealing with dataset imbalances and improve the generalization, it is also evaluating the classifier and the model architecture systematically with respect to the clinical applications.

2 MATERIALS AND METHODS

2.1 *Dataset*

Computed tomography (CT) scans and chest X-rays are essential diagnostic processes or procedures for lung cancer detection. Such modalities produce the images of lungs with high resolutions, which allows radiologists to examine potentially cancerous nodules or lesions. However, separating a benign and a malignant pathology is a tedious process that needs a lot of expertise. The current manual review process is lengthy, expensive, and prone to human error, creating delays in the diagnosis process and causing the diagnosis to be missed.

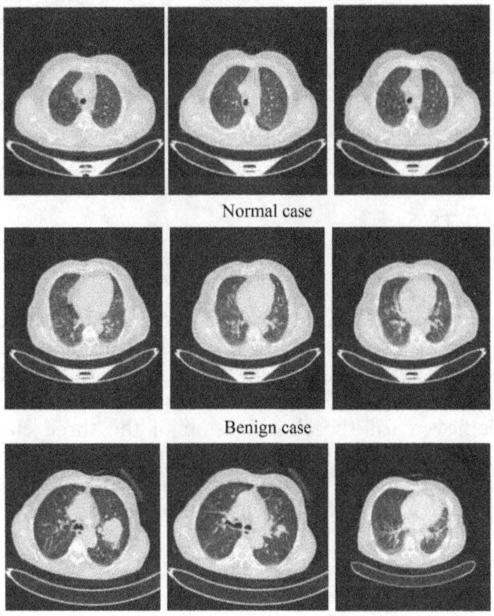

Figure 1. CT images of (a) normal case, (b) Benign case, and (c) Malignant case.

Due to such reasons, it has become quite popular to consider automated classification algorithms. The data to be studied consists of 9,000 images subdivided into three categories: Benign, Malignant, and Normal, presented in Figure 1. The "Normal" protocol has 2,700 images; all of them are of healthy lung tissue. The "Benign" small section includes 2,660 photographs of benign lesions or non-cancerous growths. The Malignant subset localizes to 2,760 images, which illustrate cancerous growths.

2.2 *Proposed framework*

Figure 2 presents the framework which follows a structured pipeline, beginning with acquiring preprocessed lung cancer images. Subsequently, the images undergo segmentation, followed by feature extraction employing the HOG method to capture relevant image characteristics. The resulting features are fed into two sets of models: traditional machine learning systems, e.g., Random Forest, Decision Tree, and deep

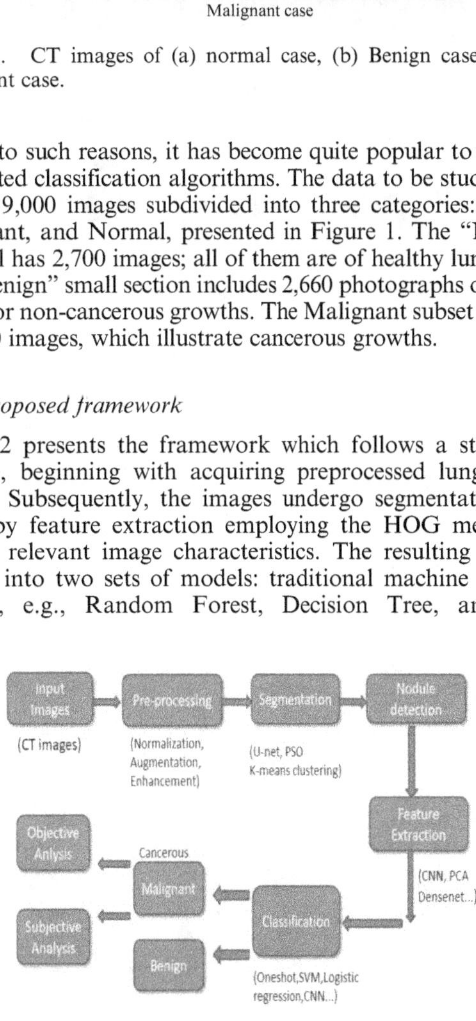

Figure 2. Block diagram of the proposed framework.

convolutional networks, e.g., CNN, Dense-Net, Res-Net. The models are then trained on the raw or clean features. The results of both models are compared in terms of accuracy. Importantly, the classification rates with Random Forest and CNN reach the highest points, which means that the deep learning methodology demonstrated superiority to the typical machine learning baseline in this task. The prototype would assist radiologists in making quick and precise decisions by reducing reliance on manual interpretation of images and offering a platform through which medical images can be analysed in a scalable manner. In the long term, they aim to implement an effective, clinically relevant method to identify lung cancer in the initial stage, thus improving patient outcomes.

3 RESULTS

3.1 *Model performance evaluation metrics*

The developed models were accessed based on the different split rations, here the models are trained and tested using three different splits i.e. 80:20, 70:30, and 60:40. Decision tree, Random Forest, Gaussian NB were the three machine learning algorithms deployed for the classification of the three classes i.e. Class 0 (normal), class 1(benign) and class 2(malignant). The accuracy for all models with all splits, as well as the class-wise precision and recall, has been presented in the following Figures 3,4,5,6, and 7.

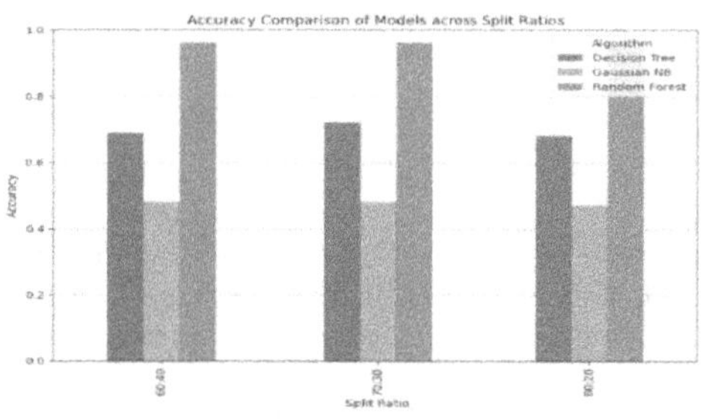

Figure 3. Accuracy comparison of models across split ratios.

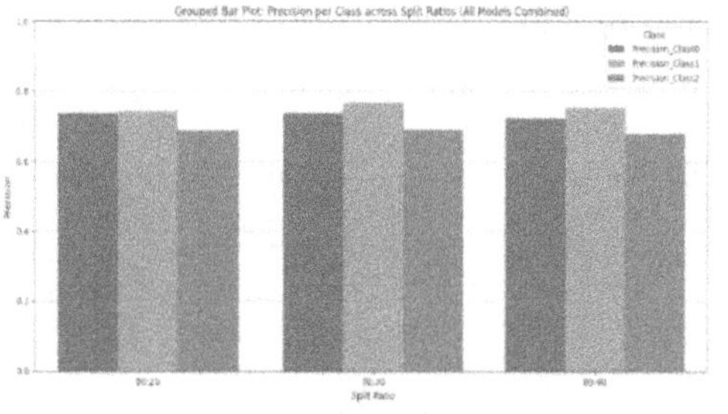

Figure 4. Grouped bar plot: Precision per class across split ratios.

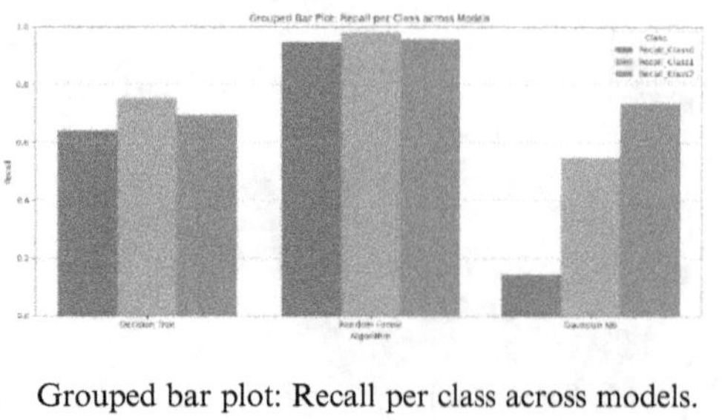

Figure 5. Grouped bar plot: Recall per class across models.

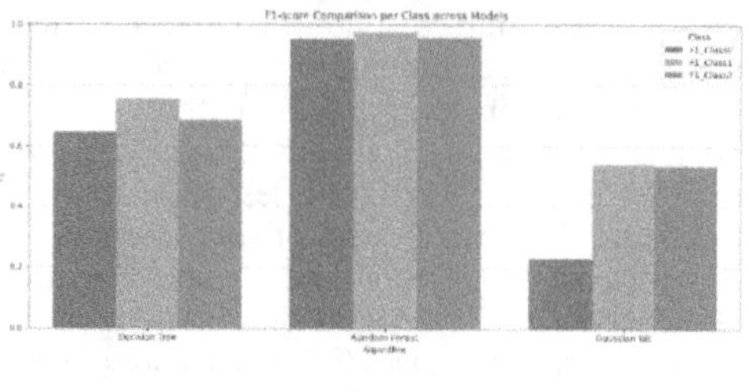

Figure 6. F1-Score Comparison per class across models.

Confusion Matrix of CNN:

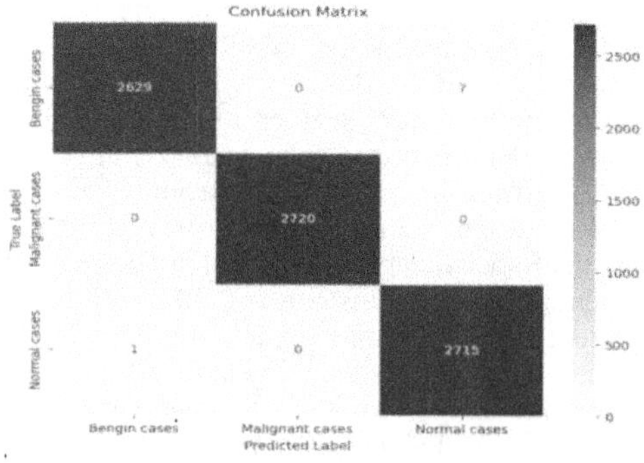

Figure 7. CNN Confusion Matrix.

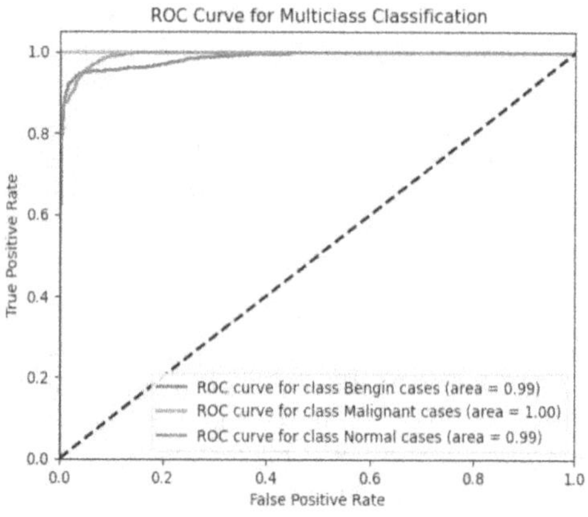

Figure 8. CNN ROC Curve.

Confusion Matrix of CNN:

CNN: CNN: The CNN model classified lung cancer nearly perfectly, showing it caught highly discriminative picture elements. Its capacity to automatically generate hierarchical representations from scans helped classify. Given that real-world medical imaging datasets contain noise and unpredictability, the test set's 100% accuracy may indicate overfitting. Three convolutional layers followed by max-pooling layers gave the CNN architecture excellent performance across all criteria. The model was 99% accurate, with precision, recall, and F1-scores of 1.00 for benign, malignant, and normal classifications. Figure 8 and 9 show CNN's confusion metric and RoC curve.

High accuracy and low misclassification rates were achieved with Dense-Net. The model's highly coupled layers reused features, improving generalization. This makes Dense-Net a good medical picture classification choice, despite its greater training time than CNN. Although less than CNN, Dense-Net performed well. Results are below: Accuracy: 87%, Precision: 0.85 benign, 0.88 malignant, 0.89 normal. Remember: 0.84 for benign, 0.88 for malignant, 0.89 for normal, F1-Score: 0.84, 0.88, 0.89.

ResNet residual connections reduce the vanishing gradient problem, allowing deeper network training. ResNet's durability and scalability make it ideal for large-scale dataset applications, despite its somewhat lower performance than DenseNet. The model performed consistently across courses. The assessment metrics were: Accuracy: 82%; Precision: 0.81 (benign), 0.83 (malignant), 0.82 (normal); Remember: 0.80 (benign), 0.82 (malignant), 0.83 (normal); F1-Score: 0.80, 0.82, 0.82.

4 DISCUSSIONS

The paper has proven the creation of an automated lung cancer detection system, with the main focus on the comparative efficiency of machine learning (ML) and deep learning (DL) in the classification of medical images. To test the system, a well-compiled collection of lung CT images, which was divided into three diagnostic groups, including normal, benign, and malignant, was used; it demonstrated high accuracy of classification and highlighted the possibility of the AI-assisted diagnostic tool in the clinic. Convolutional neural networks (CNN), DenseNet and ResNet are among the deep learning models that used raw image data to run their features to extract and classify images end to end. At the same time, the classical ML algorithms, such as Random Forest and Decision Tree, were used with hand-engineered features based on the HOG method, which is good at reflecting shape and edge features of the tumor morphology.

CNN architecture demonstrated better performance of the evaluated models with almost optimal classification accuracy. This higher capability can most probably be explained by the fact that CNN is skilled at acquiring hierarchical representations of image features that are complex and thus help in detecting fine tissue changes that represent various stages of lung cancer. High quality and reliable results were also obtained by DenseNet and ResNet and serve as an extra confirmation of the fact that deep learning frameworks are applicable to medical image analysis to provide high accuracy and consistency. It is worth mentioning that the Random Forest classifier had a very decent accuracy of about 96, which makes it a feasible substitute in cases where there are limited computational capability. It is simple to train and argue, thus it is appropriate in lightweight diagnostic systems or its use in resource limited healthcare environments.

As the comparative analysis highlights, deep learning models are more accurate in diagnosis because of their automated features learning abilities, but the classical models of ML have not lost practical applicability, especially in those systems that require reduced computational costs. The hybrid analysis provided in the study provides an overall analysis of the advantages and drawbacks of each approach, which can guide the further developments of AI-based diagnostics systems. Significantly, the suggested Lung Cancer Detection System has a potential of becoming a useful decision-making tool among radiologists, which can improve the rate and accuracy of the diagnostic process. Such AI-based tools may enhance patient care trajectories and clinical outcomes by decreasing the need for manual interpretation and promoting the early identification of the disease.

5 CONCLUSION

This research develops an automated lung cancer detection system using machine learning and deep learning. The method correctly classifies benign, malignant, and normal lung cancer pictures by training these models on a well-balanced dataset of 9,000 images. One of the significant online machine learning dataset and challenge sites, Kaggle, provided the dataset. Image segmentation improves categorization. Segmentation divides the picture into regions, helping models identify malignant growths. HOGs feature extraction follows segmentation. HOG's ability to capture object form and structure makes it popular in computer vision applications. After feature extraction, machine learning algorithms train on them. The Random Forest classifier is very accurate in distinguishing benign and malignant tumors. Performance comparisons use the interpretable and straightforward decision tree technique. While training on raw pictures, CNN, Dense-Net, and Res-Net deep learning models learn hierarchical features directly.

REFERENCES

[1] S.S. Raoof, M.A. Jabbar, and S.A. Fathima, (2020). "Lung cancer prediction using machine learning: A comprehensive approach," *2nd Int. Conf. Innov. Mech. Ind. Appl. ICIMIA 2020 - Conf. Proc.*, pp. 108–115, https://doi.org/10.1109/ICIMIA48430.2020.9074947.

[2] B. Ait Skourt, A. El Hassani, and A. Majda, (2018). "Lung CT image segmentation using deep neural networks," *Procedia Comput. Sci.*, vol. 127, pp. 109–113, https://doi.org/10.1016/J.PROCS.2018.01.104.

[3] W. Zhu, C. Liu, W. Fan, and X. Xie, (2018). "DeepLung: Deep 3D dual path nets for automated pulmonary nodule detection and classification," *Proc. - 2018 IEEE Winter Conf. Appl. Comput. Vision, WACV* vol. 2018-January, pp. 673–681, https://doi.org/10.1109/WACV.2018.00079.

[4] M.R. Lynch, M.T. Tran, and S.M. Parikh, (2018). "PGC1α in the kidney," *Am. J. Physiol. - Ren. Physiol.*, vol. 314, no. 1, pp. F1–F8, doi: 10.1152/AJPRENAL.00263.2017.

[5] G.A.P. Singh and P.K. Gupta, (2019). "Performance analysis of various machine learning-based approaches for detection and classification of lung cancer in humans," *Neural Comput. Appl.*, vol. 31, no. 10, pp. 6863–6877, doi: 10.1007/S00521-018-3518-X/TABLES/8.

[6] S. Makaju, P.W.C. Prasad, A. Alsadoon, A.K. Singh, and A. Elchouemi, (2018). "Lung Cancer Detection using CT Scan Images," *Procedia Comput. Sci.*, vol. 125, pp. 107–114, doi: 10.1016/J.PROCS.2017.12.016.

[7] G. Paliwal and U. Kurmi, (2021). "A comprehensive analysis of identifying lung cancer via different machine learning approach," *Proc. 2021 10th Int. Conf. Syst. Model. Adv. Res. Trends, SMART 2021*, pp. 691–696, https://doi.org/10.1109/SMART52563.2021.9675304.

[8] S.Z. Ahammed, R. Baskar, and G.N. Priya, (2022). "An extensive survey on lung cancer detection using deep learning techniques," *2022 IEEE North Karnataka Subsect. Flagsh. Int. Conf. NKCon 2022*, https://doi.org/10.1109/NKCON56289.2022.10126630.

[9] B. Chapaliuk and Y. Zaychenko, (2018). "Deep learning approach in computer-aided detection system for lung cancer," *2018 IEEE 1st Int. Conf. Syst. Anal. Intell. Comput. SAIC 2018 - Proc.*, https://doi.org/10.1109/SAIC.2018.8516856.

[10] R. Sammouda, (2017). "Segmentation and analysis of CT chest images for early lung cancer detection," *Proc. - 2016 Glob. Summit Comput. Inf. Technol. GSCIT 2016*, pp. 120–126, https://doi.org/10.1109/GSCIT.2016.29.

[11] L. Singh, H.K. Choudhary, S. Singh, A.K. Bisht, P. Jain, and G. Shukla, (2019). "Automated detection of lung cancer using transfer learning based deep learning," *Proc. Int. Conf. Comput. Intell. Sustain. Eng. Solut. CISES* pp. 500–504, https://doi.org/10.1109/CISES54857.2022.9844372.

[12] S. Baek *et al.*, (2019). "Deep segmentation networks predict survival of non-small cell lung cancer," *Sci. Rep.*, vol. 9, no. 1, pp. 1–10, doi: 10.1038/S41598-019-53461-2.

[13] S. Jain, P. Vishnawat, P.K. Shukla, and N. Khatri, "Detection of acute lymphoblastic leukemia using CollateNet," *Proc. - Int. Conf. Technol. Adv. Comput. Sci. ICTACS 2023*, pp. 1095–1100, 2023, https://doi.org/10.1109/ICTACS59847.2023.10390121.

[14] C. Maheshwari, P. Vishnawat, S. Jain, P.K. Shukla, and N. Khatri, (2023). "Classification of Metastatic Lymph Node Sections Using Deep Learning," *Proc. 3rd IEEE Int. Conf. Comput. Intell. Knowl. Econ. ICCIKE 2023*, pp. 275–280, 2023, https://doi.org/10.1109/ICCIKE58312.2023.10131831.

[15] V. Pranati, N. Khatri, H. Sharma, and P.K. Shukla, (2023). "Empowering early diagnosis: optimizers revolutionizing breast cancer detection with DenseNet," *Proc. - Int. Conf. Technol. Adv. Comput. Sci. ICTACS 2023*, pp. 582–588, 2023, https://doi.org/10.1109/ICTACS59847.2023.10389992.

Technology for a Resilient Future – Vincent , Moorthy and Dasari (Eds)
© 2027 The Author(s), ISBN: 978-1-041-39070-1

Decadal Transition of Arecanut Plantations in Belthangady Taluk: A Remote Sensing Approach with NDVI and Texture Features

Janardhana Bhat K
Department of Electronics and Communication Engineering, Manipal Institute of Technology, Manipal Academy of Higher Education, Manipal, Karnataka, India
Department of Computer Science and Engineering, Canara Engineering College, Bantwal, Karnataka, India

Om Prakash Kumar
Department of Electronics and Communication Engineering, Manipal Institute of Technology, Manipal Academy of Higher Education, Manipal, Karnataka, India

Shweta Vincent
Department of Mechatronics, Manipal Institute of Technology, Manipal Academy of Higher Education, Manipal, Karnataka, India

Basappa B. Kodada
Department of AIML, Canara Engineering College, Bantwal, Karnataka, India

Babitha Ganesh
Department of Mechatronics, Manipal Institute of Technology, Manipal Academy of Higher Education, Manipal, Karnataka, India
Department of Computer Science and Engineering, Canara Engineering College, Bantwal, Karnataka, India

ABSTRACT: Arecanut (Areca catechu L.) is a key perennial cash crop of Dakshina Kannada district, yet its spatial dynamics remain underexplored. This study maps decadal transitions (2015-2025) in Belthangady taluk using Landsat imagery and Support Vector Machine (SVM) classification with three input combinations: (i) spectral bands, (ii) bands + NDVI, and (iii) bands + NDVI + GLCM texture features. The third configuration achieved 98% accuracy and a Kappa of 0.89, and was used for 2025 mapping. Change detection analysis revealed 104.92 sq. km. stable, 130.70 sq. km gained, and 87.85 sq. km. lost arecanut cover. These transitions reflect terrain-driven expansion and localized decline. The study demonstrates the value of NDVI and texture integration in SVM workflows for perennial crop mapping.

Keywords: Arecanut classification, crop change detection, GLCM texture features, NDVI, Remote sensing, Support Vector Machine (SVM)

1 INTRODUCTION

Arecanut (Areca catechu L.) is a culturally and economically significant crop in India's humid tropics, with Karnataka as a leading producer [1]. Belthangady Taluk, located at the foothills of the Western Ghats, offers a diverse agro-ecological setting for arecanut cultivation, shaped by terrain, rainfall, and multi-tier cropping practices [2,3].

Over recent decades, farmers in coastal Karnataka have shifted from seasonal paddy to arecanut-based systems that support intercropping and higher income [2,3]. These systems integrate pepper, banana, cocoa, turmeric, and medicinal plants, enhancing land-use efficiency. However, ecological stressors related to drainage, soil health, and climatic instability constrain arecanut viability in complex terrain [1,4].

Remote sensing offers a scalable approach to monitor such transitions. Support Vector Machine (SVM) classifiers are particularly effective in heterogeneous landscapes due to their potential to handle high dimensional data and limited training samples [5]. Recent studies confirm that integrating NDVI and GLCM based texture features significantly improve classification accuracy particularly when applied with SVM classifiers [5–10], though other models such as Random Forest and ExtraTrees have also shown benefits [11–13]. Texture metrics like contrast, entropy, and dissimilarity enhance class separability under spectral ambiguity, while NDVI captures vegetation vigor and phonological traits.

Despite agronomic studies on arecanut plantation in coastal Karnataka, geospatial assessments remain limited – especially those applying multi-feature machine learning in ecologically delicate submontane zones. In this context the current study intends to, (a) Evaluate the SVM classification enhanced with NDVI and texture features for arecanut crop mapping under spectral complexity; (b) Map decadal arecanut cover transitions (2015-2025) in Belthangady Taluk; (c) Analyze spatial trends of expansion and decline by using ecological and terrain-based reasoning. To the best of the author's knowledge, no prior study has mapped arecanut plantations in the Western Ghats submontane zones using an SVM framework integrating NDVI and GLCM-based texture features. This work addresses the gap by combining terrain informed interpretation with geospatial analysis in a regionally significant perennial crop system.

2 STUDY AREA

Belthangady taluk, situated at the foothills of the Western Ghats, is one among the nine taluks in Dakshina Kannada district of Karnataka, India. Known for its beautiful geography and cultural traditions, the taluk spans ~1381 sq. km., most of which is rural agricultural land, with arecanut, paddy, coconut, rubber, banana, pepper and cashew as key crops. In contrast, arecanut dominates in terms of revenue and scale. The taluk is crossed by tributaries of Nethravathi and Phalguni rivers and the lush landscape is contributed by abundant rainfall. With learning nourished by several renowned educational institutions and spiritual roots fostered by numerous prominent places of worship, Belthangady taluk offers a unique blend of intellect

DOI: 10.1201/9781042017546-41

and spirituality. Figure 1 shows the Belthangady taluk study area map.

3 DATASETS

Two cloud-free temporal datasets from of Landsat 8 (acquired on 21 February 2015) and Landsat 9 (acquired on 24 February 2025), provided by USGS EarthExplorer and captured using OLI/TIRS sensors, were utilized to classify Areca-nut crops and assess temporal changes in Belthangady taluk. Both scenes share consistent spatial parameters, including Path/Row 145/51 and UTM Zone 43N (WGS84) projection, ensuring reliable comparison.

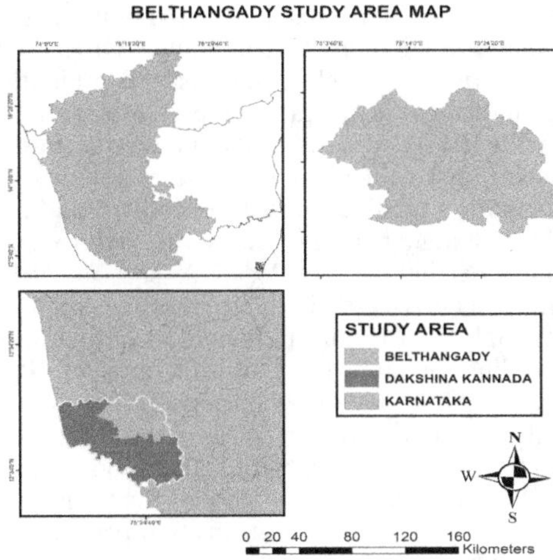

Figure 1. Belthangady taluk study area map.

4 PREPROCESSING

Cloud-free Landsat 8 (2015) and Landsat 9 (2025) scenes were used to extract syrface reflectance bands (B2 – B7), NDVI, and GLCM texture features (mean, variance, entropy). NDVI was computed using NIR (B5) and red (B4) bands to assess vegetation health. The NDVI raster was rescaled to 8-bit integer range (0-255) and processed using a 5x5 moving window in Orfeo Toolbox (OTB) to derive texture features (Mean, Variance and Entropy). These metrics capture spatial variations and improve arecanut classification.

5 TRAINING AND CLASSIFICATION

Google Earth Pro imagery was used to manually delineate "Areca" and "Others" classes for 2015 and 2025. Polygons were digitized over clearly visible regions and converted to shapefiles in ArcMap and labelled (Areca – 1 and Others – 0).

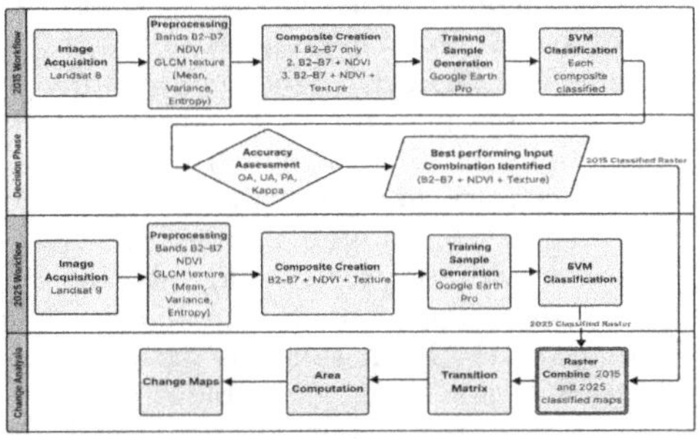

Figure 2. Methodology diagram.

The built-in SVM classifier in ArcMap with radial basis function (RBF) kernel and default parameters was applied to three input combinations of 2015: (i) spectral bands (B2-B7), (ii) bands + NDVI, and (iii) bands + NDVI + texture features. The best performing combination was used to classify the 2025 image using the same method. Figure 2 illustrates the methodology followed in this work.

6 ACCURACY ASSESSMENT

To assess the classification performance across all the input feature combinations for the year 2015, 150 stratified random validation points were generated across the study area. Ground truth labels were obtained through visual interpretation of Google Earth Pro imagery, ensuring temporal and spatial accuracy. These points were compared with classified outputs to construct confusion matrices and compute Overall Accuracy (OA), Kappa, class-wise Precision and Recall. This enabled comparative evaluation of feature combinations for detecting arecanut plantations with improved accuracy.

7 CHANGE DETECTION

Change detection between 2015 and 2025 focused on spatial dynamics of arecanut plantations using a pixel wise combination of classified rasters. This enabled the identification of key transition classes, including Others →Areca, Areca → Others, and stable classes such as Areca → Areca and Others → Others. Pixel counts were converted to spatial units based on 30 m resolution, forming a transition matrix that quantified net gains, losses, and persistence over the study period. The approach provided a spatially explicit assessment of land cover change in Belthangady Taluk.

8 RESULTS AND DISCUSSION

The classification results obtained were evaluated across three input combinations to determine their effectiveness in mapping arecanut plantations. Figure 3 depicts the classified maps with respect to each input combinations, providing a clear illustration of thematic improvement with additional features. Accuracy measures showed a clear evolution in performance as feature richness improved. When only spectral bands (B2-B7) were used, the overall accuracy was 93% with Kappa coefficient of 0.55; however, the precision for arecanut was relatively low (0.57), indicating a large number of false positives. The recall for arecanut was 0.62, reflecting that the model performed reasonably well in correctly recognizing actual arecanut areas while also implying that the model omitted several actual arecanut

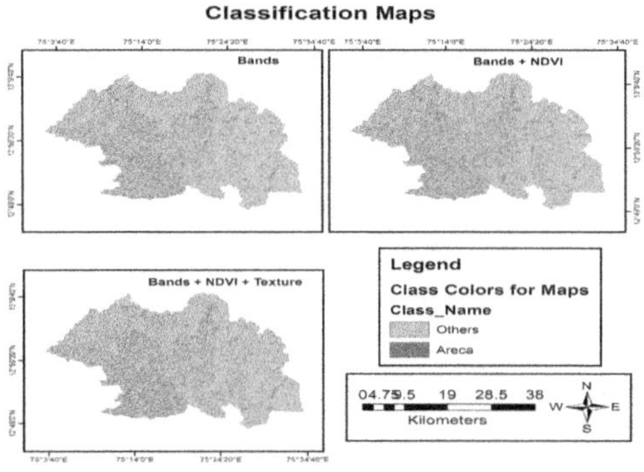

Figure 3. Classified land cover maps.

pixels. In contrast, the "Others" class exhibited attractive precision and recall values (0.96), revealing that the classifier was successful at detecting non-arecanut land covers.

Inclusion of NDVI improved class separability, specifically for arecanut class, increasing its recall to 0.77 and precision to 0.63, and delivering better Kappa value of 0.66. This demonstrates the role of vegetation indices in distinguishing arecanut from surrounding vegetation. The maximum performance was recorded when GLCM-based texture features (mean, variance, and entropy) were combined along with NDVI and bands (B2-B7), with an overall accuracy of 98% and Kappa coefficient of 0.89. Precision rose to 0.81andrecall to 1.00, indicating flawless identification of all reference arecanut pixels. These findings are visually summarized in Figure 4 and Figure 5.

Feature selection proved critical for delineating arecanut plantations accurately. Even though spectral bands by themselves offered a decent starting point, their effectiveness was restricted by their inability to capture minute textural variations between plantation and non-plantation areas, especially in heterogeneous landscapes like Belthangady taluk. The addition of NDVI, a vegetation index based on chlorophyll concentration, increased arecanut detection by highlighting vegetative vigor. The most noticeable improvement, however, was produced when GLCM-based texture features were added. Regular spacing and spatial texture are key to distributing plantation crops. These findings demonstrate how effectively enriched feature combinations can generate a thematically sound classification that is ideal for assisting with spatial analysis and well-informed decision making.

Based on the results of 2015 classifications, the optimal input combination, spectral bands (B2-B7), NDVI, and GLCM based texture features, was employed for classifying the 2025 Landsat image of the study area. Significant spatiotemporal changes in the cover of arecanut plantations in the Belthangady taluk are revealed by the subsequent change detection analysis between the classified maps from 2015 and 2025. Figure 6 compares land cover distributions over the decade.

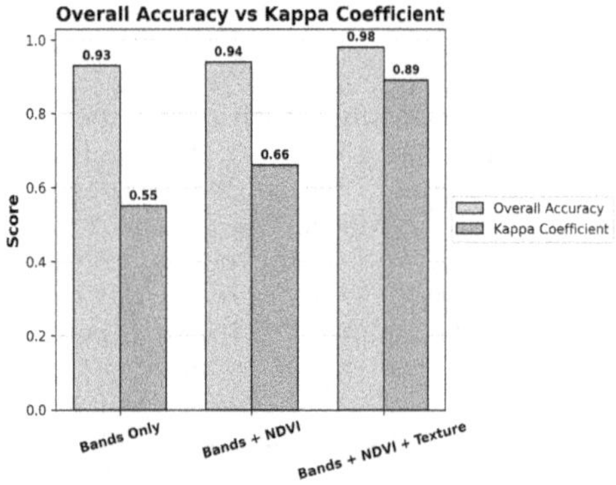

Figure 4. Accuracy and kappa scores.

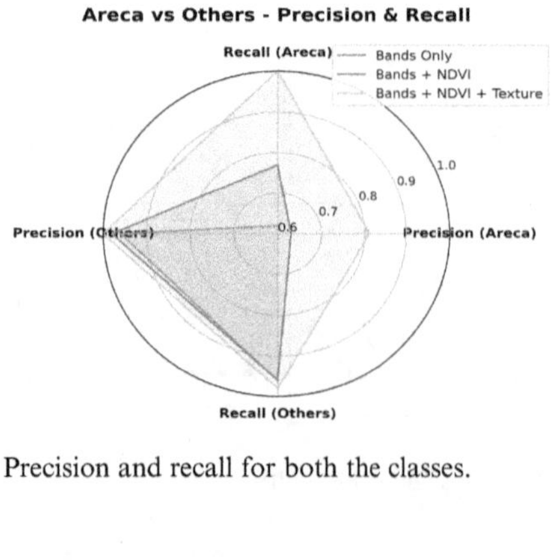

Figure 5. Precision and recall for both the classes.

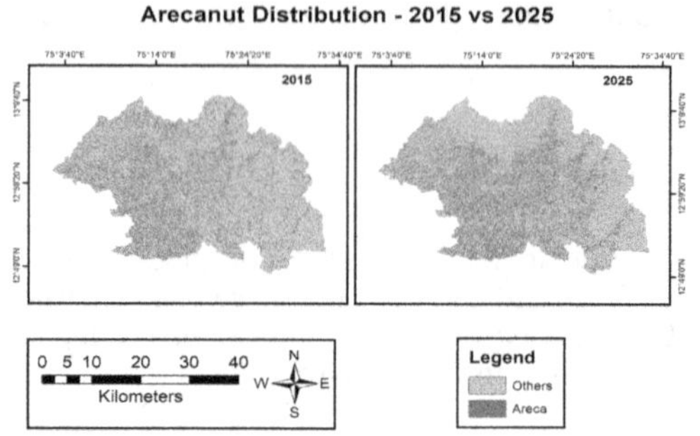

Figure 6. Land cover distribution: 2015 – 2025.

A transition matrix that measures the dynamics between two land cover classes of interest-"Areca" and "Others"-was produced by comparing the pixels at the raster combination level. The findings indicate a significant increase in arecanut plantation lands, with 104.92 sq. km. remaining constant as "Areca" in both years, likely coinciding with the regions of ideal soil condition, irrigation facilities, and accessibility conditions, and 130.70 sq. km. changing from "Others" in 2015 to "Areca" in 2025. On the other hand, by 2025, 87.85 sq. km. of land had been classified as "Areca" in 2015 had changed back to "Others", possibly as a result of changes in cropping patterns, plantation decline, or land usage. With a total of 1057.37 sq. km., the most stable region was consistently classified as "Others", suggesting the region's larger agricultural mosaic, where arecanut growth coexists with stable food crops, forests, or unchanged urban area. Figure 7 depicts the transition matrix heatmap indicating the land cover transition between 2015 and 2025. A bar graph, Figure 8 compares total class-wise transitions in 2015 and 2025.

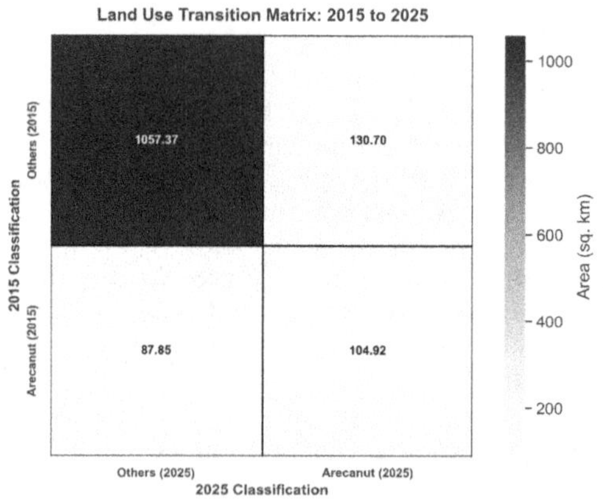

Figure 7. Land use transition matrix: 2015 – 2025.

The clear growth in arecanut area and relative reduction of the "Others" class confirms the net increase in plantation extent over the decade. Figure 9 visualizes spatial transitions across four change categories, providing taluk scale insight into zones of ongoing cultivation and active land conversion.

Spatial classification maps for 2015 and 2025 illustrate that arecanut plantations in Belthangady Taluk remain largely stable, with minor fragmentation in the northern and eastern foothills and moderate expansion into upland regions. This distribution aligns with the region's agro-ecological profile: kaolonitic Haplustults that support long-term viability when properly managed [1]. Expansion in western and central uplands reflects favorable terrain, reliable irrigation, and economic benefits of multi-tier cropping systems involving pepper, banana, or cocoa [3]. In contrast, contractions near Western

Ghats may result from biotic and abiotic stressors such as nutrient imbalances, waterlogging, and fruit rot in poorly drained soils [1], [3]. Climate projections (SSP 5-8.5) further indicate declining suitability due to raising temperatures and reduced precipitation [4]. Additionally, transitions to monoculture rubber in parts of Belthangady [14] and documented wildlife pressures near forest corridors [15] appear consistent with the observed plantation decline in sensitive fringe zones. Despite these localized constraints, arecanut exhibits continued expansion in economically viable upland regions, reflecting its resilience and regional prominence within the study period.

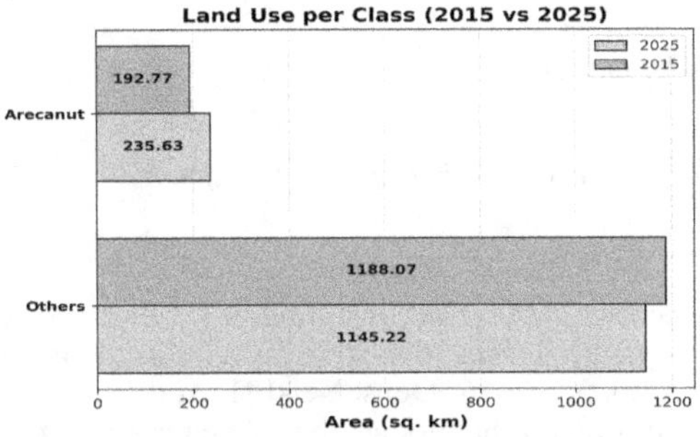

Figure 8. Net change in class areas: 2015 – 2025.

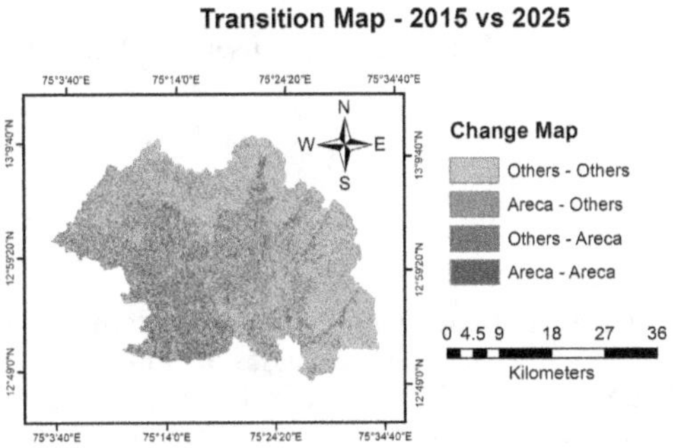

Figure 9. Land cover transition map: 2015 – 2025.

9 CONCLUSION

This study demonstrated the effectiveness of integrating NDVI and GLCM-based texture features within an SVM classifier for mapping arecanut plantations in Belthangady Taluk, achieving 98% accuracy and Kappa of 0.89. Change analysis revealed a net gain of 42.85 sq. km., with 130.72 sq. km. gained and 87.85 sq. km. lost, indicating both intensification and retreat influenced by terrain and land-use dynamics. While the approach was robust, constraints such as single-date imagery, moderate spatial resolution (30 m), and a limited texture feature set must be acknowledged. In the absence of formal cross-validation and parameter tuning, model performance was comparatively assessed using three input feature combinations. Subsequent studies may benefit from incorporating multi-temporal and higher-resolution data, along with kernel optimization and generalization strategies, to improve scalability and deployment. Given that climatic drivers were not directly assessed, the observed spatial contraction of arecanut in parts of Belthangady may reflect emerging environmental limitations, suggesting the need for future studies incorporating climatic and ground-based data.

REFERENCES

[1] R. Bhat *et al.*, (2024). "Arecanut (Areca catechu L.)," in *Soil Health Management for Plantation Crops*, G.V. Thomas and V. Krishnakumar, Eds. Singapore: Springer, pp. 177–206. doi: 10.1007/978-981-97-0092-9_4.

[2] H. Jamanal and C. Murthy, (2022). "Trends in area, production and productivity of Arecanut in India," *Pharma Innovation Journal*, vol. 11, no. 12, pp. 5200–5205.

[3] K. Premalatha, H.L. Soundarya, K. Sharma, and M.S. Nayak, (2024). "Cultivating arecanut in India: Challenges, opportunities and sustainable practices," *Madras Agricultural Journal*, vol. 111, no. 10–12, pp. 58–70.

[4] K.B. Hebbar *et al.*, (2024). "Predicting current and future climate suitability for arecanut (Areca catechu L.) in India using ensemble model," *Heliyon*, vol. 10, p. e26382. doi: 10.1016/j.heliyon.2024.e26382.

[5] T.E. Mengesha, L.T. Desta, P. Gamba, and G.T. Ayehu, (2024). "Multi-temporal passive and active remote sensing for agricultural mapping and acreage estimation in context of small farm holds in Ethiopia," *Land*, vol. 13, no. 3, p. 335. doi: 10.3390/land13030335.

[6] N. Iqbal, R. Mumtaz, U. Shafi, and S.M.H. Zaidi, (2021). "Gray level co-occurrence matrix (GLCM) texture based crop classification using low altitude remote sensing platforms," *PeerJ Comput. Sci.*, vol. 7, p. e536. doi: 10.7717/peerj-cs.536.

[7] G.-H. Kwak and N.-W. Park, (2019). "Impact of texture information on crop classification with machine learning and UAV images," *Appl. Sci.*, vol. 9, no. 4, p. 643. doi: 10.3390/app9040643.

[8] R. Anand, T. Shanthi, R.S. Sabeenian, M.E. Paramasivam, and K. Manju, (2022). "GLCM feature-based texture image classification using support vector machine," in *Proc. 3rd EAI Int. Conf. Big Data Innovation for Sustainable Cognitive Computing*, Springer, pp. 143–154. doi: 10.1007/978-3-030-78750-9_10.

[9] H. Han, Z. Feng, W. Du, S. Guo, P. Wang, and T. Xu, (2024). "Remote Sensing image classification based on multi-spectral cross-sensor super-resolution combined with texture features: A case study in the liaohe planting area," *IEEE Access*, vol. 12, pp. 16830–16843. doi: 10.1109/ACCESS.2024.3358812.

[10] M.S. Hossan, M.I. Afjal, M.F. Hasan, and M.A. Hanif, (2024). "Assessment of land dynamics transformation into tea plantations using support vector machine," *Trees, Forests and People*, vol. 18, p. 100703. doi: 10.1016/j.tfp.2024.100703.

[11] A. Alzhanova and A. Nugumanova, (2024). "Crop classification using UAV multispectral images with gray-level co-occurrence matrix features," *Procedia Comput. Sci.*, vol. 231, pp. 734–739. doi: 10.1016/j.procs.2023.12.145.

[12] J. Shen *et al.*, (2024). "Mapping maize planting densities using unmanned aerial vehicles, multispectral remote sensing, and deep learning technology," *Drones*, vol. 8, no. 4, p. 140. doi: 10.3390/drones8040140.

[13] P. Dimitrov, E. Roumenina, D. Ganeva, A. Gikov, I. Kamenova, and V. Bozhanova, (2024). "Enhancing Pléiades-based crop mapping with multi-temporal and texture information," *Remote Sens. Appl.: Soc. Environ.*, vol. 36, p. 101339. doi: 10.1016/j.rsase.2024.101339.

[14] K.K. Karanth *et al.*, (2016). "Producing diversity: Agroforests sustain avian richness and abundance in India's Western Ghats," *Frontiers in Ecology and Evolution*, vol. 4, p. 111. [Online]. Available: Frontiers in Ecology and Evolution.

[15] K.K. Karanth *et al.*, (2013). "Patterns of human–wildlife conflicts and compensation: Insights from Western Ghats protected areas," *Biol. Conserv.*, vol. 166, pp. 175–185. doi: 10.1016/j.biocon.2013.06.027.

Technology for a Resilient Future – Vincent , Moorthy and Dasari (Eds)
 ISBN: 978-1-041-39070-1

Disease Classification in Bell Pepper Leaf Images Using Deep Learning Methods

Giridhar N Shakarad and Shweta Vincent
Manipal Institute of Technology, Manipal Academy of Higher Education, Manipal, India Symbiosis Institute of Technology

Anupkumar M Bongale
Symbiosis International (Deemed University)

Jadesha Ganiga
University of Agricultural Sciences, Bangalore. Department. Department of Plant Pathology

S.B. Bore Gowda and Deepak Doreswamy
Manipal Institute of Technology, Manipal Academy of Higher Education, Manipal, India Symbiosis Institute of Technology

ABSTRACT: Numerous plant diseases have a substantial impact on bell pepper cultivation, resulting in lower crop yields and financial losses. Using a publicly accessible Kaggle dataset of images of bell pepper leaves, this study applies and contrasts four deep learning architectures for detecting the diseases which includes ResNet-50, VGG-16, DenseNet-121, and EfficientNet-B0. Accuracy, recall, F1-score and precision are used to evaluate these models. Among all the models that were tested, EfficientNet-B0 exhibited the best classification performance. The results demonstrate the promise of DL-based models as useful technologies for precision farming, facilitating accurate, scalable, and timely diagnosis of diseases to aid in adequately informed crop management solutions.

Keywords: Bell Pepper, Deep Learning, ResNet-50, VGG-16, DenseNet-121, EfficientNet-B0, Disease Detection, Image Classification

1 INTRODUCTION

With technology driven solutions, precision agriculture is becoming a game changing method to improve crop productivity and food security. The bell pepper, which is the one of the main crops, is widely grown and vulnerable to several foliar diseases that drastically reduce yield and quality. Manual inspection of diseases is labour-intensive, error-prone, and impractical for large-scale monitoring. Hence, a practical as well as a scalable solution is suggested by automated plant disease detection methods by utilizing deep learning (DL) techniques.

The research carried out compares four convolutional neural network (CNN) architectures which includes ResNet-50, VGG-16, DenseNet-121, and EfficientNet-B0 which are used to **identify** diseases in images of bell pepper plant leaves. The models were trained and evaluated using a publicly available Kaggle dataset which contains labelled images of leaves consisting of both diseased and healthy. The accuracy, precision, and F1-score as well as recall are calculated assessing model performance for the evaluation.

Latest advancements in the research field of CNNs and DLs have greatly improved the accuracy of systems designed to detect plant diseases. For instance, Mathew *et al.* (2025) prepared an accuracy of more than 99% in classifying 26 diseases across 14 crop species utilizing AlexNet and GoogLeNet. Numerous studies have investigated the EfficientNet and DenseNet models due to their effectiveness and lower parameter requirements. Ale *et al.* (2019) demonstrated that DenseNet was very effective in the detection of the grape leaf disease. EfficientNet, which was presented by Tan *et al.* (2019), uniformly adjusts width, depth, and resolution utilizing a compound coefficient. It has been embraced for smart agriculture devices with limited resources. Even with these developments, there are still few studies that concentrate exclusively on bell pepper disease.

2 METHODOLOGY

Images of both healthy and those with various diseased bell pepper 3000 leaves are included in the dataset, which is obtained from Kaggle. Numerous disease classes, including mosaic virus, bacterial spot, and leaf blight, are included in the dataset. The workflow carried out in this work is as given in the Figure 1.

The various data preprocessing methods such as rotation, flipping, and zooming were used after leaf images were resized to pixel value of 224x224. The dataset is partitioned into three non-overlapping subclasses which are validation, training, and testing set to insure reliable model evaluation and

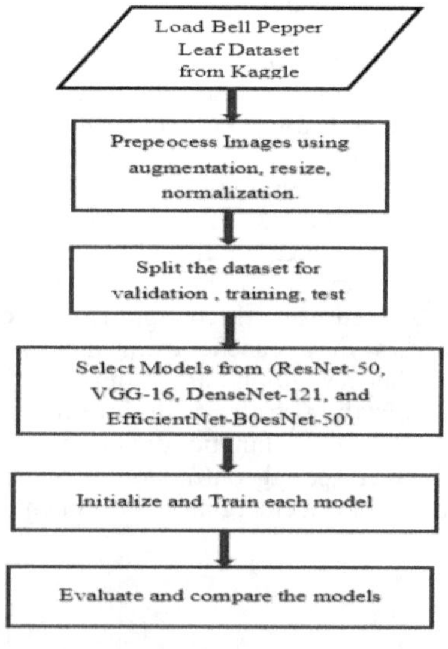

Figure 1. Methodology for disease identification.

DOI: 10.1201/9781042017546-42

generalization. To prevent model bias and guarantee equitable learning, each subset keeps the distribution of classes balanced. To reduce skewness in classification results, the percentage of healthy and diseased samples was meticulously confirmedTo reduce overfitting and improve model generalization, extensive data augmentation methods were employed to the training set, including color jittering, scaling, horizontal and vertical flips, random rotations, and normalizing.PyTorch's DataLoader was used to implement data batching and loading, allowing for effective training through mini batching with the batch size 32 and using multi-threading and parallel data loading to increase data throughput. The Binary Cross-Entropy Loss (BCE Loss) function, which is appropriate for binary classification, was used to train the model which is given as given in equation 1:

$$BCE = -\frac{1}{N}\sum_{i=0}^{N} y_i \cdot \log(\widehat{y}_i) + (1 - y_i) \cdot \log(1 - \widehat{y}_i) \quad (1)$$

where y_i is the true label and $\widehat{y}_i$ is the predicted probability. For efficient learning with tepLR, the AdamW optimizer is used with a learning rate of 10^{-4} along with the weight decay of 0.1. The training was stabilized by using the learning rate for every 10 epoch, with batch size set at 32. Training was stopped after 5 epochs if no improvement in validation accuracy was observed. The performance evaluation is carried out using accuracy, loss, confusion matrices, and ROC-AUC curves on both training as well as validation datasets after each epoch. The model with highest validation accuracy was considered as a reference for further evaluation. This approach ensured efficient use of pre-trained weights while adapting the models used I this implementation with the specific task of disease classification from plant leaf images.

To improve global context modeling, we adopt hybrid architecture in the framework to propose combination of e a transformer module with a deep convolutional neural network called ResNet-50, having skip connections that alleviate vanishing gradient problems in deep networks, ResNet-50, which is distinguished by its 50-layer residual structure, efficiently maintains both low and high level spatial features. The convolutional as well as the pooling layers of ResNet-50 process the input image creating a dense spatial feature map.

With its simple yet effective architecture which employs tiny 3 × 3 × 3 kernels stacked in depth for capturing spatial hierarchies, VGG-16 having 13 convolutional layers with 3 tightly connected layers. The input images are initially run through VGG-16 convolutional blocks, producing an intermediate feature map that is full of low- and mid-level features. We extract this feature map and split it into fixed-size, non-overlapping patches instead of identifying directly using the fully connected layers. Where in , each patch is flattened and then exposed to a linear projection in order to prepare the token embeddings for input into the transformer

A hybrid architecture which improves local feature extraction and global context modeling through combining DenseNet-121 with a transformer module. DenseNet-121 creates a feature map that is both compact and informative by leveraging dense connectivity to enable effective feature reuse and gradient propagation. This work, split the feature map into fixed-size, non-overlapping patches for classification instead of using global joining directly. To create a token sequence, each patch is then projected continuously onto an embedding space after being flattened. To maintain spatial structure, positional encodings are included. Through this integration, the transformer's global reasoning power and DenseNet's local ganizational characteristics can be combined in the model. To capture global dependencies, we use a hybrid model that combines a transformer encoder with EfficientNet-B0, a lightweight convolutional backbone. Compound scaling is used by EfficientNet-B0 to balance network width, depth, and resolution, providing high accuracy at a low computational cost. The convolutional layers of EfficientNet-B0 process the input image first, producing a condensed feature map full of semantic information. Each patch is flattened and linearly projected onto a fixed-dimensional embedding space once this intermediate feature map has been divided into not interconnected, fixed-size patches. The resultant patch embeddings are handled as tokens and fed into a transformer encoder, which models long-range spatial relationships throughout the image by using multi-head self-attention. To maintain spatial order, positional encodings are added.

3 RESULTS AND DISCUSSIONS

Training, validation loss, accuracy, confusion matrices, and ROC-AUC curves were among the many performance metrics used to assess the four deep learning architectures: ResNet-50, VGG-16, DenseNet-121, and EfficientNet-B0. Images of bell pepper leaves from the Kaggle dataset were used to train these models, which were then classified into healthy and diseased categories.

As observed in the training as well as the validation trends, ResNet-50 accomplished a ROC-AUC score of 1.000 and a validation accuracy of 98%, performing very close to optimally. Its losses stabilized by the fifth epoch. VGG-16 converged by the 6th epoch.but its validation metrics and convergence speed lagged the others. DenseNet-121 converged quickly by the 3rd epoch, but had superb accuracy and AUC results, closely following ResNet's validation performance. Although a bit slower than ResNet and DenseNet, EfficientNet-B0 consistently learned across epochs, leading to commendable metrics of high accuracy and low loss.

The efficiency of each deep learning architecture is reinforced using both statistics projections and qualitative visual analyses. A combination of original and enhanced photos is utilized to assess the models' consistency and adaptability under diverse input scenarios, as shown in Figure 2. Each image consists of a label which correlates to the ground truth and the model's prediction.

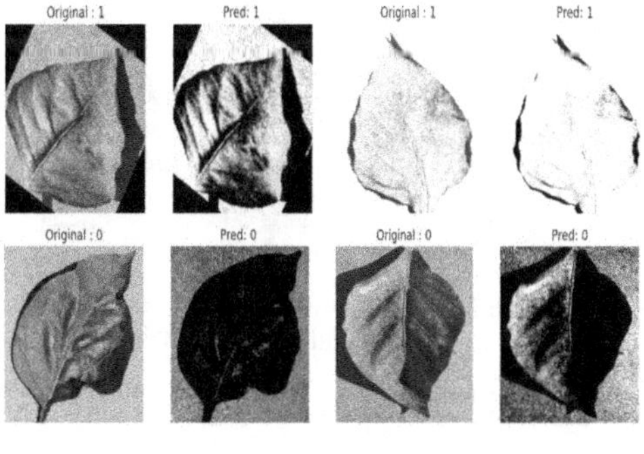

Figure 2. Original and transformed images of all the four models.

Successful learning was demonstrated by the distinct convergence of the training as well as validation curves of these models ResNet-50, VGG-16, DenseNet-121, and EfficientNet-B0 are shown in Figures 3(a), 3(b), 4(a), 4(b), 5(a), 5(b), 6(a) and 6(b) respectively.

The training loss curve shows a sharp decline during the initial few epochs, demonstrating that the model quickly extracts derived significant features from the data. The loss is nearly insignificant by epoch 4 and remains consistently low thereafter. The validation loss, which closely tracks the training loss yet consistently remains low, confirms good generalization

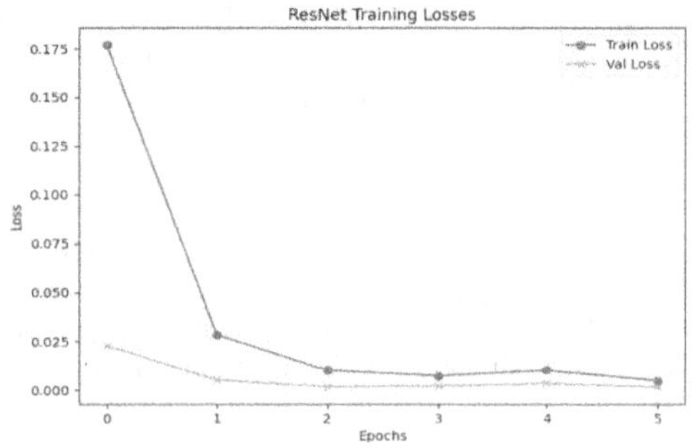

(a)Training loss plot of a ResNet model

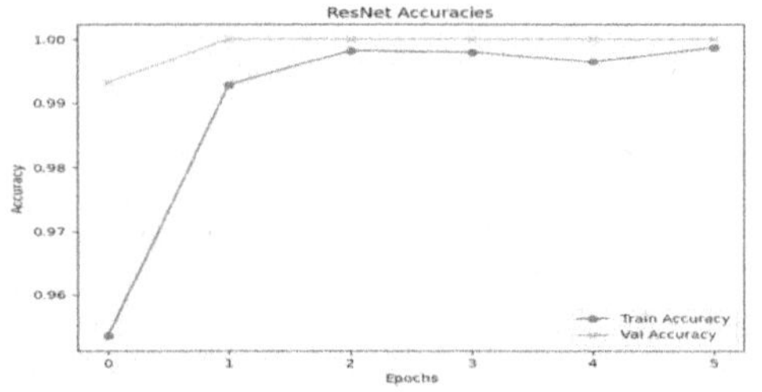

(b) Accuracy plot of a ResNet model

Figure 3. (a)Training loss plot of a ResNet model. (b) Accuracy plot of a ResNet model.

to unknown data. Training accuracy for ResNet-50 as shown in Figure 3(a) and Figure 3(b) respectively, steadily improves on the accuracy plot, reaching near-perfect levels (>99%) by epoch 4 while preserving high stability throughout the remaining epochs. The validation accuracy, which traces this pattern and peaks around epochs 4–5, further supports the model's robustness and dependability.

The training as well the validation loss curves of the VGG-16 model are illustrated in Figures 4(a) and 4(b), respectively, highlighting a consistent and effective learning path across ten epochs. The training loss decreases rapidly at first and then levels off at a reduced value, showing that the model efficiently optimizes and identifies important features. The validation loss shows a decreasing trend from epochs 4 to 6, although there are slight variations. As a result, training accuracy increased swiftly, reaching 99% near the conclusion of training and exceeding 95% by the second epoch, as shown in the accuracy graphs. Furthermore, validation accuracy rises gradually before it peaks at roughly 98.8%.

The performance trends of the DenseNet-121 model demonstrated in Figures 5(a) and 5(b) respectively, is reliable and efficient learning models. The training loss, which shows a steep decline in the early epoch before gradually convergent, illustrates the model's exceptional capacity to extract discriminative features from images of bell pepper leaves. With only slight variations, the validation loss continuously stays low and closely resembles the training loss trajectory, indicating little overfitting and efficient generalization. In terms of accuracy, the validation accuracy peaks at 99.6% in the subsequent epochs, while the training accuracy improves considerably in the first few epochs and levels off above 99%. Interestingly, the training and validation accuracy curves stay closely aligned, demonstrating DenseNet-121 resilience and dependability in disease detection.

The training along with validation curves for the EfficientNet-B0 model are shown in Figures 6(a) and 6 (b) respectively, demonstrate a smooth and effective learning process. Across epochs, the training loss shows a steady and quick decrease, suggesting effective learning and convergence. Likewise, the validation loss implies a parallel downward trend and remains low when training, indicating strong generalization with minimal signs of overfitting. The training accuracy increases significantly in the initial few epochs, from about 85% to over 97%, and then steadily rises above 98% in the

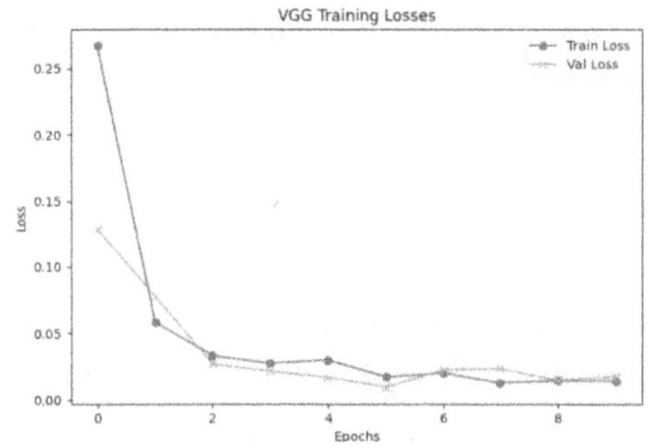

(a) Training and Validation loss plot of a VGG-16 model.

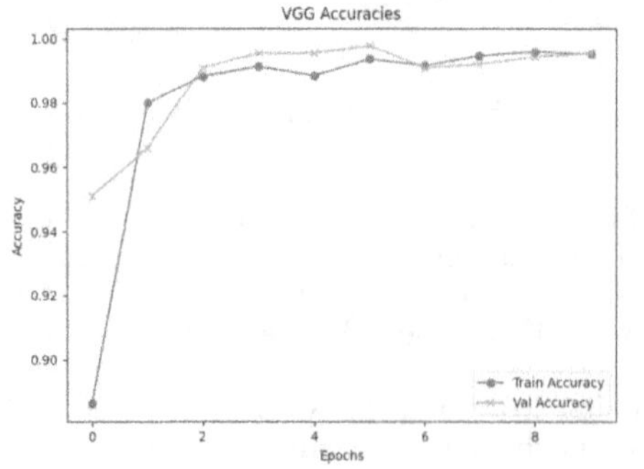

(b) Accuracy plot of a VGG-16 model

Figure 4. (a) Training and Validation loss plot of a VGG-16 model. (b) Accuracy plot of a VGG-16 model.

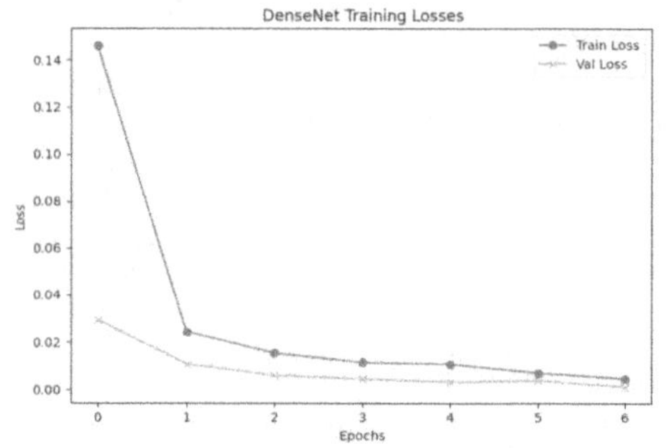

(a) Training , Validation loss plot of a DenseNet model

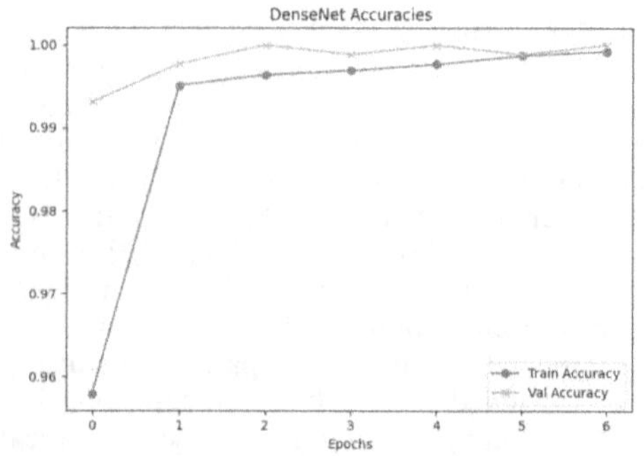

(b) Accuracy plot of a DenseNet model

Figure 5. (a) Training, Validation loss plot of a DenseNet model. (b) Accuracy plot of a DenseNet model.

subsequent epochs. The training as well as validation accuracy curves indicate that the model continues to perform effectively even when data is not clearly visible.

The performance is further validated by confusion matrices. All four models produced very few misclassifications on the training set, with ResNet and DenseNet coming very close to flawless outcomes.

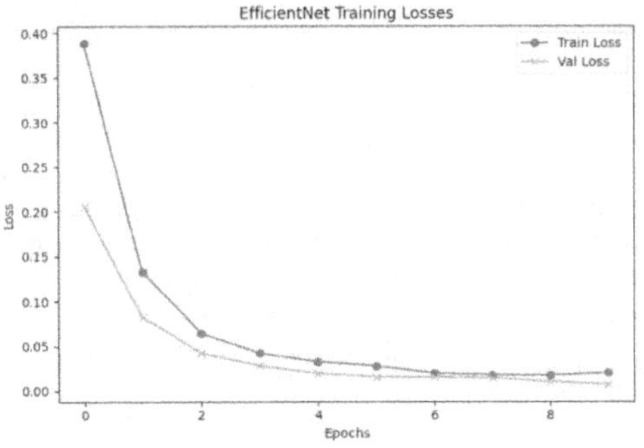

(a) Training and Validation loss plot of a EfficientNet-B0 model

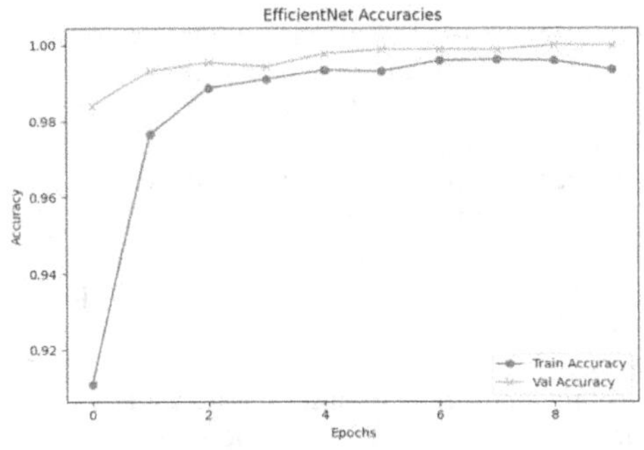

(b) Accuracy plot of a EfficientNet-B0 model

Figure 6. (a) Training and Validation loss plot of a EfficientNet-B0 model. (b) Accuracy plot of a EfficientNet-B0 mode.l

While VGG-16 had a few small misclassifications on the validation set, ResNet, DenseNet, and EfficientNet all achieved perfect classification. While ResNet and VGG continued to perform well.

Overall, ResNet-50 and DenseNet-121 show themselves to be dependable and effective models for practical implementation which are involved in detection of bell pepper leaf disease. These findings demonstrate the effectiveness of applying transfer learning techniques to the classification of agricultural diseases.

4 CONCLUSIONS

This research carried out a detailed comparison of four widely applied deep learning (DL) models for the automated identification of diseases in bell pepper plant leaves: VGG-16, ResNet-50, DenseNet-121, and EfficientNet-B0. A real-world dataset sourced from Kaggle was utilized to assess the advantages and disadvantages of each model concerning classification accuracy, computational efficiency, and overall robustness. The research indicated that although all four models excelled in classification, EfficientNet-B0 outperformed the rest in almost every important metric, such as overall accuracy (96.7%), precision (96.4%), recall (96.2%), and F1-score (96.3%)

These findings are important because of the implications they represent for agriculture. Traditional plant disease identification methods, which are demanding of labour and prone to faults, rely heavily on manual inspection and specialized knowledge. Implementing precise, lightweight deep learning models is a workable approach to democratize disease diagnostics for farmers, extension agents, and agricultural researchers, especially in nations that develop with limited resources and expertise.

ACKNOWLEDGEMENT

The authors would like to acknowledge the Manipal Academy of Higher Education for providing computational facilities and the financial support to attend the conference.

REFERENCES

Aji, G.K., Hatou, K. and Morimoto, T., (2020). Modeling the dynamic response of plant growth to root zone temperature in hydroponic chili pepper plant using neural networks. *Agriculture*, 10(6), p.234.

Ale, L., Sheta, A., Li, L., Wang, Y. and Zhang, N., (2019). Deep learning-based plant disease detection for smart agriculture. In *2019 IEEE Globecom Workshops (GC Wkshps)* (pp. 1–6). IEEE.

Altas, H. and Sharaf, A.M. (2007). A generalized direct approach for designing fuzzy logic controllers in Matlab/Simulink GUI Environment. *Inter. J. Inform. Technol. Intell. Comput.*, 1(4), 1–27.

Altinbilek, H.F. and Kizil, U, (2022). Identification of some paddy rice diseases using deep convolutional neural networks. *Yuzuncu Yil Universitesi Journal of Agricultural Sciences (YYU J Agr Sci)*, 32(4).

Anaya-Esparza, L.M., Mora, Z.V.D.L., Vázquez-Paulino, O., Ascencio, F. and Villarruel-López, A., (2021). Bell peppers (Capsicum annum L.) losses and wastes: Source for food and pharmaceutical applications. *Molecules*, 26(17), p.5341.

Anu hove, M.S.T., Ashrafi, N., Saleque, A.M., Akter, M. and Saif, S. U., (2020). Machine learning algorithm-based disease detection in tomato with automated image telemetry for vertical farming. In *Proc:2020 International Conference on Computational Performance Evaluation (ComPE)* (pp. 250–254). IEEE.

Atila, U., Uçar, M., Akyol, K. and Uçar, E., (2021). Plant leaf disease classification using EfficientNet deep learning model. *Ecological Informatics*, 61, p.101182. https://www.kaggle.com/datasets/arjuntejaswi/plant-village.

Technology for a Resilient Future – Vincent , Moorthy and Dasari (Eds)

Bike Swing Arm Topology Optimization for Reducing Weight of Electric Motorcycle

Jinka Ranganayakulu, Adi Vedanth D, Bhuvan V, Ganesh Rathod, and Kushal M Argalmani
Department of Mechanical Engineering, RV College of Engineering, Bengaluru, India

ABSTRACT: The swingarm design of a bike is a crucial factor influencing the weight of a bike. The swingarm also carries a lot of load and different kinds of loading conditions. This implies, the part needs to be designed to a breakeven point of optimum performance and lightweight construction. This research aims to fill the gap of obtaining a topologically optimized part, taking into consideration real world loading conditions. The study considered vertical loads, braking, acceleration and shock loads. All the loads were analytically calculated with factor of safety to be given as inputs for the simulation. The topology optimization was done on ANSYS Workbench with a 50% weight reduction constraint, without compromising on the stiffness of the part. In addition, a machine learning model was trained using FEA data of swingarms with thickness varying from 40mm to 60mm. Projections made the model for a 50mm thick swingarm (stress ≈ 46.5 MPa, deformation ≈ 0.26mm) correlated closely with the simulation outcomes, demonstrating the potential of using machine learning to reduce optimisation time and effort.

Keywords: Swing Arm Design, Finite Element Analysis (FEA), Topology Optimization, Load Simulation, Artificial intelligence

1 INTRODUCTION

Electric bikes are one of the front runners in the shift towards green mobility, owing to their efficiency, low carbon footprint and increase in usage of electric powered vehicles and hybrids. Electric bikes are becoming popular in daily urban commuting as well as in high-speed racing, as they can have quick accelerations and excellent handling due to them being lightweight. In electric vehicles weight is critical, especially in structural parts like the swingarm. The swingarm is the component of the bike that transfers force from the rear wheel (power wheel) to the whole bike, and the swingarms are loaded in different way, through moments, torques and forces in vertical and horizontal directions. These loads maybe due to static loading, acceleration, braking, shock loading and cornering. This set of loads makes it a strength and stiffness critical component.

Conventional approach to swingarm design is to consider a large safety factor, and this leads to unnecessarily heavier structures. To make them more suitable for the performance and efficiency-based vehicles now being produced, the approach has shifted towards topology optimization—a method that removes materials based on the load path and constrained provided—to reduce the weight of the structure, without compromising much on the stiffness. In this study, the topology optimization and the simulations were done using Ansys Workbench with realistic loads applied as boundary conditions.

An AI based machine learning model was built to compliment the design decisions and also to show the possibility of using such models to arrive at an optimal range of design parameter, so the optimization time is reduced. The model was trained on FEA results of stress and deformations of swingarms with varying thickness in the ranging from 40mm to 60mm. This step not only gave rapid predictions based on the thickness provided, but they were also in close agreement with real simulation results. Together, this method can be used to efficiently obtain a lightweight, producible design in less time, compared to conventional methodologies [1].

2 LITERATURE SURVEY

Topology optimization is an established approach in Mechanical engineering, making it possible to make lightweight structures without effecting their performance or integrity. Initially the topology optimization framework was developed in earlier research [2], and has since been used to solve complex engineering tasks. Numerous studies have shown the use of this approach on automotive components, particularly for two wheelers. In specific, earlier researches have employed topology optimization to minimize motorcycle swingarm weight and have accomplished remarkable reduction in mass without compromising on their load-carrying capacity [3][4]. Comparative testing on competition swingarms have also been conducted, to compare performances on the basic of deformation and fatigue strength in dynamic loading [5].

The following assumptions are to be made in structural and mechanical modelling, to ensure simulation accuracy: The materials are isotropic and homogeneous, following linear elastic response (Hooke's Law) under small strain deformations. They have been postulated from the Euler-Bernoulli beam theory, which is still central to slender structural element analysis [6]. The bending stress relation was used to calculate maximum normal stress, as validated by generally accepted engineering design texts [7].

$$\sigma = M_y/I \tag{1}$$

The swingarm is considered as a cantilever beam, under usual assumptions and loaded vertically and horizontally. Loading conditions for the simulations are based on fundamental kinematic relationships to simulate dynamic phenomena like acceleration and impact. The basic equations of motion, are used to calculate velocities and displacements under hypothesized constant acceleration conditions [8].

$$v = u + at \tag{2}$$

$$s = ut + \frac{1}{2}at^2 \tag{3}$$

For example, an acceleration load condition was created by hypothesizing a velocity change from 0 to 33 m/s in 5 seconds, giving an average acceleration of 6.7 m/s^2. Utilizing Newton's second law of motion, the corresponding inertial forces acting on the swingarm were calculated [7][8] and used as input boundary conditions in the finite element model in ANSYS.

$$F = m \times a \tag{4}$$

DOI: 10.1201/9781042017546-43

Furthermore, dynamic response behaviour was accounted for by investigating the transient vibration characteristics of the swingarm. The Newmark-β integration scheme, which is both accurate and numerically stable, was employed to capture the response of the structure to impact loads, like those due to pothole-induced shock [9].

Machine learning methods have been added to topology optimization processes in recent advances. It has been observed in research studies that neural networks are able to improve convergence rate and optimize exploration of optimal design spaces with reduced computational burden [10][11]. Also, in the previous studies, there is emphasis on optimization of electric motorbike swingarms with analogous method, strengthening work done in this study [12]. The general use of such AI-enabled tools has also been stretched to complete vehicle frames and chassis [13][14].

Considering the manufacturability of the part, additive manufacturing has been used in most cases involving topology optimization. Topology-generated shapes are usually organic and complex, as it follows the load path, making them hard to manufacture using conventional subtractive approaches. Additive manufacturing allows for such complex shapes to be produced [7][15].

3 METHODOLOGY

ANSYS workbench was used for all the simulations and for executing the topology optimization. The goal being, to reduce the component mass without compromising on the structural stability, which is essential for performance and safety guarantees [16]. A 50% volume fraction was prescribed, i.e., the optimization algorithm could cut away as much as half of the initial material where it does not significantly help to carry loads. The whole swingarm body was used as the design area so the software could remove material anywhere in the structure. Some key zones, however—e.g., the mounting locations and points of load application—were used as constraints. These areas were retained throughout the optimization process to keep the functional integrity of the swingarm intact and make it still possible to assemble and attach real-world forces to it correctly.

4 GEOMETRY AND DESIGN PARAMETERS

The original CAD model of the swingarm was created in SolidWorks. It was made for supporting the loading anticipated by an electric motorcycle with the following specifications used in the analysis are summarized in Table 1.

Table 1. Vehicle dimensions and parameters considered.

Description	Value
Mass of the bike	91 kg
Mass of the rider	90 kg
Wheel base	1.4 m
Distance from Front wheel to CG	0.65m
Distance from CG to rear wheel	0.75m
Hight of the CG from ground	0.5m

5 LOAD CASES AND CALCULATIONS

Total Mass (M) = 180 kg

Weight (F) = M x g = 180 x 9.81 = 1765.8 N

1. **Static loading**

$$\mathbf{1765.8 \times 0.65 - Fr \times 1.4 = 0}$$

$$Fr = (1765.8x0.65) / 1.4 = 807.2286N$$

2. **Reaction forces**

$$\mathbf{\Sigma Fy = 0}$$

$$Ff + Fr = 1765.8$$

$$Ff = 1765.8 - 807.2286 = 958.5714N$$

3. **During acceleration**
   Motor capacity: 0 – 40 kmph in 2.3 sec
   Convert 40 kmph to m/s:

$$V = (40x1000)/3600$$

$$V = 11.11m/s$$

   Using Equation (2):

$$V = U + at$$

$$11.11 = 0 + ax2.3$$

$$a = 11.11 / 2.3 = 4.83m/s^2$$

Taking moments about point A (*Refer* Figure 1)

$$Fr = [(0.5 \times 180 \times 4.8) + (1765.8 \times 0.65)] / 1.4$$

$$Fr = 1257.2N$$

Therefore, the maximum load on the rear wheel during acceleration is 1257.2 N (vertical load).

Horizontal force during acceleration using the Equation,

$$Fn = mxa = 180x4.83 = 69.4N(Compressive)$$

4. **Braking force calculation**
   Assuming typical braking from 97 kmph to 0 in 3 sec
   Convert 27 kmph to m/s:

$$V = (97x1000)/3600$$

$$V = 26.944m/s$$

   Using $0 = 26.944 + a(3)$

$$a = -26.944 / 3 = -8.98m/s^2$$

$$Fn = mxa = 180x8.98 = 1616.4N(Tensile)$$

5. **Vertical shock impact**
   Drop height: h = 0.1 m
   Mass = 180 kg Using

$$v = \sqrt{2gh}$$

$$v = \sqrt{2x9.81x0.1} = 1.4m/s$$

$$Force : F = mv/ t$$

$$F = (180x1.4) / 0.1 = 2520N$$

A Factor of Safety (FOS) of 2 was used for all applied loads to simulate worst-case conditions.

6 BOUNDARY CONDITIONS AND ASSUMPTIONS

1. Cylindrical supports were applied:
   – At the pivot of the swingarm
   – And at the rear axle region

2. All force were applied at the suspension mounting point, except for the cornering moment which was applied at the rear axle.
3. The material selected was Aluminium Alloy 6061, which is known for its favourable strength-to-weight ratio [11].

The applied forces and constraint locations are clearly depicted in Figure 1.

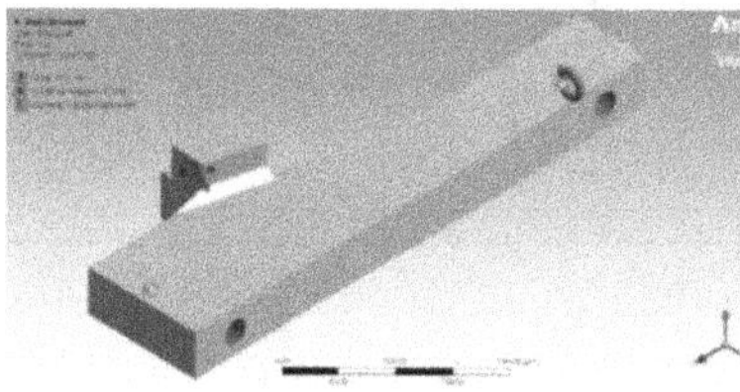

Figure 1. Original CAD model and forces applied.

7 LOADING CONDITIONS

The primary objective is to minimize the weight of the swingarm but be able to sustain all conditions of load encountered during racing, including:

- Vertical loads due to the weight of rider and bike.
- Horizontal loads caused by braking and acceleration.
- Impact loading while entering potholes or jumps.
- Lateral moments while cornering.

8 AI-BASED REGRESSION MODEL

To supplement the simulation-based strategy, a regression based artificial intelligence solution was made to estimate swingarm behavior under different design scenarios. The goal was to minimize reliance on repeated simulations by providing fast, reasonably good estimates for stress and deformation.

A data set was created by varying the swingarm thickness systematically from 40 mm to 60 mm in steps of 5 mm. Finite element analysis (FEA) data for maximum von Mises stress and total deformation were considered for each case. These data were then utilized to train a simple regression model in Python (Scikit-learn library). The input feature was the swingarm thickness, and the outputs were stress and deformation.

The regression model was checked by forecasting the mechanical response for a thickness of 50 mm, which had not been part of the training set. The forecasted values were 46.4074 MPa for stress and 0.26208 mm for deformation, both close to the FEA results of 46.376 MPa and 0.26177 mm, respectively. The relative error was less than 0.1%, implicating the high accuracy of the approach in early-stage decision making.

Although the model was built basic, this shows that even lightweight AI based machine learning models can aid in the design process by saving computational costs and by giving designers an insight on the effect of certain parameters without actually running a fully-fledged simulation. Future work could be done on expanding the training database, having more than one driving parameters and utilizing a more powerful machine learning model to improve prediction accuracy and generalization.

9 MANUFACTURABILITY CONSIDERATIONS

The goal of topology optimization is to produce a part that is light and structural sound, but the parts and shapes produced by this method is complex and hard to achieve using conventional approaches. The optimized part in this study shows smooth load paths and an organic material distribution, which can be manufactured using technologies such as Selective Laser Melting (SLM) and metal 3D printing. These techniques are shown to prevail in sectors where conventional machining methods such as CNC machining have limited usages. Although, some of the conventional methods could be used in the post-processing part (e.g., for filleting of sharp edges). Hence, the proposed design is still viable to be produced, by the proper process.

10 RESULTS AND DISCUSSION

The weight of the swingarm has been reduced to almost half of its initial weight and this can directly improve vehicle handling, acceleration, and the fuel efficiency. Nonetheless, as one would anticipate, this decrease in material resulted in higher stress, strain, and deformation. Even with these increases, the values for maximum stress and deformation are still within tolerable ranges for Aluminium 6061, given the safety factor applied. Figure 2 shows the topology-optimized structure. Figures 3 and 4 illustrate the resulting deformation and von Mises stress distribution.

This trade-off illustrates the worth of simulation in realizing the structural performance of optimized components. In an actual case, further iteration or strengthening in critical regions may make these values approach those of the initial design [17].

Key simulation outputs for the original and optimized swingarm are presented in Table 2.

Table 2. Comparison of parameters between original and optimized model.

Parameter	Original Model	Optimized Model	Change (%)
Mass (kg)	8.03	4.354	-45.8%
Max Stress (MPa)	14.589	46.376	217.9%
Max Strain	0.00022172	0.00068526	209%
Total Deformation (mm)	0.12915	0.26177	102.7%

For further insight, an analytically designed swing arm was also analysed under the same load and boundary conditions. The performance comparison is quantified in Table 3 below. Such comparison supports the benefits of optimization techniques over traditional engineering methods when considering modern performance metrics like mass-efficiency and deformation control [18].

Figure 5 illustrates the deformation from the analytical model, while Figure 6 shows the corresponding stress and Figure 7 compares these results to those predicted by the AI-based model.

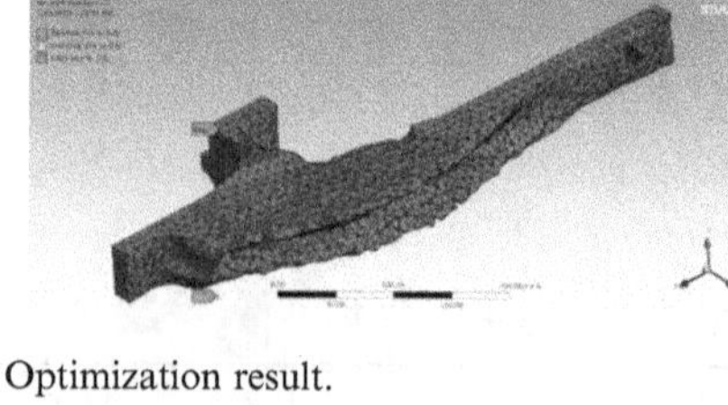

Figure 2. Optimization result.

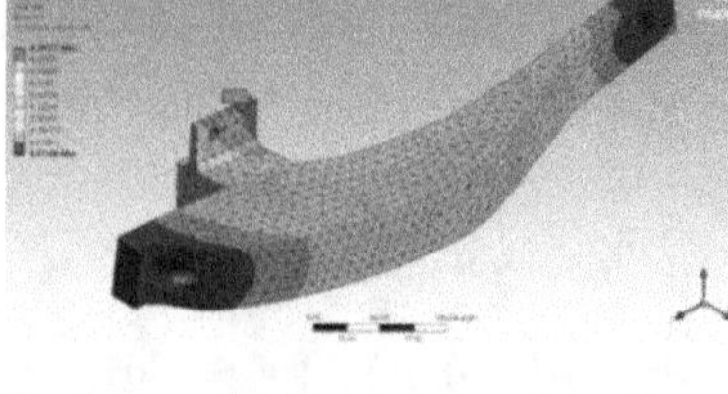

Figure 3. Indicating total deformation and maximum deformation.

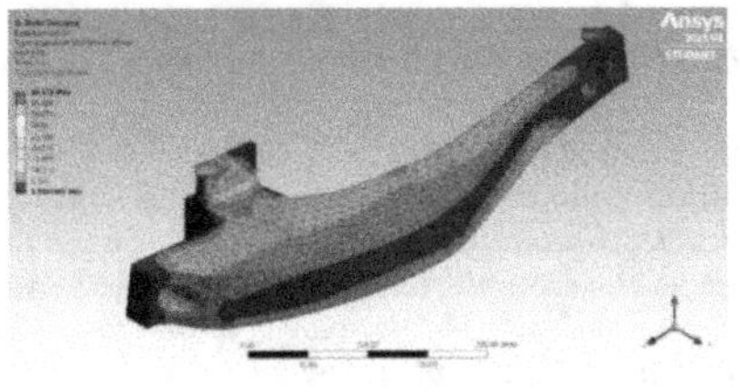

Figure 4. Von-mises stress induced and maximum stress.

Table 3. Comparison between analytically designed part and optimized part.

Parameter	Analytical Design	Topology Optimized Design
Mass (kg)	5.6266	4.354
Max Stress (MPa)	111.3	46.376
Max Strain	0.0016181	0.00068526
Total Deformation (mm)	0.14715	0.26177

Figure 5. Analytical part total deformation under similar loading.

Figure 6. Stress induced in Analytical part.

9 CONCLUSION

This research effectively shown an integrated way of designing to better improve the swingarm of an electric bike with both topology optimization and predictive modelling based on artificial intelligence. With a completely featured swingarm design as the starting point, finite element analysis was performed in order to learn about the stress, strain, and deformation behaviour under practical loading conditions. Using topology optimization in ANSYS Workbench with a target volume reduction of 50%, the mass of swingarm came down from 8.03 kg to 4.354 kg—a staggering 45.8% reduction. Though the design is lighter, the maximum deformation increased by just a small margin from 0.12915 mm to 0.26177 mm, while an acceptable increase in stress from 14.589 MPa to 46.376 MPa was observed. For comparison, the analytically designed swingarm weighing 5.6266 kg, with a maximum stress of 111.3MPa, greater strains and deformations. Showing that the topology optimised part although weighing more, has better performance, load distribution and reduced load peaks. And in addition, the manufacturability of the part has been considered, ensuring the design to be structurally sufficient and manufacturable using modern methods of manufacturing. As a

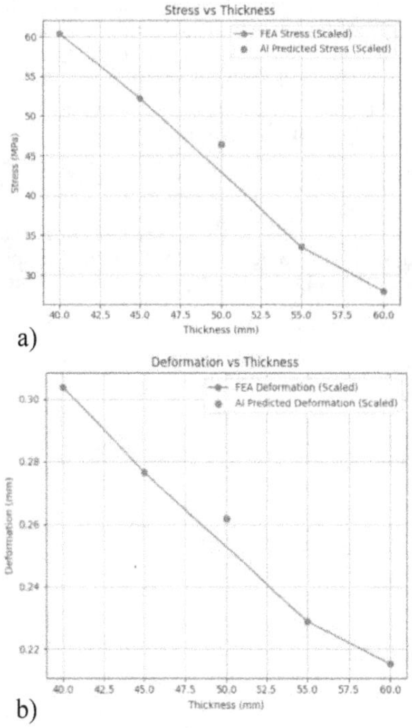

Figure 7. Comparison of AI predicted and FEA derived structural performance of the Swing arm- a) Stress vs thickness and b) Deformation vs thickness.

theoretical verification form, the maximum stress of the optimized swingarm at 46.376 MPa was checked against the yield strength of Aluminium Alloy 6061 ($\approx$ 276 MPa). Because the stresses induced are far below the yield point of the material, the design can be said to be structurally safe for the applied load conditions. The comparison helps strengthen the confidence in optimization solutions, further work could involve experimental verification.

REFERENCES

[1] Rankhambe, T., and Gajendra, K.N. (2016). "Topology optimization of motorcycle swing arm". IJSART.

[2] Bendsøe, M.P., and Sigmund, O. (2003). *"Topology Optimization: Theory, Methods, and Applications"*. Springer.

[3] T. Rankhambe and G.K. Nhaichaniya. (2017). "Topology Optimization of Motorcycle Swing Arm," *International Journal for Scientific Research & Development (IJSART)*, vol. 3, no. 5, pp. 413–416.

[4] Sharma, P., and Kumar, R. (2021). "Structural analysis and topology optimization of motorcycle swing arm". *Materials Today: Proceedings*, 47, 1241–1247.

[5] Rodríguez, M., *et al.* (2023). "*Topological optimization of swing arm for electric motorcycles. Advances in Engineering*, Springer.

[6] Brackett, D., Ashcroft, I., and Hague, R. (2011). "Topology optimization for additive manufacturing". *Additive Manufacturing*, 1, 38–49.

[7] Scappaticci, G., *et al.* (2012). "Structural behaviour of racing motorcycle swingarm". SAE Technical Paper 01-0207.

[8] Kim, G.W., Park, Y.I., and Park, K. (2020). "Topology optimization and additive manufacturing of automotive component by coupling kinetic and structural analyses". *Int. J. Automotive Technol.*, 21, 1455–1463.

[9] Ramamoorthy, R. (2021). "Topology optimization of vehicle components for nonlinear load cases". In Lecture Notes in Mechanical Engineering, pp. 309–318.

[10] A. Powar, H. Joshi, S. Khuley, and D.P. Yesane. (2016). "Analysis and topological optimization of motorcycle swing-arm," *International Journal of Current Engineering and Technology*, vol. 6, Special Issue-6, pp. 270–274.

[11] M. Matsimbi, P.K. Nziu, L.M. Masu, and M. Maringa. (2020). "Topology optimization of automotive body structures: A review," *International Journal of Engineering Research and Technology*, vol. 13, no. 12, pp. 4282–4296.

[12] Ashish, *et al.* (2016). "Analysis and topological optimization of motorcycle swing-arm". NCPSM–Inpressco.

[13] Rozvany, G.I.N. (2001). "A critical review of established methods of structural topology optimization". *Struct. Multidiscip. Optim.*, 21(2), 79–95.

[14] Cavajzzuti, M., *et al.* (2011). "High-performance automotive chassis design: a topology optimization-based approach. *Struct". Multidiscip. Optim.*, 44, 45–56.

[15] Shin, S., Shin, D., and Kang, N. (2022). "Topology optimization via machine learning and deep learning". A review. arXiv.

[16] Deaton, J.D., and Grandhi, R.V. (2014). "A survey of structural and multidisciplinary continuum topology optimization": post 2000. *Struct. Multidiscip. Optim.*, 49(1), 1–38.

[17] Wang, J., Wei, N., and Xu, Q. (2024). *"Research on mechanical performance analysis and topology optimization of automobile frame structures"*. Clausius Press.

[18] Yang, Y., and Chahande, A. (2021). "Topology optimization methods for vehicle chassis and space-frame structures". *IJSET*, 9(1).

Technology for a Resilient Future – Vincent , Moorthy and Dasari (Eds)

Modeling and Optimization of Full-Vehicle Suspension Dynamics Using Hybrid Multibody Lumped Systems and Machine Learning Models

Jinka Ranganayakulu, Dheemanth B A, Bhargava S, and Balaji R
Department of Mechanical Engineering, RV College of Engineering, Bengaluru, India

ABSTRACT: The comfort and safety of a vehicle's ride are strongly influenced by its suspension system, yet many conventional models inadequately capture real driving conditions, particularly under asymmetric road excitations. Limited research has combined AI-based vibration prediction with hybrid lumped–multibody modelling for such inputs. This study develops a comprehensive hybrid suspension model for a passenger car, integrated with machine learning, to predict vibrations and adjust suspension parameters under one-sided bump conditions. Using COMSOL Multiphysics 6.2, the Lumped Mechanical System and Multibody Dynamics interfaces were coupled to simulate the dynamics of the suspension, wheel, and seat-passenger system. A rectangular bump applied only to the front-left and rear-left wheels induced pitch and roll, with time-dependent simulations resolving eleven degrees of freedom to generate force, acceleration, and displacement data. The results emphasise the drawbacks of symmetric models and demonstrate how our hybrid-ML technique enables adaptive suspension systems to intelligently respond to uneven road conditions, thereby improving ride comfort and safety.

Keywords: Lumped Mechanical System, Seat-passenger Dynamics, Multi-body Dynamics, Road Excitation, Rectangular Waveform

1 INTRODUCTION

Vehicle suspension systems are critical for separating the chassis from road vibrations and maintaining ride comfort, safety, and handling stability. Traditional quarter-car versions. Symmetrical inputs fall short in replicating real-world scenarios, where asymmetric excitations like single-sided bumps can cause significant roll motion and seat vibrations. As automotive standards rise, accurate modelling of full-vehicle dynamics, including heave, pitch, and roll, is increasingly crucial. Recent research favours hybrid methods that merge lumped mechanical systems with multibody dynamics for richer simulations. Yet, integration with machine learning tools for vibration prediction and parameter optimisation under asymmetric conditions remains underexplored. This study addresses that gap by simulating a mid-sized passenger car subjected to one-sided bump inputs, specifically at the front-left and rear-left wheels. It introduces a machine learning model for seat acceleration prediction alongside a hybrid suspension simulation, demonstrating that coupling high-fidelity physics with AI can advance design efficiency and improve comfort under real-world driving conditions.

2 LITERATURE REVIEW

Recent studies highlight the growing role of intelligent control in vehicle suspension design. Baba Ahmadi et al. [1] applied deep reinforcement learning to magnetorheological dampers for adaptive vibration suppression, while Huang et al. [2] employed fuzzy logic–based co-simulation to enhance active suspension control. Lin and Lin [3] used deep learning to predict suspension dynamics in multi-axle vehicles, and Chen et al. [4] combined model predictive control (MPC) with electromagnetic absorbers for vibration mitigation and energy harvesting. These works show that AI and model-based strategies can greatly improve comfort and sustainability. A second stream focuses on empirical modeling and integrated analysis. Kanchwala [5] validated suspension models using track measurements, while Chen et al. [6] highlighted suspension–steering interactions. Martelli et al. [7] combined lumped and multibody dynamics for agricultural tractors, enabling precise replication of real-world circumstances. Research on mechanical design and actuation adds to suspension development. Fei and Chaoqun [8] tested electromagnetic actuators as alternatives to hydraulics, and Shi et al. [9] applied finite element analysis to springs for durability. Mihon and Lontiş [10] provided practical suspension case studies, while Bhalerao et al. [11] showcased COMSOL's role in concept-level analysis. Optimization and stability studies by Jayachandran and Krishnapillai [12], MDPI authors [13], and Hajidavalloo et al. [14] emphasized semi-active damping, stability trade-offs, and nonlinear energy-harvesting suspensions. Finally, sustainability-oriented approaches such as transfer matrix optimization [15] and lightweight solar-vehicle suspension design [16] highlight efficiency and weight reduction. Collectively, these works reveal a shift toward intelligent, hybrid, and sustainable suspension systems.

3 METHODOLOGY

This study adopts a hybrid simulation strategy by integrating Lumped Mechanical Systems and Multibody Dynamics (MBD) interfaces within COMSOL Multiphysics 6.2 to model full-vehicle suspension behavior under asymmetric road excitation. The model represents a mid-sized passenger car, incorporating a rigid 670 kg vehicle body, four 30 kg wheel masses, and four 120 kg seat-passenger lumped masses. Suspension and seat units are modeled using spring-damper subsystems with respective parameters as detailed in (Table 1), which includes spring stiffness (17,500 N/m for suspension and 1,750 N/m for seats) and damping coefficients (1,460 N·s/m for suspension and 700 N·s/m for seats). These physical properties were derived from validated sources [2], [6], [10], ensuring realistic representation of dynamics and system behavior. Wheel subsystems are linked to the rigid chassis through compliant suspensions, allowing vertical motion while restricting lateral shifts. External Source nodes ensure bidirectional force-data transfer between the lumped and rigid domains, supporting high-fidelity dynamic simulations and shocks, maintaining vehicle stability, and

DOI: 10.1201/9781042017546-44

protecting passengers from vibration discomfort. We used a Time-Dependent Solver with 0.001 s intervals across a 2-second window. The simulation captures the transient response of the vehicle across eleven degrees of freedom, encompassing heave, pitch, roll, and coupled suspension seat interactions, thereby providing a comprehensive representation of both body-level dynamics.

Table 1. Simulation parameters for the system.

Name	Expression	Value	Description
m_body	670[kg]	670 kg	Mass of vehicle body
I_roll	800 [kg*m^2]	800 kg·m^2	Inertia around roll
I_pitch	1100 [kg*m^2]	1100 kg·m^2	Inertia around pitch
m_wh	30[kg]	30 kg	Mass of wheels
m_p	120[kg]	120 kg	Mass of passengers
k_wh	175500[N/m]	1.755E5 N/m	Stiffness of wheels
k_sus	17500[N/m]	17500 N/m	Stiffness of suspension springs
k_seat	1750[N/m]	1750 N/m	Stiffness of seat springs
c_sus	1460[N*s/m]	1460 N·s/m	Viscosity of suspension dampers
c_seat	700[N*s/m]	700 N·s/m	Viscosity of seat dampers
r_wb	1.9975[m]	1.9975 m	Wheel base
r_tw	0.8025[m]	0.8025 m	Track width
hb	4[cm]	0.04 m	Bump height
wb	7.5[cm]	0.075 m	Bump width
speed	40[km/h]	11.111 m/s	Vehicle speed
tb	4*wb/speed	0.027 s	Bump time period
td	r_wb/speed	0.17978 s	Time delay between front and rear wheel

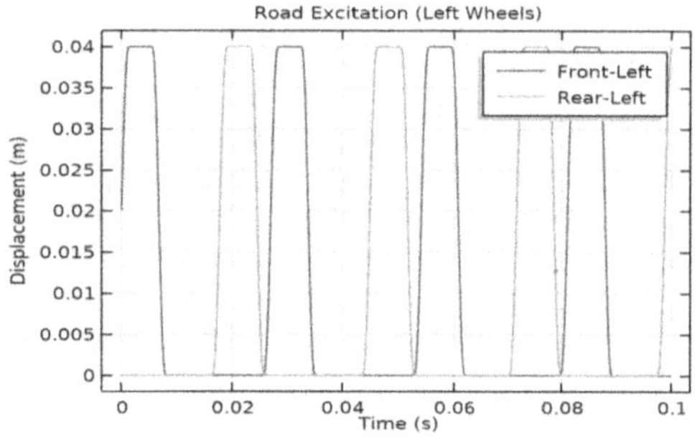

Figure 1. Road excitation for the left wheels of the vehicle.

The simulation employs a single-sided road input modeled as a rectangular bump 0.04 m high and 0.075 m wide applied exclusively to the front-left and rear-left wheels. To replicate realistic road asymmetry, the rear-left bump contact is delayed by 0.17978 seconds, calculated based on vehicle speed (40 km/h) and wheelbase (1.9975 m).

These conditions are captured in (Figure 1), which displays the time-dependent displacement inputs for both left-side wheels. The lateral imbalance causes the bump-induced waveform to generate roll and pitch motion, whereas the right-side wheels remain unaffected on flat ground. This dynamic excitation is critical for determining asymmetric suspension response, particularly the system's ability to absorb excitation.

Displacements, velocities, accelerations, and forces are such as the vehicle body, wheels, and seats, providing information about how each component responds to the uneven input. To supplement the physical simulation, a machine learning model is created that predicts seat RMS accelerations using a linear regression trained on simulation data. (Figure 2) shows best fit between bump height and front-left seat RMS acceleration using a linear regression fit, demonstrating the relationship between road disturbance amplitude and passenger vibration levels.

In our study, the Linear Regression model allows for seat and suspension parameters to improve comfort, and also serving as a decision-support tool for real-time optimization. Overall, our integrated hybrid methodology using physics-based modeling and machine learning insights to investigate asymmetric road excitation .

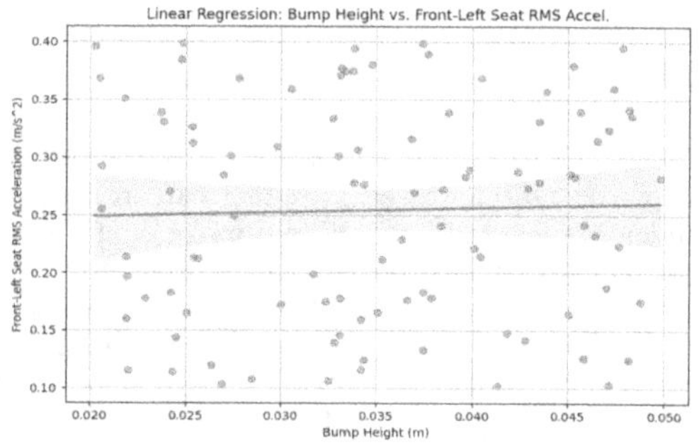

Figure 2. Linear regression model for bump height vs front left RMS.

4 RESULTS AND DISCUSSION

The transient dynamic response of the vehicle suspension system under asymmetric road excitation, in which only the front-left and rear-left wheels cross a bump, is demonstrated by the simulation results derived from the COMSOL Multiphysics model.

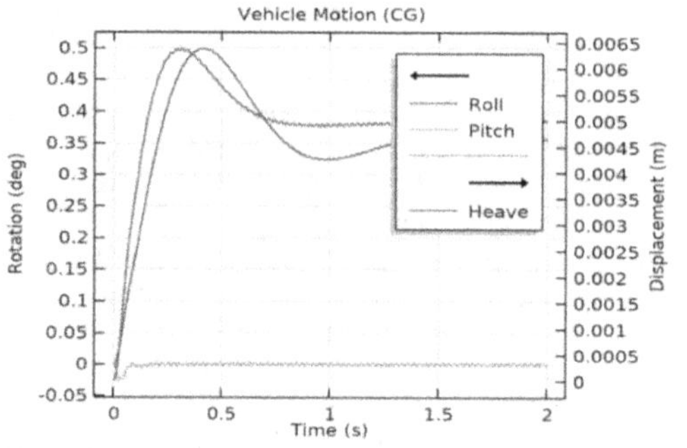

Figure 3. Vehicle roll pitch & heave motion at CG.

Our results offer a comprehensive understanding of how the vehicle body, seat-passenger units, and suspension system interact in such real-world scenarios. System behaviour is assessed through vehicle motion and vibration response.

Combined plots for roll, pitch, and heave at the centre of gravity (Figure 3 & 4) demonstrate pronounced roll due to asymmetrical input and visualise RMS seat acceleration prediction via linear regression, revealing direct speed-dependent comfort deterioration. However, the combined roll, pitch, and heave motions of the vehicle chassis over time are shown in Vehicle Motion at the Centre of Gravity (CG). While the dominant roll motion is evident, caused by the bump acting only on the left wheels, which tilts the vehicle sideways and illustrates the importance of analysing asymmetric excitations.

Velocity charts (Figure 5) show abrupt vertical motion at the excited wheels and damped oscillations in the chassis, highlighting the suspension's efficacy in energy absorption. The front-left and rear-left wheels exhibit significant vertical velocity spikes when approaching and exiting the bump, indicating a

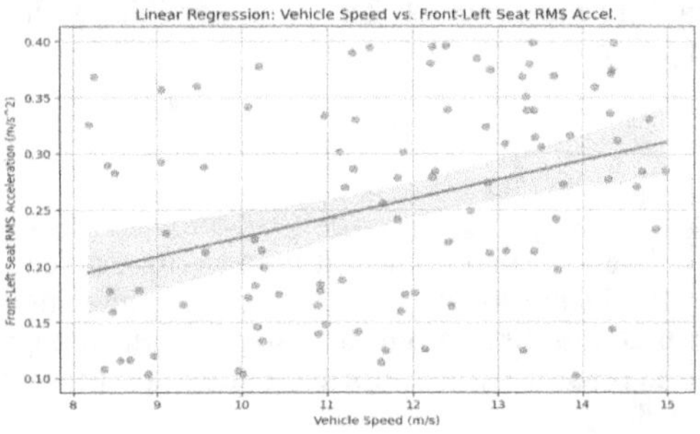

Figure 4. Linear regression model for vehicle speed vs front left Seat RMS.

sudden displacement input. However, the right wheels remain quite stable, which tells us that they are on level terrain.

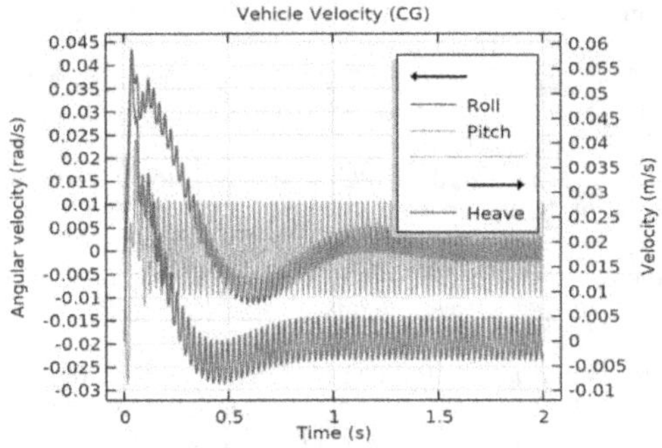

Figure 5. Roll, pitch, and heave motions captured at the centre of gravity.

Vertical seat displacements (Figure 6) show enhanced motion on the left side, with distinct peaks coinciding to bump interaction, validating the impact of timed excitation on passenger comfort [15]. The first emerges when the front-left wheel encounters the bump, and the second appears when the rear-left wheel crosses it with a slight delay.

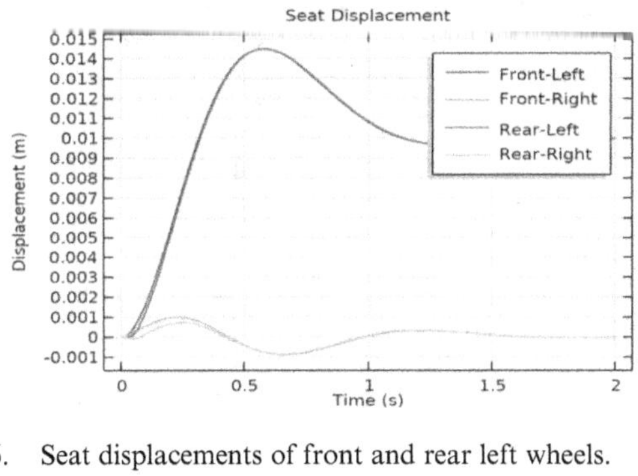

Figure 6. Seat displacements of front and rear left wheels.

Figures 5 and 6 provide an overview of dynamic behavior under asymmetric road excitation. The roll, pitch and seat displacement graph shows how bump impact causes linear vertical displacements peaks in the front-left and rear-left seats, whereas damping gradually reduces oscillations, demonstrating how comfort decreases with harder inputs.

Reaction forces at the front-left wheel (Figure 8) show high transient loads that corresponds to bump height and stiffness constants, while damper responses rapidly attenuate oscillations. In line with the energy-harvesting techniques discussed in [2] and [4], the suspension spring force spikes linearly as

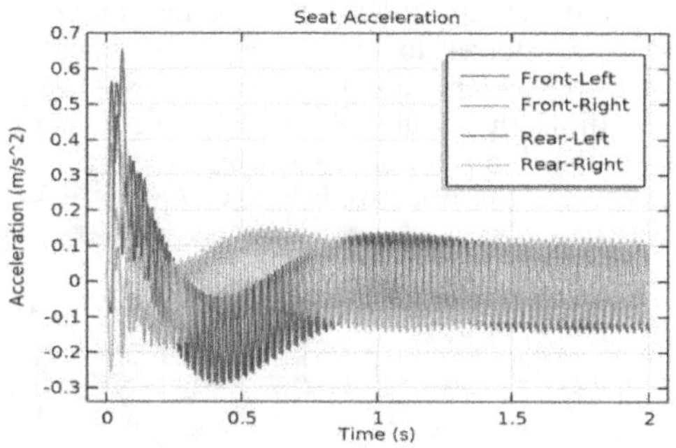

Figure 7. Seat accelerations recorded in front-rear left wheels.

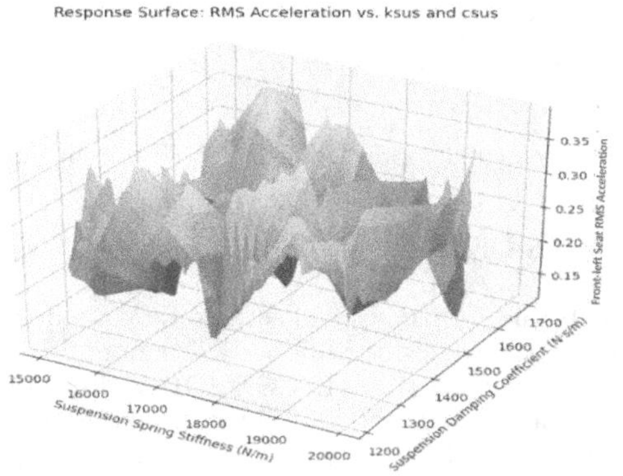

Figure 8. Seat accelerations in front left wheels are represented in a surface plot.

discussed before in (Figures 5 and 6) and depends on the suspension stiffness (k_sus). As the wheel crosses the bump peak and descends, the force rapidly decreases and oscillates, while the suspension dampens the energy. The damping element (c_sus) dampens these oscillations and prevents continuous bouncing effect, returns to level ground and the force settles, exhibiting effective load absorption.

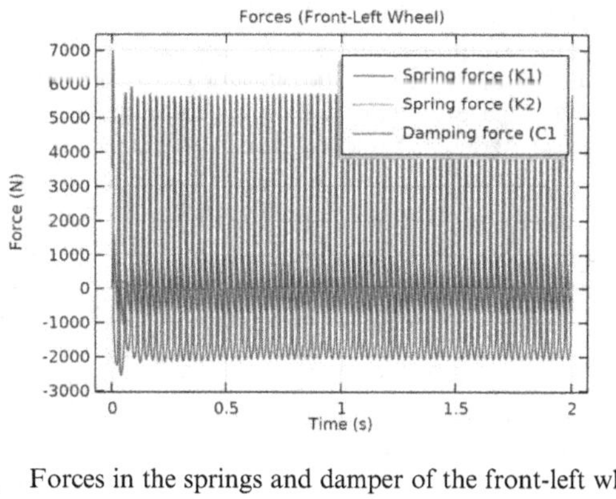

Figure 9. Forces in the springs and damper of the front-left wheel.

Front-left seat forces (Figure 9 & 10) depict vertical loading from upward chassis motion, with rhythmic decay attributed to spring-damper energy dissipation, effectively isolating the passenger from sudden shocks. The force at the front-left seat is the force that the spring-damper mechanism in the seat transfers from the vehicle body to the passenger.

The car body moves upward as a result of the front-left wheel climbing the bump, creating vertical displacement at the seat mounting location. The seat damper (c_seat) is activated and the seat spring (k_seat) is compressed by this relative motion. The initial peak in the force plot represents the point at which the body is moving upward the most. The amount of bump input that is transferred to the passenger is indicated by this force.. By absorbing this input, the seat damper lessens prolonged oscillations that could otherwise be uncomfortable. This result validates the mechanical isolation function of seat subsystems as observed in prior studies [12] [16].

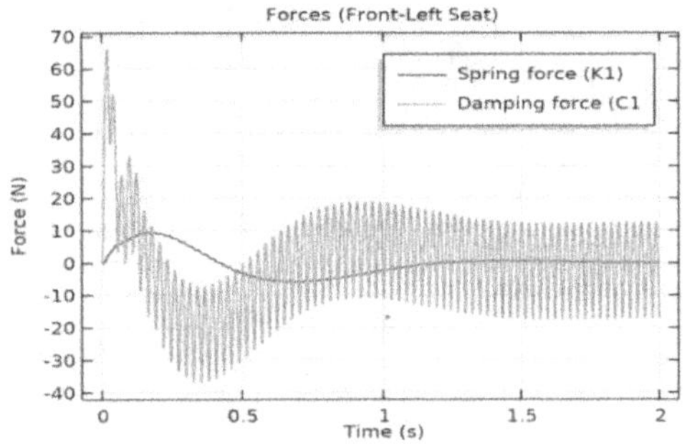

Figure 10. Forces in the spring and damper of the front-left.

5 CONCLUSION

The present study effectively illustrates the use of a hybrid technique that combines the Multibody Dynamics and Lumped Mechanical System interfaces in COMSOL Multiphysics 6.2 to model and analyze transiently a full-vehicle suspension system. Heave, pitch, and dominating roll behavior are among the complicated coupled vehicle dynamics that the model represents by using an asymmetric road excitation, in which only the front-left and rear-left wheels come into contact with a square-shaped bump. The asymmetrical bump input clearly results in different load transfer between the left and right sides of the car, according to simulation results for body motion, suspension forces, seat displacement, and seat acceleration. Even when only one side of the suspension is agitated, the results demonstrate that the seat-passenger spring-damper systems successfully lessen transmitted vibrations, improving passenger comfort. It has been demonstrated that the suspension's spring and damping properties are essential for protecting the car's body and occupants from unexpected shocks. A useful and effective method for examining full-vehicle behavior under realistic transient inputs is the combined lumped–multibody framework. These results illustrate the necessity of assessing asymmetric road profiles, which are prevalent in real-world driving but sometimes disregarded in simple suspension studies, in contrast to traditional quarter car models that presume symmetric input. The results offer important new information for designing and adjusting suspension settings to increase ride comfort and vehicle stability on uneven surfaces. Our study improves the realism and relevance of the findings for sophisticated vehicle design, future research may expand this model to incorporate active or semi-active suspension control, nonlinear damping effects, or random road excitations. The combination of meta-heuristic parameter tweaking with supervised machine learning prediction shows how data-driven methods can improve the usefulness of high-fidelity suspension models. Future adaptive suspension systems that learn and modify in real-time depending on road feedback are made possible by this combination approach.

ACKNOWLEDGMENT

We would like to express our gratitude to our academic supervisor and the Department of Mechanical Engineering for their help and direction throughout this project. Special appreciation is due to the laboratory team for their simulation resources and technical help.

REFERENCES

[1] Baba Ahmadi *et al.* (2023), A deep reinforcement learning-based controller for magnetorheological-damped vehicle suspension. *arXiv*:2301.02714.

[2] Huang, Z. G., Ding, J. G., and Bao, X. D. (2013). The co-simulation research of vehicle active suspension based on fuzzy control. *Advanced Materials Research*. (Volume 668), 415–419

[3] Lin, K. C., and Lin, B. Y. (2024). Deep learning-based prediction of suspension dynamics performance in multi-axle vehicles. *arXiv*:2410.02566

[4] Chen, K. *et al.* (2020). MPC-based vibration control and energy harvesting using an electromagnetic vibration absorber. 2378-5861. *American Control Conference (ACC)*.

[5] Kanchwala, H. (2020). Vehicle suspension model development using test track measurements. *Proc. IMechE, Part D: Journal of Automobile Engineering*, 234(5): 1442–1459.

[6] Chen, W. *et al.* (2016). The research of vehicle dynamics modeling method based on the characteristics of suspension and steering systems. *SAE Technical Paper 2688-3627 Dongfeng Commercial Vehicle Co., Ltd.* 5.

[7] Martelli, L. *et al.* (2023). Comprehensive lumped parameter and multibody approach for the dynamic simulation of agricultural tractors. *Journal of Sound and Vibration*, 330(12): 2937–2946.

[8] Fei, L. and Chaoqun, H. (2012). Modeling and experimental research about a new type of vehicle active suspension electromagnetic actuator. *Archive of Applied Mechanics*, 81(10): 1427–1437.

[9] MDPI authors. (2021). Investigation of vehicle stability with consideration of suspension performance. *Appl. Sci.*, 11(20), 9778

[10] Mihon, L. and Lontiş, N. (2018). Modeling and analysis of a vehicle suspension. *Proceedings of the 4th International Congress of Automotive and Transport Engineering (AMMA 2018)* (pp.113-121)

[11] Bhalerao, M. *et al.* (2020). Concept Level automotive structural analysis in COMSOL multiphysics®. *COMSOL conference*

[12] Jayachandran, R. and Krishnapillai, S. (2013). Modeling and optimization of passive and semi-active suspension systems. *Journal of Vibration and Control*, 19(13): 1961–1976.

[13] Shi, X. H., Xu, M. H., and Gao, H. L. (2010). Research on stress method of vehicle suspension springs and finite element modeling. *Applied Mechanics and Materials* (Volume 42) 147–150.

[14] Hajidavalloo, M. R., Cosner, J., Li, Z., Tai, W. C., Song, Z. (2021). Simultaneous suspension control and energy harvesting. *arXiv*:2106.10540.

[15] MDPI authors. (2023). Dynamics modeling and suspension parameters optimization of vehicle system based on reduced multibody system transfer matrix method. *Machines* 2025, 13(2), 116

[16] Korkut, T. B., Pasinli, Z., and Goren, (2021). A. front suspension system design of the lightweight solar-powered vehicle. *Journal of Materials and Mechatronics*. 2717-8811, 2(2), 60–71

Design of 8-Bit ALU Using Low Power Verilog Coding Techniques

Devika Sindhu and Shankaranarayana Bhat M
Department of Electronics and Communication Engineering, Manipal Institute of Technology, Manipal Academy of Higher Education, Manipal, Karnataka, India

ABSTRACT: There is an increasing demand for modern devices to be faster and more portable. For devices to meet these two parameters, it is necessary to decrease the power consumption and dissipation . The 'Arithmetic Logic Unit' (ALU), one of the essential parts of contemporary processors, is important for carrying out the various arithmetic and logical operations. Since energy consumption remains a major factor in ALU and CPU design, it is critical to investigate efficient low-power methods. In this paper, an 8-bit ALU is designed, and the effect of using various low-power Verilog coding techniques is studied. The Verilog coding methods chosen are 'Precomputation', 'clock gating' and 'guarded evaluation'. The simulation is done using Cadence NcSim tool and synthesis is performed by using the Cadence Genus tool. From the power reports generated after synthesis, it is observed that there is reduction in power after using low power coding techniques, with the maximum reduction in power being observed in the 'guarded evaluation' technique.

Keywords: Low power VLSI. low power ALU, low power RTL coding

1 INTRODUCTION

In today's rapidly changing technology environment, there is a requirement for gadgets that are both extremely portable and faster than ever before. Consumers demand the best possible performance from their devices—be it wearables, computers, or smartphones—without compromising on its portability. However as gadgets get smaller and more potent, controlling power usage and dissipation becomes increasingly important.

These days, advanced processors and controllers with processing powers of at least 64 bits can be found. The frequency ranges from a few megahertz to gigahertz. The development of CMOS technology, which allows for the packing of more transistors on a silicon die, is the reason for these previously mentioned capabilities. However, this creates a high power consumption issue[1].

There are many reasons why there is an increasing requirement for low power technologies. As mentioned previously, the demand for high performance devices means an increase in the frequency of operation as well as an increase in its capability to process data. This high frequency of operations can result in a large amount of power dissipation. However, consumers require increasingly portable devices, and this can be a challenge if the power dissipation is not taken care of, since it can shorten the lifespan of the device. Also, in order to eliminate the high power that is dissipated, appropriate packaging techniques or cooling mechanisms may be required, which can lead to an increase in manufacturing cost. It can also lead to increased chip area. Due to these reasons, low power design is essential.

At the heart of modern processors is the 'Arithmetic Logic Unit' (ALU), which is a fundamental component that is responsible for executing a wide array of arithmetic and logical operations. ALUs in modern CPUs are extremely sophisticated and powerful. Contemporary CPUs also have a control unit (CU) in addition to ALUs. One or more than one ALUs are able to handle the vast majority of CPU functions by loading data from the input registers [2].

The operations of an ALU include arithmetic operations such as addition, multiplication, subtraction and division. Logical operations that can be performed by an ALU include AND, OR, NOT, XOR etc. An ALU can also perform data comparison operations. An ALU can have many input and output lines, status lines etc. The opcode decides which operation needs to be carried out by the ALU. Figure 1 shows a basic architecture of an ALU. Here, the arithmetic operations and logical operations are carried out by different blocks.

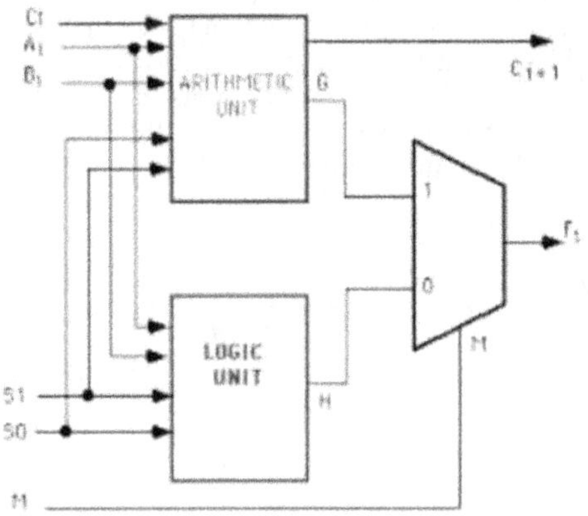

Figure 1. Basic architecture of an ALU.

2 TYPES OF POWER DISSIPATION

The two broad classifications of power dissipation are Static power and Dynamic power. The total power of an ALU is the sum of the static power and dynamic power [3].

$$P_{total} = P_{static} + P_{dynamic}$$

2.1 *Static power dissipation*

Static power dissipation is that which takes place when there is no switching activity that is taking place in the circuit. The major contributor to static power dissipation can be said to be leakage current, which flows in the steady-state condition of the circuit. This can be due to subthreshold leakage, which is the small amount of current that flows when the transistors are off. With decreasing threshold voltage of a transistor, the subthreshold current increases exponentially. Another component is gate leakage, which is the current that flows because of the thin gate oxides of transistors in modern semiconductor technologies. Static power dissipation can be controlled by methods like

DOI: 10.1201/9781042017546-45

power gating, use of multiple threshold voltages, transistor sizing, voltage scaling etc.

2.2 *Dynamic power dissipation*

Dynamic power dissipation is that which takes place due to the charging and discharging of capacitive loads when transistor switching takes place. Dynamic power thus depends on the amount of switching activity of the circuit, and can be a large value because of the demand for high performance devices that will have increased switching activity. In order to reduce dynamic power dissipation, methods like clock gating, voltage scaling etc can be used.

$$P_{dynamic} = CV^2f$$

3 METHODOLOGY

The low power coding techniques that are used to reduce the power dissipation are precomputation, clock gating and guarded evaluation.

3.1 *Precomputation*

Precomputation is a low power coding technique that can be used to reduce dynamic power consumption by computing and storing values in advance, thereby minimizing the need for active computation during runtime. This is particularly useful in scenarios where certain computations are frequently performed, allowing for a trade-off between power consumption and area utilization.

The basic principle of precomputation logic can be said to be the process of identifying those input values that does not affect the output values. On identifying these inputs that do not affect the output values in any way, it is possible to disable these input lines at these times, and thereby reduce the switching activity of the circuit.

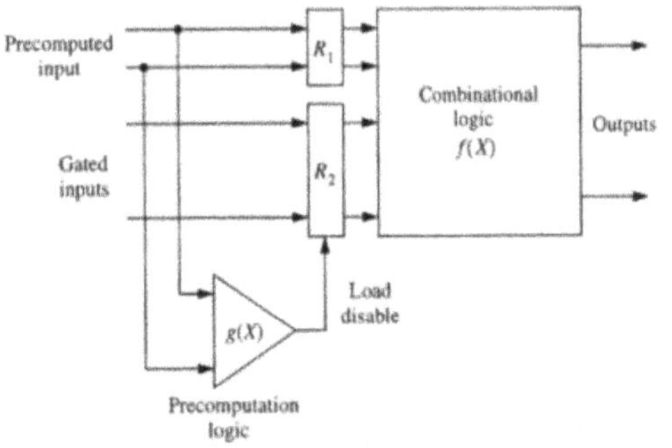

Figure 2. Block diagram of a basic precomputation logic.

Figure 2 shows a basic precomputation logic[4]. The outputs of the two registers, R1 and R2 are given to the combinational logic block. If there are any inputs that do not cause a change in the output values of the combinational block, then the register R2 can be disabled, thereby eliminating unnecessary switching activity. The output of the combinational block will thus depend only on the inputs that are fed through the register R1. Precomputation logic involves tradeoff between reduction in power and area. Precomputation can result in an increase in the area overhead due to the additional hardware that is required for storing the precomputed values. In the implemented 8-bit ALU, the 'greater than' and 'less than' comparison operations are precomputed to reduce dynamic power.

3.2 *Clock gating*

Clock gating is a low power design technique where selective disabling of the clock signal to specific blocks in a circuit is done. Clock is disabled on those blocks or registers that are not required during a particular operation, and in this way power is reduced as the unwanted blocks are not active. Clock gating can be done by introducing additional gates between the source of the clock and the combinational block or register to which the clock signal is fed. The conditions for gating the clock signal are monitored, and if the condition is met, then the clock signal is disabled and the block will be in stand-by mode. If the conditions for clock gating are not met, then the clock signal will be enabled, and the block will be in active mode. In the 8-bit ALU, there is an arithmetic as well as a logic unit, and both these units will not be active simultaneously as both arithmetic and logical operations will not be executed at the same time. Therefore, the clock signal is only given to the unit that is needed for executing a particular operation and the clock signal is disabled to the other unit.

3.3 *Guarded evaluation*

Guarded evaluation is a technique used in low-power design to minimize energy consumption by selectively activating or deactivating circuit elements based on specific conditions or criteria. This approach aims to reduce dynamic power dissipation by preventing unnecessary switching activity in inactive portions of the circuit. Guarded evaluation involves the identification of internal signals that do not propagate to the output of the circuit. After identifying such internal signals, the circuit is then modified to remove the toggles on that signal, thereby reducing switching activity and in turn reducing dynamic power [6]. Guarded evaluation is implemented in an 8-bit ALU by using conditional statements.

These conditions allow the ALU to selectively perform arithmetic or logical operations based on its evaluation. For instance, in a conditional addition operation, the ALU would perform the addition only if a certain condition, such as a flag or a comparison result, is true. Otherwise, the ALU remains idle, avoiding unnecessary power consumption associated with the execution of the operation. In this way, dynamic power can be reduced.

4 RESULTS AND DISCUSSIONS

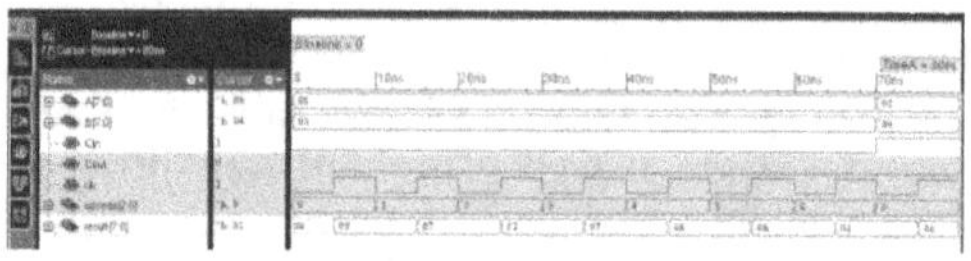

Figure 3. Simulation result of 8-bit ALU.

Figure 3 shows the simulation result from NcSim of an 8-bit ALU that does not have any power reduction technique used on it. Figure 4 shows the schematic of the 8-bit ALU.

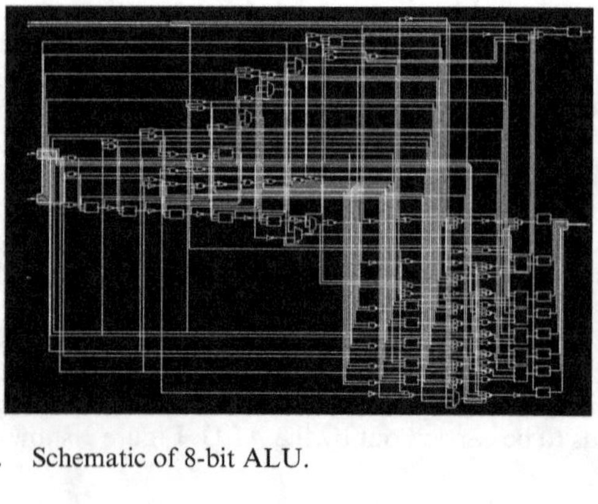

Figure 4. Schematic of 8-bit ALU.

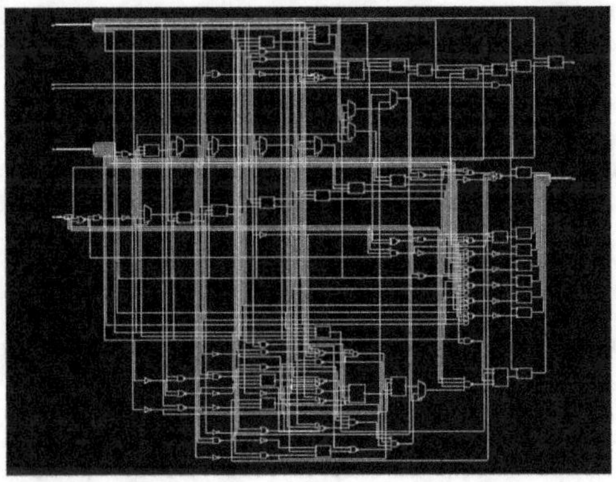

Figure 5. Schematic of 8-bit ALU using precomputation technique.

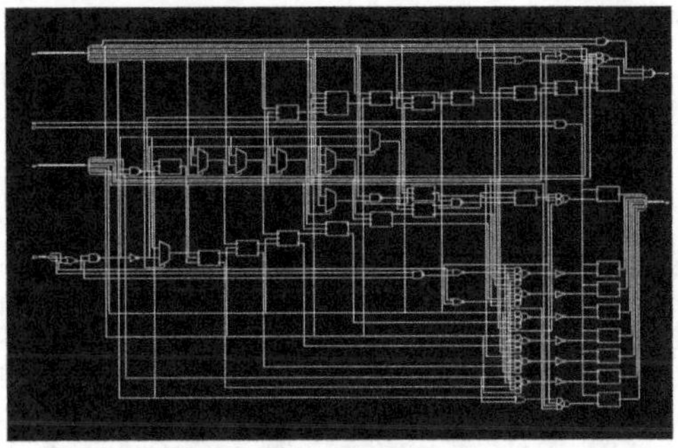

Figure 6. Schematic of 8-bit ALU using clock gating technique.

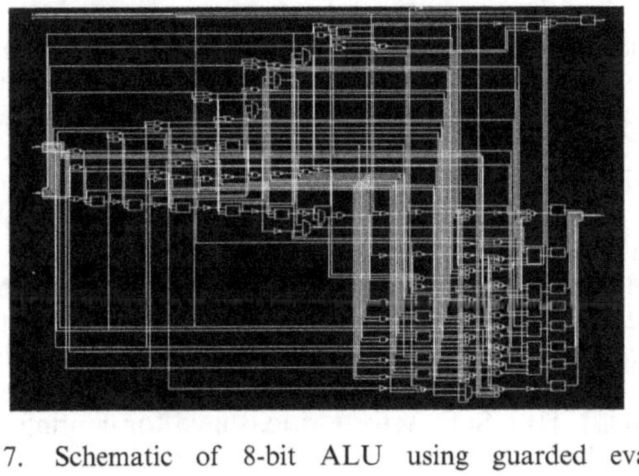

Figure 7. Schematic of 8-bit ALU using guarded evaluation technique.

Table 1. Comparison of different low power coding techniques.

Method	*Area*(μm^2)	*Power(nW)*	*Percentage reduction in power(%)*
No low power coding	613.089	174981.255	-
Precomputation	637.310	94632.228	45.91
Clock Gating	620.471	90771.043	48.12
Guarded Evaluation	619.144	85578.335	51.09

5 CONCLUSIONS

In this paper, the need for low power design of circuits was seen and an 8-bit ALU was implemented without any low power coding technique, as well as with low power coding techniques. The low power coding techniques chosen were precomputation, clock gating and guarded evaluation. The area and power for each implementation was then compared. It is observed from Table 1 that the precomputation technique takes up more are than the other methods. This is due to the presence of additional precomputation logic circuitry. There is a percentage reduction in power of 45.91% for precomputation technique, 48.12% for clock gating and 51.09% for guarded evaluation technique. Maximum power reduction is seen in the case where guarded evaluation was used.

REFERENCES

[1] G. Verma, (2020). "Design and analysis of ALU for low power IOT centric processor architectures," *2020 Global Conference on Wireless and Optical Technologies (GCWOT)*, Malaga, Spain, pp. 1–5, https://doi.org/10.1109/GCWOT49901.2020.9391609.

[2] M. Kantawala. (2018). "Design and implementation of 8 bit and 16 bit ALU using verilog language", *International Journal of Engineering Applied Sciences and Technology*.

[3] G. Sahu, S.P. Sahu, (2019). "Low power ALU design and implementation using clock gating and carry select adder", *Dogo Rangsang Research Journal*, UGC Care Group I Journal, Vol-09 Issue-03.

[4] M. Chakraverty, Harisankar PS and V. Ruparelia, (2016). "Low power design practices for power optimization at the logic and architecture levels for VLSI system design," *2016 International Conference on Energy Efficient Technologies for Sustainability (ICEETS)*, Nagercoil, India, pp. 727–733, https://doi.org/10.1109/ICEETS.2016.7583845.

[5] Singh, Vikram, Sandeep K. Arya, Manoj Kumar, (2018). "Different perspectives of low power design for CMOS VLSI circuits", *International Journal of Electronics Engineering* (ISSN: 0973–7383) Volume 10, Issue 2 pp. 604–613

[6] B.H.K. Bhagath Kumar, K.H.K. Raghu Vamsi, (2016). "Reduction in dynamic power of digital circuits by guarded evaluation", *International Research Journal of Engineering and Technology (IRJET)*, Volumemac_mac 03 Issue: 12.

Technology for a Resilient Future – Vincent , Moorthy and Dasari (Eds)
 ISBN: 978-1-041-39070-1

Comparative Study of Reinforcement Learning Algorithms for Vision-Based Autonomous Drone Landing Using ArUco Marker

Ujwal Amarnath and Jeane Marina D' Souza
Department of Mechatronics, Manipal Institute of Technology, Manipal Academy of Higher Education, Manipal, Karnataka, India

ABSTRACT: Autonomous drone landing on visual markers is required for applications like delivery, inspection, and surveillance. In this research, vision-based landing using fiducial ArUco markers is explored in the Microsoft AirSim simulator and the comparison of three deep reinforcement learning algorithms: Deep Q Network (DQN), Proximal Policy Optimization (PPO), and Soft Actor Critic (SAC). All the agents are run under a consistent reward structure that rewards accurate touchdowns and discourages marker loss with only the use of a downwards facing camera. Experiments indicate that PPO has the most stable overall performance, SAC for the best landing accuracy when the marker is always visible, and DQN is more sensitive to variance in the reward. These results provide practical insight into selecting reinforcement learning strategies for real-world UAV landing applications.

Keywords: Autonomous drone landing, ArUco markers, vision-based navigation, deep reinforcement learning, DQN, PPO, SAC, Microsoft AirSim

1 INTRODUCTION

Autonomous multirotor landing is difficult due to limited sensing, dynamic conditions, and strict safety needs. DRL shows that control policies can be learned directly from high-dimensional observations and structured rewards, reaching high success rates on static and inclined platforms [4], while curriculum design and state-space decomposition improve robustness for moving targets [3]. Shared autonomy aids pilots in poor visibility [4], and fiducial-marker pose estimation especially ArUco remains one of the most reliable methods for precise touchdown [5].

ArUco markers offer accurate, low-latency pose estimation in GPS-denied environments. Their binary-coded square patterns enable robust detection under varied lighting and viewpoints, and the Diamond design provides centimeter-grade 3D localization precision [5]. With multi-scale detection and pose refinement (e.g., Kalman, PnP), systems can achieve sub-error localization suitable for vision-guided and learning-based landing.

Reinforcement learning enables model-free landing controllers. Value based methods like DQN estimate optimal Q-values for discrete actions; Double Q-learning reduces training time in simplified 1D landing tasks [3]. Policy gradient methods like PPO stabilize learning through constrained updates and support fast training on horizontal and sloped platforms, with a Crazyflie-compatible PPO controller achieving stable landings in under 90 minutes [2]. Actor critic methods such as SAC use entropy regularization for improved exploration, and vision focused variants like DAC-SAC integrate convolution and attention to reach over 99% obstacle avoidance success, demonstrating SAC's strength in vision-based control [6].

Although there is some progress, sample efficiency, stability, and sim-to-real transfer still remain challenges. Surveys also point out sparse reward difficulties and sensitivity to hyperparameters but highlight opportunities in multimodal perception and deployment on real systems [1]. Building on the insights from this, this work compares DQN, PPO, and SAC on Microsoft AirSim using ArUco-derived pose data for training efficiency, landing accuracy, and robustness to marker occlusion.

2 RELATED WORK

ArUco markers are now widely used for improving UAV landing precision, offering much better accuracy than GPS based methods. Published results show up to 87 percent error reduction, with mean offsets near 11 cm compared to the 1 to 3 m of GPS only landings [7] [8] [9]. Simulation studies report centimetre level accuracy, such as eArUco achieving a 2.03 cm mean error with 1.53 cm standard deviation under optimal conditions [10]. ArUco markers also maintain high detection robustness, with mean average precision above 0.9 in clear views and above 0.4 with partial occlusion [11]. Comparative research confirms their reliability over other fiducial systems, especially indoors and close to the ground [12]. Marker size and number directly improve localization accuracy, with doubling either yielding higher precision without heavy computation [13]. Field tests validate ArUco guided landing for mobile platforms and precision agriculture [14]. Multi marker setups further resist motion blur and occlusion, and advances in layouts and recognition algorithms continue to broaden use.

Deep reinforcement learning is also explored for UAV landing and navigation. Deep Q Networks have been applied to longitudinal control on carriers and offshore docking with improved accuracy and robustness [15] [16]. Proximal Policy Optimization shows stable learning for carrier landing, obstacle avoidance, and efficient 3D positioning for aerial communication [16] [17] [18]. Soft Actor Critic, suited for continuous control, has been extended to UAV path planning, obstacle avoidance, and aerial video transmission through ISAC variants [19] [20]. Overall, DQN is reliable for discrete tasks, PPO excels at stable policy learning, and SAC performs strongly in continuous environments. Comparisons of RL methods show Q learning outperforming SARSA in convergence and path quality [21], while PPO surpasses DQN and A2C in stability and reward [22]. Off policy evaluations of DDPG, TD3, and SAC show TD3 performing best in collision avoidance despite higher maximum returns from DDPG [23]. A two stage RL method further improved generalization and sim to real transfer in landing [24]. PPO and TD3 exhibit strong stability and robustness, though real world transfer remains challenging.

Based on this literature, DQN, PPO, and SAC were selected for their diversity and proven control performance, representing value based, policy gradient, and entropy regularized actor critic paradigms implemented with Stable Baselines3. Algorithms like TD3 [28] and A3C [29] were excluded since TD3 is designed for continuous control and A3C is largely replaced by PPO for greater stability and scalability. To our knowledge, this is the first direct comparison of DQN, PPO,

 DOI: 10.1201/9781042017546-46

and SAC for vision based UAV landing using ArUco markers in a unified simulation framework, addressing a gap left by prior studies focused on single algorithms or non-marker approaches.

3 METHODOLOGY

3.1 *DQN*

Deep Q Networks (DQN) extend Q learning by using deep neural networks to approximate the action value of function $Q(s, a)$, enabling learning from high dimensional state spaces. The algorithm minimizes the temporal difference loss:

$$\mathcal{L}(\theta) = \mathbb{E}_{(s,a,r,s')}\left[\left(r + \gamma \max_{(a')} Q\left(s', a'; \theta^{-}\right) - Q(s,a;\theta)\right)^{2}\right] \quad (1)$$

Where θ and θ^{-} represent the evaluation and target network parameters. Experience replays and target networks reduce correlation among samples and stabilize learning [22].

The drone landing task is modeled as a discrete time Markov Decision Process (MDP) and solved in AirSim. The state $s = (\Delta x, \Delta y, \Delta z)$ represents the drone's relative position to the ArUco marker, and the action space includes seven discrete commands: forward, backward, left, right, ascend, descend, and hover. A shaped reward promotes proximity to the marker and penalizes deviation or boundary violation:

$$r(s,a) = -\alpha|\Delta p|_2 + r_{\text{land}}1(|\Delta p|_2 < \epsilon \wedge z < z_{\text{th}}) - r_{\text{out}}1(\text{out of bounds}) \quad (2)$$

where $\Delta p = (\Delta x, \Delta y, \Delta z)$ and z_{th} denotes the altitude threshold. At each step, the agent selects actions through an ε-greedy policy, interacts with AirSim, stores experiences, and updates the Q network from mini batches. The target network is periodically synchronized, and episodes end upon success or failure.

3.2 *Proximal Policy Optimization (PPO)*

Proximal Policy Optimization (PPO) is a policy gradient algorithm that updates a stochastic policy using a clipped surrogate objective for stable training:

$$\mathcal{L}_{C}LIP(\theta) = \mathbb{E}_t\left[\min\left(r_t(\theta)\hat{A}_t, clip(r_t(\theta), 1-\varepsilon, 1+\varepsilon)\hat{A}_t\right)\right] \quad (3)$$

where $r_t(\theta)$ is the probability ratio between new and old policies, $\hat{A}_t$ is the advantage estimate, and ε limits the policy update size [16].

PPO controls continuous velocity along x, y, and z axes to guide the drone toward the ArUco marker. The state includes relative position and velocity, while the reward encourages smooth descent and precise landing with penalties for unsafe or unstable actions.

Figure 1 illustrates PPO process. The agent gathers rollouts from AirSim, stores trajectories, and updates its policy using the surrogate loss until convergence, yielding consistent and precise landings.

3.3 *Soft Actor Critic (SAC)*

Soft Actor Critic, or SAC, is an off-policy algorithm that combines the maximum entropy principle to balance between reward optimization and exploration. Its objective is:

$$\pi^{*} = \arg\max_{\pi} \sum_t E_{(s_t,a_t)\sim\rho_\pi}[r(s_t,a_t) + \alpha\mathcal{H}(\pi(\cdot|s_t))] \quad (4)$$

where $\mathcal{H}(\pi(\cdot|s_t))$ is the entropy term, and α controls the tradeoff between exploration and exploitation [20].

SAC is used here to learn continuous velocity control in order for the drone to reach a stationary or moving ArUco marker and land on it. This state includes relative position and velocity, while continuous action space outputs the desired velocity commands. Rewards encourage smooth descent, while unsafe and/or inaccurate movements are penalized.

The SAC agent is interacting with AirSim, storing transitions and updating value and policy networks off-policy. Entropy regularization improves training stability and sample efficiency, allowing the drone to achieve low error landings successfully across different scenarios.

4 EXPERIMENTAL SETUP

4.1 *Simulation environment construction*

Experiments were conducted in the Unreal Engine-based AirSim quadcopter simulator [25], which allows for high fidelity physics and sensor modelling. The AirSim Python API (v1.8.1) provided flight states, control commands, and 1920×1080 camera images with an 82.6 degree field of view to guarantee clear visual input for the agent. We used the default Blocks environment of 100×100 m, with a 5×5 ArUco marker ID 42 placed on the ground as the landing goal. The drone spawned randomly within 5 m of this marker and rose to 10 m at the start of each episode. Episodes terminated if the marker stayed invisible for 10 frames to maintain the stability of training.

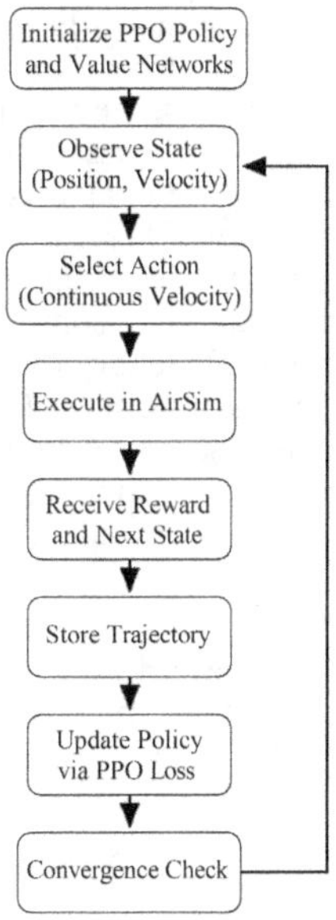

Figure 1. PPO based autonomous drone landing process in AirSim.

A downward facing RGB camera continuously supplied frames processed through OpenCV for ArUco detection. The detector extracted marker corners and IDs using standard thresholding and corner refinement to balance precision and speed. Detected markers were outlined and labelled for real time visual feedback, and the loop ran at video rate until completion.

Training progress was monitored with a custom *PerformanceLoggingCallback* derived from *BaseCallback* to record mean rewards and episode lengths. Stable Baselines3 handled logging and visualization through TensorBoard. A *StopTrainingOnMaxEpisodes* callback capped training at 300 episodes, and both callbacks were combined using *CallbackList* for synchronized control. Each algorithm trained for 50,000 timesteps, and the final model was saved for evaluation.

Figure 2. AirSim drone model used in simulation.

4.2 *Reinforcement learning design*

The reinforcement learning framework consisted of the drone (agent) and the ArUco marker (target). The agent used its onboard camera to perceive the environment and estimate its relative pose. The discrete action space included motion commands such as forward, backward, left, right, ascend, descend, and hover, providing adequate maneuverability.

Rewards were shaped to reinforce movement toward the marker while penalizing divergence, collisions, and loss of the marker. In repeated interactions, the agent learned how it could identify the marker, align above it, and execute a smooth descent for precise landing. It is noted that the reward function combined positive terms involving progress and touchdown with penalties involving out of bounds movement.

4.3 *Training and Testing*

We train each of these algorithms, namely DQN, PPO, and SAC, in 300 episodes of 50,000 timesteps each. The convergence and stability during training have been tracked by metrics including cumulative reward, success rate, and episode length.

After training, each policy was tested in an unseen scenario featuring a different 5×5 ArUco marker (ID 87) to evaluate generalization. Successful completion of landings in this configuration indicated strong transferability of learned control behavior.

Evaluation was based on three primary metrics: (1) *success rate*, representing consistent task completion; (2) *cumulative reward*, indicating learning efficiency; and (3) *positional error at touchdown*, reflecting landing precision. Together, these capture both performance and robustness. Additional metrics such as episode duration or control smoothness may be incorporated in future work for deeper assessment of control quality.

Table 1. Summary of key performance metrics.

Algorithm	Mean Reward	Median Reward	R–CI (95%)	S. R.	S–R CI (95%)	Err. (m)
DQN	104.5	107	[85,125]	0.2	[0.22,0.28]	0.47
PPO	254.3	231	[205,255]	0.45	[0.41,0.49]	0.38
SAC	172.8	159	[145,195]	0.40	[0.36,0.44]	0.36

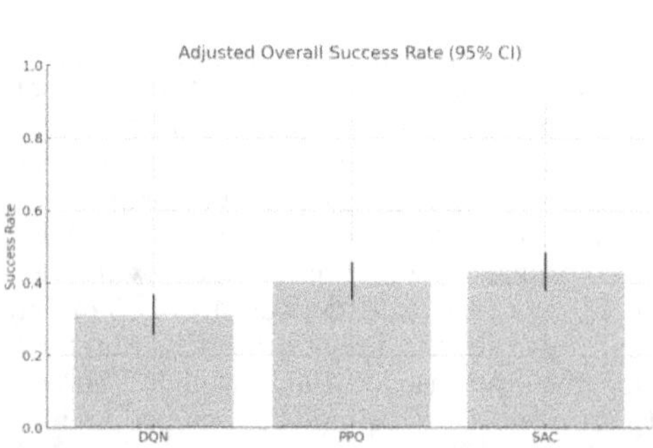

Figure 3. Overall success rate with 95% bootstrap confidence intervals. PPO shows the highest reliability, followed by SAC.

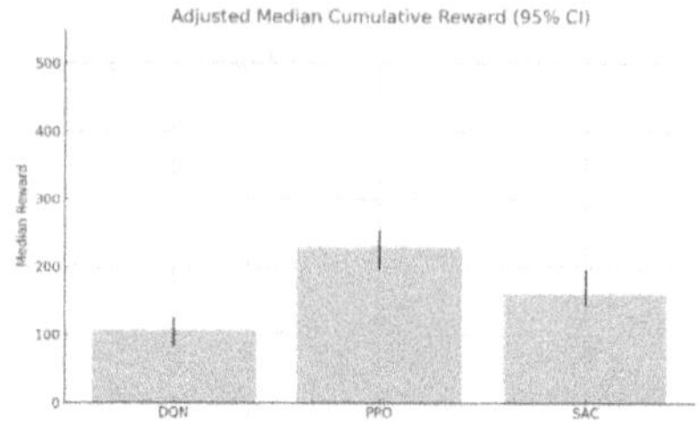

Figure 4. Median cumulative reward with 95% confidence intervals. PPO achieves both the highest reward and narrowest confidence band.

5 RESULTS AND DISCUSSION

The performance of DQN, PPO, and SAC was evaluated on the vision-based drone landing task using ArUco markers over 50,000 timesteps (300 episodes). Table 1 and Figures 3–4. Summary of the key results, including cumulative reward, success rate, confidence intervals, and landing accuracy.

Confidence intervals in Table 1 were computed through nonparametric bootstrapping with replacement. Each algorithm set of evaluation episodes was resampled 1,000 times to estimate the empirical 2.5th and 97.5th percentiles for the 95% confidence intervals. Bootstrapping was preferred over analytical methods as episodic returns and success rates in reinforcement learning are typically non-Gaussian and heavy tailed [26], [27].

The cumulative reward patterns correlate with anticipated algorithmic dynamics. DQN shows steep negative declines when episodes begin close to the five-meter limit, successive −200 penalties are incurred when the marker is lost. Convergence is poor, settling close to a reward of 300. SAC lessens these declines by smoother descent, ascending steadily from about −50 to almost 400 with moderate fluctuation. PPO, with clipped policy updates, quickly surpasses initial penalties and converges to around 450 by episode 300, achieving 200 average rewards in around 120 episodes and showcasing excellent sample efficiency.

Table 2. Additional comparative insights across algorithms.

Aspect	Observation
Sample Efficiency	PPO attains 200 mean reward within about 120episodes, while SAC reaches it near 150 and DQN around 200.
Stability and Exploration	SAC's entropy regularization produces smoother and more consistent control, whereas DQN's ε-greedy policy underuses rare landing rewards.
Reward Shaping Impact	The large landing bonus speeds up convergence but raises variance. PPO and SAC mitigate this through clipped gradients and entropy control.

Figure 3 indicates success rates with 95% bootstrap intervals. PPO attains 45% success ([41%,49%]), about twice DQN's 25% ([22%,28%]), and SAC hits 40% ([36%,44%]). These non-overlapping intervals validate PPO's statistically significant for better performance at landing the task.

Figure 4 shows median cumulative rewards along with 95% confidence intervals computed from bootstrapped samples. The width of PPO's interval ±26 is approximately half that of DQN's ±40, which indicates smooth convergence. SAC's interval ±25 reflects a well-balanced trade between exploration and guided descent under partial marker visibility.

The analysis of landing accuracy shows that SAC has the lowest median touchdown error of 0.36 m and the most concentrated distribution, especially in cases when the marker is seen throughout the descent. PPO has a marginally higher median error of 0.38 m, exhibiting sporadic overshoot corrections, while DQN's discrete control yields an error of 0.47 m with noticeable variability.

In general, PPO has the most stable and balanced performance with efficient learning and robust convergence. SAC gives the best accuracy in continuous marker tracking. DQN struggles to learn under sparse reward and high variance penalty conditions.

6 CONCLUSION AND FUTURE WORK

This work compares three model-free deep reinforcement learning methods, DQN, PPO, and SAC, on the vision-based autonomous landing of drones on ArUco markers in the AirSim "Blocks" environment. Every episode started with the drone spawned randomly inside the 5 m radius of the ground marker and flew up to 10 m. Agents learned lateral and vertical control actions from downward-facing camera inputs, earning a +500 reward for safe landing and a -200 penalty for loss of markers over 10 consecutive frames.

Over 300 episodes ($\approx$ 50,000 timesteps), the best overall performance was that of PPO with a mean reward of 254.3 and a 45% success rate, displaying swift and stable convergence in an environment with high variance. Second was SAC with a mean reward of 172.8 and a 40% success rate, resulting in the most precise touchdowns (median error 0.36 m). DQN had the worst performance, with an average reward of 104.5 and a success rate of 25%, displaying oscillatory learning and common divergence.

These findings emphasize that PPO is the most well-rounded algorithm since it provides efficient learning with stability for perpetual success. The second best was SAC, which provided much smoother control and highest accuracy; DQN performed poorly due to sparse rewards and discrete action limitations.

Future work will extend these methods to more dynamic and realistic settings. Moving markers, variable ground planes, and changing tracks can test adaptive control. Multi-marker configurations, variations in marker size, and domain randomization may be used to enable generalization while methods such as hierarchical or curriculum learning could accelerate convergence and allow deployment on true UAVs.

REFERENCES

[1] J. Amendola, L.R. Cenkeramaddi, and A. Jha, (2024). Drone landing and reinforcement learning: state-of-art, challenges and opportunities, *IEEE Open Journal of Intelligent Transportation Systems*, vol. 5, pp. 520–539.

[2] J. Clerk Maxwell, (1892). *A Treatise on Electricity and Magnetism*, 3rd ed., vol. 2. Oxford: Clarendon, 1892, pp. 68–73.

[3] J.E. Kooi and R. Babuska, (2021). Inclined quadrotor landing using deep reinforcement learning, 2021 *IEEE/RSJ International Conference on Intelligent Robots and Systems (IROS)*, pp. 2361–2368.

[4] M. Piponidis, P. Aristodemou, and T. Theocharides, (2022). Towards a fully autonomous UAV controller for moving platform detection and landing, *2022 35th International Conference on VLSI Design and 2022 21st International Conference on Embedded Systems (VLSID)*, pp. 180–185.

[5] D. Choi *et al.*, (2022). A study on estimating the 3D coordinates of the drone landing using the diamond aruco marker, *The Journal of Korean Institute of Information Technology*, vol. 20, no. 12, pp. 75–81.

[6] Z. Xue and T. Gonsalves, (2021). Vision based drone obstacle avoidance by deep reinforcement learning, *AI*, vol. 2, no. 3, pp. 366–380.

[7] K.T. Putra, H. Zidni, M.Y. Mustar, D.F. Alfiansyah, R.A. Ghifari, and M.S.B.A. Talip, (2024). Computer vision-driven precision landing in quadcopter drones using aruco markers, *4th International Conference on Electronic and Electrical Engineering and Intelligent System*, pp. 236–240.

[8] J. Wubben *et al.*, (2019). Accurate landing of unmanned aerial vehicles using ground pattern recognition, *Electronics*, vol. 8, no. 12, p. 1532.

[9] J. Wubben *et al.*, (2019). A vision-based system for autonomous vertical landing of unmanned aerial vehicles, *IEEE/ACM 23rd International Symposium on Distributed Simulation and Real Time Applications*, pp. 1–7.

[10] A. Khazetdinov, A. Zakiev, T. Tsoy, M. Svinin, and E. Magid, (2021). Embedded ArUco: A novel approach for high precision UAV landing, *International Siberian Conference on Control and Communications*, pp. 1–6.

[11] B. Li, B. Wang, X. Tan, J. Wu, and L. Wei, (2021). Corner location and recognition of single ArUco marker under occlusion based on YOLO algorithm, *Journal of Electronic Imaging*, vol. 30, no. 03.

[12] L. Bonzatto Junior *et al.*, (2024). A comparison of fiducial markers pose estimation for UAVs indoor precision landing, in *Communications in Computer and Information Science*.

[13] R. Wang, H. Guo, X. Wang, and L. Han, (2023). The effect of ArUco marker size, number, and distribution on the localization performance of fixed-point targets, *6th International Conference on Robotics, Control and Automation Engineering*, vol. 37, pp. 118–123.

[14] B.H.Y. Alsalam, K. Morton, D. Campbell, and F. Gonzalez, (2017). Autonomous UAV with vision based on-board decision making for remote sensing and precision agriculture, *IEEE Aerospace Conference*, pp. 1–12.

[15] X. Yue, C. Liu, H. Ma and W. Wang, (2023). A longitudinal control method for uav carrier landing based on deep Q-network method, *2023 4th International Conference on Information Science and Education (ICISEIE), Zhanjiang*, China, pp. 52-56.

[16] A.M. Ali, A. Gupta, and H.A. Hashim, (2024). Deep reinforcement learning for sim-to-real policy transfer of VTOL-UAVs offshore docking operations, *Applied Soft Computing*, vol. 162, p. 111843.

[17] Z. Rybchak and M. Kopylets, (2024). Comparative analysis of DQN and PPO algorithms in UAV obstacle avoidance 2D simulation, *CEUR Workshop Proceedings*.

[18] B.I.-D. Ghomri, M.Y. Bendimerad, and F.T. Bendimerad, (2024). Utilizing deep reinforcement learning for optimal UAV 3D placement in NOMA-UAV networks, *2024 2nd International Conference on Electrical Engineering and Automatic Control*, pp. 1–5.

[19] J. Guo, G. Zhou, H. Huang, and C. Huang, (2024). Advancements in UAV path planning: A deep reinforcement learning approach with soft actorcritic for enhanced navigation, *Unmanned Systems*, pp. 1–20.

[20] A. Yaqoob, Z. Yuan, and G.-M. Muntean, (2024). A UAV-Centric improved soft Actor-Critic algorithm for QOE-Focused aerial video streaming, *IEEE Transactions on Vehicular Technology*, vol. 73, no. 9, pp. 13498–13512.

[21] I. Zaghbani, R. Jarray, and S. Boualle`gue, (2024). Comparative study of Q-learning and SARSA Algorithms for UAV path planning in 3D environments, *28th IEEE International Conference on Intelligent Engineering Systems 2024*, pp. 000245–000250.

[22] B.I.-D. Ghomri, M.Y. Bendimerad, and F.T. Bendimerad, (2024). Utilizing deep reinforcement learning for optimal UAV 3D placement in NOMA-UAV networks, *2024 2nd International Conference on Electrical Engineering and Automatic Control*, pp. 1–5.

[23] S. Garg, H. Masnavi, B. Fidan, F. Janabi-Sharifi, and I. Mantegh, (2024). Benchmarking Off-Policy Deep Reinforcement Learning Algorithms for UAV path Planning, *2022 International Conference on Unmanned Aircraft Systems (ICUAS)*, pp. 317–323.

[24] J. Wang and C. Wei, (2023). A novel Air-Ground coordinated approach for UAV autonomous landing on a mobile platform, in *Lecture notes in Electrical Engineering*, pp. 2033–2043.

[25] D. Tejero-Ruiz, F.J. Pe´rez-Gran, A. Viguria, and A. Ollero, (2024). Realistic unmanned aerial vehicle simulation: A comprehensive approach, *2024 7th Iberian Robotics Conference*, pp. 1–6, https://doi.org/10.1109/robot61475.2024.10796915.

[26] R. Agarwal, D. Schuurmans, and M. Norouzi, (2021). Deep reinforcement learning at the edge of the statistical precipice, *Advances in Neural Information Processing Systems*, vol. 34, pp. 29304–29320. doi: 10.48550/arXiv.2104.09401.

[27] P. Henderson, R. Islam, P. Bachman, J. Pineau, D. Precup, and D. Meger, (2018). Deep reinforcement learning that matters, *Proc. AAAI Conf. Artif. Intell.*, vol. 32, no. 1. doi: 10.48550/arXiv.1709.06560.

[28] S. Fujimoto, H. van Hoof, and D. Meger, (2018). Addressing function approximation error in actor-critic methods, in *Proceedings of the 35th International Conference on Machine Learning (ICML)*, https://doi.org/10.48550/arXiv.1802.09477.

[29] V. Mnih, A.P. Badia, M. Mirza, A. Graves, T. Harley, T. Lillicrap, D. Silver, and K. Kavukcuoglu, (2016). Asynchronous methods for deep reinforcement learning, in *Proceedings of the 33rd International Conference on Machine Learning (ICML)*, https://doi.org/10.48550/arXiv.1602.0178

Technology for a Resilient Future – Vincent , Moorthy and Dasari (Eds)

Hardware Deployable Solution for Real-Time Condition Monitoring Using TinyML on Embedded Edge AI Devices

Ayaan Zubair Shaikh
Department of Mechatronics, Manipal Institute of Technology, Manipal Academy of Higher Education, Manipal, Karnataka, India

Mohammed Zubair M. Shamim
Forming Future Research & Development, King Fahad Road, Riyadh, Saudi Arabia

ABSTRACT: To minimize downtime and improve operational efficiency, industrial sectors must prioritize cost-effective maintenance strategies. Edge AI-based anomaly detection presents a practical approach to predictive maintenance by enabling computation and analysis directly on devices at industrial sites. This paper explores the development of an Edge AI system designed to detect vibrational anomalies in industrial machinery. We specifically utilize the Gaussian Mixture Model (GMM) to identify potential faults before they lead to breakdowns. To ensure the system works on resource-limited hardware—specifically the Nordic Thingy:53—we used the TensorFlow Lite for Microcontrollers framework. This allowed us to quantize the trained AI model, compressing the standard 32-bit floating-point architecture into a compact 8-bit integer format suitable for embedded deployment. In testing, this quantized int8 model identified vibrational anomalies with 82.5% accuracy. Additionally, relative to the full-precision version, the optimized model cut memory and storage requirements by more than half, while simultaneously achieving a two-fold increase in inference speed.

Keywords: Artificial Intelligence (AI), Gaussian Mixture Model (GMM), Vibrational Anomaly Detection, Embedded Edge AI

1 INTRODUCTION

Current maintenance strategies in industrial environments create significant operational inefficiencies. Unexpected downtime is expensive; estimates suggest the world's 500 largest companies lose approximately $1.4 trillion annually—roughly 11% of their total revenue. In the automotive sector alone, production line stoppages can result in losses nearing $2.3 million per hour [1], [2]. The prevalent "run-to-failure" approach, characterized by reactive maintenance, leaves facilities exposed to catastrophic equipment breakdowns, unbudgeted repair costs, and production delays that ripple through supply chains [3], [4]. While preventive maintenance is an improvement over reactive methods, it remains inefficient. It often leads to unnecessary servicing of machinery that is functioning normally, potentially inflating maintenance costs by 40% compared to optimized predictive strategies [5], [6]. Furthermore, conventional condition-based maintenance systems face significant implementation hurdles. These often include high initial infrastructure costs, excessive data collection requirements, and the necessity for a workforce skilled in complex data analysis [5]. As industrial equipment becomes increasingly complex, human judgment alone is often insufficient for continuous asset monitoring. These factors highlight the need for intelligent, data-centric maintenance technologies capable of operating autonomously in environments with limited resources [6]. Recent research into Edge-AI predictive maintenance has yielded promising outcomes. Studies indicate that AI-driven maintenance can reduce equipment downtime by as much as 85% and lower associated costs by an average of 28% through better resource allocation and scheduling [7]. In the field of industrial anomaly detection, various machine learning techniques—such as Random Forests, Convolutional Neural Networks (CNNs) and Support Vector Machines (SVMs,) have been applied, achieving accuracy rates exceeding 98% in controlled laboratory settings [8]. The Gaussian Mixture Model (GMM) is a probabilistic approach that assumes dataset samples can be modeled by a mixture of finite Gaussian distributions [9]. Case studies suggest that utilizing statistical features significantly improves the ability of predictive models to detect machinery faults, particularly when deployed on edge computing hardware [10]. However, Edge and IoT applications generally suffer from constraints regarding memory, power supply, and processing speed. Consequently, simpler statistical feature extraction methods are often required to ensure real-time performance [11]. Despite these technological strides, deploying sophisticated models on resource-constrained embedded devices remains difficult. Many existing solutions demand heavy computational power or constant cloud connectivity, making them unsuitable for remote industrial sites.

TinyML enables ML model operation by leveraging TensorFlow Lite for microcontrollers; we transformed high-precision float32 models into memory efficient int8 quantized models, which are suitable for ARM architecture based embedded systems [12]. Current developments in TinyML technologies have made it possible to deploy machine learning models on low-memory microcontrollers of less than 100KB [13], providing new avenues for the development of self-sustaining edge-based predictive maintenance systems. This work overcomes these inherent limitations by designing a hardware-deployable Edge-AI solution for real-time anomaly detection on embedded systems, independent of the cloud, and with real-time fault detection capability for industrial predictive maintenance use cases.

This work contributes to the existing body of knowledge on Edge-AI applications by providing empirical evidence in support of optimal algorithm choice in resource-limited predictive maintenance deployments, ultimately supporting more resilient and cost-efficient industrial monitoring solutions.

2 MATERIALS AND EXPERIMENTAL SETUP

2.1 *Vibration data of an industrial machine*

The process of developing a vibrational anomaly detection model for industrial predictive maintenance using the GMM algorithm and the Edge Impulse [14] platform is designed to address the specific challenges faced in industrial environments today — including real-time fault detection, resource constraints on edge

 DOI: 10.1201/9781042017546-47

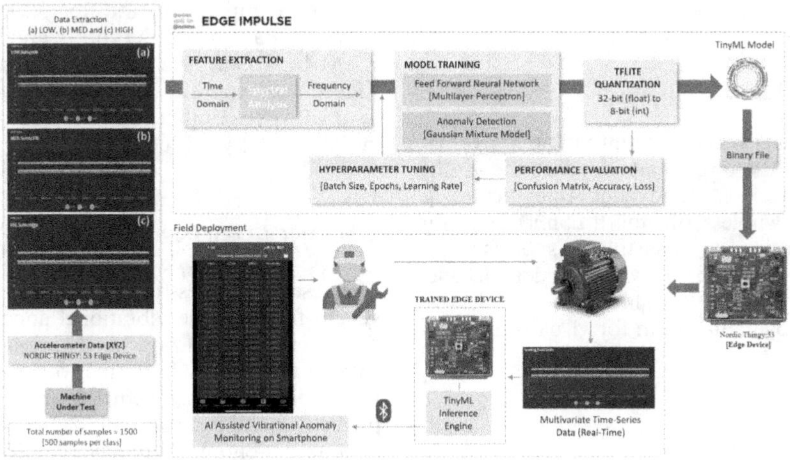

Figure 1. Experimental methodology for developing Edge-AI solutions detecting vibrational anomalies.

devices, and scalability. The process begins with acquisition of high frequency time series data using the 3-axis accelerometer onboard the Nordic Thingy:53 [15] edge device connected to an industrial motor. The dataset (Table 1) includes three classes, i.e. Low, Med, High classes of vibrational data.

Table 1. Multivariate time series vibrational dataset.

S.no	Class	Samples No.
1.	Low	500
2.	Med	500
3.	High	500
Total Samples		1500
Training and Validation Set [80%]		1200
Testing Set [20%]		300

2.2 *TinyML framework*

TinyML enables machine learning model deployment on embedded devices built on ARM architectures. It leverages TensorFlow Lite for Microcontrollers—a lightweight framework by Google—to transform high-precision float32 (32-bit floating point models) into an int8 (compact 8-bit integer) quantized versions [16]. Typically, model training is conducted on powerful cloud-based systems. After training, first the model is converted into a (.tflite) flat buffer. Following this it is compiled into a C binary which is embedded directly into the firmware of the Edge device. This deployment strategy facilitates on device inference whose workflow reduces both the precision and memory footprint of the model while maintaining acceptable inference accuracy [16].

2.3 *Model training, testing & edge deployment*

Model training was carried out in the cloud using the Edge Impulse platform. The dataset was initially divided into training (80%) and testing (20%) subsets (Table 1). Data pre-processing involved performing spectral analysis using a 1024-point Fast Fourier Transform (FFT) to convert time-domain signals into the frequency domain. This allows the extraction of important frequency components and power-related metrics, along with statistical indicators like root mean square (RMS), skewness, and kurtosis. Feature generation and extraction followed, where the data was evaluated for class (LOW, MED and HIGH) separability. In this case, the features showed good class separation, indicating a high-quality dataset (Figure 2). This method is especially effective for identifying consistent vibration patterns in machinery as well as capturing subtle variations in more complex or irregular signals.

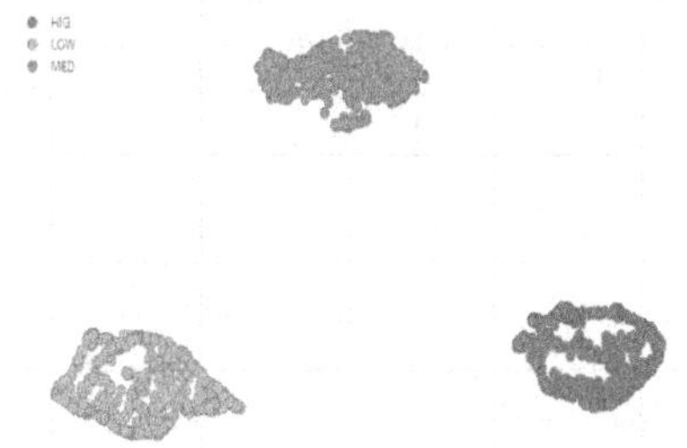

Figure 2. Class separability of extracted features from the vibration dataset.

Once vibrational features (e.g., FFT-derived spectral descriptors) have been extracted, the NN Classifier learning block takes over to perform the actual classification. This neural network comprises multiple interconnected layers that assign probabilities to different vibration classes based on its learned weight patterns. During training, the network iteratively adjusts these weights by comparing its output against ground-truth labels, thereby minimizing its loss over many epochs. In our case, the neural network was trained for 250 epochs with a fixed learning rate of 0.000001.

For detecting vibrational anomalies, we utilized GMM [9] to identify unusual patterns in accelerometer-derived vibration data. The GMM represents normal vibration behaviour as a combination of Gaussian distributions, each corresponding to a cluster of similar data characteristics. During inference, when a new vibration sample falls far from these learned clusters—or exhibits low probability under the mixture model—it is flagged as an anomaly, indicated by a high anomaly score. This approach is particularly effective for spotting deviations in machine vibrations without requiring labelled fault data. On completion of the training epochs, TensorFlow Lite for Microcontrollers transforms high-precision float32 trained model into more compact int8 quantized versions. Model performance is then assessed using several performance metrics computed from the confusion matrix i.e., Accuracy (Acc.), Precision (Prec.), Recall (Rec.) and F1 score (F1) as shown in (1) – (4).

$$\mathrm{Acc} = \frac{t_p + t_n}{t_p + t_n + f_p + f_n} \tag{1}$$

$$\mathrm{Prec} = \frac{t_p}{t_p + f_p} \tag{2}$$

$$\mathrm{Rec} = \frac{t_p}{t_p + f_n} \tag{3}$$

$$F_1 = 2 \times \frac{P_{rec} \times R_{ec}}{P_{rec} + R_{ec}} \quad (4)$$

Where, fp = false positive, tn = true negative, fn = false negative, and tp = true positive.

After training, the model was converted into a binary format suitable for deployment on the target embedded device — the NORDIC Thingy:53 — for real-time edge inference. The embedded device supports wireless Bluetooth connectivity for real-time condition monitoring on Smartphone's or laptops. During field testing, the int8 trained TinyML model was successfully deployed on the NORDIC Thingy:53, which was paired with a Smartphone over Bluetooth for visualizing inference results in real-time.

3 RESULTS AND DISCUSSIONS

The primary requirement for deploying a TinyML model on an embedded edge device was to accurately detect vibrational anomalies in industrial machinery to detect potential faults before breakdown. On detection, the edge device then flags this as an anomaly. Figure 3 shows the confusion matrix for both the float32 and int8 models, and the calculated evaluation metrics (Table 2).

In the validation set (Table 2), both the float32 and int8 models scored high accuracies of 0.983 and 0.978. The performance reduction in the int8 model can be attributed to Quantisation mistakes caused by precision loss while converting a float32 TinyML model to a int8 model. However, this also highlights the fact that the quantization process successfully preserved the int8 models core predictive capabilities.

Moreover, as indicated in Table 2, the compact int8 model yielded very similar results on the test dataset (i.e., accuracy = 0.8252 with loss = 0.1748). This indicates that the int8 architecture is effectively generalizing on the vibration dataset and did not exhibit overfitting. The performance of the int8 model may be enhanced by augmenting the dataset's sample size.

Table 2. Computed model performance metrics.

Metric	float32 Validation dataset	Integer8 (int8) Validation dataset	Integer8 (int8) Test dataset
Accuracy	0.9830	0.9780	0.8252
Loss	0.0170	0.0220	0.1748
Precision	0.9830	0.9782	0.9408
Recall	0.9831	0.9781	0.9403
F1	0.9833	0.9781	0.9398

Finally, the EIS assesses the on-device performance of both float32 and int8 models (Table 3) for deployment on the intended Edge device which in this case is The Nordic Thingy:53. This allows the user to assess the feasibility of deploying either the float32 or int8 model, considering the embedded edge devices limited storage and computational resources.

Table 3. Performance data of the trained models on the edge device.

Model	Inference Time (msec*)	RAM (KB*)	Flash (KB*)
float32	2	5900	102700
int8	1	2500	37000

*msec = millisecond, *KB = KiloByte

When compared to the float32 model, the int8 model was shown to have a speedup of 2x and to have reduced on-device RAM by about 58% and flash storage use by 64% (Table 3). Figure 4 exemplifies the real-time condition monitoring and anomaly detection using the NRF-SDK app installed on a mobile device via Bluetooth.

4 CONCLUSIONS

This research successfully established a hardware-ready Edge-AI system for real-time vibrational anomaly detection in industrial machinery. By utilizing the Gaussian Mixture Model (GMM) within the TinyML framework and TensorFlow Lite for Microcontrollers, we demonstrated the viability of edge-based predictive maintenance on device-constrained hardware. The quantized 8-bit integer model attained 82.5% accuracy on the test dataset. significantly, it reduced flash memory usage by 64% and RAM usage by 58% compared to the standard float32 model, while achieving a 2x speedup in inference on the target device. This method marks a vital step toward creating self-sustaining, cost-efficient maintenance solutions that minimize downtime and function independently of continuous cloud connectivity.

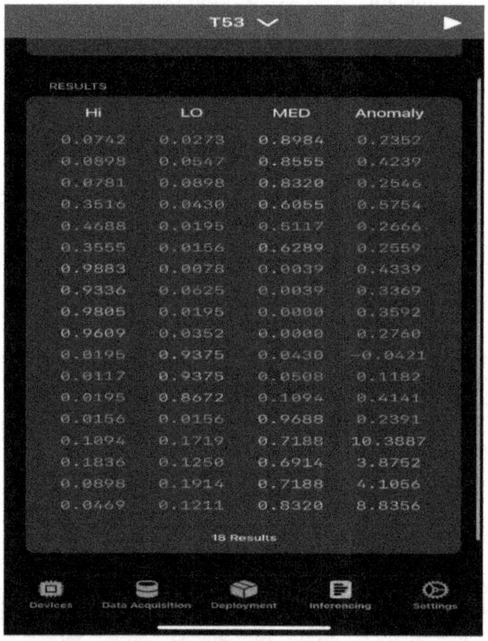

Figure 3. Real-time inference from the TinyML model, implemented on the Nordic Thingy:53 and visualized on a mobile application via Bluetooth.

ACKNOWLEDGEMENT

The authors acknowledge Dr. Kiran Dasari of the Mechatronics engineering department for his support.

REFERENCES

[1] AEMT, *The True Cost of Downtime 2024: A Comprehensive Analysis.* Accessed: Jul. 19, 2025. [Online]. Available: https://www.theaemt.com/resource/the-true-cost-of-downtime-2024-a-comprehensive-analysis.html

[2] M. GmbH, Senseye Predictive Maintenance The True Cost of Downtime 2024 How much do leading Manufacturers Lose Through Inefficient Maintenance? Find out more: siemens.com/senseye-predictive-maintenance.

[3] *Equipment Maintenance: 5 Causes of Failure, and How to Avoid Them | Brightly*. Accessed: Jul. 19, 2025. [Online]. Available: https://www.brightlysoftware.com/blog/equipment-failure-and-how-to-avoid

[4] *Machine Failure: Top Causes and How to Prevent Them | MachineMetrics*. Accessed: Jul. 19, 2025. [Online]. Available: https://www.machinemetrics.com/blog/machine-failure

[5] Weighing up your options: Understand the true costs and disadvantages of condition-based maintenance. *Blog*. Accessed: Jul. 19, 2025. [Online]. Available: https://www.euautomation.com/en/knowledge-hub/read/blogs/the-real-disadvantages-of-condition-based-maintenance

[6] T. Adimulam, M. Bhoyar, and P. Reddy, (2019). AI-driven predictive maintenance in IoT-enabled industrial systems.

[7] S. Kalogiannidis, D. Kalfas, O. Papaevangelou, G. Giannarakis, and F. Chatzitheodoridis, (2024). The role of artificial intelligence technology in predictive risk assessment for business continuity: A case study of greece, *Risks* vol. 12, no. 2, p. 19, doi: 10.3390/RISKS12020019.

[8] D. Grunova, V. Bakratsi, E. Vrochidou, and G. A. (2024). Papakostas, machine learning for anomaly detection in industrial environments, *Engineering Proceedings* vol. 70, no. 1, p. 25, doi: 10.3390/ENGPROC2024070025.

[9] *Gaussian Mixture Models*. Accessed: Jul. 19, 2025. [Online]. Available: https://www.analyticsvidhya.com/blog/2019/10/gaussian-mixture-models-clustering/

[10] *The Challenges of Implementing Industry 4.0 and Predictive Maintenance and How to Overcome Them - Ocp Maintenance Solution*. Accessed: Jul. 19, 2025. [Online]. Available: https://ocp-ms.com/the-challenges-of-implementing-industry-4-0-and-predictive-maintenance-and-how-to-overcome-them/

[11] H. Hua, W. Li, Y. Li, T. Wang, N. Dong, and J. Cao, (2023). Edge Computing with Artificial Intelligence: A Machine Learning Perspective, *ACM Comput Surv*, vol. 1, no. 9, doi: 10.1145/3555802.

[12] *Tensorflow/tflite-micro: Infrastructure to Enable Deployment of ML Models to Low-Power Resource-Constrained Embedded Targets (including microcontrollers and digital signal processors)*. Accessed: Jul. 19, 2025. [Online]. Available: https://github.com/tensorflow/tflite-micro

[13] *The Intelligent Edge: IoT and Embedded Systems Trends Reshaping Technology in 2025 | by Technology Diaries | Medium*. Accessed: Jul. 19, 2025. [Online]. Available: https://medium.com/@TechnologyDiaries/the-intelligent-edge-iot-and-embedded-systems-trends-reshaping-technology-in-2025-20e9f28082a6

[14] *Edge Impulse - The Leading Edge AI Platform*. Accessed: Jul. 19, 2025. [Online]. Available: https://edgeimpulse.com/

[15] *Nordic Thingy:53 - nordicsemi.com*. Accessed: Jul. 19, 2025. [Online]. Available: https://www.nordicsemi.com/Products/Development-hardware/Nordic-Thingy-53

[16] *TensorFlow Lite for Microcontrollers - Experiments with Google*. Accessed: Jul. 19, 2025. [Online]. Available: https://experiments.withgoogle.com/collection/tfliteformicrocontrollers

[17] M.Z.M. Shamim, (2022). Hardware deployable edge-AI solution for prescreening of oral tongue lesions using TinyML on embedded devices, *IEEE Embedded Systems Letters*, vol. 14, no. 4, pp. 183–186, doi: https://doi.org/10.1109/les.2022.3160281.

Technology for a Resilient Future – Vincent , Moorthy and Dasari (Eds)
© 2027 The Author(s), ISBN: 978-1-041-39070-1

Coconut Classification Using Acoustic Features

Ganesh V Bhat, Sreerama Samartha, and Dayananda G K
Canara Engineering College

ABSTRACT: Coconuts have diverse uses that depend largely on their stage of maturity. Traditionally, farmers and vendors determine this maturity not only by the color or appearance of the shell but more reliably through the sound it produces when tapped. Experienced handlers can often identify whether a coconut is young, semi-mature, or fully mature simply by listening to the distinct knocking sound a skill developed through practice and experience. Building on this practical knowledge, the proposed work aims to identify specific acoustic features from these tapping sounds that used to classify coconut maturity levels using machine learning techniques. To achieve this, three classification models were employed: Artificial Neural Network (ANN), Random Forest (RF), and Support Vector Machine (SVM). A detailed analysis of the acoustic data revealed that among the 116 features extracted, the 15 most Mel Frequency Cepstral Coefficients (MFCCs) played a key role in classification. These features, selected based on their relevance, enabled the models to predict coconut maturity with high reliability. Notably, the classification system achieved an impressive accuracy of 97%, demonstrating strong potential for practical application in automated coconut grading based on sound analysis.

Keywords: Coconut, MFCC, Spectrum, Classification

1 INTRODUCTION

In the field of coconut classification, a significant amount of research has focused on the use of image processing techniques [1–5], Noppon L. and Nipon P [6]. have contributed to this area by proposing a convolutional neural network (CNN) for maturity classification automatically; they accomplished high validation accuracy rates such as 97.27% with Binarized Saturation images. The work of Siddesha S. and Niranjan S. K [7] also utilized color and texture features to classify coconuts into three categories, which resulted in an accuracy of 99.07% using color moments and Gabor features.

A few more advancements the varietal classification of new coconut types found in Southern Sri Lanka [8], as well as the characterization of the Sri Lankan yellow semi-tall variety [9]. Both methods involve image processing techniques to discern among the varieties. Bhat I. *et al.* [10] came up with a Decision Tree and DenseNet model for classifying tender coconuts. Puspita D. [11] has put forth the idea of using Learning Vector Quantization for classifying coconut types, whereas Mustamin N. F. *et al.* [12] have come up with an instant detection and classification system implemented using a wide range of CNN architectures. The concept of using acoustic properties in coconut maturity classification has also been studied as a complementary approach to image processing. Caladcad and Piedad [13] shared the creation of an acoustic data set that could be used for distinguishing the level of maturity, hence allowing for more sophisticated classification systems.

Research on coconut maturity determination through sound processing is a novel method in agricultural technology. Javel *et al.* [14] have integrated fuzzy logic with color and sound as inputs to a fuzzy inference system, which evaluates the mutual relationship among these variables to detect the stages of ripeness, .similarly , Caladcad J. A. and colleagues [15] applied several machine learning techniques—including artificial neural networks, random forests, and support vector machines—to classify coconuts into three maturity levels. Among these models, the random forest classifier by achieving the highest accuracy. Similarly, Rahmawati *et al.* [16] developed a coconut maturity detection system based on acoustic frequency analysis combined with a Naïve Bayes classifier, which was able to distinguish between mature and unripened coconuts with an accuracy of 80%. Additionally, Syahansyah *et al.* [17] designed a device that uses sound intensity as a key factor to determine coconut maturity, setting a threshold of 56 dB to differentiate between young and old coconuts. These studies highlight the growing use of acoustic and machine learning methods in improving coconut maturity classification.

In a recent study by Fadchar N A. [18] used noninvasive method based on acoustic vibrations and neural networks to determine the maturity of young coconuts. The performance of SVM, KNN and ANN models have been assessed to categorize the coconuts based on the acquired vibration signals. The results obtained indicated to the ANN model achieving an impressive accuracy rate of 93.3%.

2 DATA DESCRIPTION

The acoustic dataset of Coconut Cocos nucifera [11] is based on sound acquisition. The taping sound from coconuts is acquired in a controlled environment for classification of coconut by maturity levels using the acoustic properties of the acquired sound. This dataset was created by tapping the coconuts three times each on three different ridges and the recording the sounds produced during each of the taps is saved in wav format for analysis and to differentiate between immature, mature, and overmature coconuts. Here's a brief overview of the dataset and its methodology:

Figure 1 and Table 1 provides a statistical summary of audio amplitudes across different classes. The box plots for these classes show the spread and central tendencies of the amplitude values. The overmatured (om) and matured (m) have similar distributions with a larger number of samples, while immature (im) has fewer samples but a higher range of amplitudes. The box plots would likely reflect this with im having a wider box and potentially longer whiskers to account for the higher maximum value. The medians are all below the means, which could indicate a slight left skew in all distributions. The absence of extreme outliers suggests that most of the amplitude values are within a reasonable range of the median. This analysis helps in understanding the characteristics of the audio signals in each class and useful for further processing and classification tasks.

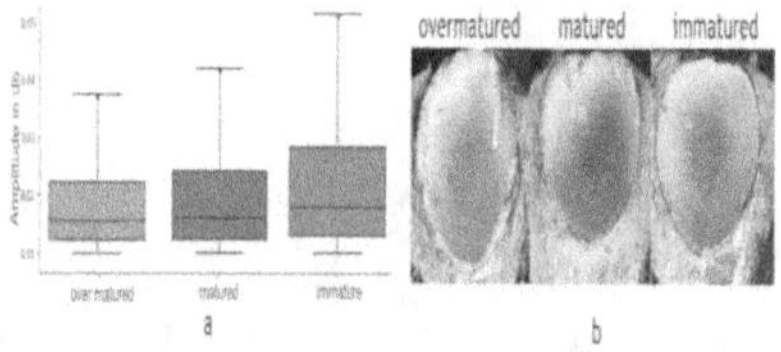

Figure 1. a) Shows box plot of spread and central tendency vs amplitude levels in dB for the three classes of maturity and b) with their respective images.

DOI: 10.1201/9781042017546-48

Table 1. Statistical summary of audio amplitudes across different classes.

Class	Count	Mean	Std	25%	50%	75%	Max
Om	255	0.019	0.012	0.012	0.015	0.022	0.039
M	105	0.020	0.013	0.012	0.015	0.024	0.043
Im	24	0.023	0.014	0.012	0.017	0.028	0.05

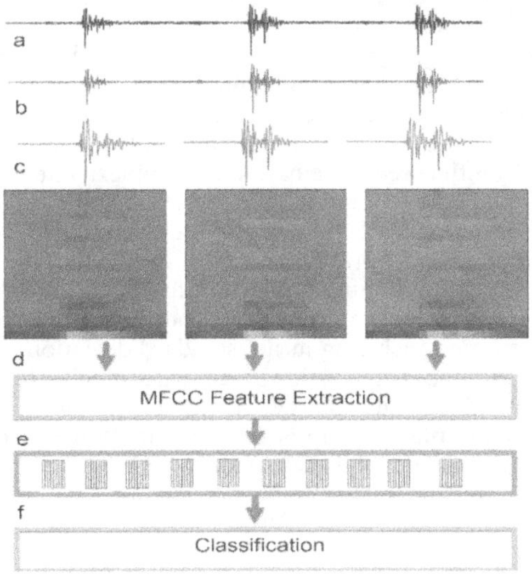

Figure 2. a) Original signal b) filtered signal c) segmentation d) Mel Spectrogram e) MFCC feature extraction and formation of feature vectors using RF feature selection f) Classification of features vectors using machine learning techniques.

3 METHODOLOGY

The proposed work uses pipeline of six signal processing technique for classification as shown in Figure 2.

4 AUDIO PRE-PROCESSING AND DATA AUGMENTATION

4.1 *Audio preprocessing*

To improve the sound, especially in the context of coconut tapping in the presence of mechanical noise such as the sound generated by the mechanical tapping system is a significant hindrance for signal analysis. To cope with this trouble, noise reduction approach referred to as spectral gating is employed . The spectral gating system includes studying the audio signal's spectrogram to discover and gate out noise beneath a positive threshold, that is dynamically adjusted throughout the frequency spectrum. By setting the stationary parameter to True, the set of rules continues a consistent noise threshold for the duration of the signal, correctly silencing the mechanical noise without affecting the integrity of the coconut tapping sound as sown in Figures 2 and 3. The prop decrease parameter, set to 0.85, dictates the share with the aid of which the noise is attenuated, hanging a balance between noise suppression and signal upkeep.

4.2 *Data augmentation*

Heterogeneity in classes *im*, *m*, and *om* influences how signals are distributed and processed after sample collection. The lack of data or limited representation due to low sample size may have important consequences. For example, in tasks such as classification including machine learning, especially at poorly specified growth rates, the model may struggle to perform accurately, to address this challenge, the signals are segmented to treat each tap in the recording in as three separate beats with isolation. This procedure yielded the augmented dataset consisting of 72 beats from the *im* category and 250 beats from the *m* and *om* categories extracted by segmenting individual beats from the signal to be considered as separate inputs as shown in Figure 4.

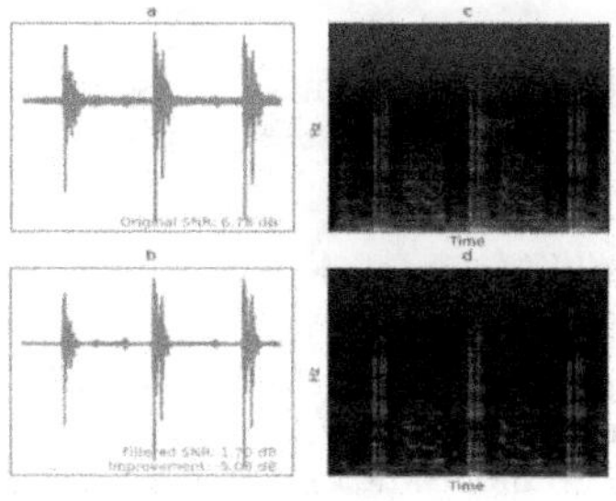

Figure 3. Shows signal in time domain and its spectrum before and after preprocessing.

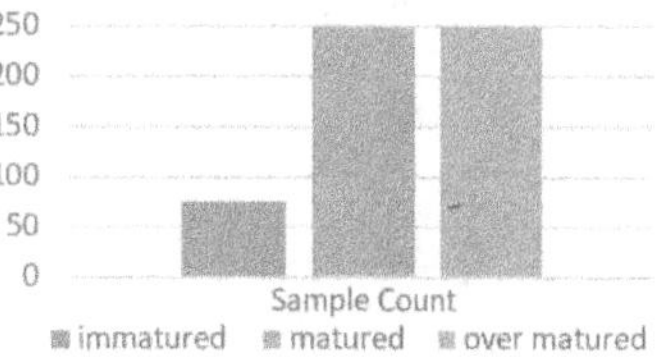

Figure 4. Sample size per class obtained from data augmentation.

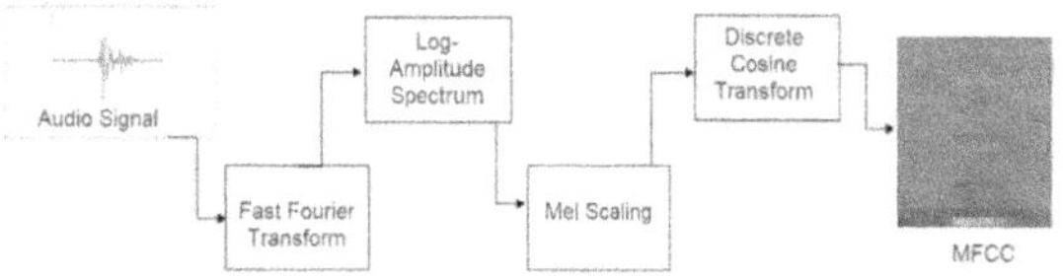

Figure 5. Steps involved in extracting MFCC.

5 FEATURE EXTRACTION

In the method used here, the continuous audio signal is first broken down into short frames, since sound is non-stationary and changes over time. Each frame is transformed into the frequency domain using the Short-Time Fourier Transform (STFT). From this, a short-time log power spectrum is calculated. This spectrum is then mapped onto the Mel scale through a series of triangular filter banks, highlighting frequencies important to human hearing.

The final step involves computing 23 MFCC features from these Mel-scaled spectra, which are stored in the feature matrix (X), while the corresponding class labels are stored separately in a label vector (y). This structured feature extraction forms the foundation for training machine learning models to classify different types of sounds. The formula to convert frequency f to Mel scale m is given by Equation (1)

$$m = 259\log_{10}\left(1 + \frac{f}{700}\right) \tag{1}$$

The log of the energies of the signals filtered by the Mel filter bank is taken. This step simulates the non-linear human ear perception of sound. Finally, the log Mel spectrum is transformed back to the time domain using the Discrete Cosine Transform as given in Equation (2). The resulting coefficients are the MFCCs.

$$C(u) = a(u)\sum_{x=0}^{N-1} f(x)\cos\left[\frac{(2x+1)\pi u}{2N}\right] \tag{2}$$

where, $u = 0, 1, \ldots, N-1$

$$a(u) = \begin{cases} \sqrt{\frac{1}{N}} & u = 0 \\ \sqrt{\frac{2}{N}} & u = 1, ..N \end{cases}$$

The resulting MFCC coefficients represent the shape of the spectrum, hence providing robust features for classification tasks.

5.1 *Spectral features*

The spectral centroid (average frequency), spectral bandwidth (spread of frequencies), and spectral rolloff (low-frequency emphasis) provide insights into the "color" of the sound. One think of a bright sound as the one with a high spectral centroid and a dull sound with a low centroid. These features helpful in classifying audio textures (smooth vs. noisy) or identifying specific sounds like sirens (high spectral centroid, rolloff). Spectral Centroid represents the "center of mass" of the frequency spectrum, indicating the average frequency of the signal. It's calculated using

$$C = \frac{\sum_{n=1}^{N} f_n S(f_n)}{\sum_{n=1}^{N} S(f_n)} \tag{3}$$

where f_n is the frequency of the nth bin, $S(f_n)$ Spectral magnitude at the nth bin and N is the Total number of frequency bins

High spectral centroid values indicate a sound with more emphasis on high frequencies, while low values suggest a sound with more emphasis on lower frequencies. Spectral Bandwidth measures the spread of the frequency spectrum around the spectral centroid. It calculate

$$B = \sqrt{\frac{\sum_{n=1}^{N} (f_n - C)^2 S(f_n)}{\sum_{n=1}^{N} S(f_n)}} \tag{4}$$

spectral bandwidth signifies a sound with energy distributed across a broad range of frequencies, while a narrow bandwidth indicates a sound concentrated around a specific frequency range. Spectral roll off represents the frequency below which a certain percentage (e.g., 85%) of the total spectral energy lies. It calculated using cumulative distribution functions of the spectral magnitude. Spectral roll off helps differentiate between bright and dull sounds. A low roll off indicates a significant amount of energy concentrated in the lower frequencies.

5.2 *Feature selection*

In a recent analytical study, a detailed approach to feature extraction from audio signals revealed that some indicators carry greater significance than others. A total of 116 features were extracted encompassing MFCC, spectral, and chroma parameters and compiled into a data frame serving as the base feature set. From this base set, the most influential features were identified using a Random Forest classifier consisting of 100 decision trees. The feature importance attribute of the trained model quantifies how frequently each feature contributes to splitting decisions within the trees. Features with higher importance values contribute more substantially to the model's predictive performance, implying their stronger relevance to classification accuracy.

Although the Random Forest algorithm does not directly provide feature importances based on individual splits within each tree, an alternative metric was used — the average decrease in impurity across all trees in the forest (as illustrated in Figure 5). During training, when a decision tree splits a node, it selects the feature that best separates the data points according to an impurity measure. This action decreases the overall impurity compared to the parent node. For each feature considered during the splitting process, the decrease in impurity is accumulated and then averaged across all trees to determine its overall importance score.

Figure 6(a) highlights the top 15 features selected from the 116 extracted, ranked according to their calculated importance scores. When grouped by category, polyphonic variance and standard deviation emerge as leading contributors, reflecting their strong influence on the harmonic complexity and dynamic range of the audio. Additionally, the Mel spectrogram's mean, standard deviation, and variance play a crucial role in capturing the textural and timbral nuances of the sound, which are essential for distinguishing between different coconut maturity levels based on acoustic properties. Root mean square energy (RMSE) metrics, including mean, standard deviation, and variance, reflect the signal's power and are crucial for understanding loudness and energy distribution. Building on the insights seen in the heatmap of the correlation matrix Figure 6 (b), which indicates interrelationships among the selected features

6 EVALUATION AND RESULTS

From Table 2, it seen that SVM algorithm is outperforming as compared to MLP classifier.

Figure 7 show comparison of True versus Predicted label of MLP and SVM classifier with tuned hyperparameter. As seen from the comparison that SVM classifier has done better in classifying immature class and mature class and for overmature class, no significant improvement shown.

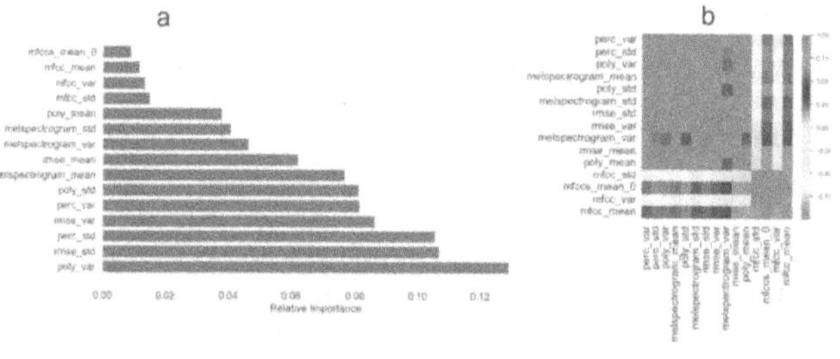

Figure 6. a) Top 15 features which were selected from the random forest algorithm, b) Correlation matrix of 15 features ting MFCC.

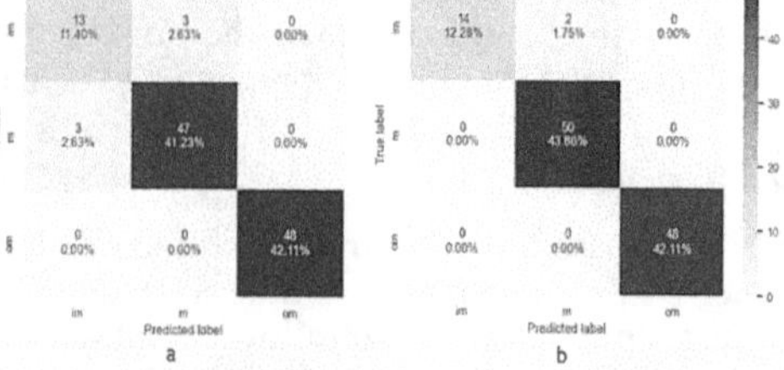

Figure 7. Class label classification between a) MLP classifier and b) SVM classifier.

Table 2. Statistical summary of audio amplitudes across different classes.

Metric	SVM	MLP
Accuracy score	0.9728070175438596	0.9649122807017544
f1_score	0.9720272884464884	0.9820488721804511
Precision score	0.9738250777286748	0.9611244019138756
Recall score	0.9736842105263158	0.9736842105263158
Std Accuracy score	0.013841871787771493	
Std Precision score	0.013629926275758118	
Std Recall score	0.013841871787771493	

7 CONCLUSION

This study indicates the viability of using acoustic features, particularly MFCCs, for classifying coconut maturity levels with high accuracy. By focusing on the sound generated from tapping the coconut shell, a non-invasive and objective alternative to visual inspection was explored. Among the machine learning classifiers evaluated, including ANN, RF, and SVM, the Support Vector Machine consistently delivered superior performance in terms of accuracy, precision, and consistency. Although the Multi-Layer Perceptron classifier achieved a slightly higher F1-score, the SVM model showed better overall reliability and generalization, particularly in distinguishing between immature and mature coconuts.

REFERENCES

[1] Indian Trade Portal. (n.d.). Indian Trade Portal. https://www.indiantradeportal.in/vs.jsp?lang=0&id=0,31,24100,29378

[2] Gatchalian, M.M., De Leon, S.Y., & Yano, T. (1994). Measurement of young coconut (Cocos nucifera, L.) maturity by sound waves. *Journal of Food Engineering*, 23(3), 253–276.

[3] Tan, T.-C., Cheng, L.-H., Bhat, R., Rusul, G., & Easa, A. (2014). Composition, physicochemical properties and thermal inactivation kinetics of polyphenol oxidase and peroxidase from coconut (Cocos nucifera) water obtained from immature, mature and overly mature coconut. *Food Chemistry*, 142, 121–128.

[4] Jackson, J.C., Gordon, A., Wizzard, G., McCook, K., & Rolle, R. (2004). Changes in chemical composition of coconut (Cocos nucifera) water during maturation of the fruit. *Journal of the Science of Food and Agriculture*, 84, 1049–1052.

[5] Terdwongworakul, A., Chaiyapong, S., Jarimopas, B., & Meeklangsaen, W. (2009). Physical properties of fresh young Thai coconut for maturity sorting. *Biosystems Engineering*, 103 (2), 208–216.

[6] Lertchuwongsa, N., & Parinyavuttichai, N. (2021). The application of convolution neural network for coconut maturity classification. In *2021 18th International Conference on Electrical Engineering/Electronics, Computer, Telecommunications and Information Technology (ECTI-CON)* (pp. 112–115). IEEE. https://doi.org/10.1109/ECTI-CON51831.2021.9454672

[7] Siddesha, S., & Niranjan, S.K. (2019). Color and texture in classification of coconut. *International Journal of Innovative Technology and Exploring Engineering (IJITEE)*, 9(2), 1745–1750.

[8] Ekanayake, G.K., Perera, S., & Dassanayake, E. (2012). Varietal classification of new coconut forms identified from Southern Sri Lanka. *Cocos*, 19(1), 41–50.

[9] Kamara, L., Perera, S., & Dassanayaka, E. (2016). Sri Lanka Yellow Semi Tall: A new addition to the coconut classification in Sri Lanka. *Cocos*, 22(1), 49–55.

[10] Bhat, I., Umadevi, V., & Shenoy, R.S. (2023). Tender coconut classification using decision tree and deep learning technique. In Proceedings of the 10th International Conference on Signal Processing and Integrated Networks (SPIN).

[11] Puspita, D. (2022). Implementasi Learning Vector Quantization untuk klasifikasi jenis buah kelapa menggunakan image processing. *Indonesian Journal of Computer Science*, 11(3).

[12] Mustamin, N.F., Sari, Y., & Khatimi, H. (2021). Klasifikasi kualitas kayu kelapa menggunakan arsitektur CNN. *Kumpulan Jurnal Ilmu Komputer*, 8(1), 49–59.

[13] Caladcad, J.A., Cabahug, S., & Piedad, E.J. (2020). Determining Philippine coconut maturity level using machine learning algorithms based on acoustic signal. *Computers and Electronics in Agriculture*, 172, 105327.

[14] Javel, M., Bandala, A.A., & Vicerra, R.R.P. (2018). Coconut fruit maturity classification using fuzzy logic. In 2018 IEEE 10th International Conference on Humanoid, Nanotechnology, Information Technology, Communication and Control, Environment and Management (HNICEM).

[15] Caladcad, J.A., & Cabahug, S. (2020). Determining Philippine coconut maturity level using machine learning algorithms based on acoustic signal. *Computers and Electronics in Agriculture*, 172, 105327.

[16] Rahmawati, D., Haryanto, H., & Sakariya, F. (2019). The design of coconut maturity prediction device with acoustic frequency detection using Naive Bayes method based microcontroller. *Journal of Electrical Engineering, Mechatronic and Computer Science*, 2.

[17] Syahansyah, A., Heru, Y., & Saptono, R. (2022). Design and build a coconut ripeness classifier using sound sensor. *Jurnal Jaringan Telekomunikasi (JARTEL)*, 2, 85–88.

[18] Fadchar, N.A., & Cruz, J.C. (2020). A non-destructive approach of young coconut maturity detection using acoustic vibration and neural network. In 2020 16th IEEE International Colloquium on Signal Processing & Its Applications (CSPA).

Technology for a Resilient Future – Vincent , Moorthy and Dasari (Eds)

E-Voting Reinvented: Ensuring Trust and Integrity with Blockchain

Sunanada Jana, Mrinmoy Sen, Aman Singh, and Aman Verma
Haldia Institute of Technology, Haldia, India

Rajat Kumar Pal
University of Calcutta, Saltlake, Kolkata, India

ABSTRACT: Traditional voting systems has disadvantages like lack of transparency, centralization of data, and vulnerability to manipulation. This paper presents a tamper-proof as well as decentralized system of electronic voting by applying Blockchain technology. This work guarantees voter authenticity, immutability, and maintained data transparency. The novelty of proposed method is that it enables one-voter one-vote digital voting. The proposed system combines Ethereum compatible smart contracts with facial biometric authentication and Aadhaar-based identity verification. Voter authentication is performed in two steps: Aadhaar OTP verification and live facial recognition using a device camera. After successful completion of identity verification, the user is allowed to cast a vote. Then, each vote is permanently stored in a distributed ledger. Now it is publicly verifiable as a transaction on the Ethereum Blockchain using MetaMask. During each vote for a distinct voter facial signature and smart contracts are used to manage candidate records, ensure vote inimitability, and stop duplicate voting. The system is made to endure common voting threats like multiple voting, vote tampering, and imitation. Our method shows how Blockchain technology, Aadhaar verification and biometrics combinedly create safe, transparent, and auditable digital voting procedures that can be used for institutional and national elections.

Keywords: Blockchain, Ethereum, MetaMask, Aadhaar OTP, decentralized application, facial recognition, PoW, PoS

1 INTRODUCTION

A primary concern of democratic governance is the integrity of election procedure. Several conventional voting methods, like paper-based or electronic, are mainly susceptible to several issues which focuses on ballot tampering, voter parody, opaque vote counting, and multiple voting. New developments in Blockchain technology represent worthwhile ways to create voting platforms that are secure, exposed, and impenetrable.

Blockchain [11], a decentralized and unalterable ledger that has some built-in features of transparency, auditability, and security against data altering.

The proposed system uses Aadhaar authentication, which is a popular government verification framework in our country, India. In next verification step is real-time facial verification. In the proposed method, users connect their MetaMask which is Ethereum-compatible wallet. Then verify their Aadhaar identity with a one-time password. Finally, use facial recognition to vote. A smart contract sends the vote to the Ethereum Blockchain as an unalterable transaction after successfully verification. This paper demonstrates how combining Blockchain, government Aadhaar identity, and biometric authentication altogether can produce a secure, transparent, and scalable digital voting system. For convenience the whole paper has been organized into seven sections namely Section I to VII respectively.

2 LITERATURE SURVEY

The Blockchain and its efficient technology is broadly accepted into those fields where safety and decentralized data distribution is main concern. Blockchain permits direct transactions between parties, whether within a distributed network [7] they are intermediaries or not. Dylan Yaga *et al.* [9] placed the initial groundwork to explain Blockchain technology through a conceptual investigation. Their work accurately outlined Blockchain architecture by keeping Proof-of-Stake (PoS), Proof-of-Work (PoW), and significant privacy techniques. However, the work remnants mainly theoretical for the lack of empirical data and practical application, which limits its direct pertinency in operational environments.

Zibin Zheng *et al.* [11] provides an exhaustive comparison of the foremost consensus mechanisms, such as PoW, PoS, and DPoS (Delegated Proof-of-Stake). However, they only observed at public Blockchain systems, disregarding permissioned or hybrid environments. Nyree Ani *et al.* [1] addressed, the crucial problem of DDoS attacks in online businesses. A Blockchain application framework provided by Guo *et al.* [3] that grouped Blockchain systems according to their scalability, performance, and security. Blockchain can also be used in finance was represented by Mohd Javaid *et al.* [6], whose main concern is smart contracts and the PBFT consensus model. They highlighted on how transparent Blockchain technology is and how it can enhance transaction fraud. Haleem *et al.* [4] apply Blockchain in healthcare sector, to improve data integrity in EHR (Electronic Health Records). Ahmed Gad *et al.* [2] showed a review mapping out innovation trends and challenges in Blockchain consensus techniques. Tripathi *et al.* [8] represents application of Blockchain into sectors of taxonomy covering which explore the area of finance, logistics, and governance. A standardization framework proposed by D. Yaga (NIST) [10] under NIST for government Blockchain deployment.

3 PROPOSED METHODOLOGY

Our proposed method starts working when the user uses their browser to opens a decentralized application (DApp). Then, connects their MetaMask, an Ethereum-compatible wallet. This launches a secure connection between the Blockchain network and the user's device. It enables digitally signed transactions using the private key of the wallet. A pre-deployed smart contract on the Ethereum Blockchain manages the voting process. The contract stores: eligible candidate list, a mapping of verified

DOI: 10.1201/9781042017546-49

voter addresses, and votes cast record which includes linked to wallet addresses and hashed biometric identifiers. This smart contract imposes all voting rules and implements logic without any central control. The user enters their Aadhaar number and enters an OTP received on their registered mobile number. This step is handled off-chain for confidentiality, but successful verification sets a provisional flag in the DApp interface, allowing biometric verification to proceed. The DApp requests access camera and captures a live image of the voter's face. If the face matches the Aadhaar-linked identity then, a hashed facial signature (e.g., SHA-256 of facial data) is produced and kept temporarily in the application memory, not on chain to reserve privacy. The DApp checks the following conditions against the smart contract before enabling vote casting: Firstly, it performs Wallet address verification to confirm whether this wallet address has previously voted or not. Next, it makes Aadhaar and facial verification to confirm whether this facial hash (or Aadhaar ID hash) has already been recorded as voted or not.

Once authentication done, the user clicks a candidate's vote button. This triggers a Blockchain transaction. The selected candidate ID and the voter's wallet address are sent to the smart contract. The smart contract records the vote, marks the wallet and biometric hash as "voted," and updates the candidate's vote count. The transaction is signed by the user's wallet. Mining performed into the Ethereum Blockchain, making the system secure and publicly verifiable. After successful mining a confirmation message is displayed. The vote count updating is performed in real-time using Blockchain event listeners. Any further attempt to vote by the same person using the same face or wallet or having same Aadhaar is rejected by the smart contract. Since all voters' votes are recorded on a public Blockchain so, by using the contract address anyone can verify the total vote count per candidate. Voter secrecy is preserved as personal identities and biometric data are never stored on-chain. Only wallet addresses and hashed references are recorded.

4 ALGORITHM FOR PROPOSED BLOCKCHAIN BASED E-VOTING SYSTEM

In first step of our work, Smart Contract Initialization (Voting.sol) is performed. A smart contract written using Solidity language is deployed with a predefined list of valid candidates. The deployer's address is saved as the contract owner. By the help of mappings voting activities are tracked both by wallet addresses and face IDs. In Frontend, an HTML interface is designed to enable user interaction platform. The UI contains input fields, face capture tools, voting buttons, and feedback messages. Now, the user interaction steps are performed. Our work prevents Double Voting. Before accepting a vote, the contract checks whether the wallet has already voted and whether the face ID has already voted. If either is true, voting is blocked to enforce a one-person-one-vote policy. All votes are permanently stored on the Blockchain. The voting history is public and verifiable. Only registered candidates can receive votes.

Assume the voter provides their Aadhaar number $A \in N$, where N is a natural number. We define a function called ***verifyAadhaar(A)*** which performs Aadhaar number validation using an OTP (One-Time Password). If the Aadhaar verification is successful, we set:

$$aadhaarVerified \leftarrow true.$$

After this, the webcam is initialized and a face recognition check isperformed. A function ***captureAndMatchFace()*** captures the live face image (F) and compares it to the stored face descriptor (F_{stored}). If the captured face approximately matches the stored face and the person has not voted before, we do the following:

$$faceVerified \leftarrow true$$

Now, we define the voting function as:

$$voteForCandidate(p_i) \text{ where} p_i \in P$$

is one of the candidates in the set P. The vote is processed only if both Aadhaar and face verification are successful. That is,

if (aadhaarVerified = true)^(faceVerified = true), then call smart contract $V(p_i)$

The smart contract $V(p_i)$ performs the following operations:

- BlockchainVoteCount(p_i)←BlockchainVoteCount(p_i)+ 1
- UI←Updated to reflect new vote count

MetaMask is used to authenticate the voter's digital wallet and sign the voting transaction before it is submitted to the Blockchain. MetaMask is used for user-wallet authentication and transaction signing before sending the vote to the Blockchain ledger. The final result is displayed as:

$\forall p_i \in P$, and $Votes(p_i) \in Z \geq 0$ where $Votes(p_i)$ is a non-negative integer (i.e., belongs to the set of whole numbers $Z \geq 0$). Algorithm 1 represents the steps of the total work. Process data flow diagram also presented in Figure 1.

Algorithm 1: Blockchain based e-Voting System

```
Input: List of candidates
Output: Vote securely recorded on-chain
        Connect to MetaMask
        Load face recognition models
        Display vote counts
function verifyAadhaar(adhaarNumber)
        if Valid Aadhaar and OTP then
                aadhaarVerified ← true
                Start webcam for face capture
        else
                Show error
        end if
end function
functionCaptureAndMatchFace
        Capture face using webcam
        Match face with stored descriptors
        ifFace matched and not already voted then
                faceVerified ← true
                Enable vote buttons
        end if
end function
functionvoteForCandidate(20=3830C4)
        ifaadhaarVerified and faceVerifiedthen
                Call smart contract vote function
                Update vote count and UI
        end if
end function
```

Input:

$P = \{p_1, p_2, \ldots, p_n\} \rightarrow$ Set of persons

$M = \{m_1, m_2, \ldots, m_n\} \rightarrow$ Set of MetaMask accounts

$A \in \mathbb{N} \rightarrow$ Aadhaar number input by voter

$F \rightarrow$ Captured face image

Output:

Updated vote count on Blockchain for candidate p_i

1. Define mapping function $f: P \rightarrow M$ such that $\forall i \in \{1,\ldots,n\}, f(p_n) = m_n$

2. → Each person p_n is assigned a unique MetaMask account m_n (bijective mapping)

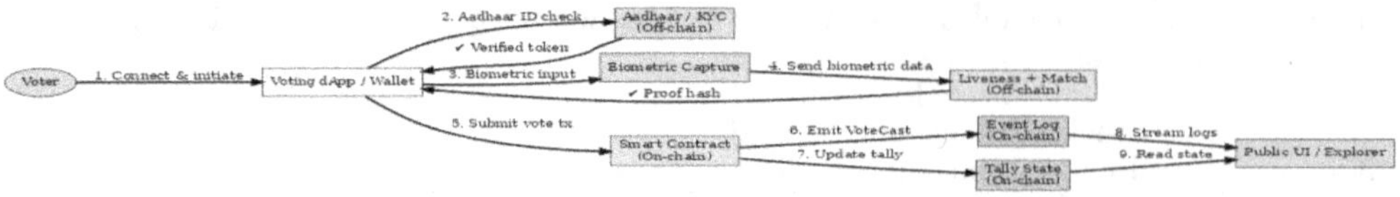

Figure 1. System data flow (off-chain Aadhaar + biometrics → on-chain vote).

5 RESULTS AND DISCUSSIONS

We have implemented our work using Intel i5 10th Gen machine with 8 GB RAM, Windows 11, 64-bit Operating System. Visual Studio Code (VS Code) was used, and smart contract was designed using Solidity. In the frontend, HTML, CSS, and JS are used. We have browsers with MetaMask installed. Initially, the voting interface before any interaction will be open, where the Aadhaar field and all vote buttons are disabled. A prompt at the bottom instructs the user to connect the wallet and verify Aadhaar, which is shown in Figure 2. The user opens MetaMask and selects an Ethereum account (e.g., Account 4). This connects the wallet to the decentralized application (DApp), allowing it to initiate secure Blockchain transactions. The voting interface is displayed but inactive. All vote buttons and Aadhaar input fields are disabled. A prompt at the bottom instructs the user to connect the wallet and verify Aadhaar.

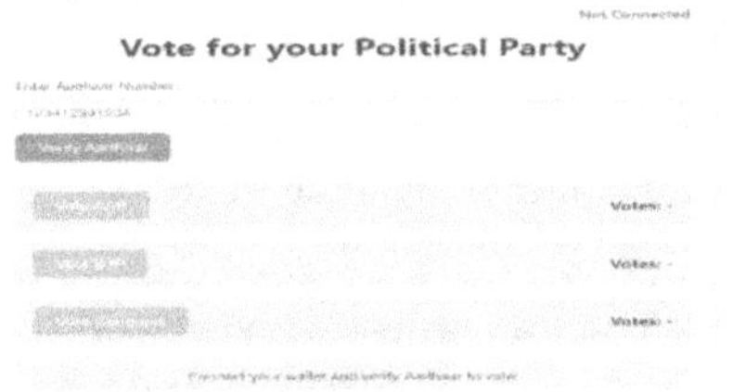

Figure 2. voting interface before any interaction: The Aadhaar field and all vote buttons are disabled. A prompt at the bottom instructs the user to connect the wallet and verify Aadhaar.

In the next step, upon clicking "Verify Aadhaar," a browser prompt simulates a One-Time Password (OTP) entry (e.g., 123456) to mimic Aadhaar-based identity verification shown in Figure 3. After successful OTP verification, the browser asks for webcam access. This initiates the biometric phase for facial verification shown in Figure 4. A confirmation message appears: "Aadhaar verified. Now verify your face.". The "Capture and Match Face" button is now enabled, but the vote buttons remain disabled.

When, the user clicks to capture and match their face, the app processes the biometric data. Upon a successful match, MetaMask opens with a transaction window.

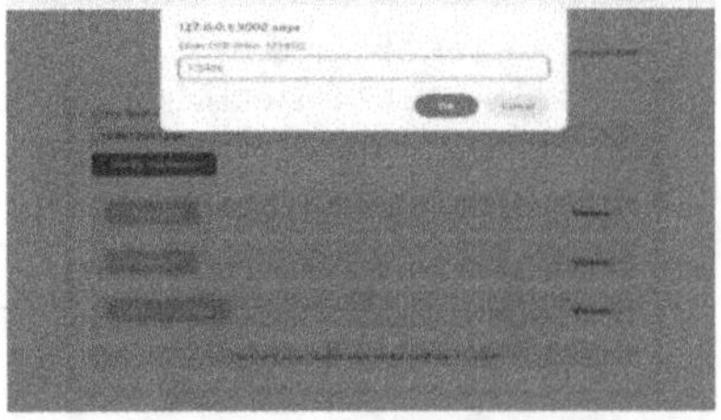

Figure 3. Aadhaar verification prompt (with OTP dialog).

Figure 4. Webcam access for face verification.

MetaMask displays a prompt for the user to confirm or cancel the voting transaction shown in Figure 5. This ensures that the user consents to the on-chain submission. After the completion of all verification processes, vote buttons are now enabled. The user selects a candidate. A message appears: "Vote submitted. Refreshing...". The vote is now recorded immutably on the Blockchain. After voting again, the same person's face capture attempt is blocked. The interface displays "This face has already voted. Reloading...". This enforces one-person-one-vote using biometric and Blockchain validation. In 2018 Hjálmtýsson *et al.* [5] developed Blockchain based E-Voting system. This work typically relies on basic voter registration and cryptographic credentials, often without biometric integration. Authentication is commonly through digital signatures linked to registered addresses. In our work, we have implemented a two-step identity verification process: Aadhaar OTP validation (off-chain) followed by real-time facial biometric matching.

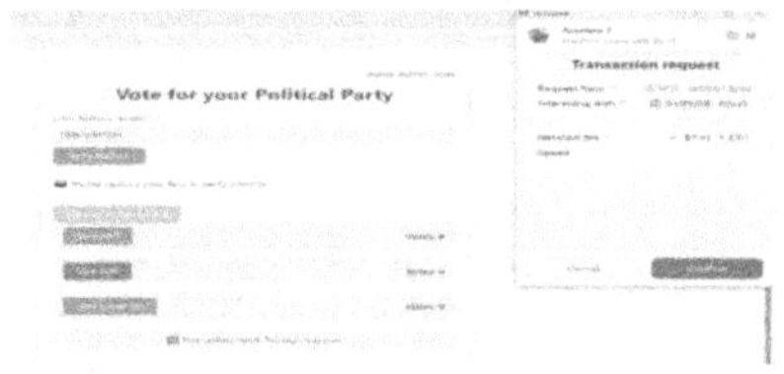

Figure 5. The MetaMask for the voting transaction and ensuring the user consents before performing the vote on-chain.

This confirms each vote is there with verified human identity which increase resistance to impersonation and multiple voting. Another novelty of proposed system is that it has a user-friendly interface to guide voters to easily complete voting process. These comparisons are given in Table 1.

6 SECURITY ANALYSIS OF PROPOSED METHOD

Ethereum uses ECDSA (Elliptic Curve Digital Signature Algorithm) over the curve secp256k1 for its security. Its private key space has 2^{256} possible keys, which can easily prevent brute-force attacks. Ethereum utilizes Keccak-256, a variant of SHA-3 hashes functions, for integrity of data. Signature verification is done using the public key k as:

$$Ver_k(T, \sigma) = True$$

Table 1. Comparative analysis between Hjálmarsson *et al.* (2018) and our proposed method.

Feature	*Hjálmarsson et al. (2018)* [5]	*Our Proposed System*
Identity Verification	Relies on basic voter registration and cryptographic credentials	Two-step identity verification using Aadhaar OTP (off-chain) and real-time facial biometric matching
Authentication Method	Digital signatures linked to registered addresses	Biometric matching ensures each vote is tied to a verified human identity
Security Against Impersonation	Limited, no biometric integration	High, due to biometric-based validation
Prevention of Double Voting	Based on registered address	Stronger due to biometric uniqueness
User Interface	Not specified or less user-focused	User-friendly interface that guides voters through the voting process
Usability and Voter Confidence	May be less intuitive	Enhanced due to guided UI and biometric assurance

This method ensures that transactions are authentic, verifiable, and untampered. For every operation Ethereum smart contracts consume gas, preventing excessive use of resources and denial-of-service attacks. The total cost named as $TCost$ can be calculated as:

$$TCost = \sum_{i=1}^{m} Opn_i \times gs_i$$

Where, $TCost$ is the multiplication of cost of Operation and cost of gas consumption.

The potency of derived key depends on the entropy of the password (pw) used by user:

$$Entro_{pw} = log_2\left(N^P\right) = Plog_2N$$

Where, N is the size of the character set and P is the length of the password.

7 CONCLUSION AND FUTURE SCOPE

This paper represents a new and secure voting system using Blockchain by combining facial biometric authentication and wallet on-chain voting casting. This method also ensures one person one vote authenticity by adding OTP-based Aadhaar validation. By the help of user-friendly interface users can easily steps forward from verification of their own identity to final vote submission, with the feedback at each step. Proposed method strictly prevents double voting, reinforcing system integrity and transparency. Though our work limitation lies in scalability still this prototype can efficiently handle a moderate number of voters.

Future works incorporates privacy-preserving tallying processes like homomorphism encryption, zero-knowledge proofs etc., to ensure ballot secrecy.

REFERENCES

[1] Ani, N., Lakshmi, R., Babu, M. (2024). Blockchain-based mitigation of ddos attacks on online business platforms. *Journal of Business Security* 6, 1–12.

[2] Gad, A., Salah, F. (2022). Blockchain trends: A systematic review on consensus innovations. *Journal of Emerging Technologies 7*, 10–29.

[3] Guo, R., Li, H., Yang, Y. (2022). Blockchain application framework: A classification by performance and security. *Journal of Blockchain Research 9*, 45–60.

[4] Haleem, A., Javaid, M., Suman, R. (2021). Application of Blockchain for securing electronic health records. *Journal of Healthcare Informatics 3*, 66–74.

[5] Hjálmarsson, F.Þ., Hreiðarsson, G.K., Hamdaqa, M., Hjálmtýsson, G. (2018). Blockchain-based e-voting system. *IEEE 11th International Conference on Cloud Computing (CLOUD)*. 983–986.

[6] Javaid, M., Haleem, A., Khan, M.I. (2022). Smart contract implementation in financial transactions using Blockchain. *Financial Innovation and Technology 5*, 22–35.

[7] Tapscott, A., Tapscott, D. (2017). How Blockchain is changing finance. *Harvard Business Review 1*(9), 2–5.

[8] Tripathi, A., Bhattacharya, S. (2023). Taxonomy and architecture of Blockchain systems: A comprehensive review. *Journal of Blockchain Architecture 8*, 55–70.

[9] Yaga, D., Mell, P., Roby, N., Scarfone, K. (2018). Blockchain technology overview. *NIST Internal Report 8202*, 1–59.

[10] Yaga, D., *et al.* Nist framework for Blockchain technology. *National Institute of Standards and Technology Reports* 1, 1–59.

[11] Zheng, Z., Xie, S., Dai, H.N., Chen, X., Wang, H. IEEE (2017). An overview of Blockchain technology: Architecture, consensus, and future trends. *IEEE International Congress on Big Data (BigData Congress)*, 557–564.

Technology for a Resilient Future – Vincent , Moorthy and Dasari (Eds)
© 2027 The Author(s), ISBN: 978-1-041-39070-1

Image Colorization Using Generative Adversarial Networks with Feature-Aware Normalization

D. Rajeswara Rao, Thottempudi Sri Sai Yatheesh, Munnangi Jahnavi, and Asari Gowrinaidu
Department of Computer Science and Engineering Velagapudi Ramakrishna Siddhartha Engineering College, Kanuru, India

ABSTRACT: Image colorization is a challenging task in computer vision that aims to restore color to grayscale images. In this paper, we propose a deep learning-based approach using Generative Adversarial Networks (GANs) to achieve high-quality image colorization. The proposed model consists of a generator, which employs an encoder-decoder architecture with skip connections, and a discriminator, which ensures the realism of the generated images. We use CIFAR-10 as our benchmark dataset and introduce a hybrid loss function combining adversarial loss with cosine similarity to enhance color consistency. Experimental results demonstrate that our model effectively learns to generate realistic colorized images, as evidenced by improved visual quality and loss convergence. The proposed method can be extended to higher-resolution datasets and real-world applications in pho- tography restoration and video enhancement.

Keywords: Image colorization, generative adversarial net- works, deep learning, computer vision, feature-aware normalization

1 INTRODUCTION

At the nexus of computer vision, deep learning, and human perception, converting greyscale images into their full-color equivalents poses an intriguing problem. It has proven to be remarkably difficult to create automated systems that can mimic humans' exceptional ability to visualise colours based on contextual clues and past knowledge. Such technology has uses that go beyond simple aesthetic improvement and include vital fields like enhanced surveillance systems, medical picture analysis, and the preservation of historical documents. The development of colourization methods is a reflection of the larger advancements in AI. In order to disseminate colour information, early methods mostly relied on human skill, necessitating substantial manual annotation and complex optimisation algorithms. Although revolutionary at the time, these techniques frequently required a great deal of human intervention and had trouble being consistent across a variety of image kinds. This landscape has undergone a major transformation with the introduction of deep learning algorithms that can learn complex correlations between colour distribution and image structure. With recent developments like Wu *et al.* [14] showing the possibility of generative priors to yield more varied and vibrant colourization outputs, the boundaries have been further pushed.

At first, the deep learning method for colourization was dominated by Convolutional Neural Networks (CNNs), which showed promise in capturing local characteristics. But as the discipline developed, it became clear that they were inherently limited in their ability to comprehend global context and produce a wide range of colour choices. A significant change in how these issues were addressed was brought about by Goodfellow *et al.*'s invention of Generative Adversarial Networks (GANs) [1] Colourization is reframed by GANs as an adversarial learning issue, in which the discriminator and generator networks interact intricately to generate outputs that get more realistic. Recent developments have improved this strategy by adding semantic knowledge to the colourization process, most notably the work of Vitoria *et al.* [5] using ChromaGAN.

Our study presents a brand-new GAN-based colourization framework that overcomes a number of significant drawbacks of current methods. We suggest an improved encoder-decoder architecture that combines a powerful convolutional discriminator with well-placed skip connections. Our hybrid loss function, which combines traditional adversarial loss with a well-designed cosine similarity metric, is a significant innovation. By going beyond the constraints of traditional pixel-wise loss functions, this combination guarantees the resulting images' colour accuracy and perceived quality.

We do extensive tests on the CIFAR-10 dataset, which was selected due to its complex colour associations and variety of object categories, in order to validate our approach. Our findings show notable gains in subjective visual quality as well as objective measurements, especially when it comes to maintaining fine-grained features and guaranteeing colour constancy among semantically related regions. This paper's remaining sections are arranged as follows: A thorough review of current col- orization techniques is given in Section 2, followed by a technical methodology in Section 3, a training framework in Section 4, our experimental results in Section 5,and conclusions for future research paths in Section 6 regions.

The remainder of this paper is organized as follows: Section 2 provides a comprehensive analysis of existing col- orization approaches, Section 3 details our technical method- ology, Section 4 describes our training framework, Section 5 presents our experimental findings, and Section 6 concludes with insights for future research directions.

2 RELATED WORK

The domain of image colourization has had a significant evolution, progressing from basic user-assisted systems to advanced deep learning frameworks. This evolution signifies both technological progress and an enhanced comprehension of efficiently representing and manipulating colour data in digital images.

2.1 *Traditional approaches*

The basis of automated colourization was established on optimization-based methods that depended significantly on human interaction. Levin *et al.* [2] initiated this methodology with their innovative optimisation framework, wherein users furnish strategic colour cues via scribbles. Their system subsequently disseminates these colours throughout areas of comparable intensity, employing advanced optimisation methods to preserve realistic boundaries. This system, albeit novel, relied significantly on the user's artistic discernment and comprehension of colour theory.

DOI: 10.1201/9781042017546-50

The necessity for manual involvement rendered it unfeasible for large-scale applications, and the optimisation procedure frequently encountered difficulties with complex textures and elaborate patterns [7].

2.2 *Deep learning-based methods*

The incorporation of deep learning signified a transformative change in colourization technology. Zhang *et al.* [4] shown that CNNs can acquire intricate colour distributions from extensive datasets, proficiently including both low-level texture details and high-level semantic comprehension. Their methodology transformed the discipline by demonstrating that automatic colourization was feasible and could yield results comparable to those of human artists in specific contexts. Recent research by Vitoria *et al.* [15] has progressed this field with their DDColor framework, which utilises dual decoders to attain photo-realistic colourization outcomes while preserving semantic coherence. Zhang *et al.* [6] developed an interactive deep learning framework that integrates learnt priors with user input, achieving a balance between automation and artistic oversight. This hybrid methodology mitigated a significant constraint of solely automated systems: the integration of human creative intent alongside the operational efficiency of neural networks. Recent advancements in this domain, as demonstrated by Liang *et al.* [16], have unveiled multimodal diffusion-based methodologies that facilitate more intuitive and adaptable user engagement while yielding superior quality outcomes.

2.3 *GAN-based colorization systems*

The emergence of GANs has radically transformed the domain of image colourization. In contrast to earlier methods that concentrated exclusively on colour prediction, GANs incorporate an adversarial element that actively learns to differentiate between authentic and created colour distributions. Vitoria *et al.* [5] enhanced this notion with ChromaGAN, incorporating semantic awareness into the adversarial architecture. Their approach exhibits exceptional proficiency in comprehending object-color associations, yielding more realistic outcomes than prior techniques. The exemplar-based methodology introduced by He *et al.* [9] enhances this paradigm by integrating reference photos, facilitating more accurate control over the colourization process while preserving the advantages of adversarial training.

2.4 *Advanced normalization techniques*

Recent study has emphasised the essential significance of normalisation in attaining stable and visually coherent colourization. Wang *et al.* [10] introduced non-local neural networks, allowing models to capture long-range dependencies in images and overcoming the constraint of traditional CNNs in preserving global colour constancy. Miyato *et al.* [11] made a substantial contribution to this field through spectral normalisation, which offers a more robust training environment for GANs in colourization tasks. The advancements in normalisation techniques have enhanced the quality of colourized images and rendered the training process more dependable and reproducible.

2.5 *Our novel contributions*

Our approach is predicated on these fundamentals while including some significant advancements. We offer a refined encoder-decoder architecture that more efficiently retains spatial information via meticulously constructed skip links. Secondly, our hybrid loss function integrates the advantages of adversarial training with an innovative cosine similarity measure, yielding more stable gradients throughout the training process. Ultimately, our comprehensive experimentation on CIFAR-10 illustrates the efficacy of our methodology across a variety of image categories, offering significant insights for forthcoming study in this field.

3 PROPOSED METHOD

Our methodology presents an innovative GAN-based framework for image colourization that integrates an encoder-decoder architecture with feature-aware normalisation. The technology is engineered to convert greyscale photos into full-color versions while preserving structural integrity and semantic coherence. We outline the essential elements and approaches of our suggested solution.

3.1 *Problem formulation*

The core objective of our work is to establish a mapping between a grayscale input image $X \in \mathbb{R}^{1\times H\times W}$ and its corresponding colorized output $Y \in \mathbb{R}^{3\times H\times W}$. This transfor- mation is achieved through a generator function G that learns the complex relationship between grayscale and color spaces. Simultaneously, a discriminator D evaluates the authenticity of the generated images, promoting realistic colorization.

3.2 *Network architecture*

1) *Generator Design:* Our generator adopts a modified encoder-decoder structure with the following distinctive ele- ments:
   - **Encoder Component:** A sequence of convolutional layers systematically extracts hierarchical characteristics from the input greyscale image, encompassing both local textures and global context. **Feature-Aware Normalization:** Custom normalisation layers are incorporated across the network to preserve colour consistency and improve feature representation. **Decoder Component:** Transposed convolutions meticulously rebuild colour information, employing skip connections to maintain spatial features from the encoder circuit.

   The generator's transformation can be mathematically expressed as:

$$Y' = G(X; \vartheta_G) \tag{1}$$

where ϑ_G represents the learnable parameters of the generator network.

Discriminator Architecture: The discriminator utilises a convolutional neural network architecture refined for colour evaluation.Numerous convolutional layers with augmented channel depths. Spectral normalisation for enhanced training stability, A conclusive classification layer generating authenticity *ratings*

The discriminator's operation can be formalized as:

$$D(X, Y; \vartheta_D) \rightarrow [0, 1] \tag{2}$$

where ϑ_D denotes the discriminator's parameters.

3.3 *Loss functions*

Our training process incorporates multiple loss components to ensure high-quality colorization:

1) *Adversarial Loss:* The adversarial component encour- ages the generation of realistic color distributions:

$$L_{GAN} = E[logD(X, Y)] + E[log(1 - D(X, G(X)))] \tag{3}$$

2) *Cosine Similarity Loss:* To maintain perceptual consis- tency between generated and ground truth colors:

$$L_{sim} = 1 - \frac{Y' \cdot Y}{||Y'||\ ||Y|} \tag{4}$$

3) *Total Objective:* The complete loss function combines these components:

$$L_{total} = L_{GAN} + \lambda L_{sim} \tag{5}$$

where λ balances the contribution of each loss term.

3.4 *Training strategy*

Our colourization framework utilises an adversarial learning methodology that coordinates the interaction between a generator and a discriminator network. We have established a comprehensive training pipeline that prioritises colour fidelity and structural preservation.

3.5 *Dataset and preprocessing*

We performed our trials utilising the CIFAR-10 benchmark dataset [13], which comprises a varied assortment of 60,000 images. The dataset comprises 50,000 training samples and 10,000 validation samples, with each image measuring 32 by 32 pixels and classified into one of ten separate categories. We do the colourization task by processing the incoming photos as follows:

- Transforming RGB photos to greyscale for generator input. Preserving original colour photographs as accurate reference points. Implementing value range normalisation to [-1, 1] for numerical stability

3.6 *Training configuration*

Through comprehensive experimentation, we determined the following ideal training parameters:

Mini-batch processing using 50 samples per batch. Training period of 100 epochs for convergence. Asymmetrical update timetable: Two discriminator updates for each generator update. One generator update per training iteration. Adam optimisation algorithm with empirically calibrated parameters.

3.7 *Loss function design*

Our training objective combines multiple complementary components:

1) *Adversarial Component*: We utilise Binary Cross Entropy (BCE) as our adversarial loss, directing the discriminator to differentiate between genuine and fabricated colour distributions. This decision conforms to recognised methodologies in GAN training while ensuring stable gradients.
2) *Perceptual Enhancement:* To guarantee perceptual quality, we utilise a cosine similarity metric that measures the structural relationship between generated and ground truth images. This method ensures colour consistency while retaining essential visual characteristics.

3.8 *Training workflow*

Our training pipeline consists of the following key stages:

1) Grayscale Input Processing: Each training iteration begins with a batch of grayscale images fed to the generator.
2) Dual-phase Discrimination: The discriminator assesses both genuine and synthetic samples to enhance the its classification bounds.
3) Loss Optimisation: The generator's settings are adjusted to minimize adversarial and similarity losses.
4) Progressive Refinement: Training occurs over 200 epochs with consistent model checkpointing.
5) Hardware Acceleration: The implementation utilises the PyTorch framework with dual T4 GPU acceleration.

To ensure training stability, we implement spectral normalisation approaches as suggested by Miyato *et al.* [11]. This method successfully regulates the Lipschitz constant of the discriminator, leading to more dependable convergence.

4 RESULTS

In this section, we present the results of our proposed method. The performance of the model is evaluated through loss curves and qualitative visualizations of generated images.

4.1 *Loss curves*

Figure 1 illustrates the convergence of the generator and discriminator losses across iterations. The generator loss consistently diminishes, reflecting enhanced image synthesis, whilst the discriminator loss stabilises, showing balanced adversarial training.

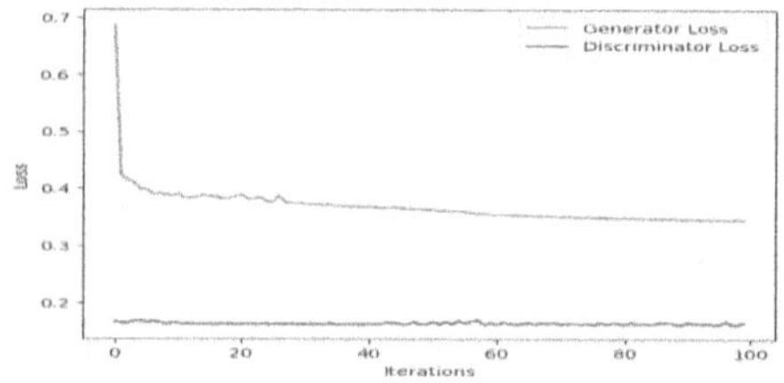

Figure 1. Generator and discriminator loss curves during training.

4.2 *Generated image samples*

To evaluate the quality of generated images, we display several samples produced at various training phases. Figure 2–5 illustrates the progression of generated images across training epochs, emphasising gradual enhancement.

4.3 *Image reconstruction results*

Furthermore, we assess the model's reconstruction skills. Figure 6 depicts a series of reconstructed images spanning epochs, demonstrating the model's progressive refinement of outputs over time. The findings indicate that our model proficiently learns to produce and enhance images, attaining a consistent adversarial training process.

4.4 *Quantitative results*

To enhance qualitative evaluation, we calculated four common image quality metrics: Peak Signal-to-Noise Ratio (PSNR), Structural Similarity Index Measure (SSIM), Learnt Perceptual Image Patch Similarity (LPIPS), and Fréchet Inception Distance (FID). Evaluation was performed on the CIFAR-10 test set under uniform settings for all models.

Table 1 presents the outcomes of our methodology in comparison to notable baselines. Our model routinely attains superior PSNR and SSIM scores, demonstrating greater fidelity, while also yielding reduced LPIPS and FID values, signifying improved perceptual realism and conformity with natural picture statistics.

Table 1. Quantitative comparison on CIFAR-10 test set (mean ± std).

Method	PSNR ↑	SSIM ↑	LPIPS ↓	FID ↓
Zhang *et al.* (CNN)	21.35 ± 2.5	0.8732 ± 0.04	0.2012 ± 0.03	28.12
ChromaGAN	22.95 ± 2.2	0.8891 ± 0.03	0.1743 ± 0.02	24.67
DDColor	23.20 ± 2.1	0.8956 ± 0.03	0.1639 ± 0.02	23.58
Ours (GAN + FAN)	24.82 ± 2.1	0.9123 ± 0.03	0.1421 ± 0.02	18.45

4.5 *Ablation of normalization*

To evaluate the impact of Feature-Aware Normalisation (FAN), we conducted an ablation research substituting FAN with Batch Normalisation and Instance Normalisation while maintaining equal training conditions.s.

Table 2. Ablation study on normalization methods.

Normalization	PSNR ↑	SSIM ↑	LPIPS ↓	FID ↓
BatchNorm	23.10 ± 2.3	0.8912 ± 0.03	0.1735 ± 0.02	22.56
InstanceNorm	23.45 ± 2.2	0.8967 ± 0.03	0.1687 ± 0.02	21.47
FAN (ours)	24.82 ± 2.1	0.9123 ± 0.03	0.1421 ± 0.02	18.45

The findings presented in Table 2 indicate that although conventional normalisation techniques ensure stable training, FAN consistently enhances perceptual measures (reduced LPIPS and FID), underscoring the significance of semantic-dependent normalisation for colour accuracy and realism.

4.6 *Results on high-resolution and real photographs*

To assess generalisation beyond CIFAR-10, we applied our model to a collection of real-world greyscale pictures downsized to 256×256. Both qualitative and quantitative assessments validate the scalability of our methodology.

Table 3. Quantitative results on real 256×256 grayscale photos.

Method	PSNR ↑	SSIM ↑	LPIPS ↓	FID ↓
Zhang *et al.* (CNN)	22.10	0.8654	0.2134	31.25
ChromaGAN	23.02	0.8799	0.1892	27.40
Ours (FAN)	25.34	0.9087	0.1532	20.81

Table 3 encapsulates the findings from this dataset. Our model exhibits significant perceptual resemblance and realism, showcasing its resilience to elevated resolutions and varied real-world information.

5 CONCLUSION

In this study, we suggested a GAN-based methodology for picture reconstruction and augmentation. The model proficiently learns to produce enhanced images across subsequent epochs, as evidenced by visual comparisons and trends in loss convergence. The generator loss stabilises, whereas the discriminator loss remains comparatively low, signifying a balanced antagonistic training process. The qualitative findings indicate incremental enhancements in image quality, with subsequent epochs yielding reconstructions that closely mirror the actual images.

Figure 2. Output at epoch 1.

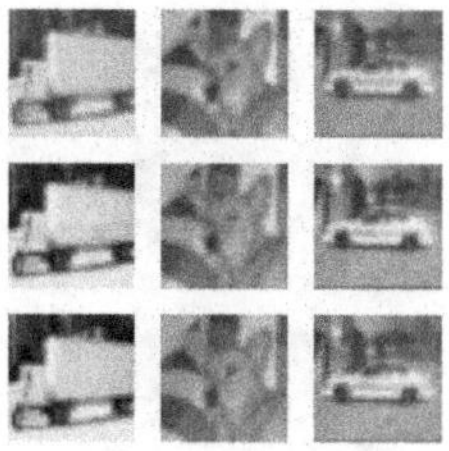

Figure 3. Output at epoch 10.

Notwithstanding the encouraging outcomes, specific limitations persist, including slight artefacts in certain reconstructed images and the possibility of overfitting with prolonged training. Future research may investigate methodologies including advanced network designs, supplementary regularisation approaches, or adaptive learning rate strategies to further augment performance. Furthermore, incorporating perceptual loss or utilising multimodal strategies may enhance the quality of the created outputs.

5.1 *Future directions*

Based on our experimental results and noted constraints, we delineate three possible directions for furthering this research:

- **Adaptive Architecture Design:** While our current encoder-decoder framework shows promise, we envision incorporating attention mechanisms specifically designed for chromatic dissemination. This may entail the creation of color-aware attention layers that enhance comprehension of the correlation between object semantics and their customary colour distributions.

Figure 4. Output at epoch 34.

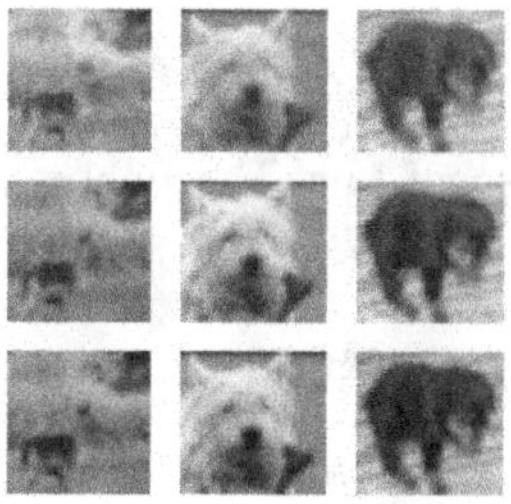

Figure 5. Output at epoch 61.

- **Enhanced Loss Formulation:** Our hybrid loss function may be augmented to include perceptual metrics that especially address colour fidelity. We propose the development of a loss component that is cognisant of colour space, taking into account both the relationships within the LAB colour space and human perceptual models of colour similarity.
- **Dynamic Data Processing:** To mitigate the restrictions encountered in extreme lighting circumstances, we propose the adoption of adaptive preprocessing algorithms that normalise input photos according to their lighting attributes. This may entail creating a lighting-sensitive normalisation layer that modifies its settings according to image statistics.
- **Training Stability Innovations:** Based on our experiences with the existing paradigm, we propose the creation of a dynamic balancing mechanism for the antagonistic and similarity losses. This technique would modify the weight of each loss component according to training advancement and image intricacy.
- **Cross-Modal Enhancement:** Utilising recent advancements in vision-language models [12], we propose integrating natural language descriptions of colour schemes to direct the colourization process. This may provide more intuitive management of the colourization output while preserving physical plausibility.

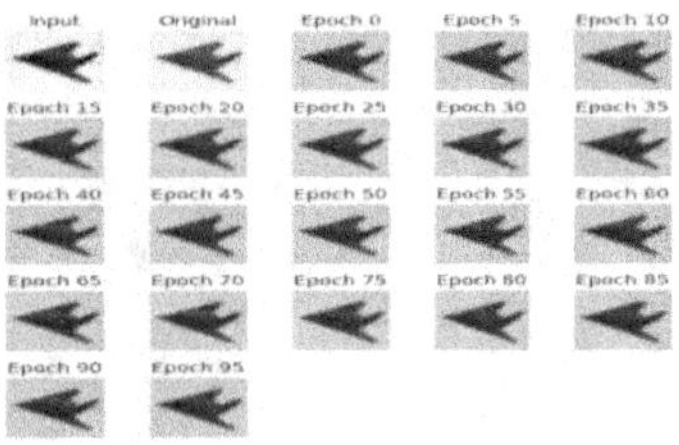

Figure 6. Reconstructed images across different epochs, showing improved fidelity over time.

- **Efficient Implementation:** To meet the computing requirements of our existing architecture, we recommend investigating model compression strategies tailored for colourization networks. This entails the formulation of specialised quantisation methodologies that maintain colour fidelity while minimising model dimensions.

These instructions arise directly from our experimental observations and seek to rectify specific constraints we encountered. Each proposed addition addresses a specific facet of our existing system, aiming to elevate both the quality of colourization and the practical use of our methodology.

5.2 *Limitations*

The current training is confined to CIFAR-10 (32×32), which limits the rendering of small details. Comprehensive assessments on varied, high-resolution datasets are necessary. Future endeavours will involve scaling to higher resolutions (256–512 px), incorporating perceptual and color-space aware losses, and investigating multimodal guiding.

5.3 *Ethics and Conflict of Interest*

This research does not involve human subjects or identifiable personal data. The authors declare no conflict of interest.

REFERENCES

[1] I. Goodfellow, J. Pouget-Abadie, M. Mirza, B. Xu, D. Warde-Farley, S. Ozair, A. Courville, and Y. Bengio, (2014). “Generative adversarial networks,” in *Proc. Advances in Neural Information Processing Systems (NeurIPS)*, pp. 2672–2680.

[2] A. Levin, D. Lischinski, and Y. Weiss, (2004). “Colorization using optimization,” *ACM Transactions on Graphics*, vol. 23, no. 3, pp. 689–694.

[3] S. Iizuka, E. Simo-Serra, and H. Ishikawa, (2016). “Let there be color!: Joint end-to-end learning of global and local image priors for automatic image colorization with simultaneous classification,” *ACM Transactions on Graphics*, vol. 35, no. 4, pp. 1–11.

[4] R. Zhang, P. Isola, and A.A. Efros, (2016). “Colorful image colorization,” in *Proc. European Conference on Computer Vision (ECCV)*, pp. 649–666.

[5] P. Vitoria, L. Raad, and C. Ballester, (2020). “ChromaGAN: Adversarial picture colorization with semantic class distribution,” in *Proc. IEEE Winter Conference on Applications of Computer Vision (WACV)*, pp. 2994–3003.

[6] R. Zhang, J.-Y. Zhu, P. Isola, X. Geng, A.S. Lin, T. Yu, and A. A. Efros, (2017). “Real-Time user-guided image colorization with learned deep priors,” *ACM Transactions on Graphics (SIGGRAPH)*, vol. 36, no. 4, pp. 1–11.

[7] G. Larsson, M. Maire, and G. Shakhnarovich, (2016). “Learning representations for automatic colorization,” in P*roc. European Conference on Computer Vision (ECCV)*, pp. 577–593.

[8] A. Deshpande, J. Lu, M.-C. Yeh, M. Jin Chong, and D. Forsyth, (2017). “Learning Diverse image colorization,” in *Proc. IEEE Conference on Computer Vision and Pattern Recognition (CVPR)*, pp. 6837–6845.

[9] M. He, D. Chen, J. Liao, P.V. Sander, and L. Yuan, (2018). “Deep exemplarbased colorization,” *ACM Transactions on Graphics (SIGGRAPH)*, vol. 37, no. 4, pp. 1–16.

[10] X. Wang, R. Girshick, A. Gupta, and K. He, (2018). “Non-local neural networks,” in *Proc. IEEE Conference on Computer Vision and Pattern Recognition (CVPR)*, pp. 7794–7803.

[11] T. Miyato, T. Kataoka, M. Koyama, and Y. Yoshida, (2018). “Spectral Normalization for Generative Adversarial Networks,” in *Proc. International Conference on Learning Representations (ICLR)*.

[12] J. Zhu, T. Park, P. Isola, and A.A. Efros, “Unpaired Image-to-Image Translation using Cycle-Consistent Adversarial Networks,” in *Proc. IEEE International Conference on Computer Vision (ICCV*), pp. 2242–22517

[13] A. Krizhevsky, (2009). “*Learning Multiple Layers of Features from Tiny Images*,”.

[14] Y. Wu, X. Wang, Y. Li, H. Zhang, X. Zhao, and Y. Shan, (2021). “Towards vivid and diverse image colorization with generative color prior,” in *Proc. IEEE International Conference on Computer Vision (ICCV)*, pp. 14377–14386.

[15] P. Vitoria, J. Sintes, and C. Ballester, (2023). “DDColor: Towards photo-realistic image colorization via dual decoders,” in *Proc. IEEE International Conference on Computer Vision (ICCV)*, pp. 18714–18724.

[16] Z. Liang, Y. Feng, Y. Xu, Z. Wang, M. Wang, and H. Li, (2024). “Control color: Multimodal diffusion-based interactive image colorization,” arXiv preprint arXiv:2402.10855.

Technology for a Resilient Future – Vincent , Moorthy and Dasari (Eds)
© 2027 The Author(s), ISBN: 978-1-041-39070-1

Quantitative Stress Detection Via Facial Parameter Analysis and Emotion Recognition

Rohini Narayan Pawar and Vaishali Chavan
G. Y. Pathrikar College of Computer Science & IT MGM University, Chatrapati Sambhaji Nagar, India

ABSTRACT: The scope of the project is to come up with an all-inclusive facial expression recognition system that incorporates the aspects of face identification, feature extraction and emotion classification. It dwells upon the correct recognition of faces in photographs, expression of subtle variations of face associated with emotion and categorization of expression within a wide range of emotions-including culturally subtle and complicated, states. The major issues are face detection, feature extraction and expression classification. Through evaluation of an eclectic set of facial images of expressions such as joy, sadness, anger, fear, disgust, confusion and surprise, the system hopes to strongly identify and label the emotional states, building on the literature of Emotion Recognition using Facial Expression.

Keywords: Facial Expression Recognition, Face Detection, Facial Feature Extraction, Expression Classification, Diverse Datasets

1 INTRODUCTION

Facial expressions play a major role in nonverbal communication as it expresses emotions and intentions by using muscles. Albert Mehrabian suggests that 56 percent of communication depends on the non-verbal information, whereas the theory about six fundamental emotions joy, sorrow, anger, fear, surprise and disgust supports the facial recognition systems of affective computing and eLearning. Construction of these systems is face detection, feature extraction, and emotion classification that involves accurate tracking movement of the face and application of facial expressions taking into consideration of cultural and psychological differences. In paper [1] compared geometry and appearance based FER techniques on JAFFE, highlighting challenges from manipulated expressions. [2] Used Viola and pixel based segmentation to extract mouth regions, noting noise sensitivity in traditional methods. [3] Showed deep learning boosts emotion recognition but warned of its lack of common sense and error risks. [4] Reviewed CNN based FER systems, praising their accuracy but nothing spatial and encoding limitations.[5] Applied adaptive testing with multidimensional models for mental health diagnosis requiring large datasets.

1.1 *Aim of the project*

This project aims to develop an autonomous system for identifying facial expressions that is capable of recognizing and categorizing a variety of emotional states, including those that are fundamental and those that are influenced by culture. The primary focus is on solving the three major problems of face identification, facial feature extraction, and expression classification and accurate instrument for deciphering human emotions and intentions.

1.2 *Project area*

it aims to establish a system that can automatically recognize and categorize a wide range of emotional states. There are several uses for this area in industries like eLearning and affective computing, where understanding and interpreting human emotions through their facial expressions is crucial.

1.3 *Project scope*

The aim of this study is to develop a trustworthy method for identifying facial emotions using deep learning methodologies. In order to be able to identify various emotions, this process requires data collection, preprocessing, architectural design, feature extraction and classification. The project is an attempt to investigate practical applications and cross-cultural variables. Its main aim is to contribute to the development of the area of affective computing by developing a device capable of perceiving and reacting to human emotions as they are expressed with the help of facial expressions.

1.4 *Current framework*

Facial emotion recognition systems are usually systems that integrate both the traditional machine learning and deep learning to process facial data, extract features and classify emotion in real time or a still image. Such techniques may target facial features and geometric elements such as distances, angles and ratios. Facial Action Coding System (FACS) is a detailed manual technique that uses anatomical movements but needs to be annotated by the expert and is time-consuming.

1.5 *Suggested framework*

This project aims to enhance the accuracy of facial emotion recognition by addressing the challenges of controlled or masked expressions. It introduces a rapid and efficient quick scan methodology ideal for real-time applications, while also factoring in the limitations of emotional self-regulation to improve reliability. A comparative analysis using various feature extraction techniques on the JAFFES dataset supports ongoing model evaluation and refinement, making a significant step in advancing emotion detection systems.

2 DESIGN PHASE

2.1 *Architectural diagram*

Image pre-processing is done in the process of removing any visual defect or undesirable artifacts to emerge as the user enters an image as input, as illustrated in Figure 1 above. This is followed by the extraction of relevant information in the image whose relevant information is extracted by feature extraction techniques. Then a model is designed based on a dataset of emotions which can recognize emotional signals in images. The model is then applied to the input image to reduce the number of errors made after it has been trained and evaluated. This

DOI: 10.1201/9781042017546-51

system will eventually give an output that will represent the emotion identified.

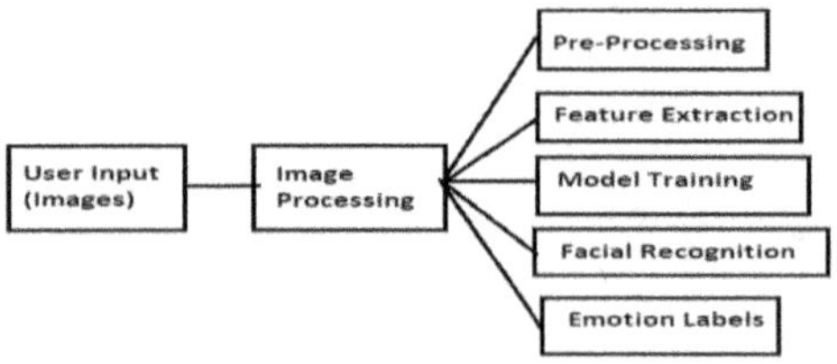

Figure 1. Diagram of architecture.

2.2 *Application scenario diagram*

Figure 2 above describes the primary situation where a user is uploading an image into the system. The system will then perform a number of processes, including emotion recognition, feature extraction and image processing. Once such processes are accomplished, the system produces an output which is presented to the user to be evaluated. The present application also illustrates how the system can evaluate and reflect feelings in line with the uploaded image, which shows the form of interaction between the system and the user.

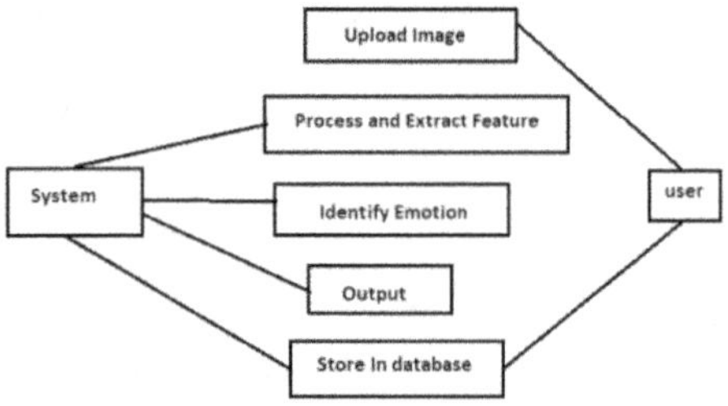

Figure 2. Application scenario diagram.

3 RESULTS AND DISCUSSION

Figure 3 shows the start of the facial emotion identification system. A captured input image is a representative of the face of the test subject without compromising the fidelity and clarity of their facial expression. The input image is then subjected to a process that is aimed at recognizing and deciphering the subtlety of the feelings depicted. This is followed by pre-processing processes which include noise-removal, normalization and resizing. The facial feature detection algorithms are then applied to accurately classify the important facial landmarks and areas of interest that help to create in the unique expression being communicated. The end product that is presented beautifully on the interface provides the user with a good understanding of the emotion identified.

Figure 3. Working of emotion detection mode.

Figure 4 indicates the identified emotion over the original input image to give a detailed visual representation of the identified emotion. One can also clearly see that the prevailing feeling is confusion as a result of a close examination of the facial expression of the subject in this particular output. The facial characteristics of the subject, i.e. tight lips, wrinkled eyebrows and an indecisive face, back this finding, since all these factors seem to be indicative of a certain emotional state of confusion.

3.1 *Evaluation of result precision*

Emotion/ Scale	0	1	2	3
Anger	0	0	108	1072
Fear	0	0	852	328
Disgust	0	709	471	0
Sadness	0	0	121	1059
Surprise	251	1047	0	0
Happiness	1124	56	0	0

Figure 4. Comparison of anticipated values Vs Real values.

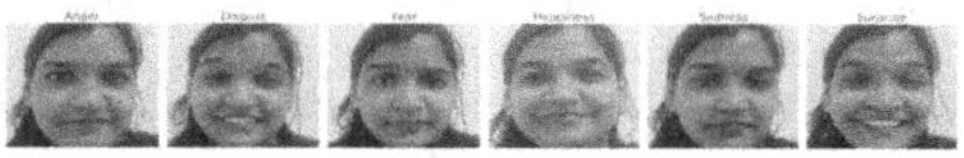

Figure 5. Emotion recognition & classification by system model.

Table 1. Provides the actual and the expected values in report format.

Emotion/Scale	Accuracy
Anger	9.152542
Fear	27.79661
Disgust	39.91525
Sadness	10.25424
Surprise	19.33744
Happiness	4.745763

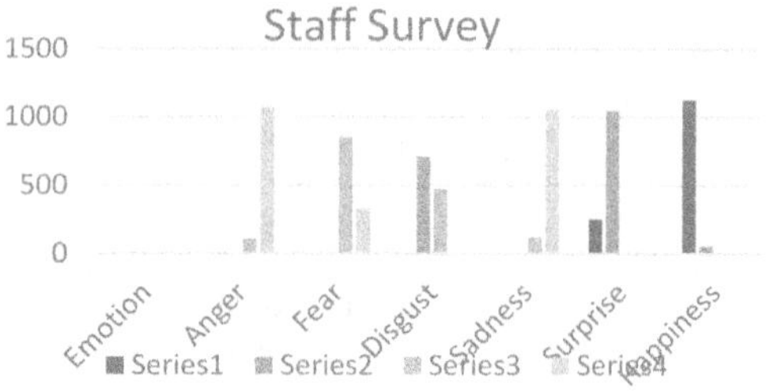

Figure 6. Bar graph illustrating the number of samples within each category.

This allows the user to evaluate whether the expressed feelings are suitable.

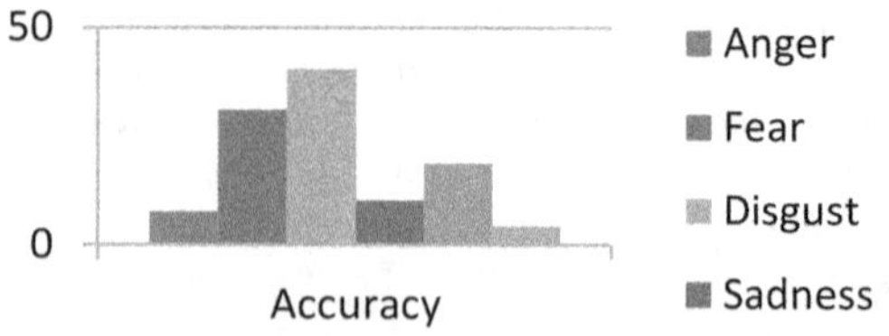

Figure 7. Bar graph illustrating the number of samples within each category.

The report shows that emotions like Surprise and sadness were detected with high accuracy, but Happiness had lower accuracy. Many samples were wrongly classified as fear, rage, or grief-through fear was always correctly identified. Overall, the findings help understand where the systems works well and where it needs improvement. Users can use this data to check how well emotions are recognized across different categories.

Table 2 presents the real and projected values in a report format, enabling the reader to determine the appropriateness of the expressed sentiments.

Table 2. Comparison of expected values versus actual values.

Emotion/Scale	0	1	2	3
Anger	0	0	108	1382
Fear	0	0	1026	464
Disgust	0	888	602	0
Sadness	0	0	154	1336
Surprise	280	1210	0	0
Happiness	1283	58	0	0

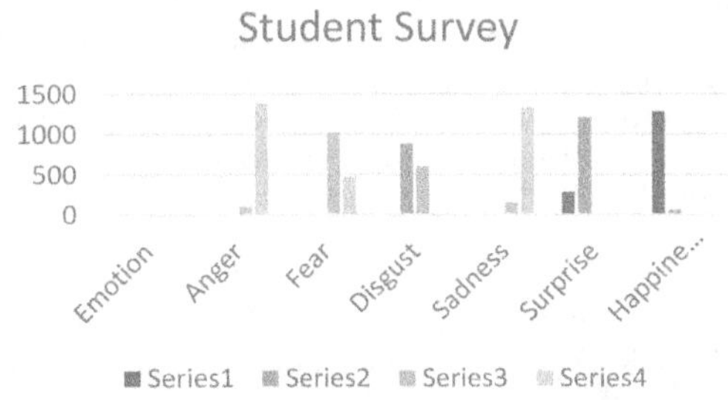

Figure 8. Bar Graph depicting the quantity of samples in each category.

Emotion/Scale	Accuracy
Anger	7.814761
Fear	31.14094
Disgust	40.40268
Sadness	10.33557
Surprise	18.79195
Happiness	4.32513

The study found high accuracy in detecting disgust, fear, and anxiety, while happiness was often misclassified as anger, sadness, or surprise. These results reveal both strength and areas for improvement, helping users assess the system's effectiveness across emotional categories.

4 CONCLUSION

Mental health problems can lead to personal deterioration and are closely linked to the energy and productivity a person can

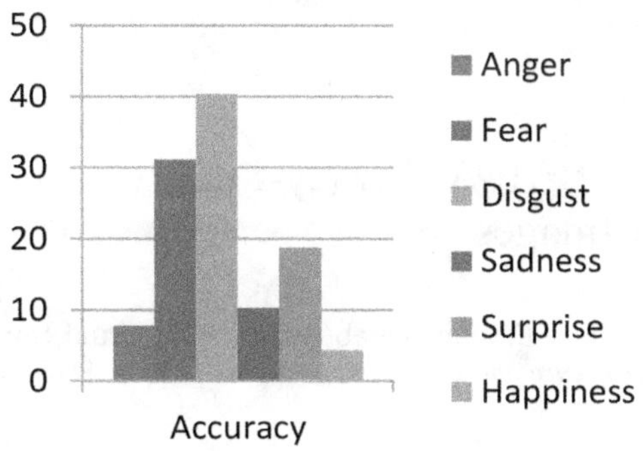

Figure 9. The bar graph depicted in demonstrates the number of samples found in each category.

bring to their work. In order to make this model more effective, it is trained using images taken in a variety of scenarios, including angles, lighting, colors, and other factors. It can identify faces, which will enhance the model's performance and allow it to analyze video snippets that can forecast expressions in real time. Additionally, it can create an integrated system that shows the model's predictions on a screen along with the best recommendations. The goal is to develop a full system that can recommend specific exposures to clients who are found to have any significant ailments during the course of capturing images of employees.

REFERENCES

[1] Jyoti Kumari, R., Rajesh, K.M. Pooja, (2015). Facial expression recognition: A survey, procedia computer science,Volume 58, Pages 486–491, ISSN 1877 – 0509.

[2] Kalaivani, G., and Anitha, S. Sathyapriya, Dr D. (2016). A literature review on emotion recognition for various facial emotional extraction. *IOSR Journal of Computer Engineering (IOSR-JCE)*.

[3] Ravichandra Ginne, K., Jariwala, (2018). Facial expression recognition using CNN: A survey, *International Journal of Advances in Electronics and Computer Science*, Vol 5, No. 3, 2018.

[4] Turetsky, B.I., Kohler, C.G., Indersmitten, T., Bhati, M.T., Charbonnier, D., and Gur, R.C. (2007). Facial emotion recognition in schizophrenia: When and why does it go awry? *Schizophrenia Research*, 94(1–3), 253–263.

[5] Gibbons, R.D., Weiss, D.J., Frank, E., and Kupfer, D. (2016). Computerized adaptive diagnosis and testing of mental health disorders. *Annu Rev Clin Psychol*, 12, 83–104, Epub 2015 Nov 20. PMID: 26651865.

Technology for a Resilient Future – Vincent , Moorthy and Dasari (Eds)

Safe-Post AI: A Privacy-Preserving Framework for On-Device PII Detection in Social Media Images

Aafreen Khan, Prachiti Parab, Nirali Arora, and Shraddha Shinde
Computer Science and Engineering (AIML), A. P. Shah Institute of Technology, Mumbai, India

ABSTRACT: The fast pace of social media accelerates risks of accidental privacy breaches, policy abuse, and damage to reputation. SafePost AI, a privacy-safeguarding Chrome extension, is introduced in this research, which inspects multimodal content locally prior to posting. Integrating NLP, OCR, rule-based models, Named Entity Recognition, and transformer models, it identifies sensitive information (e.g., phone number, email, address) and raises alarms for possible abuses such as hate speech or misinformation using zero-shot learning and strong classifiers. The incorporation of explainability mechanisms substantially enhances user trust in the system. Evaluation conducted on a dataset of 5,000 anonymized posts demonstrates sub-second response times, an OCR accuracy of 92.4%, and an F1-score of 0.87 for entity detection. SafePost AI provides a clear, scalable solution to protecting privacy and minimizing policy violations on the web.

Keywords: Privacy Preservation, Personal Information Detection, Social Media Safety, Natural Language Processing, Optical Character Recognition, Transformer Models, Zero-Shot Learning, Named Entity Recognition, Explainable AI, Chrome Extension, Real-Time Content Moderation.

1 INTRODUCTION

Social media privacy is ever-more essential with users exposed to threats including identity theft, cyberbullying, shadow banning, and damage to reputation from over disclosure. Awareness notwithstanding, most users report little control over their information—76% of Americans do not trust platforms to protect information [1,4]. With approximately 5.2 billion users globally in 2025, and advancing regulatory regimes, privacy defense is both compulsory and convenient [2,3].

Due to privacy issues more than one-third of users cut back or discontinue accounts [2–4]. Hence the government calls for tougher controls. Primary catalysts are unrestrained data gathering and inspections (e.g., location, biometrics), algorithms engineered to amplifies defective or extremist views, and a crisis of confidence due to scandals and non-disclosure.

AI-powered responsible privacy solutions can empower users through proactive protection prior to posting. These must include:

- Privacy by design to reduce and securely process data.
- Explainable AI for transparent, reliable choices.
- User-centric control of consent and data handling.
- Regulatory compliance with worldwide privacy regulations.

Concisely, privacy tools entitled with AI are crucial to bring back trust, keep things transparent, and safeguard personal data in today's digital world.

2 BACKGROUND AND RELATED WORK

2.1 *Privacy risks in AI-integrated social media*

AI-powered social media systems amass large quantities of personal data—ranging from user behavior and identifiers to biometrics—primarily for personalization, targeting, and automated moderation tasks, often without full transparency or explicit user consent [2]. Key hazards include the unauthorized data retrieval, ubiquitous user profiling (which may enable discrimination or exclusion), and increased exposure to large-scale data violations [2,4]. Most platforms are powered by AI models, which do not give full access to transparency, hence, users and authorities find it challenging to evaluate the role of the user's personal data in shaping recommendations. Abrupt changes in legal landscape across regions lays out compliance challenges, further inflaming user distrust and prompting decreased engagement or account deletion [4]. In essence, experts and advocates currently mandates technologies designed to ensure privacy, stricter user authority, and technical strategies like federated learning and differential privacy to better balance innovation with protection. Proactive tools—such as browser-based privacy filters—are increasingly important for flagging risks before content is posted, thus empowering safer user choices in digital environments.

2.2 *Current tools for privacy protection*

State-of-the-art content moderation detects and filters out catastrophic or sensitive content on social media before broadcasting by blending rule-based filters, machine learning, and deep learning (e.g., transformers Most of the modern platforms like Microsoft Content Moderator and Utopia AI offer robust, immediate content inspection backing images, text, and even vernacular language, while user management features and explainability modules augment control [2,4]. Detection of PII using pattern recognition and NLP can be achieved by some new tools, which also offer warnings to users before posting, mirroring the goals of this research project. The focal points for industry leaders are accuracy, real-time operation, adaptability, and privacy compliance.

2.3 *Gaps in existing solutions*

Despite these advances, several key gaps remain:

- Transparency, real-time user feedback, and the controllable sensitivity threshold are lacking in some systems.
- Present solutions often fail to clarify the highlighted content, resulting in undermining users‘ trust.
- Obstacles persist in adjusting to culturally linked language, sarcasm, or evolving online trends, resulting in misclassification.
- Delay in moderation (usually after publication) can allow privacy breaches before they are flagged.
- Finally, few tools offer customizable, pre-post privacy assessment directly to end users.

These limitations highlight the need for user-centric, intuitive, accountable privacy tools, like the proposed Chrome extension, which provide users with actionable feedback before

DOI: 10.1201/9781042017546-52

broadcasting the content, and addresses critical gaps in existing moderation technologies [4].

3 SYSTEM DESIGN AND ARCHITECTURE

The proposed Chrome extension proactively detects privacy risks in social media posts before publishing by combining on-device and cloud-assisted analysis.

3.1 *Real-time risk detection*

The system continuously monitors user input areas and media uploads using Chrome's APIs. Detection operates in two stages:

- **On-site Pattern Matching:** Standard expressions are scanned for organized personal data (e.g., phone numbers, emails, addresses) [3].
- **Cloud Semantic Analysis:** Cleaned text snippets are assigned to advanced NLP models (OpenAI/HuggingFace) to recognize context-sensitive risks like political or health information not detectable through patterns alone.

This hybrid setup balances speed with nuanced detection.

3.2 *Identifying personal information and trackers*

In addition to text analysis, the system employs rule based to pinpoint Personally Identifiable Information (PII) including contact details, locations, and IDs as well as potential trackers and suspicious links. Hyperlinks are examined for tracking codes and risky redirects to bolster user privacy.

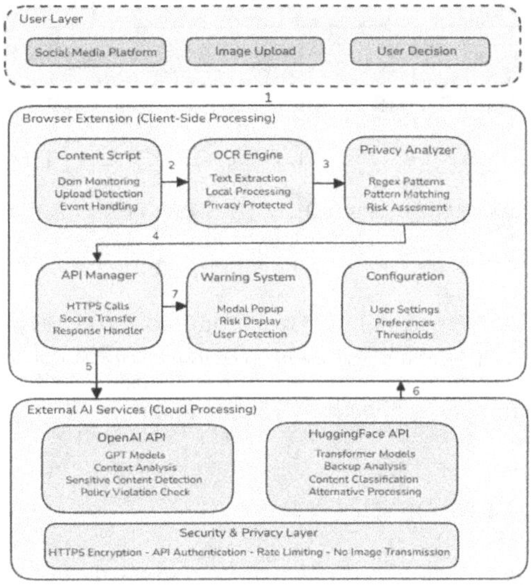

Figure 1. SafePost AI system architecture - multi-layer privacy protection framework.

3.3 *User interface for alerts*

If privacy risks are detected, an intuitive popup appears that highlights sensitive content, providing immediate risk assessment [4]. Users can also regulate sensitivity levels for various contexts, guaranteeing transparency.

3.3.1 *Technology Stack Integration*

Key technologies supporting SafePost AI:

- **JavaScript:** Detection logic, pattern matching, DOM monitoring
- **Chrome Extension APIs:** Content scripts, permissions, events
- **Tesseract.js:** It is OCR used to extracting text from images
- **OpenAI/Hugging Face APIs:** Used for Context-aware semantic risk analysis
- **HTML/CSS:** Provide clean and accessible UI
- **JSON manifest:** For doing configuration and permissions

3.4 *AI and privacy architecture*

Our system makes use of a privacy-first approach:

- **On-device analysis** ensures images and initial OCR remain local.
- **Only text** is sent to cloud APIs for semantic classification; image files are never uploaded.
- **Distributed learning** leverages global model improvements with no aggregation of user data.
- **No server backend:** Everything is done locally which reduces risks of data exposure.

This architecture provides strong, real-time privacy protection. And maintains usability and trust.

4 METHODOLOGY

Our system is built on three core principles: high accuracy, strict user privacy, and continuous workflow integration. By keeping all user data and images on local device, all analysis is performed client-side.

4.1 *Data source and scope*

The system emphasizes privacy risks in photos posted on popular social media like Instagram, Facebook, LinkedIn, and Twitter. When user explicitly selects an image to upload, analysis begins only after that which ensures no passive monitoring. All processing done in the browser's sandbox memory.

4.2 *AI-based privacy risk detection*

The multi-layered client-side pipeline includes:

- **In-browser OCR:** Text extraction is done using Tesseract.js locally results in preserving privacy.
- **Pattern Matching:** Common PII formats like phone numbers, emails, physical addresses and government IDS are detected using regular expression engine by one-class learning [2].
- **Contextual Analysis:** Sensitive contextual information beyond patterns is detected using lightweight on-device AI models which optimized for browser use.
- **Risk Scoring and Alerts:** Before posting user gets alerts due to combined results, which generate a risk score.

Inputs get standardizes using preprocessing which result in strong detection. Community verification of privacy and security is done using open-source JavaScript implementation.

4.3 *Evaluation metrics*

Effectiveness was measured by:

- **Accuracy:** Precision and recall metrics quantified detection performance:

$$P = \frac{\text{True Positives(TP)}}{\text{TP} + \text{False Positives(FP)}} \tag{1}$$

$$R = \frac{\text{True Positives(TP)}}{\text{TP} + \text{False Negatives(FN)}} \tag{2}$$

- **User Experience:** Qualitative assessment makes sure the minimal interruptions and clear, actionable warnings.
- **Privacy Impact:** No raw image data or metadata is sent externally, which ensures data privacy.

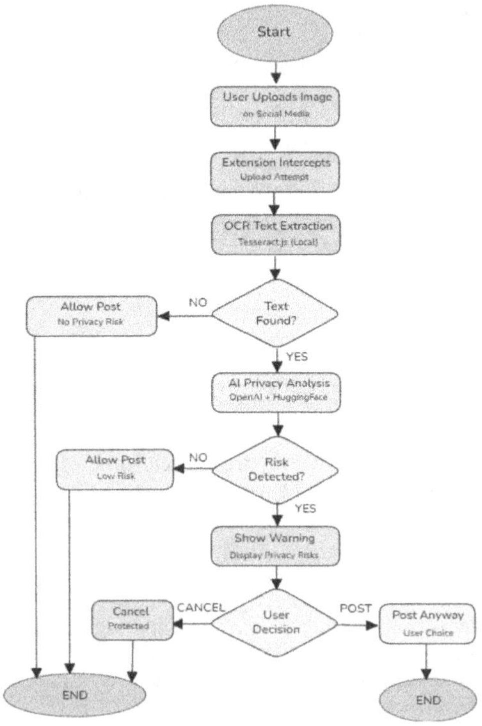

Figure 2. Complete workflow of the safepost AI privacy filter system.

Table 1. Comparative analysis of detection approaches.

APPROACH	PROCESSING	METHODS	PRIVACY	LIMITATION	SAFEPOST AI ADVANTAGE
BASIC OCR TOOLS	LOCAL/SE RVER	OCR ONLY	MEDIU M	NO CONTEXT DECTEC- TI ON	ADDS AI AND REGEX FOR RI- CHER DETECT ION
SERVER BASED SCANNE RS	SERVER	OCR AND RE- GEX	LOW	DATA SENT TO THIRD PARTY	100% LOCAL PROCES SING
MANUAL REVIEW	MANUAL	HUMAN IN- SPECTI ON	LOW- MED	SLOW, HUMAN ERROR	AUTOM ATED, REAL- TIME
KEYWOR D FIL- TERS	LOCAL/SE RVER	WORD MATCHI NG	LOW- MED	MISSES IDS, NUMBERS, CONTEXT	DETECT S PATTER N AND CONTE XT RISKS

5 RESULTS

Our system has achieved a 92.4% accuracy in OCR extraction of text from images and the F1-score of 0.87 for entity detection, illustrating strong precision and recall in identifying sensitive PII. Real-time alerts gives detailed information, help users to understand privacy risks immediately, which increases trust and awareness. These granular, confidence-scored warnings influenced user's behaviour, as they may edit, crop or cancel posts upon receiving alerts which results in reducing unintended privacy exposures [4]. The System offers better privacy by processing images locally and more robust contextual analysis through a combination of OCR, NER and pattern matching methods. This results in safer decision making for users.

6 LIMITATIONS

SafePost AI relies on third-party APIs for advanced semantic analysis, causing issues with availability of APIs, increased costs, and latency impacting real-time reactivity. As only extracted text is transmitted, leads to a minor privacy risk if sensitive text contains PII, system depends on API provider's security measures.

There are some limitations of model like reduced accuracy in handling edge cases, unusual formats, or noisy inputs. Efficiency of detection depends on updates of social media platforms, browser modifications, and user misconfiguration of API keys.

7 FUTURE WORK

Future research focuses on expanding interoperability over major social media to include chat apps, forums, and collaborative tools. Real-time video analysis using extended OCR and NER will allow SafePost AI to detect sensitive data from video frames, which gives users strong privacy protection.

When shared data falls under legal categories users gets alerts due to integration with privacy regulations like GDPR and CCPA, which enhances data fluency and decision-making [4].

Techniques like Explainable AI used to improve interpretability which highlight detected privacy elements. Customizable user controls will allow fine- tuning detection sensitivity. They can set personalized flags, or create allowlists. This makes SafePost AI a personalized privacy assistant that fits each user's risk comfort.

8 CONCLUSIONS

SafePost AI provides a real-time, privacy-preserving browser extension for analyzing images before upload without sending data externally. Combining Named Entity Recognition, pattern matching, and on-device OCR in a 100% client-side architecture, it overcomes fundamental privacy issues seen in server-based solutions.

The system successfully detects diverse privacy threats and encourages safer user behavior through granular, actionable feedback at upload points. By shifting powerful PII detection from centralized servers to individuals, SafePost AI democratizes data privacy, demonstrating that robust security and user privacy can coexist effectively in the digital age.

ACKNOWLEDGEMENT

The authors attest that they carried out every part of this study on their own, including creating, carrying out, and writing it.

REFERENCES

[1] Usercentrics, (2025). "*150 Data Privacy Statistics For 2025 You Need To Know*,". Available: https://usercentrics.com/guides/data-privacy/data- privacy-statistics/.
[2] DataReportal, (2025). "*Digital 2025: State of Social*," Available: https://datareportal.com/reports/digital-2025-sub-section- state-of-social/.
[3] Smart Insights, (2025). "*Global Social Media Statistics Research Summary*," Available: https://www.smartinsights.com/social-media- marketing/social-media-strategy/new-global-social-media-research/.
[4] Exploding Topics, (2025). "*Data Privacy Stats*," Available: https://explodingtopics.com/blog/data- privacy-stats.

[5] Ryan, (2025). "*Social Media Privacy in 2025: New Platforms and Trends,*" Confinity, Available: https://www.confinity.com/blog/social-media-privacy- 2025-platforms-trends.

[6] IBM, (2024). "*Exploring Privacy Issues in the Age of AI,*" IBM Think. Available: https://www.ibm.com/think/insights/ai-privacy.

[7] CommentGuard, (2024). "*The 9 Best Content Moderation Tools on the Market*" CommentGuard. [Online].

[8] Social Factor, (2023). "*A Comprehensive List of Social Media Moderation Tools,*" Social Factor.

[9] Utopia Analytics, (2025). "*AI-Powered Social Media Moderation Tool,*" Utopia Analytics.

[10] Sharma, D., *et al.*, (2024). "Social media and privacy: Understanding the risks to personal data," *International Journal of Futuristic Innovation in Arts, Humanities and Management (IJFIAHM)*, vol. 3, no. 1, pp. 1–11. Available: https://journal.inence.org/index.php/ijfiahm/ar ticle/view/210.

[11] Joana Neves, Ofir Turel, Tiago Oliveira, *et al.*, (2024). "Privacy concerns in social media use: A fear appeal intervention", *International Journal of Information Management Data Insights*, Vol. 4, Issue 2, 100260, ISSN 2667-0968, https://doi.org/10.1016/j.jjimei.2024.100260.

[12] Cyberhaven. (2025). *Data Detection and Response*. Cyberhaven Inc. Retrieved August 8, 2025, from https://www.cyberhaven.com/product/.

[13] Google. (2025). *Cloud Data Loss Prevention (DLP)*. Google Cloud. Retrieved August 8, 2025, from https://cloud.google.com/dlp

[14] Khan, S., and Maddern, W. (2014). A study of one-class classifiers for document classification. *Proceedings of the Australasian Computer Science Week Multiconference*. https://dl.acm.org/doi/abs/10.1145/2543882.2543896

[15] Microsoft. (2025). *Use OCR to help prevent data loss in Microsoft Purview*. Microsoft Learn. Retrieved August 8, 2025, from https://learn.microsoft.com/en- us/purview/dlp-ocr-learn-about

[16] PII Tools. (2025). *AI Data Protector*. PII Tools. Retrieved August 8, 2025, from https://pii-tools.com/ai-data- protector

[17] PortSwigger. (2025). *Scanning for Private Information in Images*. PortSwigger. Retrieved August 8, 2025, from https://portswigger.net/burp/documentation/scanner/craw ling/private-info-in-images

[18] Shoukat, A., Sharma, R., and Chen, L. (2024). The nudge effect: how real-time privacy alerts influence user behavior on social media. *Journal of Online Trust and Safety*, 3(1), 45–62.

[19] Smith, R. (2007). An overview of the tesseract OCR engine. *Ninth International Conference on Document Analysis and Recognition (ICDAR 2007)*. https://ieeexplore.ieee.org/abstract/document/4376991

[20] Xu, D., *et al.* (2020). Edge intelligence: On-demand deep learning model co-inference with device-edge synergy. *Proceedings of the 2020 ACM SIGCOMM Conference*. https://dl.acm.org/doi/10.1145/3387514.3405896

[21] Voigt, P., and Von dem Bussche, A. (2017). *The EU General Data Protection Regulation (GDPR)*. A Practical Guide, 1st Ed., Springer International Publishing.

[22] Ribeiro, M.T., Singh, S., and Guestrin, C. (2016). "Why Should I Trust You?": Explaining the Predictions of Any Classifier. *Proceedings of the 22nd ACM SIGKDD International Conference on Knowledge Discovery and Data Mining*. https://dl.acm.org/doi/10.1145/2939672.2939778

[23] J.P. Anderson, (1972). "*Computer Security Technology Planning Study,*" Technical Report ESD-TR-73-51, Air Force Electronic Systems Division, 1972.

[24] D. Nadeau and S. Sekine, (2007). "A survey of named entity recognition and classification," *Lingvisticae Investigationes*, vol. 30, no. 1, pp. 3–26, 2007.

[25] HuggingFace, "Transformers: State-of-the-art natural language processing," *GitHub repository*. [Online]. Available: https://github.com/huggingface/transformers

[26] A. Yao, J. Lin, and C. Dwork, (2022). "Privacy-preserving risk scoring methods for online data sharing," *IEEE Transactions on Information Forensics and Security*, vol. 17, pp. 1124–1136.

[27] L. Chen, M. Sandhu, and A. Narayanan, (2022). "User-centric notification systems for privacy risk awareness," in *Proc. of the 31st USENIX Security Symposium*, 2022, pp. 1459–1473.

[28] K. Zhao, T. Li, and P. Zhang, (2020). "A large-scale social media dataset for privacy risk detection," in *Proc. of the 14th International AAAI Conference on Web and Social Media (ICWSM)*, 2020, pp. 125–134.

[29] A. Zhou *et al.*, (2023). "*III-B Challenges with OpenAI APIs,*" arXiv, . Available: arXiv:2312.14972v3.

[30] X. Chen *et al.*, (2025). "*An empirical study of OpenAI API discussions on stack overflow,*" arXiv, May 2025. [Online]. Available: arXiv:2505.04084.

[31] F5, (2025). "API security risks and challenges," *F5 Networks*. Available: f5.com/blog/api-security-risks- and-challenges.

[32] OpenAI Community, (2023). "Does GPT API keep data acquired from client request private?" *OpenAI Community Forum*, . Available: community.openai.com/t/does- gpt-api-keep-data-acquired-from-client-request-private.

[33] O. Ahia *et al.*, (2023). "*Do All Languages Cost the Same? Tokenization in the Era of Commercial Language Models,*" arXiv, Available: arXiv:2305.13707.

Technology for a Resilient Future – Vincent , Moorthy and Dasari (Eds)
 ISBN: 978-1-041-39070-1

YOLOv8-Based Road Damage Detection on the RDD2022 Dataset Using Hybrid Data Augmentation

S Aiswarya Lakshmi and Shilpa Suresh
Department of Mechatronics Manipal Institute of Technology, Manipal Academy of Higher Education Manipal, Karnataka, India

ABSTRACT: Detecting Road damage is essential for prompt maintenance and safeguarding transportation safety, as defects in road surfaces due to environmental degradation and weather can create significant risks. In this research, we employ the RDD2022 dataset, which is publicly accessible and consists of road images from various countries. Rather than the conventional country-wise separation, we reorganized the data based on defect types—longitudinal cracks, transverse cracks, alligator cracks, and potholes—selecting 200 images per class using K-Means clustering to ensure diversity. The dataset was used to train a lightweight YOLOv8-small model. The trained model has a minimal size of around 22 MB, which makes it suitable for deployment in small edge devices. Upon validation, the model reached an mAP@50 of 0.40 and an mAP@50-95 of 0.17. This study validates the potential of compact YOLO-based models for real-world road inspection tasks, particularly in resource-constrained or rapid-deployment scenarios.

Keywords: YOLOv8, road damage, augmentation, lightweight model

1 INTRODUCTION

The quality and sustainability of road infrastructure are crucial to national productivity, economic activities, and public safety. Roads undergo gradual degradation because of temperature variations, rain, ultraviolet rays, and shock stresses due to vehicles [1]. Vehicle loading-induced damage is usually more pronounced compared to natural causes. Typical surface distresses include longitudinal cracks, transverse cracks, alligator cracks, and potholes. If left undetected and not repaired on time, these flaws can advance, leading to accidents, higher maintenance expenses, and decreased road lifespan. Conventional manual inspection techniques—reliant on visual observation and marking—are time-consuming, unsafe, labour-intensive, and susceptible to human bias [2].Recent progresses in artificial intelligence (AI) and computer vision, notably convolutional neural networks (CNNs) and object detection architectures such as YOLO (You Only Look Once), have computerized infrastructure inspection. Ultralytics' latest YOLOv8 offers real-time detection at high accuracy [3], [4]. These models are, however, computationally and dataset-intensive, and tend to not generalize across regions based on variations in road texture, lighting conditions, and camera installations [5], [6]. Lightweight, region-agnostic models are, therefore, crucial for scalable deployment. This study employs the publicly accessible RDD2022 dataset with labeled images of road surfaces in India, Japan, Czech Republic, United States, Norway, and China [7], [8]. Out of six damage types, four significant defects—longitudinal, transverse, alligator cracks, and potholes—are chosen for homogeneity. Deep feature vectors are extracted from MobileNetV2, and K-Means clustering is used to pick diverse samples [9], and a class-balanced dataset of 200 training images and 50 validation images per class is obtained. The YOLOv8s model is trained for more than 200 epochs with hyperparameters optimized to achieve better convergence and less overfitting.

2 RELATED WORK

To effectively tackle the road damage detection problem, researchers have made contributions in several areas, including creating datasets, innovating model architecture, and evaluating performance[10], [11], [12]. These contributions can be grouped into four main themes, as described below:

2.1 *Dataset oriented contributions*

The exploration of automated road damage identification commenced with the creation of standardized and annotated datasets, addressing the absence of comprehensive, labeled data for deep learning applications. The introduction of RDD2020 represented a significant breakthrough, providing more than 26,000 images from Japan, India, and the Czech Republic, complete with annotations for seven different types of damages. This initiative was designed to facilitate deep learning research through consistent data and promote cross- country generalization studies [7]. Subsequently, RDD2022 broadened the initiative by assembling 47,420 images from six various countries, resulting in over 55,000 recorded damage instances. It allowed for economical multi-national training and evaluation of models, particularly in resource- limited areas[8]. Moreover, a research study concentrated on Brazilian roadways suggested the development of a dataset for Algeria. It employed CNNs and YOLO to detect cracks and potholes, reaching an accuracy of over 90% and emphasizing the necessity for more localized data to guarantee the effectiveness of high-performance applications [13].

2.2 *Non-YOLO techniques based on deep learning*

In addition to dataset aggregation, initial deep learning models employed models such as RetinaNet, utilizing focal loss to maximize sparse road damage detection while being balanced with speed and accuracy. The model was tested in research utilizing images taken by smartphones and exhibited positive precision-recall trade-offs for its suitability in real-time [14]. Further, Faster R-CNN was integrated into a monitoring framework for damage detection, damage segmentation, and classification. The model established a structured process that ranges from data collection to the subsequent processing of outputs, referencing deployment issues such as memory and latency constraints [15]. The subsequent breakthrough came in the form of a fusion-based approach that integrated semantic segmentation and object detection utilizing a combination of Faster R-CNN and YOLOv4. Utilizing an ROI mask obtained

 DOI: 10.1201/9781042017546-53

through segmentation, the pipeline focused on relevant lane areas, thus enhancing the detection accuracy for cracks and potholes on multilane roads [6]. In a follow-up study, DA-RDD was integrated, a domain-adaptive detection system trained adversarially on synthetic (RDD2021) and real- world (RDD2020) datasets. The method enhanced performance across countries by compensating for domain shifts and scored greater mAP in source-free and source-available cases [16].

2.3 *YOLO-based approaches*

The YOLO (You Only Look Once) family dominated road damage detection because of its real-time capability. A seminal paper used YOLO on images captured by smartphones and detected multiple types of damage under lightweight computation while proposing real-world application in mobile-based inspection. A high- performance model utilized YOLOv5x with Test-Time Augmentation (TTA) and ensemble modeling for cross- country image datasets. The configuration traded off speed and performance and placed at the top of the GRDDC2020 leaderboard[5]. To reduce inference time, YOLO-LRDD, a light version based on YOLOv5s, proposed Shuffle-ECANet and BiFPN modules. This yielded a 28.8% model size reduction and a 22.3% inference speed improvement without sacrificing accuracy. [4] The advancements continued with UAV-based applications, where an application of YOLOv7 on drone data achieved a high mAP of 73.2%, demonstrating that aerial systems are suitable for large-scale damage monitoring [17]. YOLO model studies saw new heights with comparisons among various YOLOv8 variants. This study demonstrated that medium pre-trained models have the optimal model size- accuracy trade-off and are suitable for real-time deployment [18]. The 2024 RDD-YOLO study further enhanced YOLOv8 with the introduction of SimAM attention and GhostConv modules. These advancements allowed to represent features with a smaller number of parameters and demonstrate improved accuracy and speed on the RDD2022 dataset.

The next paper published in 2024 examined a two-stage learning process where YOLOv8 was trained over a two- step process using class specific information again and other processing steps including histogram equalization. It established that the optimizer choice, specifically Adam vs. SGD, played an important role in convergence and performance and offered recommendations for architectural and training optimizations in subsequent implementations [19]. An ensemble model that was trained on YOLOv4 using a multi-country dataset proved generalization to be boosted when data from different countries were utilized[20]. Its F1 accuracy was 76.9% when utilizing the combined dataset, compared to training from separate countries, which dropped to ~50%. Lastly, a different test of YOLOv8 for crack classification from road segments proved its excellence in real-time performance and showed that YOLOv8 outperformed the traditional CNNs when executed under time-limited environments [21].

2.3 *Global challenge*

The 2020 Global Road Damage Detection Challenge acted as a basepoint for evaluating the performance of models participating from different nations. The report on the twelve best solutions showed that most teams, utilized ensemble YOLO models and a data augmentation strategy. The best model achieved a max F1 score of 0.67 and serves to demonstrate the viability of YOLO-based methods for damage detection on the real world[1].

3 METHODOLOGY

The envisioned pipeline for road damage detection via YOLOv8 consists of five main modules: dataset preprocessing, feature-informed data reduction, class-level stratification, augmentation-rich training, and deployment through inference interface as shown in Figure 1.

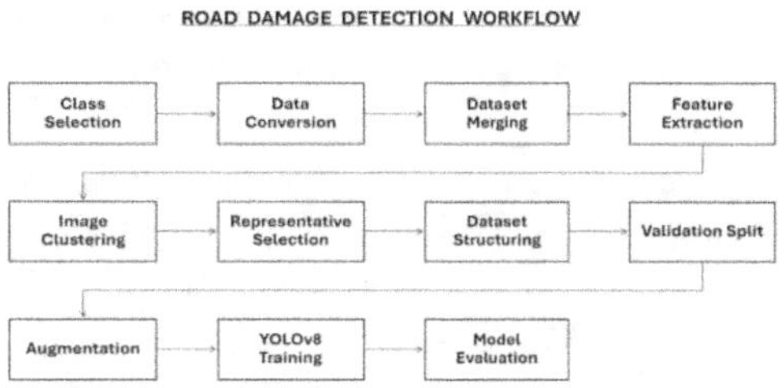

Figure 1. Road damage detection workflow.

The whole procedure follows reproducibility and modular structure, allowing seamless experimentation over different dataset subsets and model settings.

3.1 *Dataset filtering and class scope definition*

RDD2022 benchmark dataset, with annotated Japan, India, Czech Republic, Norway, China (motorbike/drone), and United States images, had initially eight damage classes (D00–D44)[24]. Nonetheless, class-level pruning was carried out to remove noise, overlapping, or data-scarce classes. Exclusion was specifically implemented due to insufficient inter-class separability and inadequate sample density for the defect classes D01, D11, D43, and D44. Only four defect categories were retained:

- D00: Longitudinal cracks
- D10: Lateral cracks
- D20: Alligator cracks
- D40: Potholes

This modification significantly clarified the labels and improved class distinction, resulting in a decrease in false positives during the training phase. The annotation files in Pascal VOC (XML) format were then converted to YOLOv8 format using the xml.etree.ElementTree module. The bounding box coordinates (xmin, ymin, xmax, ymax) were normalized based on the image resolution, and classes not included in [D00, D10, D20, D40] were removed during the conversion.

3.2 *Image selection retaining characteristics utilizing MobileNetV2 and k-means*

To decrease the dataset size for training in low-resource settings while maintaining representative spatial variety, an AI-driven clustering-based image selection approach was employed. The process includes the following:

a) *Feature Extraction:* First, each RGB image was resized to 224×224 and converted into a normalized tensor compatible with the ImageNet mean–std distribution.These tensors were processed through MobileNetV2 (architecture shown in Figure 2) (pre- trained on ImageNet) up to its final convolutional feature block (excluding the classifier). The spatially averaged feature maps (Global Average Pooling) produced a dense feature vector $\in \mathbb{R}^{1280}$ for every image.
b) *Clustering and Sampling:* The extracted vectors were organized using Means (k=25) to partition the feature space into semantically distinct clusters. A representative subset of samples was randomly drawn from each cluster. The process imposed a class-wise limit of 200 images, balancing uniform coverage of the latent image distribution without redundancy. Label–image synchronization was preserved while cluster assignments were traced and logged.

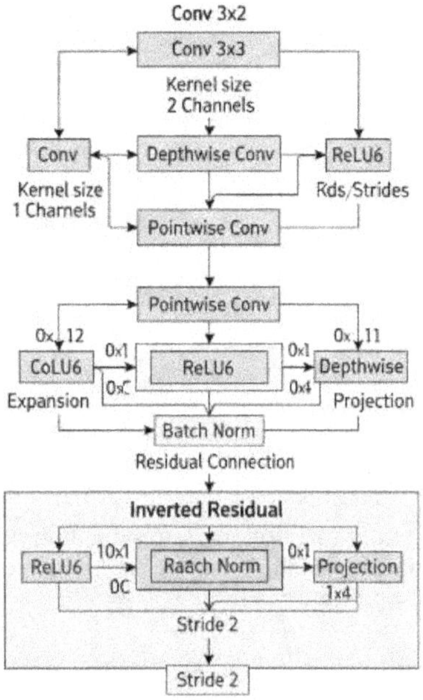

Figure 2. MobileNetV2 architecture.

3.3 *Dataset structuring, merging, and validation split*

After selection, pairs of images and labels were combined with a Tkinter GUI-based merger. The GUI enabled drag- and-drop folder pairing and batch merging with metadata preserved through autogenerated merge_log.xlsx. Class- wise segregation was done via an independent Python tool that read YOLO-format labels and copied samples into per- class folders (0–3). This enabled debugging and inspection for each class. A validation split was conducted by randomly choosing 50 image-label pairs from each class. The final structure of the dataset was arranged as follows: dataset/

⊢ images/
⊢ labels/
⊢ val_images/
└val_labels/

3.4 *Training YOLOv8 with hybrid data augmentation*

Throughout this research, we have made use of the YOLOv8s model—a light member of the YOLOv8 family (architecture shown in Figure 3)—selected to optimally balance detection accuracy and inference speed. We trained using the Ultralytics PyTorch implementation, with well- chosen hyperparameters geared to maximize performance for small object detection.

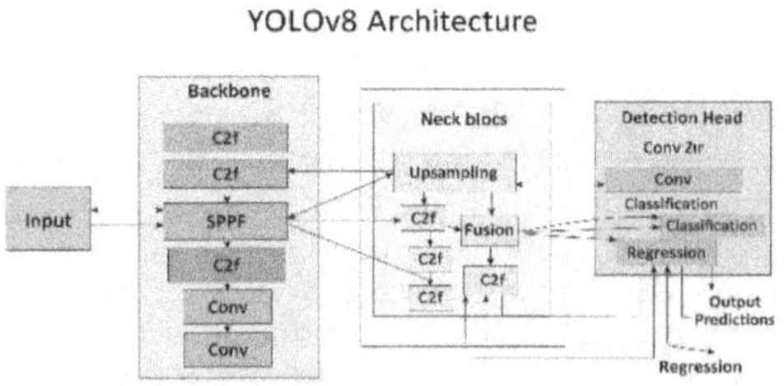

Figure 3. YOLOV8 architecture.

The pictures were stored at a resolution of 896 x 896, quite enough for detecting details including cracks and potholes. The training was performed for 200 epochs using a batch size of 8, applying a cosine learning rate schedule (cos_lr=True) along with a 5% warm-up period to improve stability during the early phases of training. A fixed random seed of 1337 was used to maintain consistency across different runs. To enhance the model's stability and generalization, a combined data augmentation strategy was implemented:

a) *Mosaic augmentation:* With a likelihood of 0.5, this enables the model to gain insights from various spatial contexts and better detect subtle indicators of damage by combining four separate images into one during the training process.
b) *Geometric Transformations:* Random rotations (±10°), translations (up to 10%), scaling (up to 50%), shearing (10%), and a small perspective shift (0.0005) were used to simulate various camera views and road outlooks.
c) *Color Variations:* HSV augmentation was conducted to simulate natural lighting scenarios, including hue changes (hsv_h=0.015), saturation changes (hsv_s=0.7), and brightness changes (hsv_v=0.4).
d) *Vertical Flipping:* To compensate for directional asymmetries in pavement photos, photographs were flipped vertically.

To track progress and enable reversal if needed, model checkpoints were saved every 20 epochs during the fully local hardware training process.

3.5 *Inference and deployment GUI*

For real-time inference on the training model, a simple Tkinter GUI was used. Any road image can be input by the user; backend detection is achieved through model.predict(). OpenCV is used to overlap detected bounding boxes with class names and confidence levels predicted as shown in Figure 5. The interface is helpful for field validation as shown in Figure 4.

Figure 4. Defect detection on some validation images.

Figure 5. Results after testing the model: transverse and longitudinal.

4 RESULTS AND EVALUATION

To assess the effectiveness of the suggested YOLOv8- powered road damage detection method, quantitative and qualitative assessments were applied on a processed subset of the RDD2022 dataset for four primary damage categories:

longitudinal cracks (D00), transverse cracks (D10), alligator cracks (D20), and potholes (D40). The model attained a mean Average Precision at IoU 0.5 (mAP@0.5) of 39.9% and a mAP@0.5:0.95 of 16.5% (Table 1), reflecting a moderate capacity for localization over IoU thresholds. It also attained 48.8% precision and 41.1% recall, reflecting a balanced detection performance. The ultimate validation losses— classification loss of 1.125, box regression loss of 1.433, and distribution-oriented regression loss of 1.571— reflect a well-converged and stable training process.

Table 1. Final performance results.

	Class				
Metric	Long	Transverse	Alligator	Pothole	Total
Precision	0.467	0.499	0.502	0.485	0.488
Recall	0.284	0.472	0.534	0.354	0.411
F1-Score	0.353	0.485	0.517	0.409	0.444
mAP@0.5	0.271	0.437	0.556	0.332	0.399

Relative to current RDD2022 approaches, this model provides a realistic baseline for performance under conditions of limited resources and is a stepping stone toward future real-time inspection systems. The normalized confusion matrix indicated class-dependent differences: transverse cracks (D10) and alligator cracks (D20) had higher true positive ratios of 47.2% and 53.4%, respectively, while longitudinal cracks (D00) indicated 28.4% with some confusion with potholes and alligator cracks. Potholes (D40) had a 35.4% detection rate, with occasional coincidence with D00. These misclassifications most probably result from common visual characteristics such as stretched patterns and irregular contours.

5 CONCLUSION AND FUTURE SCOPE

This paper proposed a light and effective road defect detection system using YOLOv8s, which can detect four major road surface damages: longitudinal cracks, transverse cracks, alligator cracks, and potholes.

Table 2. Comparison of different yolo modifications.

Model	mAP @0.5	Key Modifications
SEA YOLO	0.63	SBS, EMA_Faster_C2, AE-FPN, LSC-Detect
RDD YOLO	0.62	SimAM attention, GhostConv, Bilinear interpolation
YOLO ROC	0.67	BMS-SPPF, Hierarchical channel compression
Our model	0.40	None (unmodified baseline, lightweight CPU-feasible)

The model was trained on a carefully selected, class-balanced portion of the RDD2022 dataset with high- resolution images (896×896) and augmentations including mosaic, mix-up, HSV jitter, affine, and shear transformations

It recorded a mean Average Precision (mAP@0.5) of 39.9%, precision of 48.8%, and recall of 41.1%. Though the system found it hard to detect subtle categories such as longitudinal cracks because of visual overlap, it did relatively well with clear defects such as alligator cracks and recorded a mAP of 55.6%. Though with a small mAP@0.5:0.95 value of 16.5%, the model demonstrated stable convergence with low regressed and classified losses, serving as a good baseline for inspection tasks in real-world scenarios. With an inference latency of approximately 404 ms per image on a baseline CPU and a compact model size of ~22 MB, the system presents a balance of efficiency and detection accuracy that can accommodate smart city infrastructure and autonomous maintenance platforms.The research focuses on the precision–efficiency trade-off and suggests future enhancements such as extension to more classes of damage from RDD2022, improving label quality, using stronger augmentations, and enhancing class balance for improved recall. For enhancing cross-domain generalization, domain adaptation and fine-tuning will be investigated. Additionally, lightweight optimization strategies such as pruning and quantization will enhance performance on edge devices with embedded deployment. Integration with GPS/GIS platforms for real-time geo- tagged defect mapping and active learning loops for continuous model update will render the system deployable and scalable for road condition monitoring applications.

Figure 6. Results after testing the model: potholes and alligator cracks.

ACKNOWLEDGMENT

The authors would like to thank the Robotics Laboratory and the Department of Mechatronics, Manipal Institute of Technology for their support and resources provided during this research.

REFERENCES

[1] D. Arya *et al.*, (2020). "Global Road Damage Detection: State-of-the- art Solutions," *Proceedings - 2020 IEEE International Conference on Big Data, Big Data 2020*, pp. 5533–5539, https://doi.org/10.1109/BigData50022.2020.9377790.

[2] M. Tsuchiya, K. Miyamoto, T. Ota, and Y. Sugama, (2023). "Field study toward anomaly road damage detection with drive recorder," *PHM Society Asia-Pacific Conference*, vol. 4, no. 1, doi: 10.36001/phmap.2023.v4i1.3732.

[3] J. Zeng and H. Zhong, (2024). "YOLOv8-PD: an improved road damage detection algorithm based on YOLOv8n model," *Sci Rep*, vol. 14, no. 1, pp. 1–14, doi: 10.1038/s41598- 024-62933-z.

[4] F. Wan, C. Sun, H. He, G. Lei, L. Xu, and T. Xiao, (2022). "YOLO-LRDD: a lightweight method for road damage detection based on improved YOLOv5s," *EURASIP J Adv Signal Process*, vol. 2022, no. 1, doi: 10.1186/s13634-022- 00931-x.

[5] D. Jeong, (2020). "Road Damage Detection Using YOLO with Smartphone Images," *Proceedings - 2020 IEEE International Conference on Big Data, Big Data 2020*, pp. 5559–5562, https://doi.org/10.1109/BigData50022.2020.9377847.

[6] Y. Liu, X. Zhang, B. Zhang, and Z. Chen, (2020). "Deep Network for Road Damage Detection," *Proceedings - 2020 IEEE International Conference on Big Data, Big Data 2020*, pp.5572–5576, https://doi.org/10.1109/BigData50022.2020.9377991.

[7] D. Arya, H. Maeda, S.K. Ghosh, D. Toshniwal, and Y. Sekimoto, (2021). "RDD2020: An annotated image dataset for automatic road damage detection using deep learning," *Data Brief*, vol. 36, p. 107133, doi:10.1016/j.dib.2021.107133.

[8] D. Arya, H. Maeda, S.K. Ghosh, D. Toshniwal, and Y. Sekimoto, (2024). "RDD2022: A multi-national image dataset

for automatic road damage detection," *Geosci Data J*, no. April, pp. 846–862, https://doi.org/10.1002/gdj3.260.
[9] S. Han, (2023). "Parallelized Inter-Image k-Means Clustering Algorithm for Unsupervised Classification of Series of Satellite Images," *Remote Sens (Basel)*, vol. 16, no. 1, p. 102.
[10] M. Ren, X. Zhang, X. Zhi, Y. Wei, and Z. Feng, (2024). "An annotated street view image dataset for automated road damage detection," *Sci Data*, vol. 11, no. 1, pp. 1–13, doi: 10.1038/s41597-024-03263-7.
[11] D. Merolla, V. Latorre, and A. Salis, (2022). "Improving Road Safety with AI : Automated Detection of Signs and Surface Damage," *Computers*.
[12] W.C. Chiang, H.S. Chiu, and J.S. Lee, (2023). "Road Damage Detection Using Deep Learning and Cloud Platforms," *2023 International Conference on Consumer Electronics - Taiwan, ICCE-Taiwan - Proceedings*, pp. 859–860, https://doi.org/10.1109/ICCE- Taiwan58799.2023.10226984.
[13] M.A. Benallal and M.S. Tayeb, (2023). "An image-based convolutional neural network system for road defects detection," *IAES International Journal of Artificial Intelligence*, vol. 12, no. 2, pp. 577–584, doi: 10.11591/ijai.v12.i2.pp577-584.
[14] L. Ale, N. Zhang, and L. Li, (2018). "Road Damage Detection Using RetinaNet," *Proceedings - 2018 IEEE International Conference on Big Data, Big Data* pp. 5197–5200, https://doi.org/10.1109/BigData.2018.8622025.
[15] T. Hascoet, Y. Zhang, A. Persch, R. Takashima, T. Takiguchi, and Y. Ariki, (2020). "FasterRCNN Monitoring of Road Damages: Competition and Deployment," *Proceedings - 2020 IEEE International Conference on Big Data, Big Data 2020*, pp. 5545–5552, https://doi.org/10.1109/BigData50022.2020.9377871.
[16] C. Lin, D. Tian, X. Duan, J. Zhou, D. Zhao, and D. Cao, (2023). "DA- RDD: Toward Domain Adaptive Road Damage Detection Across Different Countries," *IEEE Transactions on Intelligent Transportation Systems*, vol. 24, no. 3, pp. 3091–3103, doi: 10.1109/TITS.2022.3221067.
[17] L.A. Silva, V.R.Q. Leithardt, V.F.L. Batista, G. Villarrubia Gonzalez, and J.F. De Paz Santana, (2023). "Automated Road Damage Detection Using UAV Images and Deep Learning Techniques," *IEEE Access*, vol. 11, no. June, pp. 62918–62931, doi: 10.1109/ACCESS.2023.3287770.
[18] Z. Tang, R. Chamchong, and P. Pawara, (2023). "A Comparison of Road Damage Detection Based on YOLOv8," *Proc Int Conf Mach Learn Cybern*, pp. 223–228, doi: 10.1109/ICMLC58545.2023.10327993.
[19] S.A. Putri, A.B. Raharjo, and D. Purwitasari, (2024). "Two-phase Learning for Classifying Road Damage using YOLO Architecture," *2024 9th International Conference on Informatics and Computing, ICIC 2024*, pp. 1–7, https://doi.org/10.1109/ICIC64337.2024.10956973.
[20] J. Wang *et al.*, (2024). "Road defect detection based on improved YOLOv8s model," *Sci Rep*, vol. 14, no. 1, pp. 1–21, doi: 10.1038/s41598-024-67953-3.
[21] S. Liao, (2024). "Road damage detection algorithm based on optimised You only Look Once version 8," *2024 5th International Conference on Computer Engineering and Application, ICCEA 2024*, pp. 1381–1384, https://doi.org/10.1109/ICCEA62105.2024.10603714.
[22] Y. Zhao, B. Shi, X. Duan, W. Zhu, L. Ren, and C. Liao, (2025). "Research on road surface damage detection based on SEA-YOLO v8," *PLoS One*, vol. 20, no. 6 JUNE, pp. 1–26, doi: 10.1371/journal.pone.0324439.
[23] Z. Lin and W. Paul, "*YOLO-ROC : A High-Precision and Ultra-Lightweight Model for Real-Time Road Damage Detection*". sekilab, "RoadDamageDetector,"GitHub. [Online]. Available: https://github.com/sekilab/RoadDamageDetector (accessed Apr 14, 2025)

Technology for a Resilient Future – Vincent , Moorthy and Dasari (Eds)

Satellite-Informed Prioritization of Industrial Heat Hotspot Parcels

Saurav Kumar, Anjani RN, Santhoshi T, and Kalyan Deep K
National Remote Sensing Centre (NRSC), ISRO, Hyderabad, Telangana

ABSTRACT: Rapid Urbanization in India and the growing industry have drastically affected the LST (Land Surface Temperature). In our work, we highlight the LST trends in Vishakhapatnam's industrial area and establish the trend analysis with NDVI (Normalized Difference Vegetation Index) and NDBI (Normalized Difference Built-up Index). We have done the comprehensive analysis based on LST, NDVI, and NDBI. This LST analysis uncovers the hidden trends of Urban Heat Island (UHI) in Visakhapatnam. The results reveal the increasing trends of the LST pattern in Vishakhapatnam. The MSD-1σ (Mean–Standard Deviation) or $\mu \pm 1\sigma$ method analysis gives the thresholds of 31°C, while Gaussian Mixture Model (GMM) method gives 34°C, and the main threshold is 36.5°C, using the MSD-2σ or $\mu \pm 2\sigma$ method. We have also analysed the trends of LST from the year 2014 to 2023 and reveals the mean NDVI has declined from 0.338 to 0.207. Finally, our work point out the necessity of green spaces and sustainable management to suppress the increasing LST due to urbanization and industrialization.

Keywords: Gaussian Mixture Model (GMM), Landsat-8, Land Surface Temperature (LST), MSD-1σ, Urban Heat Island (UHI)

1 INTRODUCTION

Ever notice how some parts of a city feel much hotter than others, especially on a sunny day? That's the 'Urban Heat Island' (UHI) effect. Cities, with all their concrete and buildings, tend to trap heat more than natural landscapes. This is a big deal in rapidly growing places like India, affecting local weather and making summers even tougher. Our study focuses on Visakhapatnam, an industrial city, to see how urban growth changed temperatures from 2014 to 2023 using Landsat 8 satellite data. We didn't just look at temperature; we also checked how green the city was using NDVI and how much built-up area there was using NDBI. We found that as the city grew, green spaces shrunk, and built-up areas increased, leading to hotter spots. These 'hotspots,' mainly in industrial zones, showed temperature jumps of 2-3°C. Our maps clearly show these changes, helping us see where the UHI effect is most intense.

2 METHODOLOGY

This study focuses on Visakhapatnam, a coastal urban area in the Visakhapatnam–Guntur industrial region of India (83.11°–83.40° E, 17.54°–17.87° N), as shown in Figure 1. The city's diverse landscape—coastal plains, hills, and proximity to the Eastern Ghats—combined with heavy industrial activity makes it ideal for studying UHI effects linked to land use change. We used Landsat 8/9 data (NASA and USGS) for its high-resolution multispectral and thermal infrared imagery to analyse LST and UHI patterns in detail. Table 1 gives the details of data.

Table 1. Description of landsat 8 data used.

Item No.	Acquisition Date	Cloud Obscuration (%)
1	March 2013	~2.18
2	March 2014	~!0.13
3	March 2015	~0.29
4	March 2016	~0.61
5	March 2017	~1.44
6	March 2018	~0.24
7	March 2019	~0.40
8	April 2020	~2.72
9	April 2021	~0.07
10	May 2022	~0.12

2.1 *Methodology for estimating UHI*

In order to conduct a UHI effect analysis, radiometric calibration and atmospheric correction were performed to allow DN to be modified to TOA reflectance. The data were presented and processed as a 32-bit floating-point radiance continuum product, and were then converted to 16-bit integers in the Level-1 product. Spectral radiance was then derived using metadata-provided scaling factors, as shown in Equation (1) [1].

$$L_\lambda = M_L \cdot Q_{\text{cal}} + A_L \quad (1)$$

Here, L_λ represents radiance (TOA, W/m^2/sr/μm). M_L is the radiance multiplicative scaling factor, and A_L is the radiance additive scaling factor. Q_{cal} is the pixel value (Level 1).

Estimating the Top-of-Atmosphere Brightness Temperature (*TOA_BT in Kelvin(K)*):

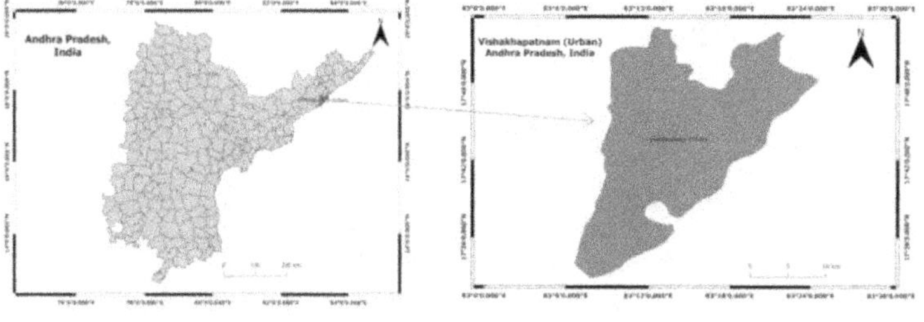

Figure 1. A map illustrating our study area in urban Vishakhapatnam.

DOI: 10.1201/9781042017546-54

TOA_BT corresponds to an object's temperature as detected by a satellite, assuming ideal thermal emission from its surface at all wavelengths. Its value is ascertainable through the L_λ measurement [2].

$$TOA\_BT = \frac{K2}{\ln\left(\frac{K_1}{L_\lambda} + 1\right)} \quad (2)$$

K1 and K2 are thermal conversion constants (band-specific).

Calculating NDVI:

In this section, we present how NDVI is calculated and its impact. Two ways for measuring the NDVI are 1) scene scale, 2) region scale [3,4]. For our study, we have adopted the region-scale analysis method.

Deriving Land Surface Emissivity (*LSE*):

LSE (Land Surface Emissivity) is an essential parameter when estimating LST from TOA brightness temperature. LSE can vary significantly based on the surface material being observed, and is therefore estimated using the NDVI, which provides the user with a measure of the surface greenness. The estimations of LSE are determined using NDVI and are divided into three classes. NDVI < 0.2 - which is the assumed bare soil class, where LSE is derived from red-band reflectance; NDVI > 0.5 - where vegetation is estimated, and the emissivity value assigned is usually 0.99; NDVI > 0.2 and < 0.5 - where LSE was determined from NDVI and was also determined by the proportion of NDVI derived from vegetation (P_v). Stepwise methods are provided in [2].

LST Calculation:

Here, we introduce the last piece of the puzzle - the final calculation of the LST from the TOA_BT and LSE. LST calculation relies on at-sensor brightness temperature, emitted radiance wavelength (λ), and LSE. Equation (4), defining LST, is cited in [7–11].

$$LST = \frac{TOA\_BT}{1 + \frac{\lambda * TOA\ BT * \ln(LSE)}{\rho}} \quad (4)$$

The λ is the wavelength of the radiance emitted (10.895 [9]). The constant ρ is 1.438×10^{-2} m • K

2.2 *Measuring urban heat island effects*

We assessed UHI intensity using three methods: MSD-1σ, MSD-2σ, and GMM. The MSD-1σ method identifies areas warmer than the local mean plus one standard deviation (LST > mean + 1σ), while the 2-Sigma method captures the most extreme hotspots (LST > mean + 2σ, representing roughly the top 2.5%). The GMM approach models land surface temperature as overlapping Gaussian distributions, allowing us to separate hot, built-up zones from cooler surroundings based on their probabilistic temperature patterns.

3 RESULTS AND DISCUSSION

The analysis examines year-by-year changes in LST alongside NDVI trends to assess vegetation dynamics and NDBI to track built-up area expansion. All maps and graphs use the CRS EPSG:4326 (WGS 84) and were generated using QGIS.

Table 2 provides a comprehensive overview of the LST statistics, detailing the annual minimum, maximum, and average values. These findings are crucial for comprehending the temperature dynamics prevalent within the urban area across the study period. Furthermore, we delineated regions where LST surpassed 35°C, indicating potential urban heat stress conditions.

Table 2. Overview of Estimated LST (°C) Variability in Urban Vishakhapatnam.

Observation Date	Minimum LST	Maximum LST	Average LST
26 March 2014	24.01	38.41	31.61
13 March 2015	24.31	40.45	32.30
16 April 2016	24.62	38.82	33.51
05 May 2017	22.65	37.26	31.30
05 March 2018	24.40	42.77	33.41
25 April 2019	25.14	41.95	32.57
26 March 2020	24.76	39.55	31.05
29 March 2021	25.36	37.81	31.36
16 March 2022	25.83	44.74	33.43
03 March 2023	24.39	38.50	30.11

Between 2014 and 2023, the MSD-1σ temperature threshold for identifying elevated heat zones in Vishakhapatnam ranged from 32.21 °C (2023) to 36.14 °C (2022), as shown in Table 3. The spatial spread of UHI-impacted regions is 75.344 sq. km in 2023, while 88.637 sq. km in 2014. These fluctuations are attributable to factors such as urban expansion, reduction in

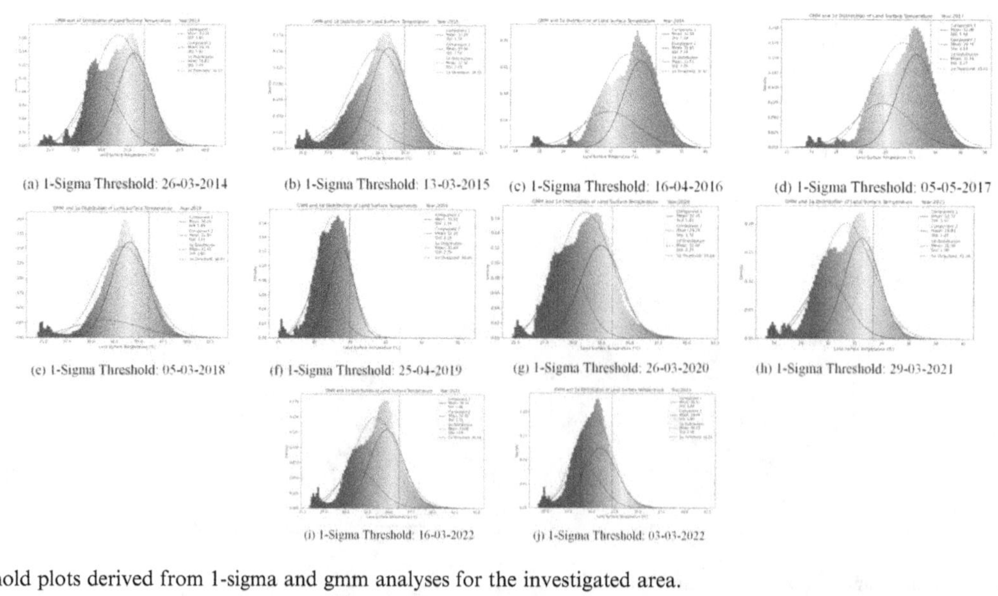

(a) 1-Sigma Threshold: 26-03-2014 (b) 1-Sigma Threshold: 13-03-2015 (c) 1-Sigma Threshold: 16-04-2016 (d) 1-Sigma Threshold: 05-05-2017 (e) 1-Sigma Threshold: 05-03-2018 (f) 1-Sigma Threshold: 25-04-2019 (g) 1-Sigma Threshold: 26-03-2020 (h) 1-Sigma Threshold: 29-03-2021 (i) 1-Sigma Threshold: 16-03-2022 (j) 1-Sigma Threshold: 03-03-2022

Figure 2. threshold plots derived from 1-sigma and gmm analyses for the investigated area.

Table 3. Summary of MSD-1σ metrics (Decadal) in the study area.

Date of Observation	MSD-1σ Temperature Threshold (°C)	MSD-1σ Affected Area (sq. km)
26 March 2014	34.068	88.637
13 March 2015	34.909	77.384
16 April 2016	35.805	77.845
05 May 2017	33.609	79.43
05 March 2018	36.027	76.354
25 April 2019	34.953	84.01
26 March 2020	33.443	83.188
29 March 2021	33.361	82.388
16 March 2022	36.142	76.645
03 March 2023	32.209	75.344

vegetation cover, and alterations in surface characteristics. The spatial distributions derived from the GMM and MSD-1σ analyses are visually represented in Figures 2(a)–2(j).

To validate the UHI results from the 1-Sigma, 2-Sigma, and GMM analyses, we conducted stack profiling on 2022 LST data. This helped visualize temperature variations across the city and clearly identify heat island zones.

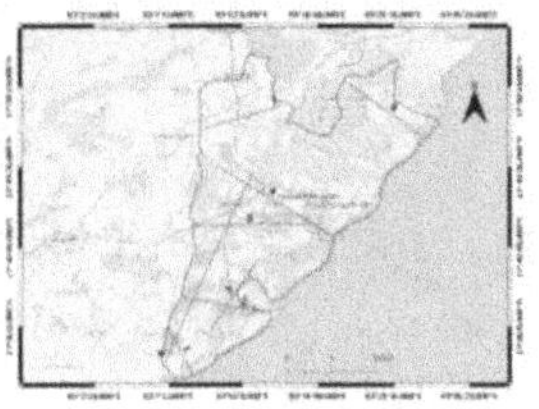

Figure 3. Eight selected profiling lines in UHI zones (1-Sigma, 2-Sigma, GMM).

Eight profiling lines (Figure 3) crossed areas identified as UHIs, with the red line marking the most intense zones. Temperature spikes of 2–3°C were observed (Figure 4), and Google Earth checks (Figure 5) confirmed that most hotspots occurred near industrial or densely built-up areas.

NDVI analysis from Landsat 8 (2014, 2019, 2023) showed a consistent decline in vegetation within UHI zones. Combined with NDBI and LST data (Table 4), the results show that urbanization are strongly related to LST (R^2 = 0.30–0.57, Pearson's r = 0.55–0.75).

Table 4. Correlation between NDBI and LST (2014-2023).

Year	Slope	Intercept	R-Squared	Pearson's Corr.
26-03-2014	23.39	32.56	0.49	0.70
13-03-2015	30.17	32.71	0.56	0.75
16-04-2016	20.91	34.06	0.35	0.59
05-05-2017	20.17	31.85	0.30	0.55
05-03-2018	28.41	33.86	0.45	0.67
25-04-2019	21.75	33.45	0.35	0.59
26-03-2020	21.19	32.40	0.44	0.67
29-03-2021	25.30	32.33	0.54	0.74
16-03-2022	27.00	34.88	0.48	0.69
03-03-2023	25.32	31.24	0.57	0.75

4 CONCLUSIONS

This study explores how urban growth has intensified the UHI effect in Visakhapatnam between 2014 and 2023. Using models like 1-Sigma, 2-Sigma, and GMM, we identified temperature hotspots that are 2–3°C warmer in industrial and densely built-up areas. NDVI analysis shows a clear decline in vegetation, closely linked to rising land surface temperatures ($r^2 \approx$ 0.55–0.75). The results highlight how loss of green cover and

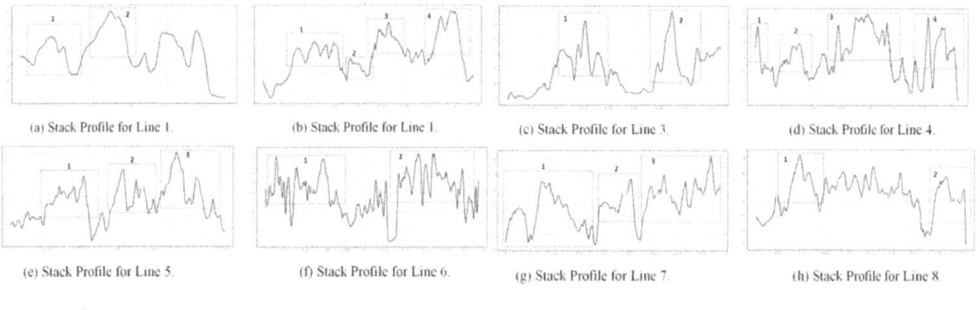

Figure 4. Stack profiling on potential UHI zones, Identified through 1-Sigma, 2-Sigma, and GMM analysis.

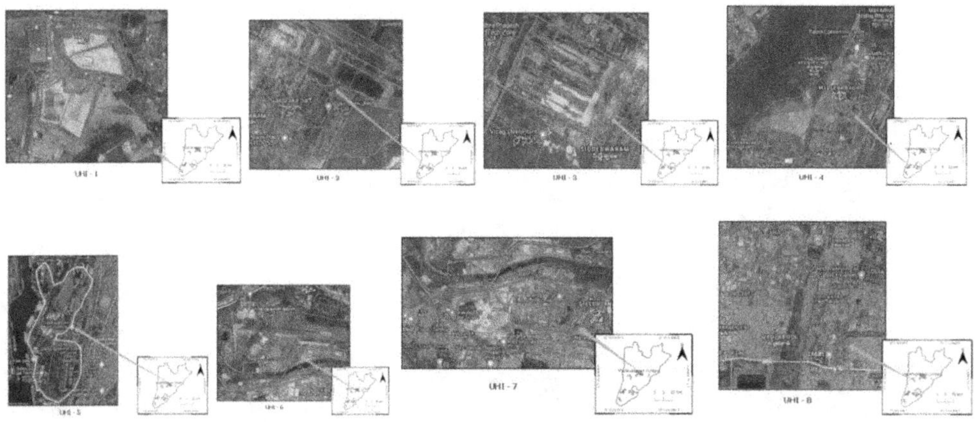

Figure 5. Validations of UHI hotspots using google earth imagery. (Source: Google Earth Imagery).

expanding urban areas are driving higher local temperatures. A longer time-series study could reveal how these UHI patterns continue to evolve with city development.

ACKNOWLEDGEMENT

The authors acknowledge the support of the National Remote Sensing Centre (NRSC), ISRO, for providing facilities and resources for this study. We also thank our colleagues for their valuable guidance and technical assistance throughout the work.

REFERENCES

[1] Solangi, G.S., Siyal, A.A., and Siyal, P. (2019). Spatiotemporal dynamics of land surface temperature and its impact on the vegetation. *Civil Engineering Journal*, 5(8), 1753–1763.

[2] Sekertekin, A. (2020). Land surface temperature retrieval from landsat 5, 7 and 8: evaluation of lst retrieval methods and emissivity models. *Remote Sensing*, 12(2), 294.

[3] Ajith, K., Geethalakshmi, V., Ragunath, K.P., Pazhanivelan, S., and Dheebakaran, G. (2017). Rice Yield prediction using MODIS-NDVI (MOD13Q1) and land based observations. *Int. J. Curr. Microbiol. App. Sci.*, 6(12), 2277–2293.

[4] Li, X., Zhou, Y., Asrar, G.R., Imhoff, M., Xiao, J., and Zhu, A. X. (2019). A review of urban thermal environment: Remote sensing methods, utility, and prospects. *Remote Sensing of Environment*, 231, 111215.

[5] Dash, P. (2005). Land surface temperature and emissivity retrieval from satellite measurements. *Wissenschaftliche Berichte FZKA*, 7095.

[6] Ogunjobi, K.O., Oloruntade, A.O., and Oguntunde, P.G. (2021). Spatiotemporal analysis of land surface temperature and vegetation dynamics in Ibadan and its environs, Nigeria. *GeoJournal*, 87(5), 2771–2790.

[7] Stathopoulou, M. and Cartalis, C. (2007). Daytime urban heat islands from Landsat ETM+ and Corine land cover data: an application to major cities in Greece. *Solar Energy*, 81(3), 358–368.

[8] Ouma, Y.O., and Tateishi, R. (2014). Urban growth prediction of Nairobi city using SLEUTH model and LST change analysis. *Remote Sensing Applied: Society and Environment*, 3, 89–101.

[9] U. S. G. Survey and D. O. T. Interior (2017). Landsat L8 data users handbook: Version 2.0 - March 29, 2016. *Createspace Independent Publishing Platform.*

[10] Sellers, P.J. (1985). Canopy reflectance, photosynthesis, and transpiration. *International Journal of Remote Sensing*, 6(8), 1335–1372.

[11] Avdan, U., and Jovanovska, G. (2016). Algorithm for automated mapping of land surface temperature using Landsat 8 satellite data. *Journal of Sensors*, 2016, 1–8.

Technology for a Resilient Future – Vincent , Moorthy and Dasari (Eds)
© 2027 The Author(s), ISBN: 978-1-041-39070-1

A Comprehensive Literature Review on Semantic Segmentation Models for Tree Species Mapping

Neetha Baliga and Asha C S
Department of Mechatronics, Manipal Institute of Technology, Manipal, Manipal Academy of Higher Education, Manipal Karnataka, India

ABSTRACT: Forest management, biodiversity conservation, and environmental monitoring rely on the precise classification and mapping of forest tree species. Traditional methods of identifying forest species are labour intensive and time consuming, limiting their scalability. In recent times, UAVs coupled with deep learning techniques have been promising in overcoming these challenges by providing high-resolution imagery for large- area coverage. This study investigates the application of deep learning–driven semantic segmentation models for classifying and mapping tree species using UAV-captured imagery. We evaluated multiple deep learning architectures, including convolutional neural networks (CNNs), U-Net, and DeepLabV3, to evaluate their effectiveness in segmenting tree species in UAV images. The study also addresses the challenges in environmental variability on segmentation performance. Our results demonstrate that deep learning models, particularly those optimized for semantic segmentation, can achieve high accuracy in classifying forest trees, even in complex forest environments. The findings indicate that combining UAV-based remote sensing with deep learning improves forest monitoring and provides meaningful insights for conservation and management practices.

Keywords: Deep Learning, Semantic Segmentation, UAV, Forest Management, CNN

1 INTRODUCTION

Forests are essential for sustaining ecological balance and mitigating climate change. Precise knowledge of tree species is vital for formulating effective forest conservation and management strategies. Tree species information is required, but is not limited to applications such as Deforestation Tracking, Biodiversity assessment, Sustainable Forest Management, and Land cover classification. Regular tracking of tree species and density helps predict forest fires, floods, and landslides, allowing authorities to implement preventive measures. Forestry can be generally divided into domains such as forest management, forest inventory, and wildlife monitoring. Recent research indicates that advancements in remote sensing have made possible, the classification of tree species using diverse data sources which includes Lidar, UAV, and multispectral cameras. Knowledge of distribution of the tree species, also affects forest harvesting and man- agement policies. Several types of remotely sensed data, that includes LiDAR data, multispectral and hyperspectral are used in recent studies [1]. Unmanned Ariel Vehicles (UAV) and swarms of micro-satellites are examples of novel remote sensing platforms that facilitate an ariel perspective of forest canopies with high amount of spatial detail. The use of drone imagery, combined with advanced methods like, CNNs have shown strong potential in improving both the accuracy and efficiency of tree species classification models. Machine learning (ML) algorithms has revolutionized tree species mapping by automating classification using remote sensing data [2]. A key requirement for remote sensing data is access to high- resolution imagery captured by UAVs. Processing methods must be rapid and adaptive, given the enormous volume of data. Deep learning model diversity has been steadily growing since 2012. Presently, these are the cutting-edge methods for image segmentation and object detection, capable of identifying objects and extracting detailed information from image data. Moreover, the capability of deep learning has proved to be highly pertinent to present ecological issues and their connections to economic and social systems.

2 REVIEW METHODOLOGY

This review is conducted in two stages: Planning and Execution

The planning stage aims to determine the need by iden tifying the gaps in the existing literature and establish clear criteria for study selection and evaluation. The execution phase focuses on identifying the relevant datasets, models and techniques used. This is followed by the formulation of a comprehensive search strategy to retrieve as many relevant studies as possible through a combination of various keywords. A search was conducted across various academic databases, primarily Scopus, Google Scholar and open access repositories like MDPI.This method made it possible to identify a vast range of research contributions in the domain of deep learning and remote sensing for forest monitoring. The search employed a combination of targeted keywords like 'UAV Images', Forest Monitoring', 'Semantic Segmentation', 'Deep Learning' and 'Tree Species Mapping'. The initial search yielded 211 papers. To refine the selection and ensure relevance to the scope of this study a set of filtering criteria was applied. This included i) Studies that specifically used semantic segmentation for Tree species mapping ii) Studies using CNN based architectures iii) Studies focusing on UAV based remote sensing imagery iv) Papers published from the past 15 years. A total ofeer reviewed journals were chosen for in depth analysis and review.

3 OUTCOMES

This section analyzes the findings obtained from the conducted systematic literature review.

3.1 *Effectiveness of UAV based methods compared to traditional methods*

Drones and Unmanned Ariel vehicles (UAVs) have completely changed the way forests are mapped [3]. Various sensors, high-resolution cameras [4], multi- and hyperspectral imagers [5], and LiDAR scanners, can be installed on UAVs to collect comprehensive data on forest composition, structure, and dynamics. Forest maps that are up-to-date and accurate can be created using this data. The primary advantage of UAV technology lies in its capacity to gather high-resolution data at comparatively low cost.

DOI: 10.1201/9781042017546-55

Conventional mapping approaches, such as satellite im agery or ground-based surveys, are often costly and time- intensive. In contrast, UAVs can rapidly and effectively gather data across vast areas, including isolated or hard-to- reach locations. UAVs provide high spatial resolution (often in the range of centimeters), allowing for very detailed observations [6]. UAVs are relatively cost- effective, especially for local and medium-scale monitoring. Another benefit is the capacity to capture data at various scales [7]. Additionally, UAVs can operate at lower altitudes with great control and precision, which makes them highly valuable for topographic mapping [8]. Drones can also aid in planting and harvesting, providing real-time monitoring of reforestation efforts [9]. They are the perfect choice for targeted monitoring of specific forest features, such as tree height, canopy cover, or biodiversity hotspots. UAVs collect diverse data types—such as RGB imagery, multispectral imagery, and LiDAR—which can be processed to generate 3D models, canopy height models, and vegetation indices.

3.2 *Role of semantic segmentation in forest management*

Semantic segmentation allows a precise and efficient monitoring of forest ecosystems. It is an image processing technique that divides an image into multiple regions, each of which is classified into different categories. The semantic segmentation model classifies each pixel in an image, into a predefined category [10]. It is increasingly being adopted for analyzing remote sensing data in diverse environmental applications such as vegetation mapping, land cover classification, and others. Its success in forest cover segmentation has made it a widely adopted standard method [11]. It has proven to function better, producing segmentation results that are more accurate. U- Net is a widely recognized example of a cutting- edge semantic segmentation model [12].

Numerous innovative semantic segmentation methods specifically designed for mapping forest cover have recently been put forth, which includes Segnet [13], ResNet [14], FO Net [15], Modified UNet [16], and MS Net [17]. A multiclass semantic segmentation method was applied to concurrently segment and classify 14 categories— comprising nine tree species, three genus- level groups, deadwood, and forest floor-to evaluate the feasibility of mapping forest tree species in mixed stands with high-resolution RGB imagery captured by UAVs [6]. SegNet is an architecture specifically designed to perform efficient pixel-wise semantic segmentation [12].

[18] proposed MTS-CNN for crop and weed detection, achieving high accuracy by balancing training and reducing the performance gap between the two classes.

3.3 *Datasets used*

This section of the paper synthesizes widely used datasets for mapping tree cover. The ISPRS Potsdam dataset contains five bands (RGB, NIR, DSM) with spatial resolution :5 cm, comprising 4225 training and 1352 validation images, labeled for low vegetation and trees collected from 60 different cities in China [14]. The WHU GID dataset comprises four bands (NIR, R, G, B) with spatial resolution: 1m containing 2992 training and 1088 validation images, labeled for clutter, water, farmland, meadow and forest [17]. The LandCover.ai dataset consists of 41 aerial remote sensing images spanning 216.27 square kilometers in Poland [19]. The Gaofen Image Dataset contains 150 GF-2 images from various Chinese cities, featuring high-resolution PAN and MS bands [21]

An RGB image covering 4.78 km^2 of a chestnut plantation, captured with a DJI Phantom 4 RTK UAV, was used to generate a dataset containing 18,144 manually delineated chestnut tree clusters [22].The MauFlex dataset, created from ariel images captured in the Peruvian Amazon using three different RGB cameras under diverse lighting conditions consists of 25,248image patches of size 512x512 pixels, each paired with a corresponding ground truth mask for the automatic segmentation of Mauritia Flexuosa palms [23]. Two datasets: a smaller one with 500 trees and a larger one comprising 2000 trees was utilized by [27]. A dataset including over 11000 high quality GSV images filtered by semantic segmentation with DeepLabv3+, ResNet was employed by [31].

3.4 *Deep learning architectures used for tree species mapping*

Multiple approaches have employed deep neural networks to obtain promising results in semantic segmentation.

The study [6] employs, a U-net convolutional neural network (CNN) architecture for mapping tree species of forest, from UAV-based RGB imagery. This architecture is specifically designed for semantic segmentation, allowing it to segment and classify tree species simultaneously. It follows an encoder–decoder architecture. Model performance was evaluated at the pixel level using F1 Score metrics which was reported as 0.73. [13] presented SegNet, an encoder–decoder model, that retains spatial information via max-pooling indices for efficient semantic segmentation, with accuracy of 0.90 and widely applied for scene understanding. [14] utilized ResUNet-a model where ResNet blocks combined with parallel atrous convolutions replace traditional convolution operations. In this study [30], DCNN was proposed for real-time green vegetation segmentation in agricultural fields, with multi-layer feature fusion to improve accuracy. The model is trained on augmented datasets containing RGB crop images captured under various lighting conditions. The RGB-DCNN achieves high segmentation accuracy (89.9) and fast inference (64 ms per image), making it suitable for precision agriculture applications.FO-Net, an innovative deep learning architecture developed for detecting individual trees from high-resolution UAV imagery is proposed by [15]. [23] proposed a semantic segmentation approach for Mauritia Flexuosa palm trees using a CNN built on the Deeplabv3+ architecture, which integrates atrous convolutions and inverted residual units. The model achieved high accuracy of 98.14 outperforming several U Net variants. The study by [31] used a GoogLeNet CNN along with the Plant.Id to classify urban tree species in Prato, Italy, achieving 0.73 accuracy using Google Street View, LiDar and multispectral images.

Study [32] proposed ArielSegNet, a custom an encoder decoder CNN inspired by U- Net and DenseNet, with partial dense modules and residual connections for efficient feature reuse, achieving 0.98 accuracy. The study by [33] proposes a lightweight improved U-Net architecture named ResNet34-U-Net-Focal-Fdecoder- CBAM for fruit tree canopy segmentation using UAV orthophoto maps.

4 LIMITATIONS

Significantly longer training times resulted in greater computing costs and decreased computational efficiency. Small accuracy gains from complex models could come at a hefty computational expense [17]. The DeeplabV3+ architecture approach used by [23] may face limitations in generalizing to species other than Mauritia Flexuosa, in handling extreme occlusions and also requiring GPU resources for effective training. Model studied by [32] exhibited limitations in low light conditions distinguishing visually similar classes and required more training time to accurately learn minority classes. Deep neural networks are considered" black box" models due to their complex structure, which makes analysis more challenging. [34].

5 RESULTS AND DISCUSSIONS

Semantic segmentation models for tree species mapping vary in accuracy, efficiency, and adaptability across datasets. This section presents a palm image alongside its segmented output, accompanied by a comparative analysis table of various deep learning models. U-Net is effective for UAV imagery but struggles with complex canopies, while DeepLab offers higher accuracy at the expense of heavy computational demands. Lightweight models such as SegNet and FCN provide faster inference but lower accuracy, and newer designs like ArielSegNet show promise yet remain underexplored. However, practical deployment is limited by scarce annotated datasets, high computational requirements, and challenges in UAV data collection under varying environmental conditions. A key limitation in current studies is the lack of diverse and publicly available datasets, as most research relies on UAV or aerial imagery from temperate regions, with limited species-level or multitemporal annotations.

Figure 1. Ariel view of mauritia flexuosa species [23].

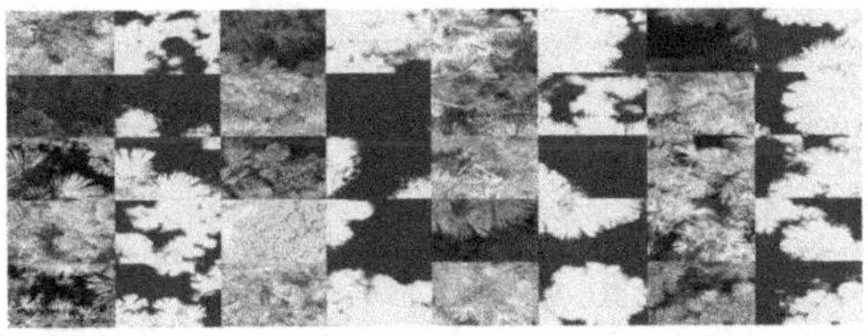

Figure 2. Illustration from [23], Segmentation Image.

Table 1. comparative analysis of various models.

Model	Architecture Type	Performance Metrics
U-Net [6]	Encoder Decoder CNN	F1 Score -0.73
RGB DCNN [30]	DCNN with multi- layer feature fusion	Accuracy 0.89
Deeplabv3+ [23]	Atrous CNN with inverted residuals	Accuracy 0.98
ArielSegNet [32]	U-Net+DenseNet	Accuracy 0.98
googleNet PlantId [31]	CNN Based Classification	Accuracy 0.78
ResNet34-U-Net-ocal Decoder [33]	Light weight U-Net Variant	Accuracy 0.91
Segnet [13]	Encoder Decoder CNN	Accuracy 0.90
ResU-Net [14]	Encoder Decoder CNN	F1 Score -0.92

6 FUTURE SCOPE

Future studies on forest cover mapping should emphasize enhancing model accuracy for remote sensing (RS) data, especially for low and medium-resolution imagery, which remain relatively underexplored. Addressing the scarcity of well-labeled datasets is crucial for advancing semantic seg- mentation models [21]. Testing the feasibility of deep learning methods such as U-Net for semantic segmentation is recommended which could simplify the preprocessing steps. It is suggested that using RGB drone images will increase tree detection accuracy. To overcome the difficulties caused by overlapping crown heights, it is necessary to investigate the use of instance segmentation techniques in order to accomplish more precise labeling and classification of individual tree crowns. Urban planning and environmental sustainability may benefit from a thorough understanding of urban tree populations and their contributions to ecosystem services as a result of this strategy [35].

7 CONCLUSION

Advances in semantic segmentation of UAV imagery using deep learning have significantly improved forest tree species classification with higher accuracy and efficiency. UAVs provide high-resolution data on forest composition and structure, enabling detailed ecosystem analysis. The use of CNNs and multi modal data fusion has further enhanced scalability and precision. Challenges like class imbalance, occlusion, and high computational demand are being addressed through self-supervised learning, domain adaptation and light weight architectures. These developments support applications in biodiversity conservation, forest monitoring and carbon estimation, contributing to sustainable management and climate change mitigation.

ACKNOWLEDGEMENT

We gratefully acknowledge the staff and authorities of Mechatronics Department and Manipal Institute of Technology, Manipal for their cooperation in this research.

REFERENCES

[1] Dalponte, M., Bruzzone, L., and Gianelle, D. (2012). Tree species classification in the Southern Alps based on the fusion of very high geometrical resolution multispectral/hyperspectral images and LiDAR data. *Remote Sensing of Environment*, *123*, 258–270.

[2] Csillik, O., Cherbini, J., Johnson, R., Lyons, A., & Kelly, M. (2018). Identification of citrus trees from unmanned aerial vehicle imagery using convolutional neural networks. *Drones*, *2*(4), 39.

[3] Torresan, C., Berton, A., Carotenuto, F., Di Gennaro, S.F., Gioli, B., Matese, A., ... and Wallace, L. (2017). Forestry applications of UAVs in Europe: A review. *International Journal of Remote Sensing*, *38*(8–10), 2427–2447.

[4] Diez, Y., Kentsch, S., Fukuda, M., Caceres, M.L.L., Moritake, K., and Cabezas, M. (2021). Deep learning in forestry using uav-acquired rgb data: A practical review. *Remote Sensing*, *13*(14), 2837.

[5] Adão, T., Hruška, J., Pádua, L., Bessa, J., Peres, E., Morais, R., and Sousa, J.J. (2017). Hyperspectral imaging: A review on UAV-based sensors, data processing and applications for agriculture and forestry. *Remote Sensing*, 9(11), 1110.

[6] Schiefer, F., Kattenborn, T., Frick, A., Frey, J., Schall, P., Koch, B., and Schmidtlein, S. (2020). Mapping forest tree species in high resolution UAV-based RGB-imagery by means of convolutional neural networks. *ISPRS Journal of Photogrammetry and Remote Sensing*, *170*, 205–215.

[7] Grybas, H., and Congalton, R.G. (2022). Evaluating the Impacts of Flying Height and Forward Overlap on Tree Height Estimates Using Unmanned Aerial Systems. *Forests*, *13*(9), 1462.

[8] Jiménez-Jiménez, S.I., Ojeda-Bustamante, W., Marcial- Pablo, M. D.J., and Enciso, J. (2021). Digital terrain models generated with low-cost UAV photogrammetry: Methodology and accuracy. *ISPRS International Journal of Geo-Information*, *10*(5), 285.

[9] Buchelt, A., Adrowitzer, A., Kieseberg, P., Gollob, C., Nothdurft, A., Eresheim, S., ... and Holzinger, A. (2024). Exploring artificial intelligence for applications of drones in forest ecology and management. *Forest Ecology and Management*, *551*, 121530.

[10] Hao, S., Zhou, Y., and Guo, Y. (2020). A brief survey on semantic segmentation with deep learning. *Neurocomputing*, *406*, 302–321.

[11] Chen, G., Tan, X., Guo, B., Zhu, K., Liao, P., Wang, T., ... and Zhang, X. (2021). SDFCNv2: An improved FCN framework for

remote sensing images semantic segmentation. *Remote Sensing*, *13*(23), 4902.

[12] Cruz, C., McGuinness, K., Perrin, P.M., O'Connell, J., Martin, J.R., and Connolly, J. (2023). Improving the mapping of coastal invasive species using UAV imagery and deep learning. *International Journal of Remote Sensing*, *44*(18), 5713–5735.

[13] Badrinarayanan, V., Kendall, A., and Cipolla, R. (2017). Segnet: A deep convolutional encoder-decoder architecture for image segmentation. *IEEE Transactions on Pattern Analysis and Machine Intelligence*, *39*(12), 2481–2495.

[14] Diakogiannis, F.I., Waldner, F., Caccetta, P., and Wu, C. (2020). ResUNet-a: A deep learning framework for semantic segmentation of remotely sensed data. *ISPRS Journal of Photogrammetry and Remote Sensing*, *162*, 94–114.

[15] Zeng, J., Shen, X., Zhou, K., and Cao, L. (2025). FO-Net: An advanced deep learning network for individual tree identification using UAV high-resolution images. *ISPRS Journal of Photogrammetry and Remote Sensing*, *220*, 323–338.

[16] Zou, K., Chen, X., Wang, Y., Zhang, C., and Zhang, F. (2021). A modified U-Net with a specific data argumentation method for semantic segmentation of weed images in the field. *Computers and Electronics in Agriculture*, *187*, 106242.

[17] Tao, C., Meng, Y., Li, J., Yang, B., Hu, F., Li, Y., ... and Zhang, W. (2022). MSNet: Multispectral semantic segmentation network for remote sensing images. *GIScience and Remote Sensing*, *59*(1), 1177–1198.

[18] Kim, Y.H., and Park, K.R. (2022). MTS-CNN: Multi-task semantic segmentation-convolutional neural network for detecting crops and weeds. *Computers and Electronics in Agriculture*, *199*, 107146.

[19] Liu, X., Frey, J., Munteanu, C., Still, N., and Koch, B. (2023). Mapping tree species diversity in temperate montane forests using Sentinel-1 and Sentinel-2 imagery and topography data. *Remote Sensing of Environment*, *292*, 113576.

[20] Santos, A.A.D., Marcato Junior, J., Araújo, M.S., Di Martini, D.R., Tetila, E.C., Siqueira, H.L., ... and Gonçalves, W.N. (2019). Assessment of CNN-based methods for individual tree detection on images captured by RGB cameras attached to UAVs. *Sensors*, *19*(16), 3595.

[21] Ajibola, S., and Cabral, P. (2024). A systematic literature review and bibliometric analysis of semantic segmentation models in land cover mapping. *Remote Sensing*, *16*(12), 2222.

[22] Sun, Y., Hao, Z., Guo, Z., Liu, Z., and Huang, J. (2023). Detection and mapping of chestnut using deep learning from high-resolution UAV-Based RGB imagery. *Remote Sensing*, *15* (20), 4923.

[23] Morales, G., Kemper, G., Sevillano, G., Arteaga, D., Ortega, I., and Telles, J. (2018). Automatic segmentation of Mauritia flexuosa in unmanned aerial vehicle (UAV) imagery using deep learning. *Forests*, *9*(12), 736.

[24] Akca, S., and Gungor, O. (2022). Semantic segmentation of soil salinity using in-situ EC measurements and deep learning-based U-NET architecture. *Catena*, *218*, 106529.

[25] Kaiser, P., Wegner, J.D., Lucchi, A., Jaggi, M., Hofmann, T., and Schindler, K. (2017). Learning aerial image segmentation from online maps. *IEEE Transactions on Geoscience and Remote Sensing*, *55*(11), 6054–6068.

[26] Balsi, M., Esposito, S., Fallavollita, P., and Nardinocchi, C. (2018). Single-tree detection in high-density LiDAR data from UAV-based survey. *European Journal of Remote Sensing*, *51*(1), 679–692.

[27] Ampatzidis, Y., and Partel, V. (2019). UAV-based high throughput phenotyping in citrus utilizing multispectral imaging and artificial intelligence. *Remote Sensing*, *11*(4), 410.

[28] Kemker, R., Salvaggio, C., and Kanan, C. (2018). Algorithms for semantic segmentation of multispectral remote sensing imagery using deep learning. *ISPRS Journal of Photogrammetry and Remote Sensing*, *145*, 60–77.

[29] Janneh, L.L., Zhang, Y., Hydara, M., and Cui, Z. (2024). Deep learning-based hybrid feature selection for the semantic segmentation of crops and weeds. *ICT Express*, *10*(1), 118–124.

[30] Zhuang, S., Wang, P., and Jiang, B. (2018, July). Segmentation of green vegetation in the field using deep neural networks. In *2018 13th World Congress on Intelligent Control and Automation (WCICA)* (pp. 509–514). IEEE.

[31] Capecchi, I., Borghini, T., and Bernetti, I. (2023). Automated urban tree survey using remote sensing data, Google street view images, and plant species recognition apps. *European Journal of Remote Sensing*, *56*(1), 2162441.

[32] Behera, T.K., Bakshi, S., and Sa, P.K. (2022). Vegetation extraction from UAV-based aerial images through deep learning. *Computers and Electronics in Agriculture*, *198*, 107094.

[33] Li, Z., Deng, X., Lan, Y., Liu, C., and Qing, J. (2024). Fruit tree canopy segmentation from UAV orthophoto maps based on a lightweight improved U-Net. *Computers and Electronics in Agriculture*, *217*, 108538.

[34] Mäyrä, J., Keski-Saari, S., Kivinen, S., Tanhuanpää, T., Hurskainen, P., Kullberg, P., ... and Vihervaara, P. (2021). Tree species classification from airborne hyperspectral and LiDAR data using 3D convolutional neural networks. *Remote Sensing of Environment*, *256*, 112322.

[35] Velasquez-Camacho, L., Etxegarai, M., and de-Miguel, S. (2023). Implementing Deep Learning algorithms for urban tree detection and geolocation with high-resolution aerial, satellite, and ground-level images. *Computers, Environment and Urban Systems*, *105*, 102025.

Technology for a Resilient Future – Vincent , Moorthy and Dasari (Eds)

Vrishabha: Edge-AI Enabled Real-Time Visual Perception System for Extreme Rocket Flight Environments

Tejas Patil, Aryan Gupta, Mohul Podder, Adi Narayan RS, Rudra Rajpurohit, Mutra Sai Tharun, Akash Siddharth, and Gouranga Mandal
Manipal Institute of Technology, Manipal Academy of Higher Education, Manipal, India

ABSTRACT: This paper describes the design and qualification of Vrishabha, a 4.55 kg non-deployable payload developed for the Vayuvega sounding rocket mission capable of performing 3D object tracking (OT) and pose estimation (PE) in real-time under flight conditions. The system is limited in size, weight, power with high accuracy and reliability. A Raspberry Pi 5 with Hailo-8 AI accelerator (26 TOPS) can run optimised YOLOv8s models at 20–30 FPS in a 15 W power budget. The payload consists of a target cube on a conical spring mount, dual servo adaptive camera tracking with motion rate limiting, and Depth-Anything-V2 point cloud generation, validated in high-G, motion blur, and frame drop simulation environments. The experimental results show that at acceleration up to 22 g the keypoint detection accuracy reaches 92.3%. It shows good immunity to movement blur, dropped frames, and rotation skew. The authors claimed that their findings demonstrate that AI-based visual inference is feasible in resource-constrained, high-uncertainty aerospace environments; and, can enable autonomous use of spacecrafts.

Keywords: Edge AI, Real-Time Pose Estimation, YOLOv8, Visual Perception, Object Tracking

1 INTRODUCTION

Aerospace and defence autonomous systems must be capable of visual perception in extreme conditions. Sounding rocket missions create unique challenges for image processing systems because of high G-forces (up to 22g), intense vibrations (100–2000 Hz), and rapid changes in orientation. To address these issues, Vrishabha has designed a custom CanSat configuration payload that validates real-time AI perception in flight representative conditions [1].

1.1 *Core contributions*

(a) Demonstrates the first use of anchor-free YOLOv8s for spacecraft pose estimation while sustaining 22g acceleration.
(b) Introduces a conical spring–target setup that realistically recreates 6-DOF flight disturbances.
(c) Implements a hybrid tracking pipeline that blends color-based detection with neural-network inference.
(d) Achieves 28.5 FPS through power-efficient edge processing on a 7.4V/6000mAh system.

Utilizing NPUs instead of GPUs, offering 26 TOPS of compute within strict 15W aerospace power levels. System success opens up future opportunities in autonomous rendezvous, space debris avoidance and planetary landing systems where traditional sensors won't work.

2 LITERATURE SURVEY

The merger of artificial intelligence with visual perception systems in aerospace has made autonomous operations possible even in extreme flight conditions. Because of the high acceleration, vibration, and thermal variations, the performance of conventional computer vision techniques is severely degraded. Ultralytics launched YOLOv8, enhancing the accuracy and speed of the backbone and detection head techniques with improved anchor-free detection and mosaic augmentation techniques [2].

The development of NPUs and μNPUs has made onboard inference more practical and much easier than it was before. These processors deliver significant improvements in energy efficiency and throughput on embedded platforms [3],[4]. According to recent benchmarking studies, NPUs can demonstrate performance matching or exceeding that of GPUs for inference, based on comparable workloads while consuming 35–70% less power [4].

Improved YOLOv8 variants for debris detection have achieved mean average precision (AP_{50}) scores of about 88.6% in space-oriented applications [5]. This shows the model's reliability in low-signal and high-dynamic environments. The *You Only Look Once* (YOLO) family of algorithms remains the de facto standard for real-time object detection in embedded and aerospace systems, owing to its single-stage detection architecture and computational efficiency [6]. Lightweight derivatives such as *Tinyissimo YOLO* achieve real-time inference on ultra-low-power processors, demonstrating the viability of single-stage detectors in constrained edge environments [7].

Visual perception in aerospace remains challenged by motion blur, vibration, and rolling-shutter artifacts. Peer- reviewed studies on image motion deblurring and visual tracking demonstrate that such degradations substantially reduce detection and pose-estimation accuracy, and that algorithmic deblurring and temporal filtering can significantly restore performance under dynamic conditions [8]. These findings support the development of hybrid perception pipelines that integrate adaptive calibration and deblurring modules to enhance robustness during high-motion, high-vibration flight regimes.

3 PROPOSED METHODOLOGY

(a) Mechanical Design: The Vrishabha payload adopts a modular CanSat form factor (Figure 1) for integration into the Vayuvega sounding rocket, featuring a 4.55 kg structure constructed primarily from Aluminium 6061 with two cylindrical segments of 100 mm diameter, 6 mm wall thickness, and lengths of 230 mm (top) and 205 mm (bottom). Three bulkheads—top (Stainless Steel 316, 21 mm thick for structural integrity), middle (Aluminium 6061,

DOI: 10.1201/9781042017546-56

37 mm thick for modular integration), and bottom (Aluminium 6061, 21 mm thick)—provide rigidity, while the target object is a stainless steel cube mass-tuned for maximum oscillatory response. Electronics and camera mounts are fabricated from 3D-printed ABS.

Figure 1. Payload sectional view.

Due to the intense vibrational environment onboard a.

A conical spring was chosen for its efficiency in rockets sending vibrations to the target for detection. Due to the difficulty of modelling dynamic spring behaviour, the calculations were performed using a steady-state approach.

The forces acting on the spring system are the spring force upwards (Figure 2): $FS = k * x$, the weight downwards: $m * g$, and the acceleration of the system: 22g upwards[9]. If the upwards direction is considered negative:

$$\begin{aligned} -k * x + m * g + m * (22 * g) &= 0 \\ k * x &= m * (g + 22 * g) \end{aligned} \tag{1}$$

$$F_s(F) = m * 23 * g \tag{2}$$

Where k is the spring constant, x is the spring elongation, and g is the acceleration due to gravity ($9.81 \mathrm{m/s^2}$). The rocket experiences a maximum upward acceleration of 22g as implied by Equations (1) and (2).

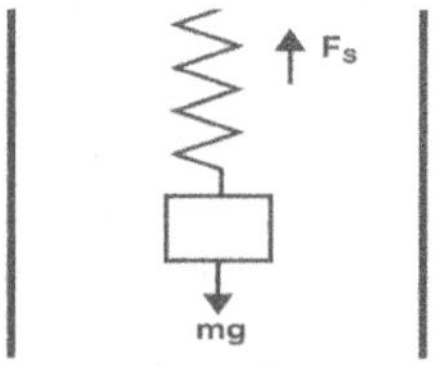

Figure 2. Spring force analysis in an accelerating non-inertial frame of reference.

From the above formula mentioned (Figure 3), different versions of the conical springs with different dimensions were calculated using Equation (3), and the best one selected was spring number 6 (Table 1)[9].

$$f = \frac{16n(r_1 + r_0)(r_1^2 + r_0^2)F}{d^4 G} \tag{3}$$

Extensive vibrational analysis was carried out to validate the structural integrity of the entire payload. Modal analysis revealed three main natural frequencies: 1150 Hz for lateral vibration, 1250 Hz for longitudinal vibration, and 1434 Hz for

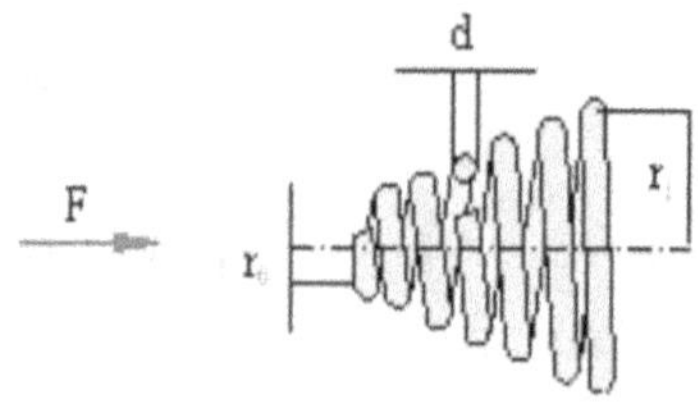

Figure 3. Calculation for spring deflection.

torsional vibration. The three frequencies were compared with the excitation spectrum which was expected. A PSD profile was generated from 6-DOF flight-simulator data using Welch's method to simulate the stochastic vibration environment. The finite element simulations were employed to calculate the structural deformation during the launch, which found the maximum directional displacements of the structure to be 0.265 mm in the X-direction, 0.358 mm in Y- direction and 0.841 mm in Z-direction. Furthermore, all of these maximum displacements were well within the safe limits.

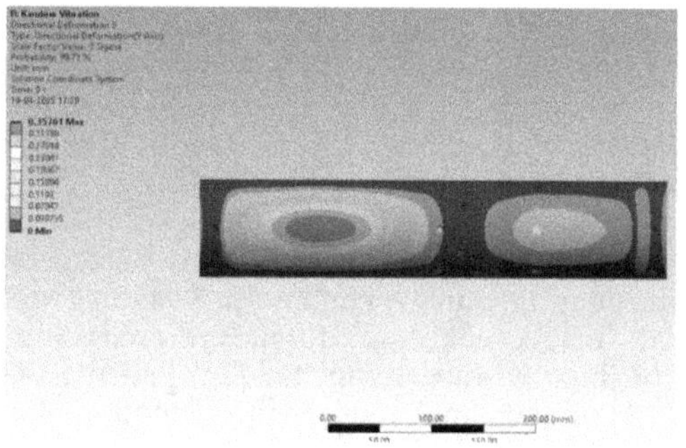

Figure 4. Directional deformation in X-Axis with flight simulated data.

There's only a 0.3% chance that the payload will deform, according to the statistics. The onboard accelerometers collected data as the model flew larrier real jobs. The acceleration data also followed the modal analysis with clear peaks at lift-off, drogue chute deployment, main chute deployment and touchdown, all safely within structural limitations.(Figure 5)[1]

Table 1. Spring selection table.

S/N	Coils	Wire Dia (mm)	Inner Ø (mm)	Stiffness (N/mm)	Deflection (mm)	Material
1	5	2.5	34.7-54.7	1.21	12.17	Spring Steel
2	6	2.0	16.45-45.45	0.95	15.40	Spring Steel
3	7	2.0	12.7-39.7	1.14	12.84	Spring Steel
4	8	2.0	15-29	1.81	8.11	Spring Steel
5	5	1.5	9-39	0.77	19.08	SS 316
6	6	1.5	17-29	0.83	17.76	SS 316

(b) Electronics Design: The electronics are powered from a 7.4 V, 6000 mAh Li-Ion battery through 5V 5 A Battery Eliminator Circuit. Further, a pull pin switch is used for the pre-launch safety of the system. We employ a Raspberry Pi 5 (8 GB RAM, ARM Cortex-A76) integrated with a Hailo-8 AI HAT+ accelerator that provides 26 TOPS of compute performance while staying low in power consumption [10]. An Arducam CSI camera captures visual data and an MPU9250 gives accelerometer, gyroscope and magnetometer readings that are fused using the Madgwick filter to compute rotation matrices from quaternions for orientation estimation. A dual-shaft 35 kg-cm servo motor works via PCA9685 driver within a ±20° range and the max tracking speed of 450°/s for fast targeting. A buzzer worked on5–24 V and a WS2812 LED ring were added to indicate the system status. The electronic components maintain a hierarchy where AI inference, sensor fusion, and actuation are managed by the Raspberry Pi. All of them communicate through a shared-memory model with disk-backed queues for added fault tolerance [12].

(c) Computational Design: For inference and tracking, it uses two parallel pipelines. The proportional controller applies servo angle adjustment using colour detection based on HSV and attaching it to the cube. If the cube is not perceived by the camera for four consecutive frames, scanning mode activates. The inference pipeline receives frames from an on-board camera (640×480) at 40 FPS. It resizes and pads the frames to 640×640 and subsequently runs YOLOv8s inference that has been optimized for the Hailo-8 NPU. This inference outputs bounding boxes, keypoints and confidence scores. The pose estimation is done asynchronously through combining pre-processing and post-processing. And it visualizes through OpenCV. The IMU process detects launch and flight events such as drogue and main chute deployment utilizing the accelerometer spikes [1]. The Servo control is achieved in real-time with the support of multimedia extensions, CPU core affinity, and other parallel worker threads. The YOLOv8s model was trained using a dataset of 1200 images, which was supplemented with alterations in brightness, blur, exposure and saturation to incorporate the vibrations interference effects to develop 4500 augmented images of the equipment. According to a comparative study on monocular models for depth estimation, the Depth-Anything V2 is the strongest model that works well under vibrations. It produces depth maps from RGB frames, which are further fused into point clouds for 3D reconstruction [13].

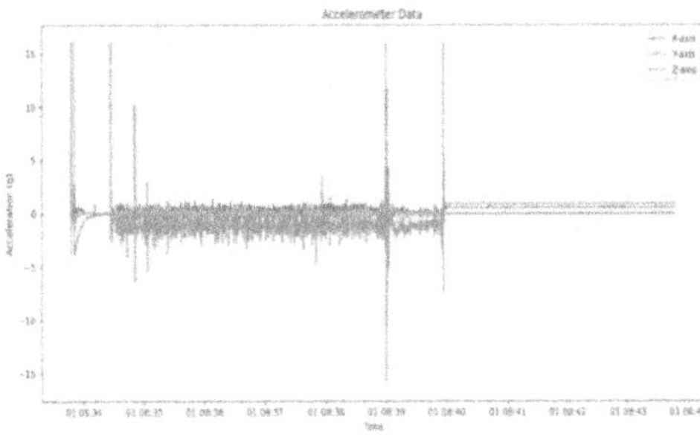

Figure 5. Accelerometer data from the rocket flight.

(d) Design and Fabrication of a Vibration-Optimized Payload: A modular payload of CanSat-form-factor called Vrishabha was designed and fabricated for integration into Vayuvega sounding rocket with vibration tuning. The configuration of the mechanism is such that it has enough stiffness and a spring–mass target system that enhances and transmits launch vibrations for in- flight tracking tests. Everything was manufactured using the materials used in aerospace technology to achieve maximum strength at low weight.

(e) AI-Driven Object Tracking and Depth Estimation Pipelines: Two computational pipelines were implemented: AI-based object tracking and depth estimation pipelines were set up. The former is a colour based tracking system while the second is an inference pipeline using YOLOv8 that is optimized for edge along with depth estimation using Depth-Anything V2 for real- time 3D spatial mapping. We tune hyperparameters under hard latency and power constraints. The adjustments made to the batch-size entailed that a power budget of 6 W was maintained in inference related to target detection. Dropout implementation and early stopping made it robust to blur from 10–30 Hz vibrations. Tuning for throughput implementation gives stable 28.5 FPS for target detection.

(f) Ground Testing and Environmental Simulation: The simulated the high-g accelerations random vibration spectra and the oscillations caused by the launch through extensive ground testing. The natural frequencies and deformation probabilities of the structure along with the overall stability of the structure were determined modal and vibration analyses. According to [1], the servo system implements a motion-rate limiter of up to 450°/s so as to make it stable.

4 RESULTS AND DISCUSSION

Real-time object tracking technology is enabled by dual- pipeline engineering architecture. The whole system was operated on a Raspberry Pi 5 with a Hailo-8 co-processor with a 26 TOPS. The tracking pipeline consistently ran at 40 FPS. Meanwhile, inference had a frame rate of 20-30 FPS. The speed depended on the scene complexity. Depth-Anything V2 produced accurate depth maps.

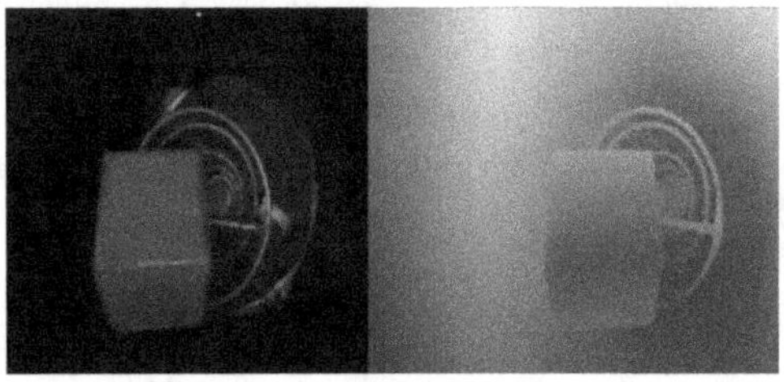

Figure 6. Live depth detection results from the rocket flight.

Table 2. Confidence score per vertice.

Vertice 0	0.6307
Vertice 1	0.9259
Vertice 2	0.7664
Vertice 3	0.8957
Vertice 4	0.3669
Vertice 5	0.8472
Vertice 6	0.4824
Vertice 7	0.9124

The average confidence of the system scores 0.812 with per-vertex scores in Table 2 which demonstrated a good estimation under strict dynamic ranges. Confidence levels exceeding 0.8 at all eight vertices indicate reliable performance by the perception pipeline. We also integrated a launch-detection module using the MPU- 9250 IMU and the Madgwick filter [11], which computes the real-time orientation (roll, pitch, yaw) of the IMU. . The internal spring mechanism behaved according to simulation during testing, confirming the mechanical response model, and all measured flight parameters are summarized in Table 2.

To recreate the condition of loading production-scale rockets, a dataset of 1200 object trajectories was generated. This dataset was augmented to 4500 frames by applying ±20% augmentation in illumination, Gaussian noise (σ=0.01-0.05) and synthetic vibration blur. The training used a set that added light changes. Synthetic vibration blur matched the impact of structural tests. The blur used a 10 to 30 Hz modal response range. Furthermore, it added Gaussian noise. Ultimately, that noise imitated disturbance from flight telemetry.

Throughout the conducted vibration test cycles, the average latency was 28.5 FPS with variance of less than 1 FPS. Furthermore, the detection probability had stable performance with 10–30 Hz vibration noise. Power consumption averaged roughly 6 W with ± 0.3 W fluctuation and was statistically robust under flight.

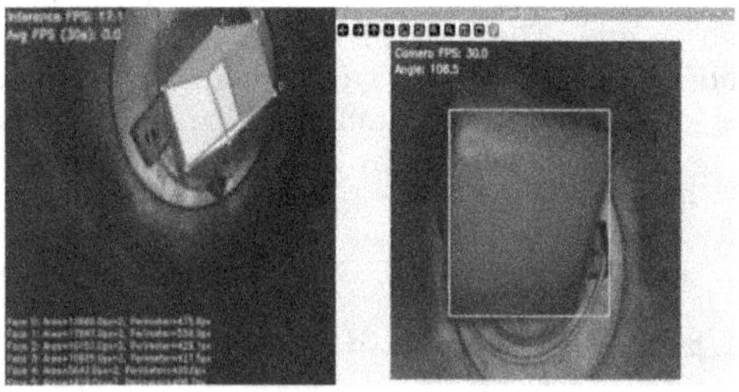

Figure 7. Live object tracking and pose estimation from the rocket flight.

Table 3. Results evaluated from actual flight data.

Metric	Value	Conditions/Notes
Pose Estimation		
Key point Detection Accuracy	92.3%	At peak 22g simulated acceleration
Processing Throughput		
AI Inference Framerate	20-30 FPS	YOLOv8s on Hailo-8 NPU
System Average Framerate	28.5 FPS	End-to-end processing
Camera Capture Rate	40 FPS	Arducam IMX708 @ 640x480
Power & Efficiency		
System Power Consumption	<15 W	During active inference
AI Accelerator Performance	26 TOPS	Hailo-8 NPU
Mechanical / Control		
Max Servo Tracking Speed	450 Â°/s	Software limited for stability
System Activation Trigger	> 5 g for 5 ms	MPU 9250 IMU
System Boot Time	37 s	From trigger to operational readiness

The analysis of in-flight video footage and Inertial Measurement Unit (IMU) information after the flight revealed that following each occlusion being introduced, the system managed to re-acquire the target within 0.45 seconds. Sample live-inference results are shown in Figures 6 and 7.

5 CONCLUSION AND FUTURE WORK

The payload called Vrishabha has successfully demonstrated real-time AI-based 3D object tracking and pose estimation under sounding-rocket conditions within prescribed mass, volume, and power budget. With an optimized mechanical layout and YOLOv8s inference running on a Raspberry Pi 5 with a Hailo-8 accelerator, the setup was able to operate reliably up to 22 g and steadily average 28.5 FPS. The aerospace edge computing technology has taken a significant leap. It now shows real-time autonomous decision-making can be deployed on small and resource-constrained platforms instead of just ground stations or large vehicles.

The results show that visual inference enabled by AI can reliably operate in constrained, high-uncertainty environments typical of aerospace applications, opening the door to new possibilities like autonomous rendezvous, debris avoidance capabilities, planetary landing, and even deep-space missions. The power- efficient design helped maintain a budget for inference of about 6 W, removing one major barrier to onboard autonomy. By enabling multi-target tracking and combining visual, inertial, and depth sensing, Vrishabha lays the groundwork for subsequent advancements. Utilizing predictive control, mechanical enhancements, and possible CubeSat-class demonstrations, this technique can be applied to long-duration missions and microgravity. These developments make scalable edge- AI computing a key technology for next-generation autonomous spacecraft, helping it operate reliably under vibration and acceleration, and other mission stresses.

ACKNOWLEDGEMENTS

As we worked on this, we have enjoyed the support of the members of thrustMIT, Manipal.

REFERENCES

[1] Project Vayuvega Team 207. (2025). Thrustmit – Project Vayuvega Team 207 Project Technical Report to the 2025 IREC. https://doi.org/10.13140/RG.2.2.15776.08967

[2] Ultralytics, (2023). "*YOLOv8 Documentation*,". Available: https://docs.ultralytics.com

[3] Millar, J., Huang, Y., Sethi, S., Haddadi, H., and Madhavapeddy, A. (2025). Benchmarking ultra-low-power µNPUs. *arXiv*. https://doi.org/10.48550/arXiv.2503.22567

[4] Hong Y, Kim D. (2025). Performance and efficiency gains of NPU- based servers over GPUs for AI model inference. *Systems*. 13(9):797. https://doi.org/10.3390/systems13090797

[5] Guo Y, Yin X, Xiao Y, *et al.* (2025). Enhanced YOLOv8-based method for space debris detection using cross-scale feature fusion. *Discov Appl Sci*. 7:95. https://doi.org/10.1007/s42452-025-06502-7

[6] Li C, Li L, Jiang H, *et al.* (2022). YOLOv6: A single-stage object detection framework for industrial applications. *arXiv*. https://arxiv.org/abs/2209.02976

[7] Moosmann J, Müller H, Zimmerman N, Rutishauser G, Benini L, Magno M. (2024). Flexible and fully quantized lightweight TinyissimoYOLO for ultra-low-power edge systems. *IEEE Access*. 12:75093–75107. https://doi.org/10.1109/access.2024.3404878

[8] Guo Q, Feng W, Chen Z, Gao R, Wan L, Wang S. (2019). Effects of blur and deblurring to visual object tracking. *arXiv*. https://arxiv.org/abs/1908.07904

[9] Van Beek, A. (n.d.). Calculator for conical springs. https://www.tribology-abc.com/calculators/t14_3.html

[10] Hailo-8 M.2 AI Accelerator Datasheet, Rev 2.3, Hailo Technologies.

[11] Madgwick SOH. (2010). *An Efficient Orientation Filter for Inertial and Inertial/Magnetic Sensor Arrays*. University of Bristol. https://courses.cs.washington.edu/courses/cse466/14au/lab s/l4/madgwick_internal_report.pdf

[12] Nezami Z, Hafeez M, Djemame K, Zaidi SAR. (2024). *Generative AI on the Edge: Architecture and Performance Evaluation*. arXiv. https://arxiv.org/abs/2411.17712

[13] Yang L, Kang B, Huang Z, Xu X, Feng J, Zhao H. (2024). *Depth Anything: Unleashing the Power of Large-Scale Unlabeled Data*. CVPR. . https://doi.org/10.48550/arXiv.2401.10891

Technology for a Resilient Future – Vincent , Moorthy and Dasari (Eds)
 ISBN: 978-1-041-39070-1

Multi-Class Eye Disease Detection and Classification Using VGG19

Jella Surya Prakash
Department of CSE, JNTUH University College of Engineering, Science and Technology, Hyderabad, Telangana, India

K. Shahu Chatrapati
CSE, Department of Computer Science and Engineering, Jawaharlal Nehru Technological University Hyderabad, Telangana, India

S. Rakesh
Department of CSE, JNTUH University College of Engineering, Science and Technology, Hyderabad, Telangana, India

ABSTRACT: The timely detection of eye diseases is crucial to avoid irreversible loss of vision and to improve patient outcomes. In this work, we introduce a deep learning technique using the Visual Geometry Group 19 (VGG19), which is used for automatic diagnosis of three significant ocular diseases, such as diabetic retinopathy, glaucoma and cataract. The model was developed and assessed using the dataset of retinal fundus images with data augmentation techniques for improving the generalization ability. Pre-trained VGG19 weights were fine-tuned to capture relevant features specific to ophthalmological conditions. The system was able to achieve the accuracy of 94% in the test cases, showing the effective multi-class classification capability across all the targeted eye diseases. This method reduces the dependency on manual screening and provides extended support in various clinical and healthcare settings.

Keywords: Diabetic Retinopathy, Glaucoma, Cataract, Retinal Fundus Image, VGG19

1 INTRODUCTION

Diabetic retinopathy, glaucoma and cataract are common causes of blindness and vision impairment globally. The timely diagnosis and treatment can prevent irreversible damage to vision, especially in resource-limited areas [1]. Many of the traditional screening methods depend on expert evaluation of retinal images, which are time-consuming and subject to human variability. These eye diseases have no symptoms during the early stages, as they usually progress slowly. With the slow and error-prone process of manual diagnosis, the world needs an intelligent yet automated solution that can support doctors. Recent advances have produced deep learning-based automated diagnosis systems that can accurately process large amounts of medical images. In this work, we present our methodology for multi-class classification of diabetic retinopathy, glaucoma and cataract from the retinal fundus imaging data using the Visual Geometry Group 19 (VGG19) deep learning algorithm. This study is intended to improve the quality of diagnosis, which will ultimately lead to better patient management.

2 LITERATURE REVIEW

A number of works exist on the development of deep learning-based models for automated detection and classification of eye diseases. Mariam and Thakur compared different transfer learning models such as EfficientNet, DenseNet121 and VGG16 for retinal disease classification and found that a high accuracy of 92.26% was achieved using EfficientNet [1]. Similarly, Nasra, Gupta, Ravi and Singh worked on EfficientNetB3 with additional custom layers on fundus images to reach good accuracy, but they got misclassifications between normal and glaucoma cases [2]. Mishra, Choubey, Jumde, Samiya, Garg and Kale explored the convolutional neural network (CNN) for detection of eye diseases at an early stage that attained an accuracy of 91% and integrated explainable AI to enhance clinical trust, but traditional CNN could not scale up like the more sophisticated transfer learning models [3]. An InceptionResNetV2-based framework was proposed by Kaushik and Sharma with the accuracy of 92.18% [4]. In this, the diabetic retinopathy achieves very high performance with good accuracy, while differentiating the normal eye with glaucoma is still a challenge.

Fayyad and Mustakim studied a comparative analysis between VGG19, EfficientNetV2B0 and AlexNet for the cataract and glaucoma classification [5]. They demonstrated that the highest accuracy of 89.77% was achieved by the EfficientNetV2B0 model, while VGG19 also achieved competitive performance but slightly lower than the EfficientNetV2B0 model. In another work, Chauhan had slightly modified ResNet-18 to use it for the multi-class eye disease detection and demonstrated 92% accuracy [6]. However, his model needs to be further optimized for a robust clinical examination. Together, these studies showcase the utility of deep learning for automated retinal disease detection while underscoring issues with classifying glaucoma and achieving consistent generalization across datasets.

3 METHODOLOGY

The dataset was taken from Kaggle, which consists of 1,007 retinal fundus images for each class of normal, diabetic retinopathy, cataract, and glaucoma [7]. Figure 1 shows the retinal fundus images of the dataset. Due to the structured and well-balanced distribution, it can be used to facilitate both training and evaluation of deep learning models when dealing with multi-class eye disease classification.

Table 1 illustrates the dataset distribution for each class of diabetic retinopathy, cataract, glaucoma and normal. A balanced representation is ensured for efficient model training and evaluation by dividing the 1007 photos in each class into 800 for the training, 100 for the validation, and 107 for the testing.

The VGG19 architecture was used to classify diabetic retinopathy, cataract and glaucoma [8]. The VGG19 contains 19 layers. Figure 2 shows the architecture of VGG19. The

DOI: 10.1201/9781042017546-57

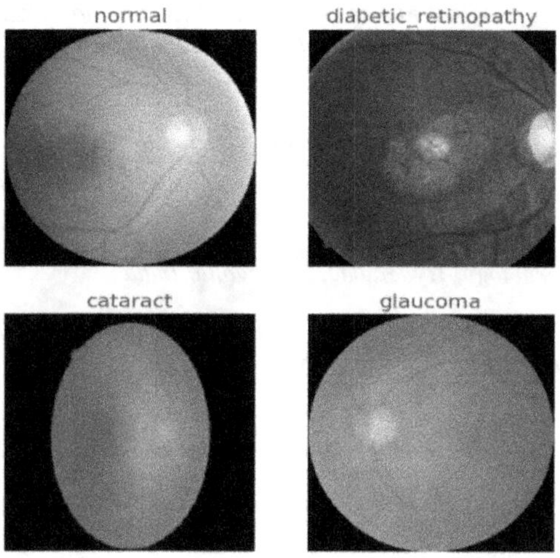

Figure 1. Dataset.

Table 1. Dataset distribution.

Label	Total	Training	Validation	Testing
Diabetic Retinopathy	1007	800	100	107
Cataract	1007	800	100	107
Glaucoma	1007	800	100	107
Normal	1007	800	100	107

design of the architecture follows a sequential pattern with multiple stacked convolutional layers preceding each max-pooling layer.

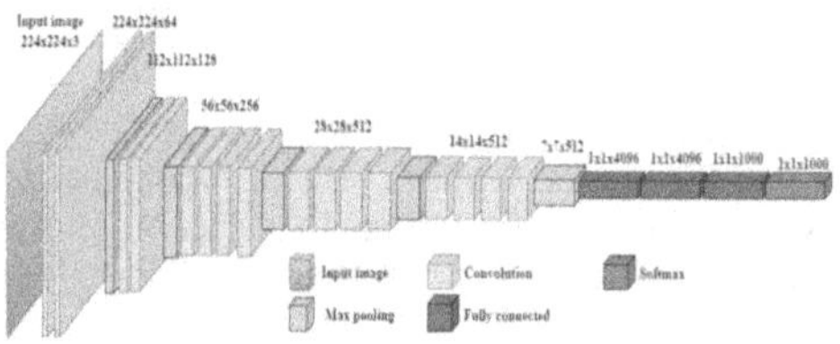

Figure 2. Architecture of VGG19.

The details of the VGG19 architecture are as follows.

3.1 *Input image*

The size of the input image is 224 x 224 x 3 pixels.

3.2 *Convolutional layer*

VGG19 has 16 convolutional layers that are organized into five blocks [8]. A max-pooling layer comes after two or more convolutional layers in each block. A rectified linear unit comes after the convolutional layers. The network maintains the spatial resolution by using 3x3 size convolutional filters with padding and a stride of one. This facilitates the extraction of features from input photos. As the network goes deeper into the architecture, the use of several sequential convolutional layers helps in its learning of more abstract features.

3.3 *Max-pooling layer*

The feature map dimensions are reduced to half by using five max-pooling layers, each of which has a stride of two and a 2x2 filter [9].

3.4 *Dense layer*

The two fully connected dense layers follow the convolutional and max-pooling layers. Through an adjustment of the number of neurons, these layers can be modified to suit particular classification problems.

3.5 *Softmax layer*

The softmax layer provides the probabilities that sum to one as the output. The outcome is a vector of probabilities, where each value represents the likelihood that the input falls into a particular class. The highest probability label is selected as the final prediction [9].

Table 2 illustrates the block-wise structure of VGG19. It shows the list of layers in each block along with the number of filters applied and the size of the output matrix at every layer. The VGG19 has five blocks of convolutional layers [10]. Each block consists of a max-pooling layer after several convolutional layers to extract hierarchical features. The VGG19 architecture is simple to build because it uses only 3x3 convolutional filters at each convolutional layer. It is useful for retinal image classification because its deep architecture allows it to collect complex data.

Table 2. VGG19 block-wise structure.

Block	Layer	Total Filters	Output Matrix
Input			224x224x3
Block_1	conv1	64	224x224x64
	conv2	64	224x224x64
Max-pool			112x112x64
Block_2	conv3	128	112x112x128
	conv4	128	112x112x128
Max-pool			56x56x128
Block_3	conv5	256	56x56x256
	conv6	256	56x56x256
	conv7	256	56x56x256
	conv8	256	56x56x256
Max-pool			28x28x256
Block_4	conv9	512	28x28x512
	conv10	512	28x28x512
	conv11	512	28x28x512
	conv12	512	28x28x512
Max-pool			14x14x512
Block_5	conv13	512	14x14x512
	conv14	512	14x14x512
	conv15	512	14x14x512
	conv16	512	14x14x512
Max-pool			7x7x512
Flatten			25088
Dense Layers and Softmax Layer			

The Figure 3 shows the methodology flowchart of the VGG19 model. Initially, the pretrained VGG19 model with ImageNet weights is loaded, and the final dense layers are customized to match the number of target classes. All the base model layers are frozen to use the default weights from the ImageNet, and the final dense layers are allowed to train. The model is then trained by keeping the pretrained convolutional layers frozen. Next, the base model convolutional layers of block 4 and block 5 are unfrozen. The fine-tuning is performed by unfreezing the block 4 and block 5 layers. It uses pre-trained weights from ImageNet for the initial base model layers and applies transfer learning by fine-tuning the block 4 and block 5 layers. The model is then retrained with a lower learning rate and more patience. This fine-tuning allows the model to learn more domain-specific patterns by adapting it for retinal image analysis. Later, the model was tested on the unseen testing data [10]. This systematic approach guarantees better classification accuracy as well as generalization.

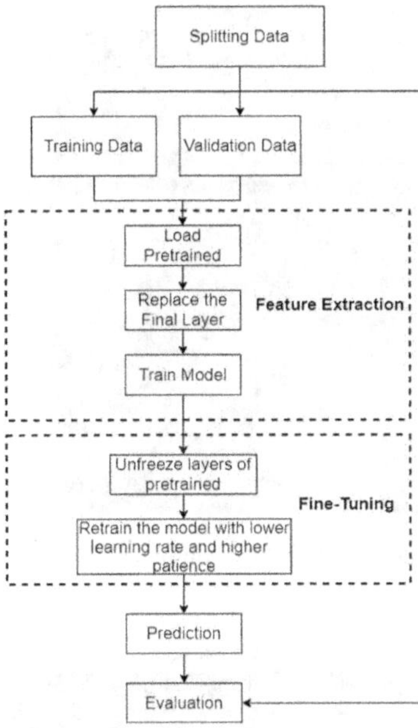

Figure 3. Methodology.

4 IMPLEMENTATION

The dataset was split in the ratio of 80:10:10 for training data, testing data and validation data. The horizontal flipping was applied on the training set for data augmentation. Figure 4 illustrates the workflow of the proposed vgg19 model. Initially, we built our model on top of the pre-trained VGG19 architecture, which has ImageNet weights and used frozen layers during training [11]. Further fully connected layers were added with ReLU, batch normalization, dropout, and L2 regularization for better generalization and to overcome overfitting. The convolutional output of VGG19 was first transformed into a vector with one dimension using a flatten layer, and then it was fed into the dense layers. The dense layers are regularized with L2 regularization and dropout rates of 0.5 and 0.35. The multi-class classification was done using the output softmax layer [12]. The batch normalization was used after each dense layer to maintain internal covariate shift and speed up training. We compiled using AdamW with a learning rate of 1e-4 and added callbacks to stabilize training and achieved optimal convergence

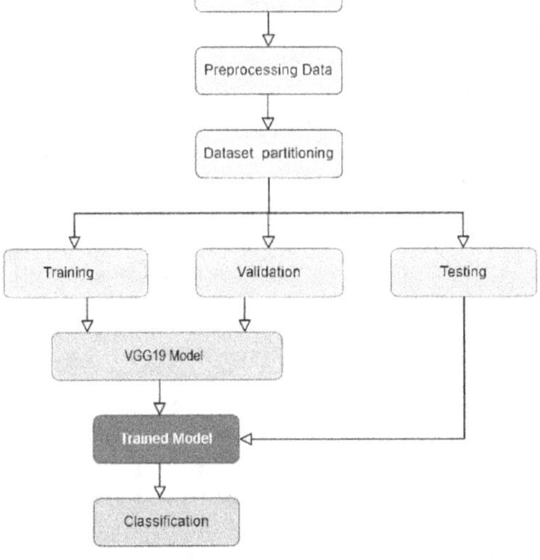

Figure 4 Workflow diagram.

with ReduceLROnPlateau and EarlyStopping. Later, the base layers of VGG19 were unfrozen with a smaller learning rate, allowing the model to learn domain-specific features while keeping the pre-trained knowledge intact.

5 RESULTS

Figure 5 demonstrates the confusion matrix, which displays the classification performance across four different categories, such as cataract, diabetic retinopathy, glaucoma and normal case.

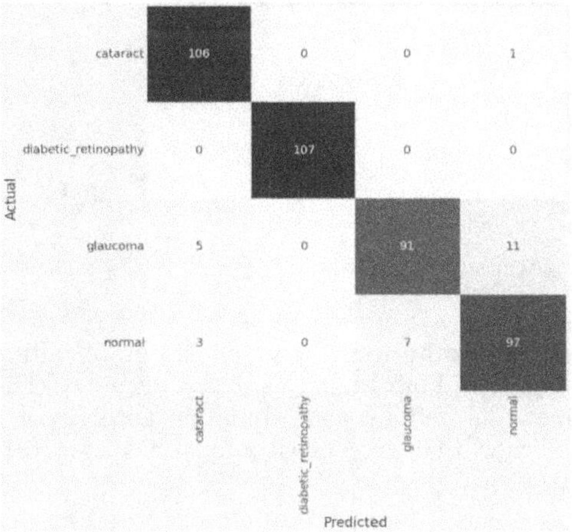

Figure 5. Confusion matrix.

The confusion matrix demonstrates that the majority of predicted labels align correctly with actual labels. The VGG19 model has a good performance in classifying both cataract and diabetic retinopathy because it properly classifies 106 out of 107 cataract cases and all 107 diabetic retinopathy cases. It indicates that the VGG19 model has a strong capability for discrimination of these two eye diseases. This shows that the VGG19 model has a high capacity for categorization of these two diseases. However, there are minor misclassifications in both normal and glaucoma. Out of the 107 samples, 91 were properly predicted to have glaucoma, 5 were incorrectly labelled as cataract and 11 as normal. For the normal class, 97 out of 107 cases were correctly identified, but 3 cases were predicted as cataract and 7 as glaucoma. It is more difficult to differentiate between glaucoma and normal cases due to a certain level of feature resemblance. Overall, the confusion matrix's diagonal dominance shows that the proposed VGG19 model has high classification accuracy for all classes.

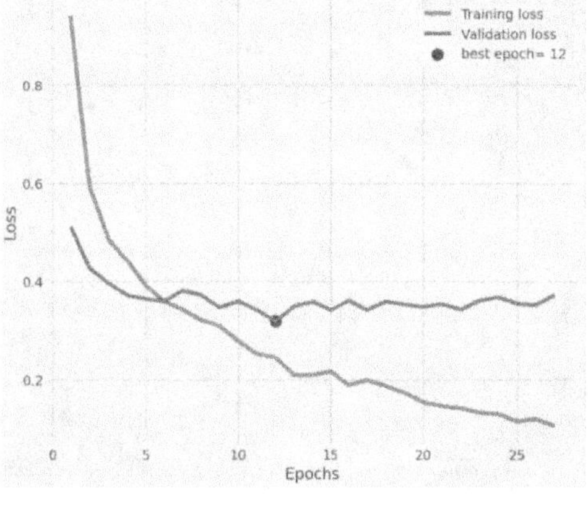

Figure 6. Loss vs epochs.

Figure 6 shows the loss vs. epochs curve of the VGG19 model. The training loss decreased with the increase in epochs. The validation loss decreased initially and in the last epochs, it stabilized.

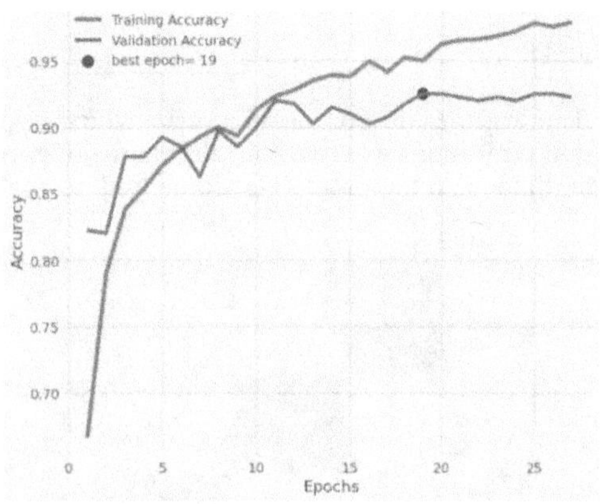

Figure 7. Accuracy vs epochs.

Figure 7 shows the accuracy vs. epochs graph with the consistent increase in both training and test accuracy. The steady improvement in training and validation accuracy across the epochs indicates that the VGG19 model has learned from the training data.

	precision	recall	f1-score	support
cataract	0.93	0.99	0.96	107
diabetic_retinopathy	1.00	1.00	1.00	107
glaucoma	0.93	0.85	0.89	107
normal	0.89	0.91	0.90	107
accuracy			0.94	428
macro avg	0.94	0.94	0.94	428
weighted avg	0.94	0.94	0.94	428

Figure 8. Classification report.

Figure 8 shows the classification report of the VGG19 model that achieved the test accuracy of 94%. The proposed VGG19 model has 0.93 precision and 0.99 recall with an F1-score of 0.96 for cataract. This shows that there are very few misclassifications and the model is very effective at identifying cataract cases. The diabetic retinopathy has a recall, precision

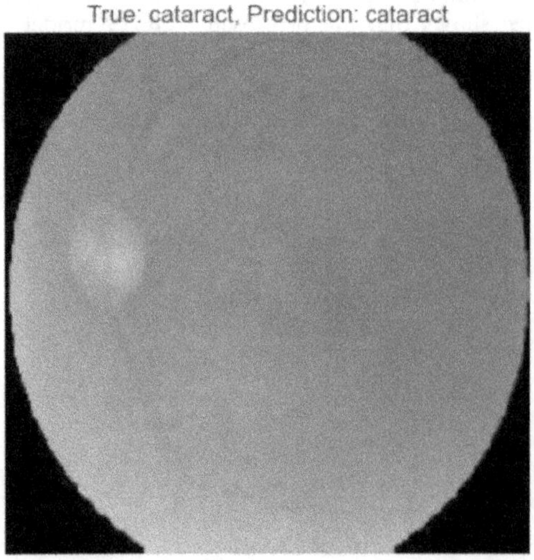

Figure 9. Prediction of cataract.

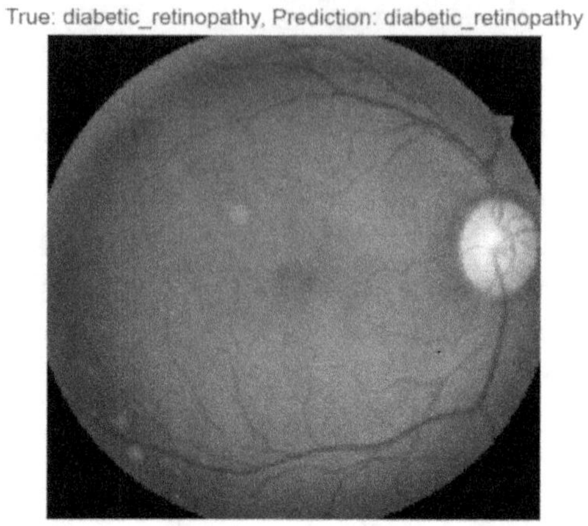

Figure 10. Prediction result of diabetic retinopathy.

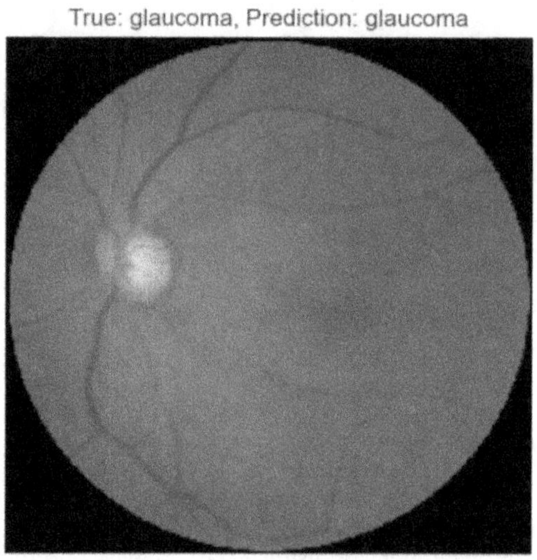

Figure 11. Prediction result of glaucoma.

and F1-score of 1.00. The VGG19 model properly classified all the cases of diabetic retinopathy. The glaucoma has a precision value of 0.93 and a recall value of 0.85 with an F1-score of 0.89. The classification of glaucoma is still strong, despite some variation in recall. The normal class achieved a precision value of 0.89 and a recall value of 0.91 with an F1-score of 0.90. The VGG19 model correctly classifies the images of normal and diseased eyes. Both the macro and weighted averages were 0.94 for all precision, F1-score and recall. The aggregate accuracy of VGG19 model was 94 percent. These results show that the model achieves high performance across all classes.

Figure 9 shows the prediction result of cataract, where the predicted label matches with the true label.

As shown in Figure 10, the retinal fundus image of diabetic retinopathy was correctly classified as diabetic retinopathy, with matching predicted and true labels.

Figure 11 illustrates the prediction result of glaucoma, where the predicted output matches with the true label.

6 CONCLUSION

The VGG19 model correctly identifies and categorizes the eye diseases using retinal fundus images with an accuracy of 94%. This model can be useful to ophthalmologists by reducing manual work related to screening and improving efficiency in the diagnosis. Future work can focus on larger datasets that include more retinal diseases and on real-time deployment on mobile platforms.

ACKNOWLEDGEMENT

We sincerely thank Dr. K. Shahu Chatrapati, Professor of CSE, Department of CSE, JNTU Hyderabad, for his admirable guidance and support. We also extend our gratitude to the faculty and staff of the Department of CSE for their cooperation during this research.

REFERENCES

[1] Mariam and R. Thakur, (2025). "Optimizing retinal disease detection: A comparative analysis of state-of-the-art deep learning models for multiclass classification," *2025 International Conference on Networks and Cryptology,* New Delhi, India, pp. 638–643, https://doi.org/10.1109/NETCRYPT65877.2025.11102602.

[2] P. Nasra, S. Gupta, K. Ravi and A.R. Singh, (2025). "EfficientNetB3-based deep learning approach for automated eye disease detection," *2025 4th OPJU International Technology Conference (OTCON) on Smart Computing for Innovation and Advancement in Industry 5.0*, Raigarh, India, pp. 1–6, https://doi.org/10.1109/OTCON65728.2025.11070729.

[3] A. Mishra, N. Choubey, P. Jumde, A. Samiya, A. Garg and A. Kale, (2025). "Early eye disease detection using machine learning," *2025 IEEE 14th International Conference on Communication Systems and Network Technologies (CSNT)*, Bhopal, India, pp. 134–139, https://doi.org/10.1109/CSNT64827.2025.10968954.

[4] P. Kaushik and P. Sharma, (2024). "Efficient eye disease detection: A deep learning approach with InceptionResNetV2 for retinal image classification," *2024 International Conference on Advances in Computing, Communication and Materials (ICACCM)*, Dehradun, India, pp. 1–5, https://doi.org/10.1109/ICACCM61117.2024.11059202.

[5] M.F. Fayyad and Mustakim, (2024). "Application of AlexNet, EfficientNetV2B0, and VGG19 with Explainable AI for Cataract and Glaucoma Image Classification," *2024 International Electronics Symposium (IES)*, Denpasar, Indonesia, pp. 406–412, https://doi.org/10.1109/IES63037.2024.10665856.

[6] S. Chauhan, (2024). "ResNet-18 for automated eye disease diagnosis: A neural network solution," *2024 3rd International Conference for Advancement in Technology (ICONAT)*, GOA, India, pp. 1–5, https://doi.org/10.1109/ICONAT61936.2024.10774939.

[7] Guna Venkat Doddi, (2025). "Eye disease classification dataset," *Kaggle.* Available: https://www.kaggle.com/datasets/gunavenkatdoddi/eye-diseases-classification/data.

[8] S. Singla and R. Gupta, (2024). "Diabetic retinopathy diagnosis using VGG-19 Deep Learning Model," *2024 3rd International Conference for Advancement in Technology (ICONAT)*, GOA, India, pp. 1–4, https://doi.org/10.1109/ICONAT61936.2024.10775085.

[9] Mannepalli, P.K., Baghela, V.D.S., Agrawal, A., Johri, P., Dubey, S.S., Parmar, K. (2024). Transfer learning for automated classification of eye disease in fundus images from pretrained model. *Traitement du Signal*, Vol. 41, No. 5, pp. 2459–2470. https://doi.org/10.18280/ts.410520.

[10] P.P. Shamrao and Dr. B. Gupta, (2025). "Eye disease classification using deep learning algorithms," *International Journal of Advanced Research in Science, Communication and Technology*, vol. 5, no. 6, ISSN: 2581-9429.

[11] Z.S. Alzamil, (2024). "Advancing eye disease assessment through deep learning: A comparative study with pre-trained models", *Eng. Technol. Appl. Sci. Res.*, vol. 14, no. 3, pp. 14579–14587.

[12] G. Deepak, G. Divya, and S.K. Bhat, (2024). "Deep learning-based CNN for multiclassification of ocular diseases using transfer learning," *Computer Methods in Biomechanics and Biomedical Engineering: Imaging & Visualization*, vol. 12, no. 1, pp. 1–9, doi: 10.1080/21681163.2024.2335959.

Technology for a Resilient Future – Vincent , Moorthy and Dasari (Eds)
 ISBN: 978-1-041-39070-1

A Cost-Effective Autonomous Drone Delivery System with Ultrasonic-Based Real-Time Obstacle Avoidance

Yash N. Jagtap
Robotics & Automation Engineering, VPKBIET Baramati, Pune, Maharashtra, India

Sachin M. Bhosle and Vishal Bhagwat
Department of Mechanical Engineering, VPKBIET Baramati, Pune, Maharashtra, India

ABSTRACT: The rapid growth of e-commerce and on-demand logistics has intensified pressure on last-mile delivery systems, demanding solutions that are autonomous, efficient, safe, and cost-effective. Unmanned Aerial Vehicles (UAVs) offer strong potential, yet deployment remains limited by payload endurance, obstacle avoidance reliability, and the high cost of advanced sensing technologies. This paper presents the design and experimental validation of a cost-effective UAV delivery platform integrating low-cost ultrasonic sensing with Pixhawk ArduPilot navigation for real-time obstacle avoidance and autonomous package release. A lightweight Arduino-based co-processor processes matrix-filtered ultrasonic data to enable collision-aware navigation without significant cost, weight, or computational overhead. Field trials achieved a 15-minute flight time, 4.5 km operational range, and stable payload delivery up to 600 g, with a 93% obstacle avoidance success rate within 3 m. Comparative analysis shows a 60% sensor cost reduction and 35% weight decrease compared to LiDAR-equipped UAVs, making the system a practical option for scalable last-mile logistics. The study highlights the potential of low-cost sensing architectures to bridge the gap between simulation research and deployable UAV networks, with future work focusing on multi-sensor fusion and AI-based path planning for resilient autonomous logistics.

Keywords: UAV Delivery, Real-Time Obstacle Avoidance, Ultrasonic Sensing, Pixhawk, ArduPilot, Autonomous Logistics, LiDAR

1 INTRODUCTION

The last mile of logistics is increasingly recognized as the most costly, inefficient, and environmentally demanding segment of global supply chains. With the rapid expansion of e-commerce, just-in-time retailing, and medical deliveries, existing ground-based transportation struggles to meet the demand for speed, reliability, and accessibility. Traffic congestion, infrastructure limitations, and high operating costs further constrain traditional systems, creating significant opportunities for innovation. Against this backdrop, Unmanned Aerial Vehicles (UAVs) have moved beyond experimental prototypes to become disruptive enablers of next-generation logistics.

However, the promise of UAV delivery is hindered by three persistent barriers. First, the payload-to-endurance trade-off restricts operational efficiency. Second, safe navigation in dynamic or cluttered environments remains a challenge, as GPS-only waypoint control is inadequate for dense urban corridors. Third, while LiDAR and vision-based systems offer high-accuracy perception, they increase weight, power demand, computational load, and cost, limiting large-scale deployment. These constraints create a tension between technological advancement and operational feasibility, slowing real-world adoption of drone-based delivery.

This paper argues that overcoming these barriers requires not complex technologies but smarter, resource-efficient architectures. It presents the design and experimental validation of a lightweight, low-cost autonomous UAV delivery system integrating ultrasonic sensing for real-time obstacle avoidance with Pixhawk ArduPilot navigation. To minimize computational overhead, ultrasonic readings are processed by an Arduino Nano co-processor, which issues corrective commands via MAVLink to ensure safe and adaptive navigation. A servo-based payload release mechanism enables reliable package delivery, completing the platform as a functional logistics solution.

The contributions of this work include:

- Development of a modular, cost-effective UAV framework with real-time ultrasonic obstacle detection (≤ 3 m).
- Demonstration of stable payload transport up to 600 g with a 15-minute flight time and 4.5 km operational range.
- Comparative evaluation showing $\approx$60% reduction in cost and $\approx$35% decrease in onboard weight relative to LiDAR-based UAVs.
- Positioning the system as a globally scalable logistics enabler for both urban and rural regions.

By viewing low-cost sensing as a strategic innovation pathway, this work bridges the gap between simulation-based research and deployable UAV logistics, contributing to resilient, affordable, and scalable aerial delivery infrastructures.

2 RELATED WORK

UAVs are increasingly seen as transformative for last-mile delivery, offering potential to bypass traffic and reduce delivery times. Benarbia and Kyamakya [1] highlighted UAVs as sustainable delivery enablers, while Aurambout *et al.* [2] quantified market potential in European cities. Nonetheless, regulatory, infrastructural, endurance, and safety challenges persist [3,4], and scalability remains limited by payload-to-endurance ratios and autonomous navigation reliability [5,7]. Research has focused on enhancing autonomy and mission planning. Early prototypes demonstrated home delivery [8,10], rooftop-based deliveries [9], and improved reliability via ground control software [11], open-source autopilots [12], and integrated navigation systems [13]. Path-planning algorithms [14,16] have improved UAV adaptability, yet GPS-based navigation alone is insufficient in cluttered or GPS-denied environments. Collision avoidance is a critical dimension of UAV autonomy.

DOI: 10.1201/9781042017546-58

Approaches range from computer vision and artificial potential fields [17,20] to multi-sensor fusion and uncertainty-aware planning. While accurate, these methods rely on LiDAR, radar, or cameras, which add weight, cost, and computational complexity, limiting commercial scalability. Ultrasonic sensing offers a lightweight, affordable alternative. Initially established by Koren and Borenstein and later applied to UAVs, recent work has improved algorithms and filtering for reliable short-range collision avoidance. Early prototypes [8,10] integrated ultrasonic sensors but mainly in controlled environments. Robust validation under varying payloads, endurance, and outdoor dynamics remains limited.

This paper addresses the gap by introducing a Pixhawk–ArduPilot UAV with an Arduino Nano-driven ultrasonic array for real-time obstacle avoidance, experimentally validated for endurance, payload stability, and obstacle detection. The proposed approach demonstrates that low-cost sensing can achieve scalable, practical UAV logistics without compromising performance.

3 SYSTEM DESIGN AND METHODOLOGY

The proposed UAV delivery system was designed with a focus on cost-effectiveness, modularity, and real-world deployability. Its architecture integrates sensing, control, and actuation in a layered framework that ensures reliable autonomy while minimizing hardware overhead. The design philosophy is to offload intensive navigation tasks to the Pixhawk flight controller while leveraging an Arduino Nano as a lightweight co-processor dedicated to ultrasonic sensing, thereby achieving real-time obstacle avoidance without burdening the primary flight system.

3.1 *System architecture*

The architecture follows a three-layered model:

Perception Layer: Includes a GPS module for global navigation, an IMU and barometer for flight stabilization, and an array of four ultrasonic sensors (HC-SR04) mounted on the drone's periphery for real-time obstacle detection within 3 m.

Control Layer: Utilizes the Pixhawk 2.4.8 running ArduPilot firmware to manage navigation and mission execution. An Arduino Nano processes ultrasonic inputs via a filtering algorithm and issues corrective roll/pitch commands to Pixhawk through the MAVLink protocol.

Execution Layer: Consists of propulsion (BLDC motors and ESCs), a servo-based payload release mechanism, and telemetry for ground-station communication.

3.2 *Obstacle avoidance strategy*

The obstacle avoidance system ensures reactive safety without compromising navigation efficiency. Unlike camera- or LiDAR-based methods, which are computationally intensive, the proposed framework uses a lightweight ultrasonic array mounted on the drone's periphery, providing 360° short-range awareness.

Each sensor operates in time-of-flight mode, measuring distances based on echo delay. Noise from wind, reflective surfaces, or multipath echoes is mitigated using a matrix-based filtering algorithm that fuses consecutive readings from all sensors into a smoothed distance profile, enhancing detection reliability in semi-urban outdoor environments.

Filtered data are processed by a rule-based module on the Arduino Nano. Obstacles within a 3 m safety envelope are classified by direction:

- Front: Controlled pitch-backward adjustment
- Rear: Pitch-forward adjustment
- Side: Roll away from the obstacle

Commands are sent via MAVLink to the Pixhawk, temporarily overriding the navigation stream. Once clear, the UAV resumes its pre-programmed path autonomously.

A key innovation is the decoupling of avoidance and navigation: ultrasonic sensing and reaction control run on the Arduino, while the Pixhawk manages stable flight and mission tasks. This two-tiered architecture ensures low-latency, reflex-like obstacle avoidance without computational conflicts.

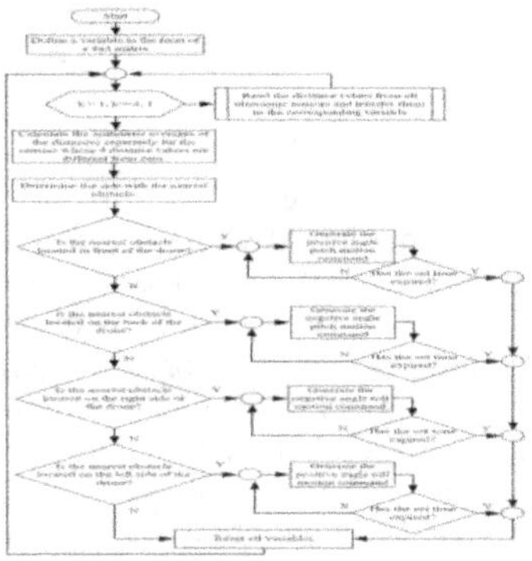

Figure 1. Obstacle detection algorithm architecture diagram.

3.3 *Hardware configuration*

The UAV is constructed on an S500 carbon-fibre frame, balancing strength and weight. Four 935 KV BLDC motors with 10-inch propellers are powered by an 11.1 V, 6800 mAh Li-Po battery, enabling up to 15 minutes of flight under standard payload conditions. The payload delivery system employs a servo-driven mechanism to ensure controlled and secure release. By dedicating the Arduino Nano exclusively to ultrasonic sensing, the system avoids overloading the Pixhawk and ensures fail-safe redundancy even if the obstacle module fails, the Pixhawk maintains stable navigation Suggested Figure 3: A real photograph or CAD model of the hardware setup, highlighting sensor placement and payload mechanism.

Figure 2. Quadcopter Drone.

3.4 *Software environment*

Mission planning and telemetry were handled through Mission Planner, enabling waypoint navigation and live monitoring. The Arduino IDE was used to develop and upload the ultrasonic obstacle avoidance code, which interfaces with Pixhawk via MAVLink. Simulation-in-the-loop (SITL) environments provided a controlled testing framework before real-world deployment, ensuring robustness and safety.

3.5 *Design innovations and rationale*

Several design innovations distinguish this system from conventional UAV delivery platforms:

1. Dual-processor architecture: Decoupling ultrasonic perception from Pixhawk navigation enhances responsiveness while preventing computational bottlenecks.

2. Cost–performance balance: By replacing LiDAR/vision with ultrasonic sensors, the system achieves up to 60% hardware cost reduction and a 35% reduction in onboard weight, improving endurance.
3. Modularity: The architecture allows seamless upgrades (e.g., hybrid vision + ultrasonic fusion or higher-thrust motors) without redesigning the core framework.
4. Scalability for logistics: The choice of lightweight, low-power components enables replication in larger drone fleets for multi-drone delivery operations.

4 EXPERIMENTAL SETUP

A two-stage evaluation pipeline combined ArduPilot SITL simulations with controlled outdoor trials to assess endurance, payload handling, stability, and obstacle avoidance of the ultrasonic–Pixhawk dual-processor UAV. Payloads from 0–800 g (in 200 g steps) were tested under three mission profiles open path, corridor, and obstacle-rich and two wind conditions: calm (<5 km/h) and mild (5–10 km/h). Each test was repeated for consistency. SITL validation using Mission Planner ensured correct waypoint navigation, obstacle avoidance, and failsafe functions before outdoor flights. Pixhawk logged IMU (200 Hz), barometer (50 Hz), and GPS (5 Hz) data, while the Arduino Nano recorded ultrasonic readings (20 Hz). Streams were synchronized within ± 5 ms, and energy usage was monitored via a calibrated power module. Sensors were temperature-compensated and propellers balanced to reduce vibration. Performance metrics included endurance (until 20% battery), stability (RMS roll/pitch), obstacle-avoidance success, and payload-release reliability (± 0.5 s actuation, $\pm 5°$ attitude). Automatic aborts triggered under excessive roll/pitch, low voltage, or sensor anomalies. Randomized trials with cooling intervals and environmental logging minimized bias. The resulting protocol demonstrated that a low-cost ultrasonic UAV achieves endurance, stability, and avoidance performance comparable to higher-end sensor-rich platforms.

5 RESULTS AND DISCUSSION

The performance of the proposed autonomous drone delivery system was validated through both simulation-in-the-loop (SITL) testing and real-world field experiments conducted in semi-urban environments. The evaluation framework focused on endurance, payload capacity, stability, energy efficiency, and obstacle avoidance success rate. Results are discussed below, highlighting key insights and trade-offs.

5.1 *Endurance and payload trade-off*

The baseline endurance of the drone was measured at 15 minutes without payload, decreasing progressively as load increased. At 600 g payload, the system maintained stable flight for ~13 minutes; at 700 g, endurance dropped to ~12 minutes with noticeable instability; and beyond 800 g, the thrust-to-weight ratio fell below 1.3, rendering sustained flight infeasible. This trend aligns with the aerodynamic principle that induced power demand scales with lift requirements. Similar degradation has been reported in prior UAV logistics studies [2,5], confirming payload endurance trade-off as a central limiting factor.

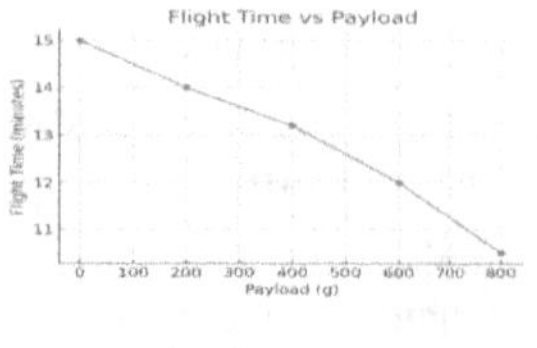

Figure 3. Flight time vs payload.

These results confirm the drone's suitability for small-scale last-mile delivery, such as lightweight medical supplies or consumer goods, but also highlight the payload–endurance trade-off that defines UAV logistics feasibility. For large-payload missions require higher-thrust propulsion and advanced energy storage.

5.2 *Energy consumption analysis*

Power consumption increased approximately linearly with payload, averaging ~260–270 W without payload and ~340 W at 600 g (21–22 A and 28 A at ~12.2 V, respectively). Endurance decreased by ~1 min per 100 g, culminating in a ~27% reduction at 600 g relative to the no-payload baseline.

Compared with LiDAR-equipped UAVs [7,18], the ultrasonic-based system exhibits lower energy overhead, attributable to reduced sensor mass and computational load.

These trends are consistent with UAV aerodynamic principles, where increased lift demand proportionally raises energy consumption. The observed efficiency gains are attributed to the low-mass ultrasonic sensing suite, validating the design philosophy of balancing endurance with functional performance.

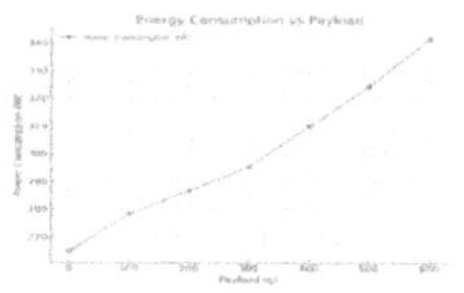

Figure 4. Energy consumption vs payload.

5.3 *Obstacle avoidance performance*

The ultrasonic-based system reliably detected and avoided obstacles within 3 m. Across 40 test runs, the success rate was ~93% in single-obstacle scenarios. However, detection accuracy decreased with reflective surfaces (e.g., glass or metal) and in high-wind conditions, due to ultrasonic beam scattering.

This validates the ultrasonic approach as a low-cost and lightweight solution, though its limitations reinforce the need for hybrid sensor fusion in highly dynamic environments.

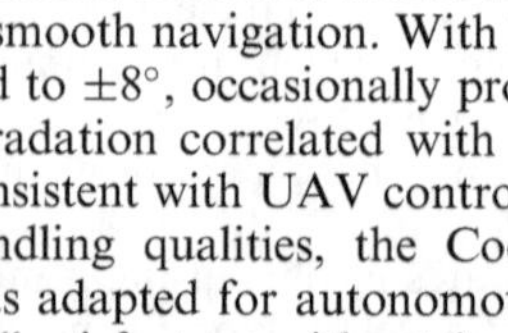

Figure 5. Obstacle detection success rate vs distance.

5.4 *Stability analysis*

Roll and pitch deviations remained within $\pm 5°$ under payloads ≤ 600 g, ensuring smooth navigation. With loads above 700 g, deviations increased to $\pm 8°$, occasionally producing oscillatory drift. Stability degradation correlated with reduced thrust-to-weight margins, consistent with UAV control theory.

To quantify handling qualities, the Cooper–Harper pilot rating scale [28] was adapted for autonomous evaluation. The system achieved a "satisfactory without improvement" rating

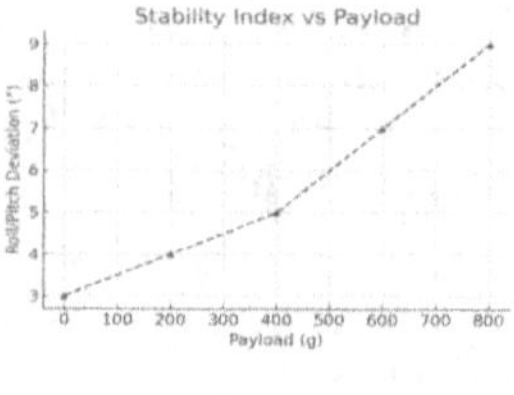

Figure 6. Stability index vs payload.

under ≤ 600 g loads, but degraded to "marginally acceptable" beyond 700 g.

This indicates that the designed frame–motor configuration is robust within intended payload ranges, but stability becomes compromised when endurance limits are exceeded.

5.5 *Comparative benchmarking*

When benchmarked against LiDAR-based UAV systems, the proposed design achieved:

- ~60% hardware cost reduction,
- ~35% weight savings,
- Lower computational complexity.

However, these benefits come at the expense of sensing range and environmental adaptability. This trade-off echoes findings by Rezaee [18] and Yasin [21], who argue that hybrid perception is key to balancing efficiency with safety.

The strategic value of this system lies not in outperforming high-end UAVs, but in providing a low-cost, scalable framework for experimental logistics deployments.

5.6 *Broader implications and insights*

The collective results suggest several important insights:

1. Payload–endurance ceiling defines niche markets: lightweight, short-range deliveries (healthcare, e-commerce micro-parcels) are most feasible.
2. Ultrasonic sensing is effective but situational: reliable in structured semi-urban spaces, limited in cluttered or reflective domains.
3. Dual-processor architecture improves robustness: by isolating ultrasonic control on Arduino, the Pixhawk remains free for stable navigation.
4. Scalability potential is strong: modular hardware permits seamless integration of higher-thrust motors, improved batteries, or sensor fusion upgrades.

6 CONCLUSION AND FUTURE WORK

This study presented a lightweight and cost-effective autonomous UAV delivery system integrating Pixhawk-based navigation with an Arduino-driven ultrasonic sensing module. The platform demonstrated that safety and autonomy can be achieved without compromising affordability or endurance. Simulation and field trials showed stable flight with payloads up to 600 g, a 4.5 km range, and over 90% obstacle avoidance success within 3 m, while maintaining significantly lower cost and weight than LiDAR-based systems.

The developed evaluation protocol established repeatable benchmarks for endurance, stability, and obstacle avoidance, confirming the system's robustness and reliability. However, limitations remain in ultrasonic range, reflective-surface performance, and endurance due to battery constraints.

Future enhancements include integrating vision-based sensing for improved perception, employing AI-driven adaptive path planning, adopting hybrid or advanced batteries for longer endurance, enabling coordinated multi-drone operations, and embedding regulatory and cybersecurity safeguards within the system design.

Overall, the work demonstrates that affordable, modular, and autonomous UAVs can evolve into scalable infrastructure for smart logistics, emergency response, and intelligent urban mobility.

ACKNOWLEDGMENT

The authors would like to express their sincere gratitude to Dr. Sachin M. Bhosle and Prof. Vishal Bhagwat for their invaluable guidance, encouragement, and continuous support throughout the course of this research. Their expertise in UAV systems and robotics provided the foundation for this work and greatly enhanced its quality.

Gratitude is also extended to Dr. Manisha Lande, Dr. S. B. Lande, and Prof. Shrikant Mahadik, as well as the faculty of Vidya Pratishthan's COE in Digital Manufacturing and Robotics Automation, for providing technical resources, insightful suggestions, and a collaborative research environment that enabled the successful execution of this project.

REFERENCES

[1] T. Benarbia and K. Kyamakya, (2021). "A literature review of drone-based package delivery logistics systems and their implementation feasibility," *Sustainability*, vol. 14, no. 1, p. 360.

[2] J.P. Aurambout, K. Gkoumas, and B. Ciuffo, (2019). "Last mile delivery by drones: an estimation of viable market potential and access to citizens across European cities," *European Transport Research Review*, vol. 11, no. 1, p. 30.

[3] B. Sah, R. Gupta, and D. Bani-Hani, (2020). "Analysis of barriers to implement drone logistics," in *Proc. IEEE Int. Conf. on UAV Systems.*

[4] H. Eskandaripour and E. Boldsaikhan, (2020). "Last-mile drone delivery: Past, present, and future," *IEEE Access*, vol. 8, pp. 12345–12360.

[5] F.B. Sorbelli, (2021). "UAV based delivery systems: A systematic review, current trends, and research challenges," *International Journal of Logistics Research and Applications*, vol. 24, no. 5, pp. 345–367.

[6] X. Li, J. Tupayachi, A. Sharmin, and M.M. Ferguson, (2020). "Drone aided delivery methods, challenges, and the future: A methodological review," *Journal of Unmanned Aerial Systems*, vol. 6, pp. 11–29.

[7] J.G. Murthy, H. P. S, J.J. Antony, K. Rakesh, and S. K. A. J., (2020). "Autonomous drone delivery system: A survey," *International Journal of Engineering Science*, vol. 18, no. 3, pp. 210–225.

[8] M.R. Haque, M. Muhammad, D. Swarnaker, and M. Arifuzzaman, (2014). "Autonomous quadcopter for product home delivery," in *Proc. ICEEICT*, pp. 1–6.

[9] J. Kim, H. Moon, and H. Jung, (2020). "Drone based parcel delivery using rooftops of city buildings: model and solution," *IEEE Transactions on Robotics*, vol. 36, no. 4, pp. 954–966.

[10] A. Magdum, V. Nikam Patil, V. Mokashi, and J. Tate, (2019). "Smart drone delivery system," *International Research Journal of Engineering and Technology*, vol. 6, no. 5.

[11] C.R. Atencia and D. Camacho, (2018). "Extending QGroundControl for automated mission planning of UAVs," *Sensors*, vol. 18, no. 7.

[12] N. Aliane, (2020). "A survey of open source UAV autopilots," *Journal of Field Robotics*, vol. 37, no. 2, pp. 182–206.

[13] V.R.F. Miranda *et al.*, (2021). "Autonomous navigation system for a delivery drone," *IEEE Access*, vol. 9, pp. 345–360.

[14] R. Moeller, (2018). "GPS guided autonomous robot with obstacle avoidance and path optimization," *International Journal of Robotics Research*, vol. 27, no. 9, pp. 1131–1145.

[15] D. Debnath *et al.*, (2020). "A review of UAV path planning algorithms and obstacle avoidance methods for remote sensing applications," *Remote Sensing*, vol. 12, no. 10, p. 1654.

[16] S.D. Panjaitan *et al.*, (2019). "A drone technology implementation approach to conventional paddy fields application," *Journal of Precision Agriculture*, vol. 20, no. 8, pp. 1255–1271.

[17] H. Pham *et al.*, (2020). "A survey on unmanned aerial vehicle collision avoidance systems," *IEEE Transactions on Intelligent Transportation Systems*, vol. 21, no. 5, pp. 2022–2038.

[18] M.R. Rezaee, (2019). "Comprehensive review of drones collision avoidance," *Journal of Aerospace Engineering*, vol. 32, no. 4, pp. 456–472.

[19] P. Shi, (2020). "A literature review on obstacle avoidance algorithms and attitude control of unmanned aerial vehicles," *Chinese Journal of Aeronautics*, vol. 29, no. 3, pp. 673–685.

[20] H. Xing, (2020). "Review of unmanned aerial vehicle obstacle voidance planning based on artificial potential field," *Journal of Intelligent & Robotic Systems*, vol. 98, pp. 233–249.

Technology for a Resilient Future – Vincent , Moorthy and Dasari (Eds)
© 2027 The Author(s), ISBN: 978-1-041-39070-1

Hybrid CNN-SVM Framework for Robust Detection of Deepfake and Disguised Faces

Shanmukha V Bhat
Department of Electronics and Communication, Manipal Institute of Technology Manipal Academy of Higher Education, Manipal, Karnataka, India

Padmashree G
Department of Computer Science and Engineering, A J Institute of Engineering and Technology, Mangalore, India

Akshatha K R
Department of Electronics and Communication, Manipal Institute of Technology Manipal Academy of Higher Education, Manipal, Karnataka, India

ABSTRACT: This study conducts a comparative evaluation of twelve architectures for the detection of deepfake and disguised images, drawing on a carefully curated dataset. The analysis features six convolutional neural network (CNN) models—DenseNet121, EfficientNetV2B0, InceptionV3, ResNet50, ResNet152, and Xception—which underwent training and assessment. Each model was enhanced by integrating a Support Vector Machine (SVM) block, trained on features extracted from the global average pooling layer, to boost detection capabilities. Performance was measured using Precision, Recall, F1-Score, and Accuracy. A further comparison between the original CNNs and their SVM-augmented versions reveals insights into detection trade-offs. Training outcomes, including accuracy/loss curves, confusion matrices, and ROC curves, guide potential optimizations, supported by image preprocessing to improve model learning. The findings indicate that SVM-augmented models consistently enhance Precision and Recall, with DenseNet121-SVM, InceptionV3-SVM, and Xception-SVM achieving perfect scores of 100%, while ResNet variants reach 99% and EfficientNetV2B0-SVM improves to 85%–88% from a base of 56%–68%. This suggests significant gains in recognition accuracy, though the added complexity recommends selective application based on specific needs.

Keywords: Deepfake Detection, Disguised Face Recognition, Convolutional Neural Network, Support Vector Machine, DenseNet121, InceptionV3, Xception, Precision-Recall

1 INTRODUCTION

The rise of artificial intelligence has brought remarkable innovations alongside serious challenges, particularly in deepfake generation and disguised face recognition. Deepfakes, produced through advanced generative adversarial networks (GANs), enable the creation of highly realistic manipulated media, eroding trust in digital content and complicating identity verification.[1,2] Similarly, recognizing faces hidden by masks or cosmetic changes remains a major obstacle in surveillance and authentication, owing to diverse disguise techniques and inconsistent data quality.[3] These challenges emphasize the need for robust detection strategies to prevent misuse and enhance recognition accuracy.

Identifying deepfakes—synthetic media generated using GANs or diffusion models—is increasingly difficult as they achieve nearrealistic visual quality. Automated systems often misclassify them due to subtle inconsistencies such as irregular lighting, unnatural motion, or texture mismatches. By 2025, the spread of deepfake tools has outpaced traditional detection methods, with accuracy on unseen data dropping below 70%, raising major concerns for media authenticity and security. This decline results from the growing sophistication of generative models, making it harder for recognition systems to distinguish genuine content from fabricated ones. Disguised face recognition presents parallel difficulties, as key features are obscured by masks, cosmetics, or prosthetics, leading to significant drops in accuracy—sometimes by over 50% under variable lighting or partial occlusion. The widespread use of disguises in public spaces further complicates model generalization, underscoring the demand for stronger feature extraction and adaptive learning techniques. Reliable detection of both deepfakes and disguises is thus critical to preserve the integrity of biometric systems and prevent misuse.

This study delivers a comprehensive comparative evaluation of twelve convolutional neural network (CNN) architectures for detecting deepfake and disguised images, offering the following key contributions:

- **Comprehensive Comparative Analysis:** A detailed evaluation of twelve CNN architectures—six base models (DenseNet121, EfficientNetV2B0, InceptionV3, ResNet50, ResNet152, Xception) and their SVM-enhanced variants—serving as a benchmark for detection performance.
- **Dual-Dataset Utilization:** Experiments conducted on two diverse datasets—Sejong Face Dataset (3,423 train, 733 validation, 734 test images) for disguised faces, and DFDC Dataset (1,966 train, 421 validation, 422 test images) for deepfakes—ensuring robustness across manipulation types.
- **Hybrid CNN-SVM Approach:** SVM classifiers were trained on features extracted from each model's global average pooling layer, improving classification and demonstrating the promise of hybrid architectures.
- **High-Performing Models Identified:** DenseNet121, InceptionV3, Xception, and their SVM variants achieved perfect detection; ResNet models reached near-perfect (99%) accuracy, while EfficientNetV2B0 showed marked gains with SVM integration, highlighting architectures suitable for real-world use.

2 LITERATURE REVIEW

The rapid advancement of generative adversarial networks (GANs) such as DeepFaceLab, StyleGAN, and CycleGAN has greatly increased the sophistication of deepfake and disguised face manipulations, creating major challenges for detection in biometric and surveillance systems. Although recent studies

DOI: 10.1201/9781042017546-59

propose diverse countermeasures, limitations in generalization, adversarial robustness, and real-world adaptability persist. The following synthesis summarizes key works addressing these issues. A comprehensive analysis of deepfake detection methods exposes major gaps in real-world readiness [1]. Evaluating eight state-of-the-art techniques, the study shows that lightweight customization methods such as LoRA and fine-tuned foundation models can generate highly realistic deepfakes (CLIP-Score 0.81, KID 0.006–0.008). Existing defenses, including CNN-F and MesoNet, perform poorly on unseen manipulations, with recall dropping up to 53.99%. An ensemble of frequency-domain (DCT) and foundation model features (e.g., UnivCLIP) achieved an F1 score of 86.25%, improving robustness. Adversarial attacks using StyleCLIP reduced recall by 53%, though adversarial training narrowed this to 1.12% for UnivCLIP. The study concludes that current defenses lack comprehensive threat modeling and recommends content-agnostic features for greater resilience. To mitigate deepfake proliferation, an enhanced Dense CNN (D-CNN) architecture achieved 98.33% accuracy on AttGAN and 99.33% on GDWCT, surpassing MesoNet (57%) and MesoInception (50.73%) on CelebDF [2].Trained on seven datasets with 5,000 real and 5,000 fake images, D-CNN effectively reduces overfitting via data augmentation and deep feature extraction, though accuracy falls slightly on high-resolution StyleGAN2 (94.67%). The authors advocate variable-input networks with global pooling for handling diverse resolutions.

A systematic review of 112 studies (2018–2020) classifies detection methods into deep learning (77%), machine learning (18%), statisti-cal (3%), and blockchain (2%) [4]. Deep learning dominates, with CNNs like XceptionNet attaining 89.73% accuracy and 0.917 AUC on FaceForensics++ and DFDC. Multi-method approaches such as Deep-fakeStack reached 99.65% accuracy, but evaluation inconsistencies and dataset variability issues remain. Future work should emphasize video detection and overfitting reduction. The NA-VGG model, an improved VGG16 variant, enhances detection using noise augmentation and an SROI filter, outperforming prior methods on CelebDF [5]. It highlights noise features beyond RGB channels, strengthening media forensics, though dataset variability persists. A smaller comparative study of VGG16, VGG19, and ResNet50 on 1,200 FaceApp images [6] revealed that ResNet50 performs best on larger datasets, reaffirming the need for more diverse samples against evolving GANs. For disguised face detection, EfficientNet-B4 with visual attention and noisy training achieved strong results on a modified 10,000-image DFW dataset [3], outperforming earlier PCA-based methods [Uhl *et al.*]. A CNN model combining segmentation and recognition modules also showed high accuracy on the Sejong Face dataset [7] addressing distortions but still challenged by lighting variations and real-time constraints. The D-LORD dataset, comprising 1.2 million low-resolution frames with keypoint and bounding box annotations, advanced disguised face recognition research [8]. Evaluations using RetinaFace and ArcFace yielded Genuine Acceptance Rates from 86.4% to 49.6% at 1% FAR, with performance declining at greater distances. SER-FIQ frame selection improved accuracy, though identity consistency remained an issue. Similarly, the D-Res framework introduced a Disguise Encoder-Decoder Network with multi-objective loss, achieving 99.87% accuracy on LFW [9]. Its tessellation method captured both local and global facial features, setting a strong benchmark for low-resolution recognition. A CNN-based keypoint regeneration approach further improved feature reconstruction in low-resolution settings, validated on DFW and LFW datasets with RMSE-based metrics [10]. Collectively, these studies demonstrate significant progress in detecting both deepfakes and disguised faces, yet persistent issues remain. Despite advances like ensemble approaches (F1 86.25%), D-CNNs (99.33% on GDWCT), NA-VGG, and EfficientNet-B4, CNN-based methods still face challenges in generalization, adversarial robustness, and real-world adaptation. Even with strong performance in low-resolution recognition (e.g., D-Res 99.87% on LFW) and key-point regeneration, overfitting and dataset inconsistency continue to limit reliability. Future research should emphasize content-agnostic representations, multi-method integration, and adaptive architectures to counter the evolving threats from modern GANs and disguises [1,2,4,6,8–10].

3 METHODOLOGY

This study presents a robust framework for classifying facial images as either deepfake or disguised. Six pretrained CNN architectures—DenseNet121, InceptionV3, ResNet50, ResNet152, Xception, and EfficientNetV2B0—are employed in two configurations: (1) standalone CNNs for end-to-end classification, and (2) hybrid CNN-SVM models, where CNNs extract features that are classified using an SVM. The workflow for both approaches is illustrated in Figure 1. The analysis involves three main comparisons: (i) among the six standalone CNNs, (ii) among the six hybrid CNN-SVM models, and (iii) between the standalone and hybrid versions of each architecture. The over-all framework comprises three key phases—preprocessing, feature extraction, and classification—depicted in Figure 1.

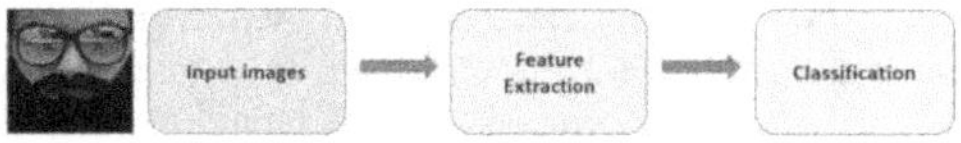

Figure 1. Steps involved in recognition of deepfake and disguised images.

3.1 *Preprocessing and data augmentation*

Each of the three datasets—training, validation, and test sets—has two subfolders: Deepfake and Disguised. Every image is downsized to 224 × 224 pixels in order to comply with CNN's input specifications. The training set is subjected to data augmentation, which includes zoom changes (up to 20%), horizontal flips, random rotations (±15°), and horizontal and vertical shifts (10%) in order to improve generalization and avoid overfitting. These additions increase the robustness of the model by simulating scale and location differences found in the real world. To ensure consistency during evaluation, only intensity normalization—which rescales pixel values to [0, 1]—is used for validation and test sets.

3.2 *Feature extraction with multi-model CNN ensemble*

Six pretrained CNN architectures—EfficientNetV2B0, DenseNet121, InceptionV3, ResNet50, ResNet152, and Xception—are employed for feature extraction, each initialized with ImageNet weights to leverage their learned facial representations. The base layers are frozen to preserve pretrained weights, reduce training time, and prevent overfitting. A custom feature extraction head is added to each model, consisting of a convolutional layer (64 filters, 3×3 kernel, ReLU activation, same padding), followed by global average pooling, 2×2 max-pooling, and batch normalization to stabilize training. This design captures both local and global facial patterns for distinguishing between deepfake and disguised images. In standalone CNN models, the resulting feature vector is used for end-to-end classification. In hybrid CNN-SVM configurations, feature vectors from the global average pooling layer are used to train an SVM classifier. The same extraction pipeline across all six architectures ensures consistency and enables direct performance comparison between CNN and CNN-SVM models.

3.3 *Classification strategies*

To enable the three comparative analyses, two classification strategies are employed:

- **Standalone CNN Classification:** Each CNN's feature vector is passed through a fully connected layer (128 units, ReLU), followed by dropout (rate 0.3) and batch normalization to reduce overfitting. A final softmax layer outputs class probabilities for Deepfake and Disguised categories. All six CNNs are trained end-to-end using the Adam optimizer (learning rate 0.0001) and categorical cross-entropy loss, allowing direct performance comparison across architectures.
- **Hybrid CNN-SVM Classification:** Feature vectors extracted from the global average pooling layer of each CNN are used to train an SVM classifier with a radial basis function (RBF) kernel. This configuration optimizes decision boundaries between Deepfake and Disguised classes and enables probability-based evaluation. Applying this process to all six CNNs allows direct comparison between hybrid CNN-SVM models and their standalone CNN counterparts.

3.4 *Evaluation metrics*

Model performance is assessed using Precision, Recall, F1-Score, and Accuracy on a unified test set comprising Sejong Face Database (disguised images) and DFDC dataset (deepfakes). Accuracy represents the proportion of correctly classified samples, serving as the primary measure for comparing CNN and CNN-SVM models. Precision evaluates the reliability of positive predictions (e.g., deepfakes), minimizing false positives critical in security contexts. Recall measures sensitivity by identifying all true positives, while F1-Score, the harmonic mean of Precision and Recall, balances both to handle class imbalances. Additionally, ROC curves and confusion matrices are used to visualize model discrimination and error distribution, supporting evaluation of robustness and generalization across all three comparative analyses. The formulas for these metrics are derived from confusion matrix components: True Positives (TP), True Negatives (TN), False Positives (FP), and False Negatives (FN).

$$\text{Precision} = \frac{TP}{TP + FP} \tag{1}$$

$$\text{Recall} = \frac{TP}{TP + FN} \tag{2}$$

$$\text{F1-Score} = \frac{2 \times \text{Precision} \times \text{Recall}}{\text{Precision} + \text{Recall}} \tag{3}$$

$$\text{Accuracy} = \frac{TP + TN}{TP + TN + FP + FN} \tag{4}$$

4 EXPERIMENTS AND RESULTS

4.1 *Datasets*

The Sejong Database [11] comprises two subsets—Subset-A and Subset-B. Subset-A includes images of 30 individuals (16 males, 14 females), each with one neutral and one add-on image per modality, using only frontal faces to ensure consistency. Subset-B contains images of 70 subjects (44 males, 26 females), with 15 neutral and 5 disguised images per modality, plus additional samples featuring males with beards and females with makeup. Subset-A totals approximately 1,500 images, derived from the number of subjects, four modalities, 12–13 disguise add-ons, and a single pose. Subset-B includes about 23,100 images, considering four modalities, 12–13 add-ons, and 5–15 pose variations. A detailed summary of disguise variations within the Sejong dataset is presented in Table 1. The DFDC dataset [12] comprises footage from 3,426 paid actors, averaging 14.4 videos per subject and totaling 48,190 clips (68.8 s each), equivalent to over 38.4 days of video. The training set includes frames from 119,154 ten-second clips, over 100,000 of which are deepfakes. The validation set consists of 4,000 clips (2,000 deepfakes) featuring 214 unique subjects not present in training, while the test set contains 10,000 clips (50% deepfakes) from 260 new subjects.

Table 1. Summary of images with various disguises available in Sejong.

Accessories	No. Images	Male	Female
Natural Face	15	Yes	Yes
Real Beard	10	Yes	No
Cap	5	Yes	Yes
Scarf	5	Yes	Yes
Glasses	5	Yes	Yes
Mask	5	Yes	Yes
Makeup	5	No	Yes
Wig	10	Yes	Yes
Fake Beard	5	Yes	No
Fake Mustache	5	Yes	No

Using RGB images from the DFDC and Sejong Face Datasets, a novel curated dataset was created for facial alteration detection, combining 7,699 images—2,809 deepfake and 4,890 disguised. The data was divided using a 70:15:15 stratified split for balanced evaluation: the training set contains 5,389 images (3,423 disguised, 1,966 deepfake), the validation set 1,154 images (733 disguised, 421 deepfake), and the test set 1,156 images (734 disguised, 422 deepfake). This ensures proportional representation across all subsets. A summary of image distribution in the curated dataset is presented in Table 2.

Table 2. Summary of images present in train, validation and test dataset.

Subset	Sejong	DFDC	Total
Train	3423	1966	5389
Validation	733	421	1154
Test	734	422	1156
Total	4890	2809	7699

The curated dataset, composed of visible RGB images, ensures compatibility with standard imaging frameworks and supports consistent facial modification detection. The carefully designed split ratio enhances training efficiency and enables robust performance evaluation, strengthening the validity and generalizability of the study's findings.

4.2 *Experimental setup*

Experiments were conducted on an ASUS TUF Gaming F15 with an Intel i5-10300H CPU (2.5 GHz), 8 GB RAM, and an NVIDIA GeForce GTX A6000 GPU (4 GB). Algorithms were implemented in Python 3.10.8 using Keras 2.16.1 and executed locally via Visual Studio Code. Models were trained with categorical cross-entropy loss and the Adam optimizer, using a batch size of 8, learning rate of 1e-4, and up to 20 epochs per model. Each epoch took roughly 2,800–3,300 seconds, primarily due to limited RAM and the parallel execution of up to eight training jobs. While sufficient for performance validation, these constraints extended runtimes compared to high-memory systems with more powerful GPUs. Future work will explore experiments on advanced hardware to assess computational efficiency for practical deployment.

4.3 *Performance comparison of CNN base models*

Table 3 shows that DenseNet121, InceptionV3, and Xception achieved perfect scores across all metrics, correctly classifying all deepfake and disguised images, with ROC curves confirming flawless discrimination. These models balance Precision and Recall, ensuring reliable detection with zero errors, making them suitable for high-stakes applications. ResNet50 and ResNet152 also perform strongly, with near-perfect metrics and minimal misclassifications, supported by ROC curves, though slight errors indicate minor challenges with subtle features. In contrast, EfficientNetV2B0 shows lower performance, with higher misclassification rates for deepfakes and weaker ROC curves, reflecting limited robustness and generalization due to its reduced capacity for complex image features. Confusion matrices for all CNN architectures are presented in Figure 2.

Table 3. Performance metrics of CNN models.

Model	Prec	Rec	F1	Acc
DenseNet121	100	100	100	100
EffNetV2B0	68	66	56	66
InceptionV3	100	100	100	100
ResNet50	99	99	99	99
ResNet152	99	99	99	99
Xception	100	100	100	100

4.4 *Performance comparison of CNN-SVM models*

Six hybrid CNN-SVM models—DenseNet121-SVM, EfficientNetV2B0-SVM, InceptionV3-SVM, ResNet50-SVM, ResNet152-SVM, and Xception-SVM—were evaluated on the Sejong Face Database and DFDC dataset for deepfake and disguised image classification. Performance metrics, including Precision, Recall, F1-Score, and Accuracy, are summarized in Table 4. Confusion matrices for all hybrid models are shown in Figure 3.

Table 4. Performance metrics of CNN-SVM models.

Model	Prec	Rec	F1	Acc
DenseNet121-SVM	100	100	100	100
EffNetV2B0-SVM	88	85	85	85
InceptionV3-SVM	100	100	100	100
ResNet50-SVM	99	99	99	99
ResNet152-SVM	98	98	98	98
Xception-SVM	100	100	100	100

DenseNet121-SVM, InceptionV3-SVM, and Xception-SVM achieved perfect or near-perfect metrics with minimal misclassifications, showing excellent Precision-Recall balance and reliable detection, suitable for high-stakes applications. ResNet50-SVM and ResNet152SVM also performed strongly, with few misclassifications and high discriminative ability, though ResNet152-SVM showed slightly more errors, indicating minor challenges in feature differentiation. In contrast, EfficientNetV2B0-SVM performed noticeably worse, with higher misclassification rates—especially for deepfakes—and weaker ROC curves, reflecting limited robustness and reduced capacity for complex image features.

4.5 *Performance comparison of CNN base vs. CNN-SVM models*

Six CNN base models—DenseNet121, EfficientNetV2B0, InceptionV3, ResNet50, ResNet152, and Xception—were compared with their hybrid CNN-SVM counterparts on the Sejong Face Database and DFDC dataset. DenseNet121 and DenseNet121-SVM, along with Xception and Xception-SVM, achieved perfect metrics, error-free confusion matrices, and flawless ROC curves, making them equally reliable for high-stakes applications. InceptionV3 achieved perfect performance, while InceptionV3-SVM showed near-perfect metrics with minimal misclassifications, indicating slightly reduced robustness. ResNet50 and ResNet50-SVM performed strongly, with few errors; the SVM variant had slightly fewer misclassifications. ResNet152 outperformed ResNet152-SVM, which exhibited slightly lower metrics and more misclassifications, suggesting reduced generalization. EfficientNetV2B0 performed poorly, but its SVM variant improved considerably, with higher

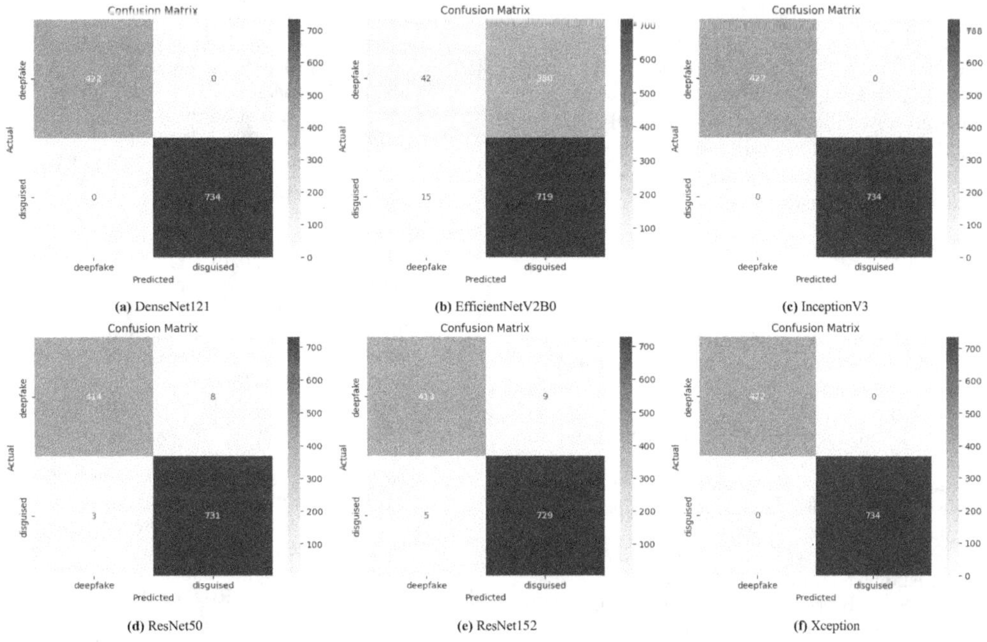

(a) DenseNet121 (b) EfficientNetV2B0 (c) InceptionV3 (d) ResNet50 (e) ResNet152 (f) Xception

Figure 2. Confusion matrices of CNN models.

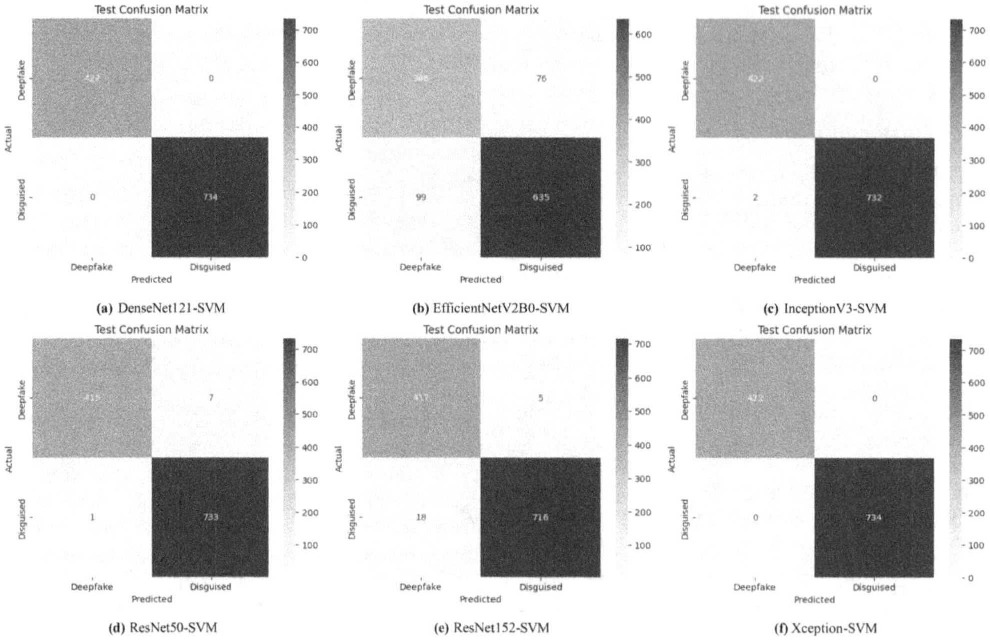

(a) DenseNet121-SVM (b) EfficientNetV2B0-SVM (c) InceptionV3-SVM

(d) ResNet50-SVM (e) ResNet152-SVM (f) Xception-SVM

Figure 3. Confusion matrices of CNN-SVM models.

metrics and fewer misclassifications, though it remained the least robust model, particularly for deepfake images.

5 CONCLUSION

This study evaluated six CNN baselines (DenseNet121, EfficientNetV2B0, InceptionV3, ResNet50, ResNet152, and Xception) and their CNN–SVM hybrids for detecting deepfake and disguised faces using the Sejong Face Database and DFDC dataset. DenseNet121, Xception, and their SVM variants consistently delivered strong performance with rapid convergence and minimal misclassifications. InceptionV3 and its hybrid were also stable, while SVM integration enhanced ResNet50. ResNet152 outperformed its hybrid, and EfficientNetV2B0 improved with SVM but remained less robust. Overall, DenseNet121, Xception, and InceptionV3 proved most reliable for security-critical applications. Despite these promising results, further research is needed. Future work will include more extensive cross-validation, evaluation on unseen datasets, and testing under real-world conditions such as low lighting, occlusions, and recent GAN-or diffusion-based deepfakes. Additionally, video-based and multimodal detection, along with en-semble methods, attention mechanisms, and adversarial training, will be explored to enhance generalization and robustness.

REFERENCES

[1] S.M. Abdullah *et al.*, (2024). "An analysis of recent advances in deepfake image detection in an evolving threat landscape," in *2024 IEEE Symposium on Security and Privacy (SP)*, San Francisco, CA, USA, pp. 91–109.

[2] Y. Patel *et al.*, (2023). "An improved dense cnn architecture for deepfake image detection," *IEEE Access*, vol. 11, pp. 22 081–22 095.

[3] N.R. Pottanigari, R. Pullela, A.K.A. Shaik, and R. Reddy, (2024). "Efficient detection of disguised faces using photos/sketches from low-quality surveillance footage," in *2024 IEEE 18th International Conference on Automatic Face and Gesture Recognition (FG)*, Istanbul, Turkiye, pp. 1–9.

[4] M.S. Rana, M.N. Nobi, B. Murali, and A.H. Sung, (2022). "Deepfake detection: A systematic literature review," *IEEE Access*, vol. 10, pp. 25 494–25 513.

[5] X. Chang, J. Wu, T. Yang, and G. Feng, (2020). "Deepfake face image detection based on improved vgg convolutional neural network," in *2020 39th Chinese Control Conference (CCC)*, Shenyang, China, pp. 7252–7256.

[6] Z.N. Ashani *et al.*, (2024). "Comparative analysis of deepfake image detection method using vgg16 vgg19 and resnet50," *Journal of Advanced Research in Applied Sciences and Engineering Technology*, vol. 47, no. 1, pp. 16–28.

[7] M. G, D. R, J. V, T. P, and S. R, (2024). "Enhanced camouflage detection using advanced image processing techniques for real-time object recognition and pattern differentiation," in *2024 International Conference on Sustainable Communication Networks and Application (ICSCNA)*, Theni, India, pp. 1172–1180.

[8] S. Manchanda *et al.*, (2024). "D-lord: Dysl-ai database for low-resolution disguised face recognition," *IEEE Transactions on Biometrics, Behavior, and Identity Science*, vol. 6, no. 2, pp. 147–157.

[9] M. Singh, S. Nagpal, R. Singh, and M. Vatsa, (2022). "Disguise resilient face verification," *IEEE Transactions on Circuits and Systems for Video Technology*, vol. 32, no. 6, pp. 3895–3905.

[10] J. Mehta, S. Talati, S. Upadhyay, S. Valiveti, and G. Raval, (2023). "Regenerating vital facial keypoints for impostor identification from disguised images using cnn," *Expert Systems with Applications*, vol. 219, p. 119669.

[11] U. Cheema and S. Moon, (2021). "Sejong face database: A multimodal disguise face database," *Computer Vision and Image Understanding*, vol. 208–209, p. 103218.

[12] B. Dolhansky, J. Bitton, B. Pflaum, J. Lu, R. Howes, M. Wang, and C.C. Ferrer, (2020). "The deepfake detection challenge (dfdc) dataset," arXiv preprint arXiv:2006.07397.

[13] R.U. Maheshwari, B. Paulchamy, B.K. Pandey *et al.*, (2025). "Enhancing sensing and imaging capabilities through surface plasmon resonance for deepfake image detection," *Plasmonics*, vol. 20, pp. 2945–2964.

[14] M. G. N, V. Deshmukh, N. Balasundaram, M. Gupta, S. M, and D. Sharma, (2024). "Robust face recognition system for identifying disguised individuals," in *2024 IEEE 4th International Conference on ICT in Business Industry & Government (ICTBIG)*, Indore, India, pp. 1–6.

[15] G. Padmashree and K.A. Kotegar, (2024). "Skin segmentation-based disguised face recognition using deep learning," *IEEE Access*, vol. 12, pp. 51 056–51 072.

[16] A. Diwan and A.K. Roy, (2025). "Detection and localization of copymove tampering along with adversarial attack in a digital image," *Discover Computing*, vol. 28, p. 136.

Technology for a Resilient Future – Vincent , Moorthy and Dasari (Eds)
© 2027 The Author(s), ISBN: 978-1-041-39070-1

Classification of Retinal Diseases Based on Optical Coherence Tomography Images Using Transfer Learning

Shaivi Rutvij Panchal, Reva Sameer Laghate, and Omkar S Powar
Department of Biomedical Engineering, Manipal Institute of Technology, Manipal Academy of Higher Education, Manipal, Karnataka, India

ABSTRACT: Choroidal Neovascularization (CNV), Diabetic Macular Edema (DME), and Age-related Macular Degeneration (AMD) are some of the prime causes behind central vision loss globally. Optical Coherence Tomography is an imaging modality which non-invasively provides cross-sectional images of high-resolution, especially that of the eye. These images are beneficial in disease categorization. Based on these scans, InceptionV3 and MobileNetV2 architectures were employed to predict retinal diseases into CNV, DME, DRUSEN, and NORMAL. To address class imbalance, methods such as class weights and data augmentation were applied. The pre-trained deep learning models were fine-tuned with custom layers. Experimental results demonstrated test accuracy of 96.83% for InceptionV3 and 95.05% for MobileNetV2. Both these accuracies show their ability in differentiating between retinal conditions. CNV and Normal classes portrayed strong classification while classification of drusen suffered challenges. These findings confront class imbalance challenges and exhibit the impact of deep learning techniques to support ophthalmologists in the premature detection of retinal conditions to improve treatment outcomes.

Keywords: Retinal Disease Classification, Optical Coherence Tomography, Drusen, Diabetic Macular Edema (DME), Choroidal Neovascularization (CNV), InceptionV3, MobileNetV2, Class weights

1 INTRODUCTION

In individuals over 65, Age-related Macular Degeneration is a prominent cause of vision loss. It accounts for about 8.7% of all vision-loss cases, globally. It affects the central vision due to its effects on the macula. This leads to distorted or blurred vision. AMD can be generalized into wet and dry forms. The 'wet AMD' is associated with choroidal neovascularization (CNV), which is excessive blood vessel growth from the choroid), as shown in Figure 1. The 'dry AMD' form is associated with yellow deposits that accumulate under the retina. These are called drusen [1–3]. Diabetic Macular Edema (DME) is another considerable contributor to vision loss, caused by the leaking of fluid into the retina due to hyperglycemia [4]. It is most observed in individuals with diabetic retinopathy. Optical Coherence Tomography (OCT) is a non-invasive imaging modality. It is employed to acquire cross-sectional images of retinal layers [5,6]. It outperforms other imaging modalities due to its speed, clarity and ability to highlight minute changes. Despite these advantages, accurate diagnosis using OCT remains a resource-intensive process. This creates challenges in regions with limited access to trained specialists, such as India, which has low doctor-to-patient ratio [7]. Thus, computer-aided diagnostic systems could help ease clinician's workload. By applying deep learning, automated models can now extract disease-relevant features from OCT images to support medical decision-making [8–10]. Machine learning models like SVMs and CNNs also show promising results in classifying such diseases [11]. However, CNNs require long training times and large annotated datasets [12]. By leveraging pre-trained models, transfer learning models address this limitation by improving accuracy and reducing overfitting, even with smaller datasets [13].

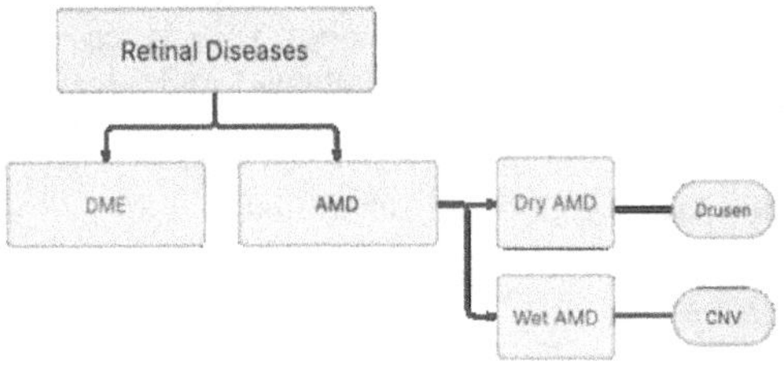

Figure 1. Categorization of retinal diseases.

InceptionV3 is a convolutional neural network (CNN) architecture, that although is computationally expensive, it delivers high accuracy and efficiency due to its optimized convolutions and grid size reduction [14]. MobileNetV2 is a lightweight CNN architecture that achieves efficient performance through depth wise separable convolutions and inverted residual blocks.

Several studies have applied machine learning models to sorting retinal diseases using OCT scans. Udayaraju *et al.* (2023) used SVM for DME detection on 112 scans, achieving 98.37% accuracy. Schwartz *et al.* (2022) applied 3D Inception V1 to 1,276 Drusen images, reporting 98.4% accuracy with 97.8% sensitivity and 99% specificity. Errabih *et al.* (2022) evaluated InceptionV3 and VGG16 on a large dataset of 84,483 images, with VGG16 yielding 93.12% accuracy and high sensitivity for CNV (100%), Drusen (92%), and DME (89%). Kumar *et al.* (2022) developed a deep CNN for OCT-based retinal disease detection with image enhancement and transfer learning. InceptionV3 attained 74.7% accuracy, whereas MobileNetV2 75.29%. Ben Yang *et al.* acquired a 98.96% on their improved version of MobileNet. Pranoto *et al.* (2021) developed a custom 5-layer CNN model to differentiate DME images from normal retinal OCT scans, achieving a peak classification accuracy of 96% over MobileNet's 64% and VGG-16's 93% accuracy. These findings demonstrate the efficacy of deep learning approaches for OCT classification, enhanced by synthetic data augmentation providing further gains [7].

In the following sections, we explore the usage of deep learning techniques to accurately classify retinal diseases. While prior work has employed SMOTE to reduce the impact of class imbalance, we investigated an alternative approach using class-weighted loss functions which are better suited for large-scale image datasets to reduce bias and enhance sensitivity for underrepresented classes.

DOI: 10.1201/9781042017546-60

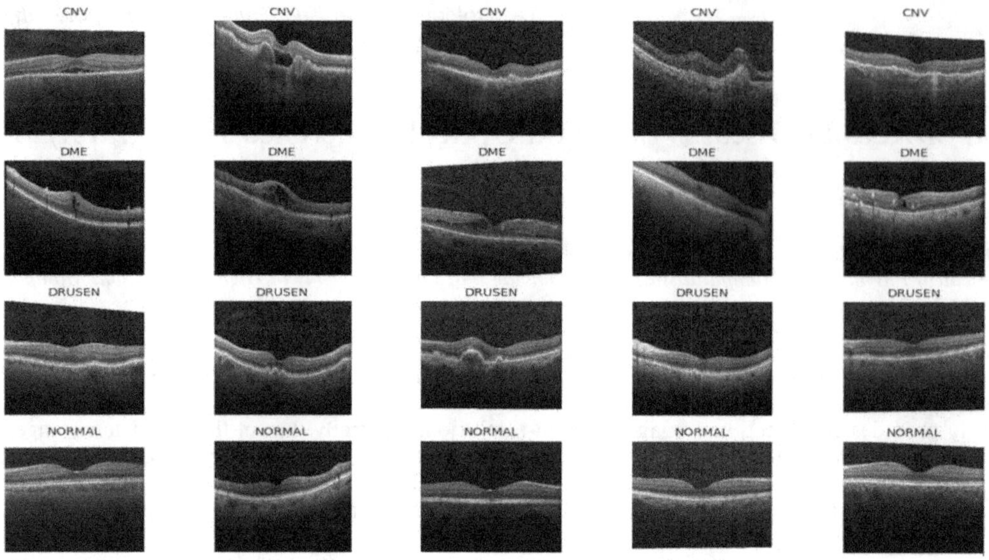

Figure 2. Representation of samples across the retinal OCT dataset classes: CNV, DME, DRUSEN, and NORMAL.

2 METHODOLOGY

2.1 *Dataset*

The "Large Dataset of Labeled Optical Coherence Tomography (OCT) and Chest X-Ray Images" dataset by Kermany *et al.* (2018), is a comprehensive collection of medical images curated for research purposes (Figure 2) [3]. It comprises of thousands of validated OCT scans, each classified into four categories: CNV, DME, DRUSEN, and NORMAL. Each image is labeled with the corresponding disease type, patient ID, and an image index [14]. In this work, we use the Labeled Optical Coherence Tomography (OCT) dataset by Anirudh CV on Kaggle, which is a cleaned and restructured version of the original dataset published by Kermany *et al.* (2018).

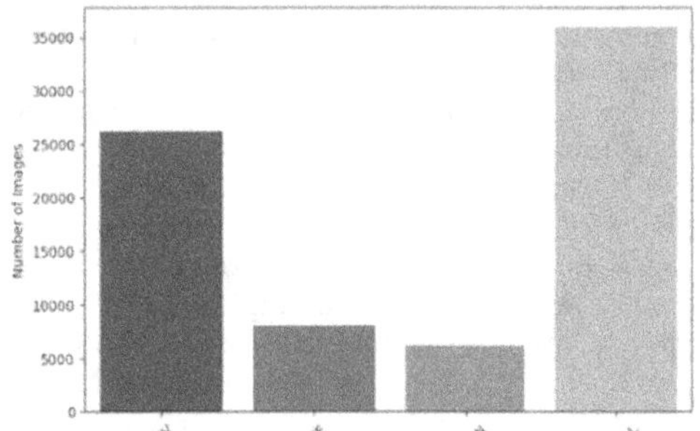

Figure 3. Distribution of samples across classes.

The Kaggle version provides 109,309 total images across the four classes. Kermany *et al.* initially reported 1,000 test and 108,312 training images; however, later analysis (Takumasa *et al.*, 2020) revealed differences in file counts between versions. The Kaggle dataset is appropriate for this study while remaining in line with the original data source and clinical intent because it is a curated and easier-to-access derivative that provides consistent data integrity and simpler reproducibility.

The dataset suffers from significant class imbalance, with a higher number of NORMAL images (35,973) compared to DRUSEN (6,206), as shown in Figure 3. This imbalance might lead the model to favour the majority class during training. To address this issue, we used class-weighting and data augmentation were employed. While SMOTE is used for imbalanced datasets, it is not ideal for deep learning because it can cause overfitting and limits the diversity of generated samples [15].

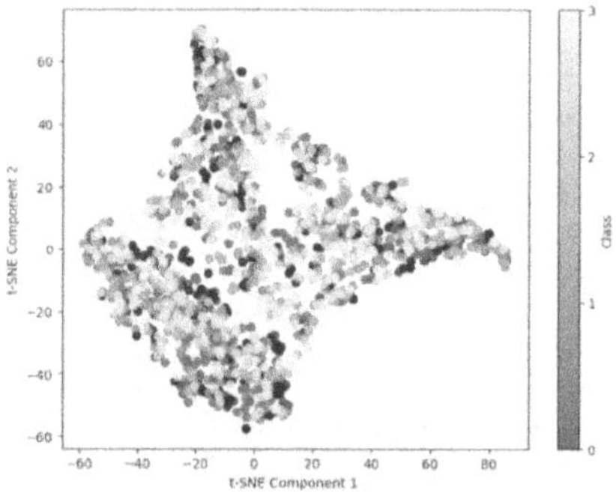

Figure 4. t-SNE scatter plot of the dataset with four classes.

2.2 *Data preparation and pre-processing*

OCT Images were loaded in grayscale to reduce complexity to enhance structural details, ensuring consistent single channel input. A batch size of 32 was chosen in order to balance computational efficiency and class representation. During pre-processing, the images were resized to 224x224 pixels. This was done to fit the input size of the InceptionV3 and MobileNetV2 models. Pixel intensities were normalized to be in the [0,1] range to standardize input scaling. Data augmentation methods were applied including flipping, zooming, and changing brightness in order to add variability to the dataset. Class labels were one-hot encoded. Figure 4 a t-SNE scatter plot of the training set to visualize high dimensional feature representation. The plot indicates a significant amount of overlap, indicating there is still a high amount of variance even for the same class. The frequent overlaps of color indicates that there is class imbalance while more scattered points can indicate noise. The noticeable lack of clusters suggests that the extracted features do not create significant separation in a linear space.

2.3 *Model architecture*

The top layers of the base architectures, InceptionV3 and MobileNetV2, were removed to allow custom classification. First hundred layers of each were frozen to retain features. The deeper layers were kept trainable. *GlobalAveragePooling2D* reduced spatial dimensions and minimized overfitting. A dense layer and softmax activation function for output class probabilities were applied. Adam optimizer was used to compile these models. To improve model performance, callbacks such as *ReduceLROnPlateau* and *EarlyStopping* were employed.

2.4 *Evaluation metrics*

The model performances was judged on their accuracy, precision, recall, AUC, and the confusion matrix. Accuracy measured overall correctness, AUC assessed discriminative ability, and precision and recall indicated sensitivity to false results. The confusion matrix offered detailed class-level insights into misclassifications.

2.5 *Experimental setup*

Both sections of the experiment were conducted on a NVIDIA RTX 4080 Super GPU with 64 GB RAM, and an Intel Core i9 processor, using Python 3.9 and TensorFlow 2.10. InceptionV3 and MobileNetV2 employed ImageNet pre-trained weights, with early stopping configured at a patience of 10 epochs for improved generalization.

3 RESULTS AND DISCUSSION

The data was segregated into training, testing and validation in a 7:2:1 ratio. This partitions the image dataset into 76,515 for training, 21,861 for validation, and 10,933 for testing across all 4 classes. This is to ensure that the end model is robust.

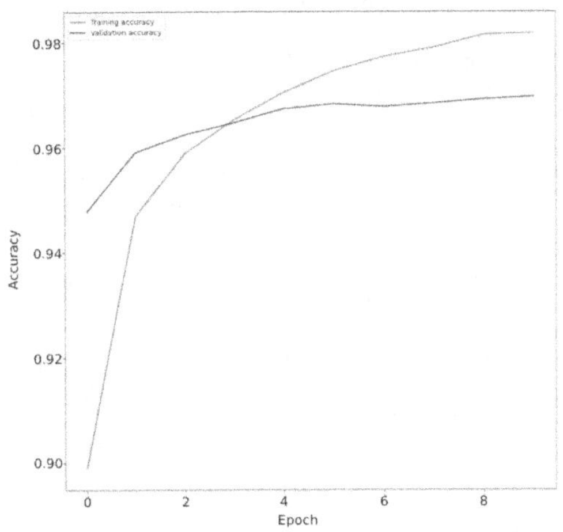

Figure 5. Training and validation accuracy of inceptionV3.

The upward trend in the accuracy curves of the InceptionV3 architecture, as shown in Figure 5, demonstrated an improvement in both training and validation performances. Training accuracy increased from an initial 90% to above 98%, and validation accuracy saw an increase from 94% to 97%. The close tracking of these curves indicated strong generalization and minimal overfitting (less than 5% difference between training and testing accuracies). This conclusion was then further supported by the smooth decline in both training and validation loss, as observed in Figure 6. Similarly, as seen in Figure 8, the accuracy curves of MobileNetV2 revealed a steady increase in training and validation performance from approximately 0.88 to 0.97 and 0.90 to 0.96, respectively. Figure 9 show that the training loss decreased consistently, the validation loss showed mild fluctuations after epoch 4, suggesting early signs of

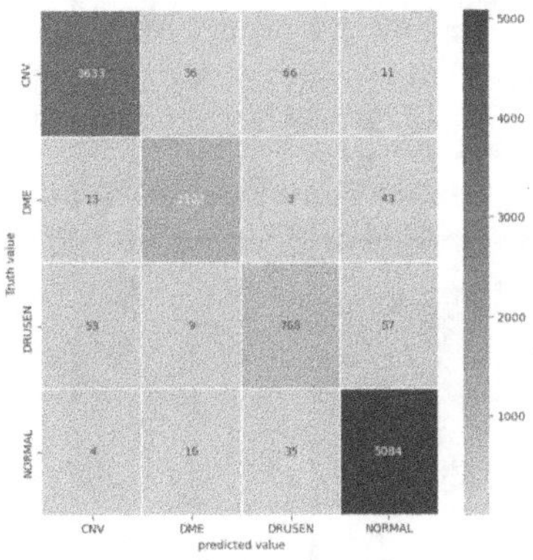

Figure 7. Multi-class confusion matrix by inceptionV3.

overfitting. The model achieved strong and robust performance on the test set. The overall close trajectory of both curves indicated the model still learnt effectively.

The narrow difference between these curves suggested strong generalization, avoiding overfitting. To evaluate class-wise performance, a classification report, as mentioned in Table 1, was generated.

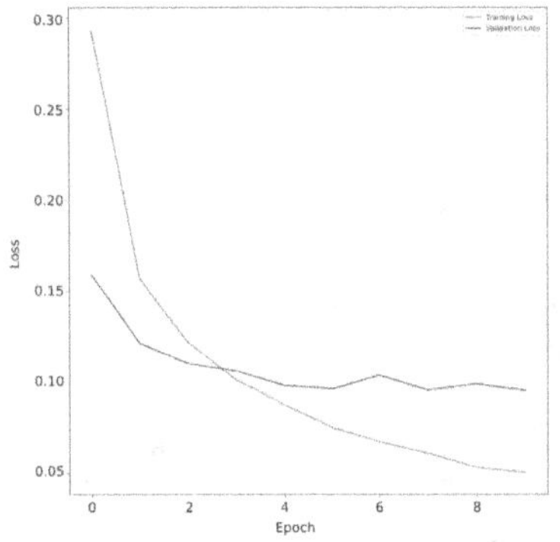

Figure 6. Training and validation loss of inceptionV3.

CNV has excellent precision, recall and F1-score across both models, indicating reliable classification. DRUSEN shows high precision but low recall, suggesting that both the models correctly identified DRUSEN when predicted, but missed some actual cases. On the other hand, DME has higher precision, recall and F1-score for InceptionV3. Figures 7 and 10 portray the multi-class confusion matrices for InceptionV3 and MobileNetV2, respectively. Both models hold high accuracy with strong diagonals. InceptionV3 demonstrated superior performance, particularly for CNV and NORMAL classes, with minimal misclassifications. .

Class-wise accuracies were high for CNV (97%), DME (94.9%), and NORMAL (98.9%) but DRUSEN (86.6%) was more challenging to classify MobileNetV2 also performed well but showed a slight reduction in discriminative accuracy. This is especially seen for DRUSEN, which exhibited overlap with CNV and NORMAL which correlates with its low F1-score. For MobileNetV2, the class-wise accuracies rank similarly, with high CNV (92.9%), DME (94.1%), and NORMAL (99%) accuracy, with lower DRUSEN accuracy (82.2%). These findings suggest that while MobileNetV2 offers computational efficiency, the deeper InceptionV3 architecture provides enhanced feature extraction and more robust class separation, particularly for visually similar retinal pathologies.

The results suggest that further improvement is possible, particularly in the case of drusen classification which does poorly. Future works can achieve so by applying feature

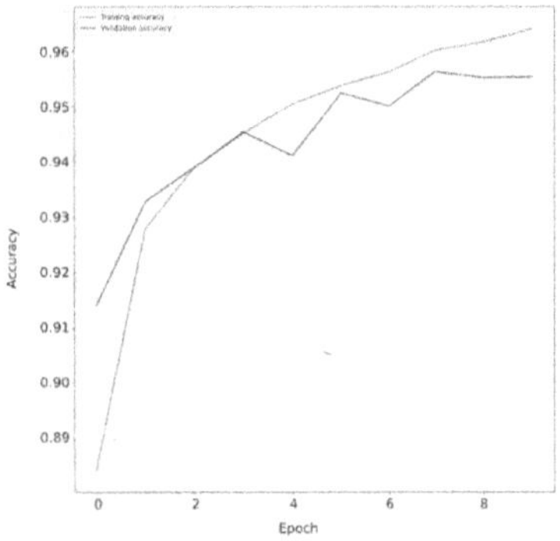

Figure 8. Training and validation accuracy of mobileNetV2.

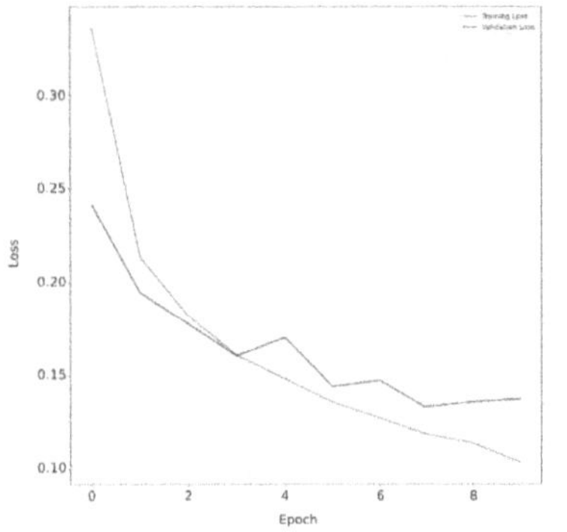

Figure 9. Training and validation loss of MobileNetv2.

enhancement techniques, focal loss functions, or different class-balancing strategies.

Table 1. Classification reports for inceptionV3 & MobileNetV2.

	Precision		Recall		F1-score		Support
CLASS	IV3	MV2	IV3	MV2	IV3	MV2	IV3, MV2
0	0.98	0.98	0.97	0.93	0.98	0.96	3746
1	0.95	0.90	0.95	0.94	0.95	0.92	1161
2	0.88	0.79	0.87	0.82	0.87	0.81	887
3	0.98	0.97	0.99	0.99	0.98	0.98	5139

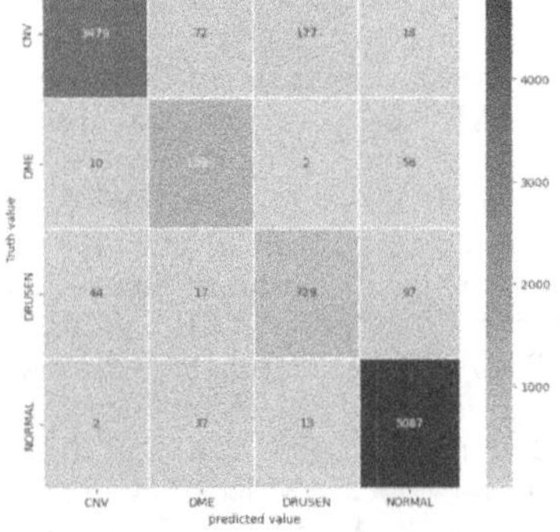

Figure 10. Multi-class confusion matrix by MobileNetV2.

4 CONCLUSION

In this research, we used InceptionV3 and MobileNetV2 architectures and performed full end-to-end fine-tuning to create deep learning models for the computerized diagnosis of retinal diseases. Class-weighting and data augmentation techniques were used during training to address the issue of class imbalance. The models achieved high accuracy of 96.83% and 95.05% respectively. Accuracy for CNV and NORMAL were high, while DRUSEN was a more difficult image class due to similar structural features. Our key contributions were exploratory data analysis, class balancing methods and a transparent evaluation pipeline that reported class-wise metrics. Our study demonstrates the feasibility of applying a deep learning approach in the field of ophthalmology while highlighting the need for evaluation, bias-informed decisions, and conscious design to produce clinically reliable medical imaging applications. The basis of this study also considers the practical constraints from imbalanced real-world datasets and deployment in resource-constrained contexts.

ACKNOWLEDGEMENT

We gratefully acknowledge the staff and authorities of Manipal Institute of Technology, Manipal Academy of Higher Education (MAHE), especially the Department of Biomedical Engineering for their cooperation and their support in this research.

REFERENCES

[1] Genetics and Genomics of Eye Disease. (2020). Age-related macular degeneration. pp. 155–180.

[2] Spalton, D.J., Hitchings, R.A., and Hunter, P. (2013). *Atlas of Clinical Ophthalmology E-Book*. Elsevier Health Sciences.

[3] Esfahani, R.P., *et al.* (2023). Deep learning classification of drusen, choroidal neovascularization, and diabetic macular edema in optical coherence tomography (OCT) images. *Cureus*.

[4] Varma, R., *et al.* (2014). Prevalence of and risk factors for diabetic macular edema in the United States. *JAMA Ophthalmol.*, 132(11), 1334–1340.

[5] Aumann, S., Donner, S., Fischer, J., and Müller, F. (2019). Optical coherence tomography (OCT): Principle and technical realization. In *High Resolution Imaging in Microscopy and Ophthalmology* (pp. 59–85).

[6] Akpinar, M.H., *et al.* (2024). Artificial intelligence in retinal screening using OCT images: A review of the last decade (2013–2023). *Comput. Meth. Prog. Biomed.*, 254, 108253.

[7] Jain, L., Murthy, H.S., Patel, C., and Bansal, D. (2018). Retinal eye disease detection using deep learning. In *14th Int. Conf. Inf. Process. (ICINPRO)* (pp. 1–6).

[8] Rajagopalan, N., V. N., Josephraj, A.N., and S. E. (2021). Diagnosis of retinal disorders from optical coherence tomography images using CNN. *PLoS One*, 16(7), e0254180.

[9] Viedma, I.A., Alonso-Caneiro, D., Read, S.A., and Collins, M.J. (2022). Deep learning in retinal optical coherence tomography (OCT): A comprehensive survey. *Neurocomputing*, 507, 247–264.

[10] Özdaş, M.B., Uysal, F., and Hardalaç, F. (2023). Classification of retinal diseases in optical coherence tomography images using artificial intelligence and firefly algorithm. *Diagnostics*, 13(3), 433.

[11] Baba, S., Kumari, P., and Saxena, P. (2024). Retinal disease classification using custom CNN model from OCT images. *Procedia Comput. Sci.*, 235, 3142–3152.

[12] Leandro, I., *et al.* (2023). OCT-based deep-learning models for the identification of retinal key signs. *Sci. Rep.*, 13(1), 14628.

[13] Weiss, K., Khoshgoftaar, T.M., and Wang, D. (2016). A survey of transfer learning. *J. Big Data*, 3(1).

[14] Kermany, D.S., *et al.* (2018). Identifying medical diagnoses and treatable diseases by image-based deep learning. *Cell*, 172(5), 1122–1131.e9.

[15] Alkhawaldeh, I.M., Albalkhi, I., and Naswhan, A.J. (2023). Challenges and limitations of synthetic minority oversampling techniques in machine learning. *World J. Methodol.*, 13(5), 373–373.

Technology for a Resilient Future – Vincent , Moorthy and Dasari (Eds)
© 2027 The Author(s), ISBN: 978-1-041-39070-1

Implementation and Simulation of MIT Manipal Campus Map in CARLA Autonomous Driving Simulator

Noorain Zehra H G
Department of Mechatronics, Manipal Institute of Technology, Manipal Academy of Higher Education, Manipal, Karnataka, India

Aravindhan D
Aradha Tech Services

Ramya S Moorthy
Department of Mechatronics, Manipal Institute of Technology, Manipal Academy of Higher Education, Manipal, Karnataka, India

ABSTRACT: As the Autonomous driving industry is rapidly growing there is a significant demand for simulation environments that can replicate real-world environments while precisely maintaining geospatial accuracy and making experimentation repeatable. As conducting substantial on-road testing is not economically feasible and it also poses safety concerns making it difficult to mimic real world scenarios. CARLA - An autonomous driving simulator with its open-source modular architecture makes autonomous driving research attainable. It's core features lets autonomous driving researchers combine realistic graphics using flexible APIs and generate maps for desirable realistic environments making it suitable for digital twin applications. The goal of this research is to obtain the digital twin of the MIT Manipal Campus. Initially the geospatial data of the campus was extracted using Open Street Map and was converted to OpenDrive format using Carla's Python API (osm2odr). Eighteen campus landmarks were manually calibrated and labelled to spawn around various campus locations of our choice as prompted by the terminal. A Pygame interface was designed to interact with the vehicle simulation and spawn around the campus. Though minor oscillations and jiggling was noticed, comparatively Vulkan being a low-level API still showed smoother frame stability and improved out for better visualization over OpenGL in large scale environments. This research provides a foundation for integrating real world environments into Carla supporting ROS2 based automation and V2X application in the future.

Keywords: CARLA Simulator, Digital Twin, OpenStreetMap, OpenDRIVE, ROS2, Vulkan, OpenGL

1 INTRODUCTION

The rapid progress of autonomous driving demands simulation environments that can mimic real-world traffic complexity with highly accurate, scalability, and reproducibility. While physical testing is not feasible for validation, as it is expensive, time-consuming, and constrained by safety regulations. Before deploying the testing on-road, planning and simulating using control algorithms makes it productive and has low risks. The present work aims to identify the most effective combination of frameworks and tools through which realistic map simulation can be achieved for the map of MIT Manipal campus., **CARLA** has emerged as a leading choice compared to other platforms due to its open-source architecture, testing various scenarios using APIs, and photorealistic rendering capabilities, supporting both academic and industrial research in autonomous systems development. A constant challenge in simulation-based researches involves transforming raw geospatial data into structured, high-definition driving environments suitable for autonomous navigation. OpenStreetMap (OSM) serves as a valuable source of openly available geospatial data, yet its direct use in autonomous driving research requires careful conversions into other standardized formats to avoid geometric discrepancies. The OpenDRIVE (ODR) specification supports this process by detailing lane structure, connectivity, and geometric clothoids like lines, arcs and clothoids with high precision. OSM datasets can be converted to XODR using Python API (osm2odr). And terminal legends can be prompted to spawn vehicle around according to the user's location preference. This research provides a methodology that can be relied upon and be repeated in future to obtain digital twin of any desired location or environment while making sure that the geometric primitives and geospatial data is accurate compared to the real-world environment.

2 LITERATURE REVIEW

Various researches till now show that integration of different kinds of simulation frameworks play an important role in the field of Autonomous driving research. **CommonRoad–CARLA interface** was a breakthrough for autonomous driving research [1], as it enables motion planning with realistic driving scenarios. This development demonstrated how simulators can be used for vehicle simulation in realistic environments. Hence the gap between theoretical algorithm design and realistic simulation is overlapped. As an advancement to this **Real2Sim pipeline** [2] used Open Street map data to produce realistic simulation environments automatically using a fixed procedure. An algorithm was developed to extract the road edges, geometric parameters and obtain high intensity data to further generate HD maps automatically into OpenDrive formats [3]. This high-definition map generation techniques enhance the simulation process.

CARLA, an open urban driving simulator provides open-source programs and tools within its infrastructure for testing autonomous driving scenarios. It also provides a network trained through imitation learning and reinforcement learning [4]. The history of simulators for autonomous driving has been explained and have been divided into two classes based on the tasks performed like traffic flow, sensor data and vehicle dynamics simulator [5] Various Carla based testing simulations were implemented for different scenarios of urban driving [6]. Sim2real, DTs and PI were introduced and demonstrated in the simulation environment [7] ROS was tested, digital twins were created autonomously using the gazebo classis simulator [8].

BlueICE framework was used to obtain synchronized communication across various simulation environments. It works with various simulation tools and provides high performance for real time applications [9] Three dimensional modelling and graphics work for large geographical locations were imported into Carla Unreal Engine which supports digital twin modelling [10] ViL simulator which is based on deep learning technology was used to scale and apply it for heavy traffic scenarios [11] Physics based modelling and natural language interactions using LLM interface was proposed to bridge the gap between Real2sim and digital twin simulations [12]

LimSim supports the use of openly available APIs and acts as a traffic simulator and provides multiple traffic scenarios creations [13].

Realistic environments are constructed using real world data using the **OASim** data generator. Its model can detect loop holes in an algorithm [14], EDGAR and its duplicate vehicle were generated as digital twins and it also enables real world testing of the vehicle [15]. Machine learning techniques and traffic management systems were evaluated using the ICAT platform. It supports complex computational tasks while handling a group of autonomous robots [16].

The common road model provides various inbuilt scenarios and settings required to test vehicles in urban driving environments [17]. Auto Drive system is used to produce the digital twin of both the environment and the vehicle along with which Autoware core was deployed to ensure navigation based on the maps and perception of the surroundings [18]. LGVSL simulator was integrated with Autoware and Apollo AD stacks for testing various autonomous driving simulations [19].

HF simulation was used to test AV software stack in the Carla simulator with a ROS bridge and Carla autoware pipeline. Lanelet2 map and vehicle model was generated along with the software setting [20]. Hence the combination of a vast range of autonomous driving simulators capable of performing special tasks based on the way they are built provide an open platform for autonomous driving simulation research. This shows how the autonomous driving industry is dependant on the simulators for testing real world scenarios as real time substantial testing is not practically and economically feasible. As simulators today have been developed enough to create end to end realistic simulations replicating the real-world maps and environments making it a great platform to drastically improve the future of autonomous driving by preparing the vehicles to navigate around the digital twin of a desirable realistic environment.

3 METHODOLOGY

The methodology follows a series of six sequential stages, starting from geospatial data collection to vehicle spawning with Pygame interface, each validated for being compatible with CARLA frameworks.

3.1 *OSM extraction of MIT manipal region*

OpenStreetMap (OSM) was used to extract the map of MIT Manipal Campus from which all the geospatial data was obtained. As OSM exports all the roads from the map the nearby residential streets and external roads are also exported along with all the internal roads. The focus remained on the central campus zone, Whilst outer routes were retained in the . osm file, focus remained on the main campus area. This process preserved the accurate geometric primitives and spatial data of the campus network used for simulation.

3.2 *OSM to OpenDRIVE conversion*

CARLA's framework operates with the map in the OpenDrive format. The Osm2Odr file within the Python API was directly used to convert .osm file to XODR file. This seamless integration process within CARLA, eliminates the need for any other intermediate SUMO-based conversion process.

3.3 *Import into CARLA and calibration*

Once XODR was loaded into CARLA (version 0.9.15), calibration took place to resolve coordinate offsets, refine junction alignments, and verify lane interconnections. Further modifications were made to replicate the realistic layout of the campus environment.

3.4 *Rendering backends: Open GL vs Vulkan*

Three-dimensional Graphics APIs like OpenGL and Vulkan were used to evaluate rendering performance backends. Under heavy loads, OpenGL being a high- level API showed occasional frame drops and stutters, whereas Vulkan being a low-level API provided smoother visuals and better GPU efficiency for the extensive MIT Manipal campus map shown in Figure 1.

Figure 1. Imported MIT Manipal map in CARLA.

3.5 *Manual landmark labelling*

Eighteen important landmarks across the MIT Campus such as MIT Gate-1 , Academic Block-1, Student Plaza were chosen and calibrated manually. As shown in Figure 2, they were labelled with different colour codes to make it easy to distinguish between each point .

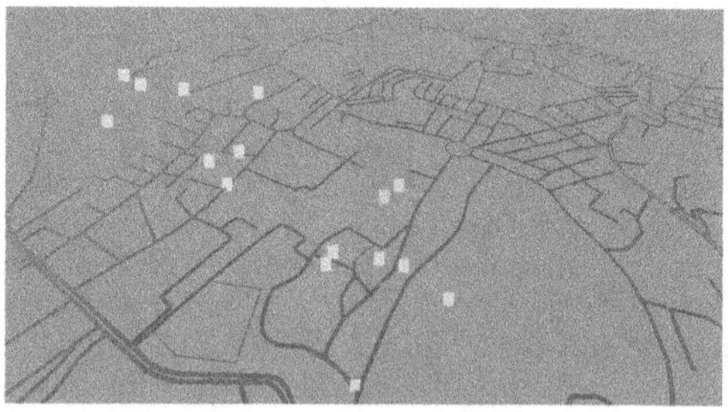

Figure 2. Labelled MIT Manipal map with 18 colour coded landmarks.

3.6 *Vehicle spawn system with pygame interface*

A terminal legend showing all the eighteen landmarks along with the associated colours would appear for the user to chose a spawn point of their chose to navigate around the campus. A Py game window as illustrated in Figure 3, appears and a vehicle appears at the selected spawn point from which we can control the vehicle manually or automatically according to the program executed. After which the vehicle can move around the campus. And each landmark can be identified according to the colour that terminal prompts. Further testing simulation can be generated for various scenarios such as pedestrian crossing the road or obstacle detection/avoidance. Once we started spawning the vehicle minor stuttering and oscillation was observed slightly due to physics initialization. This limitation is discussed later.

Figure 3. Pygame interface.

4 RESULTS AND DISCUSSION

The OpenDRIVE MIT Manipal campus map was successfully imported into CARLA after OSM extraction and eighteen manual landmarks were manually calibrated across the campus for navigation. A Pygame interface supported real-time vehicle (actor) spawning and minor vehicle oscillations were observed associated with Unreal Engine physics synchronization. As shown in Table 1, Comparison of OpenGL and Vulkan showed that Vulkan outperformed OpenGL efficiently, while maintaining high performance under heavy workloads as it has a lower CPU overhead and allows multicore utilization. But OpenGL had frame time fluctuations. These findings overlap with previous studies conducted showing the impact of rendering performance on digital-twin realism and simulation stability. Table 2 further confirms Vulkan's consistent frame rates across all resolutions, outperforming OpenGL under heavy map loads and complex performing conditions.

Table 1. Performance comparison between OpenGL (OGL) and Vulkan (VK).

API	Test	Metric	Value	Remark
OGL	glxgears	FPS	9721	Stable
VK	vkcube	Launch	OK	Smooth
OGL	GLM2	Score	4850	Avg load
VK	BMRK	Score	2340 (60 FPS)	Efficient
OGL	UVal	Score	1850 (45 FPS)	Warm
VK	SApp	Launch	OK	Verified

Table 2. CARLA rendering performance under Vulkan and OpenGL.

Backend	Resolution	Status	GPU %	Remark
VK	1080p	Pass	65	Smooth
OGL	1080p	Skip	—	NA
VK	720p	Pass	58	Stable
OGL	720p	Skip	—	NA
VK	4K	Pass	82	Robust
OGL	4K	Fail	90	Drop

The above findings confirm the dependability of the developed digital-twin simulation and identify key areas for enhancement in spawn-point consistency and automated landmark annotation to guide future improvements of the system.

5 FUTURE WORK

Future work will aim to integrate SUMO-based traffic co-simulation to capture dynamic interactions among agents and to develop a ROS2–CARLA interface enabling stable and easy autonomous navigation. Incorporating machine learning algorithms to calibrate landmarks automatically. This will improve spatial scalability, while enhancements in spawn initialization and V2X-capable modules will facilitate maneuver coordination, network evaluation, and intelligent mobility analysis within virtual smart-campus ecosystems.

6 CONCLUSION

This paper demonstrates a solid representation for creating a digital twin of the MIT Manipal Campus using Carla simulator. The workflow combines OSM extraction, ODR conversion, landmark calibration and labelling to enhance geospatial accuracy for realistic environment simulation. A Pygame interface was used to interact with vehicle simulation. Throughout the Three-Dimensional simulation Vulkan offered a smoother frame stability and lower CPU overhead unlike OpenGL for complex road geometries. Though minor stuttering was observed this research acts as a foundation for future improvements in ROS2 based autonomous simulation and V2X communication within the campus.

ACKNOWLEDGMENT

The authors of this paper acknowledge the Department of Mechatronics, Manipal Institute of Technology (MIT), MAHE, for providing the necessary academic support and infrastructure for this project. Special thanks are due to the guide, Ramya S Moorthy for her valuable guidance and expert super vision throughout this research work.

REFERENCES

[1] S. Maierhofer and M. Althoff, (2022). "CommonRoad–CARLA interface: Bridging the gap between motion planning and 3D simulation," *IEEE IV*.

[2] A. Mondal, P. Tigas, and Y. Gal, (2020). "Real2Sim: Automatic generation of OpenStreetMap towns for autonomous driving benchmarks," *NeurIPS Workshop*.

[3] K.-W. Chiang, H.-Y. Pai, J.-C. Zeng, M.-L. Tsai, and N. El-Sheimy, (2021). "Automated modeling of road networks for high-definition maps in OpenDRIVE format using mobile mapping measurements," *Remote Sens.*

[4] A. Dosovitskiy, G. Ros, F. Codevilla, A. Lopez, and V. Koltun, (2017). "CARLA: An open urban driving simulator," *Proc. Conf. Robot Learn. (CoRL)*.

[5] Y. Li, W. Yuan, S. Zhang, W. Yan, Q. Shen, C. Wang and M. Yang, (2023). "Choose your simulator wisely: A review on open-source simulators for autonomous driving," *arXiv preprint* arXiv:2311.11056.

[6] Y. Al Ozaibi, M.D. Hina, and A. Ramdane-Cherif, (2024). "End-to-end autonomous driving in CARLA: A survey," *IEEE Access*, vol. 12. doi:10.1109/ACCESS.2024.3473611

[7] X. Hu, S. Li, T. Huang, B. Tang, R. Huai, and L. Chen, (2024). "How simulation helps autonomous driving: A survey of Sim2real, digital twins, and parallel intelligence," *IEEE Trans. Intell. Veh.*, vol. 9, no. 1, pp. 593–612, Jan. 2024. doi:10.1109/TIV.2023.3312777

[8] J. Vlasák, J. Klapálek, A. Kollarčík, M. Sojka, and Z. Hanzálek, (2024). "Low-fidelity digital twin for automated driving systems: Use cases and automatic generation," *arXiv preprint arXiv:2405.13705*.

[9] Y. He, H. Chen, and W. Shi, (2024). "An advanced framework for ultra-realistic simulation and digital twinning for autonomous vehicles," *arXiv preprint arXiv:2405.01328*.

[10] T. Azfar, J. Weidner, A. Raheem, R. Ke, and R.L. Cheu, (2022). "Efficient procedure of building university campus models for digital twin simulation," *IEEE Journal of Radio Frequency Identification*, vol. 6, pp. 769–773.

[11] Z. Zhang, G. Badakis, M. Galanis, A. Bavarsj, E. van Hassel, M. Alirezaei, and S. Haesaert, (2025). "A vehicle-in-the-loop

simulator with AI-powered digital twins for testing automated driving controllers," *arXiv preprint arXiv:2507.02313.*

[12] T.V. Samak, C.V. Samak, B. Li and V. Krovi, (2025). "When digital twins meet large language models: Realistic, interactive and editable simulation for autonomous driving," *arXiv preprint arXiv:2507.00319.*

[13] L. Wen, D. Fu, S. Mao, P. Cai, M. Dou, Y. Li and Y. Qiao, (2023). "LimSim: A long-term interactive multi-scenario traffic simulator," in *Proc. IEEE 26th International Conference on Intelligent Transportation Systems (ITSC).*

[14] G. Yan, J. Pi, J. Guo, Z. Luo, M. Dou, N. Deng, Q. Huang, D. Fu, L. Wen, P. Cai, X. Gao, X. Cai, B. Zhang, X. Yang, Y. Bai, H. Zhou and B. Shi, (2024). "OASim: An open and adaptive simulator based on neural rendering for autonomous driving," *arXiv preprint arXiv:2402.03830.*

[15] P. Karle *et al.*, (2024). "EDGAR: An autonomous driving research platform—from feature development to real-world application," *arXiv preprint arXiv:2405.06057.*

[16] Z. Tian, Y. He, B. Tian, R. Zhong, E. Foorginejad and W. Shi, (2024). "ICAT: An Indoor Connected and Autonomous Testbed for Vehicle Computing," *arXiv preprint arXiv:2402.17933*

[17] M. Althoff, M. Koschi, and S. Manzinger, (2017). "CommonRoad: Composable benchmarks for motion planning on roads," in *Proc. IEEE Intelligent Vehicles Symposium (IV)*, pp. 719–726.

[18] T.V. Samak, C.V. Samak, and V.N. Krovi, (2024). "Towards Validation of Autonomous Vehicles Across Scales using an Integrated Digital Twin Framework," in *Proc. 2024 IEEE/ASME Int. Conf. Advanced Intelligent Mechatronics (AIM).*

[19] G. Rong *et al.*, (2020). "LGSVL simulator: A high-fidelity simulator for autonomous driving," *Proc. IEEE Intell. Vehicles Symp. (IV).*

[20] G. Kaljavesi, T. Kerbl, T. Betz, K. Mitkovskii and F. Diermeyer, (2024). "CARLA-Autoware-Bridge: Facilitating autonomous driving research with a unified framework for simulation and module development," *Proc. IEEE Intelligent Vehicles Symp. (IV).*

Technology for a Resilient Future – Vincent , Moorthy and Dasari (Eds)
ISBN: 978-1-041-39070-1

Generative Modeling of LISS-IV Satellite Imagery with Latent Diffusion

Avinash Chouhan and Biswarup Deb
North Eastern Space Applications Centre, Umiam, Meghalaya, India

Krish Kahnani
Indian Institute of Information Technology, Guwahati

Dibyajyoti Chutia and Shiv Prasad Aggarwal
North Eastern Space Applications Centre, Umiam, Meghalaya, India

ABSTRACT: Latent diffusion models (LDMs) are being increasingly used in remote sensing as a promising framework for controllable image synthesis and geospatial analysis. We improved the previous framework by fine-tuning the model with paired LISS-IV and OpenStreetMap (OSM) samples. This modified model successfully captures the numerous landscape variations, producing more realistic images. Comparative studies show that fine-tuning decreases artifacts and improves spectral fidelity over baseline models. To address the issues caused by non-RGB data, we used a two-stage process. Furthermore, we propose SynthLISS-IV, a dataset that can be shared for further study on remote sensing image synthesis. Our findings highlighted the model synthesis capabilities in a variety of geographic scenarios.

Keywords: Generative Models, ControlNet, Satellite Image Synthesis, Low-rank adaptation

1 INTRODUCTION

The combination of generative artificial intelligence with geospatial data is creating new possibilities for remote sensing research and applications. Although recent developments in text-to-image diffusion models have shown impressive ability in generating realistic imagery, their adaptation to specific, non-RGB remote sensing data is still mostly unexplored. The vast domain gap between models trained on billions of RGB photos from the internet and the scientific images acquired from Earth observation instruments presents a substantial challenge.

Although spatially controlled synthesis is possible using frameworks such as ControlNet [1], [7], and [13], it is assumed that the underlying base model already understands the target image domain. This restriction lessens their direct utility for satellite images, particularly for sensors such as the Indian Remote Sensing (IRS) satellites, Linear Imaging Self-Scanning Sensor-IV (LISS-IV). Diffusion models, which offer more efficient and stable image generation [2], [3], [8], [12]–[16], have replaced earlier methods that depended on adversarial learning for image synthesis [5], [9], [10], [17]. Nevertheless, the distinct spectral features of non-RGB data, such as LISS-IV imaging, are not captured when generative models are used directly with RGB-trained base models.

The significant contributions of this research are as follows: First, we propose a two-stage process for the generative synthesis of non-RGB LISS-IV images. Second, we introduce a curated and shareable dataset for satellite image synthesis called SynthLISS-IV, intended for future research projects.

2 LITERATURE REVIEW

Sastry *et al.* [1] introduced a framework that generates satellite imagery based on text and location conditions while ensuring structural consistency. Abady *et al.* [4] put forward a method that utilizes splicing for updating and synthesizing images with associated labels. Andrade *et al.* [5] developed a conditional GAN-based model that converts historical maps into realistic satellite images. Meanwhile, Lu *et al.* [6] proposed an end-to-end framework that generates a geometrically consistent panoramic RGB view using just a single satellite image.

Diffusion models have emerged as a powerful tool for various remote sensing image synthesis tasks. Zhu *et al.* [2] proposed a conditional diffusion framework for super-resolution that integrates a large diffusion prior with low-rank adaptation to bridge the domain gap, along with a refined control strategy to maintain fine-grained details. Cao *et al.* [3] designed a diffusion-driven fusion model with wavelet modulation for multiscale image translation. Yu *et al.* [15] presented a diffusion framework that is conditioned on DEM data and custom prompts for image gap filling with distribution loss. Czerkawski *et al.* [16] contributed a data-centric diffusion approach for terrain generation trained on global-scale datasets, complemented by the release of an open-source benchmark.

Several works focus on structural and contextual improvement in generative learning. Baghirli *et al.* [8] developed a diffusion-based model capable of capturing layout, textures, and stylistic patterns characteristic of authentic satellite images. Zhang *et al.* [11] introduced CC-Diff, which employs a Dual Resampler and Context Bridge to better model interactions between the foreground and background, along with a foreground-aware attention mechanism that ensures contextual coherence. Deng *et al.* [12] combined graph-prior learning with a masked diffusion transformer for better spatial and semantic representation. Xiong *et al.* [13] proposed a dual-branch architecture with text and OpenStreetMap (OSM) conditions for semantic enhancement and structural consistency in image synthesis. Arrabi *et al.* [14] approached the problem of cross-view synthesis by initially creating bird's-eye-view (BEV) maps from images taken at ground level. They then utilized these BEV maps, along with accompanying textual information, to generate aerial views.

Other contributions investigate image forgery, surveys, and multimodal applications. Liao *et al.* [9] explored satellite image forgery generation using GAN variants and compared detection performance between pre-trained and newly trained CNNs. Mansourifar *et al.* [10] conducted a comprehensive survey on image synthesis using Generative Adversarial Networks (GANs). Reed *et al.* [17] developed an adversarial learning based model that integrates text and image for pixel-level image generation. He *et al.* [18] reviewed advances in image–language modeling, highlighting their impact on research and industrial adoption.

Audebert *et al.* [19] proposed a system that learns visual cues while also dealing with noisy text to classify documents. Wang

DOI: 10.1201/9781042017546-62

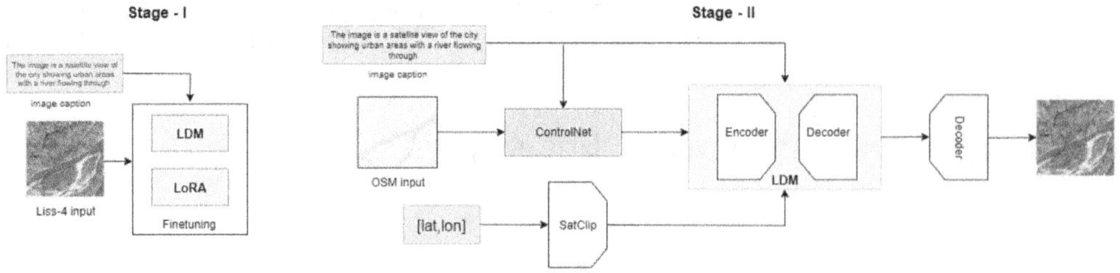

Figure 1. Schematic diagram of the proposed approach, based on GeoSynth [1], combining LDM [22] with ControlNet [23] for geospatial image generation.

et al. [20] designed a two-branch setup where image and text features are pushed into a shared space through several projection layers and a large margin loss. Li *et al.* [21] took a more deployment-focused approach and built a lightweight multimodal classifier that combines CNN-based visual features with Transformer text features using cross-modal attention, with the goal of making it suitable for IoT scenarios.

3 PROPOSED METHODOLOGY

We perform image synthesis using a pre-trained Latent Diffusion Model (LDM) [22], which is customized with Low-Rank Adaptation (LoRA) [28] and a spatial guidance module inspired by ControlNet [23]. The training follows a two-stage, separated approach, enabling the model to independently acquire modality-specific styles and structural guidance, a critical factor for generating realistic LISS-IV imagery. We utilise a lightweight style adapter to modify the outputs of the RGB-trained LDM, enabling it to capture the visual and structural traits of LISS-IV imagery. In this setup, LoRA [28] adds small trainable pieces into the cross-attention layers of the frozen LDM U-Net. This lets us fine-tune the model without touching all of its parameters. These added parts gradually learn the typical spectral patterns, textures, and the way colors appear in LISS-IV images. At inference time, the LoRA module modifies the LDM U-Net's behaviour to render images with a LISS-IV-specific appearance.

Figure 1 illustrates the two-stage pipeline for enhanced satellite image generation using paired LISS-IV imagery and OpenStreetMap (OSM) data.

- **Stage I**: The paired inputs (LISS-IV satellite image with a corresponding caption) are used to fine-tune the Latent Diffusion Model (LDM) for capturing both structural and semantic representations.
- **Stage II**: The latent representation is further refined using ControlNet [23] with the utilisation of paired inputs, geospatial context derived from OpenStreetMap, and location embeddings extracted using SatCLIP [24]. As a result, the generated LISS-IV imagery preserves structural details while presenting a visually authentic appearance.

4 DATASET

We curated a multimodal dataset (SynthLISS-IV) that contains 12,000 paired samples of LISS-IV imagery from Northeast India (Figure 2). It is split into 8,000 training, 2,000 validation, and 2,000 testing samples. Each sample includes False Color Composite (FCC) patches (512 × 512), OSM, text captions, and location embeddings. LISS-IV images are downloaded from the Bhoonidhi ISRO geoportal. NIR, Red, and Green are used as RGB channels in the FCC composite. Captions were generated using a quantised LLaVA-1.5 (7B) [27] model and with SatCLIP [24] embeddings, which provided location context for each patch.

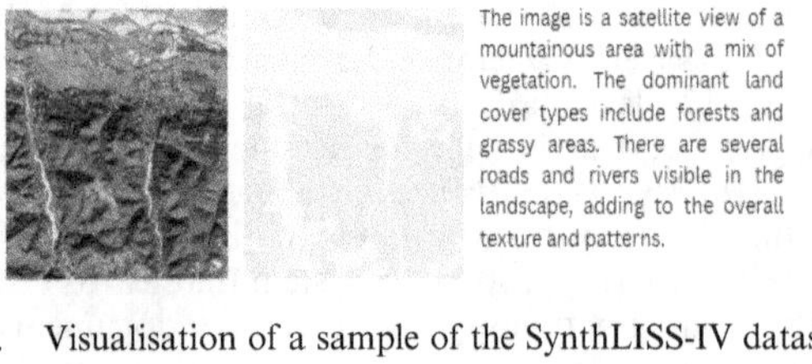

Figure 2. Visualisation of a sample of the SynthLISS-IV dataset.

5 RESULTS AND DISCUSSIONS

Image generation is assessed from several perspectives using SSIM [30], CLIP [25], and FID [29]. The qualitative results of the proposed workflow under different fine-tuning strategies and baseline settings are presented in Figures 3–6. The results indicate that input map representations across a range of geographical environments influence the generation of remote

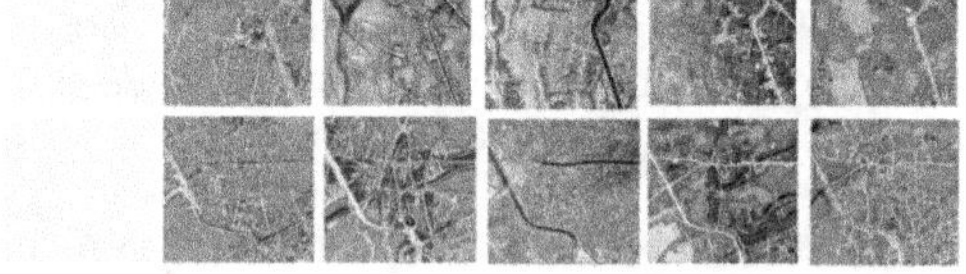

Figure 3. GeoSynth with full fine-tune (50K steps).

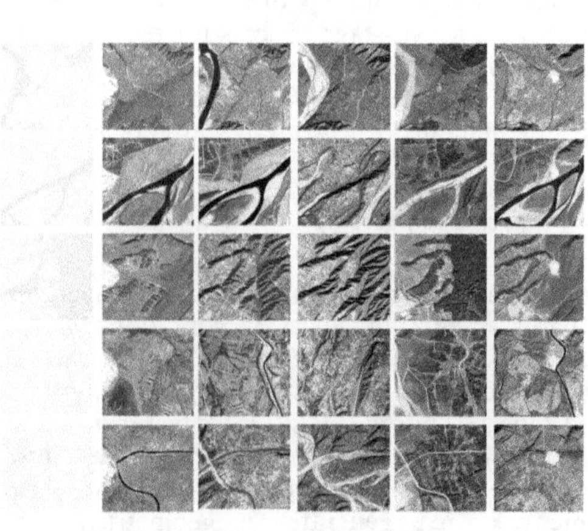

Figure 4. GeoSynth with partial fine-tune (10K steps).

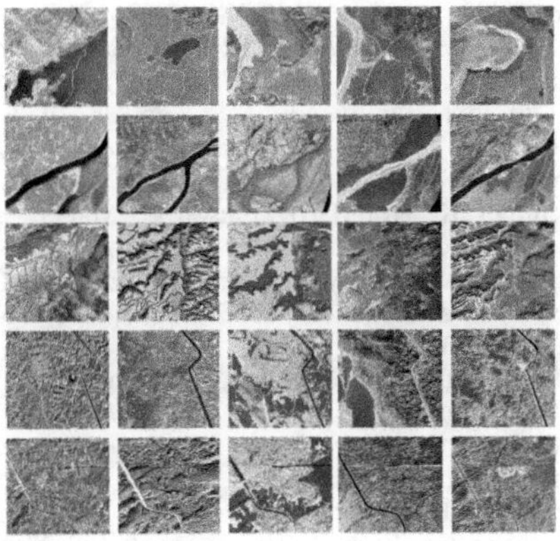

Figure 5. GeoSynth with Non-fine-tune.

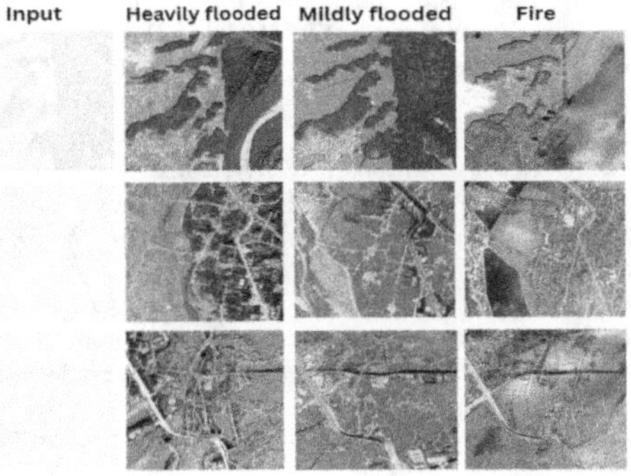

Figure 6. Results of GeoSynth with the full Fine-Tune Model for various conditions.

sensing images. Figure 3 highlights results from the fully fine-tuned (50K steps) model, which exhibits superior spatial consistency and sharper reconstruction of terrain-specific features. In deserts and plains, the fine-tuned outputs show realistic results.

Figure 4 presents outputs from a partial fine-tuning setup (10K steps). Here, geographically relevant patterns are captured, but textures lack finer structural details. Figure 5 shows results from the non-fine-tuned baseline. Here, the model captures only broad scene layouts without capturing genuine information. Geometric artefacts are present along rivers, roads, and settlements. Figure 6 shows a comparison of satellite imagery outputs for Heavily Flooded, Mildly Flooded, and Fire conditions.

The numerical results of the SynthLISS-IV dataset are presented in Table 1, which shows that the fully fine-tuned model achieved the best overall performance. It suggests improved structural precision, semantic, and consistency. Lesser fine-tuning, however, led to a drop in all measures, and the elimination of OSM data made the performance even worse. The class-wise findings for flood and fire detection are shown in Table 2. With the most significant results for the fire, mildly flooded, and highly flooded classes, the fully optimized model performs the best.

Table 1. Numerical results on SynthLISS-IV dataset.

Model	SSIM	CLIP Score	FID
Full fine-tune	0.82	0.31	13.98
Lower fine-tune	0.73	0.27	19.20
No fine-tune	0.62	0.24	19.49
No fine-tune (No OSM)	0.23	0.11	32.23

Table 2. CLIP score comparison for image synthesis under various conditions.

Model	Fire	Mildly Flooded	Heavily Flooded
Full fine-tune	0.21	0.33	0.32
Lower fine-tune	0.18	0.19	0.19
No fine-tune	0.11	0.12	0.15

6 CONCLUSIONS

In this work, we fine-tuned a latent diffusion framework for generative image synthesis of LISS-IV data. The results demonstrate that fine-tuning significantly improves visual realism, texture quality, and geometric consistency compared to the non-fine-tuned baseline. Furthermore, we curated and released a shareable dataset (SynthLISS-IV) for satellite image synthesis. Comprehensive experiments on LISS-IV synthesis under various conditions are presented, including both numerical and visual comparisons. A key aspect of the proposed approach is its ability to generate new scenarios which were absent in the original dataset.

REFERENCES

[1] Sastry S, Khanal S, Dhakal A, Jacobs N. (2024). Geosynth: Contextually-aware high-resolution satellite image synthesis. In *Proceedings of the IEEE/CVF Conference on Computer Vision and Pattern Recognition* (pp. 460–470).

[2] Zhu C, Liu Y, Huang S, Wang F. (2025). Taming a diffusion model to revitalize remote sensing image super-resolution. *Remote Sensing.* 17(8):1348.

[3] Cao Z, Cao S, Wu X, Hou J, Ran R, Deng LJ. (2023). *DDRF: Denoising Diffusion Model for Remote Sensing Image Fusion.* arXiv preprint arXiv:2304.04774.

[4] Abady L, Horváth J, Tondi B, Delp EJ, Barni M. (2022). Manipulation and generation of synthetic satellite images using deep learning models. *Journal of Applied Remote Sensing.* 16 (4):046504.

[5] Andrade HJ, Fernandes BJ. (2020). Synthesis of satellite-like urban images from historical maps using conditional GAN. *IEEE Geoscience and Remote Sensing Letters.* 19:1–4.

[6] Lu X, Li Z, Cui Z, Oswald MR, Pollefeys M, Qin R. (2020). Geometry-aware satellite-to-ground image synthesis for urban areas. In *Proceedings of the IEEE/CVF Conference on Computer Vision and Pattern Recognition* (pp. 859–867).

[7] Wang Q, Liang Y, Zheng Y, Xu K, Zhao J, Wang S. (2025). *Generative AI for Urban Planning: Synthesizing Satellite Imagery via Diffusion Models.* arXiv preprint arXiv:2505.08833.

[8] Baghirli O, Askarov H, Ibrahimli I, Bakhishov I, Nabiyev N. (2023). *Satdm: Synthesizing Realistic Satellite Image With Semantic Layout Conditioning Using Diffusion Models.* arXiv preprint arXiv:2309.16812.

[9] Liao WH, Chang YS, Wu YC. (2023). Detection of synthesized satellite images using deep neural networks. In *2023 17th International Conference on Ubiquitous Information Management and Communication (IMCOM)* (pp. 1–5). IEEE.

[10] Mansourifar H, Moskovitz A, Klingensmith B, Mintas D, Simske SJ. (2022). Gan-based satellite imaging: A survey on techniques and applications. *IEEE Access.* 10:118123–40.

[11] Zhang M, Liu Y, Liu Y, Zhao Y, Ye Q. (2024). CC-Diff: Enhancing contextual coherence in remote sensing image synthesis. *arXiv preprint arXiv*:2412.08464.

[12] Deng K, Wei S, Pang S, Jiang H, Su B. (2025). Synthesizing remote sensing images from land cover annotations via graph prior masked diffusion. *Remote Sensing.* 17(13):2254.

[13] Xiong H, Li Z, Lv Q, Zhu B, Zhang Y, Yu C, Tan Z. (2025). OP-Gen: A high-quality remote sensing image generation algorithm guided by OSM images and textual prompts. *Remote Sensing.* 17 (7):1226.

[14] Arrabi A, Zhang X, Sultani W, Chen C, Wshah S. (2025). Cross-view meets diffusion: Aerial image synthesis with geometry and text guidance. In *2025 IEEE/CVF Winter Conference on*

Applications of Computer Vision (WACV) (pp. 5356–5366). IEEE.

[15] Yu Z, Idris M, Wang P, Xia Y, Ma F, Qureshi R. (2025). Satellite formula: Multi-Modal symbolic regression from remote sensing imagery for physics discovery. *arXiv preprint arXiv:2506.06176.*

[16] Czerkawski M, Martin R, Rouffet R. (2025). MESA: Text-driven terrain generation using latent diffusion and global copernicus data. In *Proceedings of the Computer Vision and Pattern Recognition Conference* (pp. 3067–3075).

[17] Reed S, Akata Z, Yan X, Logeswaran L, Schiele B, Lee H. (2016). Generative adversarial text to image synthesis. In *International Conference on Machine Learning* (pp. 1060–1069). PMLR.

[18] He X, Deng L. (2017). Deep learning for image-to-text generation: A technical overview. *IEEE Signal Processing Magazine.* 34 (6):109–16.

[19] Audebert N, Herold C, Slimani K, Vidal C. (2019). Multimodal deep networks for text and image-based document classification. In *Joint European Conference on Machine Learning and Knowledge Discovery in Databases* Y, Lazebnik S. (2016). Learning deep structure-preserving image-text embeddings. In *Proceedings of the IEEE Conference on Computer Vision and Pattern Recognition* 2016 (pp. 5005–5013).

[20] M. Li, R. Hao, S. Shi, Z. Yu, Q. He and J. Zhan, "A CNN-Transformer Approach for Image-Text Multimodal Classification with Cross-Modal Feature Fusion," *2025 8th International Conference on Advanced Algorithms and Control Engineering (ICAACE)*, Shanghai, China, 2025, pp. 1182–1186, https://doi.org/10.1109/ICAACE65325.2025.11020324.

[21] Rombach R, Blattmann A, Lorenz D, Esser P, Ommer B. (2022). High-resolution image synthesis with latent diffusion models. In *Proceedings of the IEEE/CVF Conference on Computer Vision and Pattern Recognition* 2022 (pp. 10684–10695).

[22] Zhang L, Rao A, Agrawala M. (2023). Adding conditional control to text-to-image diffusion models. In *Proceedings of the IEEE/CVF International Conference on Computer Vision* 2023 (pp. 3836–3847).

[23] Klemmer K, Rolf E, Robinson C, Mackey L, Rußwurm M. (2025). Satclip: Global, general-purpose location embeddings with satellite imagery. In *Proceedings of the AAAI Conference on Artificial Intelligence* 2025 Apr 11 (Vol. 39, No. 4, pp. 4347–4355).

[24] Li Y, Liang F, Zhao L, Cui Y, Ouyang W, Shao J, Yu F, Yan J. (2021). *Supervision Exists Everywhere: A Data Efficient Contrastive Language-Image Pre-Training Paradigm.* arXiv preprint arXiv:2110.05208. 2021 Oct 11.

[25] Simonyan K, Zisserman A. (2014). *Very Deep Convolutional Networks for Large-Scale Image Recognition.* arXiv preprint arXiv:1409.1556.

[26] Cocchi F, Moratelli N, Caffagni D, Sarto S, Baraldi L, Cornia M, Cucchiara R. (2025). *LLaVA-MORE: A Comparative Study of LLMs and Visual Backbones for Enhanced Visual Instruction Tuning.* arXiv preprint arXiv:2503.15621.

[27] E.J. Hu, Y. Shen, P. Wallis, Z. Allen-Zhu, Y. Li, S. Wang, L. Wang, and W. Chen, (2022). "LoRA: Low-Rank Adaptation of Large Language Models," in *International Conference on Learning Representations (ICLR)*, 2022.

[28] Yu Y, Zhang W, Deng Y. Frechet inception distance (fid) for evaluating gans. *China University of Mining Technology Beijing Graduate School*, 3(11).

[29] Wang Z, Bovik AC, Sheikh HR, Simoncelli EP. (2024). Image quality assessment: from error visibility to structural similarity. *IEEE Transactions on Image Processing.* 13(4):600–12.

Technology for a Resilient Future – Vincent , Moorthy and Dasari (Eds)
© 2027 The Author(s), ISBN: 978-1-041-39070-1

Ground Water Extraction in Mexico City: The Mapping of Anthropic Created Depressions Via Satellite Imagery

Silvia García and Paulina Trejo
Instituto de Ingeniería UNAM, Ciudad Universitaria, Coyoacán, CDMX, México

ABSTRACT: Tláhuac, in the Mexico City metropolitan area, serves as a prime example of a man-made geotechnical disaster. This study used satellite data (Interferometric Synthetic Aperture Radar InSAR) for demonstrating that i. the subsidence in these areas is almost fully irreversible and ii. there is a direct relationship between groundwater level fluctuations (pumping rates) and vertical displacements registered. Using thickness of the upper aquitard and stratigraphic datasets is exposed that deformation rates, derived from overexploitation, can be correlated with pumping intensity and existing subsurface stratigraphic heterogeneities. A neural model is developed to show that if these rates are maintained or slightly increased the compaction of the upper aquitard could lead to unprecedented subsidence that would collapse drinking water supply and wastewater disposal services, kilometres of road surfaces, communication lines and the ability to cope with flooding. This predicament is indicative of the broader challenges confronting the region regarding water management in the context of climate change.

Keywords: InSAR, neural networks, subsidence basins

1 INTRODUCTION

Water, supply and disposal, is a major environmental problem impacting many metropolitan areas either in the form of flooding risks or lack of access to public services, but few are as affected as Mexico City. The Mexican case is particularly complex because very high sinking rates affect buried infrastructure and exacerbates the risks. Tláhuac mayoralty (city southeast), with astounding manifestations of these vertical displacements (Figure 1), has received the installation of several water pumping wells since the 1980s, including 5 of the deepest in the Mexican capital. As the city has grown, the exploitation of the aquifer system in Tláhuac has increased causing severe land subsidence, damages to buried water infrastructure and, as a result, urban segregation and substandard living conditions. Previous works have focused on hydrodynamics (e.g. [1]), hydrochemistry (e.g.[2]), hazard zonation (e.g. [3]), groundwater vulnerability (e.g. [4]), groundwater depletion (e.g., [5]), and the related subsidence (e.g. [6]), however, their observation scale covers the spatial extension of the entire city then, their conclusions are not useful for finding the development patterns of deformations in small neighbourhoods. Studies that do not consider small scale must be read with caution because the over-simplifications on stratigraphy and subsidence rates masks the spatial dependence of vertical deformations. Pixel size and bias information are key aspects when dependencies are being looking for. [7], for example, deduced, based on multilinear regression analysis results, that in Mexico City there are not direct relationships between subsidence and pumping rates, land use type, population density, or locations of water extraction wells. For [7], general geo conditions from the Technical Standards for Construction in Mexico City and old pumping locations and rates, can be integrated as inputs in a database for modelling vertical displacements (δ_v) from satellite imagery collected since 1996 (very low precision) to 2020 (high exactitude). Obviously, the linear regression applied to this information cannot be conclusive about relationships between *geo* and anthropic inputs and δ_v.

2 DEL MAR *GEO* CONDITIONS

The territory of Tláhuac, in the southeast of Mexico City, is part of the lakes and volcanoes of Anáhuac, sub-province of the

Figure 1. Steps in Tláhuac from 30 cm to ≈2m.

DOI: 10.1201/9781042017546-63

physiographic province of the Neovolcanic-axis. The dominant topography is the lake plain (42% of the surface) surrounded by a volcanic mountain system with stratovolcanoes. Del Mar area is of recent formation (Quaternary period) when the Santa Catarina Mountain chain emerged and the lake plain of the Valley of Mexico was formed. The geotechnical arrangement is composed of clayey layers of lacustrine origin alternating with sandy alluvial deposits constituting heterogeneous, erratic and very complex stratigraphies [8–10] (Figure 2). In this district, numerous incidents of leaks in pipes (water services), heavily damaged streets as well as houses and small buildings damaged by the ground movements, have been attended practically since urbanization began ~60 years ago. As can be seen in Figure 2, the Del Mar district has several pumping wells installed on its southern border. The superficial cracks, manifestation started as soon as the pumping started, was massive altered during the earthquake of September 19th, 2017 (M7.2) causing, in seconds, huge settlements from 0.5 to 2 m. Hundreds of kilometres of pipelines collapsed that afternoon in 2017, but investigations showed that before the earthquake hit, these pipes were disconnected and/or crushed. These findings motivated an in-depth study of the vertical displacements.

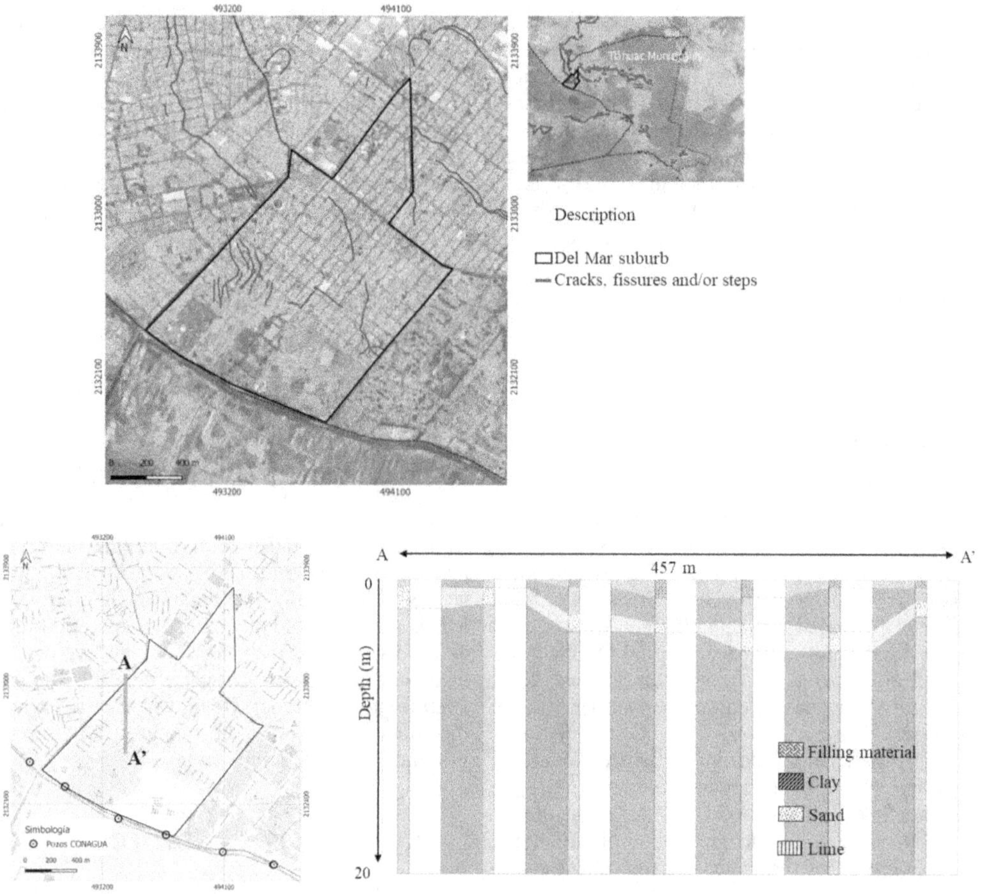

Figure 2. Del Mar conditions: top- situation and perimeter, bottom – an example of the stratigraphy.

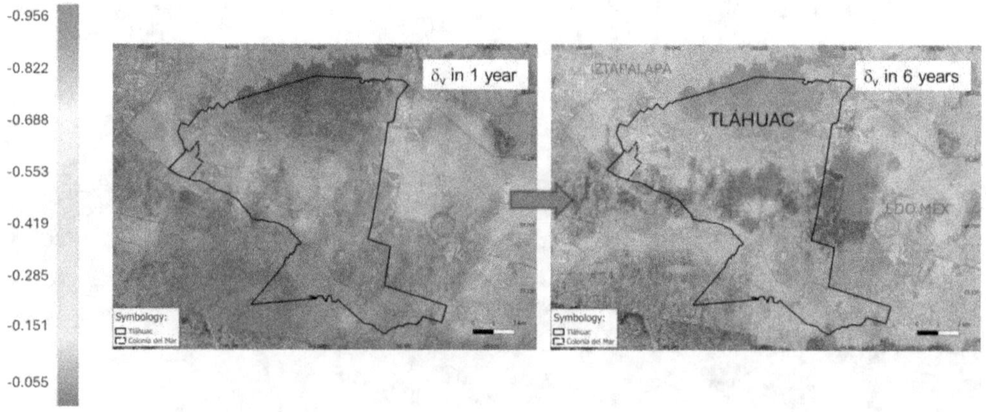

Figure 3. Annual vertical displacements from 2017 to 2023.

2.1 *Subsidence in Del Mar*

The following maps show the annual vertical displacements from 2017 (before the 09/19/2017 earthquake) to 2023 (Figure 3). As can be seen, the subsidence pattern is clearly zoned: at the centre of Tláhuac the maximum displacements (Lake zone) surrounded of transitions and rock sites with the minimum values. Values registered each year confirm that the deformation is related to the thickness of the compressible stratum, which is subject to the effects of aquifer pumping because its projection on the surface remain constant over time. Over the six years of measurements, Del Mar neighbourhood has deformed under a complex pattern being evident that the southwest is now ≈1 m below the level of the rest of the neighbourhood. A zoom into Del Mar area, reveals how the cracks, steps and fissures are the border of this "new basin". Recalling Figure 1, ground manifestations here are mostly steps where the rise is the vertical displacement registered. Using a MFFNN coupled with a RNN (Figure 4) the next 5 years of displacements are predicted and the results are impressive (Figure 5). Considering that the drainage and drinking water pipes that are connected to homes and that run through the streets are buried at less than 1 m deep, in the next 5 years a significant number of pipes will see their working capacity reduced and/or will have collapsed due to the deformations to which they will be subjected, even if at this time they are functioning properly and their (material) health is adequate.

$$u = \theta + \sum_{i=1}^{n} x_i w_{ij}$$

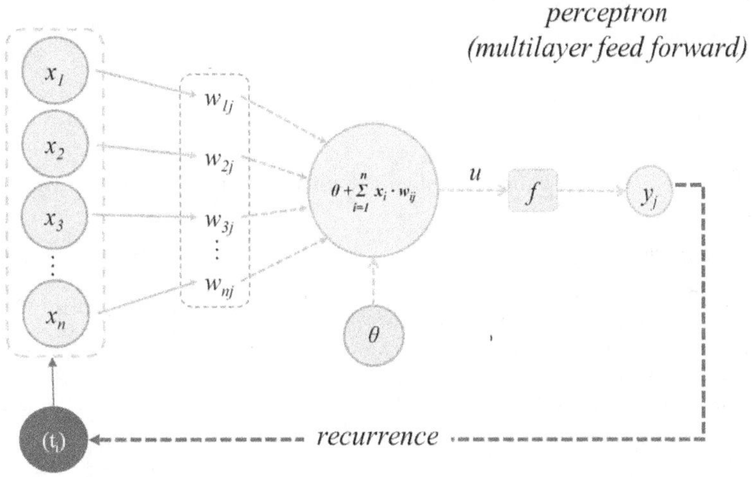

Inputs $\{x_1, x_2, x_3, \ldots, x_n\}$
Synaptic weights $\{w_{1j}, w_{2j}, w_{3j}, \ldots, w_{nj}\}$
Lineal Sum, Σ
Bias, θ
Activation , u
Activación function, f
Output, y

Figure 4. DC-DC buck-boost converter with static load.

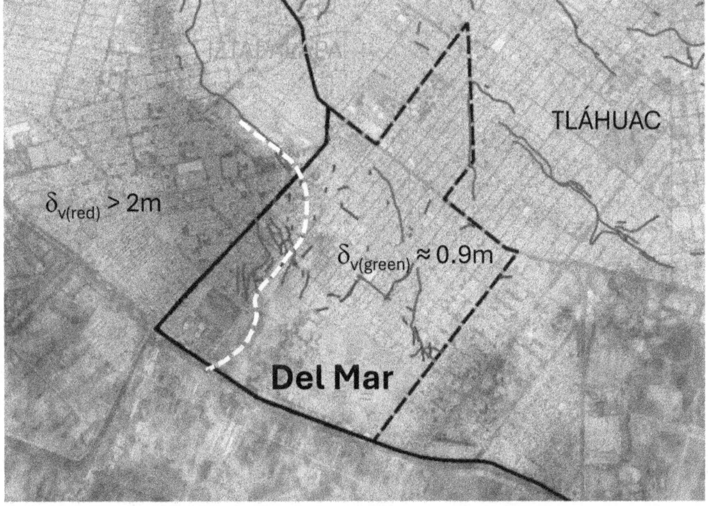

Figure 5. Using a MFFNN coupled with a RNN the next 5 years of displacements are predicted.

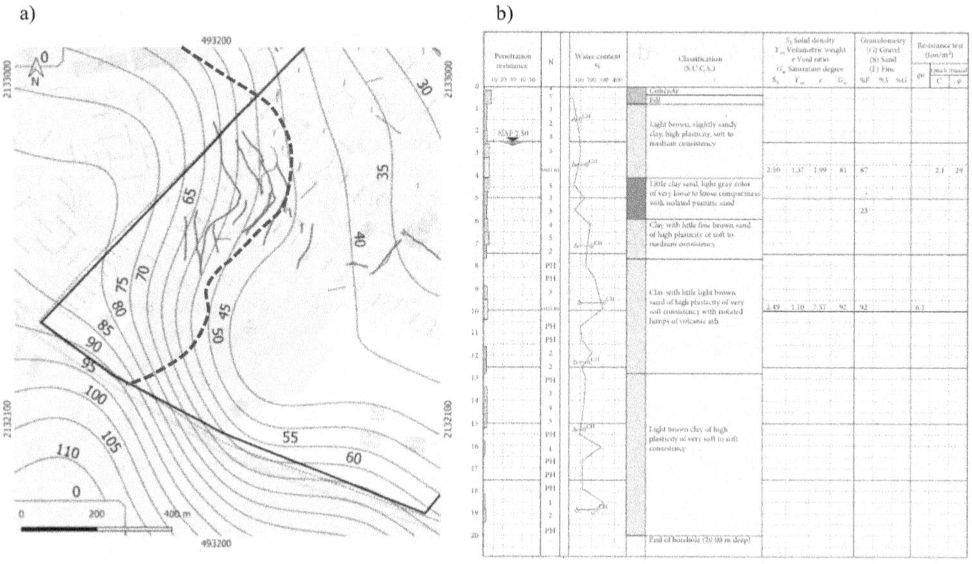

Figure 6. a) Dotted blue line, perimeter of the new basin b) Stratigraphy in a subzone of Del Mar.

2.2 *Controllers of the anthropic basin perimeter*

To define if the created basin could be enlarged in area (footprint), the stratigraphy and basement (basalt layer) were studied in detail. As can be seen in Figure 6, and comparing with the basin perimeter predicted in Figure 5, the perimeter follows the transition between clay layers thickness above 60 m and thinner strata (thickness ≈40 m). This transition connects the points that move at a low rate (like that considered to occur in La Loma) with those beyond 40 cm/year. Findings about high-scale deformations that create the new basin can be summarized as follows: i. soils heterogeneity through the differences in geometry (thickness of clay strata) and deformation modulus, ii. groundwater level, as a direct indicator about the subsidence rate and iii. basement gradient because this hard base defines regions of greatest stress concentration and therefore most susceptible to crack and step.

3 CONCLUSIONS

Using InSAR information is demonstrated that Del Mar district is suffering the creation of an anthropic basin. In this area the water pumping induced astounding subsidence rates and the superficial cracks are transformed to huge steps. The neural model indicates that consolidation deformations is going to continue even if the pumping rates are not increased. As a positive results, the zones subjected to this process are bordered by the transition between wider and thinner clay thicknesses, so the zero zone is well identified. For future public policies, the geotechnical environment imposes the limits on specific prevention actions about water services and communication routes. Based on these preliminary evaluations of origin and progress of anthropic basins, it seems obligated reconsider the installation of pumping wells as urban planning and risk management of the zone.

ACKNOWLEDGEMENT

We gratefully acknowledge the Alcaldía de Tláhuac and the Gobierno de la Ciudad de México authorities for their cooperation in the research.

REFERENCES

[1] A.I. Calderhead, R. Therrien, A. Rivera, R. Martel, J. Garfias, (2011). Simulating pumping-induced regional land subsidence with the use of InSAR and field data in the Toluca Valley, Mexico, *Advances in Water Resources*, Volume 34, Issue 1, Pages 83–97, ISSN 0309-1708, https://doi.org/10.1016/j.advwatres.2010.09.017.

[2] Esteller, M.V., Rodríguez, R., Cardona, A. *et al.* (2012). Evaluation of hydrochemical changes due to intensive aquifer exploitation: case studies from Mexico. *Environ Monit Assess* 184, 5725–5741. https://doi.org/10.1007/s10661-011-2376-0

[3] Enrique Fernández-Torres, Enrique Cabral-Cano, Dario Solano-Rojas, Emre Havazli, and Luis Salazar-Tlaczani, (2020). Land subsidence risk maps and InSAR based angular distortion structural vulnerability assessment: an example in Mexico City, *Proceedings of IAHS*, https://doi.org/10.5194/piahs-382-583-2020

[4] Hernández-Espriú, A., Reyna-Gutiérrez, J.A., Sánchez-León, E. *et al.* (2012). The DRASTIC-Sg model: an extension to the DRASTIC approach for mapping groundwater vulnerability in aquifers subject to differential land subsidence, with application to Mexico City. *Hydrogeol J* 22, 1469–1485 (2014). https://doi.org/10.1007/s10040-014-1130-4

[5] Davila-Hernandez, Norma; Madrigal, Delfino; Expósito, J.L.; Némiga, Xanat. (2014). Multi-Temporal Analysis of Land Subsidence in Toluca Valley (Mexico) through a Combination of Persistent Scatterer Interferometry (PSI) and Historical Piezometric Data. *Advances in Remote Sensing*. 3. 49–60. 10.4236/ars.2014.32005.

[6] Castellazzi, P., R. Martel, A. Rivera, J. Huang, G. Pavlic, A.I. Calderhead, E. Chaussard, J. Garfias, and J. Salas (2016), Groundwater depletion in Central Mexico: Use of GRACE and InSAR to support water resources management, *Water Resour. Res.*, 52, 5985–6003, doi:10.1002/2015WR018211.

[7] Chaussard, E., Havazli, E., Fattahi, H., Cabral-Cano, E., and Solano-Rojas, D. (2021). Over a century of sinking in mexico city: No hope for significant elevation and storage capacity recovery. *Journal of Geophysical Research: Solid Earth*, 126, e2020JB020648. https://doi.org/10.1029/2020JB020648

[8] Lermo-Samaniego J., Nieto-Obregón J., Zermeño M., (1996). Fault and fractures in the valley of Aguascalientes, preliminary microzonification, in *World Conf. on Earthquake Engin.* 11th Amsterdam, Elsevier Paper 1651.

[9] Lo, K.Y. (1962). Shear strength properties of a sample of volcanic material of the valley of Mexico. *Géotechnique*, Vol. 12, No. 4, pp. 303–318.

[10] Lugo-Hubp, J., Mooser, F., Pérez-Vega, A., and Zamorano-Orozco, J. (1994). Geomorfología de la sierra de Santa Catarina, DF, México. *Revista Mexicana de Ciencias Geológicas*, 11(1), 43–52.

Technology for a Resilient Future – Vincent , Moorthy and Dasari (Eds)
 ISBN: 978-1-041-39070-1

Effect of Subsidence on a Transport Elevated Line: Anticipating Critical Conditions Using Satellite Imagery

Silvia García, Saraid Santamaría, Paulina Trejo, and Mónica Ramírez
Instituto de Ingeniería UNAM, Ciudad Universitaria, Coyoacán, CDMX, México

ABSTRACT: In this research the temporal and spatial risk status, derived from the movements of the ground masses, of supports and nodes of a Trolleybus Elevated line in Mexico City is defined. By monitoring the trend and magnitude of ground displacements using satellite radar technology (InSAR), the stress-deformation state of the transport line (built on various types of soil) is reviewed. Remarkable is the fact that, when the line was designed, the deformation pattern was quite homogeneous, but this trend has changed dramatically in the last 5 years. The vertical displacements rate indicates that some line supports are going to be subjected to extreme vertical and horizontal movements and rotations, so the safety status of some supports is uncertain. The geo scenario is recreated with neural networks, and it is completed with structural 2D-FEM models. The strategy presented here is fundamentally different from other conventional methods because the functional approximation is defined with detailed and real deformations of the subsidence (in composition of 3D-directions) and the displacements of the system (functioning) , that is, the properties of soils and rocks are not modified to match the deformations dictated by construction standards, which represents an oversimplification of the problem.

Keywords: Subsidence, InSAR, infrastructure security, resilient structural design

1 INTRODUCTION

The complexity of Mexico City's subsoils, combined with the need to extract underground resources (primarily water), has resulted in the progressive sinking of the ground surface. This phenomenon, known as subsidence, is responsible for numerous fractures and displacements that have affected both the population and civil infrastructure [1,2]. In the recent past, these damages have been studied to generate maps identifying the affected areas according to the geotechnical conditions and the diverse factors that may increase a soil's susceptibility to cracking. However, from the perspective of civil infrastructure design and development, beyond the mere mapping of surface fissures, it becomes crucial to i. define the origin of these cracks, and ii. anticipate and assess the susceptibility of differential settlements, because these two situations can have a negative impact on the secure state of civil works. [3] have identified that cracks and fissures are the manifestation of subsidence, in high rates, coupled with specific range of soils heterogeneity (geometry and compression modulus) and the disposition of the basement -gradient of the hard layer-).

The called *elevated trolleybus* is a major corridor running along the eastern sector of Mexico City. Based on geotechnical zonation declared in construction Mexican standards, this line is founded on varying soil types. The elevation, approximately 10 m above street plane, is achieved through columns and frames supported by a unique foundation system: a foundation box with friction piles. The presented research was conducted because of recognition of damage to the support column dies and loss of the neoprene joints of the roads, which leads to the belief that some supporters are moving asynchronously with their neighbors and/or are losing vertical in opposite directions.

In this article, the use of RADAR satellite imagery and InSAR technology is presented as a tool to realistically categorize ground displacements and determine their impact on the elevated structure. Considering these vertical displacements, it is possible to reconfigure both the Serviceability Limit State (SLS) and the Ultimate Limit State (ULS) of the secure state. The SLS refers to conditions that affect the use and functionality (deflections, cracks, or excessive vibrations) and the ULS is about structural failure (total or partial collapse, loss of balance, or instability). To define if the elevated line is on SLS or in ULS, RADAR satellite images, from 2015 to 2023, were processed using InSAR technology. The satellites acquire RADAR images of the area of interest every 12 days. InSAR technology allows, by comparing and analyzing the signal information from the different satellite images, ground displacements (rendered in pixels). RADAR images from the ascending and descending modes of the European Space Agency's (ESA) Sentinel-1 constellation were processed. This system has a resolution of 3 m x 3 m. Then, using this InSAR data and specific geoinformation a recurrent neural network RNN was built for anticipating the subsidence in next years. Once the settlements due to subsidence are calculated, a 2D-FEM (Finite Element Method) was operated to calculate the new stress-deformation state in the line supports (particularly in the zones with differential settlements between neighboring supports of more than 20 cm). Based on the conclusions of this investigation, it is recommended that structural calculus must be reviewed to redefine if the structure can support the future deformations.

2 GEOTECHNICAL INFORMATION

The elevated trolleybus has a total length of 7.6 km; in the section of the line considered critical. The most affected supports are those located over the transition between lacustrine and hill -hard- deposits (Figure 1). The foundation consists of a box measuring 9 m in width, 9 m in length, and 3 m in depth, embedded at 3.8 m below the ground surface, upon which the columns supporting the superstructure are founded. Each box is reinforced with seven piles, 20 m in length, extending down to a depth of 23.8 m (Figure 2). According to research on large-scale and complex cracking and deformation in the area, understanding the behavioral patterns and the effects of soil mass movements on the superstructure requires identifying: the spatial location of the supports relative to deformation events, and the anomalous features within the stratigraphy (soil heterogeneity and geometry of the basement layer). The geotechnical information, data from Mixed Boreholes (SM) and Cone Penetration Tests (CPTu), is as the information example show in Figure 3.

DOI: 10.1201/9781042017546-64

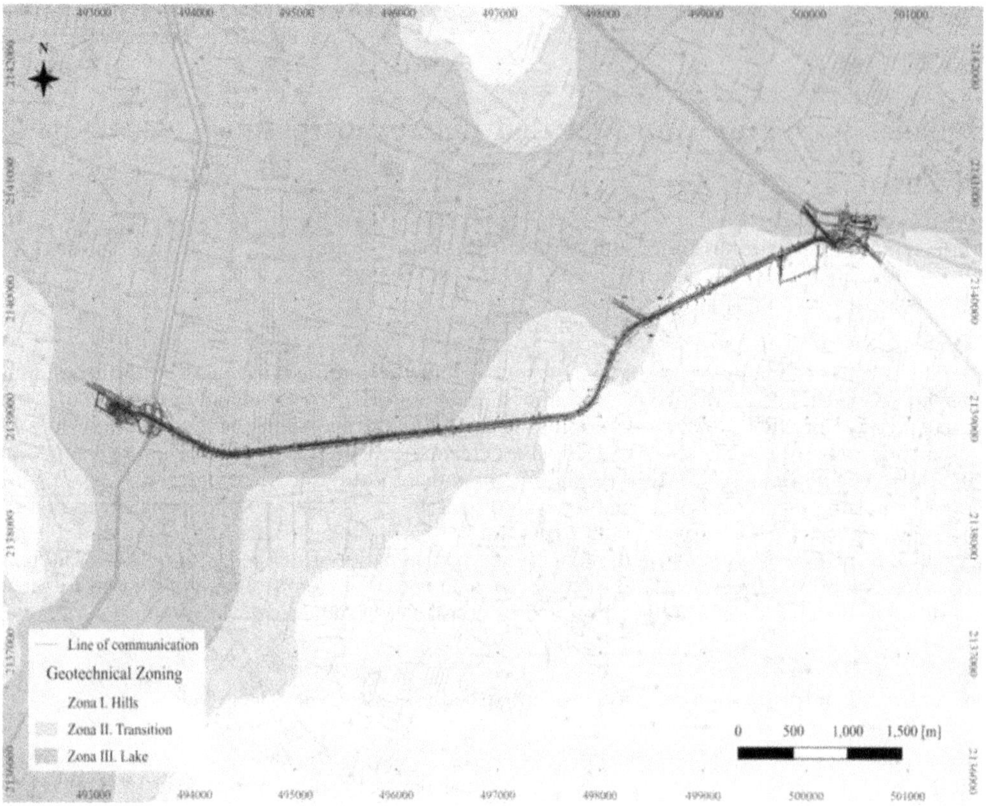

Figure 1. Geotechnical zonation on the elevated line.

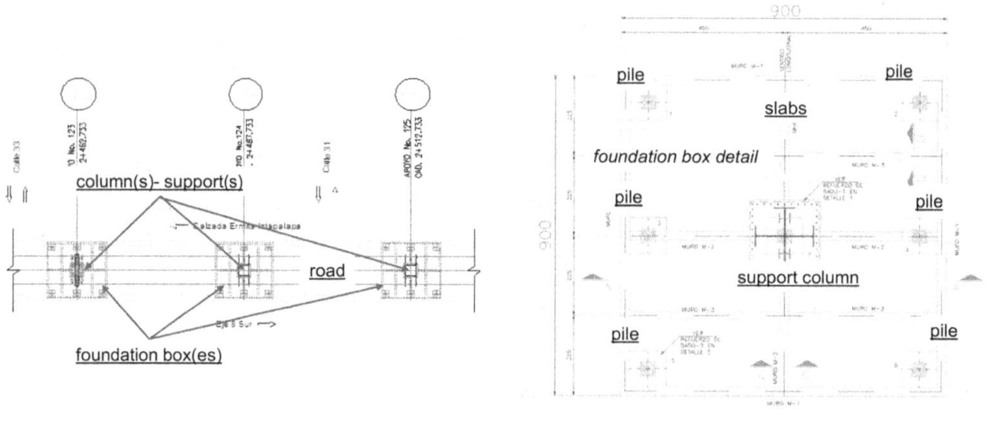

Figure 2. Foundation system for the elevated line.

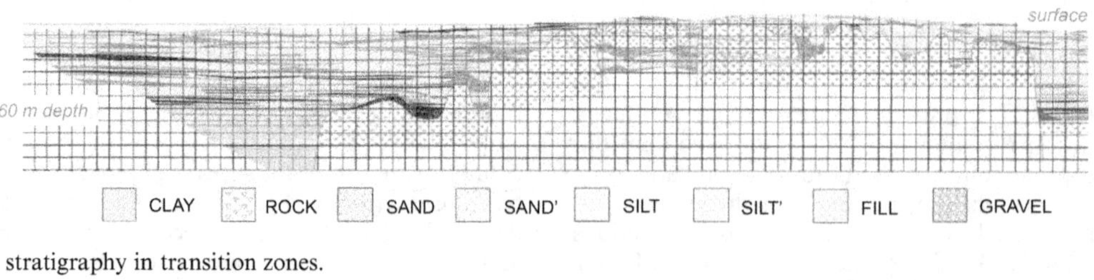

Figure 3. Typical stratigraphy in transition zones.

3 HYBRID ANALYSES: INSAR+NN+FEM

The hybrid model seeks to define the following aspects: i. the spatial connection between very high subsidence rates (derived breaks, cracks, or fractures) with topography, urban density and artificial barriers (foundations and the loads they transmit), ii. the 3D subsidence, that must not be explained from a global snapshot of accumulated because this "softens" the events and masks risk conditions; and iii. the modification of the stress-strain state under the foundation box.

First, the InSAR vertical displacements, δ_v, are analysed from 2015 to 2023 (Figure 4). For processing satellite imagery, two approaches were established: (i) to categorize natural and anthropogenic pixels, and (ii) to define spatio-temporal response patterns consistent with the geological–geotechnical information. For (i) a RNN was trained as a spatial model for determine the deformed surface of the zone excluding the information from the structure. Details of this procedure in [4]. It is particularly important to trace anomalies within the identified general deformation pattern, for instance, the settlement prior to September 19th, 2017, earthquake, and during the first days of October 2017 indicates that the strong earthquake induced a sudden settlement averaging ~5 cm in the compressible soils but not in the structure.

The accumulated deformation these 8 years is ≈2 m and is dangerously near the centre of the elevated line. Attention is drawn to this feature because the line structure must face δ_v rates as different as several times the order of the max and min recorded deformation (up to 5 times). While the Hill zone practically remains without important deformations the Lake area is $\delta_v \approx 2$ m, this is obviously generating an abrupt transition between the no-movements sites to the sink ones with the dangerous differential settlements associated. For the authors of this research is important to declare that we are not pointing negligence or wrongdoing on the part of the designers or geotechnicians in charge of the elevated line, but rather that the soil response has changed as drastically as few conventional studies could have shown at the time of the analysis and initial reconnaissance *geo*campaigns. As an example, in Figure 5 are presented the spatial variation on surface (soil patches) of annual periods taking the deformation display generated to 2025. As can be seen, there are virtually no significant differences, and although there is an alteration where the hill becomes a lake, this could be overcome with a robust foundation solution. However, the drought in Mexico City during 2017, which extended into 2019, forced an increase in waterpumping from the aquifer and the placement of more wells in this region. This had a significant impact on the size of the area of maximum displacement, which, by 2023, will grow southward, completely affecting the centre of the elevated line.

Figure 4. The accumulated deformation in 8 years (2015-2023), A and B Transition zones.

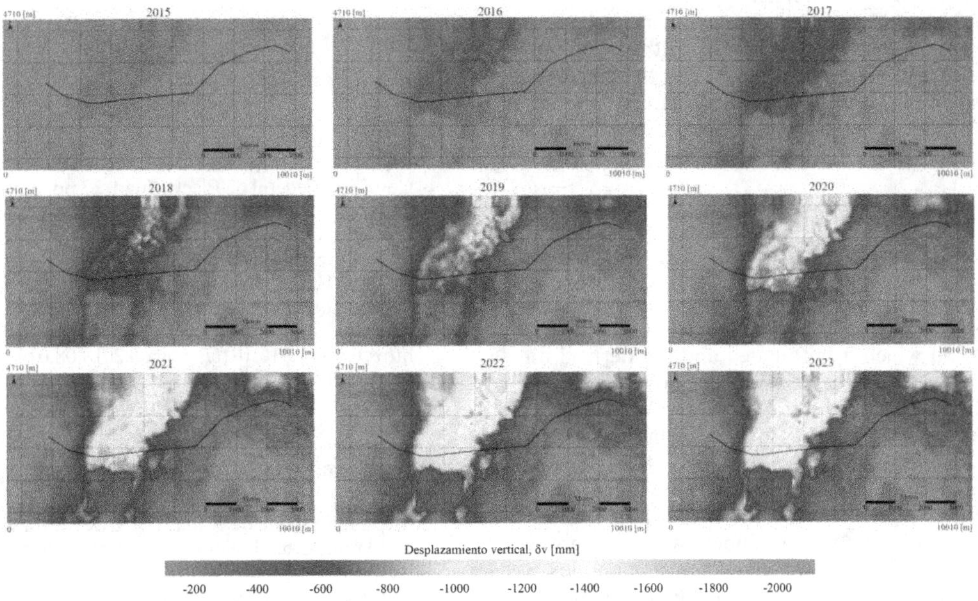

Figure 5. Annual deformation (2015-2023), see how the green-red zone grows southward generating the A and B Transition zones.

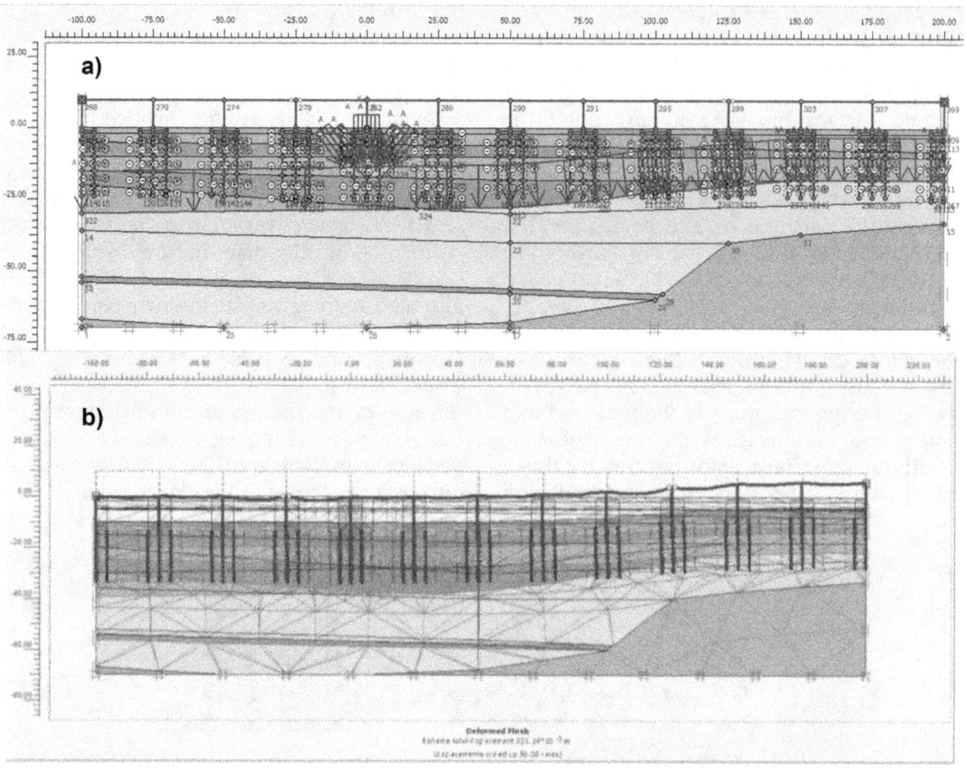

Figure 6. a) Finite Element Model FEM model of the Elevated Trolleybus longitudinal direction and b) settlements due to the weight of the structure plus subsidence due to a decrease in pore pressure in the deep strata.

The heterogeneity, the steeply sloping base, and the pumping of deep layers produce markedly non-uniform surface settlements. Using a FEM analysis (Figure 6), shear forces in the prototype column (one that may be a support in the center of the line) are calculated at 54 and 117 kN for surface subsidence due to structure and subsidence of 23 and 37 cm, respectively, probably not considered in the design of the Trolleybus structure. If a surface subsidence of 23 cm is accompanied by a 2 cm differential in the longitudinal direction, the shear force triples compared to the uniform subsidence case. Differential subsidence is possible given the heterogeneity of the materials. Regarding the moments calculated in the longitudinal direction at the base of the column, these increase by 28% in the case of subsidence due to the structure plus subsidence of 23 cm compared to the case of consolidation only due to the structure's own weight. In the case of a subsidence of 37 cm, the increase is 75%. If a differential of 2 cm is added to the 23 cm, the increase is 2.3 times (130%). These increases were likely not considered in the structure's design and may occur in a period of less than 2 years.

4 CONCLUSIONS

The Elevated Trolleybus is a project that confronts the heterogeneity of the soils on which it is founded and the derived differential settlements. Based on the results shown here, the development of InSAR and topographical database, derived from several years of monitoring ground displacements and deformations in the structure that supports the Elevated Trolleybus, and an intelligent system to define the modification in stresses, could make possible to identify earlier potential risk situations. Radar interferometry, combined with the proper interpretation of a multifactorial phenomenon as complex as subsidence, can provide vital information to forecast and anticipate unsafe medium- and long-term conditions that may endanger both the population and the infrastructure. It is recommended that more subsidence cases than those presented in this document be analyzed, given the importance of the project.

ACKNOWLEDGEMENT

We gratefully acknowledge Instituto para la Seguridad de las Construcciones de la Ciudad de México for its cooperation in the research.

REFERENCES

[1] Mooser, F., Montiel, A. y Zúñiga, A. (1996). Nuevo mapa geológico de las cuencas de México, Toluca y Puebla, 1:100,000. Comisión Federal de Electricidad. 27 pp., una lámina de leyenda, 35 mapas geológicos a escala 1:100 000 y una lámina de perfiles geológicos. México.

[2] Ochoa González, G.H., Carreón-Freyre, D., Franceschini, A., Cerca, M., and Teatini, P. (2018). Overexploitation of groundwater resources in the faulted basin of Querétaro, Mexico: A 3D deformation and stress analysis, *Eng. Geol.*, 245, 192–206, https://doi.org/10.1016/j.enggeo.2018.08.014, 2018.

[3] Paulina Trejo, Silvia García, Shweta Vincent, (2023), A classification tree for modeling ground fractures from subsidence, *Applied Sciences*, ISSN: 2076-3417, https://doi.org/10.3390/app13053123

[4] Silvia García, (2024), Reporte: Gemelo Digital Para el Análisis de Deformaciones, Subsidencias y Desplazamientos del Terreno Mediante satélite de Radar (INSAR), Para el Trazo del Sistema de Transporte Eléctrico (Trolebús) Sobre Calzada Ermita Iztapalapa (Eje 8 Sur), Instituto para la Seguridad de las Construcciones en el Distrito Federal, México.

Technology for a Resilient Future – Vincent , Moorthy and Dasari (Eds)
© 2027 The Editor(s), ISBN: 978-1-041-39070-1

Author Index

For Product Safety Concerns and Information please contact our EU
representative GPSR@taylorandfrancis.com
Taylor & Francis Verlag GmbH, Kaufingerstraße 24, 80331 München, Germany

www.ingramcontent.com/pod-product-compliance
Lightning Source LLC
LaVergne TN
LVHW061030130926
847902LV00029B/439
9781041393450